KU-455-710

OFFICE OF POPULATION CENSUSES AND SURVEYS

1991 Census

County report

Laid before Parliament pursuant to Section 4(1)
Census Act 1920

Hampshire

part 1

volume 2 of 2

Part 1 of this report has been bound as two separate volumes. For the convenience of the reader, sections 1 to 16 of the text of the report, together with the Annexes, have been reproduced in full in both volumes. The main tables are divided between the volumes, although all titles are listed in section 16 of the text.

London: HMSO

© *Crown copyright 1993*

First published 1993

ISBN 0 11 691401 7

Two of two volumes not to be sold separately

HMSO
Standing order service

Placing a standing order with HMSO BOOKS enables a
customer to receive future titles in this series automatically
as published. This saves the time, trouble and expense of
placing individual orders and avoids the problem of
knowing when to do so. For details please write to HMSO
BOOKS (PC 13A/1), Publications Centre, PO Box 276,
London SW8 5DT quoting reference 02 02 009. The
standing order service also enables customers to receive
automatically as published all material of their choice
which additionally saves extensive catalogue research. The
scope and selectivity of the service has been extended by
new techniques, and there are more than 3,500
classifications to choose from. A special leaflet describing
the service in detail may be obtained on request.

Cover illustration by Guy Eves

Contents

1 Introduction

1.1 This volume is the first part of the Report for Hampshire from the Census of Great Britain which took place on 21 April 1991. It is published and laid before Parliament under the authority of, and to meet the requirements of, section 4(1) of the Census Act 1920.

1.2 The 1991 Census was the nineteenth in a series begun in 1801, and carried out every tenth year except 1941, and the ninth in which there have been reports for each county.

1.3 The Report contains statistical tables on all topics covered by the 1991 Census. Part 1 includes the results based on processing all Census returns, prefaced by a summary of the main results. Part 2 includes results based on the subsequent processing of a one in ten sample of the returns, and is published separately and later. Each of the main tables is presented for the county as a whole and for each local authority district within the county.

1.4 A similar Report is being made for each county in England and Wales, and for each Region and Islands Area in Scotland. These are being published in a series during 1992 and 1993. To complete the series, there will be a Report for Great Britain as a whole, including figures for Scotland as a whole, Wales as a whole, and for each of the standard statistical regions in England.

1.5 The contents of the Reports were designed, after extensive consultations, to meet needs for statistical facts in consistent form over the whole country on population, housing, employment, health, education, and transport. The series of Reports will serve: local and health authorities; the elected representatives of the community; business and commerce; academic research; education and teaching; local community groups; and, taking the series of Reports as a whole, central government and other national organisations.

1.6 In addition, the forms of table included in this Report were designed to be the basis of standard sets of *statistical abstracts* available, under the terms of section 4(2) of the Census Act 1920, for areas such as wards which are smaller than a local authority. Thus the results of the Census can be analysed for counties, for local authority areas, and for still smaller local areas with comparability throughout Great Britain.

1.7 The text of this Report gives brief background information on the 1991 Census, an introduction to the detailed content of the report, and guidance to assist the user. It also includes a summary of the complete programme of reports and other results from the Census. There is guidance on how to obtain further information.

1.8 This Report was made possible by the co-operation of the households and other members of the public in Hampshire in responding to the Census, by the hard work of the many members of the temporary Census field staff who delivered and collected the Census forms, and by other help given locally. The Registrar General is most grateful for all these contributions. They will be repaid by the value of the results of the Census both to people and organisations in Hampshire and more widely.

2   The 1991 Census

2.1   The Census was held on Sunday 21 April 1991, when every household in Great Britain was required by law to complete a census form. In England there were five questions on housing and 19 questions on each person, while in Wales there was one additional question, and in Scotland two further questions. People in communal establishments such as hospitals, hotels, and prisons were also included. The forms were delivered shortly before Census day by some 118,000 'enumerators', each responsible for a precisely defined area, and then collected in the following days. Enumeration went well over Britain as a whole, although some households, mainly in inner city areas, proved difficult to contact.

2.2   The first results of the Census were published in July 1991 in *Preliminary Reports* for England and Wales and for Scotland. These results were derived from summary records made by the field staff. The main processing of the Census began in June 1991. The publication of County and Region Reports is scheduled to be completed during 1993.

2.3   Preparations for the Census began well in advance, and included trials in the field. Consultation on the topics to be included took place in 1987/8 and the Government issued its plans in a Parliamentary White Paper in July 1988[1]. Parliament debated and approved plans for the Census at the end of 1989 and they became law shortly afterwards. Consultation on the form of statistical output began in August 1988, and, for the County Reports, was completed by mid 1990.

*The 1991 Census Reports to Parliament will be concluded by a **General Report** covering all aspects of the conduct of the Census; in the meantime more information may be obtained from the addresses given in section 13.*

3   Local results from the Census

3.1   Results have been published for local areas of Great Britain from every census since the first in 1801. Reports for each county have been published from censuses in this century. These reports have covered most of the questions asked in each successive census, but there were innovations in the way the 1991 Census County Reports were prepared.

3.2   The Census Offices planned from the outset that the 1991 County Reports should provide results from *all* the topics covered by the Census, and that there should be a single base of standard statistical tables for the Reports and for the associated statistical abstracts which would be made available for smaller areas. It was therefore possible, for the

first time, to consult with users of local statistics with a focus on one main objective.

3.3   The Census Offices prepared initial proposals for the local statistics based on those produced from the 1981 Census, and invited comment from advisory groups representing government departments and local and health authorities. Meetings, which were open to all those with an interest, were also held in various parts of the country to discuss the proposals, and written comments were invited. The form of the local statistics was then developed and refined through two further rounds of consultations.

3.4   It was decided to produce two tiers of local statistics. The upper tier is the set of main tables appearing in this Report - they are also known as the 'Local Base Statistics'. This upper tier is also available as statistical abstracts for wards in England and Wales and for postcode sectors in Scotland, provided that the wards or sectors are above a minimum population size. The lower tier - known as the 'Small Area Statistics' (SAS) - is a set of some 80 tables which, for comparability, are either whole or abbreviated versions of the upper tier tables. The SAS are available as statistical abstracts for smaller areas. More information is given in Annex B.

4   The range of information in the Report

4.1   This Report gives Census results for Hampshire, and for the local authority districts within it, *as constituted on 21 April 1991*. The county and district boundaries are shown on the map which forms section 14. There have been changes in the boundaries of Basingstoke and Dean, East Hampshire, Eastleigh, Hart, Havant, Rushmoor, Test Valley, and Winchester districts since the Census on 5 April 1981, and these are summarised in Annex A which follows the main tables.

4.2   The starting point of the topics covered in this Report is the Census form itself. There are facsimiles of the forms used in the Census in the volume of *1991 Census Definitions* - see section 7. All the topics in the 1981 Census were included in the 1991 Census, with the exception of a separate question on outside WCs. However, the answer categories in questions like tenure and economic position (whether in work, etc) were updated. There were also new questions on ethnic group, limiting long-term illness, term-time address of students and schoolchildren, and central heating; a question on weekly hours worked was reintroduced; and information was collected to give a count of dwellings and building types. As in the 1981 and previous censuses, a number of 'hard to code' questions, such as occupation, name and business of employer, and workplace, have been processed only for a 10 per cent sample of households - see section 8.2.

---

[1]*1991 Census of Population* (Cm 430). HMSO, 1988 ISBN 010 104302 3

4.3   The Census questions for all people, whether they were in households or in communal establishments like hospitals and hotels, were:

age (date of birth)
sex
marital status
relationship to head of household*/position in
  establishment
whereabouts on Census night - asked in households only
usual address
term-time address of students and schoolchildren
usual address one year ago (migration)
country of birth
ethnic group
long-term illness;

and for all those aged 16 or over:

economic activity in preceding week and employment
  status (self-employed, employee, etc)
hours worked weekly*
occupation*
industry of employment (name and business of
  employer)*
address of work-place*
means of daily journey to work*
higher qualifications*.

* Analysed for a 10 per cent sample of the population - see section 8.

In Wales there was a question on the Welsh language and in Scotland a question on Gaelic.

4.4   In addition, the person filling in the form in each household was asked about:

number of rooms
'shared' accommodation
tenure
amenities (WC, bath, central heating)
number of cars and vans available
lowest floor of accommodation - Scotland only.

The name and address of the household was recorded on the form, but, apart from the postcode of the address, this information was not included in the processing operation.

4.5   If a household was absent, or no contact was made with a household which appeared to be present on Census day, the census enumerators recorded the type of accommodation and an estimate of the number of rooms and the number of residents. Absent households were asked to complete a census form voluntarily on return. Where they did so, the data from the forms have been included in the results; where they did not, data about such households have been imputed.

4.6   Each topic on the Census form is covered by tables in this Report. But one of the strengths of the Census is the facility to derive additional variables from a number of

questions asked at one time. Examples of derived variables for individuals are 'socio-economic group' and 'social class' (based on occupation) and, for households, an example is the type of household by composition.

---

5   Finding information in the Report

The tables

5.1   Each Report contains the following tables:

Summary tables in (Part 1)

A to L   All parts of Great Britain

M   Areas in Wales or Scotland only
  (Welsh or Gaelic language)

Main tables in (Part 1)

1 to 66   All parts of Great Britain

67   Areas in Wales or Scotland only
  (Welsh or Gaelic language)

68-70   Areas in Scotland only
  (special housing tables)

Main tables in (Part 2)

71-99   All parts of Great Britain

The *main tables* are either *cross-tabulations*, that is where each element in the population is counted only once in the matrix of table *cells*, or groupings of two or more cross-tabulations of related statistics. Some additional counts are given in *single cells* which do not form part of the matrix of a cross-tabulation.

5.2   Each of the main tables has a short *key word title* which appears at the head of each page and indicates the main feature of the table, but not necessarily every aspect included. These key word titles are listed in table number order in section 16. The tables are grouped into six main subject areas:

in part 1 of the Report:

1-18   Demographic and economic characteristics

19-27   Housing

28-53   Households and household composition

54-66   Household spaces and dwellings

67-70   Scotland and Wales only tables;

and, in part 2 of the Report:

71-99   Socio-economic characteristics (tables based on the 10 per cent sample)

The *Topic and key word index* in section 16 shows where topics and cross-tabulations of topics are found.

Table conventions

5.3   In each table, the figures for the county as a whole are given first, with the local authority areas following in alphabetical order. In the larger tables, the margins are repeated for each area. To make the table content clear, the wording in the table margins is as comprehensive as possible, and abbreviations have been kept to a minimum. There are also a number of standard conventions used in the tables.

Margins (row and column headings)

The *population base* or *bases* for each table - see section 6, are shown in the banner heading over the column headings; when the table contains two or more bases, these are separated by semi-colons.

Indentation in row headings indicates that counts in that row are *sub-totals* of counts in the previous non-indented rows (equivalent to the sub-divisions of column headings).

Text set in italics signifies either that no counts will appear for that row/column, or that counts in that row/column are a *sub-set* of a previous row/column and should not be added to other rows/columns when totalling.

Total rows/columns are indicated by text in capital letters.

Counts

Counts based on full processing (Tables 1 to 70) are given without modification; a cell where the count is zero, but where a non-zero count was possible, is shown with a dash, whereas a cell for which a non-zero count is impossible is left blank. Some cells obviously duplicating others are also left blank.

Counts based on the one in ten sample of returns (Tables 71 to 99) are given as the count obtained in the sample without modification; the count must be multiplied by ten to provide an estimated figure for the enumerated population as a whole; a cell with no member of the sample population is shown with a dash, but this is not necessarily an estimate of a nil value in the population as a whole. (part 2 of the Report gives fuller guidance.)

Cross-tabulations, that is where an element of the population is counted only once, are separated by *ruled lines* within tables, as are single cell counts; where a table has a total row or column common to a number of cross-tabulations, it is usually shown only for the first cross-tabulation.

6   The populations covered in the Report

6.1   Each cross-tabulation in this Report has a *population base*, that is the total population distributed among the tabulation cells - using the term 'population' in the wider statistical sense of the items being counted. Most of the bases count people or households, but some count other items, and many tabulations have bases which are sub-sets of populations as a whole.

6.2   The tabulations count people in an area in one of two basic ways - those who were *present* on Census night, and those who were *resident* whether or not they were present. The method of counting people present is unchanged from previous censuses; the method of enumerating people resident was revised for the 1991 Census to provide a more complete count.

6.3   The Census placed a legal obligation on every household in which someone was present on Census night, and on every person present in a communal establishment, to complete a census form whether they were resident there or a visitor resident elsewhere in Great Britain or outside Britain. Additionally in 1991, for the first time in a British census, there was an arrangement to enumerate, on a voluntary basis, households where nobody was present on Census night - 'wholly absent households'. Census forms and reply paid envelopes were left for completion on the return of such households. (This part of the enumeration was on a voluntary basis because members of the absent households either would have fulfilled their legal obligation by filling in forms if they were elsewhere in Britain, or, if they were outside Britain, had no such obligation.)

6.4   In all cases of wholly absent households, or where no contact was made with a household which appeared to have been present on Census day, the census enumerator recorded the type of accommodation and an estimate of the number of rooms and residents. Where a wholly absent household did not subsequently return a form or where no contact was made with a household, values for the fully processed parts of the Census form were imputed during computer processing using the basic information returned and data on households nearby. The number of people in an area, included either on the basis of voluntary returns or by imputation, is shown in Table 1, with more detail in Table 18; the number of households included by imputation is shown in Table 19.

6.5   The addition of data from wholly absent households and non-contacted households is an improvement compared with the 1981 Census, when people from absent households were only enumerated where they were present on Census night (if in Britain). In 1981, people in wholly absent households, although included in the counts of people present, were excluded from the tables with a base of residents in the 1981 County Reports. The change to the base does, however, slightly affect comparisons between 1981 and 1991 - see section 10.

Population bases

6.6   The main population bases used in cross-tabulations in this Report are defined in full in the volume *1991 Census Definitions* - see section 7. In summary they are as follows:

Persons present in the area on the night of 21 April 1991.

Residents of the area, who are:

* people both present and resident in a household or communal establishment;

* people resident in, but absent on the night of 21 April 1991, from a household in which one or more other people were present (people resident in communal establishments but absent on Census night are *not* included since the Census forms for communal establishments covered only those people present on Census night);

* people resident in wholly absent households who returned a census form; and

* people imputed as resident in wholly absent households and in households where no contact was made (Tables A to M and 1 to 70 only).

Households with residents.

Households with people present but no residents.

Household spaces occupied by a household, or unoccupied.

Dwellings - structurally separate premises (a building or part of one) designed for occupation by a single household.

Figure 1 below shows the relationship between the elements in the population bases of *persons present* and *residents*.

6.7   In addition, there are bases of: *families* of resident persons; units of *non-permanent accommodation*; units of *converted or shared accommodation*; *rooms*; *cars in* (available to) *households*; and *communal establishments*.

6.8   Many tabulations count sub-sets of the main bases, for example, residents in households (that is, excluding those in communal establishments). Two tabulations - Tables 10 and 26 - combine more than one sub-set by including both students who were residents and those whose usual addresses were elsewhere. *Bases should therefore be checked before making comparisons between tabulations.*

Fig 1   Inter-relationship of population bases

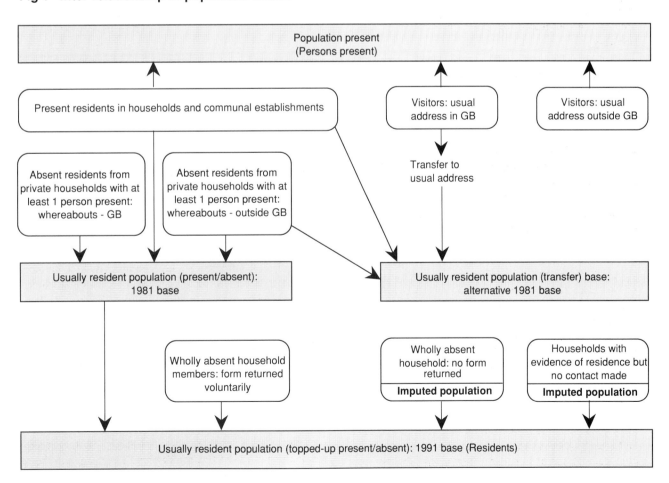

7 Definitions and explanatory notes

7.1 Definitions of all the terms used in the tables in this Report are given in *1991 Census Definitions* published by HMSO[2]. There are too many such definitions for them to be included in the text of this Report, although the terms used in the summary tables in section 15 are defined in Annex C after the main tables.

7.2 The margins of tables in this Report have been made as self-explanatory as possible, with as few abbreviations as possible. But they do not provide a complete definition of the statistics tabulated, and reference should also be made to the *1991 Census Definitions*. Reference may also need to be made to the volumes of *Definitions* for previous censuses if comparisons are being made, or to the appropriate definitions of terms in non-census sources.

7.3 Explanatory notes for the main tables, where they are necessary, are given in Annex C after the main tables.

8 The '10 per cent' sample
(Tables 71-99 in part 2 of the Report)

8.1 The answers to certain census questions, mainly those which are difficult to code because of a wide range of written responses, have been processed for a sample of a nominal one in ten returns. The questions are identified in the list in section 4. The sample is drawn from the edited records prepared during the processing of all the returns. Thus the processing of the sample follows after the full processing, and the results are published somewhat later.

8.2 The sample is drawn by randomly selecting one complete enumerated (but not imputed) household from each 'stratum' of ten sequentially numbered forms, together with one person randomly selected from each stratum of ten sequentially numbered individual forms in communal establishments. This method of sampling avoids the types of bias that can occur in field sampling, and the stratification improves the geographical spread of households included in the sample. However, the clustering of people within households tends to reduce the precision of estimates for variables such as migration or mode of travel to work where the characteristics of individuals within the same household tend to be inter-dependent. Data are not imputed for the sampled topics. *Imputed wholly absent households - see section 6 - are therefore not included in the '10 per cent' tables and the sample is therefore slightly fewer than 10 per cent of the households included in the '100 per cent' tables.* The 'sampling fraction' varies slightly from one area to another according to the proportion of imputed wholly absent households in the area.

9 Evaluation of the results

9.1 The results presented in this Report will inevitably contain some inaccuracies arising from deficiencies and errors in coverage or response. The main causes are:

(a) failure to identify all residential accommodation;

(b) failure to identify all households and household spaces within accommodation;

(c) failure to enumerate all persons present or resident within households or communal establishments;

(d) errors in the estimates of numbers of persons in wholly absent households or where no contact was made;

(e) mis-classification of accommodation, for example, classifying wholly absent households as vacant, or vice versa;

(f) errors of double counting persons recorded as resident at more than one address;

(g) incorrect information supplied by filling in the forms, including missing responses; and

(h) errors introduced when processing the forms, including the imputation of data.

Steps are taken to assess the prevalence of these inaccuracies; but, because of the impracticability of conducting a very large number of one-to-one checks, the results are fairly broad estimates. These provide the basis of allowances for inaccuracies in the Census when the Registrar General's mid-year population estimates are made, and provide users of the Census with indications of the degree of confidence that may be placed in the Census results. The figures in Census Reports themselves are *not* adjusted.

9.2 The main check on the completeness and quality of response to the 1991 Census is provided by a Census Validation Survey (CVS). This was a voluntary sample survey conducted soon after the Census in 1,200 Census Enumeration Districts by interviewers employed in the Social Survey by the Office of Population Censuses and Surveys (OPCS). The sampling fraction for the CVS was higher in Inner and Outer London, and in the Metropolitan Counties and Glasgow.

9.3 The checks on *coverage* assessed whether:

(a) any household spaces in accommodation in the sampled areas had been missed;

(b) any of a sample of unoccupied household spaces had been mis-classified;

---

[2]OPCS/GRO(S). *1991 Census Definitions, Great Britain.* HMSO, 1992

(c) any household in a sample of multi-occupied buildings had been missed; and whether

(d) anyone was present on Census night in a sample of households reported to have been wholly absent.

A sample of households where no contact had been made was also checked. On the basis of the coverage checks, estimates of under- or over-enumeration are being made for Inner London, Outer London, Glasgow, other Metropolitan Counties as a whole, the remaining parts of England and Wales as a whole, and the remaining parts of Scotland as a whole.

9.4 The check on the *quality* of response is provided by a further sample of households taken in the sampled Enumeration Districts. As well as checking whether everybody in the household had been included on the Census form (as part of the coverage check), the interviewer checked the accuracy of responses on the form by asking further questions, noting any explanations for differences. Analyses of gross and net differences will be prepared.

9.5 All estimates from the CVS will, of course, be subject to sampling error. Also, the CVS cannot provide a complete check on coverage and quality, even for the households included in the sample, because of changes in the circumstances of respondents between the Census and the CVS and because of incomplete response to the CVS. Despite these inherent limitations, the CVS is expected to provide much valuable information about the coverage and quality of the Census.

9.6 Results of the CVS are published as they become available, starting in summer 1992 with the first results on coverage. The full report on the CVS is scheduled to be published early in 1994. The *Census Newsletter* - see section 13, will include summaries of the main findings.

9.7 The Registrar General's mid-year estimates for local authorities in 1991 and subsequent years will take the Census counts of usual residents given in the County Reports as the starting point. The Census counts will be adjusted as necessary, the main adjustments being as follows:

(a) allowances for any estimated under- (or over-) enumeration indicated by the CVS and any other appropriate evidence;

(b) allowances for differences in the definition of 'residents' between the Census and the estimates; in particular, students are included in the estimates at term-time addresses (an extra question was included in the 1991 Census to provide a better basis for this adjustment);

(c) allowances in respect of armed forces personnel and their dependants; and

(d) the lapse of time between the Census and mid-year 1991.

The counts of residents in this Report and the 1991 mid-year population estimates will therefore not be identical. Differences should be interpreted in the light of the adjustments described above.

---

10 Comparisons of results with those of earlier censuses

10.1 The population of Hampshire at successive censuses from 1891 to 1991 is given in summary Table A in section 15. Comparisons between 1981 and 1991 are also given for selected variables in other tables in section 15.

10.2 Further comparisons between censuses are affected by changes in: the geographic base; the topics included in the censuses; and the definition of counts presented in the tables. The detail of changes over the long series of censuses is complex, and there is no single guide for users. Reports since the 1901 Census have listed intercensal boundary changes - on the lines of Annex A in this Report, and the *Guide to Census Reports*[3] describes the general changes in censuses up to 1966.

10.3 A guide to the detailed comparability of the 1971 and 1981 Census Small Area Statistics was issued after the 1981 Census (OPCS *1981 User Guide 84*[4]), but it does not cover comparison between 1971 and 1981 County Reports where they differ from the Small Area Statistics for those years. There is a similar guide on the detailed comparability of 1981 Small Area Statistics and 1991 Local and Small Area Statistics (OPCS/GRO(S) *1991 User Guide 28*[5]), and, although the Guide is not specific to the 1981 County Reports - the content of which differed somewhat from the Small Area Statistics, OPCS *1981 User Guide 86*[6] gives the link between 1981 SAS and 1981 County Report tables. It is therefore possible to determine where comparisons can be made between figures in the 1981 and 1991 County Report tables, and where comparisons must be qualified.

[3]OPCS/GRO(S). *Guide to Census reports, Great Britain 1801-1966.* HMSO, 1977. ISBN 0 11 690638 3

[4]OPCS. *Guide to Statistical Comparability 1971-81: England and Wales.* User Guide 84, OPCS Census Customer Services, 1984

[5]OPCS. *Guide to Statistical Comparability of 1981 Small Area Statistics and 1991 Local Base and Small Area Statistics - Prospectus.* User Guide 28, OPCS Census Customer Services, 1992

[6]OPCS. *1981 Small Area Statistics/County Reports. A guide to comparison.* User Guide 86, OPCS Census Customer Services, 1982

11 Further results from the 1991 Census

11.1 The results of the Census are made available in two ways:

    (a)   in printed reports made to Parliament and sold by HMSO bookshops (or, in a few cases, directly from the Census Offices); or

    (b)   in statistical abstracts available, on request and for a charge, from the Census Offices.

11.2 The results also tend to fall into two broad types: local statistics which cover the full range of census topics - such as this Report - or a summary selection of all topics; and topic statistics which focus on a particular census topic in more detail, mainly at national and regional level. There are also other products which provide further information from the Census. All the main results and products are described in *Prospectuses* in the OPCS/GRO(S) 1991 *User Guide* series, available from the addresses given in section 13. A brief guide to sources of comparable local statistics for other areas, and to sources of more detailed results on particular census topics, together with relevant *Prospectuses,* is included at Annex B.

12 Copyright and reproduction of material from this Report

12.1 All text, statistical and other material in this Report and information of any kind derived from the statistics or other material in the Report is CROWN COPYRIGHT and may be reproduced only with the permission of the Office of Population Censuses and Surveys (OPCS).

12.2 OPCS is prepared to allow extracts of statistics or other material from this Report to be reproduced without a licence provided that these form part of a larger work not primarily designed to reproduce the extracts *and* provided that any extract of statistics represents only a limited part of a table or tables *and* provided that Crown Copyright and the source are prominently acknowledged. OPCS reserves its rights in all circumstances and should be consulted in any case of uncertainty. Enquiries about the reproduction of material should be directed to OPCS at the address given in section 13, and reproduction may require a licence and payment of fees.

13 Further information

14 Reference map

13.1 Any *queries* about the content of this Report or on the interpretation of the results in the Report should be made to:

Census Division
OPCS
St Catherine's House
10 Kingsway
London WC2B 6JP

telephone 071 396 2008

13.2 All *Prospectuses/User Guides* mentioned in this Report may be obtained (by those in England and Wales, or outside Great Britain) from:

Census Customer Services
OPCS
Segensworth Road
Titchfield
Fareham
Hants PO15 5RR

telephone 0329 813800

or (by those in Scotland) from:

Census Customer Services
General Register Office for Scotland
Ladywell House
Ladywell Road
Edinburgh EH12 7TF

telephone 031 314 4254

Census Customer Services will also arrange the supply of any statistical abstracts required.

Request to reproduce material from this Report - see section 12, should be made to Census Customer Services at OPCS.

Reports published by HMSO may be purchased from the addresses shown on the back cover of this Report.

Census Newsletter

*News on all aspects of the Census, including the availability of results, is provided by the **Census Newsletter** issued several times a year by the Census Offices and distributed without charge. Names may be added to the mailing list by contacting Census Customer Services. It is also possible to register with Census Customer Services as a user of the Census to obtain details of relevant products automatically and to ensure inclusion in consultation over future developments.*

14.1 The map on the following page shows the boundaries of districts covered by this Report, and the boundaries of neighbouring counties. The map is reproduced from the Ordnance Survey 1:250,000 map with the permission of the Controller of Her Majesty's Stationery Office, Crown Copyright reserved.

14.2 The highlighted county/county district boundary lines were drawn by OPCS and reflect, as accurately as possible, the boundaries as constituted at 21 April 1991. As the base maps supplied by Ordnance Survey may not always reflect the latest boundary changes, the county boundary lines on the base map and the highlighted boundaries will not always correspond exactly.

358

15 Summary of 1991 Census results for Hampshire

The Tables A to L in this section were first published in 1992: Hampshire, County Monitor in September 1992.

15.1 This section of the Report contains a summary of the final figures of the population and housing in Hampshire and its districts. The statistics in the summary tables are derived largely from the main tables in the Report, and there is a short commentary on each summary table. In addition, the section contains: population counts from 1891 to 1991; selected measures of changes between 1981 to 1991; and a size in hectares and population density figures.

Comparisons between 1981 and 1991; terms and abbreviations

15.2 Section 6 explains the differences between the population bases used in the 1981 and 1991 Reports. The difference has necessitated the use of particular population bases in the parts of the summary tables showing change, and these are explained in Annex C after the main tables. Annex C also explains the terms and conventions used in the summary tables.

Population present on Census night (Tables A and B)

15.3 The figures of population *present* in an area include visitors to a household on Census night and exclude any residents who were away from the area on Census night. The 1991 Census showed that the population present on Census night in Hampshire was 1,523,742, an increase of about 64,800 compared with the rounded figure for 1981 - see Annex C. This represents an increase of 0.43 per cent per year in the population of the county during the decade, compared with virtually no change for England and Wales as a whole (based on preliminary figures), and with an increase of 0.61 per cent per year for the county over the period 1971-81.

15.4 The period in which there was the greatest rate of change in the county over the last century was 1961-71, with an increase of 1.78 per cent per year. The changing size of the population present from 1891 to 1991 is illustrated by the diagram below.

Resident population (Tables C and D)

15.5 The number of people *resident* in Hampshire on Census night (that is, excluding visitors but including residents who were recorded as absent on Census night) was 1,541,547 (Table D). There was an increase of 4.2 per cent since 1981 (using the 1981 population base in each year - see Annex C). This change results principally from there being more births than deaths in the county and a net gain due to migration.

Population present 1891-1991 Hampshire

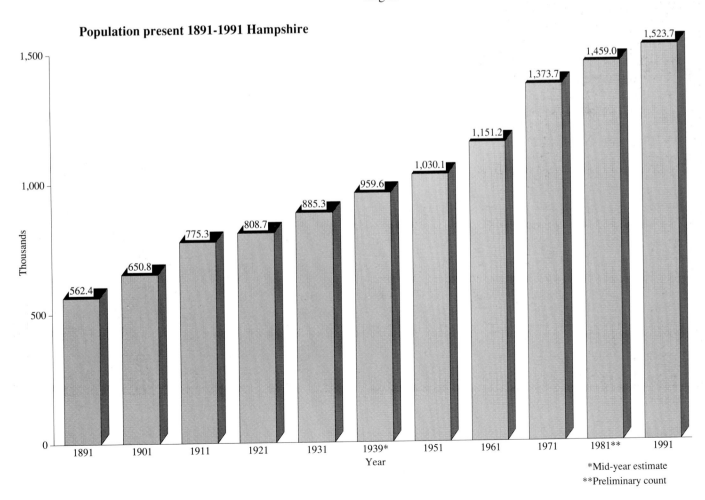

*Mid-year estimate
**Preliminary count

Percentage change in resident population (1981 population base) 1981-91: districts in Hampshire

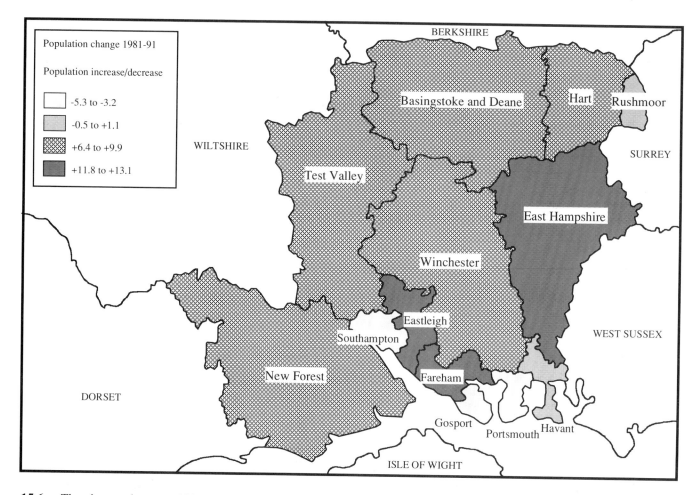

15.6   The changes between 1981 and 1991 in the resident population of the districts in Hampshire varied from an increase of 13.1 per cent in East Hampshire to a decrease of 5.3 per cent in Southampton. These changes are illustrated by the map above. The shading classes in the map have been chosen to highlight the pattern of population change in Hampshire, and will not necessarily be the same as those used for other counties.

15.7   The district with the largest proportion of people resident in communal establishments was Rushmoor, with a figure of 4.1 per cent; this compares with 1.9 per cent for Hampshire as a whole.

Density of population (Table D)

15.8   People in Hampshire were living at an average density of 4.1 persons per hectare on Census night, compared with a provisional figure of 3.2 for England and Wales as a whole. Portsmouth was the most densely populated district (41.6 persons per hectare) and Winchester the least densely populated (1.5).

15.9   OPCS acknowledges the use of hectare figures supplied by Ordnance Survey in this table.

Children and young adults (Tables E and K)

15.10   At the 1991 Census, children (people aged under 16) made up 20.1 per cent of the population resident in

Hampshire. The proportion was highest in Gosport (21.4 per cent) and lowest in New Forest (18.0 per cent).

15.11   The proportion of the total population in households who were young adults (people aged 16-24) was highest in Rushmoor (14.3 per cent) and lowest in New Forest (10.6 per cent). The proportion of young adults in households who were lone parents in 1991 was highest in Southampton (2.8 per cent).

15.12   Winchester had the highest proportion of people aged 16-24 resident in households who were full-time students, 38.5 per cent, compared with 25.4 per cent for the county as a whole. Southampton was the district with the highest proportion of young adults who were unemployed, 12.7 per cent, compared with the county figure of 8.9 per cent.

Pensioners (Tables E and L)

15.13   People of pensionable age (that is, 65 years and over for men and 60 years and over for women) made up 18.0 per cent of the population of Hampshire in 1991, an increase of 1.1 percentage points since 1981 (using the 1981 population base in each year - see Annex C). The proportion of men and women who were aged 75 years and over increased, respectively, by 0.5 percentage points and 0.8 percentage points between 1981 and 1991. The proportion who were aged 85 years and over increased by 0.4 percentage points in the intercensal period.

15.14 The proportion of people of pensionable age in 1991 was highest in New Forest (24.7 per cent) and lowest in Hart (12.6 per cent).

15.15 In 1991, the total number of households containing at least one pensioner in Hampshire was 194,381. This was 32.2 per cent of all households in the county, a decrease of 0.9 percentage points over the figure in 1981. New Forest, with 40.9 per cent, was the district with the highest proportion of such households in 1991.

15.16 Of all households in Hampshire in 1991, 23.9 per cent consisted only of pensioners; an increase of 0.9 percentage points since 1981. The district with the highest proportion of households with at least one pensioner and which either lacked or shared basic amenities (bath/shower; inside WC) was Portsmouth, with 3.2 per cent.

Economic characteristics (Table F)

15.17 In Hampshire, 82.0 per cent of men aged 16-64 and 66.2 per cent of women aged 16-59 were in employment (full-time or part-time employees, self-employed, or on a Government scheme) at some time in the week before the Census. This was a fall of 3.6 percentage points for men and a rise of 9.0 percentage points for women since 1981 (using the 1981 population base, and the 1981 definition of students, in each year - see Annex C). At the 1991 Census 7.6 per cent of men and 3.5 per cent of women were unemployed (that is, seeking work, prevented by temporary sickness from seeking work, or waiting to take up a job already accepted). The remaining 10.4 per cent of men and 30.3 per cent of women were economically inactive. (See Annex C for further definitions.)

15.18 The proportion of men aged 16-64 who were economically active but unemployed in the week before the Census in 1991 was highest in Southampton (12.5 per cent) and lowest in Hart (4.4 per cent). The corresponding figures for women were 5.0 per cent in Portsmouth and 2.7 per cent in East Hampshire, Hart, Test Valley and Winchester.

Tenure (Table G)

15.19 The 1991 Census showed that 72.6 per cent of households in Hampshire were living in owner occupied accommodation (either owned outright or buying) and 15.6 per cent in accommodation that was rented from a local authority or new town association. This represents a rise of 10.2 percentage points and a fall of 7.9 percentage points respectively since 1981 (using the 1981 population base in each year - see Annex C). The proportion in owner occupied accommodation ranged from 86.0 per cent in Fareham to 60.9 per cent in Southampton.

Amenities (Table G)

15.20 In the county as a whole, 1.1 per cent of households lacked, or had to share with another household, the use of either a bath/shower or an inside WC. This represented an improvement since 1981 when the figure was 2.3 percentage points higher (using the 1981 population base in each year - see Annex C). The district with the highest proportion of

such households was Portsmouth (2.6 per cent). The lowest proportion was in Basingstoke and Deane, and Test Valley, with 0.5 per cent.

15.21 The 1991 Census showed that 15.7 per cent of households in Hampshire had no central heating in any rooms though over nine-tenths of these had exclusive use of bath/shower and WC. The district with the highest proportion of accommodation without central heating was Portsmouth (36.2 per cent) and the lowest was in Hart with 6.6 per cent.

15.22 Portsmouth had the highest proportion of households with no car available in 1991 (40.0 per cent). Hart had the highest proportion with two or more cars (50.7 per cent). These compare with respective figures of 24.0 per cent and 31.3 per cent for Hampshire as a whole in 1991. Car availability had generally increased since the 1981 Census when the proportion of households with no car was 6.8 percentage points higher, and that with two or more cars 11.6 percentage points lower, than in 1991.

Overcrowding (Table G)

15.23 In 1991, 1.6 per cent of households in the county were living at a density of more than one person per room. This represents a decrease of 0.8 percentage points since 1981 (using the 1981 population base in each year - see Annex C). This figure varied throughout the county from a high of 3.0 per cent in Southampton to 0.9 per cent in Fareham and Hart.

Dwellings (Table H)

15.24 There were 627,550 dwellings in Hampshire in 1991. Of these, 28.4 per cent were detached household spaces, 24.4 per cent semi-detached, and 28.8 per cent terraced housing. 0.3 per cent of dwellings were shared - see Annex C.

Household composition (Table I)

15.25 There were 603,257 households in Hampshire at the 1991 Census. Of these, 13.0 per cent had at least one child aged under 5, 4.6 per cent had three or more children aged under 16, and 24.1 per cent had one person living alone. Compared with the 1981 Census, the proportion of households with a young family had decreased by 0.2 percentage points; the proportion with large families decreased by 0.9 percentage points; and the proportion of single person households increased by 4.0 percentage points (using the 1981 population base in each year - see Annex C). Rushmoor was the district with the highest proportion of households with a young family, while Basingstoke and Deane had the greatest proportion with large families and Portsmouth the largest proportion of single person households.

Limiting long-term illness (Tables E and I)

15.26 A question on long-term illness was asked in the 1991 Census for the first time. Portsmouth had the highest proportion of households containing at least one person with a long-term illness (24.5 per cent) while Hart, with 15.6 per cent, had the lowest. These figures compare with 20.6 per cent for the county as a whole.

15.27   In Hampshire, 10.8 per cent of people had a long-term illness. This figure ranged from 13.9 per cent of persons in Portsmouth, the district with the highest proportion, to 7.3 per cent in Hart, the district with the lowest.

Ethnic group (Table J)

15.28   The 1991 Census included, for the first time, a question on ethnic group. In Hampshire the White group formed 98.1 per cent of the population.

Summary Tables

Explanatory notes for the tables
begin on the first page of
Annex C, after the main tables

Table A Population present 1891 - 1991

Notes: (1) From 1961 to 1991 the figures relate to the county as
constituted at 21 April 1991 and from 1891 to 1951
as closely as is possible.
(2) § Based on preliminary counts (rounded to the nearest
hundred) - see notes.

Date of census	Population present	Intercensal increase or decrease (−)	
		Amount	Per cent per year
1891, April 5/6	562,429		
1901, March 31/April 1	650,796	88,367	1.47
1911, April 2/3	775,302	124,505	1.77
1921, June 19/20	808,677	33,376	0.41
1931, April 26/27	885,252	76,574	0.92
1939, Mid-year estimate	959,647	74,395	0.99
1951, April 8/9	1,030,108	70,461	0.60
1961, April 23/24	1,151,249	121,140	1.11
1971, April 25/26	1,373,713	222,465	1.78
1981, April 5/6	1,459,000 §	85,300 §	0.61
1991, April 21/22	1,523,742	64,800 §	0.43

Table B Population present 1971 - 91

Notes: (1) All figures relate to the areas as constituted at 21 April 1991.
(2) Changes since 1981 are denoted by:
    * boundary
    † name
    # denotes that the district has been granted borough status.
(3) § Based on preliminary counts (rounded to the nearest hundred) - see notes.

Area	Population present							Intercensal increase or decrease (−)		
	1971	1981 §			1991			Amount §	Per cent per year	
	Total persons	Total persons	Males	Females	Total persons	Males	Females	1981 - 1991	1971 - 1981	1981 - 1991
HAMPSHIRE *	**1,373,713**	**1,459,000**	**719,200**	**739,800**	**1,523,742**	**746,383**	**777,359**	**64,800**	**0.61**	**0.43**
Districts										
Basingstoke & Deane *	104,105	130,600	64,300	66,300	141,823	70,179	71,644	11,200	2.31	0.82
East Hampshire *	79,458	89,800	44,500	45,300	101,606	49,701	51,905	11,800	1.24	1.24
Eastleigh *	78,421	92,500	45,700	46,800	103,742	50,904	52,838	11,300	1.67	1.15
Fareham	80,403	88,300	43,800	44,400	97,496	47,795	49,701	9,200	0.94	0.99
Gosport	76,116	77,300	38,500	38,700	73,185	35,502	37,683	− 4,100	0.15	− 0.54
Hart *	58,461	72,200	36,400	35,800	79,083	39,839	39,244	6,900	2.15	0.91
Havant *	109,343	116,700	56,400	60,200	118,078	56,869	61,209	1,400	0.65	0.12
New Forest	130,989	145,100	70,000	75,200	158,898	76,193	82,705	13,800	1.04	0.91
Portsmouth *	197,431	179,400	88,100	91,300	177,142	86,747	90,395	− 2,300	− 0.96	− 0.13
Rushmoor *	78,086	81,500	41,800	39,700	80,850	40,808	40,042	− 700	0.44	− 0.09
Southampton	215,118	204,400	99,900	104,500	195,906	95,868	100,038	− 8,500	− 0.51	− 0.42
Test Valley *	79,920	90,900	45,500	45,300	99,348	49,428	49,920	8,500	1.30	0.89
Winchester *	85,862	90,200	44,000	46,200	96,585	46,550	50,035	6,300	0.50	0.68

Table C   Resident population - 1981 base

Note: The 1981 population base excludes households wholly absent on Census night.

Area	Residents (1981 population base)		Percentage increase or decrease (–) 1981 - 91		
	1981	1991	Total	By births and deaths	Migration and other changes
HAMPSHIRE	**1,443,345**	**1,504,638**	**4.2**	**3.2**	**1.1**
Districts					
Basingstoke & Deane	129,618	141,610	9.3	6.0	3.2
East Hampshire	89,405	101,108	13.1	3.2	9.9
Eastleigh	92,138	103,596	12.4	5.4	7.1
Fareham	87,061	97,309	11.8	3.0	8.8
Gosport	76,757	73,241	– 4.6	6.7	– 11.3
Hart	71,996	79,138	9.9	6.0	3.9
Havant	116,101	117,342	1.1	4.1	– 3.0
New Forest	143,251	156,299	9.1	– 1.7	10.8
Portsmouth	175,382	169,834	– 3.2	1.0	– 4.1
Rushmoor	80,871	80,479	– 0.5	8.8	– 9.3
Southampton	201,989	191,297	– 5.3	2.7	– 8.0
Test Valley	90,211	99,184	9.9	3.1	6.8
Winchester	88,565	94,201	6.4	– 1.5	7.8

Table D   Resident population and area

Note: A hectare is equivalent to 2.471 acres.

Area	Area (hectares)	Persons per hectare	Total persons = 100 per cent	Residents				
				Males	Females	In households	In communal establishments	
							Number	Percentage of total
HAMPSHIRE *	**377,872**	**4.1**	**1,541,547**	**755,484**	**786,063**	**1,512,038**	**29,509**	**1.9**
Districts								
Basingstoke & Deane	63,381	2.3	144,790	71,771	73,019	143,278	1,512	1.0
East Hampshire	51,492	2.0	103,460	50,695	52,765	101,335	2,125	2.1
Eastleigh	7,977	13.3	105,999	52,215	53,784	105,298	701	0.7
Fareham *	7,424	13.4	99,262	48,552	50,710	97,607	1,655	1.7
Gosport *	2,526	29.7	75,061	36,576	38,485	73,704	1,357	1.8
Hart	21,525	3.8	80,921	40,796	40,125	79,014	1,907	2.4
Havant *	5,536	21.6	119,697	57,825	61,872	118,297	1,400	1.2
New Forest *	75,299	2.1	160,456	77,000	83,456	157,604	2,852	1.8
Portsmouth *	4,027	43.4	174,697	84,805	89,892	169,730	4,967	2.8
Rushmoor	3,905	21.1	82,526	41,648	40,878	79,121	3,405	4.1
Southampton	4,984	39.5	196,864	96,382	100,482	193,866	2,998	1.5
Test Valley	63,698	1.6	101,428	50,494	50,934	99,463	1,965	1.9
Winchester	66,098	1.5	96,386	46,725	49,661	93,721	2,665	2.8

* The Ordnance Survey area measurement (hectares) was revised after publication in the County Monitor. The figure in the persons per hectare column has been adjusted as necessary.

Table E Residents by age

Note: The 1981 population base excludes households wholly absent on Census night.

Area	Total persons = 100 per cent	Percentage aged:									75 and over		Percentage of all persons with limiting long-term illness
		0 - 4	5 - 15	16 - 17	18 - 29	30 - 44	45 up to pensionable age	Pensionable age to 74	75 - 84	85 and over	Males	Females	
HAMPSHIRE	**1,541,547**	**6.7**	**13.4**	**2.6**	**18.4**	**21.8**	**19.2**	**11.1**	**5.4**	**1.5**	**2.4**	**4.5**	**10.8**
Districts					*Residents - 1991 population base*								
Basingstoke & Deane	144,790	6.9	14.2	2.7	20.0	23.4	19.3	8.7	3.9	1.0	1.7	3.1	8.6
East Hampshire	103,460	6.6	14.1	2.7	16.7	22.7	20.1	10.2	5.2	1.6	2.4	4.4	9.4
Eastleigh	105,999	6.9	14.1	2.5	17.7	23.7	19.1	10.3	4.4	1.2	2.0	3.6	9.3
Fareham	99,262	6.4	12.9	2.6	16.2	22.7	21.3	11.5	5.2	1.3	2.4	4.2	10.2
Gosport	75,061	7.4	14.0	2.7	20.5	21.6	16.8	10.5	5.2	1.4	2.2	4.4	11.1
Hart	80,921	6.4	14.9	3.0	18.2	24.1	20.7	7.7	3.8	1.1	1.6	3.3	7.3
Havant	119,697	6.8	14.3	2.7	16.5	20.7	20.4	12.1	5.0	1.4	2.2	4.2	12.3
New Forest	160,456	5.7	12.3	2.4	14.6	20.3	19.9	14.7	7.7	2.3	3.7	6.4	12.2
Portsmouth	174,697	7.1	12.0	2.1	21.2	20.0	17.1	12.2	6.5	1.9	2.8	5.6	13.9
Rushmoor	82,526	8.0	13.0	2.5	24.7	22.4	16.2	8.1	4.0	1.1	1.7	3.4	9.0
Southampton	196,864	7.1	12.9	2.3	20.1	20.6	17.9	11.8	5.7	1.5	2.5	4.7	12.7
Test Valley	101,428	6.4	13.9	2.8	17.5	22.8	20.3	10.1	4.8	1.3	2.2	3.9	9.4
Winchester	96,386	5.6	13.2	2.9	15.4	21.7	21.3	11.9	6.1	1.9	2.8	5.2	10.4
Hampshire					*Residents - 1981 population base*								
1981	1,443,345	6.2	16.6	3.6	17.8	20.5	18.7	11.1	4.4	1.1	1.9	3.6	10.8
1991	1,504,638	6.7	13.6	2.6	18.4	21.8	19.1	10.9	5.3	1.5	2.4	4.4	10.8

Table F Economic characteristics

Notes: (1) * 1991 base counts include students who were also in employment, or seeking work, in the week before the Census. 1981 base counts categorise <u>all</u> students as economically inactive.
(2)   The 1981 population base excludes households wholly absent on Census night.

Area	Total males aged 16 - 64 = 100 per cent	Percentage of males aged 16 - 64							
		Economically active*						Economically inactive	Students (economically active or inactive)
		Total	Employees		Self-employed	On a Government scheme	Unemployed		
			Full-time	Part-time					
Residents - 1991 population base									
HAMPSHIRE	**500,537**	**89.6**	**65.4**	**2.3**	**13.5**	**0.8**	**7.6**	**10.4**	**5.3**
Districts									
Basingstoke & Deane	49,376	91.7	70.3	2.0	12.5	0.7	6.2	8.3	4.6
East Hampshire	33,549	89.9	64.0	2.3	18.0	0.6	5.0	10.1	6.2
Eastleigh	34,902	90.8	68.2	2.3	13.7	0.5	6.0	9.2	4.9
Fareham	32,483	90.2	67.9	2.3	13.2	0.9	5.9	9.8	5.2
Gosport	23,987	90.9	70.3	1.9	9.0	1.6	8.1	9.1	4.3
Hart	28,396	91.2	70.0	2.4	13.8	0.6	4.4	8.8	6.4
Havant	37,197	88.5	61.8	2.2	13.4	1.0	10.0	11.5	5.0
New Forest	47,820	88.6	61.0	2.7	17.2	0.6	7.0	11.4	5.0
Portsmouth	55,763	88.5	62.6	2.2	11.3	1.2	11.2	11.5	4.8
Rushmoor	29,050	92.7	73.5	1.7	11.3	0.6	5.6	7.3	3.9
Southampton	63,137	87.1	59.7	2.2	11.6	1.1	12.5	12.9	5.8
Test Valley	33,945	90.8	67.7	2.1	14.8	0.7	5.5	9.2	5.3
Winchester	30,932	87.8	62.8	2.9	16.2	0.7	5.2	12.2	7.3
Residents - 1981 population base									
Hampshire									
1981	461,244	91.6	73.0	1.6	10.2		6.8	8.4	5.3
1991	487,992	88.8	65.3	1.6	13.5	0.8	7.6	11.2	5.3

Total females aged 16 - 59 = 100 per cent	Percentage of females aged 16 - 59								Area
	Economically active*						Economi-cally inactive	Students (economi-cally active or inactive)	
	Total	Employees		Self-employed	On a Government scheme	Unemployed			
		Full-time	Part-time						
454,333	**69.7**	**37.2**	**24.4**	**4.1**	**0.5**	**3.5**	**30.3**	**5.8**	**HAMPSHIRE**
									Districts
45,327	73.7	43.8	22.8	3.7	0.4	3.0	26.3	5.4	Basingstoke & Deane
30,833	69.2	36.2	24.1	5.9	0.4	2.7	30.8	6.5	East Hampshire
31,977	71.7	37.9	26.7	3.7	0.4	2.8	28.3	5.4	Eastleigh
29,714	70.4	37.3	25.5	4.2	0.6	2.9	29.6	5.8	Fareham
22,190	69.7	37.3	24.3	2.8	0.9	4.3	30.3	4.9	Gosport
25,095	69.7	37.0	24.8	4.8	0.3	2.7	30.3	7.2	Hart
35,033	67.2	35.0	24.3	3.4	0.7	3.8	32.8	5.4	Havant
43,989	67.7	32.2	26.5	5.6	0.4	3.0	32.3	5.9	New Forest
49,632	69.2	37.4	23.0	3.1	0.6	5.0	30.8	4.8	Portsmouth
25,223	73.5	44.6	22.2	2.8	0.4	3.5	26.5	4.8	Rushmoor
56,784	67.0	35.2	23.6	2.9	0.6	4.8	33.0	5.6	Southampton
30,346	70.8	37.7	25.1	4.7	0.6	2.7	29.2	5.8	Test Valley
28,190	69.0	34.7	25.1	6.0	0.5	2.7	31.0	8.5	Winchester
414,064	59.5	31.6	22.0	2.5		3.4	40.5	5.7	1981
444,122	68.6	37.0	23.5	4.0	0.5	3.5	31.4	5.8	1991

Table G Tenure and amenities: selected categories

Note: The 1981 population base excludes households wholly absent on Census night.

Area	Total households = 100 per cent	Owner occupied (owned outright or buying)	Rented privately, from a housing association, or with a job	Rented from a local authority or new town	Over 1.0 person per room	Lacking or sharing use of bath/shower and/or inside WC — With central heating	Lacking or sharing use of bath/shower and/or inside WC — No central heating	Exclusive use of bath/shower and inside WC — With central heating	Exclusive use of bath/shower and inside WC — No central heating	No car	2 or more cars
					Households with residents - 1991 population base						
HAMPSHIRE	**603,257**	**72.6**	**11.8**	**15.6**	**1.6**	**0.5**	**0.6**	**83.7**	**15.1**	**24.0**	**31.3**
Districts											
Basingstoke & Deane	54,323	71.1	10.9	18.1	1.4	0.3	0.2	92.0	7.5	19.1	37.6
East Hampshire	39,158	77.9	11.0	11.1	1.5	0.5	0.3	89.2	9.9	15.5	42.3
Eastleigh	41,219	81.4	7.1	11.5	1.1	0.4	0.3	88.1	11.2	17.9	36.3
Fareham	38,369	86.0	6.0	8.0	0.9	0.4	0.2	87.6	11.8	17.4	36.5
Gosport	29,356	70.1	12.5	17.4	1.3	0.4	0.3	81.9	17.4	29.3	20.0
Hart	29,073	81.0	11.0	8.0	0.9	0.3	0.3	93.1	6.3	11.3	50.7
Havant	46,151	72.6	6.1	21.3	2.2	0.6	0.2	78.6	20.5	25.2	28.7
New Forest	65,411	81.0	9.5	9.5	1.1	0.5	0.4	88.5	10.6	18.1	34.3
Portsmouth	72,590	67.1	16.2	16.6	2.0	0.7	1.9	63.1	34.3	40.0	16.1
Rushmoor	30,523	67.0	16.6	16.4	2.0	1.0	0.6	91.4	7.0	21.8	31.4
Southampton	81,140	60.9	15.4	23.8	3.0	1.0	1.1	76.7	21.2	35.3	19.7
Test Valley	38,391	70.4	13.2	16.5	1.0	0.2	0.3	91.5	8.0	18.4	38.0
Winchester	37,553	69.5	14.6	15.9	1.0	0.4	0.4	90.0	9.2	19.4	39.1
					Households with residents - 1981 population base						
Hampshire											
1981	512,524	62.4	13.9	23.7	2.4	3.4		96.6		30.7	20.1
1991	582,749	72.6	11.6	15.8	1.6	0.5	0.6	83.7	15.2	23.9	31.7

Table H Dwellings

Note: No comparable statistics available for 1981.

Area	Total dwellings = 100 per cent	Percentage of dwellings					
		Unshared dwellings					Shared dwellings
		Detached house	Semi-detached house	Terraced house	Purpose-built flat	In converted or partly converted accomm-odation	
HAMPSHIRE	**627,550**	**28.4**	**24.4**	**28.8**	**15.5**	**2.6**	**0.3**
Districts							
Basingstoke & Deane	56,055	31.5	23.1	34.0	10.3	0.9	0.1
East Hampshire	40,479	43.4	24.0	20.2	10.4	1.9	0.1
Eastleigh	42,578	34.9	29.2	23.6	11.2	0.9	0.1
Fareham	39,654	34.4	34.0	21.5	9.5	0.6	0.1
Gosport	31,258	11.4	25.6	41.3	20.5	1.2	0.1
Hart	29,903	46.1	25.5	19.3	8.1	1.0	0.1
Havant	48,043	28.9	24.9	28.9	16.0	1.1	0.1
New Forest	68,872	48.2	22.1	17.3	10.6	1.7	0.1
Portsmouth	76,360	3.3	12.7	52.8	22.8	7.7	0.7
Rushmoor	31,276	16.7	31.6	30.4	18.4	2.4	0.5
Southampton	84,446	14.4	26.9	25.3	28.2	4.4	0.8
Test Valley	39,845	37.7	24.9	26.4	9.3	1.6	0.1
Winchester	38,781	38.8	24.7	22.5	11.2	2.6	0.1

Table I Household composition: selected categories

Notes: (1) * See introductory notes for the definition of a 'dependant'.
(2) The 1981 population base excludes households wholly absent on Census night.

Area	Total households = 100 per cent	Percentage of households with:					
		Child(ren) aged under 5	3 or more children aged under 16	Only 1 person aged 16 or over with child(ren) aged 0 - 15	1 person living alone	1 or more person(s) with limiting long-term illness	Only 'dependants' *
Households with residents - 1991 population base							
HAMPSHIRE	**603,257**	**13.0**	**4.6**	**3.0**	**24.1**	**20.6**	**6.6**
Districts							
Basingstoke & Deane	54,323	14.0	5.1	2.5	20.3	17.4	5.2
East Hampshire	39,158	13.3	4.9	2.4	21.6	18.2	5.2
Eastleigh	41,219	13.6	4.6	2.6	21.6	18.3	5.6
Fareham	38,369	12.7	4.0	2.2	20.4	19.2	5.6
Gosport	29,356	14.6	4.9	3.7	23.4	21.5	7.0
Hart	29,073	13.5	5.0	2.0	18.7	15.6	4.2
Havant	46,151	13.4	5.4	3.8	22.6	23.8	7.4
New Forest	65,411	10.7	3.7	2.3	24.8	22.1	7.0
Portsmouth	72,590	13.0	4.2	4.0	30.3	24.5	9.1
Rushmoor	30,523	16.2	4.8	3.4	21.5	18.0	5.6
Southampton	81,140	13.0	5.0	4.2	29.8	23.3	8.1
Test Valley	38,391	13.0	4.5	2.6	21.1	18.7	5.5
Winchester	37,553	10.9	4.4	1.8	24.9	19.4	6.3
Households with residents - 1981 population base							
Hampshire							
1981	512,524	13.4	5.6	2.0	19.2		
1991	582,749	13.2	4.7	3.0	23.2	20.7	6.6

Table J Ethnic group of residents

Note: No comparable statistics available for 1981.

Area	Total persons = 100 per cent	Ethnic group - percentage									
		White	Black Carib-bean	Black African	Black other	Indian	Pakis-tani	Bangla-deshi	Chinese	Other groups	
										Asian	Other
HAMPSHIRE	**1,541,547**	**98.1**	**0.2**	**0.1**	**0.2**	**0.5**	**0.1**	**0.1**	**0.2**	**0.2**	**0.3**
Districts											
Basingstoke & Deane	144,790	97.8	0.4	0.1	0.3	0.5	0.1	0.1	0.2	0.2	0.4
East Hampshire	103,460	99.0	0.1	0.1	0.1	0.1	0.0	0.1	0.1	0.1	0.2
Eastleigh	105,999	98.4	0.1	0.0	0.1	0.7	0.0	0.1	0.3	0.1	0.2
Fareham	99,262	99.1	0.1	0.0	0.1	0.2	0.0	0.0	0.2	0.1	0.2
Gosport	75,061	98.9	0.1	0.1	0.1	0.1	0.0	0.1	0.2	0.1	0.2
Hart	80,921	97.9	0.1	0.1	0.1	0.2	0.0	0.1	0.2	1.0	0.3
Havant	119,697	99.1	0.1	0.1	0.1	0.2	0.0	0.1	0.2	0.1	0.2
New Forest	160,456	99.3	0.0	0.0	0.1	0.1	0.0	0.0	0.1	0.1	0.2
Portsmouth	174,697	97.4	0.1	0.1	0.2	0.4	0.0	0.6	0.4	0.2	0.5
Rushmoor	82,526	97.4	0.4	0.1	0.2	0.4	0.3	0.0	0.3	0.3	0.4
Southampton	196,864	95.1	0.4	0.2	0.3	2.0	0.5	0.3	0.4	0.3	0.6
Test Valley	101,428	98.9	0.1	0.0	0.1	0.3	0.0	0.0	0.2	0.1	0.2
Winchester	96,386	99.0	0.1	0.0	0.1	0.1	0.0	0.1	0.1	0.2	0.3

Table K Young adults: selected categories

Notes: (1) * 1991 base counts include students who were also in employment, or seeking work, in the week before the Census. 1981 base counts categorise <u>all</u> students as economically inactive.
(2) The 1981 population base excludes households wholly absent on Census night.

Area	Total persons aged 16 - 24 in households = 100 per cent	Percentage of persons aged 16 - 24 in households who are:					
		Married	The only adult in household with child(ren) aged 0 - 15	Students (economically active or inactive)	Economically active*	On a Government scheme	Unemployed*
Residents - 1991 population base							
HAMPSHIRE	**190,983**	**11.5**	**1.5**	**25.4**	**72.6**	**1.9**	**8.9**
Districts							
Basingstoke & Deane	19,722	10.9	0.7	23.0	76.0	1.5	7.4
East Hampshire	12,048	9.6	0.8	32.5	67.6	1.4	6.4
Eastleigh	12,774	11.8	0.9	25.7	74.5	1.7	7.1
Fareham	11,260	8.8	0.8	28.7	72.8	2.4	7.8
Gosport	9,837	19.3	1.9	20.0	75.6	3.1	9.5
Hart	10,351	7.2	0.4	33.8	69.0	1.1	6.3
Havant	14,496	9.7	2.0	24.4	71.8	2.5	10.8
New Forest	16,736	10.3	1.2	28.1	71.5	1.7	8.1
Portsmouth	22,653	13.6	2.2	19.3	75.3	2.2	12.1
Rushmoor	11,277	17.0	1.8	19.1	76.8	1.1	7.2
Southampton	26,388	12.6	2.8	21.6	72.5	2.4	12.7
Test Valley	12,403	11.2	1.2	27.5	71.9	1.6	6.7
Winchester	11,038	6.9	0.8	38.5	63.7	1.5	7.1
Residents - 1981 population base							
Hampshire							
1981	195,663	22.7		23.0	68.8		8.3
1991	186,966	11.4	1.5	25.5	68.0	1.9	8.8

Table L Pensioners: selected categories

Note: The 1981 population base excludes households wholly absent on Census night.

Area	All households			Households with pensioners				
	Total households = 100 per cent	Percentage with:		Total households = 100 per cent	Total pensioners	Percentage of households which:		
		1 pensioner living alone	2 or more pensioners and no other person(s)			Lack or share use of bath/ shower and/or inside WC	Have no central heating	Have no car
Households and residents - 1991 population base								
HAMPSHIRE	**603,257**	**13.8**	**10.1**	**194,381**	**264,449**	**1.4**	**20.2**	**45.7**
Districts								
Basingstoke & Deane	54,323	10.4	7.9	14,021	19,003	0.6	11.0	45.0
East Hampshire	39,158	13.0	10.0	12,192	16,684	1.5	14.5	35.9
Eastleigh	41,219	11.8	9.4	11,943	16,375	1.0	15.7	42.9
Fareham	38,369	12.3	11.0	12,172	16,962	1.3	16.9	39.9
Gosport	29,356	14.2	9.5	9,175	12,362	1.3	22.0	51.9
Hart	29,073	9.9	7.6	7,237	9,776	0.7	12.0	33.7
Havant	46,151	13.7	11.0	15,618	21,396	1.3	21.5	43.2
New Forest	65,411	16.6	15.1	26,773	37,783	1.3	12.2	33.6
Portsmouth	72,590	16.9	9.9	25,502	33,837	3.2	43.7	62.1
Rushmoor	30,523	11.0	7.1	7,707	10,269	1.3	11.8	48.1
Southampton	81,140	15.6	9.5	27,089	36,102	1.4	26.6	57.7
Test Valley	38,391	12.4	9.5	11,575	15,801	0.8	12.9	40.2
Winchester	37,553	15.7	11.0	13,377	18,099	1.0	12.6	39.8
Households and residents - 1981 population base								
Hampshire								
1981	512,524	12.7	10.1	169,158	230,991	5.4		54.0
1991	582,749	13.6	10.1	186,926	254,717	1.4	20.4	45.8

Tables by key word title

Summary tables

A   Population present 1891-1991
B   Population present 1971-91
C   Resident population 1981 base
D   Resident population and area
E   Residents by age
F   Economic characteristics
G   Tenure and amenities: selected categories
H   Dwellings
I   Household composition: selected categories
J   Ethnic group of residents
K   Young adults: selected categories
L   Pensioners: selected categories
M   Born in Wales/Welsh speakers (Wales only)

Main tables (Part 1)

I   *Demographic and Economic characteristics*

1   Population bases
2   Age and marital status
3   Communal establishments
4   Medical and care establishments
5   Hotels and other establishments

6   Ethnic group
7   Country of birth
8   Economic position
9   Economic position and ethnic group
10   Term-time address

11   Persons present
12   Long-term illness in households
13   Long-term illness in communal establishments
14   Long-term illness and economic position

15   Migrants
16   Wholly moving households
17   Ethnic group of migrants
18   Imputed residents

II   *Housing*

19   Imputed households
20   Tenure and amenities
21   Car availability
22   Rooms and household size
23   Persons per room

24   Residents 18 and over
25   Visitor households
26   Students in households
27   Households: 1971/81/91 bases

III   *Households and household composition*

28   Dependants in households
29   Dependants and long-term illness
30   'Carers'
31   Dependent children in households
32   Children aged 0-15 in households

33   Women in 'couples': economic position
34   Economic position of household residents
35   Age and marital status of household residents
36   'Earners' and dependent children
37   Young adults

38   Single years of age
39   Headship
40   Lone 'parents'
41   Shared accommodation
42   Household composition and housing

43   Household composition and ethnic group
44   Household composition and long-term illness
45   Migrant household heads
46   Households with dependent children: housing
47   Households with pensioners: housing

48   Households with dependants: housing
49   Ethnic group: housing
50   Country of birth: household heads and residents
51   Country of birth and ethnic group
52   Language indicators
53   'Lifestages'

IV   *Household spaces and dwellings*

54   Occupancy (occupied, vacant and other accommodation)
55   Household spaces and occupancy
56   Household space type and occupancy
57   Household space type: rooms and household size
58   Household space type: tenure and amenities

59   Household space type: household composition
60   Dwellings and household spaces
61   Dwelling type and occupancy
62   Occupancy and tenure of dwellings

63   Dwelling type and tenure
64   Tenure of dwellings and household spaces
65   Occupancy of dwellings and household spaces
66   Shared dwellings

Topic and key word index (Part 1)

The numerical and alpha references in this index refer to county report and summary tables respectively

Absent residents
    in households *1*
    students *10*
    imputed *18, 19*

Absent households *19*

Adults
    amenities in households *42*
    economically active *36, 37*
    ethnic group of head of household *43*
    in employment *36*
    in household with long-term illness *44*
    tenure of household *46*
    unemployed *37*
    with/without (dependent) children *31, 36, 37, 42, 43,*
      46, 59

Age
    all residents *2, 52, (E)*
    'carers' *30*
    children aged 0-15 *32, 40*
    country of birth *50, 52*
    dependants *28-30, 48*
    dependent children *31, 46, 68*
    economic position *8, 14*
    ethnic group *6, 43*
    head of household *39, 45, 53*
    headship *39*
    imputed residents *18*
    in communal establishments (not in households) *4, 5,*
      11, 13
    lifestage *53*
    long-term illness *12-14, 44, (E)*
    marital status *2, 35, 37, 39*
    migrants *15, 45*
    non-dependants *30*
    not in households *4, 5, 11, 13, 67*
    pensioners *47, (E)*
    persons present *11, 13*
    single years of age *38*
    students *10*
    Welsh speakers (Wales only) *67*
    young adults *37*
    1981/1991 population base *(E)*

Amenities
    ethnic group of head of household *49*
    household composition *42*
    household space type *58*
    households with dependants *48*
    households with dependent children *46*
    households with pensioners *47, (L)*
    imputed households *19*
    no car *20*
    non permanent accommodation *20*
    selected categories *(G)*

Amenities - *continued*
    shared accommodation *41*
    student households *26*
    tenure *20*
    visitor households *25*
    1981/1991 population base *(G)*

Area (hectares) *(D)*

Availability of cars - see *Car availability*

Bath/shower - see *Amenities*

Bedsit - see *Household space type*

Born
    in Ireland *6, 7, 9, 17, 43, 50, 51*
    in New Commonwealth *7, 50-52*
    in Scotland *7, 50, 51, (M)*
    in UK *6, 7, 50, 51*
    in Wales *7, 50, 51, 67, (M)*
    outside UK *7, 10, 50, 51*

Campers *3, 5*

Car availability
    no car
        amenities *20*
        ethnic group of head of household *49*
        household composition *42*
        households with dependants *48*
        households with dependent children *46*
        household with pensioners *47, (L)*
        imputed households *19*
        number of persons aged 17 and over in household
         21
        shared accommodation *41*
        tenure *20*
    number of cars *21*
    total cars *21, 25, 26*
    two or more cars *42, (G)*
    1981/1991 population base *(G)*

'Carers' *30*

Central heating - see *Amenities*

Communal establishments *3-5, 13*

Converted flat - see *Household space type*

Converted/shared accommodation - see *Dwelling type*

New Commonwealth head of household *49-52*

No car - see *Car availability*

No central heating - see *Amenities*

Non-dependants *28-30, 48*

Non-permanent accommodation
    amenities *20, 58*
    household composition *59*
    household size *57*
    number of rooms *57*
    occupancy type *56, 61*
    persons per room *23, 57*
    tenure *58, 63*

Not in households
    age *4, 5, 11*
    economic activity *5*
    ethnic group *4, 5*
    long-term illness *4, 13*
    migrants *4, 5*
    non-staff *4, 5*
    persons of pensionable age *4, 5*
    persons present *3, 11*
    residents *1, 4, 5, (D)*
    staff *11*
    students *10*
    type of establishment *3-5*
    visitors (not resident) *1, 3*
    Welsh language (Wales only) *67*

Not self-contained/shared accommodation
    amenities *58*
    dependants *48*
    dwelling type *60*
    ethnic group of head of household *49*
    household composition *42, 47, 59*
    household size *41, 57*
    household spaces in shared dwellings *66*
    households with dependent children *46, 59*
    no car *41*
    number of rooms *41, 57*
    occupancy type *56, 61, 65*
    pensioners *47, 59*
    persons per room *41, 57*
    students *26*
    tenure *58, 63, 64*
    visitor households *25*

Number of persons in household (household size)
    amenities *41, 42, 48*
    ethnic group of head of household *43*
    household space type *57*
    imputed households *19*
    in employment *28, 36, 44*
    in shared accommodation *41*
    number of dependants/non-dependants *29, 30*
    number of persons aged 18 and over *24*
    number of rooms *22*
    number of students *26*
    tenure *22, 42*

Number of persons in household (household size) - *continued*
    with migrant head *57*
    1971/81/91 population bases *27*

Occupancy type
    dwellings *61, 62, 64, 65*
    household spaces *54-56, 65*
    household space type *56, 61*
    rooms *54*
    tenure *62, 64*

On a Government scheme - see *Government scheme, on a*

Owner occupied - see *Tenure*

Part-time employees - see *Economic position*

Permanently sick *8, 9, 14, 34*

Persons aged
    17 and over *21*
    18 and over *24*

Persons of pensionable age
    age *43, 47, 50, 53, 59, (E)*
    'carers' *30*
    country of birth *50, 52*
    dependants *28, 30*
    ethnic group of head of household *43*
    household space type *59*
    housing characteristics *47, 48, (L)*
    imputed residents *18*
    migrant head of household *59*
    no car *47, 48*
    with long-term illness *14, 47*
    1981/1991 population base *(E), (L)*

Persons per hectare *(D)*

Persons per room
    ethnic group of head of household *49*
    household composition *42, 46-48*
    household size *41*
    household space type *57*
    households with migrant head *57*
    non-permanent accommodation *23*
    not self-contained accommodation *41*
    tenure *23*
    1981/1991 population base *(G)*

Persons present
    in households *1, 11, 25-27*
    not in households *1, 3, 11, 13*
    1891-1991 *(A)*
    1971-1991 *(B)*

Persons sleeping rough *3, 5*

Population bases *1, 27*

Present residents *1, 3-5, 11, 13*

Full table titles

The following notes describe how to interpret the titles, which are constructed in standard forms. Titles of simple tables which are generally a *cross-tabulation* with a single variable in the rows, but possibly have more than one variable in the columns, follow the form:

(row variable) "by" (column variable(s))

Table 7 is an example.

Titles of tables with more than one variable in the rows have the general form:

(row variables) "all by" (column variable(s))

Where cross-tabulations share a common set of total counts, this 'concatenation' is separated by a comma. Different tabulations *within* a table are separated by a semi-colon (for example, where a set of counts shares only the same population base but no common variables). Table 47 illustrates these features:

An example of a complex table illustrates these features.

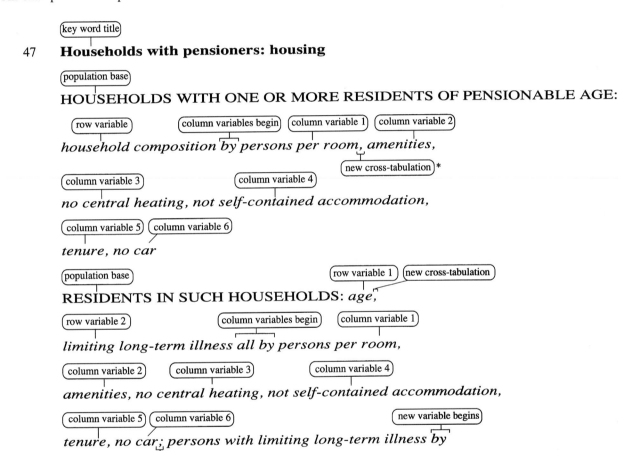

* refers to all commas

Where row or column variables are 'nested', that is where one variable is broken down by another along one axis of a table, they are separated by the word "by". Where this 'nesting' occurs in the rows axis, the 'nested' variables will be followed by "all by". Table 73 illustrates these features:

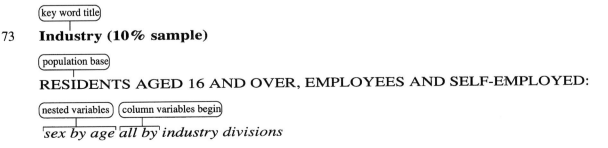

383

Main tables (Part 1)

I Demographic and Economic characteristics

Main tables (Part 1) - *continued*

Main tables (Part 1) - *continued*

Main tables (Part 1) - *continued*

III *Households and household composition*

Main tables (Part 1) - *continued*

Main tables (Part 1) - *continued*

IV *Household spaces and dwellings*

Main tables (Part 1) - *continued*

V *Wales only tables*

Main Tables (Part 2)

VI *10 per cent topics*

Page numbers for tables are given in Part 2 of the report published separately and later.

Main tables (Part 2) - *continued*

74 **Occupation (10% sample)**

RESIDENTS AGED 16 AND OVER, EMPLOYEES AND SELF-EMPLOYED: *Standard Occupational Classification sub-major groups by sex, by age*

75 **Hours worked (10% sample)**

RESIDENTS AGED 16 AND OVER, EMPLOYEES AND SELF-EMPLOYED: *sex, by age, sex by marital status, limiting long-term illness by sex all by hours worked weekly*

76 **Occupation and industry (10% sample)**

RESIDENTS AGED 16 AND OVER, EMPLOYEES AND SELF-EMPLOYED: *Standard Occupational Classification sub-major groups, working outside district of usual residence all by industry divisions, working outside district of usual residence*

77 **Industry and hours worked (10% sample)**

RESIDENTS AGED 16 AND OVER, EMPLOYEES AND SELF-EMPLOYED: *hours worked weekly by industry divisions*

78 **Occupation and hours worked (10% sample)**

RESIDENTS AGED 16 AND OVER, EMPLOYEES AND SELF-EMPLOYED: *Standard Occupational Classification sub-major groups, working outside district of usual residence all by hours worked weekly*

79 **Industry and employment status (10% sample)**

RESIDENTS AGED 16 AND OVER, EMPLOYEES AND SELF-EMPLOYED: *sex, by employment status all by industry divisions*

80 **Working parents: hours worked (10% sample)**

WOMEN IN COUPLE FAMILIES AND LONE PARENTS IN EMPLOYMENT: *family composition by hours worked weekly*

81 **Occupation and employment status (10% sample)**

RESIDENTS AGED 16 AND OVER, EMPLOYEES AND SELF-EMPLOYED: *sex, by employment status all by Standard Occupational Classification major groups*

82 **Travel to work and SEG (10% sample)**

RESIDENTS AGED 16 AND OVER, EMPLOYEES AND SELF-EMPLOYED: *socio-economic group, working outside district of usual residence, car availability by means of transport to work, working outside district of usual residence*

83 **Travel to work and car availability (10% sample)**

HOUSEHOLDS WITH RESIDENTS AGED 16 AND OVER, EMPLOYEES AND SELF-EMPLOYED: *car availability by number of resident employees or self-employed aged 16 and over by means of transport to work*

84 **Qualified manpower (10% sample)**

RESIDENTS AGED 18 AND OVER: *level of highest qualification, by age, economic position all by sex*

Main tables (Part 2) - *continued*

85 **Ethnic group of qualified manpower (10% sample)**

RESIDENTS AGED 16 AND OVER: *whether qualified, by age, economic position all by ethnic group, born in Ireland*

86 **SEG of households and families (10% sample)**

HOUSEHOLDS WITH RESIDENTS: *socio-economic group by tenure, migrant head of household, no car*
RESIDENTS IN HOUSEHOLDS: *total, economically active, dependent children all by tenure, migrant head of household, no car, in families, in lone parent with dependent child(ren) families; socio-economic group by economically active, dependent children, adults with limiting long-term illness*
FAMILIES OF RESIDENT PERSONS: *socio-economic group by total, lone parent families with dependent child(ren) by socio-economic group*

87 **Family type and tenure (10% sample)**

HOUSEHOLDS WITH RESIDENTS: *household and family composition by tenure, migrant head of household, car availability*
RESIDENTS IN HOUSEHOLDS: *dependent children aged 0-17 in lone parent families by tenure, migrant head of household, car availability; household and family composition by total, dependent children*

88 **'Concealed' families (10% sample)**

FAMILIES OF RESIDENT PERSONS: *family composition by age of head of household; composition of concealed families by age of head of family*

89 **Family composition (10% sample)**

FAMILIES OF RESIDENT PERSONS: *family composition, in households with two or more families by type of family*

90 **Social class of households (10% sample)**

HOUSEHOLDS WITH RESIDENTS: *social class based on occupation of household head, household head on a Government scheme, economic position of economically inactive heads*
RESIDENTS IN HOUSEHOLDS: *social class based on occupation of household head, household head on a Government scheme, economic position of economically inactive heads all by age, females in couples*

91 **Social class and economic position (10% sample)**

RESIDENTS AGED 16 AND OVER IN HOUSEHOLDS: *social class based on occupation, on a Government scheme, economic position of the economically inactive all by economic position, by sex, females in a couple*

92 **SEG and economic position (10% sample)**

ECONOMICALLY ACTIVE RESIDENTS: *socio-economic group, on a Government scheme all by economic position by sex , migrants, by sex*

93 **SEG, social class and ethnic group (10% sample)**

RESIDENTS AGED 16 AND OVER, EMPLOYEES AND SELF-EMPLOYED: *socio-economic group, social class based on occupation all by ethnic group, born in Ireland*

Main tables (Part 2) - *continued*

94 **Former industry of unemployed (10% sample)**

RESIDENTS ON A GOVERNMENT SCHEME OR UNEMPLOYED: *sex, by industry division of most recent job in last 10 years*

95 **Former occupation of unemployed (10% sample)**

RESIDENTS ON A GOVERNMENT SCHEME OR UNEMPLOYED: *sex by Standard Occupational Classification major group of most recent job in last 10 years*

96 **Armed forces (10% sample)**

RESIDENT ARMED FORCES, IN EMPLOYMENT: *age by whether in households by sex; age of migrants by type of move by whether in households*

97 **Armed forces: households (10% sample)**

RESIDENTS IN HOUSEHOLDS WITH HEAD IN EMPLOYMENT IN ARMED FORCES: *household heads: age, migrants all by marital status by sex; all persons: age, migrants all by marital status, by sex*

98 **Occupation orders: 1980 classification (10% sample)**

RESIDENTS AGED 16 AND OVER, EMPLOYEES AND SELF-EMPLOYED: *1980 occupation orders by sex*

99 **Occupation: Standard Occupational Classification (10% sample)**

RESIDENTS AGED 16 AND OVER, EMPLOYEES AND SELF EMPLOYED: *Standard Occupational Classification minor groups by sex*

Main Tables (28-66)

Explanatory notes for tables appear in Annex C, after the tables. Notes are in the numerical order of the tables.

Table 28 Dependants in households

28. Households with residents; residents in households

Household composition	TOTAL HOUSE-HOLDS	No non-dependants	1 male non-dependant		1 female non-dependant		1 male and 1 female non-dependants		
			Not in employment	In employment	Not in employment	In employment	Neither in employment	1 in employment	Both in employment
a	b	c	d	e	f	g	h	i	j

HAMPSHIRE

TOTAL HOUSEHOLDS	603,257	39,977	21,469	37,843	74,670	33,555	46,717	85,943	154,142
Households with no dependants	340,397		15,214	31,059	47,984	21,396	38,706	33,075	82,516
Households with 1 dependant									
Age of dependant									
0 - 4	28,257	12	54	94	2,440	849	1,349	11,124	9,319
5 - 15	32,783	14	184	453	1,759	2,327	702	4,020	10,162
16 - 18	10,647	55	50	215	200	535	151	1,028	2,639
19 up to pensionable age	16,819	4,016	757	1,968	3,410	2,053	466	904	791
Pensionable age and over	49,345	25,570	4,535	2,186	11,316	1,683	441	1,118	672
Households with at least 2 dependants									
Age of youngest dependant 0 - 4 and age of oldest									
0 - 4	16,075	6	23	37	1,050	135	1,054	8,547	4,408
5 - 15	31,738	7	71	80	2,696	641	2,092	13,416	10,443
16 - 18	1,016	2	3	2	80	23	66	280	220
19 up to pensionable age	1,235	54	50	205	399	69	36	81	33
Pensionable age and over	338	3	2	5	28	10	22	74	64
Age of youngest dependant 5 - 15 and age of oldest									
5 - 15	47,336	15	185	398	1,993	2,532	1,254	9,720	26,345
16 - 18	10,671	7	26	124	280	536	224	1,948	5,429
19 up to pensionable age	2,188	193	84	385	453	310	43	139	144
Pensionable age and over	892	27	11	21	89	62	35	142	242
Age of youngest dependant 16 - 18 and age of oldest									
16 - 18	1,043	3	3	16	22	61	12	170	527
19 up to pensionable age	475	44	14	73	69	58	8	46	39
Pensionable age and over	195	18	3	8	15	13	5	19	43
Age of youngest dependant 19 up to pensionable age and age of oldest									
19 up to pensionable age	990	588	32	86	71	43	21	33	32
Pensionable age and over	1,822	1,251	53	110	169	82	11	31	22
Age of youngest dependant pensionable age and over	8,995	8,092	115	318	147	137	19	28	52
TOTAL PERSONS	1,512,038	50,847	28,716	47,161	113,027	51,757	109,622	274,097	441,384
Persons in households with dependants									
Non-dependants	435,950		6,255	6,784	26,686	12,159	16,022	105,736	143,252
Dependants	430,937	50,847	7,247	9,318	38,357	18,202	16,188	102,211	133,100

2 same sex non-dependants			3 or more non-dependants			Household composition
Neither in employment	1 in employment	Both in employment	None in employment	1 in employment	2 or more in employment	
k	l	m	n	o	p	a
2,751	**6,019**	**9,020**	**2,487**	**10,558**	**78,106**	**TOTAL HOUSEHOLDS**
1,851	3,701	6,791	1,629	6,742	49,733	Households with no dependants
						Households with 1 dependant
						Age of dependant
100	226	108	108	449	2,025	0 - 4
122	315	519	158	823	11,225	5 - 15
31	145	179	63	541	4,815	16 - 18
115	458	516	66	233	1,066	19 up to pensionable age
169	493	253	43	128	738	Pensionable age and over
						Households with at least 2 dependants
						Age of youngest dependant 0 - 4 and age of oldest
35	57	36	52	146	489	0 - 4
100	160	79	123	421	1,409	5 - 15
9	17	2	21	68	223	16 - 18
27	29	12	29	71	140	19 up to pensionable age
8	8	5	11	22	76	Pensionable age and over
						Age of youngest dependant 5 - 15 and age of oldest
71	193	250	102	470	3,808	5 - 15
19	50	75	35	282	1,636	16 - 18
31	83	89	19	50	165	19 up to pensionable age
10	16	6	5	35	191	Pensionable age and over
						Age of youngest dependant 16 - 18 and age of oldest
4	5	5	6	34	175	16 - 18
11	17	35	7	15	39	19 up to pensionable age
3	3	3	-	7	55	Pensionable age and over
						Age of youngest dependant 19 up to pensionable age and age of oldest
14	12	16	6	8	28	19 up to pensionable age
12	14	16	4	10	37	Pensionable age and over
						Age of youngest dependant pensionable age and over
9	17	25	-	3	33	
6,978	**15,327**	**21,089**	**9,591**	**39,590**	**302,852**	**TOTAL PERSONS**
						Persons in households with dependants
1,800	4,636	4,458	2,768	12,107	93,287	Non-dependants
1,476	3,289	3,049	1,602	6,344	39,707	Dependants

Table 28   Dependants in households – **continued**

28. Households with residents; residents in households

Household composition	TOTAL HOUSE-HOLDS	No non-dependants	1 male non-dependant		1 female non-dependant		1 male and 1 female non-dependants		
			Not in employment	In employment	Not in employment	In employment	Neither in employment	1 in employment	Both in employment
a	b	c	d	e	f	g	h	i	j

Basingstoke & Deane

TOTAL HOUSEHOLDS	54,323	2,807	1,346	3,567	4,786	2,987	3,207	7,837	16,628
Households with no dependants	30,576		909	2,985	3,092	1,948	2,650	2,784	9,052
Households with 1 dependant									
Age of dependant									
0 - 4	2,740	-	1	8	128	82	80	1,133	987
5 - 15	3,229	1	5	39	115	211	42	382	1,024
16 - 18	1,078	2	6	16	12	49	12	75	276
19 up to pensionable age	1,247	254	50	173	207	171	46	62	62
Pensionable age and over	3,472	1,810	331	183	690	117	30	95	57
Households with at least 2 dependants									
Age of youngest dependant 0 - 4 and age of oldest									
0 - 4	1,553	-	2	4	65	7	63	824	499
5 - 15	3,082	1	4	7	220	77	165	1,263	1,095
16 - 18	92	-	1	-	11	4	3	22	23
19 up to pensionable age	101	2	6	16	21	7	3	5	4
Pensionable age and over	25	-	-	-	1	1	4	3	7
Age of youngest dependant 5 - 15 and age of oldest									
5 - 15	4,755	-	11	31	135	203	82	923	2,872
16 - 18	1,106	2	3	14	21	49	22	204	563
19 up to pensionable age	175	13	2	37	25	27	1	14	16
Pensionable age and over	87	5	-	3	5	3	1	16	28
Age of youngest dependant 16 - 18 and age of oldest									
16 - 18	105	-	-	2	4	5	-	19	55
19 up to pensionable age	33	1	-	9	3	5	-	4	1
Pensionable age and over	12	1	-	-	-	1	-	1	3
Age of youngest dependant 19 up to pensionable age and age of oldest									
19 up to pensionable age	65	43	1	5	6	3	2	2	1
Pensionable age and over	134	90	4	11	13	7	1	1	-
Age of youngest dependant pensionable age and over	656	582	10	24	12	10	-	5	3
TOTAL PERSONS	143,278	3,594	1,853	4,381	7,347	4,551	7,570	25,446	47,484
Persons in households with dependants									
Non-dependants	42,678		437	582	1,694	1,039	1,114	10,106	15,152
Dependants	39,918	3,594	507	814	2,561	1,564	1,156	9,772	14,228

2 same sex non-dependants			3 or more non-dependants			Household composition
Neither in employment	1 in employment	Both in employment	None in employment	1 in employment	2 or more in employment	
k	l	m	n	o	p	a
159	**467**	**901**	**142**	**879**	**8,610**	**TOTAL HOUSEHOLDS**
102	271	692	84	539	5,468	Households with no dependants
						Households with 1 dependant
						Age of dependant
5	13	14	2	33	254	0 - 4
10	30	46	10	71	1,243	5 - 15
2	10	23	4	47	544	16 - 18
7	33	51	2	15	114	19 up to pensionable age
8	45	20	5	16	65	Pensionable age and over
						Households with at least 2 dependants
						Age of youngest dependant 0 - 4 and age of oldest
2	7	2	9	17	52	0 - 4
9	13	8	8	41	171	5 - 15
1	-	-	1	4	22	16 - 18
2	5	1	3	3	23	19 up to pensionable age
1	1	-	-	1	6	Pensionable age and over
						Age of youngest dependant 5 - 15 and age of oldest
5	16	22	10	45	400	5 - 15
1	2	8	-	37	180	16 - 18
3	10	5	2	3	17	19 up to pensionable age
-	2	1	2	1	20	Pensionable age and over
						Age of youngest dependant 16 - 18 and age of oldest
-	1	-	-	4	15	16 - 18
-	3	2	-	1	4	19 up to pensionable age
-	1	-	-	-	5	Pensionable age and over
						Age of youngest dependant 19 up to pensionable age and age of oldest
-	-	1	-	-	1	19 up to pensionable age
-	2	1	-	1	3	Pensionable age and over
						Age of youngest dependant pensionable age and over
1	2	4	-	-	3	
417	**1,222**	**2,080**	**561**	**3,322**	**33,450**	**TOTAL PERSONS**
						Persons in households with dependants
114	392	418	186	1,076	10,368	Non-dependants
99	288	278	115	581	4,361	Dependants

Table 28 Dependants in households – **continued**

28. Households with residents; residents in households

Household composition	TOTAL HOUSE-HOLDS	No non-dependants	1 male non-dependant		1 female non-dependant		1 male and 1 female non-dependants		
			Not in employment	In employment	Not in employment	In employment	Neither in employment	1 in employment	Both in employment
a	b	c	d	e	f	g	h	i	j

East Hampshire

Household composition	b	c	d	e	f	g	h	i	j
TOTAL HOUSEHOLDS	39,158	2,024	1,090	2,214	4,432	2,060	2,902	6,159	11,238
Households with no dependants	22,141		765	1,820	2,993	1,334	2,532	2,301	5,885
Households with 1 dependant									
Age of dependant									
0 - 4	1,746	1	6	6	115	48	53	748	626
5 - 15	2,162	1	10	33	63	119	34	302	722
16 - 18	849	-	-	16	9	32	10	95	233
19 up to pensionable age	775	157	27	92	177	108	20	45	40
Pensionable age and over	2,798	1,372	242	114	732	95	20	61	51
Households with at least 2 dependants									
Age of youngest dependant 0 - 4 and age of oldest									
0 - 4	1,110	-	1	3	27	3	59	631	324
5 - 15	2,192	1	3	6	117	42	90	1,003	790
16 - 18	78	-	-	-	3	2	4	30	13
19 up to pensionable age	50	-	1	17	17	1	1	7	1
Pensionable age and over	24	-	-	1	3	-	1	6	5
Age of youngest dependant 5 - 15 and age of oldest									
5 - 15	3,400	4	10	33	105	179	62	706	1,964
16 - 18	919	-	1	14	15	45	11	180	486
19 up to pensionable age	114	7	4	26	22	20	1	5	9
Pensionable age and over	64	3	1	2	7	2	-	9	19
Age of youngest dependant 16 - 18 and age of oldest									
16 - 18	100	1	-	3	1	6	2	20	46
19 up to pensionable age	36	1	2	4	5	5	-	5	9
Pensionable age and over	15	1	-	-	-	-	-	2	7
Age of youngest dependant 19 up to pensionable age and age of oldest									
19 up to pensionable age	44	23	4	3	2	5	-	2	2
Pensionable age and over	83	51	5	3	6	5	2	1	2
Age of youngest dependant pensionable age and over	458	401	8	18	13	9	-	-	4
TOTAL PERSONS	101,335	2,547	1,469	2,791	6,403	3,198	6,551	19,912	32,599
Persons in households with dependants									
Non-dependants	29,949		325	394	1,439	726	740	7,716	10,706
Dependants	28,711	2,547	379	577	1,971	1,138	747	7,594	10,123

2 same sex non-dependants			3 or more non-dependants			Household composition
Neither in employment	1 in employment	Both in employment	None in employment	1 in employment	2 or more in employment	
k	l	m	n	o	p	a
132	346	495	127	687	5,252	**TOTAL HOUSEHOLDS**
97	207	363	82	439	3,323	Households with no dependants
						Households with 1 dependant
						Age of dependant
2	10	6	5	18	102	0 - 4
5	21	29	12	66	745	5 - 15
2	9	14	2	57	370	16 - 18
4	22	23	4	9	47	19 up to pensionable age
13	24	18	6	7	43	Pensionable age and over
						Households with at least 2 dependants
						Age of youngest dependant 0 - 4 and age of oldest
-	5	5	-	8	44	0 - 4
1	15	4	5	15	100	5 - 15
-	2	-	-	7	17	16 - 18
-	1	-	-	1	3	19 up to pensionable age
-	-	1	1	1	5	Pensionable age and over
						Age of youngest dependant 5 - 15 and age of oldest
2	19	20	9	23	264	5 - 15
1	4	3	1	27	131	16 - 18
1	-	6	-	2	11	19 up to pensionable age
1	1	1	-	1	17	Pensionable age and over
						Age of youngest dependant 16 - 18 and age of oldest
-	-	1	-	5	15	16 - 18
-	2	-	-	-	3	19 up to pensionable age
-	-	-	-	1	4	Pensionable age and over
						Age of youngest dependant 19 up to pensionable age and age of oldest
-	2	1	-	-	-	19 up to pensionable age
2	1	-	-	-	5	Pensionable age and over
						Age of youngest dependant pensionable age and over
1	1	-	-	-	3	
312	899	1,178	464	2,515	20,497	**TOTAL PERSONS**
						Persons in households with dependants
70	278	264	143	780	6,368	Non-dependants
48	207	188	70	371	2,751	Dependants

Table 28 Dependants in households – **continued**

28. Households with residents; residents in households

Household composition	TOTAL HOUSE-HOLDS	No non-dependants	1 male non-dependant		1 female non-dependant		1 male and 1 female non-dependants		
			Not in employment	In employment	Not in employment	In employment	Neither in employment	1 in employment	Both in employment
a	b	c	d	e	f	g	h	i	j
Eastleigh									
TOTAL HOUSEHOLDS	41,219	2,295	1,196	2,701	4,306	2,240	2,979	6,216	12,103
Households with no dependants	23,144		820	2,230	2,785	1,398	2,561	2,232	6,409
Households with 1 dependant									
Age of dependant									
0 - 4	2,062	1	2	8	123	52	73	854	784
5 - 15	2,264	1	9	28	86	142	30	274	774
16 - 18	764	1	2	18	12	41	10	81	184
19 up to pensionable age	1,008	200	51	142	225	135	33	43	49
Pensionable age and over	2,951	1,451	279	145	695	117	32	80	39
Households with at least 2 dependants									
Age of youngest dependant 0 - 4 and age of oldest									
0 - 4	1,195	-	1	2	63	9	60	676	350
5 - 15	2,205	-	-	6	121	50	103	1,041	764
16 - 18	61	-	-	1	5	-	3	14	17
19 up to pensionable age	56	-	-	12	20	7	-	6	2
Pensionable age and over	16	-	-	1	-	-	-	4	3
Age of youngest dependant 5 - 15 and age of oldest									
5 - 15	3,728	-	12	34	102	197	58	755	2,245
16 - 18	731	-	-	9	17	43	8	119	395
19 up to pensionable age	139	13	5	31	17	25	3	12	7
Pensionable age and over	47	-	2	-	4	2	2	9	17
Age of youngest dependant 16 - 18 and age of oldest									
16 - 18	73	-	-	-	1	3	-	10	48
19 up to pensionable age	31	2	-	6	5	4	-	1	3
Pensionable age and over	13	-	-	1	1	1	-	-	3
Age of youngest dependant 19 up to pensionable age and age of oldest									
19 up to pensionable age	63	39	2	4	6	2	1	3	3
Pensionable age and over	108	78	4	2	13	2	-	-	3
Age of youngest dependant pensionable age and over	560	509	7	21	5	10	2	2	4
TOTAL PERSONS	105,298	2,967	1,615	3,349	6,391	3,526	6,753	20,091	34,739
Persons in households with dependants									
Non-dependants	30,934		376	471	1,521	842	836	7,968	11,388
Dependants	29,847	2,967	419	648	2,085	1,286	795	7,659	10,533

2 same sex non-dependants			3 or more non-dependants			Household composition
Neither in employment	1 in employment	Both in employment	None in employment	1 in employment	2 or more in employment	
k	l	m	n	o	p	a
145	**311**	**596**	**116**	**621**	**5,394**	**TOTAL HOUSEHOLDS**
103	178	444	78	416	3,490	Households with no dependants
						Households with 1 dependant
						Age of dependant
6	8	11	11	26	103	0 - 4
4	17	38	8	49	804	5 - 15
-	13	12	2	32	356	16 - 18
3	30	26	-	11	60	19 up to pensionable age
14	29	20	1	8	41	Pensionable age and over
						Households with at least 2 dependants
						Age of youngest dependant 0 - 4 and age of oldest
1	3	-	4	6	20	0 - 4
3	12	5	4	14	82	5 - 15
-	2	-	-	6	13	16 - 18
-	1	-	1	3	4	19 up to pensionable age
1	-	-	-	-	7	Pensionable age and over
						Age of youngest dependant 5 - 15 and age of oldest
5	11	20	3	27	259	5 - 15
1	3	9	1	15	111	16 - 18
1	3	6	2	3	11	19 up to pensionable age
-	-	-	-	1	10	Pensionable age and over
						Age of youngest dependant 16 - 18 and age of oldest
-	-	1	-	2	8	16 - 18
1	1	3	-	-	5	19 up to pensionable age
-	-	-	-	1	6	Pensionable age and over
						Age of youngest dependant 19 up to pensionable age and age of oldest
1	-	-	1	-	1	19 up to pensionable age
1	-	1	-	1	3	Pensionable age and over
						Age of youngest dependant pensionable age and over
-	-	-	-	-	-	
353	**803**	**1,398**	**427**	**2,260**	**20,626**	**TOTAL PERSONS**
						Persons in households with dependants
84	266	304	118	646	6,114	Non-dependants
63	181	206	64	323	2,618	Dependants

Table 28 Dependants in households – **continued**

28. Households with residents; residents in households

a Household composition	TOTAL HOUSE-HOLDS b	No non-dependants c	1 male non-dependant		1 female non-dependant		1 male and 1 female non-dependants		
			Not in employment d	In employment e	Not in employment f	In employment g	Neither in employment h	1 in employment i	Both in employment j
Fareham									
TOTAL HOUSEHOLDS	38,369	2,166	1,112	2,083	4,352	1,830	3,173	5,811	10,733
Households with no dependants	21,864		707	1,661	2,836	1,108	2,838	2,291	5,732
Households with 1 dependant									
Age of dependant									
0 - 4	1,736	1	2	7	74	55	59	726	642
5 - 15	2,197	-	11	33	74	139	34	285	718
16 - 18	806	-	2	19	5	48	8	75	215
19 up to pensionable age	979	159	53	142	239	115	29	65	57
Pensionable age and over	2,945	1,351	313	117	813	90	28	83	54
Households with at least 2 dependants									
Age of youngest dependant 0 - 4 and age of oldest									
0 - 4	1,016	-	1	3	36	7	36	570	310
5 - 15	1,986	-	4	6	97	29	80	881	763
16 - 18	49	-	-	-	2	1	-	12	14
19 up to pensionable age	66	1	1	15	24	4	1	3	6
Pensionable age and over	18	1	-	-	1	1	1	6	4
Age of youngest dependant 5 - 15 and age of oldest									
5 - 15	3,046	2	5	19	77	158	48	669	1,789
16 - 18	676	-	1	8	17	36	6	113	374
19 up to pensionable age	96	9	2	17	23	12	-	5	7
Pensionable age and over	55	1	1	1	4	2	1	10	16
Age of youngest dependant 16 - 18 and age of oldest									
16 - 18	51	-	-	1	1	3	1	6	27
19 up to pensionable age	28	1	-	5	6	2	1	3	1
Pensionable age and over	10	-	-	-	1	-	1	2	1
Age of youngest dependant 19 up to pensionable age and age of oldest									
19 up to pensionable age	52	34	-	6	3	2	1	1	-
Pensionable age and over	111	83	1	3	9	7	-	5	-
Age of youngest dependant pensionable age and over	582	523	8	20	10	11	-	-	3
TOTAL PERSONS	97,607	2,850	1,552	2,644	6,322	2,878	6,941	18,285	30,638
Persons in households with dependants									
Non-dependants	28,236		405	422	1,516	722	670	7,040	10,002
Dependants	26,606	2,850	440	561	1,970	1,048	595	6,663	9,172

2 same sex non-dependants			3 or more non-dependants			Household composition
Neither in employment	1 in employment	Both in employment	None in employment	1 in employment	2 or more in employment	
k	l	m	n	o	p	a
117	353	528	123	657	5,331	**TOTAL HOUSEHOLDS**
83	214	395	86	433	3,480	Households with no dependants
						Households with 1 dependant
						Age of dependant
4	10	5	5	25	121	0 - 4
4	17	31	9	52	790	5 - 15
3	13	10	4	36	368	16 - 18
6	22	30	2	12	48	19 up to pensionable age
5	31	12	2	8	38	Pensionable age and over
						Households with at least 2 dependants
						Age of youngest dependant 0 - 4 and age of oldest
2	3	3	2	15	28	0 - 4
4	8	10	4	27	73	5 - 15
-	-	-	2	6	12	16 - 18
-	3	-	-	-	8	19 up to pensionable age
-	1	-	-	2	1	Pensionable age and over
						Age of youngest dependant 5 - 15 and age of oldest
2	13	19	4	16	225	5 - 15
1	5	4	2	13	96	16 - 18
2	6	2	1	5	5	19 up to pensionable age
-	2	1	-	3	13	Pensionable age and over
						Age of youngest dependant 16 - 18 and age of oldest
-	-	1	-	1	10	16 - 18
1	2	3	-	1	2	19 up to pensionable age
-	-	-	-	1	4	Pensionable age and over
						Age of youngest dependant 19 up to pensionable age and age of oldest
-	1	1	-	-	3	19 up to pensionable age
-	1	-	-	-	2	Pensionable age and over
						Age of youngest dependant pensionable age and over
-	1	1	-	1	4	
287	905	1,246	449	2,403	20,207	**TOTAL PERSONS**
						Persons in households with dependants
68	278	266	121	704	6,022	Non-dependants
53	199	190	61	352	2,452	Dependants

Table 28 Dependants in households – **continued**

28. Households with residents; residents in households

Household composition	TOTAL HOUSE-HOLDS	No non-dependants	1 male non-dependant		1 female non-dependant		1 male and 1 female non-dependants		
			Not in employment	In employment	Not in employment	In employment	Neither in employment	1 in employment	Both in employment
a	b	c	d	e	f	g	h	i	j

Gosport

TOTAL HOUSEHOLDS	**29,356**	**2,046**	**1,028**	**1,686**	**3,850**	**1,548**	**2,179**	**4,439**	**7,617**
Households with no dependants	15,890		713	1,324	2,394	939	1,755	1,572	4,037
Households with 1 dependant									
Age of dependant									
0 - 4	1,609	-	5	4	170	50	63	680	502
5 - 15	1,785	-	16	23	114	131	51	237	565
16 - 18	518	1	3	16	14	31	7	47	142
19 up to pensionable age	816	187	41	111	163	90	24	40	36
Pensionable age and over	2,426	1,308	223	97	546	60	15	61	38
Households with at least 2 dependants									
Age of youngest dependant 0 - 4 and age of oldest									
0 - 4	813	-	1	-	63	9	69	457	182
5 - 15	1,766	-	3	11	156	38	116	765	559
16 - 18	44	1	-	-	5	-	4	11	14
19 up to pensionable age	59	2	2	18	21	3	1	4	1
Pensionable age and over	9	-	1	-	-	-	-	2	2
Age of youngest dependant 5 - 15 and age of oldest									
5 - 15	2,312	1	7	19	129	139	56	458	1,252
16 - 18	455	1	1	7	27	25	9	77	233
19 up to pensionable age	145	9	4	32	19	18	4	12	13
Pensionable age and over	31	1	2	1	3	-	3	4	9
Age of youngest dependant 16 - 18 and age of oldest									
16 - 18	36	-	-	-	-	3	-	5	23
19 up to pensionable age	20	3	-	2	5	1	-	2	2
Pensionable age and over	6	-	-	-	1	1	-	-	2
Age of youngest dependant 19 up to pensionable age and age of oldest									
19 up to pensionable age	40	27	-	4	3	-	-	2	-
Pensionable age and over	79	58	-	2	10	2	-	1	1
Age of youngest dependant pensionable age and over	497	447	6	15	7	8	2	2	4
TOTAL PERSONS	**73,704**	**2,623**	**1,384**	**2,214**	**5,964**	**2,479**	**5,226**	**14,308**	**21,742**
Persons in households with dependants									
Non-dependants	21,974		315	362	1,456	609	848	5,734	7,160
Dependants	21,918	2,623	356	528	2,114	931	868	5,430	6,508

2 same sex non-dependants			3 or more non-dependants			Household composition
Neither in employment	1 in employment	Both in employment	None in employment	1 in employment	2 or more in employment	
k	l	m	n	o	p	a
110	**294**	**490**	**117**	**470**	**3,482**	**TOTAL HOUSEHOLDS**
75	172	358	64	299	2,188	Households with no dependants
						Households with 1 dependant
						Age of dependant
4	9	5	6	29	82	0 - 4
5	14	31	12	37	549	5 - 15
-	11	8	4	26	208	16 - 18
2	24	33	2	7	56	19 up to pensionable age
9	29	12	1	9	18	Pensionable age and over
						Households with at least 2 dependants
						Age of youngest dependant 0 - 4 and age of oldest
2	3	1	2	5	19	0 - 4
3	7	6	13	18	71	5 - 15
-	-	-	-	1	8	16 - 18
-	-	-	2	1	4	19 up to pensionable age
-	-	-	1	1	2	Pensionable age and over
						Age of youngest dependant 5 - 15 and age of oldest
5	13	19	6	21	187	5 - 15
1	-	6	1	10	57	16 - 18
2	9	8	1	3	11	19 up to pensionable age
-	-	-	1	1	6	Pensionable age and over
						Age of youngest dependant 16 - 18 and age of oldest
-	-	-	-	1	4	16 - 18
1	1	-	1	1	1	19 up to pensionable age
-	-	-	-	-	2	Pensionable age and over
						Age of youngest dependant 19 up to pensionable age and age of oldest
1	-	1	-	-	2	19 up to pensionable age
-	1	1	-	-	3	Pensionable age and over
						Age of youngest dependant pensionable age and over
-	1	1	-	-	4	
279	**757**	**1,165**	**465**	**1,718**	**13,380**	**TOTAL PERSONS**
						Persons in households with dependants
70	244	264	168	536	4,208	Non-dependants
59	169	185	101	255	1,791	Dependants

Table 28 Dependants in households – **continued**

28. Households with residents; residents in households

Household composition	TOTAL HOUSE-HOLDS	No non-dependants	1 male non-dependant		1 female non-dependant		1 male and 1 female non-dependants		
			Not in employment	In employment	Not in employment	In employment	Neither in employment	1 in employment	Both in employment
a	b	c	d	e	f	g	h	i	j

Hart

TOTAL HOUSEHOLDS	**29,073**	**1,207**	**572**	**1,796**	**2,458**	**1,430**	**1,659**	**4,954**	**8,793**
Households with no dependants	16,092		403	1,498	1,691	927	1,420	1,671	4,469
Households with 1 dependant									
Age of dependant									
0 - 4	1,323	-	-	1	51	34	29	619	458
5 - 15	1,682	-	1	26	32	91	24	216	508
16 - 18	742	1	-	10	12	22	11	75	176
19 up to pensionable age	481	74	15	87	93	59	14	31	26
Pensionable age and over	1,706	839	140	86	391	82	12	51	24
Households with at least 2 dependants									
Age of youngest dependant 0 - 4 and age of oldest									
0 - 4	910	-	-	2	20	4	32	543	270
5 - 15	1,614	-	1	4	54	20	49	806	586
16 - 18	47	-	-	-	1	-	2	16	13
19 up to pensionable age	26	-	-	8	4	1	2	1	2
Pensionable age and over	15	-	-	-	-	-	-	5	2
Age of youngest dependant 5 - 15 and age of oldest									
5 - 15	3,054	-	5	22	60	136	41	725	1,763
16 - 18	788	-	1	7	12	25	11	161	425
19 up to pensionable age	78	4	2	23	12	9	2	5	5
Pensionable age and over	45	1	-	-	4	4	4	8	11
Age of youngest dependant 16 - 18 and age of oldest									
16 - 18	85	-	-	-	1	3	4	17	45
19 up to pensionable age	22	-	-	5	2	4	1	1	1
Pensionable age and over	17	-	-	1	1	2	-	2	4
Age of youngest dependant 19 up to pensionable age and age of oldest									
19 up to pensionable age	26	14	1	4	4	-	-	-	1
Pensionable age and over	57	39	1	4	5	3	-	-	2
Age of youngest dependant pensionable age and over	263	235	2	8	8	4	1	1	2
TOTAL PERSONS	**79,014**	**1,512**	**762**	**2,213**	**3,492**	**2,199**	**3,787**	**16,348**	**25,869**
Persons in households with dependants									
Non-dependants	24,281		169	298	767	503	478	6,566	8,648
Dependants	22,158	1,512	190	417	1,034	769	469	6,440	8,283

2 same sex non-dependants			3 or more non-dependants			Household composition
Neither in employment	1 in employment	Both in employment	None in employment	1 in employment	2 or more in employment	
k	l	m	n	o	p	a
102	239	474	75	567	4,747	**TOTAL HOUSEHOLDS**
78	149	363	52	354	3,017	Households with no dependants
						Households with 1 dependant
						Age of dependant
4	7	4	1	19	96	0 - 4
1	17	32	3	27	704	5 - 15
2	8	8	6	60	351	16 - 18
5	13	15	1	8	40	19 up to pensionable age
2	13	19	1	6	40	Pensionable age and over
						Households with at least 2 dependants
						Age of youngest dependant 0 - 4 and age of oldest
-	7	3	-	2	27	0 - 4
3	8	4	3	12	64	5 - 15
-	-	-	-	4	11	16 - 18
2	-	1	-	1	4	19 up to pensionable age
-	-	-	1	-	7	Pensionable age and over
						Age of youngest dependant 5 - 15 and age of oldest
3	8	11	6	35	239	5 - 15
1	2	7	-	28	108	16 - 18
-	3	4	-	3	6	19 up to pensionable age
-	1	-	-	1	11	Pensionable age and over
						Age of youngest dependant 16 - 18 and age of oldest
-	-	-	-	3	12	16 - 18
-	1	2	-	2	3	19 up to pensionable age
1	-	-	-	1	5	Pensionable age and over
						Age of youngest dependant 19 up to pensionable age and age of oldest
-	1	-	1	-	-	19 up to pensionable age
-	-	1	-	1	1	Pensionable age and over
						Age of youngest dependant pensionable age and over
-	1	-	-	-	1	
243	614	1,101	276	2,114	18,484	**TOTAL PERSONS**
						Persons in households with dependants
48	180	222	71	660	5,671	Non-dependants
39	136	153	41	330	2,345	Dependants

Table 28　Dependants in households – **continued**

28. Households with residents; residents in households

Household composition	TOTAL HOUSE-HOLDS	No non-dependants	1 male non-dependant		1 female non-dependant		1 male and 1 female non-dependants		
			Not in employment	In employment	Not in employment	In employment	Neither in employment	1 in employment	Both in employment
a	b	c	d	e	f	g	h	i	j
Havant									
TOTAL HOUSEHOLDS	46,151	3,413	1,704	2,459	6,280	2,448	4,194	6,351	10,730
Households with no dependants	24,555		1,102	1,858	3,670	1,394	3,247	2,552	5,527
Households with 1 dependant									
Age of dependant									
0 - 4	1,998	-	7	4	196	72	119	665	644
5 - 15	2,668	-	12	45	184	207	89	290	745
16 - 18	875	2	4	19	14	52	14	99	220
19 up to pensionable age	1,668	366	86	189	367	210	50	86	86
Pensionable age and over	4,060	2,040	404	173	964	135	44	77	58
Households with at least 2 dependants									
Age of youngest dependant 0 - 4 and age of oldest									
0 - 4	1,167	-	3	2	106	11	113	575	274
5 - 15	2,745	2	8	7	321	46	278	1,062	803
16 - 18	93	-	-	-	14	1	8	24	17
19 up to pensionable age	141	10	12	13	41	5	3	9	3
Pensionable age and over	35	-	-	1	4	1	1	6	10
Age of youngest dependant 5 - 15 and age of oldest									
5 - 15	3,725	1	20	38	265	179	174	707	1,882
16 - 18	819	-	2	13	25	48	35	142	383
19 up to pensionable age	230	23	19	26	52	38	7	14	12
Pensionable age and over	83	2	-	6	10	10	5	12	18
Age of youngest dependant 16 - 18 and age of oldest									
16 - 18	68	-	1	1	1	6	-	13	34
19 up to pensionable age	49	5	4	6	6	5	1	4	4
Pensionable age and over	22	2	3	2	1	2	2	1	3
Age of youngest dependant 19 up to pensionable age and age of oldest									
19 up to pensionable age	113	70	5	8	11	3	-	4	3
Pensionable age and over	189	123	7	17	14	11	1	5	2
Age of youngest dependant pensionable age and over	848	767	5	31	14	12	3	4	2
TOTAL PERSONS	118,297	4,469	2,452	3,289	10,288	4,000	10,409	20,308	31,154
Persons in households with dependants									
Non-dependants	35,149		602	601	2,610	1,054	1,894	7,598	10,406
Dependants	35,889	4,469	748	830	4,008	1,552	2,021	7,606	9,694

2 same sex non-dependants			3 or more non-dependants			Household composition
Neither in employment	1 in employment	Both in employment	None in employment	1 in employment	2 or more in employment	
k	l	m	n	o	p	a
225	**489**	**552**	**193**	**916**	**6,197**	**TOTAL HOUSEHOLDS**
119	259	359	99	546	3,823	Households with no dependants
						Households with 1 dependant
						Age of dependant
13	22	5	12	39	200	0 - 4
11	32	49	16	84	904	5 - 15
1	14	19	4	40	373	16 - 18
11	44	43	10	20	100	19 up to pensionable age
18	41	23	3	8	72	Pensionable age and over
						Households with at least 2 dependants
						Age of youngest dependant 0 - 4 and age of oldest
3	7	2	7	15	49	0 - 4
18	13	6	18	48	115	5 - 15
2	4	-	4	6	13	16 - 18
5	4	3	3	12	18	19 up to pensionable age
-	1	-	1	3	7	Pensionable age and over
						Age of youngest dependant 5 - 15 and age of oldest
8	22	23	15	52	339	5 - 15
2	5	6	-	31	127	16 - 18
3	13	6	1	1	15	19 up to pensionable age
1	-	-	-	5	14	Pensionable age and over
						Age of youngest dependant 16 - 18 and age of oldest
-	-	-	-	1	11	16 - 18
3	1	4	-	2	4	19 up to pensionable age
1	1	-	-	-	4	Pensionable age and over
						Age of youngest dependant 19 up to pensionable age and age of oldest
3	1	2	-	1	2	19 up to pensionable age
2	2	1	-	1	3	Pensionable age and over
						Age of youngest dependant pensionable age and over
1	3	1	-	1	4	
642	**1,318**	**1,362**	**785**	**3,538**	**24,283**	**TOTAL PERSONS**
						Persons in households with dependants
212	460	386	300	1,175	7,851	Non-dependants
192	340	258	177	667	3,327	Dependants

Table 28 Dependants in households – **continued**

28. Households with residents; residents in households

Household composition	TOTAL HOUSE-HOLDS	No non-dependants	1 male non-dependant		1 female non-dependant		1 male and 1 female non-dependants		
			Not in employment	In employment	Not in employment	In employment	Neither in employment	1 in employment	Both in employment
a	b	c	d	e	f	g	h	i	j

New Forest

TOTAL HOUSEHOLDS	**65,411**	**4,599**	**2,544**	**3,384**	**9,632**	**3,154**	**7,319**	**9,242**	**15,067**
Households with no dependants	38,245		1,743	2,776	6,403	1,992	6,597	3,905	8,073
Households with 1 dependant									
Age of dependant									
0 - 4	2,483	1	2	9	193	70	100	1,047	828
5 - 15	3,192	-	17	50	150	188	61	434	980
16 - 18	1,093	4	6	20	21	46	13	121	282
19 up to pensionable age	1,684	280	87	161	460	199	64	97	81
Pensionable age and over	6,408	3,036	637	220	1,823	187	76	129	73
Households with at least 2 dependants									
Age of youngest dependant 0 - 4 and age of oldest									
0 - 4	1,489	1	-	3	80	12	100	831	411
5 - 15	2,793	-	7	6	152	44	157	1,266	997
16 - 18	88	-	-	-	3	1	5	34	18
19 up to pensionable age	99	7	2	15	32	5	3	7	3
Pensionable age and over	31	1	-	-	2	-	2	4	2
Age of youngest dependant 5 - 15 and age of oldest									
5 - 15	4,738	-	12	34	180	252	105	1,075	2,648
16 - 18	1,131	2	1	6	16	65	16	229	552
19 up to pensionable age	204	10	7	28	48	44	3	10	13
Pensionable age and over	97	2	1	2	10	12	5	12	29
Age of youngest dependant 16 - 18 and age of oldest									
16 - 18	125	-	1	2	4	3	1	26	57
19 up to pensionable age	41	1	-	7	7	5	1	4	3
Pensionable age and over	21	1	-	-	3	1	1	1	4
Age of youngest dependant 19 up to pensionable age and age of oldest									
19 up to pensionable age	93	58	1	6	9	6	5	1	5
Pensionable age and over	176	114	9	10	19	10	2	4	2
Age of youngest dependant pensionable age and over	1,180	1,081	11	29	17	12	2	5	6
TOTAL PERSONS	**157,604**	**5,914**	**3,411**	**4,184**	**13,694**	**4,922**	**15,973**	**28,703**	**43,125**
Persons in households with dependants									
Non-dependants	43,318		801	608	3,229	1,162	1,444	10,674	13,988
Dependants	43,144	5,914	867	800	4,062	1,768	1,335	10,219	12,991

	2 same sex non-dependants			3 or more non-dependants			Household composition
	Neither in employment	1 in employment	Both in employment	None in employment	1 in employment	2 or more in employment	
	k	l	m	n	o	p	a
	372	609	693	305	1,104	7,387	**TOTAL HOUSEHOLDS**
	277	388	507	233	750	4,601	Households with no dependants
							Households with 1 dependant
							Age of dependant
	6	21	10	8	30	158	0 - 4
	12	26	47	12	83	1,132	5 - 15
	5	12	16	9	60	478	16 - 18
	17	52	35	6	24	121	19 up to pensionable age
	25	61	18	6	14	103	Pensionable age and over
							Households with at least 2 dependants
							Age of youngest dependant 0 - 4 and age of oldest
	1	2	4	2	6	36	0 - 4
	7	13	7	5	38	94	5 - 15
	-	1	-	1	7	18	16 - 18
	2	1	-	3	7	12	19 up to pensionable age
	-	3	-	3	5	9	Pensionable age and over
							Age of youngest dependant 5 - 15 and age of oldest
	8	11	18	6	39	350	5 - 15
	3	7	6	6	19	203	16 - 18
	2	6	13	2	3	15	19 up to pensionable age
	2	-	2	-	6	14	Pensionable age and over
							Age of youngest dependant 16 - 18 and age of oldest
	-	-	-	2	7	22	16 - 18
	2	1	4	1	3	2	19 up to pensionable age
	-	-	-	-	1	9	Pensionable age and over
							Age of youngest dependant 19 up to pensionable age and age of oldest
	1	1	-	-	-	-	19 up to pensionable age
	-	-	1	-	2	3	Pensionable age and over
							Age of youngest dependant pensionable age and over
	2	3	5	-	-	7	
	889	1,508	1,643	1,075	3,990	28,573	**TOTAL PERSONS**
							Persons in households with dependants
	190	442	372	232	1,112	9,064	Non-dependants
	145	290	257	127	553	3,816	Dependants

Table 28 Dependants in households – **continued**

28. Households with residents; residents in households

Household composition	TOTAL HOUSE-HOLDS	No non-dependants	1 male non-dependant		1 female non-dependant		1 male and 1 female non-dependants		
			Not in employment	In employment	Not in employment	In employment	Neither in employment	1 in employment	Both in employment
a	b	c	d	e	f	g	h	i	j

Portsmouth

TOTAL HOUSEHOLDS	**72,590**	**6,626**	**3,483**	**5,439**	**10,768**	**4,772**	**5,499**	**8,703**	**15,441**
Households with no dependants	41,098		2,550	4,472	6,844	3,094	4,183	3,495	8,710
Households with 1 dependant									
Age of dependant									
0 - 4	3,595	3	11	15	442	126	258	1,193	1,077
5 - 15	3,666	5	40	52	334	367	108	412	1,062
16 - 18	799	16	8	21	38	53	19	67	194
19 up to pensionable age	2,637	803	122	277	466	303	62	147	94
Pensionable age and over	7,405	4,222	639	356	1,420	237	71	151	81
Households with at least 2 dependants									
Age of youngest dependant 0 - 4 and age of oldest									
0 - 4	1,776	2	3	6	174	26	161	839	463
5 - 15	3,678	1	14	6	481	103	348	1,320	1,105
16 - 18	124	1	-	-	9	6	17	27	25
19 up to pensionable age	227	10	11	28	65	13	11	20	3
Pensionable age and over	58	1	1	1	5	5	4	13	9
Age of youngest dependant 5 - 15 and age of oldest									
5 - 15	4,344	1	33	47	302	301	203	815	2,137
16 - 18	791	-	3	9	42	54	29	134	366
19 up to pensionable age	305	33	9	52	63	26	11	20	21
Pensionable age and over	126	7	1	2	15	9	6	15	32
Age of youngest dependant 16 - 18 and age of oldest									
16 - 18	69	1	-	1	3	8	-	9	30
19 up to pensionable age	59	13	1	6	8	7	1	4	5
Pensionable age and over	31	7	-	1	1	1	-	7	8
Age of youngest dependant 19 up to pensionable age and age of oldest									
19 up to pensionable age	175	98	8	14	12	5	4	4	7
Pensionable age and over	295	204	9	21	16	14	1	9	5
Age of youngest dependant pensionable age and over	1,332	1,198	20	52	28	14	2	2	7
TOTAL PERSONS	**169,730**	**8,286**	**4,579**	**6,736**	**16,604**	**7,225**	**13,713**	**27,277**	**42,998**
Persons in households with dependants									
Non-dependants	46,625		933	967	3,924	1,678	2,632	10,416	13,462
Dependants	49,819	8,286	1,096	1,297	5,836	2,453	2,715	9,871	12,116

2 same sex non-dependants			3 or more non-dependants			Household composition
Neither in employment	1 in employment	Both in employment	None in employment	1 in employment	2 or more in employment	
k	l	m	n	o	p	a
460	**904**	**1,279**	**415**	**1,286**	**7,515**	**TOTAL HOUSEHOLDS**
302	563	1,008	273	787	4,817	Households with no dependants
						Households with 1 dependant
						Age of dependant
15	55	14	25	78	283	0 - 4
22	40	49	21	104	1,050	5 - 15
5	10	19	6	35	308	16 - 18
16	76	77	14	37	143	19 up to pensionable age
28	71	33	5	19	72	Pensionable age and over
						Households with at least 2 dependants
						Age of youngest dependant 0 - 4 and age of oldest
9	11	2	10	20	50	0 - 4
19	18	9	16	67	171	5 - 15
1	2	1	5	5	25	16 - 18
6	6	4	8	20	22	19 up to pensionable age
2	-	1	-	4	12	Pensionable age and over
						Age of youngest dependant 5 - 15 and age of oldest
13	24	25	16	65	362	5 - 15
2	2	3	6	19	122	16 - 18
5	12	14	5	11	23	19 up to pensionable age
4	3	-	-	2	30	Pensionable age and over
						Age of youngest dependant 16 - 18 and age of oldest
3	-	1	2	5	6	16 - 18
1	2	5	2	2	2	19 up to pensionable age
-	-	-	-	1	5	Pensionable age and over
						Age of youngest dependant 19 up to pensionable age and age of oldest
5	3	6	1	3	5	19 up to pensionable age
2	4	4	-	2	4	Pensionable age and over
						Age of youngest dependant pensionable age and over
-	2	4	-	-	3	
1,199	**2,283**	**2,927**	**1,658**	**4,971**	**29,274**	**TOTAL PERSONS**
						Persons in households with dependants
316	682	542	464	1,597	9,012	Non-dependants
279	475	369	283	883	3,860	Dependants

Table 28 Dependants in households – **continued**

28. Households with residents; residents in households

Household composition	TOTAL HOUSE-HOLDS	No non-dependants	1 male non-dependant		1 female non-dependant		1 male and 1 female non-dependants		
			Not in employment	In employment	Not in employment	In employment	Neither in employment	1 in employment	Both in employment
a	b	c	d	e	f	g	h	i	j

Rushmoor

Household composition	TOTAL HOUSE-HOLDS	No non-dependants	Not in employment	In employment	Not in employment	In employment	Neither in employment	1 in employment	Both in employment
TOTAL HOUSEHOLDS	**30,523**	**1,709**	**875**	**2,158**	**2,944**	**1,744**	**1,603**	**4,508**	**9,091**
Households with no dependants	16,878		615	1,799	1,793	1,073	1,233	1,466	4,887
Households with 1 dependant									
Age of dependant									
0 - 4	1,928	1	1	9	171	43	62	816	659
5 - 15	1,741	1	7	18	100	144	31	187	599
16 - 18	478	3	2	15	10	23	2	34	124
19 up to pensionable age	726	179	24	112	112	99	11	34	58
Pensionable age and over	2,039	1,094	188	105	386	87	13	50	32
Households with at least 2 dependants									
Age of youngest dependant 0 - 4 and age of oldest									
0 - 4	1,121	-	4	3	74	8	71	575	332
5 - 15	1,772	-	8	4	132	39	98	747	628
16 - 18	57	-	1	-	1	1	4	19	14
19 up to pensionable age	61	7	3	19	16	7	1	-	2
Pensionable age and over	18	-	-	-	3	1	1	4	5
Age of youngest dependant 5 - 15 and age of oldest									
5 - 15	2,428	1	10	17	89	147	58	460	1,394
16 - 18	548	-	1	7	11	30	11	84	300
19 up to pensionable age	116	16	5	22	27	14	2	7	8
Pensionable age and over	44	-	-	1	2	4	1	8	13
Age of youngest dependant 16 - 18 and age of oldest									
16 - 18	49	-	-	1	1	1	1	10	21
19 up to pensionable age	21	-	1	4	1	3	-	4	3
Pensionable age and over	10	2	-	-	1	2	-	-	3
Age of youngest dependant 19 up to pensionable age and age of oldest									
19 up to pensionable age	38	14	1	6	3	4	2	2	3
Pensionable age and over	75	56	1	3	7	5	-	1	1
Age of youngest dependant pensionable age and over	375	335	3	13	4	9	1	-	5
TOTAL PERSONS	**79,121**	**2,179**	**1,188**	**2,646**	**4,646**	**2,779**	**3,975**	**14,789**	**25,828**
Persons in households with dependants									
Non-dependants	23,535		260	359	1,151	671	740	6,084	8,408
Dependants	22,636	2,179	313	488	1,702	1,035	769	5,773	7,646

2 same sex non-dependants			3 or more non-dependants			Household composition
Neither in employment	1 in employment	Both in employment	None in employment	1 in employment	2 or more in employment	
k	l	m	n	o	p	a
89	271	686	83	406	4,356	**TOTAL HOUSEHOLDS**
60	180	555	44	280	2,893	Households with no dependants
						Households with 1 dependant
						Age of dependant
6	8	10	6	20	116	0 - 4
5	14	36	5	29	565	5 - 15
-	7	11	2	16	229	16 - 18
-	11	29	3	2	52	19 up to pensionable age
7	27	13	-	2	35	Pensionable age and over
						Households with at least 2 dependants
						Age of youngest dependant 0 - 4 and age of oldest
2	-	3	4	10	35	0 - 4
5	8	2	9	16	76	5 - 15
-	1	1	1	-	14	16 - 18
1	-	-	-	1	4	19 up to pensionable age
-	-	1	1	1	1	Pensionable age and over
						Age of youngest dependant 5 - 15 and age of oldest
1	8	14	3	18	208	5 - 15
1	2	3	3	7	88	16 - 18
-	2	3	1	1	8	19 up to pensionable age
-	2	-	-	1	12	Pensionable age and over
						Age of youngest dependant 16 - 18 and age of oldest
-	-	-	1	-	13	16 - 18
1	-	2	-	-	2	19 up to pensionable age
-	-	-	-	1	1	Pensionable age and over
						Age of youngest dependant 19 up to pensionable age and age of oldest
-	-	1	-	-	2	19 up to pensionable age
-	-	-	-	-	1	Pensionable age and over
						Age of youngest dependant pensionable age and over
-	1	2	-	1	1	
226	667	1,545	348	1,493	16,812	**TOTAL PERSONS**
						Persons in households with dependants
58	182	262	128	404	4,828	Non-dependants
48	125	173	82	214	2,089	Dependants

Table 28 Dependants in households – **continued**

28. Households with residents; residents in households

Household composition	TOTAL HOUSE-HOLDS	No non-dependants	1 male non-dependant		1 female non-dependant		1 male and 1 female non-dependants		
			Not in employment	In employment	Not in employment	In employment	Neither in employment	1 in employment	Both in employment
a	b	c	d	e	f	g	h	i	j

Southampton

Household composition	b	c	d	e	f	g	h	i	j
TOTAL HOUSEHOLDS	81,140	6,603	4,299	5,930	11,970	5,208	6,555	10,201	16,404
Households with no dependants	46,428		3,312	5,021	7,339	3,462	4,912	4,178	9,193
Households with 1 dependant									
Age of dependant									
0 - 4	3,818	3	12	13	579	134	319	1,272	997
5 - 15	4,045	3	44	47	378	335	139	454	1,099
16 - 18	1,049	21	12	17	31	61	24	103	222
19 up to pensionable age	3,120	1,032	141	274	546	345	77	145	122
Pensionable age and over	7,143	3,985	634	314	1,435	240	57	155	79
Households with at least 2 dependants									
Age of youngest dependant 0 - 4 and age of oldest									
0 - 4	2,016	2	5	7	269	26	212	950	426
5 - 15	4,219	1	14	9	623	89	451	1,591	1,075
16 - 18	161	-	1	1	18	1	10	36	24
19 up to pensionable age	240	8	8	24	104	13	7	12	5
Pensionable age and over	58	-	-	1	6	1	6	14	12
Age of youngest dependant 5 - 15 and age of oldest									
5 - 15	5,299	1	41	40	403	325	278	1,036	2,566
16 - 18	1,043	2	8	10	42	56	40	182	480
19 up to pensionable age	393	41	20	50	106	52	6	26	19
Pensionable age and over	120	5	1	2	17	7	6	15	27
Age of youngest dependant 16 - 18 and age of oldest									
16 - 18	88	-	1	1	2	6	2	7	38
19 up to pensionable age	86	13	5	8	14	11	2	7	5
Pensionable age and over	19	2	-	2	3	1	-	2	3
Age of youngest dependant 19 up to pensionable age and age of oldest									
19 up to pensionable age	206	121	6	19	9	12	4	9	5
Pensionable age and over	325	233	8	19	30	8	2	4	1
Age of youngest dependant pensionable age and over	1,264	1,130	26	51	16	23	1	3	6
TOTAL PERSONS	193,866	8,277	5,509	7,168	19,278	7,775	16,556	32,243	46,273
Persons in households with dependants									
Non-dependants	53,382		987	909	4,631	1,746	3,286	12,046	14,422
Dependants	56,894	8,277	1,210	1,238	7,308	2,567	3,446	11,841	13,465

2 same sex non-dependants			3 or more non-dependants			Household composition
Neither in employment	1 in employment	Both in employment	None in employment	1 in employment	2 or more in employment	
k	l	m	n	o	p	a
556	1,000	1,274	524	1,572	9,044	**TOTAL HOUSEHOLDS**
348	645	979	335	983	5,721	Households with no dependants
						Households with 1 dependant
						Age of dependant
26	40	14	24	82	303	0 - 4
33	47	59	34	115	1,258	5 - 15
9	17	24	10	48	450	16 - 18
31	87	87	16	61	156	19 up to pensionable age
25	67	39	7	20	86	Pensionable age and over
						Households with at least 2 dependants
						Age of youngest dependant 0 - 4 and age of oldest
10	3	6	7	28	65	0 - 4
19	26	7	32	77	205	5 - 15
5	4	-	7	16	38	16 - 18
7	6	1	7	18	20	19 up to pensionable age
1	1	2	2	2	10	Pensionable age and over
						Age of youngest dependant 5 - 15 and age of oldest
14	27	21	19	71	457	5 - 15
5	9	11	10	25	163	16 - 18
11	10	11	3	9	29	19 up to pensionable age
-	3	1	1	6	29	Pensionable age and over
						Age of youngest dependant 16 - 18 and age of oldest
1	1	-	-	4	25	16 - 18
1	1	5	3	3	8	19 up to pensionable age
1	1	-	-	-	4	Pensionable age and over
						Age of youngest dependant 19 up to pensionable age and age of oldest
3	2	1	3	3	9	19 up to pensionable age
5	1	3	4	1	6	Pensionable age and over
						Age of youngest dependant pensionable age and over
1	2	3	-	-	2	
1,439	2,503	2,945	2,136	6,114	35,650	**TOTAL PERSONS**
						Persons in households with dependants
416	710	590	623	1,900	11,116	Non-dependants
327	503	397	378	1,053	4,884	Dependants

Table 28 Dependants in households – **continued**

28. Households with residents; residents in households

Household composition	TOTAL HOUSE-HOLDS	No non-dependants	1 male non-dependant		1 female non-dependant		1 male and 1 female non-dependants		
			Not in employment	In employment	Not in employment	In employment	Neither in employment	1 in employment	Both in employment
a	b	c	d	e	f	g	h	i	j

Test Valley

TOTAL HOUSEHOLDS	38,391	2,102	1,055	2,285	4,134	1,982	2,604	5,886	10,788
Households with no dependants	21,504		738	1,852	2,688	1,265	2,228	2,249	5,594
Households with 1 dependant									
Age of dependant									
0 - 4	1,811	1	1	5	132	42	81	747	625
5 - 15	2,322	-	8	34	76	156	33	298	760
16 - 18	782	3	2	14	9	36	9	67	214
19 up to pensionable age	861	152	31	108	178	105	18	61	45
Pensionable age and over	2,815	1,392	242	144	685	108	21	61	41
Households with at least 2 dependants									
Age of youngest dependant 0 - 4 and age of oldest									
0 - 4	1,043	1	2	1	43	10	51	577	309
5 - 15	1,987	1	5	4	137	36	91	900	672
16 - 18	61	-	-	-	4	4	3	17	12
19 up to pensionable age	58	5	2	11	19	2	1	2	1
Pensionable age and over	15	-	-	-	3	-	-	2	1
Age of youngest dependant 5 - 15 and age of oldest									
5 - 15	3,432	3	11	39	87	165	47	713	2,028
16 - 18	797	-	2	9	16	24	12	160	419
19 up to pensionable age	110	11	2	21	27	10	3	6	5
Pensionable age and over	45	-	2	1	3	3	-	10	10
Age of youngest dependant 16 - 18 and age of oldest									
16 - 18	92	1	-	3	2	5	-	11	47
19 up to pensionable age	21	3	-	6	3	1	1	2	1
Pensionable age and over	9	1	-	1	1	1	-	1	-
Age of youngest dependant 19 up to pensionable age and age of oldest									
19 up to pensionable age	44	27	1	3	3	1	-	1	1
Pensionable age and over	93	62	2	6	13	3	2	-	1
Age of youngest dependant pensionable age and over	489	439	4	23	5	5	3	1	2
TOTAL PERSONS	99,463	2,693	1,414	2,884	6,156	3,038	5,929	18,751	31,177
Persons in households with dependants									
Non-dependants	29,566		317	433	1,446	717	752	7,274	10,388
Dependants	27,798	2,693	359	599	2,022	1,056	721	6,979	9,601

2 same sex non-dependants			3 or more non-dependants			Household composition
Neither in employment	1 in employment	Both in employment	None in employment	1 in employment	2 or more in employment	
k	l	m	n	o	p	a
145	359	566	130	660	5,695	**TOTAL HOUSEHOLDS**
104	228	408	97	417	3,636	Households with no dependants
						Households with 1 dependant
						Age of dependant
6	16	4	2	29	120	0 - 4
5	17	45	11	59	820	5 - 15
-	14	4	3	37	370	16 - 18
8	21	35	3	14	82	19 up to pensionable age
6	23	19	4	5	64	Pensionable age and over
						Households with at least 2 dependants
						Age of youngest dependant 0 - 4 and age of oldest
2	1	2	3	7	34	0 - 4
4	8	5	2	20	102	5 - 15
-	1	-	-	3	17	16 - 18
1	-	2	2	-	10	19 up to pensionable age
1	1	-	-	2	5	Pensionable age and over
						Age of youngest dependant 5 - 15 and age of oldest
3	12	22	2	32	268	5 - 15
-	5	5	1	25	119	16 - 18
1	7	5	-	4	8	19 up to pensionable age
1	1	-	-	4	10	Pensionable age and over
						Age of youngest dependant 16 - 18 and age of oldest
-	1	1	-	-	21	16 - 18
-	1	3	-	-	-	19 up to pensionable age
-	-	-	-	-	4	Pensionable age and over
						Age of youngest dependant 19 up to pensionable age and age of oldest
-	1	2	-	1	3	19 up to pensionable age
-	1	1	-	1	1	Pensionable age and over
						Age of youngest dependant pensionable age and over
3	-	3	-	-	1	
355	914	1,350	448	2,454	21,900	**TOTAL PERSONS**
						Persons in households with dependants
82	262	316	103	771	6,705	Non-dependants
65	196	218	47	385	2,857	Dependants

Table 28 Dependants in households – **continued**

28. Households with residents; residents in households

Household composition	TOTAL HOUSE-HOLDS	No non-dependants	1 male non-dependant		1 female non-dependant		1 male and 1 female non-dependants		
			Not in employment	In employment	Not in employment	In employment	Neither in employment	1 in employment	Both in employment
a	b	c	d	e	f	g	h	i	j
Winchester									
TOTAL HOUSEHOLDS	37,553	2,380	1,165	2,141	4,758	2,152	2,844	5,636	9,509
Households with no dependants	21,982		837	1,763	3,456	1,462	2,550	2,379	4,948
Households with 1 dependant									
Age of dependant									
0 - 4	1,408	-	4	5	66	41	53	624	490
5 - 15	1,830	2	4	25	53	97	26	249	606
16 - 18	814	1	3	14	13	41	12	89	157
19 up to pensionable age	817	173	29	100	177	114	18	48	35
Pensionable age and over	3,177	1,670	263	132	736	128	22	64	45
Households with at least 2 dependants									
Age of youngest dependant 0 - 4 and age of oldest									
0 - 4	866	-	-	1	30	3	27	499	258
5 - 15	1,699	-	-	4	85	28	66	771	606
16 - 18	61	-	-	-	4	2	3	18	16
19 up to pensionable age	51	2	2	9	15	1	2	5	-
Pensionable age and over	16	-	-	-	-	-	2	5	2
Age of youngest dependant 5 - 15 and age of oldest									
5 - 15	3,075	1	8	25	59	151	42	678	1,805
16 - 18	867	-	2	11	19	36	14	163	453
19 up to pensionable age	83	4	3	20	12	15	-	3	9
Pensionable age and over	48	-	-	-	5	4	1	14	13
Age of youngest dependant 16 - 18 and age of oldest									
16 - 18	102	-	-	1	1	9	1	17	56
19 up to pensionable age	28	1	1	5	4	5	-	5	1
Pensionable age and over	10	1	-	-	1	-	1	-	2
Age of youngest dependant 19 up to pensionable age and age of oldest									
19 up to pensionable age	31	20	2	4	-	-	2	2	1
Pensionable age and over	97	60	2	9	14	5	-	-	2
Age of youngest dependant pensionable age and over	491	445	5	13	8	10	2	3	4
TOTAL PERSONS	93,721	2,936	1,528	2,662	6,442	3,187	6,239	17,636	27,758
Persons in households with dependants									
Non-dependants	26,323		328	378	1,302	690	588	6,514	9,122
Dependants	25,599	2,936	363	521	1,684	1,035	551	6,364	8,740

2 same sex non-dependants			3 or more non-dependants			Household composition
Neither in employment	1 in employment	Both in employment	None in employment	1 in employment	2 or more in employment	
k	l	m	n	o	p	a
139	377	486	137	733	5,096	TOTAL HOUSEHOLDS
103	247	360	102	499	3,276	Households with no dependants
						Households with 1 dependant
						Age of dependant
3	7	6	1	21	87	0 - 4
5	23	27	5	47	661	5 - 15
2	7	11	7	47	410	16 - 18
5	23	32	3	13	47	19 up to pensionable age
9	32	7	2	6	61	Pensionable age and over
						Households with at least 2 dependants
						Age of youngest dependant 0 - 4 and age of oldest
1	5	3	2	7	30	0 - 4
5	11	6	4	28	85	5 - 15
-	-	-	-	3	15	16 - 18
1	2	-	-	4	8	19 up to pensionable age
2	-	-	1	-	4	Pensionable age and over
						Age of youngest dependant 5 - 15 and age of oldest
2	9	16	3	26	250	5 - 15
-	4	4	4	26	131	16 - 18
-	2	6	1	2	6	19 up to pensionable age
1	1	-	1	3	5	Pensionable age and over
						Age of youngest dependant 16 - 18 and age of oldest
-	2	-	1	1	13	16 - 18
-	1	2	-	-	3	19 up to pensionable age
-	-	3	-	-	2	Pensionable age and over
						Age of youngest dependant 19 up to pensionable age and age of oldest
-	-	-	-	-	-	19 up to pensionable age
-	1	2	-	-	2	Pensionable age and over
						Age of youngest dependant pensionable age and over
-	-	1	-	-	-	
337	934	1,149	499	2,698	19,716	TOTAL PERSONS
						Persons in households with dependants
72	260	252	111	746	5,960	Non-dependants
59	180	177	56	377	2,556	Dependants

Table 29 Dependants and long-term illness   County, districts

29. Households with residents; dependants in households

Household composition	TOTAL HOUSEHOLDS	TOTAL DEPENDANTS	Aged 0 - 15		Aged 16 - 18		Aged 19 up to pensionable age with long-term illness and permanently sick/retired	Pensionable age and over with long-term illness and permanently sick/retired
			With long-term illness	With no long-term illness	Single, in full-time education and economically inactive	With long-term illness and permanently sick/retired		
a	b	c	d	e	f	g	h	i

HAMPSHIRE

Household composition	b	c	d	e	f	g	h	i
TOTAL HOUSEHOLDS	603,257	430,937	6,054	302,742	26,012	148	25,068	70,913
1 or more non-dependants, no dependants	340,397							
1 dependant, living alone	29,667	29,667	2	24	50	5	4,016	25,570
2 dependants, no non-dependants	9,887	19,774	12	164	47	6	2,352	17,193
3 or more dependants, no non-dependants	423	1,406	26	264	46	1	610	459
1 non-dependant with 1 or more dependant(s)	51,884	73,124	1,291	35,738	2,779	32	11,389	21,895
2 non-dependants with 1 or more dependant(s)	137,952	259,313	3,981	231,607	14,732	60	4,609	4,324
3 or more non-dependants with 1 or more dependant(s)	33,047	47,653	742	34,945	8,358	44	2,092	1,472

Basingstoke & Deane

Household composition	b	c	d	e	f	g	h	i
TOTAL HOUSEHOLDS	54,323	39,918	547	29,812	2,608	18	1,863	5,070
1 or more non-dependants, no dependants	30,576							
1 dependant, living alone	2,067	2,067	-	1	1	1	254	1,810
2 dependants, no non-dependants	702	1,404	-	14	2	1	152	1,235
3 or more dependants, no non-dependants	38	123	-	17	2	-	63	41
1 non-dependant with 1 or more dependant(s)	3,752	5,446	76	2,791	249	4	837	1,489
2 non-dependants with 1 or more dependant(s)	13,648	25,821	391	23,243	1,461	5	361	360
3 or more non-dependants with 1 or more dependant(s)	3,540	5,057	80	3,746	893	7	196	135

East Hampshire

Household composition	b	c	d	e	f	g	h	i
TOTAL HOUSEHOLDS	39,158	28,711	317	21,100	2,196	9	1,171	3,918
1 or more non-dependants, no dependants	22,141							
1 dependant, living alone	1,531	1,531	-	2	-	-	157	1,372
2 dependants, no non-dependants	470	940	-	12	3	-	90	835
3 or more dependants, no non-dependants	23	76	-	13	2	-	27	34
1 non-dependant with 1 or more dependant(s)	2,884	4,065	53	1,920	196	-	580	1,316
2 non-dependants with 1 or more dependant(s)	9,887	18,907	216	16,874	1,319	8	226	264
3 or more non-dependants with 1 or more dependant(s)	2,222	3,192	48	2,279	676	1	91	97

Eastleigh

Household composition	b	c	d	e	f	g	h	i
TOTAL HOUSEHOLDS	41,219	29,847	365	21,872	1,827	8	1,508	4,267
1 or more non-dependants, no dependants	23,144							
1 dependant, living alone	1,654	1,654	-	2	1	-	200	1,451
2 dependants, no non-dependants	618	1,236	-	6	1	-	145	1,084
3 or more dependants, no non-dependants	23	77	1	12	1	-	45	18
1 non-dependant with 1 or more dependant(s)	3,210	4,438	70	2,073	199	1	739	1,356
2 non-dependants with 1 or more dependant(s)	10,423	19,437	253	17,591	1,045	4	269	275
3 or more non-dependants with 1 or more dependant(s)	2,147	3,005	41	2,188	580	3	110	83

Fareham

Household composition	b	c	d	e	f	g	h	i
TOTAL HOUSEHOLDS	38,369	26,606	316	18,843	1,719	4	1,400	4,324
1 or more non-dependants, no dependants	21,864							
1 dependant, living alone	1,511	1,511	-	1	-	-	159	1,351
2 dependants, no non-dependants	631	1,262	-	6	-	-	147	1,109
3 or more dependants, no non-dependants	24	77	-	17	3	-	24	33
1 non-dependant with 1 or more dependant(s)	3,065	4,019	56	1,615	179	-	704	1,465
2 non-dependants with 1 or more dependant(s)	9,162	16,872	227	15,125	965	3	272	280
3 or more non-dependants with 1 or more dependant(s)	2,112	2,865	33	2,079	572	1	94	86

Table 29 Dependants and long-term illness – **continued** County, districts

29. Households with residents; dependants in households

Household composition	TOTAL HOUSEHOLDS	TOTAL DEPENDANTS	Aged 0 - 15 With long-term illness	Aged 0 - 15 With no long-term illness	Aged 16 - 18 Single, in full-time education and economically inactive	Aged 16 - 18 With long-term illness and permanently sick/retired	Aged 19 up to pensionable age with long-term illness and permanently sick/retired	Pensionable age and over with long-term illness and permanently sick/retired
a	b	c	d	e	f	g	h	i
Gosport								
TOTAL HOUSEHOLDS	29,356	21,918	403	15,581	1,150	6	1,225	3,553
1 or more non-dependants, no dependants	15,890							
1 dependant, living alone	1,496	1,496	-	-	1	-	187	1,308
2 dependants, no non-dependants	530	1,060	2	6	2	1	103	946
3 or more dependants, no non-dependants	20	67	2	13	3	-	38	11
1 non-dependant with 1 or more dependant(s)	2,742	3,929	91	2,092	159	2	563	1,022
2 non-dependants with 1 or more dependant(s)	7,160	13,219	255	11,865	655	1	232	211
3 or more non-dependants with 1 or more dependant(s)	1,518	2,147	53	1,605	330	2	102	55
Hart								
TOTAL HOUSEHOLDS	29,073	22,158	255	16,962	1,834	5	726	2,376
1 or more non-dependants, no dependants	16,092							
1 dependant, living alone	914	914	-	-	1	-	74	839
2 dependants, no non-dependants	282	564	-	3	-	-	63	498
3 or more dependants, no non-dependants	11	34	-	3	-	-	14	17
1 non-dependant with 1 or more dependant(s)	1,737	2,410	27	1,134	119	1	359	770
2 non-dependants with 1 or more dependant(s)	8,071	15,520	193	13,907	1,098	3	144	175
3 or more non-dependants with 1 or more dependant(s)	1,966	2,716	35	1,915	616	1	72	77
Havant								
TOTAL HOUSEHOLDS	46,151	35,889	662	24,458	2,074	14	2,563	6,118
1 or more non-dependants, no dependants	24,555							
1 dependant, living alone	2,408	2,408	-	-	2	-	366	2,040
2 dependants, no non-dependants	963	1,926	1	16	5	-	267	1,637
3 or more dependants, no non-dependants	42	135	6	31	2	-	54	42
1 non-dependant with 1 or more dependant(s)	4,867	7,138	157	3,612	260	9	1,205	1,895
2 non-dependants with 1 or more dependant(s)	10,478	20,111	405	17,703	1,162	4	468	369
3 or more non-dependants with 1 or more dependant(s)	2,838	4,171	93	3,096	643	1	203	135
New Forest								
TOTAL HOUSEHOLDS	65,411	43,144	510	28,362	2,709	15	2,415	9,133
1 or more non-dependants, no dependants	38,245							
1 dependant, living alone	3,321	3,321	-	1	4	-	280	3,036
2 dependants, no non-dependants	1,248	2,496	3	11	2	-	230	2,250
3 or more dependants, no non-dependants	30	97	2	16	5	-	29	45
1 non-dependant with 1 or more dependant(s)	5,800	7,497	79	2,874	242	4	1,205	3,093
2 non-dependants with 1 or more dependant(s)	13,555	25,237	364	22,325	1,565	4	465	514
3 or more non-dependants with 1 or more dependant(s)	3,212	4,496	62	3,135	891	7	206	195
Portsmouth								
TOTAL HOUSEHOLDS	72,590	49,819	771	32,407	2,025	17	3,975	10,624
1 or more non-dependants, no dependants	41,098							
1 dependant, living alone	5,049	5,049	-	8	13	3	803	4,222
2 dependants, no non-dependants	1,517	3,034	2	34	15	3	406	2,574
3 or more dependants, no non-dependants	60	203	5	38	8	1	90	61
1 non-dependant with 1 or more dependant(s)	7,502	10,682	207	5,538	321	1	1,622	2,993
2 non-dependants with 1 or more dependant(s)	14,025	25,825	474	22,923	1,084	4	730	610
3 or more non-dependants with 1 or more dependant(s)	3,339	5,026	83	3,866	584	5	324	164

Table 29 Dependants and long-term illness – **continued**   County, districts

29. Households with residents; dependants in households

Household composition	TOTAL HOUSEHOLDS	Dependants						
		TOTAL DEPENDANTS	Aged 0 - 15		Aged 16 - 18		Aged 19 up to pensionable age with long-term illness and permanently sick/retired	Pensionable age and over with long-term illness and permanently sick/retired
			With long-term illness	With no long-term illness	Single, in full-time education and economically inactive	With long-term illness and permanently sick/retired		
a	b	c	d	e	f	g	h	i
Rushmoor								
TOTAL HOUSEHOLDS	30,523	22,636	340	16,982	1,247	10	1,099	2,958
1 or more non-dependants, no dependants	16,878							
1 dependant, living alone	1,278	1,278	1	1	3	-	179	1,094
2 dependants, no non-dependants	403	806	-	7	2	-	83	714
3 or more dependants, no non-dependants	28	95	6	27	3	-	33	26
1 non-dependant with 1 or more dependant(s)	2,441	3,538	59	1,967	129	2	522	859
2 non-dependants with 1 or more dependant(s)	7,867	14,534	237	13,176	711	6	202	202
3 or more non-dependants with 1 or more dependant(s)	1,628	2,385	37	1,804	399	2	80	63
Southampton								
TOTAL HOUSEHOLDS	81,140	56,894	964	38,294	2,661	24	4,701	10,250
1 or more non-dependants, no dependants	46,428							
1 dependant, living alone	5,044	5,044	1	5	21	-	1,032	3,985
2 dependants, no non-dependants	1,479	2,958	2	32	12	-	462	2,450
3 or more dependants, no non-dependants	80	275	3	50	11	-	129	82
1 non-dependant with 1 or more dependant(s)	8,273	12,323	320	6,751	365	6	1,913	2,968
2 non-dependants with 1 or more dependant(s)	15,735	29,979	529	26,698	1,391	8	774	579
3 or more non-dependants with 1 or more dependant(s)	4,101	6,315	109	4,758	861	10	391	186
Test Valley								
TOTAL HOUSEHOLDS	38,391	27,798	317	20,329	1,917	7	1,259	3,969
1 or more non-dependants, no dependants	21,504							
1 dependant, living alone	1,548	1,548	-	1	2	1	152	1,392
2 dependants, no non-dependants	527	1,054	1	12	3	-	109	929
3 or more dependants, no non-dependants	27	91	1	24	5	-	41	20
1 non-dependant with 1 or more dependant(s)	2,913	4,036	60	1,941	165	-	577	1,293
2 non-dependants with 1 or more dependant(s)	9,537	17,780	213	15,977	1,111	5	246	228
3 or more non-dependants with 1 or more dependant(s)	2,335	3,289	42	2,374	631	1	134	107
Winchester								
TOTAL HOUSEHOLDS	37,553	25,599	287	17,740	2,045	11	1,163	4,353
1 or more non-dependants, no dependants	21,982							
1 dependant, living alone	1,846	1,846	-	2	1	-	173	1,670
2 dependants, no non-dependants	517	1,034	1	5	-	1	95	932
3 or more dependants, no non-dependants	17	56	-	3	1	-	23	29
1 non-dependant with 1 or more dependant(s)	2,698	3,603	36	1,430	196	2	563	1,376
2 non-dependants with 1 or more dependant(s)	8,404	16,071	224	14,200	1,165	5	220	257
3 or more non-dependants with 1 or more dependant(s)	2,089	2,989	26	2,100	682	3	89	89

Table 30 'Carers'   County, districts

30. Households with residents; residents in households with dependants

Number, sex and age of non-dependants	TOTAL HOUSE-HOLDS	Households with no dependants	Households with 1 or more dependants						Persons in households with dependants	
			Age of youngest dependant 0-15 and age of oldest			Age of youngest dependant 16 up to pensionable age and age of oldest		Age of youngest dependant pensionable age and over	Non-dependants	Depen-dants
			0-15	16 up to pension-able age	Pension-able age and over	16 up to pension-able age	Pension-able age and over			
a	b	c	d	e	f	g	h	i	j	k
HAMPSHIRE										
TOTAL HOUSEHOLDS	603,257	340,397	156,189	15,110	1,230	29,974	2,017	58,340	435,950	430,937
No non-dependants	39,977		54	256	30	4,706	1,269	33,662		50,847
1 male	59,312	46,273	1,579	879	39	3,214	174	7,154	13,039	16,565
16 - 44	28,067	23,772	1,246	677	25	1,173	94	1,080	4,295	7,025
45 - 64	16,401	12,156	308	199	9	1,823	53	1,853	4,245	4,952
65 and over	14,844	10,345	25	3	5	218	27	4,221	4,499	4,588
1 female	108,225	69,380	16,422	2,150	189	6,522	279	13,283	38,845	56,559
16 - 44	31,209	12,232	15,483	1,754	111	1,078	55	496	18,977	35,014
45 - 59	15,574	9,588	879	373	56	3,221	103	1,354	5,986	7,283
60 and over	61,442	47,560	60	23	22	2,223	121	11,433	13,882	14,262
1 male and 1 female	286,802	154,297	113,955	8,643	579	6,867	131	2,330	265,010	251,499
Both of pensionable age	36,145	35,549	61	4	-	302	5	224	1,192	634
1 under, 1 of pensionable age	20,496	18,466	365	61	24	549	25	1,006	4,060	2,411
Both under pensionable age	230,161	100,282	113,529	8,578	555	6,016	101	1,100	259,758	248,454
2 of same sex	17,790	12,343	2,371	443	53	1,563	51	966	10,894	7,814
Both of pensionable age	1,212	1,116	2	-	-	16	2	76	192	105
1 under, 1 of pensionable age	3,503	2,478	237	28	27	205	11	517	2,050	1,225
Both under pensionable age	13,075	8,749	2,132	415	26	1,342	38	373	8,652	6,484
3 or more	91,151	58,104	21,808	2,739	340	7,102	113	945	108,162	47,653
All of pensionable age	348	335	-	-	-	6	-	7	40	14
1 or more under pensionable age	90,803	57,769	21,808	2,739	340	7,096	113	938	108,122	47,639
Basingstoke & Deane										
TOTAL HOUSEHOLDS	54,323	30,576	15,359	1,474	112	2,528	146	4,128	42,678	39,918
No non-dependants	2,807		2	17	5	300	91	2,392		3,594
1 male	4,913	3,894	112	79	3	262	15	548	1,019	1,321
16 - 44	2,560	2,231	98	61	3	76	9	82	329	569
45 - 64	1,314	967	13	18	-	165	3	148	347	400
65 and over	1,039	696	1	-	-	21	3	318	343	352
1 female	7,773	5,040	1,243	165	10	465	21	829	2,733	4,125
16 - 44	2,549	1,120	1,165	138	8	82	3	33	1,429	2,684
45 - 59	1,205	767	74	25	1	236	10	92	438	547
60 and over	4,019	3,153	4	2	1	147	8	704	866	894
1 male and 1 female	27,672	14,486	11,434	880	59	617	6	190	26,372	25,156
Both of pensionable age	2,615	2,570	3	-	-	26	-	16	90	47
1 under, 1 of pensionable age	1,706	1,526	27	8	1	50	2	92	360	208
Both under pensionable age	23,351	10,390	11,404	872	58	541	4	82	25,922	24,901
2 of same sex	1,527	1,065	202	38	5	133	4	80	924	665
Both of pensionable age	66	60	-	-	-	1	-	5	12	7
1 under, 1 of pensionable age	278	197	16	5	1	10	2	47	162	98
Both under pensionable age	1,183	808	186	33	4	122	2	28	750	560
3 or more	9,631	6,091	2,366	295	30	751	9	89	11,630	5,057
All of pensionable age	17	17	-	-	-	-	-	-	-	-
1 or more under pensionable age	9,614	6,074	2,366	295	30	751	9	89	11,630	5,057

Table 30 'Carers' – **continued**   County, districts

30. Households with residents; residents in households with dependants

Number, sex and age of non-dependants	TOTAL HOUSE-HOLDS	Households with no dependants	Households with 1 or more dependants						Persons in households with dependants	
			Age of youngest dependant 0 - 15 and age of oldest			Age of youngest dependant 16 up to pensionable age and age of oldest		Age of youngest dependant pensionable age and over		
			0 - 15	16 up to pension-able age	Pension-able age and over	16 up to pension-able age	Pension-able age and over		Non-depen-dants	Depen-dants
a	b	c	d	e	f	g	h	i	j	k
East Hampshire										
TOTAL HOUSEHOLDS	**39,158**	**22,141**	**10,610**	**1,161**	**88**	**1,804**	**98**	**3,256**	**29,949**	**28,711**
No non-dependants	2,024		7	7	3	182	52	1,773		2,547
1 male	**3,304**	**2,585**	**111**	**63**	**4**	**151**	**8**	**382**	**719**	**956**
16 - 44	1,480	1,223	94	45	4	61	3	50	257	439
45 - 64	903	693	16	18	-	82	2	92	210	257
65 and over	921	669	1	-	-	8	3	240	252	260
1 female	**6,492**	**4,327**	**818**	**125**	**12**	**350**	**11**	**849**	**2,165**	**3,109**
16 - 44	1,570	636	744	99	8	63	3	17	934	1,769
45 - 59	981	629	67	25	4	178	3	75	352	439
60 and over	3,941	3,062	7	1	-	109	5	757	879	901
1 male and 1 female	**20,299**	**10,718**	**8,114**	**748**	**40**	**529**	**14**	**136**	**19,162**	**18,464**
Both of pensionable age	2,423	2,397	2	-	-	12	2	10	52	28
1 under, 1 of pensionable age	1,369	1,252	30	2	1	34	1	49	234	138
Both under pensionable age	16,507	7,069	8,082	746	39	483	11	77	18,876	18,298
2 of same sex	**973**	**667**	**144**	**18**	**4**	**80**	**3**	**57**	**612**	**443**
Both of pensionable age	81	75	-	-	-	-	-	6	12	6
1 under, 1 of pensionable age	233	165	21	3	2	9	1	32	136	82
Both under pensionable age	659	427	123	15	2	71	2	19	464	355
3 or more	**6,066**	**3,844**	**1,416**	**200**	**25**	**512**	**10**	**59**	**7,291**	**3,192**
All of pensionable age	29	27	-	-	-	1	-	1	6	2
1 or more under pensionable age	6,037	3,817	1,416	200	25	511	10	58	7,285	3,190
Eastleigh										
TOTAL HOUSEHOLDS	**41,219**	**23,144**	**11,454**	**987**	**63**	**1,939**	**121**	**3,511**	**30,934**	**29,847**
No non-dependants	2,295		2	13	-	242	78	1,960		2,967
1 male	**3,897**	**3,050**	**102**	**58**	**3**	**225**	**7**	**452**	**847**	**1,067**
16 - 44	1,988	1,699	87	45	2	74	4	77	289	464
45 - 64	998	728	14	13	1	136	2	104	270	311
65 and over	911	623	1	-	-	15	1	271	288	292
1 female	**6,546**	**4,183**	**945**	**134**	**6**	**434**	**17**	**827**	**2,363**	**3,371**
16 - 44	1,893	796	889	105	4	61	1	37	1,097	2,000
45 - 59	991	587	55	29	2	226	4	88	404	490
60 and over	3,662	2,800	1	-	-	147	12	702	862	881
1 male and 1 female	**21,298**	**11,202**	**8,841**	**586**	**35**	**469**	**6**	**159**	**20,192**	**18,987**
Both of pensionable age	2,359	2,307	5	-	-	27	-	20	104	53
1 under, 1 of pensionable age	1,380	1,263	21	2	2	23	-	69	234	142
Both under pensionable age	17,559	7,632	8,815	584	33	419	6	70	19,854	18,792
2 of same sex	**1,052**	**725**	**144**	**26**	**1**	**91**	**2**	**63**	**654**	**450**
Both of pensionable age	68	61	-	-	-	-	1	6	14	8
1 under, 1 of pensionable age	196	143	11	-	1	11	-	30	106	61
Both under pensionable age	788	521	133	26	-	80	1	27	534	381
3 or more	**6,131**	**3,984**	**1,420**	**170**	**18**	**478**	**11**	**50**	**6,878**	**3,005**
All of pensionable age	18	17	-	-	-	-	-	1	3	1
1 or more under pensionable age	6,113	3,967	1,420	170	18	478	11	49	6,875	3,004

30. Households with residents; residents in households with dependants

Number, sex and age of non-dependants	TOTAL HOUSE-HOLDS	Households with no dependants	Households with 1 or more dependants						Persons in households with dependants	
			Age of youngest dependant 0-15 and age of oldest			Age of youngest dependant 16 up to pensionable age and age of oldest		Age of youngest dependant pensionable age and over	Non-depen-dants	Depen-dants
			0-15	16 up to pension-able age	Pension-able age and over	16 up to pension-able age	Pension-able age and over			
a	b	c	d	e	f	g	h	i	j	k

Fareham

TOTAL HOUSEHOLDS	**38,369**	**21,864**	**9,981**	**887**	**73**	**1,916**	**121**	**3,527**	**28,236**	**26,606**
No non-dependants	2,166		3	10	2	194	83	1,874		2,850
1 male	**3,195**	**2,368**	**91**	**44**	**2**	**228**	**4**	**458**	**827**	**1,001**
16 - 44	1,419	1,174	71	39	1	77	2	55	245	396
45 - 64	906	636	18	5	-	138	-	109	270	289
65 and over	870	558	2	-	1	13	2	294	312	316
1 female	**6,182**	**3,944**	**746**	**119**	**8**	**424**	**17**	**924**	**2,238**	**3,018**
16 - 44	1,462	567	702	98	4	62	4	25	895	1,585
45 - 59	925	563	41	18	2	209	9	83	362	436
60 and over	3,795	2,814	3	3	2	153	4	816	981	997
1 male and 1 female	**19,717**	**10,861**	**7,610**	**541**	**38**	**490**	**9**	**168**	**17,712**	**16,430**
Both of pensionable age	2,541	2,499	3	-	-	21	-	18	84	42
1 under, 1 of pensionable age	1,421	1,303	19	1	2	31	2	63	236	142
Both under pensionable age	15,755	7,059	7,588	540	36	438	7	87	17,392	16,246
2 of same sex	**998**	**692**	**135**	**23**	**4**	**93**	**1**	**50**	**612**	**442**
Both of pensionable age	62	56	1	-	-	1	-	4	12	6
1 under, 1 of pensionable age	190	135	14	2	1	12	1	25	110	69
Both under pensionable age	746	501	120	21	3	80	-	21	490	367
3 or more	**6,111**	**3,999**	**1,396**	**150**	**19**	**487**	**7**	**53**	**6,847**	**2,865**
All of pensionable age	28	28	-	-	-	-	-	-	-	-
1 or more under pensionable age	6,083	3,971	1,396	150	19	487	7	53	6,847	2,865

Gosport

TOTAL HOUSEHOLDS	**29,356**	**15,890**	**8,285**	**703**	**40**	**1,430**	**85**	**2,923**	**21,974**	**21,918**
No non-dependants	2,046		1	13	1	218	58	1,755		2,623
1 male	**2,714**	**2,037**	**89**	**64**	**4**	**177**	**2**	**341**	**677**	**884**
16 - 44	1,235	1,007	68	50	-	65	-	45	228	395
45 - 64	782	550	19	13	3	105	2	90	232	267
65 and over	697	480	2	1	1	7	-	206	217	222
1 female	**5,398**	**3,333**	**999**	**118**	**3**	**310**	**14**	**621**	**2,065**	**3,045**
16 - 44	1,646	494	968	100	-	55	2	27	1,152	2,067
45 - 59	722	466	29	16	2	148	6	55	256	304
60 and over	3,030	2,373	2	2	1	107	6	539	657	674
1 male and 1 female	**14,235**	**7,364**	**6,012**	**383**	**20**	**330**	**4**	**122**	**13,742**	**12,806**
Both of pensionable age	1,556	1,536	5	-	-	9	-	6	40	22
1 under, 1 of pensionable age	947	844	19	2	1	23	1	57	206	123
Both under pensionable age	11,732	4,984	5,988	381	19	298	3	59	13,496	12,661
2 of same sex	**894**	**605**	**127**	**26**	**-**	**82**	**2**	**52**	**578**	**413**
Both of pensionable age	42	38	-	-	-	-	-	4	8	4
1 under, 1 of pensionable age	164	116	8	-	-	12	-	28	96	51
Both under pensionable age	688	451	119	26	-	70	2	20	474	358
3 or more	**4,069**	**2,551**	**1,057**	**99**	**12**	**313**	**5**	**32**	**4,912**	**2,147**
All of pensionable age	20	20	-	-	-	-	-	-	-	-
1 or more under pensionable age	4,049	2,531	1,057	99	12	313	5	32	4,912	2,147

Table 30 'Carers' – **continued**   County, districts

30. Households with residents; residents in households with dependants

Number, sex and age of non-dependants	TOTAL HOUSE-HOLDS	Households with no dependants	Households with 1 or more dependants						Persons in households with dependants	
			Age of youngest dependant 0 - 15 and age of oldest			Age of youngest dependant 16 up to pensionable age and age of oldest		Age of youngest dependant pensionable age and over		
			0 - 15	16 up to pension-able age	Pension-able age and over	16 up to pension-able age	Pension-able age and over		Non-depen-dants	Depen-dants
a	b	c	d	e	f	g	h	i	j	k
Hart										
TOTAL HOUSEHOLDS	29,073	16,092	8,583	939	60	1,356	74	1,969	24,281	22,158
No non-dependants	1,207		-	4	1	89	39	1,074		1,512
1 male	**2,368**	**1,901**	**62**	**41**	**-**	**122**	**6**	**236**	**467**	**607**
16 - 44	1,228	1,069	47	26	-	44	4	38	159	264
45 - 64	661	496	15	15	-	71	2	62	165	200
65 and over	479	336	-	-	-	7	-	136	143	143
1 female	**3,888**	**2,618**	**502**	**64**	**8**	**200**	**11**	**485**	**1,270**	**1,803**
16 - 44	1,041	479	460	45	4	33	2	18	562	1,022
45 - 59	663	438	42	19	4	97	5	58	225	282
60 and over	2,184	1,701	-	-	-	70	4	409	483	499
1 male and 1 female	**15,406**	**7,560**	**6,669**	**645**	**30**	**403**	**8**	**91**	**15,692**	**15,192**
Both of pensionable age	1,371	1,351	2	-	-	9	-	9	40	20
1 under, 1 of pensionable age	916	847	15	4	-	17	1	32	138	85
Both under pensionable age	13,119	5,362	6,652	641	30	377	7	50	15,514	15,087
2 of same sex	**815**	**590**	**112**	**20**	**1**	**55**	**2**	**35**	**450**	**328**
Both of pensionable age	55	55	-	-	-	-	-	-	-	-
1 under, 1 of pensionable age	126	83	14	2	1	8	-	18	86	56
Both under pensionable age	634	452	98	18	-	47	2	17	364	272
3 or more	**5,389**	**3,423**	**1,238**	**165**	**20**	**487**	**8**	**48**	**6,402**	**2,716**
All of pensionable age	9	8	-	-	-	-	-	1	3	1
1 or more under pensionable age	5,380	3,415	1,238	165	20	487	8	47	6,399	2,715
Havant										
TOTAL HOUSEHOLDS	46,151	24,555	12,303	1,283	118	2,773	211	4,908	35,149	35,889
No non-dependants	3,413		3	33	2	443	125	2,807		4,469
1 male	**4,163**	**2,960**	**146**	**85**	**7**	**323**	**29**	**613**	**1,203**	**1,578**
16 - 44	1,816	1,393	111	65	5	125	18	99	423	707
45 - 64	1,254	856	33	20	2	174	8	161	398	481
65 and over	1,093	711	2	-	-	24	3	353	382	390
1 female	**8,728**	**5,064**	**1,587**	**224**	**25**	**675**	**28**	**1,125**	**3,664**	**5,560**
16 - 44	2,576	717	1,505	186	15	107	9	37	1,859	3,592
45 - 59	1,379	777	75	35	7	347	10	128	602	724
60 and over	4,773	3,570	7	3	3	221	9	960	1,203	1,244
1 male and 1 female	**21,275**	**11,326**	**8,420**	**657**	**52**	**618**	**14**	**188**	**19,898**	**19,321**
Both of pensionable age	2,908	2,864	6	2	-	22	-	14	88	49
1 under, 1 of pensionable age	1,707	1,526	24	8	4	56	1	88	362	214
Both under pensionable age	16,660	6,936	8,390	647	48	540	13	86	19,448	19,058
2 of same sex	**1,266**	**737**	**234**	**53**	**2**	**146**	**7**	**87**	**1,058**	**790**
Both of pensionable age	84	75	-	-	-	1	-	8	18	10
1 under, 1 of pensionable age	267	179	22	1	2	17	4	42	176	106
Both under pensionable age	915	483	212	52	-	128	3	37	864	674
3 or more	**7,306**	**4,468**	**1,913**	**231**	**30**	**568**	**8**	**88**	**9,326**	**4,171**
All of pensionable age	22	21	-	-	-	-	-	1	3	1
1 or more under pensionable age	7,284	4,447	1,913	231	30	568	8	87	9,323	4,170

Table 30 'Carers' – **continued**　　　　　　　　　　　　　　　　　　　County, districts

30. Households with residents; residents in households with dependants

Number, sex and age of non-dependants	TOTAL HOUSE-HOLDS	Households with no dependants	Households with 1 or more dependants						Persons in households with dependants	
			Age of youngest dependant 0-15 and age of oldest			Age of youngest dependant 16 up to pensionable age and age of oldest		Age of youngest dependant pensionable age and over		
			0-15	16 up to pension-able age	Pension-able age and over	16 up to pension-able age	Pension-able age and over		Non-depen-dants	Depen-dants
a	b	c	d	e	f	g	h	i	j	k

New Forest

TOTAL HOUSEHOLDS	**65,411**	**38,245**	**14,695**	**1,522**	**128**	**3,036**	**197**	**7,588**	**43,318**	**43,144**
No non-dependants	4,599		2	19	3	343	115	4,117		5,914
1 male	**5,928**	**4,519**	**140**	**59**	**3**	**291**	**19**	**897**	**1,409**	**1,667**
16 - 44	2,289	1,950	99	41	3	88	8	100	339	531
45 - 64	1,586	1,161	36	16	-	171	7	195	425	481
65 and over	2,053	1,408	5	2	-	32	4	602	645	655
1 female	**12,786**	**8,395**	**1,321**	**214**	**24**	**760**	**33**	**2,039**	**4,391**	**5,830**
16 - 44	2,498	965	1,205	169	9	89	7	54	1,533	2,775
45 - 59	1,756	1,018	110	44	10	369	10	195	738	891
60 and over	8,532	6,412	6	1	5	302	16	1,790	2,120	2,164
1 male and 1 female	**31,628**	**18,575**	**11,040**	**893**	**54**	**761**	**14**	**291**	**26,106**	**24,545**
Both of pensionable age	6,167	6,064	7	-	-	54	2	40	206	110
1 under, 1 of pensionable age	2,634	2,369	52	8	1	72	1	131	530	304
Both under pensionable age	22,827	10,142	10,981	885	53	635	11	120	25,370	24,131
2 of same sex	**1,674**	**1,172**	**193**	**41**	**7**	**146**	**1**	**114**	**1,004**	**692**
Both of pensionable age	219	198	-	-	-	7	-	14	42	22
1 under, 1 of pensionable age	400	286	20	3	2	26	-	63	228	133
Both under pensionable age	1,055	688	173	38	5	113	1	37	734	537
3 or more	**8,796**	**5,584**	**1,999**	**296**	**37**	**735**	**15**	**130**	**10,408**	**4,496**
All of pensionable age	58	55	-	-	-	2	-	1	10	3
1 or more under pensionable age	8,738	5,529	1,999	296	37	733	15	129	10,398	4,493

Portsmouth

TOTAL HOUSEHOLDS	**72,590**	**41,098**	**17,059**	**1,447**	**184**	**3,739**	**326**	**8,737**	**46,625**	**49,819**
No non-dependants	6,626		12	44	8	931	211	5,420		8,286
1 male	**8,922**	**7,022**	**227**	**112**	**5**	**458**	**31**	**1,067**	**1,900**	**2,393**
16 - 44	4,347	3,678	172	95	3	177	17	205	669	1,046
45 - 64	2,508	1,888	52	17	1	248	10	292	620	719
65 and over	2,067	1,456	3	-	1	33	4	570	611	628
1 female	**15,540**	**9,938**	**2,656**	**278**	**34**	**903**	**32**	**1,699**	**5,602**	**8,289**
16 - 44	5,118	2,074	2,534	238	26	165	2	79	3,044	5,533
45 - 59	2,096	1,310	114	36	7	428	18	183	786	925
60 and over	8,326	6,554	8	4	1	310	12	1,437	1,772	1,831
1 male and 1 female	**29,643**	**16,388**	**11,501**	**684**	**79**	**647**	**30**	**314**	**26,510**	**24,702**
Both of pensionable age	3,780	3,700	7	-	-	35	1	37	160	87
1 under, 1 of pensionable age	2,228	1,966	34	9	4	71	12	132	524	315
Both under pensionable age	23,635	10,722	11,460	675	75	541	17	145	25,826	24,300
2 of same sex	**2,643**	**1,873**	**325**	**58**	**10**	**229**	**10**	**138**	**1,540**	**1,123**
Both of pensionable age	182	166	1	-	-	3	1	11	32	20
1 under, 1 of pensionable age	484	339	29	3	4	35	1	73	290	167
Both under pensionable age	1,977	1,368	295	55	6	191	8	54	1,218	936
3 or more	**9,216**	**5,877**	**2,338**	**271**	**48**	**571**	**12**	**99**	**11,073**	**5,026**
All of pensionable age	47	45	-	-	-	1	-	1	6	3
1 or more under pensionable age	9,169	5,832	2,338	271	48	570	12	98	11,067	5,023

30. Households with residents; residents in households with dependants

Number, sex and age of non-dependants	TOTAL HOUSE-HOLDS	Households with no dependants	Age of youngest dependant 0 - 15 and age of oldest			Age of youngest dependant 16 up to pensionable age and age of oldest		Age of youngest dependant pensionable age and over	Persons in households with dependants	
			0 - 15	16 up to pension-able age	Pension-able age and over	16 up to pension-able age	Pension-able age and over		Non-depen-dants	Depen-dants
a	b	c	d	e	f	g	h	i	j	k
Rushmoor										
TOTAL HOUSEHOLDS	30,523	16,878	8,990	782	62	1,312	85	2,414	23,535	22,636
No non-dependants	1,709		3	23	-	196	58	1,429		2,179
1 male	**3,033**	**2,414**	**81**	**58**	**1**	**166**	**4**	**309**	**619**	**801**
16 - 44	1,674	1,436	66	48	1	74	2	47	238	388
45 - 64	769	577	14	10	-	86	2	80	192	222
65 and over	590	401	1	-	-	6	-	182	189	191
1 female	**4,688**	**2,866**	**947**	**107**	**10**	**257**	**15**	**486**	**1,822**	**2,737**
16 - 44	1,651	579	900	86	4	45	6	31	1,072	1,917
45 - 59	695	431	41	20	4	141	2	56	264	315
60 and over	2,342	1,856	6	1	2	71	7	399	486	505
1 male and 1 female	**15,202**	**7,586**	**6,717**	**452**	**32**	**309**	**5**	**101**	**15,232**	**14,188**
Both of pensionable age	1,200	1,185	5	-	-	5	-	5	30	15
1 under, 1 of pensionable age	893	797	16	3	3	30	2	42	192	117
Both under pensionable age	13,109	5,604	6,696	449	29	274	3	54	15,010	14,056
2 of same sex	**1,046**	**795**	**122**	**14**	**3**	**62**	**-**	**50**	**502**	**346**
Both of pensionable age	39	34	-	-	-	-	-	5	10	5
1 under, 1 of pensionable age	180	123	15	1	3	10	-	28	114	69
Both under pensionable age	827	638	107	13	-	52	-	17	378	272
3 or more	**4,845**	**3,217**	**1,120**	**128**	**16**	**322**	**3**	**39**	**5,360**	**2,385**
All of pensionable age	12	12	-	-	-	-	-	-	-	-
1 or more under pensionable age	4,833	3,205	1,120	128	16	322	3	39	5,360	2,385
Southampton										
TOTAL HOUSEHOLDS	81,140	46,428	19,397	1,837	178	4,549	344	8,407	53,382	56,894
No non-dependants	6,603		10	51	5	1,187	235	5,115		8,277
1 male	**10,229**	**8,333**	**232**	**122**	**4**	**484**	**29**	**1,025**	**1,896**	**2,448**
16 - 44	5,151	4,469	188	98	3	203	18	172	682	1,121
45 - 64	2,770	2,155	38	24	1	247	8	297	615	716
65 and over	2,308	1,709	6	-	-	34	3	556	599	611
1 female	**17,178**	**10,801**	**3,161**	**392**	**31**	**1,037**	**42**	**1,714**	**6,377**	**9,875**
16 - 44	6,076	2,432	3,029	325	19	190	9	72	3,644	6,875
45 - 59	2,294	1,396	122	62	9	503	15	187	898	1,107
60 and over	8,808	6,973	10	5	3	344	18	1,455	1,835	1,893
1 male and 1 female	**33,160**	**18,283**	**12,865**	**847**	**80**	**772**	**12**	**301**	**29,754**	**28,752**
Both of pensionable age	4,421	4,338	8	1	-	49	-	25	166	90
1 under, 1 of pensionable age	2,512	2,244	44	10	1	79	2	132	536	320
Both under pensionable age	26,227	11,701	12,813	836	79	644	10	144	29,052	28,342
2 of same sex	**2,830**	**1,972**	**352**	**80**	**8**	**270**	**11**	**137**	**1,716**	**1,227**
Both of pensionable age	155	146	-	-	-	2	-	7	18	9
1 under, 1 of pensionable age	519	360	38	5	3	35	1	77	318	192
Both under pensionable age	2,156	1,466	314	75	5	233	10	53	1,380	1,026
3 or more	**11,140**	**7,039**	**2,777**	**345**	**50**	**799**	**15**	**115**	**13,639**	**6,315**
All of pensionable age	41	40	-	-	-	1	-	-	3	1
1 or more under pensionable age	11,099	6,999	2,777	345	50	798	15	115	13,636	6,314

Table 30 'Carers' – **continued**   County, districts

30. Households with residents; residents in households with dependants

Number, sex and age of non-dependants	TOTAL HOUSE-HOLDS	Households with no dependants	Households with 1 or more dependants					Age of youngest dependant pensionable age and over	Persons in households with dependants	
			Age of youngest dependant 0 - 15 and age of oldest			Age of youngest dependant 16 up to pensionable age and age of oldest			Non-dependants	Depen-dants
			0 - 15	16 up to pension-able age	Pension-able age and over	16 up to pension-able age	Pension-able age and over			
a	b	c	d	e	f	g	h	i	j	k
Test Valley										
TOTAL HOUSEHOLDS	38,391	21,504	10,595	1,026	60	1,800	102	3,304	29,566	27,798
No non-dependants	2,102		6	16	-	186	63	1,831		2,693
1 male	**3,340**	**2,590**	**110**	**47**	**3**	**168**	**9**	**413**	**750**	**958**
16 - 44	1,480	1,242	82	33	-	56	2	65	238	375
45 - 64	988	726	27	14	1	100	5	115	262	326
65 and over	872	622	1	-	2	12	2	233	250	257
1 female	**6,116**	**3,953**	**884**	**106**	**9**	**343**	**18**	**803**	**2,163**	**3,078**
16 - 44	1,657	638	824	89	5	64	3	34	1,019	1,840
45 - 59	888	572	55	17	-	159	6	79	316	388
60 and over	3,571	2,743	5	-	4	120	9	690	828	850
1 male and 1 female	**19,278**	**10,071**	**7,932**	**641**	**23**	**478**	**4**	**129**	**18,414**	**17,301**
Both of pensionable age	2,212	2,180	3	-	-	15	-	14	64	33
1 under, 1 of pensionable age	1,304	1,176	38	3	3	31	-	53	256	154
Both under pensionable age	15,762	6,715	7,891	638	20	432	4	62	18,094	17,114
2 of same sex	**1,070**	**740**	**152**	**27**	**4**	**91**	**2**	**54**	**660**	**479**
Both of pensionable age	79	76	-	-	-	1	-	2	6	4
1 under, 1 of pensionable age	234	176	14	2	3	12	1	26	116	75
Both under pensionable age	757	488	138	25	1	78	1	26	538	400
3 or more	**6,485**	**4,150**	**1,511**	**189**	**21**	**534**	**6**	**74**	**7,579**	**3,289**
All of pensionable age	28	27	-	-	-	1	-	-	3	1
1 or more under pensionable age	6,457	4,123	1,511	189	21	533	6	74	7,576	3,288
Winchester										
TOTAL HOUSEHOLDS	37,553	21,982	8,878	1,062	64	1,792	107	3,668	26,323	25,599
No non-dependants	2,380		3	6	-	195	61	2,115		2,936
1 male	**3,306**	**2,600**	**76**	**47**	**-**	**159**	**11**	**413**	**706**	**884**
16 - 44	1,400	1,201	63	31	-	53	7	45	199	330
45 - 64	962	723	13	16	-	100	2	108	239	283
65 and over	944	676	-	-	-	6	2	260	268	271
1 female	**6,910**	**4,918**	**613**	**104**	**9**	**364**	**20**	**882**	**1,992**	**2,719**
16 - 44	1,472	735	558	76	5	62	4	32	737	1,355
45 - 59	979	634	54	27	4	180	5	75	345	435
60 and over	4,459	3,549	1	1	-	122	11	775	910	929
1 male and 1 female	**17,989**	**9,877**	**6,800**	**686**	**37**	**444**	**5**	**140**	**16,224**	**15,655**
Both of pensionable age	2,592	2,558	5	1	-	18	-	10	68	38
1 under, 1 of pensionable age	1,479	1,353	26	1	1	32	-	66	252	149
Both under pensionable age	13,918	5,966	6,769	684	36	394	5	64	15,904	15,468
2 of same sex	**1,002**	**710**	**129**	**19**	**4**	**85**	**6**	**49**	**584**	**416**
Both of pensionable age	80	76	-	-	-	-	-	4	8	4
1 under, 1 of pensionable age	232	176	15	1	4	8	-	28	112	66
Both under pensionable age	690	458	114	18	-	77	6	17	464	346
3 or more	**5,966**	**3,877**	**1,257**	**200**	**14**	**545**	**4**	**69**	**6,817**	**2,989**
All of pensionable age	19	18	-	-	-	-	-	1	3	1
1 or more under pensionable age	5,947	3,859	1,257	200	14	545	4	68	6,814	2,988

Table 31 Dependent children in households

Note: * May include a small number of households with no adults

31. Households with residents; residents in households

Households with the following adults	Households with no dependent children	Households with dependent children						Persons in households				
		All households	With 1 dependent child		With 2 or more dependent children			With no dependent child(ren)		With dependent child(ren)		
			Aged 0-4	Aged 5 and over	All aged 0-4	All aged 5 and over	1 or more aged 0-4 and 1 or more aged 5 and over	All persons	Persons economically active	Dependent children	Adults	Persons economically active
a	b	c	d	e	f	g	h	i	j	k	l	m

HAMPSHIRE

a	b	c	d	e	f	g	h	i	j	k	l	m
ALL HOUSEHOLDS*	418,448	184,809	28,955	45,603	16,287	60,547	33,417	786,368	475,168	334,808	390,862	300,679
1 male	54,815	2,052	151	923	60	762	156	54,815	35,411	3,349	2,052	1,581
1 female	90,429	18,344	3,315	4,924	1,192	5,465	3,448	90,429	23,159	32,351	18,344	8,264
2 (1 male and 1 female)	188,932	128,863	22,032	19,469	14,117	46,366	26,879	377,864	215,642	247,335	257,726	201,539
2 (same sex)	15,320	3,078	457	1,389	130	719	383	30,640	20,487	4,799	6,156	4,259
3 or more (male(s) and female(s))	66,348	31,977	2,916	18,643	766	7,152	2,500	224,143	173,871	46,262	105,400	84,202
3 or more (same sex)	2,604	380	72	191	16	58	43	8,477	6,598	545	1,184	834

Basingstoke & Deane

a	b	c	d	e	f	g	h	i	j	k	l	m
ALL HOUSEHOLDS*	36,161	18,162	2,806	4,475	1,561	6,094	3,226	71,058	48,917	32,967	39,253	31,313
1 male	4,447	156	9	67	6	62	12	4,447	3,221	268	156	133
1 female	6,552	1,412	211	397	72	419	313	6,552	2,051	2,558	1,412	739
2 (1 male and 1 female)	16,916	12,855	2,216	1,857	1,390	4,794	2,598	33,832	22,310	24,750	25,710	20,641
2 (same sex)	1,245	266	33	131	11	60	31	2,490	1,857	413	532	392
3 or more (male(s) and female(s))	6,777	3,429	328	1,998	81	753	269	23,013	18,838	4,918	11,323	9,314
3 or more (same sex)	224	39	9	23	1	4	2	724	640	51	120	94

East Hampshire

a	b	c	d	e	f	g	h	i	j	k	l	m
ALL HOUSEHOLDS*	26,303	12,855	1,786	3,133	1,118	4,522	2,296	50,260	30,976	23,613	27,462	21,352
1 male	3,013	146	12	60	4	61	9	3,013	1,944	242	146	119
1 female	5,428	938	163	227	30	354	164	5,428	1,416	1,702	938	505
2 (1 male and 1 female)	12,622	9,371	1,441	1,445	1,018	3,520	1,947	25,244	14,986	18,184	18,742	14,743
2 (same sex)	810	189	20	82	10	54	23	1,620	1,046	304	378	268
3 or more (male(s) and female(s))	4,311	2,179	144	1,304	56	527	148	14,575	11,269	3,133	7,180	5,658
3 or more (same sex)	119	24	5	14	-	1	4	380	315	33	78	59

Table 31 Dependent children in households – continued

Note: * May include a small number of households with no adults

31. Households with residents; residents in households

Households with the following adults	Households with no dependent children	Households with dependent children						Persons in households				
		With 1 dependent child			With 2 or more dependent children			With no dependent child(ren)		With dependent child(ren)		
		All households	Aged 0 - 4	Aged 5 and over	All aged 0 - 4	All aged 5 and over	1 or more aged 0 - 4 and 1 or more aged 5 and over	All persons	Persons economically active	Dependent children	Adults	Persons economically active
a	b	c	d	e	f	g	h	i	j	k	l	m
Eastleigh												
ALL HOUSEHOLDS*	27,837	13,382	2,090	3,157	1,209	4,630	2,296	53,086	33,646	24,064	28,148	22,217
1 male	3,507	133	10	58	3	55	7	3,507	2,419	220	133	114
1 female	5,377	1,075	175	286	72	366	176	5,377	1,478	1,884	1,075	567
2 (1 male and 1 female)	13,426	9,863	1,725	1,401	1,092	3,685	1,960	26,852	16,186	18,700	19,726	15,691
2 (same sex)	902	193	25	88	4	54	22	1,804	1,239	295	386	290
3 or more (male(s) and female(s))	4,491	2,096	151	1,309	38	467	131	15,121	11,976	2,940	6,769	5,506
3 or more (same sex)	134	19	3	13	-	3	-	425	348	22	59	49
Fareham												
ALL HOUSEHOLDS*	26,536	11,833	1,770	3,110	1,033	3,852	2,068	51,428	31,048	20,878	25,301	19,974
1 male	2,789	124	9	66	4	35	10	2,789	1,780	194	124	105
1 female	5,033	865	129	269	44	294	129	5,033	1,160	1,443	865	498
2 (1 male and 1 female)	13,212	8,583	1,441	1,371	925	3,073	1,773	26,424	14,797	16,137	17,166	13,631
2 (same sex)	849	174	20	79	8	45	22	1,698	1,147	272	348	250
3 or more (male(s) and female(s))	4,542	2,069	169	1,316	50	400	134	15,134	11,873	2,806	6,753	5,454
3 or more (same sex)	111	15	1	9	2	3	-	350	291	20	45	36
Gosport												
ALL HOUSEHOLDS*	19,750	9,606	1,638	2,423	822	2,883	1,840	36,718	22,126	17,134	19,852	15,248
1 male	2,423	117	9	59	1	34	14	2,423	1,521	182	117	91
1 female	4,442	1,115	222	295	72	327	199	4,442	1,006	1,930	1,115	478
2 (1 male and 1 female)	9,075	6,705	1,259	1,089	714	2,153	1,490	18,150	10,533	12,626	13,410	10,442
2 (same sex)	746	165	20	72	6	49	18	1,492	1,040	264	330	238
3 or more (male(s) and female(s))	2,941	1,487	128	900	29	314	116	9,817	7,688	2,100	4,835	3,964
3 or more (same sex)	123	14	-	7	-	4	3	394	338	26	45	35

Table 31　Dependent children in households – continued

Note: * May include a small number of households with no adults

31. Households with residents; residents in households

Households with the following adults	Households with no dependent children	Households with dependent children						Persons in households				
		All households	With 1 dependent child		With 2 or more dependent children			With no dependent child(ren)		With dependent child(ren)		
			Aged 0-4	Aged 5 and over	All aged 0-4	All aged 5 and over	1 or more aged 0-4 and 1 or more aged 5 and over	All persons	Persons economically active	Dependent children	Adults	Persons economically active
a	b	c	d	e	f	g	h	i	j	k	l	m
Hart												
ALL HOUSEHOLDS*	18,627	10,446	1,343	2,533	916	3,978	1,676	37,266	25,264	19,051	22,697	17,813
1 male	2,123	81	1	38	2	35	5	2,123	1,577	138	81	75
1 female	3,309	580	85	159	24	237	75	3,309	978	1,015	580	350
2 (1 male and 1 female)	8,702	7,696	1,112	1,046	847	3,215	1,476	17,404	11,277	14,986	15,392	12,107
2 (same sex)	680	143	15	68	10	34	16	1,360	989	224	286	217
3 or more (male(s) and female(s))	3,697	1,927	128	1,212	32	452	103	12,692	10,111	2,660	6,302	5,029
3 or more (same sex)	116	18	2	9	1	5	1	378	332	27	56	35
Havant												
ALL HOUSEHOLDS*	31,439	14,712	2,079	3,775	1,192	4,758	2,908	59,973	34,357	27,194	31,130	23,445
1 male	3,638	191	12	84	5	75	15	3,638	2,227	311	191	145
1 female	6,792	1,760	273	463	117	525	382	6,792	1,557	3,231	1,760	681
2 (1 male and 1 female)	14,576	9,653	1,451	1,539	974	3,459	2,230	29,152	15,160	19,035	19,306	14,892
2 (same sex)	960	313	43	139	13	73	45	1,920	1,209	502	626	398
3 or more (male(s) and female(s))	5,329	2,759	291	1,538	83	620	227	18,013	13,833	4,056	9,153	7,261
3 or more (same sex)	144	31	9	10	-	5	7	458	371	50	94	68
New Forest												
ALL HOUSEHOLDS*	47,794	17,617	2,535	4,488	1,507	6,146	2,941	88,584	45,575	31,581	37,439	28,877
1 male	5,414	179	11	94	3	58	13	5,414	3,079	263	179	145
1 female	10,816	1,491	267	409	93	521	201	10,816	2,131	2,555	1,491	725
2 (1 male and 1 female)	23,216	12,605	1,995	1,965	1,347	4,789	2,509	46,432	21,771	24,037	25,210	19,626
2 (same sex)	1,541	257	38	126	7	58	28	3,082	1,722	389	514	360
3 or more (male(s) and female(s))	6,629	3,055	220	1,879	55	714	187	22,275	16,444	4,291	9,977	7,967
3 or more (same sex)	178	22	3	11	1	4	3	565	428	35	68	54

Table 31 Dependent children in households – continued

Note: * May include a small number of households with no adults

31. Households with residents; residents in households

Households with the following adults	Households with no dependent children	Households with dependent children						Persons in households				
		All households	With 1 dependent child		With 2 or more dependent children			With no dependent child(ren)		With dependent child(ren)		
			Aged 0-4	Aged 5 and over	All aged 0-4	All aged 5 and over	1 or more aged 0-4 and 1 or more aged 5 and over	All persons	Persons economically active	Dependent children	Adults	Persons economically active
a	b	c	d	e	f	g	h	i	j	k	l	m
Portsmouth												
ALL HOUSEHOLDS*	52,953	19,637	3,717	4,778	1,811	5,401	3,930	94,056	54,105	35,203	40,471	29,989
1 male	8,518	277	27	127	9	94	20	8,518	5,378	447	277	197
1 female	13,470	2,912	575	817	201	719	600	13,470	3,482	5,064	2,912	1,177
2 (1 male and 1 female)	21,144	12,716	2,563	1,957	1,483	3,817	2,896	42,288	23,523	24,044	25,432	19,602
2 (same sex)	2,409	398	89	156	22	75	56	4,818	3,157	622	796	511
3 or more (male(s) and female(s))	6,988	3,249	441	1,681	91	686	350	23,540	17,546	4,917	10,872	8,394
3 or more (same sex)	424	58	19	22	3	8	6	1,422	1,019	76	182	108
Rushmoor												
ALL HOUSEHOLDS*	20,138	10,385	1,968	2,332	1,132	3,096	1,857	38,835	27,033	18,569	21,717	16,916
1 male	2,792	111	10	44	7	37	13	2,792	1,984	184	111	81
1 female	3,761	1,036	216	280	83	283	174	3,761	1,148	1,767	1,036	464
2 (1 male and 1 female)	8,956	7,467	1,557	1,022	986	2,372	1,530	17,912	12,094	14,013	14,934	11,732
2 (same sex)	934	157	25	78	5	31	18	1,868	1,451	235	314	238
3 or more (male(s) and female(s))	3,515	1,585	155	889	49	371	121	11,925	9,872	2,330	5,252	4,352
3 or more (same sex)	180	23	4	15	2	1	1	577	484	30	70	49
Southampton												
ALL HOUSEHOLDS*	58,501	22,639	3,947	5,447	2,051	6,680	4,514	105,045	61,234	41,919	46,902	33,971
1 male	10,033	289	26	122	12	104	25	10,033	6,373	495	289	173
1 female	14,118	3,420	717	830	296	844	733	14,118	3,899	6,141	3,420	1,148
2 (1 male and 1 female)	23,186	14,451	2,629	2,184	1,610	4,762	3,266	46,372	25,461	28,369	28,902	21,653
2 (same sex)	2,440	466	86	202	20	94	64	4,880	3,308	726	932	585
3 or more (male(s) and female(s))	8,148	3,905	470	2,052	106	860	417	27,709	20,843	6,039	13,125	10,255
3 or more (same sex)	576	75	16	33	5	13	8	1,933	1,350	109	234	157

Table 31 Dependent children in households – **continued**

Note: * May include a small number of households with no adults

31. Households with residents; residents in households

Households with the following adults	Households with no dependent children	Households with dependent children						Persons in households				
		All households	With 1 dependent child		With 2 or more dependent children			With no dependent child(ren)		With dependent child(ren)		
			Aged 0 - 4	Aged 5 and over	All aged 0 - 4	All aged 5 and over	1 or more aged 0 - 4 and 1 or more aged 5 and over	All persons	Persons economically active	Dependent children	Adults	Persons economically active
a	b	c	d	e	f	g	h	i	j	k	l	m
Test Valley												
ALL HOUSEHOLDS*	**25,809**	**12,582**	**1,841**	**3,208**	**1,057**	**4,399**	**2,077**	**50,077**	**31,761**	**22,563**	**26,823**	**21,098**
1 male	3,016	141	6	58	3	65	9	3,016	1,984	235	141	113
1 female	5,072	997	175	284	54	301	183	5,072	1,328	1,738	997	502
2 (1 male and 1 female)	12,011	9,010	1,466	1,420	945	3,469	1,710	24,022	14,393	17,099	18,020	14,282
2 (same sex)	916	192	27	88	5	54	18	1,832	1,194	298	384	275
3 or more (male(s) and female(s))	4,663	2,207	165	1,343	48	501	150	15,724	12,526	3,128	7,197	5,867
3 or more (same sex)	131	26	1	13	1	5	6	411	336	46	84	59
Winchester												
ALL HOUSEHOLDS*	**26,600**	**10,953**	**1,435**	**2,744**	**878**	**4,108**	**1,788**	**49,982**	**29,126**	**20,072**	**23,667**	**18,466**
1 male	3,102	107	9	46	1	47	4	3,102	1,924	170	107	90
1 female	6,259	743	107	208	34	275	119	6,259	1,525	1,323	743	430
2 (1 male and 1 female)	11,890	7,888	1,177	1,173	786	3,258	1,494	23,780	13,151	15,355	15,776	12,497
2 (same sex)	888	165	16	80	9	38	22	1,776	1,128	255	330	237
3 or more (male(s) and female(s))	4,317	2,030	126	1,222	48	487	147	14,605	11,052	2,944	6,662	5,181
3 or more (same sex)	144	16	-	12	-	2	2	460	346	20	49	31

Table 32   Children aged 0 - 15 in households   County, districts

Note: * May include a small number of households with no persons aged 16 and over

32. Households with residents; residents in households

Households with the following persons aged 16 and over	Households with no person aged 0-15	Households with persons aged 0-15						Persons in households					
		All households	With one person aged 0-15		With two or more persons aged 0-15			With no person aged 0-15		With person(s) aged 0-15			
			Aged 0-4	Aged 5-15	All aged 0-4	All aged 5-15	1 or more aged 0-4 and 1 or more aged 5-15	All persons	Persons economically active	Persons aged 0-15	Persons aged 16 and over	Persons economically active
a	b	c	d	e	f	g	h	i	j	k	l	m

HAMPSHIRE

ALL HOUSEHOLDS*	430,728	172,529	29,266	42,545	16,336	51,325	33,057	830,237	499,739	308,796	373,005	276,108
1 male	54,841	1,607	151	656	60	589	151	54,841	35,411	2,661	1,607	1,187
1 female	90,453	16,588	3,316	4,171	1,192	4,566	3,343	90,453	23,159	29,162	16,588	7,031
2 (1 male and 1 female)	189,434	116,335	22,050	15,796	14,117	38,036	26,336	378,868	216,048	222,171	232,670	179,801
2 (same sex)	15,846	3,022	471	1,376	131	650	394	31,692	20,912	4,659	6,044	3,762
3 or more (male(s) and female(s))	77,281	34,518	3,190	20,322	813	7,413	2,780	265,036	197,209	49,472	114,841	83,544
3 or more (same sex)	2,873	405	76	210	17	56	46	9,347	7,000	578	1,255	783

Basingstoke & Deane

ALL HOUSEHOLDS*	37,378	16,945	2,834	4,203	1,563	5,149	3,196	75,481	51,519	30,359	37,438	28,711
1 male	4,447	115	9	46	6	43	11	4,447	3,221	198	115	95
1 female	6,553	1,257	211	335	72	341	298	6,553	2,051	2,260	1,257	622
2 (1 male and 1 female)	16,959	11,605	2,217	1,515	1,390	3,930	2,553	33,918	22,347	22,216	23,210	18,428
2 (same sex)	1,286	265	36	124	11	57	37	2,572	1,893	421	530	343
3 or more (male(s) and female(s))	7,884	3,663	352	2,160	83	774	294	27,185	21,319	5,210	12,210	9,149
3 or more (same sex)	249	38	9	22	1	4	2	806	688	51	116	74

East Hampshire

ALL HOUSEHOLDS*	27,299	11,859	1,806	2,936	1,121	3,723	2,273	53,866	32,934	21,417	26,052	19,394
1 male	3,013	112	12	44	4	43	9	3,013	1,944	185	112	86
1 female	5,428	824	163	185	30	287	159	5,428	1,416	1,484	824	418
2 (1 male and 1 female)	12,650	8,246	1,441	1,116	1,018	2,768	1,903	25,300	15,010	15,907	16,492	12,823
2 (same sex)	841	194	20	86	10	56	22	1,682	1,071	310	388	245
3 or more (male(s) and female(s))	5,228	2,452	163	1,487	59	565	178	17,996	13,148	3,491	8,159	5,768
3 or more (same sex)	139	24	6	17	-	-	1	447	345	27	77	54

Table 32 Children aged 0 - 15 in households – continued

Note: * May include a small number of households with no persons aged 16 and over

32. Households with residents; residents in households

Households with the following persons aged 16 and over	Households with no person aged 0-15	Households with persons aged 0-15						Persons in households				
		All households	With one person aged 0-15		With two or more persons aged 0-15			With no person aged 0-15		With person(s) aged 0-15		
			Aged 0-4	Aged 5-15	All aged 0-4	All aged 5-15	1 or more aged 0-4 and 1 or more aged 5-15	All persons	Persons economically active	Persons aged 0-15	Persons aged 16 and over	Persons economically active
a	b	c	d	e	f	g	h	i	j	k	l	m
Eastleigh												
ALL HOUSEHOLDS*	28,715	12,504	2,109	2,934	1,214	3,975	2,272	56,226	35,442	22,237	26,835	20,421
1 male	3,508	103	10	38	3	46	6	3,508	2,419	176	103	85
1 female	5,377	953	175	233	72	302	171	5,377	1,478	1,664	953	472
2 (1 male and 1 female)	13,466	8,979	1,725	1,137	1,092	3,097	1,928	26,932	16,221	16,957	17,958	14,135
2 (same sex)	935	184	25	85	4	46	24	1,870	1,270	278	368	244
3 or more (male(s) and female(s))	5,278	2,258	170	1,422	43	481	142	18,060	13,680	3,131	7,376	5,430
3 or more (same sex)	151	25	3	18	-	3	1	479	374	29	77	55
Fareham												
ALL HOUSEHOLDS*	27,428	10,941	1,784	2,810	1,038	3,260	2,049	54,587	32,869	19,159	23,861	18,153
1 male	2,789	92	9	45	4	24	10	2,789	1,780	144	92	76
1 female	5,033	752	129	216	44	237	126	5,033	1,160	1,252	752	408
2 (1 male and 1 female)	13,248	7,745	1,442	1,086	925	2,544	1,748	26,496	14,831	14,546	15,490	12,137
2 (same sex)	887	164	21	73	8	40	22	1,774	1,182	257	328	218
3 or more (male(s) and female(s))	5,343	2,169	181	1,379	55	411	143	18,094	13,600	2,934	7,151	5,281
3 or more (same sex)	128	16	1	11	2	2	-	401	316	20	48	33
Gosport												
ALL HOUSEHOLDS*	20,328	9,028	1,651	2,247	823	2,481	1,826	38,714	23,267	15,984	19,006	14,107
1 male	2,423	91	9	41	1	26	14	2,423	1,521	145	91	65
1 female	4,443	1,009	222	249	72	272	194	4,443	1,006	1,740	1,009	408
2 (1 male and 1 female)	9,106	6,143	1,259	901	714	1,807	1,462	18,212	10,559	11,555	12,286	9,444
2 (same sex)	780	169	20	78	6	43	22	1,560	1,071	268	338	212
3 or more (male(s) and female(s))	3,438	1,596	141	966	30	328	131	11,634	8,747	2,243	5,222	3,940
3 or more (same sex)	138	19	-	12	-	4	3	442	363	30	60	38

Table 32 Children aged 0 - 15 in households – continued

Note: * May include a small number of households with no persons aged 16 and over

32. Households with residents; residents in households

Households with the following persons aged 16 and over	Households with no person aged 0-15	Households with persons aged 0-15						Persons in households				
			With one person aged 0-15		With two or more persons aged 0-15			With no person aged 0-15		With person(s) aged 0-15		
		All households	Aged 0-4	Aged 5-15	All aged 0-4	All aged 5-15	1 or more aged 0-4 and 1 or more aged 5-15	All persons	Persons economically active	Persons aged 0-15	Persons aged 16 and over	Persons economically active
a	b	c	d	e	f	g	h	i	j	k	l	m
Hart												
ALL HOUSEHOLDS*	**19,491**	**9,582**	**1,356**	**2,362**	**917**	**3,285**	**1,662**	**40,411**	**26,963**	**17,217**	**21,386**	**16,114**
1 male	2,124	63	1	28	2	27	5	2,124	1,577	111	63	57
1 female	3,309	504	85	125	24	196	74	3,309	978	882	504	300
2 (1 male and 1 female)	8,724	6,753	1,112	793	847	2,555	1,446	17,448	11,292	13,102	13,506	10,480
2 (same sex)	702	133	15	64	10	28	16	1,404	1,006	208	266	187
3 or more (male(s) and female(s))	4,505	2,108	141	1,340	33	474	120	15,712	11,760	2,884	6,984	5,052
3 or more (same sex)	127	21	2	12	1	5	1	414	350	30	63	38
Havant												
ALL HOUSEHOLDS*	**32,447**	**13,704**	**2,113**	**3,456**	**1,198**	**4,069**	**2,868**	**63,525**	**36,337**	**25,120**	**29,652**	**21,465**
1 male	3,639	151	12	60	5	59	15	3,639	2,227	250	151	109
1 female	6,793	1,601	273	395	117	449	367	6,793	1,557	2,936	1,601	570
2 (1 male and 1 female)	14,620	8,675	1,455	1,214	974	2,848	2,184	29,240	15,198	17,085	17,350	13,225
2 (same sex)	1,008	301	46	134	13	65	43	2,016	1,249	479	602	350
3 or more (male(s) and female(s))	6,221	2,939	317	1,640	89	643	250	21,311	15,704	4,311	9,844	7,148
3 or more (same sex)	166	34	10	13	-	4	7	526	402	52	104	63
New Forest												
ALL HOUSEHOLDS*	**49,066**	**16,345**	**2,565**	**4,215**	**1,511**	**5,147**	**2,907**	**93,165**	**48,094**	**28,872**	**35,567**	**26,358**
1 male	5,416	141	11	68	3	46	13	5,416	3,079	211	141	113
1 female	10,818	1,336	267	345	93	434	197	10,818	2,131	2,287	1,336	606
2 (1 male and 1 female)	23,256	11,272	1,997	1,568	1,347	3,907	2,453	46,512	21,801	21,406	22,544	17,363
2 (same sex)	1,593	247	38	127	7	47	28	3,186	1,765	360	494	316
3 or more (male(s) and female(s))	7,781	3,320	248	2,093	59	708	212	26,594	18,855	4,561	10,968	7,907
3 or more (same sex)	202	27	3	14	1	5	4	639	463	44	84	53

Table 32 Children aged 0 - 15 in households – continued

Note: * May include a small number of households with no persons aged 16 and over

32. Households with residents; residents in households

		Households with persons aged 0 - 15						Persons in households				
			With one person aged 0 - 15		With two or more persons aged 0 - 15			With no person aged 0 - 15		With person(s) aged 0 - 15		
Households with the following persons aged 16 and over	Households with no person aged 0 - 15	All households	Aged 0 - 4	Aged 5 - 15	All aged 0 - 4	All aged 5 - 15	1 or more aged 0 - 4 and 1 or more aged 5 - 15	All persons	Persons economically active	Persons aged 0 - 15	Persons aged 16 and over	Persons economically active
a	b	c	d	e	f	g	h	i	j	k	l	m
Portsmouth												
ALL HOUSEHOLDS*	**53,900**	**18,690**	**3,752**	**4,515**	**1,819**	**4,717**	**3,887**	**97,306**	**55,869**	**33,178**	**39,246**	**28,225**
1 male	8,523	231	27	95	9	80	20	8,523	5,378	383	231	158
1 female	13,478	2,689	576	717	201	610	585	13,478	3,482	4,660	2,689	1,039
2 (1 male and 1 female)	21,208	11,823	2,565	1,697	1,483	3,253	2,825	42,416	23,571	22,213	23,646	18,055
2 (same sex)	2,478	402	92	154	23	75	58	4,956	3,201	626	804	470
3 or more (male(s) and female(s))	7,763	3,473	469	1,825	98	691	390	26,425	19,181	5,198	11,690	8,398
3 or more (same sex)	450	60	20	22	3	7	8	1,508	1,056	82	186	105
Rushmoor												
ALL HOUSEHOLDS*	**20,689**	**9,834**	**1,988**	**2,255**	**1,136**	**2,622**	**1,833**	**40,800**	**28,191**	**17,322**	**20,999**	**15,758**
1 male	2,793	83	10	26	7	28	12	2,793	1,984	142	83	56
1 female	3,763	957	216	248	83	238	172	3,763	1,148	1,619	957	406
2 (1 male and 1 female)	8,975	6,849	1,557	863	986	1,950	1,493	17,950	12,106	12,747	13,698	10,638
2 (same sex)	965	163	25	86	5	29	18	1,930	1,480	235	326	217
3 or more (male(s) and female(s))	3,995	1,757	175	1,018	53	374	137	13,728	10,957	2,541	5,868	4,397
3 or more (same sex)	198	22	4	13	2	2	1	636	516	31	67	44
Southampton												
ALL HOUSEHOLDS*	**59,728**	**21,412**	**3,990**	**5,060**	**2,059**	**5,840**	**4,463**	**109,379**	**63,627**	**39,258**	**45,229**	**31,578**
1 male	10,045	239	26	94	12	84	23	10,045	6,373	410	239	138
1 female	14,127	3,193	717	731	296	736	713	14,127	3,899	5,721	3,193	1,015
2 (1 male and 1 female)	23,251	13,287	2,635	1,838	1,610	4,002	3,202	46,502	25,509	25,912	26,574	19,668
2 (same sex)	2,503	441	89	191	20	82	59	5,006	3,351	666	882	496
3 or more (male(s) and female(s))	9,187	4,162	503	2,172	113	920	454	31,641	23,096	6,413	14,091	10,111
3 or more (same sex)	615	80	17	31	6	15	11	2,058	1,399	122	250	150

Table 32 Children aged 0 - 15 in households – continued

Note: * May include a small number of households with no persons aged 16 and over

32. Households with residents; residents in households

Households with the following persons aged 16 and over	Households with no person aged 0-15	Households with persons aged 0-15						Persons in households				
		All households	With one person aged 0-15		With two or more persons aged 0-15			With no person aged 0-15		With person(s) aged 0-15		
			Aged 0-4	Aged 5-15	All aged 0-4	All aged 5-15	1 or more aged 0-4 and 1 or more aged 5-15	All persons	Persons economically active	Persons aged 0-15	Persons aged 16 and over	Persons economically active
a	b	c	d	e	f	g	h	i	j	k	l	m
Test Valley												
ALL HOUSEHOLDS*	26,710	11,681	1,865	3,021	1,058	3,685	2,052	53,316	33,612	20,646	25,501	19,247
1 male	3,018	110	6	42	3	50	9	3,018	1,984	185	110	86
1 female	5,072	895	175	238	54	254	174	5,072	1,328	1,557	895	429
2 (1 male and 1 female)	12,041	8,054	1,467	1,141	945	2,821	1,680	24,082	14,418	15,224	16,108	12,603
2 (same sex)	949	188	27	88	5	46	22	1,898	1,222	288	376	248
3 or more (male(s) and female(s))	5,478	2,401	188	1,497	49	507	160	18,760	14,296	3,331	7,927	5,826
3 or more (same sex)	152	27	1	15	1	4	6	486	364	46	85	55
Winchester												
ALL HOUSEHOLDS*	27,549	10,004	1,453	2,531	879	3,372	1,769	53,461	31,015	18,027	22,233	16,577
1 male	3,103	76	9	29	1	33	4	3,103	1,924	121	76	63
1 female	6,259	618	107	154	34	210	113	6,259	1,525	1,100	618	338
2 (1 male and 1 female)	11,930	6,904	1,178	927	786	2,554	1,459	23,860	13,185	13,301	13,808	10,802
2 (same sex)	919	171	17	86	9	36	23	1,838	1,151	263	342	216
3 or more (male(s) and female(s))	5,180	2,220	142	1,323	49	537	169	17,896	12,866	3,224	7,351	5,137
3 or more (same sex)	158	12	-	10	-	1	1	505	364	14	38	21

Table 33 Women in 'couples': economic position

33. Females resident in households of one male aged 16 or over and one female aged 16 or over with or without persons aged 0 - 15; number of persons aged 0 - 15 in such households

In households with:	TOTAL FEMALES	Economically active females					Economically inactive females
		Employees		Self-employed	Other	Economically active students	
		Full-time	Part-time				
a	b	c	d	e	f	g	h

HAMPSHIRE

In households with:							
No persons aged 0 - 15	189,434	62,440	25,151	5,813	3,880	153	92,150
Person(s) aged 0 - 4 only	36,167	3,764	9,319	1,229	1,089	6	20,766
Person(s) aged 5 - 15 only	53,832	11,251	24,137	3,055	1,219	73	14,170
Persons aged 0 - 4 and 5 - 15	26,336	1,503	8,251	1,155	401	14	15,026
TOTAL PERSONS AGED 0 - 15	222,171	27,687	79,973	10,437	4,618	184	99,456
Persons aged 0 - 4	83,118	6,065	22,268	3,046	1,840	23	49,899

Basingstoke & Deane

No persons aged 0 - 15	16,959	7,425	2,056	495	309	11	6,674
Person(s) aged 0 - 4 only	3,607	449	964	133	88	1	1,973
Person(s) aged 5 - 15 only	5,445	1,325	2,435	326	115	5	1,244
Persons aged 0 - 4 and 5 - 15	2,553	162	861	114	41	-	1,375
TOTAL PERSONS AGED 0 - 15	22,216	3,246	8,323	1,101	425	9	9,121
Persons aged 0 - 4	8,193	699	2,368	314	160	1	4,652

East Hampshire

No persons aged 0 - 15	12,650	4,194	1,755	583	213	11	5,905
Person(s) aged 0 - 4 only	2,459	243	600	127	61	-	1,428
Person(s) aged 5 - 15 only	3,884	821	1,673	299	66	8	1,025
Persons aged 0 - 4 and 5 - 15	1,903	104	589	119	16	2	1,075
TOTAL PERSONS AGED 0 - 15	15,907	1,983	5,607	1,032	238	22	7,047
Persons aged 0 - 4	5,814	402	1,507	308	97	2	3,500

Eastleigh

No persons aged 0 - 15	13,466	5,000	1,808	359	233	13	6,066
Person(s) aged 0 - 4 only	2,817	263	822	96	65	1	1,571
Person(s) aged 5 - 15 only	4,234	810	2,120	233	86	4	985
Persons aged 0 - 4 and 5 - 15	1,928	106	621	66	25	-	1,110
TOTAL PERSONS AGED 0 - 15	16,957	1,973	6,755	739	303	11	7,187
Persons aged 0 - 4	6,281	415	1,820	211	103	1	3,732

Fareham

No persons aged 0 - 15	13,248	4,201	1,744	436	241	6	6,626
Person(s) aged 0 - 4 only	2,367	271	608	103	71	-	1,314
Person(s) aged 5 - 15 only	3,630	813	1,593	203	79	12	942
Persons aged 0 - 4 and 5 - 15	1,748	99	589	98	19	2	943
TOTAL PERSONS AGED 0 - 15	14,546	1,986	5,308	764	280	35	6,208
Persons aged 0 - 4	5,427	422	1,530	253	105	2	3,117

Gosport

No persons aged 0 - 15	9,106	3,149	1,136	181	269	3	4,371
Person(s) aged 0 - 4 only	1,973	211	470	33	98	-	1,161
Person(s) aged 5 - 15 only	2,708	618	1,167	119	99	4	705
Persons aged 0 - 4 and 5 - 15	1,462	88	469	29	23	-	853
TOTAL PERSONS AGED 0 - 15	11,555	1,528	3,988	333	350	7	5,356
Persons aged 0 - 4	4,475	350	1,140	77	145	-	2,763

33. Females resident in households of one male aged 16 or over and one female aged 16 or over with or without persons aged 0 - 15; number of persons aged 0 - 15 in such households

In households with:	TOTAL FEMALES	Economically active females					Economically inactive females
		Employees		Self-employed	Other	Economically active students	
		Full-time	Part-time				
a	b	c	d	e	f	g	h

Hart

No persons aged 0 - 15	8,724	3,344	1,220	352	167	6	3,641
Person(s) aged 0 - 4 only	1,959	207	464	74	44	-	1,170
Person(s) aged 5 - 15 only	3,348	636	1,505	205	62	7	940
Persons aged 0 - 4 and 5 - 15	1,446	67	455	79	18	-	827
TOTAL PERSONS AGED 0 - 15	**13,102**	**1,544**	**4,772**	**719**	**224**	**14**	**5,843**
Persons aged 0 - 4	4,567	335	1,158	205	75	-	2,794

Havant

No persons aged 0 - 15	14,620	4,103	1,986	370	276	8	7,885
Person(s) aged 0 - 4 only	2,429	274	607	75	75	-	1,398
Person(s) aged 5 - 15 only	4,062	896	1,728	205	103	7	1,130
Persons aged 0 - 4 and 5 - 15	2,184	142	636	78	43	1	1,285
TOTAL PERSONS AGED 0 - 15	**17,085**	**2,283**	**5,767**	**689**	**410**	**17**	**7,936**
Persons aged 0 - 4	6,140	479	1,560	192	155	2	3,754

New Forest

No persons aged 0 - 15	23,256	5,421	2,972	886	348	9	13,629
Person(s) aged 0 - 4 only	3,344	259	889	146	76	-	1,974
Person(s) aged 5 - 15 only	5,475	973	2,519	375	99	5	1,509
Persons aged 0 - 4 and 5 - 15	2,453	105	796	135	36	2	1,381
TOTAL PERSONS AGED 0 - 15	**21,406**	**2,256**	**8,057**	**1,217**	**377**	**15**	**9,499**
Persons aged 0 - 4	7,711	411	2,146	359	147	2	4,648

Portsmouth

No persons aged 0 - 15	21,208	7,001	2,654	487	541	30	10,525
Person(s) aged 0 - 4 only	4,048	476	1,079	83	177	3	2,233
Person(s) aged 5 - 15 only	4,950	1,077	2,158	215	132	3	1,368
Persons aged 0 - 4 and 5 - 15	2,825	171	908	92	57	3	1,597
TOTAL PERSONS AGED 0 - 15	**22,213**	**2,755**	**7,709**	**751**	**602**	**15**	**10,396**
Persons aged 0 - 4	9,091	740	2,480	212	285	8	5,374

Rushmoor

No persons aged 0 - 15	8,975	4,152	1,021	178	259	5	3,365
Person(s) aged 0 - 4 only	2,543	282	694	48	91	-	1,428
Person(s) aged 5 - 15 only	2,813	675	1,281	120	75	2	662
Persons aged 0 - 4 and 5 - 15	1,493	105	486	68	27	-	807
TOTAL PERSONS AGED 0 - 15	**12,747**	**1,720**	**4,629**	**474**	**310**	**3**	**5,614**
Persons aged 0 - 4	5,420	442	1,532	149	147	-	3,150

Southampton

No persons aged 0 - 15	23,251	7,017	3,347	518	623	30	11,746
Person(s) aged 0 - 4 only	4,245	413	1,002	109	151	-	2,570
Person(s) aged 5 - 15 only	5,840	1,062	2,641	242	136	5	1,759
Persons aged 0 - 4 and 5 - 15	3,202	164	882	100	56	1	2,000
TOTAL PERSONS AGED 0 - 15	**25,912**	**2,727**	**8,719**	**872**	**587**	**10**	**13,007**
Persons aged 0 - 4	9,998	671	2,394	268	265	1	6,400

33. Females resident in households of one male aged 16 or over and one female aged 16 or over with or without persons aged 0 - 15; number of persons aged 0 - 15 in such households

In households with:	TOTAL FEMALES	Economically active females					Economically inactive females
		Employees		Self-employed	Other	Economically active students	
		Full-time	Part-time				
a	b	c	d	e	f	g	h

Test Valley

No persons aged 0 - 15	12,041	4,104	1,644	459	224	10	5,610
Person(s) aged 0 - 4 only	2,412	228	656	81	45	-	1,402
Person(s) aged 5 - 15 only	3,962	851	1,766	249	100	6	996
Persons aged 0 - 4 and 5 - 15	1,680	116	517	64	23	2	960
TOTAL PERSONS AGED 0 - 15	**15,224**	**2,063**	**5,543**	**765**	**289**	**15**	**6,564**
Persons aged 0 - 4	5,450	394	1,491	185	84	2	3,296

Winchester

No persons aged 0 - 15	11,930	3,329	1,808	509	177	11	6,107
Person(s) aged 0 - 4 only	1,964	188	464	121	47	1	1,144
Person(s) aged 5 - 15 only	3,481	694	1,551	264	67	5	905
Persons aged 0 - 4 and 5 - 15	1,459	74	442	113	17	1	813
TOTAL PERSONS AGED 0 - 15	**13,301**	**1,623**	**4,796**	**981**	**223**	**11**	**5,678**
Persons aged 0 - 4	4,551	305	1,142	313	72	2	2,719

Table 34 Economic position of household residents

County, districts

34. Residents aged 16 and over in households

Economic position	TOTAL PERSONS	Males		Females		Students (economically active or inactive)
		Single, widowed or divorced	Married	Single, widowed or divorced	Married	
a	b	c	d	e	f	g

HAMPSHIRE

Economic position	TOTAL PERSONS	Single, widowed or divorced	Married	Single, widowed or divorced	Married	Students
TOTAL PERSONS AGED 16 AND OVER	1,203,242	212,596	369,161	249,476	372,009	52,025
Economically active	775,847	161,855	285,514	122,902	205,576	9,229
Employees - full time	490,897	110,005	210,598	83,319	86,975	670
- part time	134,958	7,606	7,492	23,192	96,668	8,273
Self-employed - with employees	27,466	3,646	17,159	1,231	5,430	16
- without employees	62,436	15,470	33,693	3,590	9,683	44
On a Government scheme	6,387	2,837	1,139	1,841	570	
Unemployed	53,703	22,291	15,433	9,729	6,250	226
Economically active students (included above)	*9,229*	*4,010*	*123*	*4,921*	*175*	
Economically inactive	427,395	50,741	83,647	126,574	166,433	42,796
Students	42,796	21,383	585	19,897	931	42,796
Permanently sick	26,739	5,668	9,591	5,866	5,614	
Retired	206,755	22,269	71,586	62,956	49,944	
Other inactive	151,105	1,421	1,885	37,855	109,944	

Basingstoke & Deane

Economic position	TOTAL PERSONS	Single, widowed or divorced	Married	Single, widowed or divorced	Married	Students
TOTAL PERSONS AGED 16 AND OVER	112,919	20,276	35,257	22,022	35,364	4,723
Economically active	80,230	16,403	29,341	12,589	21,897	828
Employees - full time	54,638	12,086	22,546	9,297	10,709	56
- part time	12,523	679	735	1,925	9,184	751
Self-employed - with employees	2,472	325	1,579	93	475	2
- without employees	5,697	1,387	3,069	318	923	2
On a Government scheme	528	232	99	143	54	
Unemployed	4,372	1,694	1,313	813	552	17
Economically active students (included above)	*828*	*349*	*3*	*468*	*8*	
Economically inactive	32,689	3,873	5,916	9,433	13,467	3,895
Students	3,895	1,906	22	1,915	52	3,895
Permanently sick	1,962	395	633	466	468	
Retired	15,046	1,479	5,121	4,541	3,905	
Other inactive	11,786	93	140	2,511	9,042	

East Hampshire

Economic position	TOTAL PERSONS	Single, widowed or divorced	Married	Single, widowed or divorced	Married	Students
TOTAL PERSONS AGED 16 AND OVER	79,918	13,072	25,628	15,381	25,837	4,078
Economically active	52,328	9,666	20,483	7,660	14,519	648
Employees - full time	32,067	6,453	14,465	5,082	6,067	62
- part time	9,147	501	542	1,518	6,586	563
Self-employed - with employees	2,625	337	1,681	113	494	1
- without employees	5,663	1,318	2,978	382	985	1
On a Government scheme	304	120	66	87	31	
Unemployed	2,522	937	751	478	356	21
Economically active students (included above)	*648*	*282*	*14*	*336*	*16*	
Economically inactive	27,590	3,406	5,145	7,721	11,318	3,430
Students	3,430	1,762	18	1,608	42	3,430
Permanently sick	1,256	238	455	277	286	
Retired	12,293	1,322	4,551	3,582	2,838	
Other inactive	10,611	84	121	2,254	8,152	

34. Residents aged 16 and over in households

Economic position	TOTAL PERSONS	Males		Females		Students (economically active or inactive)
		Single, widowed or divorced	Married	Single, widowed or divorced	Married	
a	b	c	d	e	f	g

Eastleigh

Economic position	TOTAL PERSONS	Single, widowed or divorced	Married	Single, widowed or divorced	Married	Students
TOTAL PERSONS AGED 16 AND OVER	83,061	13,771	26,805	15,641	26,844	3,456
Economically active	55,863	10,775	21,334	8,239	15,515	710
Employees - full time	36,218	7,689	16,214	5,844	6,471	37
- part time	10,152	557	462	1,506	7,627	658
Self-employed - with employees	1,867	213	1,243	63	348	-
- without employees	4,300	1,020	2,428	198	654	3
On a Government scheme	330	156	33	110	31	
Unemployed	2,996	1,140	954	518	384	12
Economically active students (included above)	*710*	*322*	*2*	*377*	*9*	
Economically inactive	27,198	2,996	5,471	7,402	11,329	2,746
Students	2,746	1,373	23	1,292	58	2,746
Permanently sick	1,573	291	605	318	359	
Retired	13,026	1,266	4,734	3,661	3,365	
Other inactive	9,853	66	109	2,131	7,547	

Fareham

Economic position	TOTAL PERSONS	Single, widowed or divorced	Married	Single, widowed or divorced	Married	Students
TOTAL PERSONS AGED 16 AND OVER	78,448	12,086	25,926	14,381	26,055	3,412
Economically active	51,022	9,198	20,140	7,203	14,481	726
Employees - full time	33,020	6,397	15,419	4,925	6,279	64
- part time	9,030	466	467	1,442	6,655	643
Self-employed - with employees	1,855	214	1,183	53	405	1
- without employees	3,896	885	2,128	192	691	4
On a Government scheme	458	193	84	142	39	
Unemployed	2,763	1,043	859	449	412	14
Economically active students (included above)	*726*	*299*	*15*	*392*	*20*	
Economically inactive	27,426	2,888	5,786	7,178	11,574	2,686
Students	2,686	1,334	27	1,268	57	2,686
Permanently sick	1,441	237	580	281	343	
Retired	13,529	1,253	5,070	3,554	3,652	
Other inactive	9,770	64	109	2,075	7,522	

Gosport

Economic position	TOTAL PERSONS	Single, widowed or divorced	Married	Single, widowed or divorced	Married	Students
TOTAL PERSONS AGED 16 AND OVER	57,720	9,698	17,892	12,019	18,111	2,099
Economically active	37,374	7,537	14,022	5,860	9,955	417
Employees - full time	24,755	5,222	11,252	3,852	4,429	37
- part time	6,277	306	262	1,172	4,537	368
Self-employed - with employees	841	113	494	38	196	1
- without employees	2,029	505	1,103	103	318	3
On a Government scheme	576	221	152	163	40	
Unemployed	2,896	1,170	759	532	435	8
Economically active students (included above)	*417*	*154*	*12*	*242*	*9*	
Economically inactive	20,346	2,161	3,870	6,159	8,156	1,682
Students	1,682	829	17	793	43	1,682
Permanently sick	1,299	260	467	259	313	
Retired	9,913	1,013	3,294	3,115	2,491	
Other inactive	7,452	59	92	1,992	5,309	

34. Residents aged 16 and over in households

Economic position	TOTAL PERSONS	Males		Females		Students (economically active or inactive)
		Single, widowed or divorced	Married	Single, widowed or divorced	Married	
a	b	c	d	e	f	g

Hart

Economic position	TOTAL PERSONS	Single, widowed or divorced	Married	Single, widowed or divorced	Married	Students
TOTAL PERSONS AGED 16 AND OVER	61,797	10,344	20,100	11,174	20,179	3,610
Economically active	43,077	7,977	17,055	6,097	11,948	710
Employees - full time	28,053	5,662	13,051	4,300	5,040	44
- part time	7,504	495	363	1,096	5,550	653
Self-employed - with employees	1,728	197	1,104	74	353	-
- without employees	3,629	852	1,920	180	677	3
On a Government scheme	220	77	59	58	26	
Unemployed	1,943	694	558	389	302	10
Economically active students (included above)	*710*	*329*	*4*	*364*	*13*	
Economically inactive	18,720	2,367	3,045	5,077	8,231	2,900
Students	2,900	1,480	7	1,378	35	2,900
Permanently sick	740	129	268	142	201	
Retired	7,390	721	2,712	2,260	1,697	
Other inactive	7,690	37	58	1,297	6,298	

Havant

Economic position	TOTAL PERSONS	Single, widowed or divorced	Married	Single, widowed or divorced	Married	Students
TOTAL PERSONS AGED 16 AND OVER	93,177	15,567	28,916	19,447	29,247	3,762
Economically active	57,802	11,793	21,499	9,115	15,395	678
Employees - full time	35,418	7,587	15,415	5,962	6,454	39
- part time	10,282	522	570	1,801	7,389	613
Self-employed - with employees	1,912	243	1,200	75	394	-
- without employees	4,542	1,145	2,550	230	617	5
On a Government scheme	589	255	104	190	40	
Unemployed	5,059	2,041	1,660	857	501	21
Economically active students (included above)	*678*	*279*	*11*	*372*	*16*	
Economically inactive	35,375	3,774	7,417	10,332	13,852	3,084
Students	3,084	1,559	31	1,427	67	3,084
Permanently sick	2,680	443	1,085	560	592	
Retired	16,919	1,638	6,097	4,819	4,365	
Other inactive	12,692	134	204	3,526	8,828	

New Forest

Economic position	TOTAL PERSONS	Single, widowed or divorced	Married	Single, widowed or divorced	Married	Students
TOTAL PERSONS AGED 16 AND OVER	128,732	19,646	41,552	25,668	41,866	4,949
Economically active	74,452	14,299	28,866	10,898	20,389	924
Employees - full time	43,414	9,273	19,801	6,928	7,412	59
- part time	14,479	805	952	2,377	10,345	836
Self-employed - with employees	3,799	450	2,338	191	820	3
- without employees	7,592	1,659	4,227	498	1,208	4
On a Government scheme	456	233	65	126	32	
Unemployed	4,712	1,879	1,483	778	572	22
Economically active students (included above)	*924*	*427*	*5*	*481*	*11*	
Economically inactive	54,280	5,347	12,686	14,770	21,477	4,025
Students	4,025	1,904	41	2,009	71	4,025
Permanently sick	2,549	504	1,034	509	502	
Retired	29,211	2,801	11,394	7,814	7,202	
Other inactive	18,495	138	217	4,438	13,702	

34. Residents aged 16 and over in households

Economic position	TOTAL PERSONS	Males		Females		Students (economically active or inactive)
		Single, widowed or divorced	Married	Single, widowed or divorced	Married	
a	b	c	d	e	f	g

Portsmouth

TOTAL PERSONS AGED 16 AND OVER	136,552	28,504	36,738	34,059	37,251	4,923
Economically active	84,094	21,577	26,961	15,962	19,594	781
Employees - full time	52,521	14,248	19,564	10,492	8,217	73
- part time	13,997	886	714	3,004	9,393	685
Self-employed - with employees	2,240	406	1,253	158	423	-
- without employees	5,923	1,736	3,097	378	712	2
On a Government scheme	922	450	161	253	58	
Unemployed	8,491	3,851	2,172	1,677	791	21
Economically active students (included above)	781	354	16	393	18	
Economically inactive	52,458	6,927	9,777	18,097	17,657	4,142
Students	4,142	2,142	84	1,809	107	4,142
Permanently sick	4,374	1,072	1,425	1,055	822	
Retired	27,273	3,485	8,039	9,739	6,010	
Other inactive	16,669	228	229	5,494	10,718	

Rushmoor

TOTAL PERSONS AGED 16 AND OVER	61,799	11,779	18,640	12,536	18,844	2,345
Economically active	43,949	9,621	15,572	7,139	11,617	422
Employees - full time	30,388	7,109	12,290	5,322	5,667	19
- part time	6,676	374	283	1,102	4,917	394
Self-employed - with employees	931	153	577	34	167	2
- without employees	3,167	918	1,707	142	400	-
On a Government scheme	268	96	68	67	37	
Unemployed	2,519	971	647	472	429	7
Economically active students (included above)	422	188	4	226	4	
Economically inactive	17,850	2,158	3,068	5,397	7,227	1,923
Students	1,923	902	40	911	70	1,923
Permanently sick	1,216	255	406	280	275	
Retired	8,108	922	2,552	2,675	1,959	
Other inactive	6,603	79	70	1,531	4,923	

Southampton

TOTAL PERSONS AGED 16 AND OVER	154,608	32,368	42,590	36,701	42,949	6,575
Economically active	95,205	24,224	31,317	17,437	22,227	955
Employees - full time	58,015	15,427	22,363	11,523	8,702	59
- part time	16,507	958	938	3,242	11,369	856
Self-employed - with employees	2,259	351	1,381	118	409	2
- without employees	6,969	2,059	3,684	395	831	8
On a Government scheme	1,019	529	122	307	61	
Unemployed	10,436	4,900	2,829	1,852	855	30
Economically active students (included above)	955	396	21	510	28	
Economically inactive	59,403	8,144	11,273	19,264	20,722	5,620
Students	5,620	2,869	229	2,348	174	5,620
Permanently sick	5,046	1,325	1,693	1,135	893	
Retired	28,735	3,676	9,032	9,421	6,606	
Other inactive	20,002	274	319	6,360	13,049	

34. Residents aged 16 and over in households

Economic position	TOTAL PERSONS	Males		Females		Students (economically active or inactive)
		Single, widowed or divorced	Married	Single, widowed or divorced	Married	
a	b	c	d	e	f	g

Test Valley

TOTAL PERSONS AGED 16 AND OVER	78,817	13,307	25,169	14,950	25,391	3,583
Economically active	52,859	10,132	20,359	7,636	14,732	681
Employees - full time	33,742	7,157	15,000	5,226	6,359	49
- part time	9,264	503	525	1,494	6,742	612
Self-employed - with employees	2,318	309	1,466	93	450	2
- without employees	4,476	980	2,492	258	746	3
On a Government scheme	388	141	63	111	73	
Unemployed	2,671	1,042	813	454	362	15
Economically active students (included above)	*681*	*306*	*2*	*363*	*10*	
Economically inactive	25,958	3,175	4,810	7,314	10,659	2,902
Students	2,902	1,487	16	1,330	69	2,902
Permanently sick	1,332	286	478	290	278	
Retired	11,868	1,304	4,213	3,525	2,826	
Other inactive	9,856	98	103	2,169	7,486	

Winchester

TOTAL PERSONS AGED 16 AND OVER	75,694	12,178	23,948	15,497	24,071	4,510
Economically active	47,592	8,653	18,565	7,067	13,307	749
Employees - full time	28,648	5,695	13,218	4,566	5,169	72
- part time	9,120	554	679	1,513	6,374	641
Self-employed - with employees	2,619	335	1,660	128	496	2
- without employees	4,553	1,006	2,310	316	921	6
On a Government scheme	329	134	63	84	48	
Unemployed	2,323	929	635	460	299	28
Economically active students (included above)	*749*	*325*	*14*	*397*	*13*	
Economically inactive	28,102	3,525	5,383	8,430	10,764	3,761
Students	3,761	1,836	30	1,809	86	3,761
Permanently sick	1,271	233	462	294	282	
Retired	13,444	1,389	4,777	4,250	3,028	
Other inactive	9,626	67	114	2,077	7,368	

35. Residents in households

Age	TOTAL PERSONS	Males					Females				
		Total	Single	Married	Widowed	Divorced	Total	Single	Married	Widowed	Divorced
a	b	c	d	e	f	g	h	i	j	k	l

HAMPSHIRE

Age	TOTAL PERSONS	Total	Single	Married	Widowed	Divorced	Total	Single	Married	Widowed	Divorced
ALL AGES	**1,512,038**	**740,181**	**319,989**	**369,161**	**18,044**	**32,987**	**771,857**	**277,662**	**372,009**	**76,741**	**45,445**
0 - 4	103,087	52,622	52,622				50,465	50,465			
5 - 9	95,999	49,587	49,587				46,412	46,412			
10 - 14	91,725	47,023	47,023				44,702	44,702			
15	17,985	9,192	9,192				8,793	8,793			
16 - 17	38,506	19,792	19,747	30	4	11	18,714	18,637	73	4	-
18 - 19	41,443	20,970	20,818	138	3	11	20,473	19,794	653	6	20
20 - 24	111,034	55,497	48,432	6,752	6	307	55,537	40,080	14,410	47	1,000
25 - 29	121,322	60,577	30,299	28,082	30	2,166	60,745	19,163	37,262	127	4,193
30 - 34	113,337	57,194	14,031	39,005	69	4,089	56,143	7,443	42,674	235	5,791
35 - 39	103,083	51,441	7,231	39,456	125	4,629	51,642	3,784	41,299	372	6,187
40 - 44	116,480	57,973	5,225	46,957	241	5,550	58,507	2,727	47,901	752	7,127
45 - 49	98,078	49,108	3,466	40,581	345	4,716	48,970	1,793	40,053	1,255	5,869
50 - 54	82,687	41,549	2,576	34,686	547	3,740	41,138	1,523	33,273	2,008	4,334
55 - 59	76,512	38,121	2,297	32,179	846	2,799	38,391	1,604	29,951	3,487	3,349
60 - 64	74,498	36,311	2,379	30,385	1,503	2,044	38,187	1,913	27,281	6,362	2,631
65 - 69	71,593	32,651	1,992	26,798	2,423	1,438	38,942	2,137	24,023	10,701	2,081
70 - 74	59,077	25,489	1,400	20,352	2,927	810	33,588	1,964	16,861	13,373	1,390
75 - 79	47,649	19,042	912	14,131	3,556	443	28,607	1,960	10,246	15,539	862
80 - 84	30,400	10,903	526	7,085	3,122	170	19,497	1,589	4,602	12,892	414
85 - 89	13,350	4,131	181	2,168	1,731	51	9,219	882	1,232	6,942	163
90 and over	4,193	1,008	53	376	566	13	3,185	297	215	2,639	34

Basingstoke & Deane

Age	TOTAL PERSONS	Total	Single	Married	Widowed	Divorced	Total	Single	Married	Widowed	Divorced
ALL AGES	**143,278**	**70,994**	**31,421**	**35,257**	**1,366**	**2,950**	**72,284**	**27,386**	**35,364**	**5,594**	**3,940**
0 - 4	9,952	5,009	5,009				4,943	4,943			
5 - 9	9,302	4,747	4,747				4,555	4,555			
10 - 14	9,201	4,742	4,742				4,459	4,459			
15	1,904	963	963				941	941			
16 - 17	3,935	1,969	1,965	3	-	1	1,966	1,962	4	-	-
18 - 19	4,316	2,174	2,157	14	1	2	2,142	2,080	58	2	2
20 - 24	11,471	5,762	5,093	645	-	24	5,709	4,187	1,423	3	96
25 - 29	12,803	6,443	3,243	2,963	3	234	6,360	2,009	3,904	14	433
30 - 34	11,298	5,750	1,397	3,944	6	403	5,548	675	4,303	22	548
35 - 39	10,354	5,141	623	4,056	10	452	5,213	333	4,276	41	563
40 - 44	12,008	6,017	422	5,040	21	534	5,991	207	5,056	62	666
45 - 49	9,858	4,909	233	4,199	36	441	4,949	144	4,130	110	565
50 - 54	7,910	4,094	179	3,539	46	330	3,816	117	3,223	151	325
55 - 59	6,885	3,507	159	3,039	92	217	3,378	132	2,706	282	258
60 - 64	6,032	3,078	158	2,651	132	137	2,954	111	2,186	478	179
65 - 69	5,424	2,530	147	2,068	210	105	2,894	115	1,824	836	119
70 - 74	4,127	1,785	80	1,457	218	30	2,342	125	1,170	957	90
75 - 79	3,285	1,316	53	984	247	32	1,969	118	687	1,103	61
80 - 84	2,058	712	34	483	189	6	1,346	104	317	900	25
85 - 89	859	277	14	148	113	2	582	49	84	441	8
90 and over	296	69	3	24	42	-	227	20	13	192	2

35. Residents in households

Age	TOTAL PERSONS	Males					Females				
		Total	Single	Married	Widowed	Divorced	Total	Single	Married	Widowed	Divorced
a	b	c	d	e	f	g	h	i	j	k	l

East Hampshire

Age	TOTAL PERSONS	Total	Single	Married	Widowed	Divorced	Total	Single	Married	Widowed	Divorced
ALL AGES	101,335	49,670	21,038	25,628	1,169	1,835	51,665	18,531	25,837	4,652	2,645
0 - 4	6,821	3,462	3,462				3,359	3,359			
5 - 9	6,673	3,477	3,477				3,196	3,196			
10 - 14	6,603	3,347	3,347				3,256	3,256			
15	1,320	684	684				636	636			
16 - 17	2,676	1,402	1,401	-	1	-	1,274	1,270	4	-	-
18 - 19	2,849	1,452	1,447	5	-	-	1,397	1,358	37	-	2
20 - 24	6,523	3,292	2,941	336	1	14	3,231	2,411	773	3	44
25 - 29	7,074	3,495	1,798	1,601	2	94	3,579	1,066	2,294	7	212
30 - 34	7,512	3,691	823	2,647	9	212	3,821	445	3,053	19	304
35 - 39	7,182	3,585	448	2,880	8	249	3,597	239	2,999	15	344
40 - 44	8,675	4,276	314	3,583	18	361	4,399	194	3,706	38	461
45 - 49	7,308	3,637	187	3,151	26	273	3,671	127	3,070	89	385
50 - 54	5,931	2,938	149	2,537	38	214	2,993	120	2,483	139	251
55 - 59	5,105	2,575	119	2,241	52	163	2,530	97	2,010	217	206
60 - 64	4,760	2,399	120	2,063	104	112	2,361	133	1,735	357	136
65 - 69	4,403	2,034	119	1,703	135	77	2,369	150	1,482	606	131
70 - 74	3,672	1,617	90	1,327	165	35	2,055	134	1,079	770	72
75 - 79	3,090	1,220	59	889	250	22	1,870	136	679	988	67
80 - 84	1,968	737	32	485	213	7	1,231	109	318	785	19
85 - 89	897	265	14	145	104	2	632	78	93	452	9
90 and over	293	85	7	35	43	-	208	17	22	167	2

Eastleigh

Age	TOTAL PERSONS	Total	Single	Married	Widowed	Divorced	Total	Single	Married	Widowed	Divorced
ALL AGES	105,298	51,982	21,919	26,805	1,056	2,202	53,316	18,915	26,844	4,733	2,824
0 - 4	7,318	3,766	3,766				3,552	3,552			
5 - 9	6,935	3,575	3,575				3,360	3,360			
10 - 14	6,697	3,390	3,390				3,307	3,307			
15	1,287	675	675				612	612			
16 - 17	2,690	1,364	1,363	-	-	1	1,326	1,321	5	-	-
18 - 19	2,801	1,442	1,431	11	-	-	1,359	1,328	31	-	-
20 - 24	7,283	3,672	3,208	443	-	21	3,611	2,550	1,013	1	47
25 - 29	8,654	4,233	1,982	2,086	3	162	4,421	1,232	2,872	9	308
30 - 34	8,485	4,278	899	3,064	2	313	4,207	472	3,348	16	371
35 - 39	7,968	4,015	472	3,207	10	326	3,953	227	3,246	27	453
40 - 44	8,617	4,333	340	3,583	15	395	4,284	174	3,584	46	480
45 - 49	6,931	3,514	180	3,017	18	299	3,417	98	2,881	87	351
50 - 54	5,794	2,971	163	2,528	44	236	2,823	78	2,351	137	257
55 - 59	5,012	2,508	107	2,195	46	160	2,504	75	2,035	200	194
60 - 64	4,998	2,451	119	2,134	75	123	2,547	86	1,911	421	129
65 - 69	4,632	2,140	110	1,803	150	77	2,492	131	1,561	707	93
70 - 74	3,622	1,591	68	1,294	184	45	2,031	95	1,011	842	83
75 - 79	2,838	1,153	40	877	205	31	1,685	84	625	935	41
80 - 84	1,678	605	21	400	175	9	1,073	76	282	708	7
85 - 89	810	254	8	142	100	4	556	42	74	433	7
90 and over	248	52	2	21	29	-	196	15	14	164	3

35. Residents in households

Age	TOTAL PERSONS	Males					Females				
		Total	Single	Married	Widowed	Divorced	Total	Single	Married	Widowed	Divorced
a	b	c	d	e	f	g	h	i	j	k	l

Fareham

Age	TOTAL PERSONS	Total	Single	Married	Widowed	Divorced	Total	Single	Married	Widowed	Divorced
ALL AGES	97,607	47,806	18,936	25,926	1,070	1,874	49,801	16,543	26,055	4,632	2,571
0 - 4	6,351	3,258	3,258				3,093	3,093			
5 - 9	5,910	3,023	3,023				2,887	2,887			
10 - 14	5,803	2,936	2,936				2,867	2,867			
15	1,095	577	577				518	518			
16 - 17	2,458	1,252	1,248	3	-	1	1,206	1,200	5	1	-
18 - 19	2,646	1,340	1,332	7	-	1	1,306	1,292	14	-	-
20 - 24	6,156	3,193	2,915	262	-	16	2,963	2,218	695	1	49
25 - 29	6,901	3,344	1,519	1,704	2	119	3,557	1,001	2,340	8	208
30 - 34	7,365	3,689	712	2,718	1	258	3,676	394	2,959	13	310
35 - 39	6,843	3,400	386	2,774	4	236	3,443	201	2,880	22	340
40 - 44	8,114	4,033	277	3,418	12	326	4,081	132	3,473	42	434
45 - 49	7,088	3,501	180	3,013	26	282	3,587	92	3,023	81	391
50 - 54	5,783	2,882	129	2,489	32	232	2,901	78	2,422	138	263
55 - 59	5,590	2,770	105	2,467	52	146	2,820	82	2,342	216	180
60 - 64	5,175	2,542	115	2,232	82	113	2,633	111	1,977	405	140
65 - 69	4,878	2,206	74	1,907	151	74	2,672	113	1,765	685	109
70 - 74	3,713	1,664	58	1,394	174	38	2,049	83	1,116	776	74
75 - 79	2,965	1,236	48	936	230	22	1,729	78	674	930	47
80 - 84	1,828	671	30	455	178	8	1,157	51	305	780	21
85 - 89	731	231	8	127	94	2	500	35	61	400	4
90 and over	214	58	6	20	32	-	156	17	4	134	1

Gosport

Age	TOTAL PERSONS	Total	Single	Married	Widowed	Divorced	Total	Single	Married	Widowed	Divorced
ALL AGES	73,704	35,862	15,464	17,892	824	1,682	37,842	13,430	18,111	3,778	2,523
0 - 4	5,529	2,801	2,801				2,728	2,728			
5 - 9	5,102	2,662	2,662				2,440	2,440			
10 - 14	4,546	2,376	2,376				2,170	2,170			
15	807	433	433				374	374			
16 - 17	1,911	988	986	2	-	-	923	919	4	-	-
18 - 19	2,018	943	924	18	-	1	1,075	1,010	65	-	-
20 - 24	5,908	2,836	2,166	658	1	11	3,072	1,842	1,155	1	74
25 - 29	6,861	3,426	1,330	1,930	2	164	3,435	776	2,352	7	300
30 - 34	6,087	3,137	614	2,280	4	239	2,950	301	2,264	15	370
35 - 39	4,805	2,427	319	1,870	4	234	2,378	141	1,860	19	358
40 - 44	5,176	2,607	204	2,125	18	260	2,569	99	2,088	28	354
45 - 49	4,095	2,050	167	1,650	15	218	2,045	67	1,635	58	285
50 - 54	3,410	1,707	93	1,412	36	166	1,703	61	1,355	83	204
55 - 59	3,481	1,668	94	1,394	43	137	1,813	62	1,383	163	205
60 - 64	3,397	1,606	90	1,352	72	92	1,791	85	1,257	309	140
65 - 69	3,235	1,447	79	1,199	97	72	1,788	86	1,109	506	87
70 - 74	2,794	1,150	65	900	129	56	1,644	91	824	654	75
75 - 79	2,306	876	33	666	157	20	1,430	83	483	825	39
80 - 84	1,423	488	19	322	138	9	935	55	201	653	26
85 - 89	627	187	6	98	81	2	440	31	67	336	6
90 and over	186	47	3	16	27	1	139	9	9	121	-

35. Residents in households

Age	TOTAL PERSONS	Males					Females				
		Total	Single	Married	Widowed	Divorced	Total	Single	Married	Widowed	Divorced
a	b	c	d	e	f	g	h	i	j	k	l

Hart

Age	TOTAL PERSONS	Total	Single	Married	Widowed	Divorced	Total	Single	Married	Widowed	Divorced
ALL AGES	79,014	39,369	17,320	20,100	683	1,266	39,645	14,748	20,179	2,942	1,776
0 - 4	5,211	2,721	2,721				2,490	2,490			
5 - 9	5,413	2,819	2,819				2,594	2,594			
10 - 14	5,523	2,855	2,855				2,668	2,668			
15	1,070	530	530				540	540			
16 - 17	2,403	1,284	1,283	1	-	-	1,119	1,118	-	1	-
18 - 19	2,455	1,286	1,282	4	-	-	1,169	1,149	20	-	-
20 - 24	5,493	2,788	2,571	207	1	9	2,705	2,161	513	3	28
25 - 29	5,747	2,924	1,558	1,293	2	71	2,823	930	1,735	6	152
30 - 34	5,889	2,899	667	2,083	2	147	2,990	329	2,448	6	207
35 - 39	6,024	2,964	337	2,436	8	183	3,060	134	2,665	15	246
40 - 44	7,266	3,557	206	3,103	15	233	3,709	113	3,271	36	289
45 - 49	6,234	3,133	134	2,769	22	208	3,101	81	2,695	59	266
50 - 54	4,964	2,564	83	2,303	28	150	2,400	49	2,049	97	205
55 - 59	3,969	2,085	63	1,872	44	106	1,884	49	1,563	146	126
60 - 64	3,110	1,577	63	1,386	62	66	1,533	43	1,174	237	79
65 - 69	2,613	1,257	61	1,064	87	45	1,356	69	872	348	67
70 - 74	2,067	887	33	736	94	24	1,180	53	628	458	41
75 - 79	1,670	648	28	494	114	12	1,022	78	324	581	39
80 - 84	1,218	414	20	259	127	8	804	58	170	561	15
85 - 89	499	138	3	72	59	4	361	27	43	278	13
90 and over	176	39	3	18	18	-	137	15	9	110	3

Havant

Age	TOTAL PERSONS	Total	Single	Married	Widowed	Divorced	Total	Single	Married	Widowed	Divorced
ALL AGES	118,297	57,375	24,474	28,916	1,360	2,625	60,922	21,689	29,247	5,991	3,995
0 - 4	8,103	4,060	4,060				4,043	4,043			
5 - 9	7,884	4,116	4,116				3,768	3,768			
10 - 14	7,612	3,949	3,949				3,663	3,663			
15	1,521	767	767				754	754			
16 - 17	3,216	1,634	1,632	2	-	-	1,582	1,579	2	1	-
18 - 19	3,366	1,717	1,703	12	-	2	1,649	1,607	39	-	3
20 - 24	7,914	3,922	3,496	398	1	27	3,992	2,940	959	5	88
25 - 29	8,184	4,012	1,999	1,830	-	183	4,172	1,281	2,553	12	326
30 - 34	8,258	4,104	913	2,890	8	293	4,154	499	3,123	21	511
35 - 39	7,810	3,825	520	2,916	6	383	3,985	274	3,093	25	593
40 - 44	8,657	4,219	384	3,410	21	404	4,438	217	3,550	75	596
45 - 49	7,496	3,709	230	3,080	28	371	3,787	141	3,038	99	509
50 - 54	6,808	3,257	145	2,781	37	294	3,551	85	2,883	186	397
55 - 59	6,758	3,240	133	2,809	67	231	3,518	105	2,766	340	307
60 - 64	6,778	3,314	144	2,871	126	173	3,464	123	2,533	548	260
65 - 69	6,192	2,891	112	2,454	200	125	3,301	165	2,081	887	168
70 - 74	4,767	2,084	80	1,689	234	81	2,683	132	1,374	1,057	120
75 - 79	3,564	1,441	48	1,097	260	36	2,123	125	816	1,116	66
80 - 84	2,132	757	28	506	210	13	1,375	101	331	908	35
85 - 89	974	280	12	143	117	8	694	73	87	522	12
90 and over	303	77	3	28	45	1	226	14	19	189	4

35. Residents in households

Age	TOTAL PERSONS	Males					Females				
		Total	Single	Married	Widowed	Divorced	Total	Single	Married	Widowed	Divorced
a	b	c	d	e	f	g	h	i	j	k	l

New Forest

Age	TOTAL PERSONS	Total	Single	Married	Widowed	Divorced	Total	Single	Married	Widowed	Divorced
ALL AGES	157,604	75,958	29,153	41,552	2,310	2,943	81,646	26,102	41,866	9,605	4,073
0 - 4	9,170	4,684	4,684				4,486	4,486			
5 - 9	8,968	4,612	4,612				4,356	4,356			
10 - 14	8,980	4,582	4,582				4,398	4,398			
15	1,754	882	882				872	872			
16 - 17	3,822	1,895	1,891	2	1	1	1,927	1,925	2	-	-
18 - 19	3,836	1,918	1,910	8	-	-	1,918	1,877	40	-	1
20 - 24	9,078	4,611	4,078	515	-	18	4,467	3,240	1,162	4	61
25 - 29	10,103	5,027	2,556	2,341	-	130	5,076	1,494	3,290	9	283
30 - 34	10,095	5,063	1,234	3,525	5	299	5,032	633	3,946	22	431
35 - 39	10,297	4,970	664	3,932	5	369	5,327	407	4,360	49	511
40 - 44	11,925	5,879	462	4,844	18	555	6,046	262	5,067	91	626
45 - 49	9,945	4,980	343	4,196	35	406	4,965	165	4,125	117	558
50 - 54	8,753	4,265	234	3,655	50	326	4,488	149	3,700	230	409
55 - 59	8,687	4,246	221	3,644	88	293	4,441	197	3,557	359	328
60 - 64	9,320	4,408	246	3,778	172	212	4,912	268	3,636	736	272
65 - 69	9,997	4,607	208	3,952	288	159	5,390	310	3,561	1,286	233
70 - 74	8,487	3,790	150	3,190	354	96	4,697	285	2,634	1,600	178
75 - 79	7,115	2,958	102	2,303	505	48	4,157	320	1,765	1,975	97
80 - 84	4,569	1,728	60	1,197	453	18	2,841	270	779	1,731	61
85 - 89	2,025	687	27	397	254	9	1,338	144	197	980	17
90 and over	678	166	7	73	82	4	512	44	45	416	7

Portsmouth

Age	TOTAL PERSONS	Total	Single	Married	Widowed	Divorced	Total	Single	Married	Widowed	Divorced
ALL AGES	169,730	82,143	38,140	36,738	2,465	4,800	87,587	32,800	37,251	10,893	6,643
0 - 4	12,266	6,235	6,235				6,031	6,031			
5 - 9	10,426	5,341	5,341				5,085	5,085			
10 - 14	8,747	4,440	4,440				4,307	4,307			
15	1,739	885	885				854	854			
16 - 17	3,544	1,820	1,811	5	1	3	1,724	1,699	24	1	-
18 - 19	4,272	2,163	2,149	14	-	-	2,109	2,004	98	4	3
20 - 24	14,837	7,314	6,283	984	-	47	7,523	5,422	1,958	7	136
25 - 29	16,282	8,159	4,283	3,520	6	350	8,123	2,943	4,498	14	668
30 - 34	13,110	6,816	1,952	4,228	13	623	6,294	1,103	4,317	26	848
35 - 39	10,363	5,282	1,080	3,533	18	651	5,081	540	3,627	50	864
40 - 44	10,841	5,546	796	4,015	30	705	5,295	369	3,876	93	957
45 - 49	9,409	4,741	611	3,456	36	638	4,668	268	3,488	160	752
50 - 54	8,248	4,101	456	3,046	59	540	4,147	230	3,044	251	622
55 - 59	7,931	3,903	420	2,948	118	417	4,028	245	2,806	436	541
60 - 64	8,202	3,878	444	2,912	195	327	4,324	300	2,721	862	441
65 - 69	8,653	3,758	369	2,782	371	236	4,895	336	2,687	1,528	344
70 - 74	7,913	3,266	285	2,424	419	138	4,647	292	2,106	2,027	222
75 - 79	6,340	2,436	176	1,699	479	82	3,904	329	1,235	2,209	131
80 - 84	4,214	1,392	87	862	413	30	2,822	264	585	1,889	84
85 - 89	1,821	540	32	261	236	11	1,281	133	153	969	26
90 and over	572	127	5	49	71	2	445	46	28	367	4

35. Residents in households

Age	TOTAL PERSONS	Males					Females				
		Total	Single	Married	Widowed	Divorced	Total	Single	Married	Widowed	Divorced
a	b	c	d	e	f	g	h	i	j	k	l

Rushmoor

Age	TOTAL PERSONS	Total	Single	Married	Widowed	Divorced	Total	Single	Married	Widowed	Divorced
ALL AGES	79,121	39,324	18,217	18,640	744	1,723	39,797	15,358	18,844	3,234	2,361
0 - 4	6,588	3,367	3,367				3,221	3,221			
5 - 9	5,241	2,667	2,667				2,574	2,574			
10 - 14	4,595	2,411	2,411				2,184	2,184			
15	898	460	460				438	438			
16 - 17	1,942	995	992	2	1	-	947	941	6	-	-
18 - 19	2,198	1,048	1,037	10	-	1	1,150	1,087	60	-	3
20 - 24	7,137	3,493	2,843	630	-	20	3,644	2,372	1,209	2	61
25 - 29	8,800	4,561	2,122	2,308	-	131	4,239	1,232	2,750	7	250
30 - 34	7,091	3,679	908	2,521	3	247	3,412	416	2,623	8	365
35 - 39	5,379	2,760	363	2,115	5	277	2,619	161	2,137	13	308
40 - 44	5,724	2,901	278	2,302	5	316	2,823	138	2,278	44	363
45 - 49	4,520	2,279	157	1,865	12	245	2,241	79	1,831	56	275
50 - 54	3,957	2,035	128	1,702	25	180	1,922	73	1,526	90	233
55 - 59	3,324	1,669	113	1,400	41	115	1,655	90	1,234	181	150
60 - 64	3,055	1,458	120	1,170	74	94	1,597	71	1,096	290	140
65 - 69	2,797	1,294	109	1,031	100	54	1,503	77	908	422	96
70 - 74	2,238	955	60	745	124	26	1,283	65	608	562	48
75 - 79	1,875	720	49	522	138	11	1,155	68	386	661	40
80 - 84	1,136	398	25	235	133	5	738	38	141	543	16
85 - 89	488	141	4	76	60	1	347	23	46	266	12
90 and over	138	33	4	6	23	-	105	10	5	89	1

Southampton

Age	TOTAL PERSONS	Total	Single	Married	Widowed	Divorced	Total	Single	Married	Widowed	Divorced
ALL AGES	193,866	95,085	44,377	42,590	2,671	5,447	98,781	37,593	42,949	11,166	7,073
0 - 4	13,886	7,099	7,099				6,787	6,787			
5 - 9	12,166	6,321	6,321				5,845	5,845			
10 - 14	11,079	5,640	5,640				5,439	5,439			
15	2,127	1,067	1,067				1,060	1,060			
16 - 17	4,577	2,404	2,395	6	-	3	2,173	2,161	12	-	-
18 - 19	5,265	2,694	2,664	27	1	2	2,571	2,451	115	-	5
20 - 24	16,546	8,187	7,079	1,030	2	76	8,359	6,001	2,130	10	218
25 - 29	17,214	8,701	4,680	3,660	6	355	8,513	3,124	4,681	18	690
30 - 34	14,592	7,434	2,295	4,498	8	633	7,158	1,288	4,869	37	964
35 - 39	12,496	6,423	1,167	4,476	26	754	6,073	643	4,464	53	913
40 - 44	13,036	6,543	919	4,750	34	840	6,493	466	4,849	105	1,073
45 - 49	11,007	5,548	653	4,106	40	749	5,459	314	4,132	164	849
50 - 54	9,618	4,934	535	3,691	81	627	4,684	261	3,508	263	652
55 - 59	9,402	4,623	448	3,583	112	480	4,779	256	3,467	544	512
60 - 64	9,815	4,753	471	3,671	222	389	5,062	296	3,391	974	401
65 - 69	9,832	4,500	380	3,496	352	272	5,332	270	3,112	1,593	357
70 - 74	8,126	3,442	267	2,575	454	146	4,684	296	2,161	2,008	219
75 - 79	6,529	2,586	165	1,800	539	82	3,943	245	1,275	2,283	140
80 - 84	4,137	1,503	101	908	458	36	2,634	232	590	1,755	57
85 - 89	1,859	564	28	275	259	2	1,295	115	166	994	20
90 and over	557	119	3	38	77	1	438	43	27	365	3

35. Residents in households

Age	TOTAL PERSONS	Males					Females				
		Total	Single	Married	Widowed	Divorced	Total	Single	Married	Widowed	Divorced
a	b	c	d	e	f	g	h	i	j	k	l

Test Valley

Age	TOTAL PERSONS	Total	Single	Married	Widowed	Divorced	Total	Single	Married	Widowed	Divorced
ALL AGES	99,463	49,237	20,945	25,169	1,136	1,987	50,226	17,626	25,391	4,523	2,686
0 - 4	6,518	3,405	3,405				3,113	3,113			
5 - 9	6,337	3,288	3,288				3,049	3,049			
10 - 14	6,496	3,421	3,421				3,075	3,075			
15	1,295	647	647				648	648			
16 - 17	2,771	1,436	1,434	1	-	1	1,335	1,332	3	-	-
18 - 19	2,811	1,476	1,472	3	1	-	1,335	1,281	53	-	1
20 - 24	6,821	3,463	3,015	433	-	15	3,358	2,384	899	6	69
25 - 29	7,132	3,568	1,763	1,692	2	111	3,564	1,034	2,285	8	237
30 - 34	7,288	3,595	806	2,534	6	249	3,693	424	2,925	18	326
35 - 39	7,062	3,450	434	2,729	13	274	3,612	219	2,977	22	394
40 - 44	8,572	4,195	302	3,538	16	339	4,377	177	3,704	47	449
45 - 49	7,336	3,688	198	3,159	22	309	3,648	96	3,095	85	372
50 - 54	5,800	2,984	152	2,549	35	248	2,816	91	2,353	116	256
55 - 59	5,114	2,676	179	2,279	48	170	2,438	83	1,978	208	169
60 - 64	4,650	2,309	151	1,957	91	110	2,341	133	1,701	373	134
65 - 69	4,228	1,903	98	1,579	150	76	2,325	123	1,456	627	119
70 - 74	3,596	1,576	88	1,245	198	45	2,020	115	1,036	796	73
75 - 79	2,815	1,158	53	873	204	28	1,657	105	579	924	49
80 - 84	1,834	699	25	461	203	10	1,135	79	267	766	23
85 - 89	777	249	13	117	117	2	528	49	73	393	13
90 and over	210	51	1	20	30	-	159	16	7	134	2

Winchester

Age	TOTAL PERSONS	Total	Single	Married	Widowed	Divorced	Total	Single	Married	Widowed	Divorced
ALL AGES	93,721	45,376	18,585	23,948	1,190	1,653	48,345	16,941	24,071	4,998	2,335
0 - 4	5,374	2,755	2,755				2,619	2,619			
5 - 9	5,642	2,939	2,939				2,703	2,703			
10 - 14	5,843	2,934	2,934				2,909	2,909			
15	1,168	622	622				546	546			
16 - 17	2,561	1,349	1,346	3	-	-	1,212	1,210	2	-	-
18 - 19	2,610	1,317	1,310	5	-	2	1,293	1,270	23	-	-
20 - 24	5,867	2,964	2,744	211	-	9	2,903	2,352	521	1	29
25 - 29	5,567	2,684	1,466	1,154	2	62	2,883	1,041	1,708	8	126
30 - 34	6,267	3,059	811	2,073	2	173	3,208	464	2,496	12	236
35 - 39	6,500	3,199	418	2,532	8	241	3,301	265	2,715	21	300
40 - 44	7,869	3,867	321	3,246	18	282	4,002	179	3,399	45	379
45 - 49	6,851	3,419	193	2,920	29	277	3,432	121	2,910	90	311
50 - 54	5,711	2,817	130	2,454	36	197	2,894	131	2,376	127	260
55 - 59	5,254	2,651	136	2,308	43	164	2,603	131	2,104	195	173
60 - 64	5,206	2,538	138	2,208	96	96	2,668	153	1,963	372	180
65 - 69	4,709	2,084	126	1,760	132	66	2,625	192	1,605	670	158
70 - 74	3,955	1,682	76	1,376	180	50	2,273	198	1,114	866	95
75 - 79	3,257	1,294	58	991	228	17	1,963	191	718	1,009	45
80 - 84	2,205	799	44	512	232	11	1,406	152	316	913	25
85 - 89	983	318	12	167	137	2	665	83	88	478	16
90 and over	322	85	6	28	47	4	237	31	13	191	2

36. Households with residents; resident adults; dependent children

Households with the following adults			TOTAL HOUSEHOLDS	Households with the following dependent children				TOTAL DEPENDENT CHILDREN
Number	Economically active	In employment		0	1	2	3 or more	
a	b	c	d	e	f	g	h	i
HAMPSHIRE								
None	None	None	115		76	30	9	167
One	None	None	97,225	86,674	4,365	3,980	2,206	19,764
One	One	None	6,910	6,115	480	237	78	1,212
One	One	One	61,505	52,455	4,468	3,660	922	14,724
Two or more	None	None	70,317	67,997	1,066	719	535	4,417
Two or more	One	None	10,913	4,584	2,007	2,370	1,952	13,605
Two or more	One	One	95,658	45,327	16,658	22,684	10,989	98,325
Two or more	Two or more	None	2,591	1,551	474	330	236	1,965
Two or more	Two or more	One	16,755	10,372	3,137	2,268	978	10,925
Two or more	Two or more	Two or more	241,268	143,373	41,827	43,017	13,051	169,704
TOTAL HOUSEHOLDS			603,257	418,448	74,558	79,295	30,956	334,808
TOTAL ADULTS			1,177,230	786,368	168,007	160,425	62,430	
Economically active			775,847	475,168	131,674	125,074	43,931	
In employment			722,144	441,368	122,091	118,617	40,068	
Basingstoke & Deane								
None	None	None	5		2	2	1	9
One	None	None	6,423	5,727	252	264	180	1,400
One	One	None	404	339	27	23	15	120
One	One	One	5,740	4,933	405	319	83	1,306
Two or more	None	None	4,723	4,596	53	40	34	252
Two or more	One	None	729	295	128	150	156	972
Two or more	One	One	8,488	3,690	1,615	2,120	1,063	9,361
Two or more	Two or more	None	163	87	30	30	16	149
Two or more	Two or more	One	1,509	889	274	247	99	1,097
Two or more	Two or more	Two or more	26,139	15,605	4,495	4,601	1,438	18,301
TOTAL HOUSEHOLDS			54,323	36,161	7,281	7,796	3,085	32,967
TOTAL ADULTS			110,311	71,058	16,957	16,013	6,283	
Economically active			80,230	48,917	13,801	12,925	4,587	
In employment			75,858	46,245	13,016	12,349	4,248	
East Hampshire								
None	None	None	8		2	5	1	15
One	None	None	5,541	5,081	182	172	106	889
One	One	None	240	206	26	4	4	48
One	One	One	3,744	3,154	254	268	68	1,007
Two or more	None	None	4,316	4,195	57	43	21	210
Two or more	One	None	499	219	84	105	91	608
Two or more	One	One	6,833	3,037	1,216	1,750	830	7,488
Two or more	Two or more	None	103	60	23	13	7	72
Two or more	Two or more	One	889	538	178	123	50	585
Two or more	Two or more	Two or more	16,985	9,813	2,897	3,245	1,030	12,691
TOTAL HOUSEHOLDS			39,158	26,303	4,919	5,728	2,208	23,613
TOTAL ADULTS			77,722	50,260	11,306	11,705	4,451	
Economically active			52,328	30,976	8,884	9,216	3,252	
In employment			49,806	29,430	8,397	8,901	3,078	

Table 36 'Earners' and dependent children – **continued**   County, districts

36. Households with residents; resident adults; dependent children

Households with the following adults			TOTAL HOUSEHOLDS	Households with the following dependent children				TOTAL DEPENDENT CHILDREN
Number	Economically active	In employment		0	1	2	3 or more	
a	b	c	d	e	f	g	h	i
Eastleigh								
None	None	None	3		3	-	-	3
One	None	None	5,514	4,987	218	201	108	979
One	One	None	308	269	23	13	3	58
One	One	One	4,270	3,628	288	295	59	1,067
Two or more	None	None	4,515	4,415	52	31	17	172
Two or more	One	None	580	252	102	139	87	677
Two or more	One	One	6,746	2,966	1,216	1,773	791	7,328
Two or more	Two or more	None	117	77	22	9	9	70
Two or more	Two or more	One	1,073	649	203	165	56	722
Two or more	Two or more	Two or more	18,093	10,594	3,120	3,421	958	12,988
TOTAL HOUSEHOLDS			41,219	27,837	5,247	6,047	2,088	24,064
TOTAL ADULTS			81,234	53,086	11,773	12,179	4,196	
Economically active			55,863	33,646	9,447	9,709	3,061	
In employment			52,867	31,736	8,916	9,331	2,884	
Fareham								
None	None	None	3		1	1	1	6
One	None	None	5,268	4,882	153	167	66	706
One	One	None	202	171	19	12	-	43
One	One	One	3,341	2,769	301	229	42	888
Two or more	None	None	4,960	4,842	53	40	25	216
Two or more	One	None	498	254	90	96	58	480
Two or more	One	One	6,409	3,069	1,109	1,570	661	6,392
Two or more	Two or more	None	112	73	19	13	7	66
Two or more	Two or more	One	984	616	188	129	51	615
Two or more	Two or more	Two or more	16,592	9,860	2,947	2,978	807	11,466
TOTAL HOUSEHOLDS			38,369	26,536	4,880	5,235	1,718	20,878
TOTAL ADULTS			76,729	51,428	11,165	10,648	3,488	
Economically active			51,022	31,048	8,989	8,424	2,561	
In employment			48,259	29,267	8,461	8,116	2,415	
Gosport								
None	None	None	3		1	1	1	6
One	None	None	5,001	4,338	289	253	121	1,198
One	One	None	327	264	41	19	3	88
One	One	One	2,769	2,263	255	191	60	826
Two or more	None	None	3,281	3,188	47	26	20	168
Two or more	One	None	572	223	104	137	108	769
Two or more	One	One	4,677	2,026	924	1,180	547	5,094
Two or more	Two or more	None	146	70	40	21	15	136
Two or more	Two or more	One	991	583	227	124	57	663
Two or more	Two or more	Two or more	11,589	6,795	2,133	2,043	618	8,186
TOTAL HOUSEHOLDS			29,356	19,750	4,061	3,995	1,550	17,134
TOTAL ADULTS			56,570	36,718	8,831	7,951	3,070	
Economically active			37,374	22,126	6,922	6,151	2,175	
In employment			34,478	20,421	6,336	5,769	1,952	

Table 36 'Earners' and dependent children – **continued** County, districts

36. Households with residents; resident adults; dependent children

Households with the following adults			TOTAL HOUSEHOLDS	Households with the following dependent children				TOTAL DEPENDENT CHILDREN
Number	Economically active	In employment		0	1	2	3 or more	
a	b	c	d	e	f	g	h	i

Hart

None	None	None	1		1	-	-	1
One	None	None	3,113	2,877	94	97	45	441
One	One	None	148	130	5	11	2	33
One	One	One	2,832	2,425	184	183	40	679
Two or more	None	None	2,438	2,370	39	20	9	110
Two or more	One	None	309	124	58	80	47	382
Two or more	One	One	5,403	2,163	980	1,569	691	6,356
Two or more	Two or more	None	64	41	6	8	9	52
Two or more	Two or more	One	751	475	127	117	32	468
Two or more	Two or more	Two or more	14,014	8,022	2,382	2,810	800	10,529
TOTAL HOUSEHOLDS			**29,073**	**18,627**	**3,876**	**4,895**	**1,675**	**19,051**
TOTAL ADULTS			**59,963**	**37,266**	**9,191**	**10,096**	**3,410**	
Economically active			43,077	25,264	7,287	8,007	2,519	
In employment			41,134	24,020	6,952	7,752	2,410	

Havant

None	None	None	5		2	2	1	9
One	None	None	7,771	6,646	389	468	268	2,232
One	One	None	609	532	45	22	10	123
One	One	One	4,001	3,252	398	281	70	1,187
Two or more	None	None	6,076	5,817	115	80	64	508
Two or more	One	None	1,275	493	206	309	267	1,759
Two or more	One	One	7,305	3,675	1,154	1,583	893	7,301
Two or more	Two or more	None	273	139	53	41	40	274
Two or more	Two or more	One	1,357	773	251	205	128	1,089
Two or more	Two or more	Two or more	17,479	10,112	3,241	3,132	994	12,712
TOTAL HOUSEHOLDS			**46,151**	**31,439**	**5,854**	**6,123**	**2,735**	**27,194**
TOTAL ADULTS			**91,103**	**59,973**	**13,306**	**12,362**	**5,462**	
Economically active			57,802	34,357	10,329	9,425	3,691	
In employment			52,743	31,442	9,447	8,693	3,161	

New Forest

None	None	None	8		5	3	-	11
One	None	None	11,820	11,020	365	309	126	1,392
One	One	None	503	442	34	22	5	93
One	One	One	5,577	4,768	382	340	87	1,333
Two or more	None	None	11,151	10,941	101	73	36	369
Two or more	One	None	1,065	560	154	209	142	1,049
Two or more	One	One	10,414	5,304	1,686	2,382	1,042	9,856
Two or more	Two or more	None	224	139	36	33	16	157
Two or more	Two or more	One	1,502	974	253	195	80	904
Two or more	Two or more	Two or more	23,147	13,646	4,007	4,297	1,197	16,417
TOTAL HOUSEHOLDS			**65,411**	**47,794**	**7,023**	**7,863**	**2,731**	**31,581**
TOTAL ADULTS			**126,023**	**88,584**	**15,941**	**15,975**	**5,523**	
Economically active			74,452	45,575	12,466	12,433	3,978	
In employment			69,740	42,487	11,680	11,874	3,699	

Table 36 'Earners' and dependent children – **continued** County, districts

36. Households with residents; resident adults; dependent children

Households with the following adults			TOTAL HOUSEHOLDS	Households with the following dependent children				TOTAL DEPENDENT CHILDREN
Number	Economically active	In employment		0	1	2	3 or more	
a	b	c	d	e	f	g	h	i
Portsmouth								
None	None	None	27		21	6	-	33
One	None	None	14,943	13,128	793	639	383	3,351
One	One	None	1,467	1,294	119	42	12	240
One	One	One	8,767	7,566	634	441	126	1,920
Two or more	None	None	8,558	8,225	147	104	82	665
Two or more	One	None	1,770	683	368	362	357	2,366
Two or more	One	One	9,956	5,164	1,681	2,074	1,037	9,286
Two or more	Two or more	None	486	305	86	56	39	337
Two or more	Two or more	One	2,381	1,505	463	279	134	1,475
Two or more	Two or more	Two or more	24,235	15,083	4,183	3,816	1,153	15,530
TOTAL HOUSEHOLDS			**72,590**	**52,953**	**8,495**	**7,819**	**3,323**	**35,203**
TOTAL ADULTS			**134,527**	**94,056**	**18,333**	**15,513**	**6,625**	
Economically active			84,094	54,105	13,954	11,694	4,341	
In employment			75,603	48,697	12,420	10,777	3,709	
Rushmoor								
None	None	None	6		5	-	1	10
One	None	None	4,023	3,421	281	222	99	1,055
One	One	None	295	260	17	13	5	58
One	One	One	3,382	2,872	252	199	59	838
Two or more	None	None	2,450	2,320	51	44	35	263
Two or more	One	None	424	129	88	118	89	634
Two or more	One	One	4,809	1,964	1,013	1,262	570	5,448
Two or more	Two or more	None	105	61	20	15	9	80
Two or more	Two or more	One	896	538	182	119	57	605
Two or more	Two or more	Two or more	14,133	8,573	2,391	2,482	687	9,578
TOTAL HOUSEHOLDS			**30,523**	**20,138**	**4,300**	**4,474**	**1,611**	**18,569**
TOTAL ADULTS			**60,552**	**38,835**	**9,410**	**9,030**	**3,277**	
Economically active			43,949	27,033	7,475	7,119	2,322	
In employment			41,430	25,493	7,011	6,796	2,130	
Southampton								
None	None	None	33		27	5	1	40
One	None	None	16,267	13,879	1,000	862	526	4,523
One	One	None	1,934	1,789	90	41	14	226
One	One	One	9,659	8,483	605	457	114	1,887
Two or more	None	None	9,413	8,886	222	158	147	1,078
Two or more	One	None	2,253	895	456	483	419	2,929
Two or more	One	One	11,562	5,908	1,893	2,349	1,412	11,367
Two or more	Two or more	None	607	387	103	64	53	421
Two or more	Two or more	One	2,690	1,767	466	318	139	1,573
Two or more	Two or more	Two or more	26,722	16,507	4,532	4,136	1,547	17,875
TOTAL HOUSEHOLDS			**81,140**	**58,501**	**9,394**	**8,873**	**4,372**	**41,919**
TOTAL ADULTS			**151,947**	**105,045**	**20,550**	**17,576**	**8,776**	
Economically active			95,205	61,234	15,319	12,957	5,695	
In employment			84,769	54,409	13,588	11,840	4,932	

Table 36 'Earners' and dependent children – **continued**   County, districts

36. Households with residents; resident adults; dependent children

Households with the following adults			TOTAL HOUSEHOLDS	Households with the following dependent children				TOTAL DEPENDENT CHILDREN
Number	Economically active	In employment		0	1	2	3 or more	
a	b	c	d	e	f	g	h	i
Test Valley								
None	None	None	9		3	4	2	19
One	None	None	5,299	4,776	219	195	109	975
One	One	None	223	195	17	10	1	43
One	One	One	3,704	3,117	287	240	60	955
Two or more	None	None	4,011	3,889	65	31	26	219
Two or more	One	None	526	243	96	113	74	577
Two or more	One	One	6,535	3,019	1,163	1,615	738	6,806
Two or more	Two or more	None	102	58	25	12	7	79
Two or more	Two or more	One	933	573	172	146	42	603
Two or more	Two or more	Two or more	17,049	9,939	3,002	3,217	891	12,287
TOTAL HOUSEHOLDS			38,391	25,809	5,049	5,583	1,950	22,563
TOTAL ADULTS			76,900	50,077	11,496	11,388	3,939	
Economically active			52,859	31,761	9,167	9,079	2,852	
In employment			50,188	30,127	8,629	8,729	2,703	
Winchester								
None	None	None	4		3	1	-	5
One	None	None	6,242	5,912	130	131	69	623
One	One	None	250	224	17	5	4	39
One	One	One	3,719	3,225	223	217	54	831
Two or more	None	None	4,425	4,313	64	29	19	187
Two or more	One	None	413	214	73	69	57	403
Two or more	One	One	6,521	3,342	1,008	1,457	714	6,242
Two or more	Two or more	None	89	54	11	15	9	72
Two or more	Two or more	One	799	492	153	101	53	526
Two or more	Two or more	Two or more	15,091	8,824	2,497	2,839	931	11,144
TOTAL HOUSEHOLDS			37,553	26,600	4,179	4,864	1,910	20,072
TOTAL ADULTS			73,649	49,982	9,748	9,989	3,930	
Economically active			47,592	29,126	7,634	7,935	2,897	
In employment			45,269	27,594	7,238	7,690	2,747	

Table 37   Young adults   County, districts

37. Residents aged 16 - 24 in households

Age	TOTAL PERSONS		Married		Lone 'parent' aged 16 - 24 with child(ren) aged 0 - 15		Economically active		On a Government scheme		Unemployed		Students (including those economically active)	
	Males	Females	Males	Females	Males	Females	Males	Females	Males	Females	Males	Females	Males	Females
a	b	c	d	e	f	g	h	i	j	k	l	m	n	o

HAMPSHIRE

Age	Males	Females	Males	Females	Males	Females	Males	Females	Males	Females	Males	Females	Males	Females
ALL AGES 16 - 24	96,259	94,724	6,920	15,136	67	2,786	74,683	63,927	2,185	1,452	11,295	5,748	24,502	24,061
16	9,769	9,317	9	11	2	4	3,221	2,992	344	247	592	382	7,521	7,585
17	10,023	9,397	21	62	2	26	6,197	5,349	788	571	987	609	4,903	5,237
18	10,359	10,043	40	168	3	74	7,487	6,637	451	317	1,267	760	3,680	3,924
19	10,611	10,430	98	485	7	163	8,395	7,631	183	97	1,543	816	2,463	2,326
20	10,897	10,985	289	990	2	304	8,827	7,946	100	61	1,489	740	2,136	1,994
21	10,976	10,431	635	1,723	5	415	9,282	7,646	97	42	1,479	641	1,736	1,384
22	11,091	11,136	1,136	2,775	12	559	9,903	8,342	80	42	1,353	663	1,133	903
23	11,019	11,298	1,879	3,901	19	559	10,336	8,654	75	40	1,307	591	575	464
24	11,514	11,687	2,813	5,021	15	682	11,035	8,730	67	35	1,278	546	355	244

Basingstoke & Deane

Age	Males	Females	Males	Females	Males	Females	Males	Females	Males	Females	Males	Females	Males	Females
ALL AGES 16 - 24	9,905	9,817	662	1,485	2	143	7,951	7,044	186	112	934	526	2,208	2,336
16	970	989	-	-	1	-	320	327	41	23	43	29	752	803
17	999	977	3	4	-	-	650	557	79	44	93	62	444	544
18	1,092	1,060	6	16	1	2	817	721	29	23	124	78	339	403
19	1,082	1,082	8	42	-	8	886	814	11	6	139	78	219	220
20	1,119	1,144	27	88	-	12	911	918	8	7	127	70	197	172
21	1,073	1,065	48	184	-	23	948	824	3	2	108	53	133	108
22	1,189	1,144	105	274	-	30	1,110	938	10	2	113	67	76	44
23	1,158	1,159	172	360	-	35	1,111	965	3	2	90	48	33	31
24	1,223	1,197	293	517	-	33	1,198	980	2	3	97	41	15	11

East Hampshire

Age	Males	Females	Males	Females	Males	Females	Males	Females	Males	Females	Males	Females	Males	Females
ALL AGES 16 - 24	6,146	5,902	341	814	3	96	4,362	3,788	96	70	500	267	2,005	1,907
16	702	627	-	-	-	-	198	180	17	13	28	12	578	536
17	700	647	-	4	-	-	331	293	33	27	45	25	435	439
18	764	690	1	7	-	3	493	386	21	13	58	32	335	350
19	688	707	4	30	-	10	490	490	10	8	64	38	218	203
20	703	701	14	50	-	15	527	476	5	-	77	38	181	187
21	680	595	30	84	-	10	553	456	1	2	60	38	138	95
22	642	638	59	155	-	22	567	481	4	2	69	33	70	60
23	615	632	96	202	2	12	572	513	2	4	60	31	34	25
24	652	665	137	282	1	24	631	513	3	1	39	20	16	12

Eastleigh

Age	Males	Females	Males	Females	Males	Females	Males	Females	Males	Females	Males	Females	Males	Females
ALL AGES 16 - 24	6,478	6,296	454	1,049	3	116	5,094	4,428	125	94	596	311	1,648	1,631
16	671	661	-	-	-	-	199	207	20	14	24	16	544	559
17	693	665	-	5	-	1	452	390	47	41	56	42	333	385
18	710	716	6	11	-	3	516	471	30	19	70	42	278	301
19	732	643	5	20	1	10	578	482	8	8	63	38	174	132
20	735	666	9	50	1	14	618	519	6	2	84	29	114	102
21	701	714	40	120	1	16	611	562	7	4	80	39	95	75
22	715	720	70	199	-	20	655	586	1	2	67	32	61	46
23	777	783	142	301	-	23	743	636	3	2	75	41	33	20
24	744	728	182	343	-	29	722	575	3	2	77	32	16	11

Table 37 Young adults – **continued**

County, districts

37. Residents aged 16 - 24 in households

Age	TOTAL PERSONS		Married		Lone 'parent' aged 16 - 24 with child(ren) aged 0 - 15		Economically active		On a Government scheme		Unemployed		Students (including those economically active)	
	Males	Females	Males	Females	Males	Females	Males	Females	Males	Females	Males	Females	Males	Females
a	b	c	d	e	f	g	h	i	j	k	l	m	n	o

Fareham

Age	Males	Females	Males	Females	Males	Females	Males	Females	Males	Females	Males	Females	Males	Females
ALL AGES 16 - 24	5,785	5,475	272	714	4	84	4,437	3,760	154	114	595	282	1,597	1,631
16	615	596	1	3	-	-	195	191	20	20	23	17	494	508
17	637	610	2	2	-	-	376	345	61	56	49	28	337	373
18	677	640	1	3	1	3	490	426	34	25	77	37	264	292
19	663	666	6	11	1	1	512	498	4	6	89	36	176	173
20	719	693	13	45	-	10	584	527	5	4	86	45	143	130
21	652	524	19	72	-	11	568	410	6	1	87	32	88	72
22	604	609	37	141	-	17	546	482	9	2	67	35	56	47
23	598	563	68	193	1	18	566	433	6	-	54	25	24	29
24	620	574	125	244	1	24	600	448	9	-	63	27	15	7

Gosport

Age	Males	Females	Males	Females	Males	Females	Males	Females	Males	Females	Males	Females	Males	Females
ALL AGES 16 - 24	4,767	5,070	678	1,224	5	181	3,915	3,521	161	141	603	334	957	1,013
16	467	443	1	-	-	1	165	150	27	25	28	15	346	356
17	521	480	1	4	1	3	333	293	52	54	67	34	225	245
18	440	505	1	20	-	8	344	366	28	37	64	42	127	168
19	503	570	17	45	-	6	420	438	15	6	81	56	95	95
20	514	569	32	89	1	19	455	429	12	4	68	38	64	69
21	544	569	78	159	1	29	498	434	8	3	79	46	42	39
22	571	626	120	222	1	34	524	459	5	6	79	39	38	25
23	557	658	178	334	-	33	539	496	8	2	55	25	13	10
24	650	650	250	351	1	48	637	456	6	4	82	39	7	6

Hart

Age	Males	Females	Males	Females	Males	Females	Males	Females	Males	Females	Males	Females	Males	Females
ALL AGES 16 - 24	5,358	4,993	212	533	-	45	3,858	3,281	70	46	420	227	1,787	1,716
16	634	548	-	-	-	-	192	170	13	8	20	11	520	476
17	650	571	1	-	-	-	355	279	24	16	43	25	387	391
18	644	584	2	3	-	2	414	349	12	12	45	33	319	303
19	642	585	2	17	-	1	465	399	12	7	63	29	199	190
20	572	580	5	28	-	5	440	403	5	2	47	28	143	163
21	591	498	22	46	-	7	476	375	3	-	58	30	118	101
22	569	521	41	87	-	8	500	404	-	-	48	26	68	57
23	501	554	50	142	-	7	477	465	1	-	52	27	23	25
24	555	552	89	210	-	15	539	437	-	1	44	18	10	10

Havant

Age	Males	Females	Males	Females	Males	Females	Males	Females	Males	Females	Males	Females	Males	Females
ALL AGES 16 - 24	7,273	7,223	412	1,000	6	277	5,673	4,736	191	165	1,086	479	1,791	1,751
16	839	803	1	-	-	-	272	271	18	27	62	41	632	625
17	795	779	1	2	-	3	501	474	73	69	89	53	381	390
18	844	825	2	8	-	4	623	567	47	37	119	78	266	284
19	873	824	10	31	-	10	714	631	20	5	167	73	178	149
20	816	861	20	73	-	20	692	635	7	4	152	48	129	123
21	809	764	38	99	-	42	709	551	8	7	127	46	101	73
22	817	788	57	167	1	70	742	548	4	3	141	52	73	59
23	737	791	111	270	3	62	706	545	10	6	113	44	17	27
24	743	788	172	350	2	66	714	514	4	7	116	44	14	21

Table 37 Young adults – **continued**

County, districts

37. Residents aged 16 - 24 in households

Age	TOTAL PERSONS		Married		Lone 'parent' aged 16 - 24 with child(ren) aged 0 - 15		Economically active		On a Government scheme		Unemployed		Students (including those economically active)	
	Males	Females	Males	Females	Males	Females	Males	Females	Males	Females	Males	Females	Males	Females
a	b	c	d	e	f	g	h	i	j	k	l	m	n	o

New Forest

ALL AGES 16 - 24	8,424	8,312	525	1,204	4	204	6,484	5,487	193	98	922	440	2,271	2,438
16	949	984	1	1	-	1	308	271	34	12	39	25	750	850
17	946	943	1	1	-	4	561	521	67	42	67	43	495	546
18	954	984	4	12	-	7	687	616	40	25	109	65	366	417
19	964	934	4	28	-	14	780	696	24	8	124	65	210	212
20	961	906	19	70	-	22	797	664	7	7	120	64	169	171
21	937	813	45	138	-	30	813	598	11	2	130	39	123	115
22	933	901	74	226	1	38	840	708	5	1	108	55	97	70
23	854	869	130	309	2	37	804	667	3	1	117	42	42	39
24	926	978	247	419	1	51	894	746	2	-	108	42	19	18

Portsmouth

ALL AGES 16 - 24	11,297	11,356	1,003	2,080	12	496	9,181	7,866	309	189	1,808	937	2,309	2,055
16	888	843	1	4	1	-	350	314	47	35	100	89	603	606
17	932	881	4	20	1	4	652	560	96	73	136	95	365	368
18	986	974	6	27	1	12	763	692	68	41	184	120	276	280
19	1,177	1,135	8	71	2	31	953	836	31	10	247	123	244	202
20	1,269	1,302	50	120	-	51	1,053	902	19	5	235	113	224	200
21	1,432	1,399	99	234	2	72	1,179	1,011	19	12	230	89	242	157
22	1,468	1,581	171	397	1	92	1,291	1,169	9	5	237	117	169	125
23	1,526	1,609	260	555	3	103	1,404	1,224	10	6	231	104	110	67
24	1,619	1,632	404	652	1	131	1,536	1,158	10	2	208	87	76	50

Rushmoor

ALL AGES 16 - 24	5,536	5,741	642	1,275	8	199	4,618	4,043	72	51	488	329	1,048	1,103
16	510	470	2	2	-	-	183	175	9	15	36	22	381	366
17	485	477	-	4	-	1	328	262	21	16	57	24	206	262
18	535	570	1	16	-	6	398	395	19	14	49	46	174	190
19	513	580	9	44	-	12	440	439	3	1	57	37	85	97
20	591	660	26	104	-	19	508	499	4	1	58	52	87	86
21	617	621	64	148	-	19	561	479	5	-	69	35	50	53
22	697	763	120	241	3	44	658	577	2	1	47	43	37	29
23	781	764	194	293	3	48	758	586	4	2	67	34	16	9
24	807	836	226	423	2	50	784	631	5	1	48	36	12	11

Southampton

ALL AGES 16 - 24	13,285	13,103	1,063	2,257	19	716	10,447	8,691	389	236	2,273	1,075	3,031	2,666
16	1,153	1,073	1	-	-	2	405	359	55	31	124	68	823	812
17	1,251	1,100	5	12	-	6	873	707	149	84	185	128	485	482
18	1,305	1,172	9	27	-	17	1,023	832	68	41	239	114	341	337
19	1,389	1,399	18	88	3	50	1,132	1,005	28	19	298	154	263	257
20	1,483	1,507	47	156	-	91	1,187	1,031	17	19	295	139	298	234
21	1,581	1,597	79	262	1	122	1,277	1,068	19	8	303	136	314	225
22	1,629	1,646	178	407	5	128	1,378	1,148	17	15	264	108	229	159
23	1,730	1,769	306	567	5	148	1,553	1,246	20	12	272	114	157	102
24	1,764	1,840	420	738	5	152	1,619	1,295	16	7	293	114	121	58

Table 37 Young adults – **continued**

County, districts

37. Residents aged 16 - 24 in households

Age	TOTAL PERSONS		Married		Lone 'parent' aged 16 - 24 with child(ren) aged 0 - 15		Economically active		On a Government scheme		Unemployed		Students (including those economically active)	
	Males	Females	Males	Females	Males	Females	Males	Females	Males	Females	Males	Females	Males	Females
a	b	c	d	e	f	g	h	i	j	k	l	m	n	o

Test Valley

Age	Males	Females	Males	Females	Males	Females	Males	Females	Males	Females	Males	Females	Males	Females
ALL AGES 16 - 24	6,375	6,028	437	955	-	146	4,864	4,052	128	76	557	274	1,750	1,661
16	707	665	-	-	-	-	246	209	28	14	33	19	538	558
17	729	670	1	3	-	4	435	379	41	32	58	23	384	401
18	762	696	-	13	-	4	522	465	28	17	67	39	294	268
19	714	639	3	40	-	6	574	477	11	6	77	41	168	155
20	758	717	21	79	-	16	604	526	4	1	72	43	165	123
21	706	667	47	119	-	23	590	492	4	-	77	30	118	81
22	665	641	74	162	-	37	607	474	6	1	58	34	51	47
23	636	635	108	239	-	21	607	495	3	1	59	20	20	24
24	698	698	183	300	-	35	679	535	3	4	56	25	12	4

Winchester

Age	Males	Females	Males	Females	Males	Females	Males	Females	Males	Females	Males	Females	Males	Females
ALL AGES 16 - 24	5,630	5,408	219	546	1	83	3,799	3,230	111	60	513	267	2,100	2,153
16	664	615	1	1	-	-	188	168	15	10	32	18	560	530
17	685	597	2	1	-	-	350	289	45	17	42	27	426	411
18	646	627	1	5	-	3	397	351	27	13	62	34	301	331
19	671	666	4	18	-	4	451	426	6	7	74	48	234	241
20	657	679	6	38	-	10	451	417	1	5	68	33	222	234
21	653	605	26	58	-	11	499	386	3	1	71	28	174	190
22	592	558	30	97	-	19	485	368	8	2	55	22	108	135
23	549	512	64	136	-	12	496	383	2	2	62	36	53	56
24	513	549	85	192	1	24	482	442	4	3	47	21	22	25

Table 38   Single years of age

County, districts

38. Residents in households

Age	TOTAL PERSONS	Males	Females	Age	TOTAL PERSONS	Males	Females
a	b	c	d	a	b	c	d
	HAMPSHIRE				HAMPSHIRE – *continued*		
ALL AGES	1,512,038	740,181	771,857				
0	20,786	10,662	10,124	45	20,720	10,358	10,362
1	20,932	10,743	10,189	46	21,249	10,627	10,622
2	20,437	10,403	10,034	47	19,767	9,986	9,781
3	20,878	10,621	10,257	48	19,215	9,649	9,566
4	20,054	10,193	9,861	49	17,127	8,488	8,639
5	19,687	10,178	9,509	50	15,994	8,133	7,861
6	19,488	10,067	9,421	51	17,141	8,621	8,520
7	18,921	9,786	9,135	52	16,830	8,393	8,437
8	18,749	9,623	9,126	53	16,630	8,250	8,380
9	19,154	9,933	9,221	54	16,092	8,152	7,940
10	19,525	9,942	9,583	55	15,816	7,945	7,871
11	19,261	9,905	9,356	56	15,578	7,766	7,812
12	18,168	9,295	8,873	57	14,779	7,455	7,324
13	17,280	8,843	8,437	58	14,872	7,251	7,621
14	17,491	9,038	8,453	59	15,467	7,704	7,763
15	17,985	9,192	8,793	60	15,640	7,740	7,900
16	19,086	9,769	9,317	61	15,224	7,379	7,845
17	19,420	10,023	9,397	62	14,895	7,354	7,541
18	20,402	10,359	10,043	63	14,221	6,929	7,292
19	21,041	10,611	10,430	64	14,518	6,909	7,609
20	21,882	10,897	10,985	65	14,304	6,787	7,517
21	21,407	10,976	10,431	66	14,201	6,612	7,589
22	22,227	11,091	11,136	67	14,243	6,419	7,824
23	22,317	11,019	11,298	68	14,204	6,308	7,896
24	23,201	11,514	11,687	69	14,641	6,525	8,116
25	23,822	11,901	11,921	70	15,162	6,651	8,511
26	24,464	12,048	12,416	71	14,321	6,239	8,082
27	24,741	12,450	12,291	72	10,000	4,317	5,683
28	24,299	12,069	12,230	73	9,141	3,888	5,253
29	23,996	12,109	11,887	74	10,453	4,394	6,059
30	23,665	11,968	11,697	75	9,940	4,200	5,740
31	23,042	11,684	11,358	76	10,564	4,202	6,362
32	22,724	11,503	11,221	77	9,852	3,923	5,929
33	22,235	11,169	11,066	78	9,084	3,617	5,467
34	21,671	10,870	10,801	79	8,209	3,100	5,109
35	20,544	10,442	10,102	80	7,627	2,862	4,765
36	20,763	10,337	10,426	81	6,783	2,450	4,333
37	20,760	10,398	10,362	82	6,177	2,155	4,022
38	20,551	10,152	10,399	83	5,301	1,940	3,361
39	20,465	10,112	10,353	84	4,512	1,496	3,016
40	20,747	10,469	10,278	85	3,885	1,247	2,638
41	21,559	10,567	10,992	86	3,266	1,020	2,246
42	22,767	11,308	11,459	87	2,557	805	1,752
43	24,964	12,398	12,566	88	2,048	620	1,428
44	26,443	13,231	13,212	89	1,594	439	1,155
				90 and over	4,193	1,008	3,185

Table 38 Single years of age – **continued**

County, districts

38. Residents in households

Age	TOTAL PERSONS	Males	Females	Age	TOTAL PERSONS	Males	Females
a	b	c	d	a	b	c	d
	Basingstoke & Deane				Basingstoke & Deane – *continued*		
ALL AGES	143,278	70,994	72,284				
0	2,017	1,010	1,007	45	2,116	1,072	1,044
1	2,073	1,068	1,005	46	2,125	1,018	1,107
2	1,957	1,000	957	47	1,988	1,002	986
3	1,975	950	1,025	48	1,967	1,005	962
4	1,930	981	949	49	1,662	812	850
5	1,925	977	948	50	1,573	815	758
6	1,915	980	935	51	1,653	868	785
7	1,812	959	853	52	1,663	837	826
8	1,844	930	914	53	1,545	817	728
9	1,806	901	905	54	1,476	757	719
10	1,894	990	904	55	1,523	810	713
11	1,946	1,004	942	56	1,422	712	710
12	1,838	947	891	57	1,310	665	645
13	1,740	869	871	58	1,290	641	649
14	1,783	932	851	59	1,340	679	661
15	1,904	963	941	60	1,343	717	626
16	1,959	970	989	61	1,235	625	610
17	1,976	999	977	62	1,181	595	586
18	2,152	1,092	1,060	63	1,139	592	547
19	2,164	1,082	1,082	64	1,134	549	585
20	2,263	1,119	1,144	65	1,101	553	548
21	2,138	1,073	1,065	66	1,021	481	540
22	2,333	1,189	1,144	67	1,082	488	594
23	2,317	1,158	1,159	68	1,096	490	606
24	2,420	1,223	1,197	69	1,124	518	606
25	2,588	1,314	1,274	70	1,063	480	583
26	2,607	1,309	1,298	71	1,044	480	564
27	2,572	1,321	1,251	72	701	290	411
28	2,514	1,221	1,293	73	633	259	374
29	2,522	1,278	1,244	74	686	276	410
30	2,364	1,194	1,170	75	702	297	405
31	2,341	1,216	1,125	76	702	289	413
32	2,237	1,150	1,087	77	659	257	402
33	2,176	1,113	1,063	78	656	265	391
34	2,180	1,077	1,103	79	566	208	358
35	2,069	1,040	1,029	80	545	219	326
36	2,045	1,022	1,023	81	472	163	309
37	2,102	1,032	1,070	82	426	139	287
38	2,076	1,031	1,045	83	338	100	238
39	2,062	1,016	1,046	84	277	91	186
40	2,161	1,117	1,044	85	262	92	170
41	2,231	1,104	1,127	86	217	73	144
42	2,326	1,143	1,183	87	169	58	111
43	2,572	1,280	1,292	88	114	28	86
44	2,718	1,373	1,345	89	97	26	71
				90 and over	296	69	227

Table 38   Single years of age – **continued**   County, districts

38. Residents in households

Age	TOTAL PERSONS	Males	Females	Age	TOTAL PERSONS	Males	Females
a	b	c	d	a	b	c	d
	East Hampshire				East Hampshire – *continued*		
ALL AGES	101,335	49,670	51,665				
0	1,324	682	642	45	1,476	712	764
1	1,370	694	676	46	1,594	774	820
2	1,319	649	670	47	1,520	790	730
3	1,373	697	676	48	1,420	710	710
4	1,435	740	695	49	1,298	651	647
5	1,350	714	636	50	1,161	564	597
6	1,355	705	650	51	1,252	612	640
7	1,321	689	632	52	1,225	599	626
8	1,260	643	617	53	1,160	600	560
9	1,387	726	661	54	1,133	563	570
10	1,300	670	630	55	1,055	547	508
11	1,437	740	697	56	1,065	541	524
12	1,367	669	698	57	992	508	484
13	1,238	640	598	58	976	471	505
14	1,261	628	633	59	1,017	508	509
15	1,320	684	636	60	1,012	541	471
16	1,329	702	627	61	957	479	478
17	1,347	700	647	62	930	473	457
18	1,454	764	690	63	936	472	464
19	1,395	688	707	64	925	434	491
20	1,404	703	701	65	878	397	481
21	1,275	680	595	66	848	387	461
22	1,280	642	638	67	899	413	486
23	1,247	615	632	68	878	410	468
24	1,317	652	665	69	900	427	473
25	1,311	640	671	70	978	439	539
26	1,381	696	685	71	867	367	500
27	1,458	696	762	72	587	260	327
28	1,488	737	751	73	556	263	293
29	1,436	726	710	74	684	288	396
30	1,441	719	722	75	606	257	349
31	1,498	732	766	76	675	255	420
32	1,471	704	767	77	623	254	369
33	1,583	779	804	78	623	251	372
34	1,519	757	762	79	563	203	360
35	1,416	683	733	80	470	180	290
36	1,443	709	734	81	430	167	263
37	1,407	721	686	82	417	147	270
38	1,488	722	766	83	345	134	211
39	1,428	750	678	84	306	109	197
40	1,493	769	724	85	263	83	180
41	1,659	779	880	86	206	57	149
42	1,697	818	879	87	180	55	125
43	1,871	932	939	88	141	37	104
44	1,955	978	977	89	107	33	74
				90 and over	293	85	208

Table 38 Single years of age – **continued**

County, districts

38. Residents in households

Age	TOTAL PERSONS	Males	Females	Age	TOTAL PERSONS	Males	Females
a	b	c	d	a	b	c	d
Eastleigh				**Eastleigh** – *continued*			
ALL AGES	105,298	51,982	53,316				
0	1,497	774	723	45	1,437	718	719
1	1,487	768	719	46	1,582	840	742
2	1,443	754	689	47	1,430	714	716
3	1,474	744	730	48	1,310	667	643
4	1,417	726	691	49	1,172	575	597
5	1,378	730	648	50	1,123	588	535
6	1,382	720	662	51	1,239	632	607
7	1,390	696	694	52	1,190	621	569
8	1,325	684	641	53	1,152	579	573
9	1,460	745	715	54	1,090	551	539
10	1,456	727	729	55	1,073	570	503
11	1,430	713	717	56	1,009	476	533
12	1,279	646	633	57	1,018	509	509
13	1,265	659	606	58	948	488	460
14	1,267	645	622	59	964	465	499
15	1,287	675	612	60	1,066	520	546
16	1,332	671	661	61	987	471	516
17	1,358	693	665	62	987	494	493
18	1,426	710	716	63	970	494	476
19	1,375	732	643	64	988	472	516
20	1,401	735	666	65	954	448	506
21	1,415	701	714	66	920	440	480
22	1,435	715	720	67	934	447	487
23	1,560	777	783	68	879	396	483
24	1,472	744	728	69	945	409	536
25	1,659	829	830	70	925	386	539
26	1,757	826	931	71	879	399	480
27	1,788	888	900	72	589	267	322
28	1,728	838	890	73	568	255	313
29	1,722	852	870	74	661	284	377
30	1,778	896	882	75	593	246	347
31	1,715	864	851	76	636	267	369
32	1,691	848	843	77	618	253	365
33	1,678	852	826	78	501	195	306
34	1,623	818	805	79	490	192	298
35	1,589	810	779	80	426	151	275
36	1,625	831	794	81	369	144	225
37	1,613	820	793	82	357	127	230
38	1,572	767	805	83	274	100	174
39	1,569	787	782	84	252	83	169
40	1,561	769	792	85	238	72	166
41	1,591	784	807	86	204	64	140
42	1,694	866	828	87	128	40	88
43	1,917	976	941	88	135	43	92
44	1,854	938	916	89	105	35	70
				90 and over	248	52	196

Table 38 Single years of age – **continued**

County, districts

38. Residents in households

Age	TOTAL PERSONS	Males	Females	Age	TOTAL PERSONS	Males	Females
a	b	c	d	a	b	c	d
Fareham				Fareham – *continued*			
ALL AGES	97,607	47,806	49,801				
0	1,229	632	597	45	1,549	751	798
1	1,253	664	589	46	1,558	768	790
2	1,281	631	650	47	1,422	729	693
3	1,315	692	623	48	1,372	673	699
4	1,273	639	634	49	1,187	580	607
5	1,213	616	597	50	1,114	541	573
6	1,193	592	601	51	1,213	612	601
7	1,167	585	582	52	1,123	553	570
8	1,144	617	527	53	1,157	583	574
9	1,193	613	580	54	1,176	593	583
10	1,229	607	622	55	1,141	548	593
11	1,181	619	562	56	1,094	551	543
12	1,133	565	568	57	1,098	567	531
13	1,111	568	543	58	1,118	523	595
14	1,149	577	572	59	1,139	581	558
15	1,095	577	518	60	1,119	543	576
16	1,211	615	596	61	1,150	575	575
17	1,247	637	610	62	999	516	483
18	1,317	677	640	63	917	436	481
19	1,329	663	666	64	990	472	518
20	1,412	719	693	65	1,003	479	524
21	1,176	652	524	66	968	446	522
22	1,213	604	609	67	934	412	522
23	1,161	598	563	68	941	417	524
24	1,194	620	574	69	1,032	452	580
25	1,292	628	664	70	1,020	473	547
26	1,333	632	701	71	927	415	512
27	1,383	667	716	72	592	272	320
28	1,403	680	723	73	560	239	321
29	1,490	737	753	74	614	265	349
30	1,537	737	800	75	606	280	326
31	1,520	765	755	76	664	274	390
32	1,488	748	740	77	611	269	342
33	1,421	728	693	78	583	232	351
34	1,399	711	688	79	501	181	320
35	1,387	728	659	80	465	168	297
36	1,374	676	698	81	386	125	261
37	1,383	687	696	82	369	143	226
38	1,352	656	696	83	340	132	208
39	1,347	653	694	84	268	103	165
40	1,400	678	722	85	205	76	129
41	1,429	726	703	86	183	53	130
42	1,580	772	808	87	138	44	94
43	1,741	876	865	88	118	38	80
44	1,964	981	983	89	87	20	67
				90 and over	214	58	156

Table 38 Single years of age – **continued**

38. Residents in households

Age	TOTAL PERSONS	Males	Females	Age	TOTAL PERSONS	Males	Females
a	b	c	d	a	b	c	d
Gosport				**Gosport** – *continued*			
ALL AGES	**73,704**	**35,862**	**37,842**				
0	1,133	550	583	45	916	484	432
1	1,119	565	554	46	894	446	448
2	1,113	567	546	47	781	384	397
3	1,078	566	512	48	766	393	373
4	1,086	553	533	49	738	343	395
5	1,031	537	494	50	640	332	308
6	1,075	561	514	51	693	342	351
7	1,002	511	491	52	651	323	328
8	983	524	459	53	719	349	370
9	1,011	529	482	54	707	361	346
10	998	509	489	55	679	315	364
11	944	491	453	56	721	347	374
12	859	428	431	57	669	311	358
13	887	477	410	58	675	324	351
14	858	471	387	59	737	371	366
15	807	433	374	60	699	319	380
16	910	467	443	61	739	349	390
17	1,001	521	480	62	704	361	343
18	945	440	505	63	616	284	332
19	1,073	503	570	64	639	293	346
20	1,083	514	569	65	634	299	335
21	1,113	544	569	66	603	249	354
22	1,197	571	626	67	698	322	376
23	1,215	557	658	68	650	293	357
24	1,300	650	650	69	650	284	366
25	1,260	612	648	70	730	297	433
26	1,373	681	692	71	643	284	359
27	1,406	710	696	72	480	179	301
28	1,423	729	694	73	469	201	268
29	1,399	694	705	74	472	189	283
30	1,326	655	671	75	499	195	304
31	1,256	691	565	76	521	195	326
32	1,275	642	633	77	441	180	261
33	1,139	587	552	78	432	155	277
34	1,091	562	529	79	413	151	262
35	1,067	576	491	80	333	120	213
36	973	503	470	81	298	104	194
37	916	467	449	82	306	98	208
38	933	433	500	83	257	93	164
39	916	448	468	84	229	73	156
40	864	455	409	85	193	46	147
41	991	479	512	86	167	49	118
42	1,059	518	541	87	113	41	72
43	1,125	571	554	88	85	24	61
44	1,137	584	553	89	69	27	42
				90 and over	186	47	139

Table 38 Single years of age – **continued**

County, districts

38. Residents in households

Age	TOTAL PERSONS	Males	Females	Age	TOTAL PERSONS	Males	Females
a	b	c	d	a	b	c	d
Hart				**Hart** – *continued*			
ALL AGES	**79,014**	**39,369**	**39,645**				
0	1,007	553	454	45	1,285	637	648
1	1,086	580	506	46	1,380	675	705
2	1,002	504	498	47	1,264	638	626
3	1,075	543	532	48	1,237	626	611
4	1,041	541	500	49	1,068	557	511
5	1,086	591	495	50	976	507	469
6	1,052	552	500	51	1,028	535	493
7	1,058	546	512	52	1,027	527	500
8	1,087	531	556	53	988	508	480
9	1,130	599	531	54	945	487	458
10	1,123	566	557	55	879	450	429
11	1,131	596	535	56	811	423	388
12	1,143	601	542	57	802	440	362
13	1,059	530	529	58	770	367	403
14	1,067	562	505	59	707	405	302
15	1,070	530	540	60	714	370	344
16	1,182	634	548	61	658	340	318
17	1,221	650	571	62	592	278	314
18	1,228	644	584	63	564	302	262
19	1,227	642	585	64	582	287	295
20	1,152	572	580	65	550	275	275
21	1,089	591	498	66	511	248	263
22	1,090	569	521	67	521	253	268
23	1,055	501	554	68	510	237	273
24	1,107	555	552	69	521	244	277
25	1,110	583	527	70	543	228	315
26	1,136	571	565	71	517	235	282
27	1,165	588	577	72	329	136	193
28	1,186	597	589	73	312	134	178
29	1,150	585	565	74	366	154	212
30	1,204	589	615	75	331	150	181
31	1,171	593	578	76	384	148	236
32	1,184	560	624	77	338	121	217
33	1,172	586	586	78	332	130	202
34	1,158	571	587	79	285	99	186
35	1,106	544	562	80	293	104	189
36	1,192	585	607	81	272	96	176
37	1,240	614	626	82	253	87	166
38	1,278	637	641	83	215	75	140
39	1,208	584	624	84	185	52	133
40	1,231	588	643	85	163	39	124
41	1,266	641	625	86	124	49	75
42	1,429	683	746	87	85	20	65
43	1,639	795	844	88	71	19	52
44	1,701	850	851	89	56	11	45
				90 and over	176	39	137

Table 38 Single years of age – **continued**

County, districts

38. Residents in households

Age	TOTAL PERSONS	Males	Females	Age	TOTAL PERSONS	Males	Females
a	b	c	d	a	b	c	d
	Havant			Havant – *continued*			
ALL AGES	**118,297**	**57,375**	**60,922**				
0	1,542	777	765	45	1,604	763	841
1	1,650	859	791	46	1,584	797	787
2	1,587	786	801	47	1,505	745	760
3	1,653	828	825	48	1,468	727	741
4	1,671	810	861	49	1,335	677	658
5	1,666	898	768	50	1,273	604	669
6	1,553	802	751	51	1,367	644	723
7	1,570	818	752	52	1,486	713	773
8	1,522	753	769	53	1,368	670	698
9	1,573	845	728	54	1,314	626	688
10	1,705	849	856	55	1,338	658	680
11	1,558	827	731	56	1,384	634	750
12	1,491	775	716	57	1,330	619	711
13	1,430	738	692	58	1,301	628	673
14	1,428	760	668	59	1,405	701	704
15	1,521	767	754	60	1,422	709	713
16	1,642	839	803	61	1,393	676	717
17	1,574	795	779	62	1,373	668	705
18	1,669	844	825	63	1,280	643	637
19	1,697	873	824	64	1,310	618	692
20	1,677	816	861	65	1,223	583	640
21	1,573	809	764	66	1,220	591	629
22	1,605	817	788	67	1,247	568	679
23	1,528	737	791	68	1,243	566	677
24	1,531	743	788	69	1,259	583	676
25	1,580	761	819	70	1,274	560	714
26	1,606	748	858	71	1,188	519	669
27	1,623	795	828	72	852	377	475
28	1,664	829	835	73	701	321	380
29	1,711	879	832	74	752	307	445
30	1,683	835	848	75	734	319	415
31	1,681	835	846	76	822	326	496
32	1,652	831	821	77	717	293	424
33	1,639	808	831	78	702	287	415
34	1,603	795	808	79	589	216	373
35	1,570	764	806	80	548	206	342
36	1,650	813	837	81	490	191	299
37	1,546	742	804	82	421	138	283
38	1,561	763	798	83	356	130	226
39	1,483	743	740	84	317	92	225
40	1,532	777	755	85	278	93	185
41	1,585	753	832	86	245	66	179
42	1,755	838	917	87	198	54	144
43	1,826	909	917	88	150	43	107
44	1,959	942	1,017	89	103	24	79
				90 and over	303	77	226

Table 38 Single years of age – **continued**

County, districts

38. Residents in households

Age	TOTAL PERSONS	Males	Females	Age	TOTAL PERSONS	Males	Females
a	b	c	d	a	b	c	d
New Forest				**New Forest** – *continued*			
ALL AGES	**157,604**	**75,958**	**81,646**				
0	1,836	943	893	45	2,061	1,049	1,012
1	1,786	925	861	46	2,162	1,102	1,060
2	1,819	908	911	47	2,071	1,046	1,025
3	1,880	983	897	48	1,959	949	1,010
4	1,849	925	924	49	1,692	834	858
5	1,731	883	848	50	1,686	850	836
6	1,795	895	900	51	1,778	869	909
7	1,769	943	826	52	1,705	828	877
8	1,840	926	914	53	1,791	851	940
9	1,833	965	868	54	1,793	867	926
10	1,900	992	908	55	1,778	890	888
11	1,926	969	957	56	1,785	861	924
12	1,729	865	864	57	1,679	850	829
13	1,688	870	818	58	1,705	827	878
14	1,737	886	851	59	1,740	818	922
15	1,754	882	872	60	1,881	892	989
16	1,933	949	984	61	1,822	810	1,012
17	1,889	946	943	62	1,874	956	918
18	1,938	954	984	63	1,821	850	971
19	1,898	964	934	64	1,922	900	1,022
20	1,867	961	906	65	1,968	926	1,042
21	1,750	937	813	66	2,042	1,001	1,041
22	1,834	933	901	67	1,953	897	1,056
23	1,723	854	869	68	1,971	884	1,087
24	1,904	926	978	69	2,063	899	1,164
25	1,925	982	943	70	2,218	1,021	1,197
26	2,021	1,015	1,006	71	2,039	881	1,158
27	2,040	1,050	990	72	1,364	622	742
28	2,113	1,006	1,107	73	1,293	555	738
29	2,004	974	1,030	74	1,573	711	862
30	2,033	1,037	996	75	1,526	658	868
31	1,942	962	980	76	1,560	622	938
32	2,109	1,074	1,035	77	1,461	600	861
33	1,979	974	1,005	78	1,345	570	775
34	2,032	1,016	1,016	79	1,223	508	715
35	2,006	946	1,060	80	1,189	480	709
36	1,978	959	1,019	81	968	354	614
37	2,041	998	1,043	82	912	342	570
38	2,103	1,026	1,077	83	828	324	504
39	2,169	1,041	1,128	84	672	228	444
40	2,077	1,011	1,066	85	578	210	368
41	2,168	1,076	1,092	86	492	155	337
42	2,265	1,128	1,137	87	399	147	252
43	2,646	1,322	1,324	88	300	102	198
44	2,769	1,342	1,427	89	256	73	183
				90 and over	678	166	512

Table 38 Single years of age – **continued**

38. Residents in households

Age	TOTAL PERSONS	Males	Females	Age	TOTAL PERSONS	Males	Females
a	b	c	d	a	b	c	d
Portsmouth				**Portsmouth** – *continued*			
ALL AGES	**169,730**	**82,143**	**87,587**				
0	2,529	1,330	1,199	45	2,078	1,062	1,016
1	2,503	1,233	1,270	46	2,031	1,004	1,027
2	2,400	1,214	1,186	47	1,794	922	872
3	2,527	1,304	1,223	48	1,842	944	898
4	2,307	1,154	1,153	49	1,664	809	855
5	2,267	1,122	1,145	50	1,578	785	793
6	2,219	1,170	1,049	51	1,733	861	872
7	2,082	1,074	1,008	52	1,634	798	836
8	1,985	1,027	958	53	1,685	828	857
9	1,873	948	925	54	1,618	829	789
10	1,927	983	944	55	1,639	805	834
11	1,792	891	901	56	1,557	779	778
12	1,805	924	881	57	1,494	744	750
13	1,627	812	815	58	1,596	780	816
14	1,596	830	766	59	1,645	795	850
15	1,739	885	854	60	1,677	833	844
16	1,731	888	843	61	1,654	784	870
17	1,813	932	881	62	1,698	816	882
18	1,960	986	974	63	1,560	716	844
19	2,312	1,177	1,135	64	1,613	729	884
20	2,571	1,269	1,302	65	1,637	750	887
21	2,831	1,432	1,399	66	1,705	760	945
22	3,049	1,468	1,581	67	1,716	734	982
23	3,135	1,526	1,609	68	1,796	728	1,068
24	3,251	1,619	1,632	69	1,799	786	1,013
25	3,278	1,604	1,674	70	1,867	785	1,082
26	3,373	1,688	1,685	71	1,992	829	1,163
27	3,400	1,762	1,638	72	1,374	577	797
28	3,180	1,574	1,606	73	1,280	518	762
29	3,051	1,531	1,520	74	1,400	557	843
30	2,873	1,530	1,343	75	1,286	535	751
31	2,769	1,426	1,343	76	1,441	560	881
32	2,622	1,385	1,237	77	1,358	532	826
33	2,488	1,278	1,210	78	1,183	433	750
34	2,358	1,197	1,161	79	1,072	376	696
35	2,122	1,117	1,005	80	1,027	354	673
36	2,144	1,052	1,092	81	952	316	636
37	2,102	1,071	1,031	82	842	262	580
38	2,003	1,018	985	83	740	264	476
39	1,992	1,024	968	84	653	196	457
40	1,929	998	931	85	534	165	369
41	2,077	1,039	1,038	86	441	129	312
42	2,104	1,086	1,018	87	348	99	249
43	2,251	1,167	1,084	88	294	93	201
44	2,480	1,256	1,224	89	204	54	150
				90 and over	572	127	445

Table 38 Single years of age – **continued**   County, districts

38. Residents in households

Age	TOTAL PERSONS	Males	Females	Age	TOTAL PERSONS	Males	Females
a	b	c	d	a	b	c	d
Rushmoor				**Rushmoor** – *continued*			
ALL AGES	**79,121**	**39,324**	**39,797**				
0	1,427	717	710	45	962	481	481
1	1,373	669	704	46	925	482	443
2	1,279	648	631	47	944	461	483
3	1,325	711	614	48	882	451	431
4	1,184	622	562	49	807	404	403
5	1,094	562	532	50	820	425	395
6	1,054	540	514	51	823	404	419
7	1,052	535	517	52	780	402	378
8	1,012	514	498	53	771	398	373
9	1,029	516	513	54	763	406	357
10	1,027	544	483	55	702	349	353
11	978	508	470	56	693	363	330
12	906	469	437	57	614	298	316
13	834	450	384	58	630	307	323
14	850	440	410	59	685	352	333
15	898	460	438	60	627	296	331
16	980	510	470	61	648	312	336
17	962	485	477	62	593	279	314
18	1,105	535	570	63	586	268	318
19	1,093	513	580	64	601	303	298
20	1,251	591	660	65	573	289	284
21	1,238	617	621	66	580	266	314
22	1,460	697	763	67	567	263	304
23	1,545	781	764	68	541	252	289
24	1,643	807	836	69	536	224	312
25	1,801	909	892	70	598	265	333
26	1,852	942	910	71	541	242	299
27	1,796	909	887	72	372	160	212
28	1,732	919	813	73	308	114	194
29	1,619	882	737	74	419	174	245
30	1,619	857	762	75	409	157	252
31	1,509	772	737	76	405	161	244
32	1,423	714	709	77	378	144	234
33	1,314	677	637	78	343	139	204
34	1,226	659	567	79	340	119	221
35	1,087	590	497	80	312	122	190
36	1,090	549	541	81	256	87	169
37	1,095	558	537	82	199	69	130
38	1,007	497	510	83	199	61	138
39	1,100	566	534	84	170	59	111
40	1,063	550	513	85	130	39	91
41	1,065	528	537	86	130	37	93
42	1,119	577	542	87	103	34	69
43	1,186	579	607	88	70	20	50
44	1,291	667	624	89	55	11	44
				90 and over	138	33	105

Table 38 Single years of age – **continued**

County, districts

38. Residents in households

Age	TOTAL PERSONS	Males	Females	Age	TOTAL PERSONS	Males	Females
a	b	c	d	a	b	c	d
Southampton				Southampton – *continued*			
ALL AGES	**193,866**	**95,085**	**98,781**				
0	2,866	1,438	1,428	45	2,324	1,174	1,150
1	2,867	1,452	1,415	46	2,303	1,149	1,154
2	2,807	1,486	1,321	47	2,151	1,095	1,056
3	2,761	1,384	1,377	48	2,195	1,088	1,107
4	2,585	1,339	1,246	49	2,034	1,042	992
5	2,558	1,315	1,243	50	1,884	1,016	868
6	2,540	1,334	1,206	51	1,948	1,012	936
7	2,329	1,215	1,114	52	1,948	976	972
8	2,352	1,210	1,142	53	1,951	941	1,010
9	2,387	1,247	1,140	54	1,887	989	898
10	2,421	1,191	1,230	55	1,807	871	936
11	2,316	1,191	1,125	56	1,893	994	899
12	2,140	1,109	1,031	57	1,744	870	874
13	2,035	1,037	998	58	1,892	920	972
14	2,167	1,112	1,055	59	2,066	968	1,098
15	2,127	1,067	1,060	60	1,987	955	1,032
16	2,226	1,153	1,073	61	1,983	949	1,034
17	2,351	1,251	1,100	62	1,996	951	1,045
18	2,477	1,305	1,172	63	1,902	944	958
19	2,788	1,389	1,399	64	1,947	954	993
20	2,990	1,483	1,507	65	1,981	937	1,044
21	3,178	1,581	1,597	66	2,006	925	1,081
22	3,275	1,629	1,646	67	1,921	845	1,076
23	3,499	1,730	1,769	68	1,955	886	1,069
24	3,604	1,764	1,840	69	1,969	907	1,062
25	3,559	1,773	1,786	70	2,015	870	1,145
26	3,550	1,780	1,770	71	1,887	783	1,104
27	3,553	1,807	1,746	72	1,446	597	849
28	3,328	1,657	1,671	73	1,320	579	741
29	3,224	1,684	1,540	74	1,458	613	845
30	3,058	1,564	1,494	75	1,320	532	788
31	2,993	1,524	1,469	76	1,444	572	872
32	2,954	1,546	1,408	77	1,399	531	868
33	2,831	1,404	1,427	78	1,218	507	711
34	2,756	1,396	1,360	79	1,148	444	704
35	2,492	1,343	1,149	80	1,032	391	641
36	2,539	1,260	1,279	81	964	346	618
37	2,591	1,319	1,272	82	847	313	534
38	2,436	1,271	1,165	83	707	264	443
39	2,438	1,230	1,208	84	587	189	398
40	2,525	1,308	1,217	85	549	164	385
41	2,563	1,279	1,284	86	423	144	279
42	2,523	1,293	1,230	87	350	93	257
43	2,597	1,237	1,360	88	294	93	201
44	2,828	1,426	1,402	89	243	70	173
				90 and over	557	119	438

Table 38 Single years of age – **continued**

County, districts

38. Residents in households

Age	TOTAL PERSONS	Males	Females	Age	TOTAL PERSONS	Males	Females
a	b	c	d	a	b	c	d
Test Valley				**Test Valley** – *continued*			
ALL AGES	**99,463**	**49,237**	**50,226**				
0	1,314	706	608	45	1,514	750	764
1	1,281	661	620	46	1,637	846	791
2	1,340	707	633	47	1,510	757	753
3	1,372	698	674	48	1,400	705	695
4	1,211	633	578	49	1,275	630	645
5	1,270	667	603	50	1,095	572	523
6	1,247	632	615	51	1,196	615	581
7	1,288	666	622	52	1,186	603	583
8	1,253	666	587	53	1,217	620	597
9	1,279	657	622	54	1,106	574	532
10	1,354	712	642	55	1,142	590	552
11	1,377	728	649	56	1,095	568	527
12	1,317	703	614	57	983	528	455
13	1,267	648	619	58	946	485	461
14	1,181	630	551	59	948	505	443
15	1,295	647	648	60	1,020	505	515
16	1,372	707	665	61	939	471	468
17	1,399	729	670	62	925	457	468
18	1,458	762	696	63	877	418	459
19	1,353	714	639	64	889	458	431
20	1,475	758	717	65	887	431	456
21	1,373	706	667	66	847	380	467
22	1,306	665	641	67	838	392	446
23	1,271	636	635	68	801	347	454
24	1,396	698	698	69	855	353	502
25	1,409	736	673	70	928	409	519
26	1,377	646	731	71	872	405	467
27	1,410	713	697	72	619	277	342
28	1,455	748	707	73	537	213	324
29	1,481	725	756	74	640	272	368
30	1,504	738	766	75	648	269	379
31	1,450	700	750	76	623	266	357
32	1,436	716	720	77	563	226	337
33	1,506	747	759	78	512	209	303
34	1,392	694	698	79	469	188	281
35	1,393	689	704	80	468	185	283
36	1,420	709	711	81	409	162	247
37	1,414	707	707	82	357	115	242
38	1,436	682	754	83	333	135	198
39	1,399	663	736	84	267	102	165
40	1,517	744	773	85	223	73	150
41	1,529	684	845	86	184	63	121
42	1,681	840	841	87	156	48	108
43	1,874	921	953	88	124	36	88
44	1,971	1,006	965	89	90	29	61
				90 and over	210	51	159

Table 38 Single years of age – **continued**

County, districts

38. Residents in households

Age	TOTAL PERSONS	Males	Females	Age	TOTAL PERSONS	Males	Females
a	b	c	d	a	b	c	d
Winchester				Winchester – continued			
ALL AGES	93,721	45,376	48,345				
0	1,065	550	515	45	1,398	705	693
1	1,084	605	479	46	1,474	726	748
2	1,090	549	541	47	1,387	703	684
3	1,070	521	549	48	1,397	711	686
4	1,065	530	535	49	1,195	574	621
5	1,118	566	552	50	1,071	534	537
6	1,108	584	524	51	1,218	615	603
7	1,081	549	532	52	1,212	613	599
8	1,142	598	544	53	1,126	506	620
9	1,193	642	551	54	1,084	549	535
10	1,191	602	589	55	1,060	542	518
11	1,245	628	617	56	1,049	517	532
12	1,161	594	567	57	1,046	546	500
13	1,099	545	554	58	1,025	490	535
14	1,147	565	582	59	1,074	556	518
15	1,168	622	546	60	1,073	540	533
16	1,279	664	615	61	1,059	538	521
17	1,282	685	597	62	1,043	510	533
18	1,273	646	627	63	1,053	510	543
19	1,337	671	666	64	978	440	538
20	1,336	657	679	65	915	420	495
21	1,258	653	605	66	930	438	492
22	1,150	592	558	67	933	385	548
23	1,061	549	512	68	943	402	541
24	1,062	513	549	69	988	439	549
25	1,050	530	520	70	1,003	438	565
26	1,098	514	584	71	925	400	525
27	1,147	544	603	72	695	303	392
28	1,085	534	551	73	604	237	367
29	1,187	562	625	74	728	304	424
30	1,245	617	628	75	680	305	375
31	1,197	604	593	76	687	267	420
32	1,182	585	597	77	686	263	423
33	1,309	636	673	78	654	244	410
34	1,334	617	717	79	550	215	335
35	1,240	612	628	80	519	182	337
36	1,290	669	621	81	517	195	322
37	1,310	662	648	82	471	175	296
38	1,306	649	657	83	369	128	241
39	1,354	607	747	84	329	119	210
40	1,394	705	689	85	269	95	174
41	1,405	695	710	86	250	81	169
42	1,535	746	789	87	190	72	118
43	1,719	833	886	88	152	44	108
44	1,816	888	928	89	122	26	96
				90 and over	322	85	237

Table 39   Headship

County, districts

Notes: (1) * May include a small number of heads aged under 16
       (2) ** May include a small number of persons in households with heads aged under 16

39. Residents in households

Age	TOTAL PERSONS	Males				Females			
		Total	Single	Married	Widowed or divorced	Total	Single	Married	Widowed or divorced
a	b	c	d	e	f	g	h	i	j

HAMPSHIRE

Heads of households

Age	TOTAL PERSONS	Total	Single	Married	Widowed or divorced	Total	Single	Married	Widowed or divorced
All ages 16 and over*	603,257	434,882	51,440	343,555	39,887	168,375	33,784	30,736	103,855
16 - 19*	2,265	941	843	90	8	1,324	1,223	85	16
20 - 24	25,351	15,738	10,201	5,419	118	9,613	7,262	1,750	601
25 - 29	54,319	40,179	14,430	24,471	1,278	14,140	6,871	4,483	2,786
30 - 44	174,909	140,212	14,942	115,027	10,243	34,697	6,945	12,689	15,063
45 - 59	143,990	117,016	5,231	101,556	10,229	26,974	2,965	6,769	17,240
60 - 64	44,933	33,943	1,830	29,131	2,982	10,990	1,415	1,312	8,263
65 - 74	85,339	54,684	2,663	45,339	6,682	30,655	3,267	2,075	25,313
75 - 84	58,539	27,662	1,112	20,163	6,387	30,877	2,882	1,294	26,701
85 and over	13,612	4,507	188	2,359	1,960	9,105	954	279	7,872

All persons in households by head's age, sex and marital status

Age	TOTAL PERSONS	Total	Single	Married	Widowed or divorced	Total	Single	Married	Widowed or divorced
All ages 16 and over**	1,512,038	1,203,131	88,684	1,048,093	66,354	308,907	57,617	85,666	165,624
16 - 19**	4,830	1,980	1,701	266	13	2,850	2,604	221	25
20 - 24	56,992	35,396	20,487	14,673	236	21,596	15,320	4,705	1,571
25 - 29	137,851	103,338	26,914	73,719	2,705	34,513	13,464	13,208	7,841
30 - 44	572,952	477,221	24,962	430,290	21,969	95,731	12,082	42,270	41,379
45 - 59	393,602	339,870	7,271	313,889	18,710	53,732	4,101	16,779	32,852
60 - 64	91,591	75,892	2,372	69,247	4,273	15,699	1,698	2,526	11,475
65 - 74	149,423	110,989	3,370	99,045	8,574	38,434	3,883	3,646	30,905
75 - 84	86,850	51,032	1,368	42,129	7,535	35,818	3,354	1,932	30,532
85 and over	17,947	7,413	239	4,835	2,339	10,534	1,111	379	9,044

Basingstoke & Deane

Heads of households

Age	TOTAL PERSONS	Total	Single	Married	Widowed or divorced	Total	Single	Married	Widowed or divorced
All ages 16 and over*	54,323	41,021	4,831	32,828	3,362	13,302	2,706	2,716	7,880
16 - 19*	134	60	51	7	2	74	66	4	4
20 - 24	2,364	1,578	1,040	529	9	786	596	148	42
25 - 29	5,697	4,296	1,576	2,583	137	1,401	687	433	281
30 - 44	17,617	14,425	1,416	11,986	1,023	3,192	609	1,217	1,366
45 - 59	13,754	11,506	367	10,215	924	2,248	234	590	1,424
60 - 64	3,689	2,911	125	2,559	227	778	80	96	602
65 - 74	6,230	4,084	181	3,400	503	2,146	202	125	1,819
75 - 84	3,981	1,867	65	1,394	408	2,114	172	87	1,855
85 and over	857	294	10	155	129	563	60	16	487

All persons in households by head's age, sex and marital status

Age	TOTAL PERSONS	Total	Single	Married	Widowed or divorced	Total	Single	Married	Widowed or divorced
All ages 16 and over**	143,278	117,451	8,440	102,983	6,028	25,827	4,705	7,824	13,298
16 - 19**	297	136	113	21	2	161	144	9	8
20 - 24	5,296	3,563	2,110	1,432	21	1,733	1,230	387	116
25 - 29	14,221	10,865	2,937	7,630	298	3,356	1,335	1,242	779
30 - 44	58,114	49,190	2,303	44,643	2,244	8,924	1,044	4,104	3,776
45 - 59	39,287	34,594	498	32,301	1,795	4,693	331	1,506	2,856
60 - 64	7,895	6,719	165	6,197	357	1,176	106	192	878
65 - 74	11,136	8,423	227	7,520	676	2,713	253	224	2,236
75 - 84	5,892	3,476	76	2,917	483	2,416	191	134	2,091
85 and over	1,140	485	11	322	152	655	71	26	558

Table 39 Headship – continued

Notes: (1) * May include a small number of heads aged under 16
(2) ** May include a small number of persons in households with heads aged under 16

39. Residents in households

Age	TOTAL PERSONS	Males				Females			
		Total	Single	Married	Widowed or divorced	Total	Single	Married	Widowed or divorced
a	b	c	d	e	f	g	h	i	j

East Hampshire

Heads of households

All ages 16 and over*	39,158	29,150	2,812	23,953	2,385	10,008	1,882	2,028	6,098
16 - 19*	115	48	44	4	-	67	64	3	-
20 - 24	1,153	759	484	272	3	394	311	63	20
25 - 29	2,938	2,253	774	1,426	53	685	324	225	136
30 - 44	12,002	9,934	900	8,421	613	2,068	374	876	818
45 - 59	10,157	8,348	259	7,473	616	1,809	209	537	1,063
60 - 64	2,908	2,272	94	1,989	189	636	102	81	453
65 - 74	5,237	3,431	168	2,896	367	1,806	218	135	1,453
75 - 84	3,767	1,799	71	1,306	422	1,968	205	89	1,674
85 and over	881	306	18	166	122	575	75	19	481

All persons in households by head's age, sex and marital status

All ages 16 and over**	101,335	83,029	4,918	74,089	4,022	18,306	3,000	5,665	9,641
16 - 19**	285	125	105	20	-	160	154	6	-
20 - 24	2,564	1,713	992	716	5	851	639	156	56
25 - 29	7,328	5,707	1,432	4,160	115	1,621	601	640	380
30 - 44	40,147	34,345	1,534	31,477	1,334	5,802	614	2,938	2,250
45 - 59	28,778	25,040	383	23,480	1,177	3,738	288	1,380	2,070
60 - 64	6,153	5,208	133	4,793	282	945	129	161	655
65 - 74	9,341	7,063	220	6,369	474	2,278	264	234	1,780
75 - 84	5,578	3,323	97	2,732	494	2,255	223	126	1,906
85 and over	1,161	505	22	342	141	656	88	24	544

Eastleigh

Heads of households

All ages 16 and over*	41,219	31,186	3,422	25,161	2,603	10,033	1,848	1,900	6,285
16 - 19*	120	52	47	5	-	68	62	6	-
20 - 24	1,595	1,092	722	364	6	503	383	97	23
25 - 29	3,914	3,026	1,052	1,864	110	888	415	290	183
30 - 44	13,203	10,974	1,040	9,159	775	2,229	428	815	986
45 - 59	9,931	8,344	288	7,389	667	1,587	145	399	1,043
60 - 64	2,924	2,279	84	2,032	163	645	63	79	503
65 - 74	5,394	3,517	139	2,974	404	1,877	179	129	1,569
75 - 84	3,341	1,631	41	1,227	363	1,710	131	73	1,506
85 and over	797	271	9	147	115	526	42	12	472

All persons in households by head's age, sex and marital status

All ages 16 and over**	105,298	87,112	5,796	76,978	4,338	18,186	2,982	5,258	9,946
16 - 19**	252	109	96	13	-	143	126	17	-
20 - 24	3,393	2,327	1,385	929	13	1,066	751	254	61
25 - 29	9,488	7,461	1,892	5,347	222	2,027	748	798	481
30 - 44	43,316	37,255	1,690	33,935	1,630	6,061	699	2,704	2,658
45 - 59	27,422	24,350	399	22,755	1,196	3,072	176	967	1,929
60 - 64	5,956	5,046	104	4,717	225	910	75	163	672
65 - 74	9,396	7,090	174	6,411	505	2,306	206	237	1,863
75 - 84	5,011	3,027	45	2,574	408	1,984	153	103	1,728
85 and over	1,064	447	11	297	139	617	48	15	554

Table 39 Headship – **continued**

County, districts

Notes: (1) * May include a small number of heads aged under 16
(2) ** May include a small number of persons in households with heads aged under 16

39. Residents in households

Age	TOTAL PERSONS	Males				Females			
		Total	Single	Married	Widowed or divorced	Total	Single	Married	Widowed or divorced
a	b	c	d	e	f	g	h	i	j

Fareham

Heads of households

All ages 16 and over*	38,369	29,130	2,427	24,366	2,337	9,239	1,369	1,836	6,034
16 - 19*	78	38	29	8	1	40	36	3	1
20 - 24	967	629	423	202	4	338	239	76	23
25 - 29	2,914	2,308	705	1,530	73	606	262	225	119
30 - 44	11,543	9,595	766	8,229	600	1,948	327	798	823
45 - 59	10,136	8,461	251	7,590	620	1,675	141	451	1,083
60 - 64	3,076	2,398	93	2,145	160	678	79	85	514
65 - 74	5,443	3,694	99	3,206	389	1,749	148	110	1,491
75 - 84	3,494	1,760	51	1,319	390	1,734	94	75	1,565
85 and over	718	247	10	137	100	471	43	13	415

All persons in households by head's age, sex and marital status

All ages 16 and over**	97,607	81,076	4,198	72,945	3,933	16,531	2,189	5,022	9,320
16 - 19**	172	84	55	28	1	88	80	7	1
20 - 24	2,154	1,400	856	537	7	754	509	186	59
25 - 29	7,353	5,973	1,310	4,525	138	1,380	454	622	304
30 - 44	38,086	32,786	1,277	30,199	1,310	5,300	525	2,614	2,161
45 - 59	27,618	24,236	366	22,696	1,174	3,382	198	1,097	2,087
60 - 64	6,279	5,331	119	4,993	219	948	90	154	704
65 - 74	9,685	7,551	135	6,927	489	2,134	177	200	1,757
75 - 84	5,290	3,286	66	2,747	473	2,004	109	123	1,772
85 and over	970	429	14	293	122	541	47	19	475

Gosport

Heads of households

All ages 16 and over*	29,356	20,732	2,199	16,590	1,943	8,624	1,463	1,682	5,479
16 - 19*	125	53	38	15	-	72	66	6	-
20 - 24	1,669	1,091	524	562	5	578	387	150	41
25 - 29	3,226	2,412	607	1,702	103	814	279	322	213
30 - 44	8,684	6,858	594	5,750	514	1,826	276	657	893
45 - 59	6,159	4,893	202	4,201	490	1,266	104	284	878
60 - 64	2,063	1,509	72	1,301	136	554	66	72	416
65 - 74	3,929	2,442	113	2,015	314	1,487	142	103	1,242
75 - 84	2,850	1,264	42	936	286	1,586	109	73	1,404
85 and over	651	210	7	108	95	441	34	15	392

All persons in households by head's age, sex and marital status

All ages 16 and over**	73,704	57,474	3,930	50,327	3,217	16,230	2,648	4,647	8,935
16 - 19**	303	129	87	42	-	174	156	18	-
20 - 24	3,933	2,565	1,100	1,457	8	1,368	878	383	107
25 - 29	8,812	6,661	1,144	5,280	237	2,151	599	962	590
30 - 44	28,976	23,787	1,009	21,664	1,114	5,189	472	2,186	2,531
45 - 59	15,897	13,470	283	12,329	858	2,427	133	657	1,637
60 - 64	4,097	3,319	102	3,035	182	778	76	137	565
65 - 74	6,713	4,888	137	4,363	388	1,825	165	177	1,483
75 - 84	4,139	2,309	58	1,934	317	1,830	131	109	1,590
85 and over	834	346	10	223	113	488	38	18	432

Table 39 Headship – continued

Notes: (1) * May include a small number of heads aged under 16
       (2) ** May include a small number of persons in households with heads aged under 16

39. Residents in households

Age	TOTAL PERSONS	Males				Females			
		Total	Single	Married	Widowed or divorced	Total	Single	Married	Widowed or divorced
a	b	c	d	e	f	g	h	i	j

Hart

Heads of households

Age	TOTAL PERSONS	Total	Single	Married	Widowed or divorced	Total	Single	Married	Widowed or divorced
All ages 16 and over*	29,073	22,770	2,271	18,948	1,551	6,303	1,047	1,412	3,844
16 - 19*	50	26	24	2	-	24	21	3	-
20 - 24	859	579	414	163	2	280	213	52	15
25 - 29	2,381	1,906	724	1,140	42	475	232	163	80
30 - 44	9,749	8,318	754	7,128	436	1,431	219	665	547
45 - 59	8,542	7,307	196	6,655	456	1,235	101	370	764
60 - 64	1,867	1,496	52	1,331	113	371	32	50	289
65 - 74	2,986	2,013	67	1,724	222	973	95	67	811
75 - 84	2,151	972	36	720	216	1,179	103	35	1,041
85 and over	488	153	4	85	64	335	31	7	297

All persons in households by head's age, sex and marital status

Age	TOTAL PERSONS	Total	Single	Married	Widowed or divorced	Total	Single	Married	Widowed or divorced
All ages 16 and over**	79,014	67,328	3,997	60,652	2,679	11,686	1,703	3,955	6,028
16 - 19**	105	54	47	7	-	51	43	8	-
20 - 24	1,895	1,290	843	444	3	605	444	131	30
25 - 29	5,801	4,763	1,351	3,323	89	1,038	400	441	197
30 - 44	32,903	28,951	1,276	26,756	919	3,952	367	2,155	1,430
45 - 59	25,090	22,564	275	21,445	844	2,526	146	952	1,428
60 - 64	3,994	3,451	73	3,212	166	543	36	94	413
65 - 74	5,423	4,177	86	3,781	310	1,246	112	111	1,023
75 - 84	3,160	1,814	42	1,510	262	1,346	119	53	1,174
85 and over	643	264	4	174	86	379	36	10	333

Havant

Heads of households

Age	TOTAL PERSONS	Total	Single	Married	Widowed or divorced	Total	Single	Married	Widowed or divorced
All ages 16 and over*	46,151	32,958	2,960	26,913	3,085	13,193	2,271	2,461	8,461
16 - 19*	136	52	43	9	-	84	79	4	1
20 - 24	1,543	835	516	305	14	708	503	145	60
25 - 29	3,476	2,445	810	1,545	90	1,031	440	354	237
30 - 44	12,983	10,146	955	8,441	750	2,837	487	974	1,376
45 - 59	11,626	9,305	310	8,192	803	2,321	192	573	1,556
60 - 64	4,043	3,113	110	2,742	261	930	84	111	735
65 - 74	7,156	4,709	147	3,999	563	2,447	231	176	2,040
75 - 84	4,210	2,041	57	1,523	461	2,169	186	100	1,883
85 and over	978	312	12	157	143	666	69	24	573

All persons in households by head's age, sex and marital status

Age	TOTAL PERSONS	Total	Single	Married	Widowed or divorced	Total	Single	Married	Widowed or divorced
All ages 16 and over**	118,297	92,915	5,359	82,253	5,303	25,382	4,279	6,974	14,129
16 - 19**	280	105	81	24	-	175	162	12	1
20 - 24	3,849	2,052	1,089	930	33	1,797	1,193	421	183
25 - 29	9,763	6,881	1,635	5,063	183	2,882	975	1,179	728
30 - 44	44,226	35,939	1,708	32,456	1,775	8,287	988	3,298	4,001
45 - 59	31,642	26,994	419	25,115	1,460	4,648	284	1,385	2,979
60 - 64	8,337	6,989	150	6,436	403	1,348	100	223	1,025
65 - 74	12,659	9,644	186	8,728	730	3,015	271	285	2,459
75 - 84	6,267	3,794	71	3,178	545	2,473	220	141	2,112
85 and over	1,274	517	20	323	174	757	86	30	641

Table 39 Headship – **continued**

County, districts

Notes: (1) * May include a small number of heads aged under 16
(2) ** May include a small number of persons in households with heads aged under 16

39. Residents in households

Age	TOTAL PERSONS	Males				Females			
		Total	Single	Married	Widowed or divorced	Total	Single	Married	Widowed or divorced
a	b	c	d	e	f	g	h	i	j

New Forest

Heads of households

All ages 16 and over*	65,411	47,478	4,251	39,024	4,203	17,933	3,137	3,103	11,693
16 - 19*	151	63	57	5	1	88	82	6	-
20 - 24	1,756	1,139	719	411	9	617	447	136	34
25 - 29	4,195	3,254	1,138	2,039	77	941	447	326	168
30 - 44	16,532	13,523	1,245	11,383	895	3,009	574	1,197	1,238
45 - 59	14,975	12,270	465	10,881	924	2,705	305	727	1,673
60 - 64	5,427	4,133	181	3,630	322	1,294	195	171	928
65 - 74	11,792	7,988	299	6,905	784	3,804	467	301	3,036
75 - 84	8,510	4,354	116	3,334	904	4,156	469	192	3,495
85 and over	2,073	754	31	436	287	1,319	151	47	1,121

All persons in households by head's age, sex and marital status

All ages 16 and over**	157,604	127,446	7,131	113,685	6,630	30,158	4,811	8,192	17,155
16 - 19**	332	124	106	16	2	208	191	17	-
20 - 24	3,846	2,510	1,397	1,095	18	1,336	896	355	85
25 - 29	10,433	8,210	2,045	6,006	159	2,223	816	941	466
30 - 44	54,618	46,358	2,134	42,324	1,900	8,260	969	3,943	3,348
45 - 59	40,718	35,478	629	33,162	1,687	5,240	395	1,729	3,116
60 - 64	10,997	9,179	250	8,463	466	1,818	243	336	1,239
65 - 74	20,915	16,211	383	14,826	1,002	4,704	551	520	3,633
75 - 84	12,960	8,113	147	6,914	1,052	4,847	568	292	3,987
85 and over	2,785	1,263	40	879	344	1,522	182	59	1,281

Portsmouth

Heads of households

All ages 16 and over*	72,590	47,435	8,467	33,421	5,547	25,155	5,894	4,110	15,151
16 - 19*	463	190	181	7	2	273	247	18	8
20 - 24	4,432	2,636	1,822	794	20	1,796	1,431	277	88
25 - 29	7,917	5,442	2,232	2,998	212	2,475	1,292	709	474
30 - 44	18,897	14,017	2,166	10,471	1,380	4,880	1,127	1,594	2,159
45 - 59	14,670	11,048	960	8,707	1,381	3,622	441	802	2,379
60 - 64	5,110	3,519	337	2,766	416	1,591	224	173	1,194
65 - 74	11,092	6,491	522	4,960	1,009	4,601	499	322	3,780
75 - 84	8,085	3,501	216	2,429	856	4,584	478	180	3,926
85 and over	1,924	591	31	289	271	1,333	155	35	1,143

All persons in households by head's age, sex and marital status

All ages 16 and over**	169,730	123,865	14,726	100,181	8,958	45,865	10,252	11,441	24,172
16 - 19**	917	384	365	15	4	533	473	48	12
20 - 24	9,838	5,925	3,733	2,154	38	3,913	2,960	732	221
25 - 29	19,952	13,950	4,278	9,230	442	6,002	2,546	2,150	1,306
30 - 44	58,700	45,499	3,629	39,034	2,836	13,201	2,045	5,314	5,842
45 - 59	37,263	30,219	1,330	26,477	2,412	7,044	628	1,994	4,422
60 - 64	9,923	7,657	430	6,656	571	2,266	279	326	1,661
65 - 74	18,724	12,852	646	10,912	1,294	5,872	584	562	4,726
75 - 84	11,857	6,414	273	5,101	1,040	5,443	555	261	4,627
85 and over	2,556	965	42	602	321	1,591	182	54	1,355

Table 39 Headship – **continued**

Notes: (1) * May include a small number of heads aged under 16
(2) ** May include a small number of persons in households with heads aged under 16

39. Residents in households

Age	TOTAL PERSONS	Males				Females			
		Total	Single	Married	Widowed or divorced	Total	Single	Married	Widowed or divorced
a	b	c	d	e	f	g	h	i	j

Rushmoor

Heads of households

All ages 16 and over*	30,523	22,577	3,290	17,411	1,876	7,946	1,664	1,543	4,739
16 - 19*	140	44	38	6	-	96	86	10	-
20 - 24	1,868	1,243	698	535	10	625	441	142	42
25 - 29	4,090	3,187	1,081	2,032	74	903	409	337	157
30 - 44	9,715	7,998	939	6,473	586	1,717	331	575	811
45 - 59	6,739	5,463	244	4,736	483	1,276	143	264	869
60 - 64	1,861	1,374	105	1,133	136	487	41	56	390
65 - 74	3,314	2,085	124	1,701	260	1,229	109	79	1,041
75 - 84	2,302	1,032	56	720	256	1,270	82	67	1,121
85 and over	494	151	5	75	71	343	22	13	308

All persons in households by head's age, sex and marital status

All ages 16 and over**	79,121	63,678	5,978	54,406	3,294	15,443	3,080	4,335	8,028
16 - 19**	295	82	71	11	-	213	189	24	-
20 - 24	4,345	2,873	1,409	1,445	19	1,472	983	384	105
25 - 29	10,608	8,332	2,145	5,991	196	2,276	833	965	478
30 - 44	31,515	26,801	1,649	23,892	1,260	4,714	586	1,899	2,229
45 - 59	18,737	16,154	333	14,899	922	2,583	196	702	1,685
60 - 64	3,758	3,044	127	2,729	188	714	50	105	559
65 - 74	5,877	4,288	169	3,775	344	1,589	125	152	1,312
75 - 84	3,351	1,865	69	1,509	287	1,486	95	88	1,303
85 and over	635	239	6	155	78	396	23	16	357

Southampton

Heads of households

All ages 16 and over*	81,140	54,646	9,255	39,085	6,306	26,494	6,558	4,104	15,832
16 - 19*	565	242	226	14	2	323	307	14	2
20 - 24	4,923	2,806	1,995	781	30	2,117	1,648	306	163
25 - 29	8,321	5,704	2,380	3,114	210	2,617	1,446	659	512
30 - 44	21,789	16,297	2,443	12,304	1,550	5,492	1,391	1,657	2,444
45 - 59	17,261	13,374	1,074	10,680	1,620	3,887	559	806	2,522
60 - 64	6,075	4,418	376	3,521	521	1,657	223	164	1,270
65 - 74	12,021	7,414	517	5,817	1,080	4,607	457	280	3,870
75 - 84	8,223	3,779	218	2,561	1,000	4,444	400	177	3,867
85 and over	1,962	612	26	293	293	1,350	127	41	1,182

All persons in households by head's age, sex and marital status

All ages 16 and over**	193,866	144,646	15,418	119,123	10,105	49,220	11,773	11,594	25,853
16 - 19**	1,161	494	447	43	4	667	629	35	3
20 - 24	10,888	6,146	3,949	2,139	58	4,742	3,442	878	422
25 - 29	20,860	14,406	4,258	9,735	413	6,454	2,970	2,027	1,457
30 - 44	69,006	54,113	3,906	47,006	3,201	14,893	2,519	5,564	6,810
45 - 59	44,786	37,207	1,471	32,925	2,811	7,579	802	1,955	4,822
60 - 64	11,960	9,608	460	8,433	715	2,352	252	312	1,788
65 - 74	20,714	14,876	641	12,874	1,361	5,838	555	494	4,789
75 - 84	11,962	6,831	258	5,372	1,201	5,131	463	270	4,398
85 and over	2,529	965	28	596	341	1,564	141	59	1,364

Table 39 Headship – **continued** County, districts

Notes: (1) * May include a small number of heads aged under 16
(2) ** May include a small number of persons in households with heads aged under 16

39. Residents in households

Age	TOTAL PERSONS	Males				Females			
		Total	Single	Married	Widowed or divorced	Total	Single	Married	Widowed or divorced
a	b	c	d	e	f	g	h	i	j

Test Valley

Heads of households

All ages 16 and over*	38,391	28,755	2,745	23,564	2,446	9,636	1,741	1,913	5,982
16 - 19*	105	37	35	2	-	68	61	7	-
20 - 24	1,323	846	497	345	4	477	349	96	32
25 - 29	3,022	2,310	752	1,494	64	712	326	246	140
30 - 44	11,699	9,606	840	8,144	622	2,093	363	842	888
45 - 59	10,167	8,569	323	7,583	663	1,598	149	462	987
60 - 64	2,788	2,143	91	1,879	173	645	101	74	470
65 - 74	5,033	3,263	136	2,719	408	1,770	187	108	1,475
75 - 84	3,508	1,722	60	1,269	393	1,786	155	62	1,569
85 and over	746	259	11	129	119	487	50	16	421

All persons in households by head's age, sex and marital status

All ages 16 and over**	99,463	81,547	4,730	72,624	4,193	17,916	2,903	5,423	9,590
16 - 19**	236	78	72	6	-	158	141	17	-
20 - 24	3,014	1,910	952	950	8	1,104	750	273	81
25 - 29	7,758	6,011	1,397	4,470	144	1,747	628	707	412
30 - 44	38,865	33,034	1,443	30,242	1,349	5,831	589	2,796	2,446
45 - 59	28,483	25,231	484	23,469	1,278	3,252	201	1,175	1,876
60 - 64	5,858	4,952	124	4,561	267	906	118	130	658
65 - 74	8,932	6,691	178	5,984	529	2,241	230	200	1,811
75 - 84	5,305	3,212	67	2,674	471	2,093	185	102	1,806
85 and over	1,012	428	13	268	147	584	61	23	500

Winchester

Heads of households

All ages 16 and over*	37,553	27,044	2,510	22,291	2,243	10,509	2,204	1,928	6,377
16 - 19*	83	36	30	6	-	47	46	1	-
20 - 24	899	505	347	156	2	394	314	62	18
25 - 29	2,228	1,636	599	1,004	33	592	312	194	86
30 - 44	10,496	8,521	884	7,138	499	1,975	439	822	714
45 - 59	9,873	8,128	292	7,254	582	1,745	242	504	999
60 - 64	3,102	2,378	110	2,103	165	724	125	100	499
65 - 74	5,712	3,553	151	3,023	379	2,159	333	140	1,686
75 - 84	4,117	1,940	83	1,425	432	2,177	298	84	1,795
85 and over	1,043	347	14	182	151	696	95	21	580

All persons in households by head's age, sex and marital status

All ages 16 and over**	93,721	75,564	4,063	67,847	3,654	18,157	3,292	5,336	9,529
16 - 19**	195	76	56	20	-	119	116	3	-
20 - 24	1,977	1,122	672	445	5	855	645	165	45
25 - 29	5,474	4,118	1,090	2,959	69	1,356	559	534	263
30 - 44	34,480	29,163	1,404	26,662	1,097	5,317	665	2,755	1,897
45 - 59	27,881	24,333	401	22,836	1,096	3,548	323	1,280	1,945
60 - 64	6,384	5,389	135	5,022	232	995	144	193	658
65 - 74	9,908	7,235	188	6,575	472	2,673	390	250	2,033
75 - 84	6,078	3,568	99	2,967	502	2,510	342	130	2,038
85 and over	1,344	560	18	361	181	784	108	26	650

Table 40 Lone 'parents'

40. Lone 'parents' aged 16 and over in households of one person aged 16 and over with person(s) aged 0 - 15; persons aged 0 - 15 in such households

Age of child(ren)	TOTAL LONE 'PARENTS'	Male lone 'parents'							Female lone 'parents'						
		Total male lone 'parents'	Economically active					Econom-ically inactive	Total female lone 'parents'	Economically active					Econom-ically inactive
			Employees		Self-employed	Other	Econom-ically active students			Employees		Self-employed	Other	Econom-ically active students	
			Full-time	Part-time						Full-time	Part-time				
a	b	c	d	e	f	g	h	i	j	k	l	m	n	o	p
HAMPSHIRE															
Total households	**18,195**	**1,607**	**802**	**62**	**187**	**136**	**3**	**420**	**16,588**	**2,514**	**3,433**	**412**	**672**	**26**	**9,557**
Child(ren) aged 0 - 4 only	4,719	211	102	6	23	17	1	63	4,508	369	530	54	168	3	3,387
Child(ren) aged 5 - 15 only	9,982	1,245	638	51	152	107	2	297	8,737	2,012	2,473	301	407	22	3,544
Child(ren) aged 0 - 4 and 5 - 15	3,494	151	62	5	12	12	-	60	3,343	133	430	57	97	1	2,626
TOTAL CHILDREN AGED 0 - 15	**31,823**	**2,661**	**1,279**	**102**	**295**	**218**	**3**	**767**	**29,162**	**3,756**	**5,869**	**686**	**1,059**	**44**	**17,792**
Children aged 0 - 4	10,303	473	204	15	47	44	1	163	9,830	536	1,107	126	305	6	7,756
Basingstoke & Deane															
Total households	**1,372**	**115**	**66**	**1**	**18**	**10**	**-**	**20**	**1,257**	**274**	**259**	**32**	**57**	**-**	**635**
Child(ren) aged 0 - 4 only	298	15	9	-	3	-	-	3	283	41	37	8	9	-	188
Child(ren) aged 5 - 15 only	765	89	53	1	13	9	-	13	676	214	180	13	34	-	235
Child(ren) aged 0 - 4 and 5 - 15	309	11	4	-	2	1	-	4	298	19	42	11	14	-	212
TOTAL CHILDREN AGED 0 - 15	**2,458**	**198**	**104**	**1**	**29**	**17**	**-**	**47**	**2,260**	**398**	**451**	**52**	**109**	**-**	**1,250**
Children aged 0 - 4	758	39	18	-	6	1	-	14	719	64	86	20	25	-	524
East Hampshire															
Total households	**936**	**112**	**59**	**5**	**17**	**5**	**-**	**26**	**824**	**139**	**209**	**37**	**33**	**-**	**406**
Child(ren) aged 0 - 4 only	209	16	6	-	3	-	-	7	193	14	32	3	8	-	136
Child(ren) aged 5 - 15 only	559	87	49	5	12	5	-	16	472	112	150	32	22	-	156
Child(ren) aged 0 - 4 and 5 - 15	168	9	4	-	2	-	-	3	159	13	27	2	3	-	114
TOTAL CHILDREN AGED 0 - 15	**1,669**	**185**	**92**	**9**	**30**	**5**	**-**	**49**	**1,484**	**223**	**362**	**66**	**51**	**-**	**782**
Children aged 0 - 4	443	33	12	-	8	-	-	13	410	28	64	6	11	-	301

Table 40 Lone 'parents' – continued

40. Lone 'parents' aged 16 and over in households of one person aged 16 and over with person(s) aged 0 - 15; persons aged 0 - 15 in such households

Age of child(ren)	TOTAL LONE 'PARENTS'	Male lone 'parents'							Female lone 'parents'						
		Total male lone 'parents'	Economically active					Economically inactive	Total female lone 'parents'	Economically active					Economically inactive
			Employees		Self-employed	Other	Economically active students			Employees		Self-employed	Other	Economically active students	
			Full-time	Part-time						Full-time	Part-time				
a	b	c	d	e	f	g	h	i	j	k	l	m	n	o	p
Eastleigh															
Total households	**1,056**	**103**	**64**	**5**	**9**	**7**	**-**	**18**	**953**	**164**	**246**	**33**	**29**	**2**	**481**
Child(ren) aged 0 - 4 only	260	13	7	-	3	-	-	3	247	17	39	3	7	-	181
Child(ren) aged 5 - 15 only	619	84	53	4	5	7	-	15	535	138	170	27	18	2	182
Child(ren) aged 0 - 4 and 5 - 15	177	6	4	1	1	-	-	-	171	9	37	3	4	-	118
TOTAL CHILDREN AGED 0 - 15	**1,840**	**176**	**108**	**9**	**17**	**10**	**-**	**32**	**1,664**	**251**	**429**	**55**	**48**	**4**	**881**
Children aged 0 - 4	546	23	13	1	5	-	-	4	523	28	87	6	12	-	390
Fareham															
Total households	**844**	**92**	**54**	**3**	**11**	**8**	**-**	**16**	**752**	**170**	**180**	**36**	**22**	**1**	**344**
Child(ren) aged 0 - 4 only	186	13	8	-	2	-	-	3	173	26	28	7	6	-	106
Child(ren) aged 5 - 15 only	522	69	41	3	8	8	-	9	453	137	134	25	12	1	145
Child(ren) aged 0 - 4 and 5 - 15	136	10	5	-	1	-	-	4	126	7	18	4	4	-	93
TOTAL CHILDREN AGED 0 - 15	**1,396**	**144**	**81**	**4**	**18**	**11**	**-**	**30**	**1,252**	**249**	**298**	**57**	**31**	**2**	**617**
Children aged 0 - 4	394	30	16	-	3	-	-	11	364	33	54	12	10	-	255
Gosport															
Total households	**1,100**	**91**	**40**	**5**	**8**	**12**	**-**	**26**	**1,009**	**138**	**195**	**24**	**51**	**-**	**601**
Child(ren) aged 0 - 4 only	304	10	3	1	-	2	-	4	294	19	29	7	9	-	230
Child(ren) aged 5 - 15 only	588	67	28	3	7	10	-	19	521	112	137	16	33	-	223
Child(ren) aged 0 - 4 and 5 - 15	208	14	9	1	1	-	-	3	194	7	29	1	9	-	148
TOTAL CHILDREN AGED 0 - 15	**1,885**	**145**	**69**	**10**	**11**	**14**	**-**	**41**	**1,740**	**212**	**337**	**40**	**75**	**-**	**1,076**
Children aged 0 - 4	626	28	13	2	1	2	-	10	598	28	67	11	19	-	473

Table 40 Lone 'parents' – continued

40. Lone 'parents' aged 16 and over in households of one person aged 16 and over with person(s) aged 0 - 15; persons aged 0 - 15 in such households

Age of child(ren)	TOTAL LONE 'PARENTS'	Male lone 'parents'							Female lone 'parents'						
		Total male lone 'parents'	Economically active					Economically inactive	Total female lone 'parents'	Economically active					Economically inactive
			Employees		Self-employed	Other	Economically active students			Employees		Self-employed	Other	Economically active students	
			Full-time	Part-time						Full-time	Part-time				
a	b	c	d	e	f	g	h	i	j	k	l	m	n	o	p
Hart															
Total households	567	63	38	1	16	2	-	6	504	115	139	30	16	-	204
Child(ren) aged 0 - 4 only	112	3	2	-	1	-	-	-	109	15	19	4	2	-	69
Child(ren) aged 5 - 15 only	376	55	33	1	14	2	-	5	321	95	111	20	13	-	82
Child(ren) aged 0 - 4 and 5 - 15	79	5	3	-	1	-	-	1	74	5	9	6	1	-	53
TOTAL CHILDREN AGED 0 - 15	993	111	67	1	22	4	-	17	882	186	239	51	29	-	377
Children aged 0 - 4	234	13	9	-	2	-	-	2	221	22	29	12	4	-	154
Havant															
Total households	1,752	151	71	4	20	14	1	42	1,601	196	282	27	65	3	1,031
Child(ren) aged 0 - 4 only	407	17	4	-	2	3	-	8	390	34	39	6	14	-	297
Child(ren) aged 5 - 15 only	963	119	61	4	17	8	1	29	844	155	210	17	41	3	421
Child(ren) aged 0 - 4 and 5 - 15	382	15	6	-	1	3	-	5	367	7	33	4	10	-	313
TOTAL CHILDREN AGED 0 - 15	3,186	250	113	5	31	28	1	73	2,936	282	468	42	107	4	2,037
Children aged 0 - 4	994	40	11	-	4	10	-	15	954	46	80	12	28	-	788
New Forest															
Total households	1,477	141	66	9	26	12	-	28	1,336	180	331	45	50	3	730
Child(ren) aged 0 - 4 only	374	14	11	-	1	-	-	2	360	31	46	5	12	-	266
Child(ren) aged 5 - 15 only	893	114	50	8	25	10	-	21	779	141	254	36	33	3	315
Child(ren) aged 0 - 4 and 5 - 15	210	13	5	1	-	2	-	5	197	8	31	4	5	-	149
TOTAL CHILDREN AGED 0 - 15	2,498	211	96	14	38	20	-	43	2,287	270	584	74	80	5	1,279
Children aged 0 - 4	738	33	18	3	2	2	-	8	705	40	93	10	23	-	539

Table 40 Lone 'parents' – continued

40. Lone 'parents' aged 16 and over in households of one person aged 16 and over with person(s) aged 0 - 15; persons aged 0 - 15 in such households

Age of child(ren)	TOTAL LONE 'PARENTS'	Male lone 'parents'							Female lone 'parents'						
		Total male lone 'parents'	Economically active					Econom-ically inactive	Total female lone 'parents'	Economically active					Econom-ically inactive
			Employees		Self-employed	Other	Econom-ically active students			Employees		Self-employed	Other	Econom-ically active students	
			Full-time	Part-time						Full-time	Part-time				
a	b	c	d	e	f	g	h	i	j	k	l	m	n	o	p
Portsmouth															
Total households	**2,920**	**231**	**93**	**16**	**16**	**33**	**1**	**73**	**2,689**	**348**	**521**	**40**	**130**	**10**	**1,650**
Child(ren) aged 0 - 4 only	813	36	16	3	2	6	-	9	777	55	90	5	40	2	587
Child(ren) aged 5 - 15 only	1,502	175	73	13	12	26	1	51	1,327	273	362	25	76	8	591
Child(ren) aged 0 - 4 and 5 - 15	605	20	4	-	2	1	-	13	585	20	69	10	14	-	472
TOTAL CHILDREN AGED 0 - 15	**5,043**	**383**	**146**	**25**	**29**	**47**	**1**	**136**	**4,660**	**500**	**873**	**62**	**185**	**16**	**3,040**
Children aged 0 - 4	1,780	72	26	4	6	11	-	25	1,708	83	185	17	64	3	1,359
Rushmoor															
Total households	**1,040**	**83**	**41**	**2**	**8**	**5**	-	**27**	**957**	**175**	**181**	**23**	**27**	-	**551**
Child(ren) aged 0 - 4 only	316	17	9	-	3	-	-	5	299	21	30	-	7	-	241
Child(ren) aged 5 - 15 only	540	54	28	2	5	4	-	15	486	146	126	18	14	-	182
Child(ren) aged 0 - 4 and 5 - 15	184	12	4	-	-	1	-	7	172	8	25	5	6	-	128
TOTAL CHILDREN AGED 0 - 15	**1,761**	**142**	**63**	**5**	**12**	**7**	-	**55**	**1,619**	**268**	**305**	**44**	**48**	-	**954**
Children aged 0 - 4	633	40	14	-	5	1	-	20	593	32	63	5	18	-	475
Southampton															
Total households	**3,432**	**239**	**97**	**6**	**13**	**22**	**1**	**101**	**3,193**	**328**	**520**	**35**	**132**	**5**	**2,178**
Child(ren) aged 0 - 4 only	1,051	38	17	1	2	6	1	12	1,013	51	96	4	42	1	820
Child(ren) aged 5 - 15 only	1,645	178	74	3	10	13	-	78	1,467	260	357	28	75	3	747
Child(ren) aged 0 - 4 and 5 - 15	736	23	6	2	1	3	-	11	713	17	67	3	15	1	611
TOTAL CHILDREN AGED 0 - 15	**6,131**	**410**	**154**	**12**	**21**	**46**	**1**	**177**	**5,721**	**478**	**869**	**57**	**200**	**9**	**4,117**
Children aged 0 - 4	2,325	85	33	4	4	16	1	28	2,240	72	197	7	64	3	1,900

Table 40 Lone 'parents' – continued

40. Lone 'parents' aged 16 and over in households of one person aged 16 and over with person(s) aged 0 - 15; persons aged 0 - 15 in such households

Age of child(ren)	TOTAL LONE 'PARENTS'	Male lone 'parents'							Female lone 'parents'						
		Total male lone 'parents'	Economically active				Econom-ically active students	Econom-ically inactive	Total female lone 'parents'	Economically active				Econom-ically active students	Econom-ically inactive
			Employees		Self-employed	Other				Employees		Self-employed	Other		
			Full-time	Part-time						Full-time	Part-time				
a	b	c	d	e	f	g	h	i	j	k	l	m	n	o	p

Test Valley

a	b	c	d	e	f	g	h	i	j	k	l	m	n	o	p
Total households	**1,005**	**110**	**64**	**2**	**17**	**3**	-	**24**	**895**	**172**	**203**	**22**	**32**	**1**	**466**
Child(ren) aged 0 - 4 only	238	9	5	-	1	-	-	3	229	24	26	1	5	-	173
Child(ren) aged 5 - 15 only	584	92	55	2	16	2	-	17	492	140	153	20	20	1	159
Child(ren) aged 0 - 4 and 5 - 15	183	9	4	-	-	1	-	4	174	8	24	1	7	-	134
TOTAL CHILDREN AGED 0 - 15	**1,742**	**185**	**107**	**4**	**25**	**4**	-	**45**	**1,557**	**262**	**351**	**34**	**53**	**2**	**857**
Children aged 0 - 4	514	22	11	-	1	1	-	9	492	33	61	3	14	-	381

Winchester

a	b	c	d	e	f	g	h	i	j	k	l	m	n	o	p
Total households	**694**	**76**	**49**	**3**	**8**	**3**	-	**13**	**618**	**115**	**167**	**28**	**28**	**1**	**280**
Child(ren) aged 0 - 4 only	151	10	5	1	-	-	-	4	141	21	19	1	7	-	93
Child(ren) aged 5 - 15 only	426	62	40	2	8	3	-	9	364	89	129	24	16	1	106
Child(ren) aged 0 - 4 and 5 - 15	117	4	4	-	-	-	-	-	113	5	19	3	5	-	81
TOTAL CHILDREN AGED 0 - 15	**1,221**	**121**	**79**	**3**	**12**	**5**	-	**22**	**1,100**	**177**	**303**	**52**	**43**	**2**	**525**
Children aged 0 - 4	318	15	10	1	-	-	-	4	303	27	41	5	13	-	217

Table 41 Shared accommodation

41. Households with residents not in self-contained accommodation; rooms in such households

Households with the following persons	TOTAL HOUSE-HOLDS	Over one person per room	Exclusive use of bath/shower			Shared use of bath/shower			No bath/shower			Central heating			No car	TOTAL ROOMS
			Exclusive use of inside WC	Shared use of inside WC	No inside WC	Exclusive use of inside WC	Shared use of inside WC	No inside WC	Exclusive use of inside WC	Shared use of inside WC	No inside WC	All rooms	Some rooms	No rooms		
a	b	c	d	e	f	g	h	i	j	k	l	m	n	o	p	q
HAMPSHIRE																
TOTAL HOUSEHOLDS	**6,318**	**980**	**3,130**	**108**	**13**	**96**	**2,912**	**9**	**20**	**9**	**21**	**3,144**	**436**	**2,738**	**3,887**	**12,014**
1 person	4,334		2,048	88	10	53	2,089	8	16	5	17	1,986	286	2,062	2,941	6,657
2 persons	1,306	603	703	12	3	32	545	-	3	4	4	729	93	484	663	3,116
3 or more persons	678	377	379	8	-	11	278	1	1	-	-	429	57	192	283	2,241
Basingstoke & Deane																
TOTAL HOUSEHOLDS	**203**	**31**	**88**	**1**	**-**	**-**	**114**	**-**	**-**	**-**	**-**	**154**	**10**	**39**	**94**	**463**
1 person	136		50	1	-	-	85	-	-	-	-	96	8	32	72	241
2 persons	43	22	25	-	-	-	18	-	-	-	-	39	-	4	18	118
3 or more persons	24	9	13	-	-	-	11	-	-	-	-	19	2	3	4	104
East Hampshire																
TOTAL HOUSEHOLDS	**158**	**36**	**94**	**3**	**1**	**4**	**55**	**-**	**1**	**-**	**-**	**117**	**24**	**17**	**64**	**429**
1 person	74		43	2	1	3	24	-	1	-	-	46	18	10	40	138
2 persons	45	19	26	-	-	1	18	-	-	-	-	38	3	4	19	108
3 or more persons	39	17	25	1	-	-	13	-	-	-	-	33	3	3	5	183
Eastleigh																
TOTAL HOUSEHOLDS	**167**	**17**	**81**	**1**	**-**	**2**	**82**	**-**	**1**	**-**	**-**	**112**	**17**	**38**	**84**	**294**
1 person	122		61	-	-	1	59	-	1	-	-	87	12	23	68	172
2 persons	27	10	12	1	-	-	14	-	-	-	-	15	3	9	11	64
3 or more persons	18	7	8	-	-	1	9	-	-	-	-	10	2	6	5	58
Fareham																
TOTAL HOUSEHOLDS	**77**	**8**	**46**	**3**	**-**	**1**	**27**	**-**	**-**	**-**	**-**	**46**	**11**	**20**	**42**	**177**
1 person	46		28	2	-	-	16	-	-	-	-	26	6	14	32	73
2 persons	25	7	14	1	-	1	9	-	-	-	-	15	4	6	9	73
3 or more persons	6	1	4	-	-	-	2	-	-	-	-	5	1	-	1	31

Table 41 Shared accommodation – continued

41. Households with residents not in self-contained accommodation; rooms in such households

Households with the following persons	TOTAL HOUSE-HOLDS	Over one person per room	Exclusive use of bath/shower			Shared use of bath/shower			No bath/shower			Central heating			No car	TOTAL ROOMS
			Exclusive use of inside WC	Shared use of inside WC	No inside WC	Exclusive use of inside WC	Shared use of inside WC	No inside WC	Exclusive use of inside WC	Shared use of inside WC	No inside WC	All rooms	Some rooms	No rooms		
a	b	c	d	e	f	g	h	i	j	k	l	m	n	o	p	q
Gosport																
TOTAL HOUSEHOLDS	89	11	52	-	1	1	35	-	-	-	-	39	16	34	47	202
1 person	56		32	-	1	-	23	-	-	-	-	26	5	25	33	100
2 persons	23	8	15	-	-	1	7	-	-	-	-	8	8	7	10	65
3 or more persons	10	3	5	-	-	-	5	-	-	-	-	5	3	2	4	37
Hart																
TOTAL HOUSEHOLDS	70	3	31	-	-	5	34	-	-	-	-	57	5	8	15	213
1 person	44		14	-	-	2	28	-	-	-	-	37	3	4	9	89
2 persons	16	2	9	-	-	3	4	-	-	-	-	12	2	2	5	67
3 or more persons	10	1	8	-	-	-	2	-	-	-	-	8	-	2	1	57
Havant																
TOTAL HOUSEHOLDS	197	80	84	4	4	5	100	-	3	-	1	111	11	75	113	416
1 person	70		37	1	4	1	28	-	2	-	1	29	7	34	49	116
2 persons	70	39	29	2	-	3	35	-	1	-	-	48	1	21	37	148
3 or more persons	57	41	18	1	-	1	37	-	-	-	-	34	3	20	27	152
New Forest																
TOTAL HOUSEHOLDS	234	38	121	4	4	8	100	-	1	-	-	163	27	44	111	640
1 person	121		60	4	4	4	52	-	1	-	-	73	14	34	73	236
2 persons	66	15	36	-	-	4	26	-	-	-	-	50	7	9	25	228
3 or more persons	47	23	25	-	-	-	22	-	-	-	-	40	6	1	13	176
Portsmouth																
TOTAL HOUSEHOLDS	1,905	228	996	47	5	32	800	6	7	-	11	580	103	1,222	1,305	3,731
1 person	1,352		674	39	4	19	594	5	6	-	10	373	67	912	1,005	2,208
2 persons	405	160	236	4	1	9	153	-	1	-	1	144	23	238	224	993
3 or more persons	148	68	86	4	-	4	53	1	-	-	-	63	13	72	76	530

Table 41 Shared accommodation – continued

41. Households with residents not in self-contained accommodation; rooms in such households

Households with the following persons	TOTAL HOUSE-HOLDS	Over one person per room	Exclusive use of bath/shower			Shared use of bath/shower			No bath/shower			Central heating			No car	TOTAL ROOMS
			Exclusive use of inside WC	Shared use of inside WC	No inside WC	Exclusive use of inside WC	Shared use of inside WC	No inside WC	Exclusive use of inside WC	Shared use of inside WC	No inside WC	All rooms	Some rooms	No rooms		
a	b	c	d	e	f	g	h	i	j	k	l	m	n	o	p	q
Rushmoor																
TOTAL HOUSEHOLDS	581	143	260	4	1	6	304	-	2	1	3	381	28	172	352	862
1 person	381		147	4	1	3	224	-	1	-	1	225	19	137	255	482
2 persons	124	88	69	-	-	3	49	-	1	1	2	92	6	26	64	198
3 or more persons	76	55	44	-	-	-	31	-	1	-	-	64	3	9	33	182
Southampton																
TOTAL HOUSEHOLDS	2,337	344	1,100	37	3	30	1,148	3	5	7	4	1,170	165	1,002	1,528	3,873
1 person	1,728		785	31	1	19	878	3	4	4	3	820	113	795	1,204	2,413
2 persons	411	209	199	4	2	7	194	-	1	3	1	232	33	146	222	903
3 or more persons	198	135	116	2	-	4	76	-	-	-	-	118	19	61	102	557
Test Valley																
TOTAL HOUSEHOLDS	98	9	67	2	2	2	24	-	-	-	1	79	6	13	37	253
1 person	64		40	2	2	1	18	-	-	-	1	52	3	9	30	114
2 persons	16	6	14	-	-	-	2	-	-	-	-	14	1	1	5	52
3 or more persons	18	3	13	-	-	1	4	-	-	-	-	13	2	3	2	87
Winchester																
TOTAL HOUSEHOLDS	202	32	110	2	-	-	89	-	-	-	1	135	13	54	95	461
1 person	140		77	2	-	-	60	-	-	-	1	96	11	33	71	275
2 persons	35	18	19	-	-	-	16	-	-	-	-	22	2	11	14	99
3 or more persons	27	14	14	-	-	-	13	-	-	-	-	17	-	10	10	87

Table 42 Household composition and housing

Note: * May include a small number of households with no resident adults

42. Households with residents; dependent children in households

TOTAL HOUSE-HOLDS	Over 1 and up to 1.5 persons per room	Over 1.5 persons per room	Lacking or sharing use of bath/shower and/or inside WC	No central heating	Lacking or sharing use of bath/shower and/or inside WC and/or no central heating	Not self-contained accomm-odation	Household composition — Adults	Dependent children
a	b	c	d	e	f	g	h	i
HAMPSHIRE								
603,257	7,174	2,618	7,073	95,028	98,312	6,318	ALL HOUSEHOLDS*	
83,475	-	-	2,073	18,350	19,370	543	1 adult of pensionable age	0
61,769	-	-	2,675	13,573	14,807	3,765	1 adult under pensionable age	0
20,396	257	325	315	3,999	4,212	391	1 adult any age	1 or more
188,932	-	1,038	1,117	28,311	28,719	857	2 adults (1 male and 1 female)	0
128,863	4,189	712	409	12,859	13,080	399		1 or more
15,320	-	116	166	3,320	3,370	144	2 adults (same sex)	0
3,078	88	20	12	514	518	10		1 or more
66,348	356	98	210	9,746	9,829	101	3 or more adults (male(s) and female(s))	0
31,977	2,246	283	68	3,796	3,834	55		1 or more
2,604	12	20	18	469	475	24	3 or more adults (same sex)	0
380	26	5	-	65	65	2		1 or more
334,808	20,502	3,312	1,164	38,975	39,661	1,218	TOTAL DEPENDENT CHILDREN AGED 0 - 18	
103,087	7,220	1,615	650	13,409	13,801	752	Dependent children aged 0 - 4	
205,709	12,554	1,585	466	23,489	23,752	406	Dependent children aged 5 - 15	
20,342	630	88	35	1,738	1,760	41	Dependent children aged 16 - 17	
Basingstoke & Deane								
54,323	594	181	293	4,187	4,352	203	ALL HOUSEHOLDS*	
5,659	-	-	56	676	699	13	1 adult of pensionable age	0
5,340	-	-	124	654	736	123	1 adult under pensionable age	0
1,568	24	18	19	136	151	13	1 adult any age	1 or more
16,916	-	74	46	1,355	1,373	31	2 adults (1 male and 1 female)	0
12,855	313	48	20	588	600	14		1 or more
1,245	-	4	12	127	130	3	2 adults (same sex)	0
266	7	-	-	17	17	-		1 or more
6,777	24	7	12	446	456	6	3 or more adults (male(s) and female(s))	0
3,429	224	28	3	170	172	-		1 or more
224	-	2	-	14	14	-	3 or more adults (same sex)	0
39	2	-	-	3	3	-		1 or more
32,967	1,719	274	70	1,663	1,711	43	TOTAL DEPENDENT CHILDREN AGED 0 - 18	
9,952	601	107	34	592	615	21	Dependent children aged 0 - 4	
20,407	1,060	156	35	980	1,004	20	Dependent children aged 5 - 15	
2,048	49	8	1	71	72	1	Dependent children aged 16 - 17	
East Hampshire								
39,158	418	152	344	4,030	4,237	158	ALL HOUSEHOLDS*	
5,103	-	-	148	825	925	19	1 adult of pensionable age	0
3,338	-	-	78	452	493	55	1 adult under pensionable age	0
1,084	14	13	9	140	147	11	1 adult any age	1 or more
12,622	-	59	62	1,213	1,244	31	2 adults (1 male and 1 female)	0
9,371	258	56	23	563	581	27		1 or more
810	-	1	8	137	139	5	2 adults (same sex)	0
189	6	3	1	17	18	1		1 or more
4,311	24	4	11	507	510	2	3 or more adults (male(s) and female(s))	0
2,179	112	15	3	157	160	6		1 or more
119	2	-	-	15	15	-	3 or more adults (same sex)	0
24	2	1	-	4	4	1		1 or more
23,613	1,161	192	53	1,604	1,645	64	TOTAL DEPENDENT CHILDREN AGED 0 - 18	
6,821	380	98	28	517	541	28	Dependent children aged 0 - 4	
14,596	734	89	20	995	1,008	28	Dependent children aged 5 - 15	
1,658	40	4	4	72	75	6	Dependent children aged 16 - 17	

	Tenure							No car	2 or more cars
Owner occupied		Rented privately		Rented with a job or business	Rented from a housing association	Rented from a local authority or new town			
Owned outright	Buying	Furnished	Unfurnished						
j	k	l	m	n	o	p		q	r

j	k	l	m	n	o	p	q	r
146,621	**291,358**	**22,247**	**19,113**	**17,834**	**11,951**	**94,133**	**144,615**	**188,907**
42,859	4,898	1,293	4,932	847	5,438	23,208	61,889	479
8,580	31,145	7,955	2,537	1,868	1,442	8,242	18,861	3,706
1,170	7,299	1,127	655	418	644	9,083	10,441	731
66,234	82,940	5,209	5,920	5,051	2,472	21,106	29,324	56,539
4,418	95,536	2,443	2,497	6,604	1,017	16,348	10,065	58,549
4,261	6,052	1,364	666	334	197	2,446	4,379	4,531
342	1,493	108	78	74	59	924	972	776
15,526	38,101	1,536	1,292	1,581	388	7,924	5,544	42,583
2,814	22,709	396	434	973	215	4,436	2,437	19,538
361	988	737	81	73	67	297	529	1,318
47	168	34	14	9	8	100	110	148
14,120	**228,501**	**6,555**	**6,296**	**14,805**	**3,523**	**61,008**	**44,721**	**141,716**
2,304	66,928	3,246	2,592	5,421	1,343	21,253	16,632	37,194
9,163	142,313	2,969	3,362	8,575	2,034	37,293	26,063	89,247
1,961	14,953	228	282	638	123	2,157	1,694	11,474
9,010	**29,599**	**1,254**	**1,385**	**2,032**	**1,228**	**9,815**	**10,361**	**20,420**
2,283	357	74	278	130	458	2,079	4,320	40
549	3,040	358	166	251	120	856	1,245	339
91	553	34	30	31	87	742	768	75
4,157	8,707	355	448	611	247	2,391	2,178	5,947
328	9,692	138	247	538	188	1,724	769	6,575
211	605	79	35	47	17	251	266	471
19	133	6	4	5	7	92	83	70
1,151	4,020	125	123	260	53	1,045	458	4,559
191	2,378	28	45	147	45	595	236	2,187
21	94	56	7	8	5	33	31	139
8	18	1	1	3	1	7	6	15
1,051	**22,894**	**327**	**575**	**1,315**	**623**	**6,182**	**3,586**	**15,905**
180	6,845	160	226	372	188	1,981	1,205	4,353
680	14,102	151	309	848	407	3,910	2,197	9,926
136	1,516	13	33	71	26	253	157	1,237
10,192	**20,296**	**1,001**	**1,258**	**1,629**	**435**	**4,347**	**6,087**	**16,560**
2,989	266	89	311	84	211	1,153	3,271	54
577	1,915	201	148	199	51	247	549	299
101	464	51	53	30	10	375	350	61
4,518	5,917	309	384	463	90	941	1,126	5,169
430	7,159	176	171	561	46	828	294	5,711
283	292	53	49	27	4	102	184	313
29	110	5	1	3	3	38	24	66
1,018	2,531	65	98	162	10	427	200	3,166
225	1,583	26	33	88	8	216	65	1,639
15	44	24	8	12	2	14	16	68
4	10	2	2	-	-	6	7	12
1,344	**17,079**	**447**	**463**	**1,284**	**119**	**2,877**	**1,393**	**13,701**
221	4,818	190	166	411	42	973	482	3,593
871	10,543	238	269	801	71	1,803	850	8,512
183	1,288	15	21	56	5	90	50	1,161

Table 42 Household composition and housing – **continued**

Note: * May include a small number of households with no resident adults

42. Households with residents; dependent children in households

TOTAL HOUSE-HOLDS	Over 1 and up to 1.5 persons per room	Over 1.5 persons per room	Lacking or sharing use of bath/shower and/or inside WC	No central heating	Lacking or sharing use of bath/shower and/or inside WC and/or no central heating	Not self-contained accommodation	Household composition	
							Adults	Dependent children
a	b	c	d	e	f	g	h	i

Eastleigh

TOTAL HOUSE-HOLDS	b	c	d	e	f	g	Adults	children
41,219	**362**	**102**	**278**	**4,746**	**4,895**	**167**	ALL HOUSEHOLDS*	
4,874	-	-	97	791	847	11	1 adult of pensionable age	0
4,010	-	-	88	647	694	111	1 adult under pensionable age	0
1,208	5	7	9	196	200	11	1 adult any age	1 or more
13,426	-	43	47	1,606	1,625	18	2 adults (1 male and 1 female)	0
9,863	235	25	15	700	709	8		1 or more
902	-	3	7	150	153	1	2 adults (same sex)	0
193	5	1	-	18	18	-		1 or more
4,491	16	8	14	470	480	4	3 or more adults (male(s) and female(s))	0
2,096	99	15	1	150	151	2		1 or more
134	2	-	-	17	17	1	3 or more adults (same sex)	0
19	-	-	-	1	1	-		1 or more
24,064	**1,037**	**109**	**31**	**1,862**	**1,881**	**28**	**TOTAL DEPENDENT CHILDREN AGED 0 - 18**	
7,318	362	55	15	742	750	14	Dependent children aged 0 - 4	
14,919	631	51	14	1,022	1,032	13	Dependent children aged 5 - 15	
1,420	38	2	1	85	85	-	Dependent children aged 16 - 17	

Fareham

TOTAL HOUSE-HOLDS	b	c	d	e	f	g	Adults	children
38,369	**282**	**55**	**229**	**4,621**	**4,767**	**77**	ALL HOUSEHOLDS*	
4,723	-	-	127	933	1,028	13	1 adult of pensionable age	0
3,099	-	-	24	557	565	33	1 adult under pensionable age	0
989	5	1	6	157	161	5	1 adult any age	1 or more
13,212	-	30	46	1,500	1,527	19	2 adults (1 male and 1 female)	0
8,583	148	8	6	559	561	3		1 or more
849	-	-	2	157	158	1	2 adults (same sex)	0
174	3	-	2	22	22	-		1 or more
4,542	14	1	12	520	527	3	3 or more adults (male(s) and female(s))	0
2,069	112	14	3	199	201	-		1 or more
111	-	1	1	16	16	-	3 or more adults (same sex)	0
15	-	-	-	1	1	-		1 or more
20,878	**808**	**64**	**25**	**1,706**	**1,717**	**12**	**TOTAL DEPENDENT CHILDREN AGED 0 - 18**	
6,351	290	30	13	586	592	8	Dependent children aged 0 - 4	
12,808	497	32	11	1,006	1,011	4	Dependent children aged 5 - 15	
1,334	19	1	1	100	100	-	Dependent children aged 16 - 17	

Gosport

TOTAL HOUSE-HOLDS	b	c	d	e	f	g	Adults	children
29,356	**306**	**68**	**217**	**5,193**	**5,315**	**89**	ALL HOUSEHOLDS*	
4,161	-	-	110	1,047	1,114	6	1 adult of pensionable age	0
2,704	-	-	43	657	673	49	1 adult under pensionable age	0
1,232	1	16	17	202	218	4	1 adult any age	1 or more
9,075	-	18	27	1,596	1,606	16	2 adults (1 male and 1 female)	0
6,705	192	24	10	830	837	6		1 or more
746	-	3	2	188	189	4	2 adults (same sex)	0
165	4	-	-	33	33	-		1 or more
2,941	14	1	4	452	454	1	3 or more adults (male(s) and female(s))	0
1,487	92	6	2	160	162	1		1 or more
123	1	-	1	26	26	1	3 or more adults (same sex)	0
14	2	-	-	1	1	-		1 or more
17,134	**910**	**116**	**36**	**2,101**	**2,132**	**16**	**TOTAL DEPENDENT CHILDREN AGED 0 - 18**	
5,529	324	47	21	799	819	7	Dependent children aged 0 - 4	
10,455	559	66	12	1,201	1,209	6	Dependent children aged 5 - 15	
951	22	1	2	85	87	2	Dependent children aged 16 - 17	

Tenure							No car	2 or more cars
Owner occupied		Rented privately		Rented with a job or business	Rented from a housing association	Rented from a local authority or new town		
Owned outright	Buying	Furnished	Unfurnished					
j	k	l	m	n	o	p	q	r
9,538	**24,015**	**956**	**883**	**332**	**770**	**4,725**	**7,366**	**14,981**
2,492	328	49	270	32	386	1,317	3,587	21
595	2,607	303	82	53	72	298	790	252
81	639	51	24	4	38	371	421	52
4,440	6,954	249	310	101	168	1,204	1,585	4,566
325	8,372	132	96	68	53	817	403	5,013
245	433	69	23	9	15	108	196	318
27	120	1	3	-	1	41	42	65
1,098	2,834	58	59	44	20	378	243	3,150
200	1,661	19	13	18	10	175	77	1,457
30	56	24	1	3	7	13	19	77
5	11	-	1	-	-	2	2	10
1,008	**19,467**	**316**	**233**	**163**	**161**	**2,716**	**1,774**	**11,642**
160	5,757	165	111	50	76	999	674	3,111
657	12,229	133	108	97	84	1,611	1,016	7,379
147	1,139	12	12	14	-	96	67	871
11,328	**21,671**	**782**	**719**	**546**	**254**	**3,069**	**6,683**	**13,998**
3,132	304	56	163	25	149	894	3,408	28
587	1,965	190	77	39	23	218	581	213
56	566	44	26	22	4	271	330	43
5,555	6,358	211	201	121	55	711	1,469	4,410
291	7,316	120	136	247	6	467	338	4,340
282	389	50	30	12	8	78	182	280
23	114	2	6	5	1	23	40	56
1,159	2,950	66	58	51	6	252	238	3,200
221	1,646	16	20	22	1	143	81	1,357
22	49	26	2	2	1	9	15	60
-	12	-	-	-	-	3	1	10
880	**17,027**	**316**	**328**	**549**	**15**	**1,763**	**1,445**	**10,075**
142	5,065	135	150	236	8	615	485	2,721
558	10,563	167	162	296	4	1,058	874	6,315
128	1,087	11	15	11	3	79	71	784
6,491	**14,090**	**865**	**784**	**1,383**	**631**	**5,112**	**8,600**	**5,879**
2,087	259	59	172	29	382	1,173	3,288	19
386	1,453	209	74	64	27	491	952	128
43	422	51	35	78	16	587	716	30
2,947	4,082	250	198	403	155	1,040	1,795	1,677
135	4,553	122	228	676	21	970	963	1,601
196	324	61	17	14	7	127	263	162
20	66	3	4	6	3	63	67	31
597	1,796	63	32	45	7	401	357	1,520
72	1,076	15	20	66	9	229	157	665
7	51	32	4	2	4	23	35	40
-	7	-	-	-	-	7	6	6
378	**10,681**	**299**	**554**	**1,560**	**92**	**3,570**	**3,519**	**3,961**
42	3,159	136	235	658	38	1,261	1,331	911
257	6,678	152	304	859	49	2,156	2,039	2,592
60	696	9	15	37	3	131	123	367

Table 42 Household composition and housing – **continued**

Note: * May include a small number of households with no resident adults

42. Households with residents; dependent children in households

TOTAL HOUSE-HOLDS	Over 1 and up to 1.5 persons per room	Over 1.5 persons per room	Lacking or sharing use of bath/shower and/or inside WC	No central heating	Lacking or sharing use of bath/shower and/or inside WC and/or no central heating	Not self-contained accomm-odation	Household composition Adults	Dependent children
a	b	c	d	e	f	g	h	i
				Hart				
29,073	220	46	150	1,922	1,996	70	ALL HOUSEHOLDS*	
2,876	-	-	34	381	388	5	1 adult of pensionable age	0
2,556	-	-	56	199	237	39	1 adult under pensionable age	0
661	7	4	6	65	69	5	1 adult any age	1 or more
8,702	-	15	22	596	609	11	2 adults (1 male and 1 female)	0
7,696	126	22	16	261	266	3		1 or more
680	-	-	4	95	96	1	2 adults (same sex)	0
143	2	-	-	15	15	-		1 or more
3,697	13	-	9	235	239	4	3 or more adults (male(s) and female(s))	0
1,927	71	5	2	64	65	1		1 or more
116	1	-	1	10	11	1	3 or more adults (same sex)	0
18	-	-	-	1	1	-		1 or more
19,051	596	74	46	740	759	10	TOTAL DEPENDENT CHILDREN AGED 0 - 18	
5,211	198	33	14	246	250	4	Dependent children aged 0 - 4	
12,006	382	40	30	454	468	4	Dependent children aged 5 - 15	
1,393	12	-	1	37	37	1	Dependent children aged 16 - 17	
				Havant				
46,151	834	198	389	9,594	9,869	197	ALL HOUSEHOLDS*	
6,321	-	-	189	1,391	1,550	8	1 adult of pensionable age	0
4,109	-	-	68	1,097	1,131	61	1 adult under pensionable age	0
1,951	36	34	45	613	648	42	1 adult any age	1 or more
14,576	-	46	33	2,753	2,768	34	2 adults (1 male and 1 female)	0
9,653	487	77	42	1,689	1,715	44		1 or more
960	-	10	4	257	259	4	2 adults (same sex)	0
313	14	2	-	73	73	-		1 or more
5,329	36	4	6	1,150	1,154	1	3 or more adults (male(s) and female(s))	0
2,759	260	23	2	530	530	2		1 or more
144	-	1	-	30	30	-	3 or more adults (same sex)	0
31	1	1	-	8	8	-		1 or more
27,194	2,523	337	132	5,616	5,705	131	TOTAL DEPENDENT CHILDREN AGED 0 - 18	
8,103	823	171	97	1,849	1,913	101	Dependent children aged 0 - 4	
17,017	1,605	159	35	3,509	3,534	29	Dependent children aged 5 - 15	
1,650	84	7	-	228	228	1	Dependent children aged 16 - 17	
				New Forest				
65,411	526	180	590	7,182	7,507	234	ALL HOUSEHOLDS*	
10,856	-	-	259	1,514	1,689	35	1 adult of pensionable age	0
5,374	-	-	120	936	987	86	1 adult under pensionable age	0
1,670	9	19	30	247	273	29	1 adult any age	1 or more
23,216	-	73	91	2,300	2,327	36	2 adults (1 male and 1 female)	0
12,605	335	48	39	896	924	36		1 or more
1,541	-	6	13	241	243	3	2 adults (same sex)	0
257	2	2	2	35	36	-		1 or more
6,629	22	10	24	721	730	2	3 or more adults (male(s) and female(s))	0
3,055	155	20	9	258	262	5		1 or more
178	1	2	3	32	34	2	3 or more adults (same sex)	0
22	2	-	-	2	2	-		1 or more
31,581	1,479	235	109	2,516	2,591	88	TOTAL DEPENDENT CHILDREN AGED 0 - 18	
9,170	531	95	52	894	935	51	Dependent children aged 0 - 4	
19,702	885	131	51	1,480	1,509	35	Dependent children aged 5 - 15	
2,125	56	8	5	115	119	2	Dependent children aged 16 - 17	

Tenure							No car	2 or more cars
Owner occupied		Rented privately		Rented with a job or business	Rented from a housing association	Rented from a local authority or new town		
Owned outright	Buying	Furnished	Unfurnished					
j	k	l	m	n	o	p	q	r
6,072	17,484	915	719	1,252	301	2,330	3,287	14,753
1,681	185	56	155	26	172	601	1,856	23
356	1,611	242	67	89	34	157	340	250
72	342	39	26	19	12	151	155	49
2,649	4,602	218	264	330	50	589	572	4,208
215	6,277	141	111	596	13	343	108	5,103
173	319	53	24	22	7	82	109	312
17	84	6	3	6	-	27	24	56
749	2,438	92	54	104	3	257	91	3,068
144	1,569	28	14	58	1	113	24	1,588
13	45	38	1	2	9	8	8	83
3	11	2	-	-	-	2	-	12
743	15,090	370	277	1,308	43	1,220	555	12,296
102	3,965	158	100	471	22	393	187	3,071
479	9,584	193	159	783	20	788	347	7,811
127	1,158	16	11	45	1	35	16	1,056
11,465	22,044	1,195	717	486	400	9,844	11,636	13,267
3,262	470	80	192	44	166	2,107	4,636	22
583	1,974	337	87	69	60	999	1,331	200
88	607	95	37	18	17	1,089	1,156	69
5,558	6,251	314	199	119	80	2,055	2,356	3,862
280	6,922	198	108	134	41	1,970	973	3,907
297	358	45	28	10	8	214	297	236
26	140	12	4	3	2	126	118	64
1,147	3,286	63	38	59	13	723	440	3,288
194	1,959	25	22	27	12	520	287	1,534
28	63	24	2	2	1	24	26	73
2	14	2	-	1	-	12	12	12
907	17,339	502	275	343	145	7,683	4,994	9,776
146	4,803	267	114	123	53	2,597	1,775	2,537
583	10,998	219	148	194	86	4,789	3,006	6,164
134	1,202	11	10	21	6	266	186	804
23,921	29,067	1,613	2,217	1,499	858	6,236	11,848	22,450
7,236	632	160	601	98	420	1,709	6,683	78
1,216	2,852	460	257	200	49	340	956	431
169	696	87	65	25	51	577	590	89
11,395	8,599	456	739	448	194	1,385	2,300	7,449
664	9,828	232	245	431	80	1,125	471	6,772
677	516	69	72	32	12	163	353	496
40	143	7	6	8	1	52	41	99
2,107	3,527	84	161	172	32	546	298	4,787
372	2,188	37	64	71	12	311	126	2,136
44	69	19	6	12	6	22	25	99
1	13	1	-	1	-	6	4	14
1,985	23,131	604	642	962	231	4,026	2,179	16,222
292	6,551	245	243	300	108	1,431	852	4,032
1,318	14,602	327	353	581	109	2,412	1,223	10,370
287	1,540	26	36	64	11	161	91	1,377

Table 42 Household composition and housing – **continued**

Note: * May include a small number of households with no resident adults

42. Households with residents; dependent children in households

TOTAL HOUSE-HOLDS	Over 1 and up to 1.5 persons per room	Over 1.5 persons per room	Lacking or sharing use of bath/shower and/or inside WC	No central heating	Lacking or sharing use of bath/shower and/or inside WC and/or no central heating	Not self-contained accomm-odation	Household composition — Adults	Dependent children
a	b	c	d	e	f	g	h	i
					Portsmouth			
72,590	980	442	1,905	26,293	26,787	1,905	ALL HOUSEHOLDS*	
12,232	-	-	559	5,497	5,628	208	1 adult of pensionable age	0
9,756	-	-	710	3,988	4,192	1,141	1 adult under pensionable age	0
3,189	48	56	63	1,129	1,152	87	1 adult any age	1 or more
21,144	-	180	341	7,594	7,670	282	2 adults (1 male and 1 female)	0
12,716	536	96	77	3,380	3,406	75		1 or more
2,409	-	30	65	1,019	1,033	53	2 adults (same sex)	0
398	16	6	2	135	135	5		1 or more
6,988	60	18	63	2,391	2,405	33	3 or more adults (male(s) and female(s))	0
3,249	316	53	17	982	987	11		1 or more
424	2	3	6	149	149	7	3 or more adults (same sex)	0
58	2	-	-	21	21	-		1 or more
35,203	2,827	564	233	10,156	10,241	236	TOTAL DEPENDENT CHILDREN AGED 0 - 18	
12,266	1,014	253	137	3,671	3,723	143	Dependent children aged 0 - 4	
20,912	1,727	289	86	5,987	6,016	84	Dependent children aged 5 - 15	
1,602	75	16	7	405	408	7	Dependent children aged 16 - 17	
					Rushmoor			
30,523	424	199	492	2,341	2,635	581	ALL HOUSEHOLDS*	
3,351	-	-	76	453	483	27	1 adult of pensionable age	0
3,202	-	-	272	445	608	351	1 adult under pensionable age	0
1,147	10	46	24	46	67	57	1 adult any age	1 or more
8,956	-	70	61	731	767	75	2 adults (1 male and 1 female)	0
7,467	253	46	37	269	296	48		1 or more
934	-	8	5	106	110	7	2 adults (same sex)	0
157	4	2	1	7	8	1		1 or more
3,515	20	7	9	208	214	4	3 or more adults (male(s) and female(s))	0
1,585	134	18	5	53	58	5		1 or more
180	1	1	2	20	21	3	3 or more adults (same sex)	0
23	2	1	-	1	1	-		1 or more
18,569	1,194	217	94	623	700	153	TOTAL DEPENDENT CHILDREN AGED 0 - 18	
6,588	455	127	50	234	272	97	Dependent children aged 0 - 4	
10,734	703	83	41	340	376	49	Dependent children aged 5 - 15	
971	29	4	2	41	43	5	Dependent children aged 16 - 17	
					Southampton			
81,140	1,644	820	1,700	18,125	18,940	2,337	ALL HOUSEHOLDS*	
12,667	-	-	274	3,460	3,573	166	1 adult of pensionable age	0
11,484	-	-	947	3,090	3,556	1,544	1 adult under pensionable age	0
3,709	83	96	74	921	973	115	1 adult any age	1 or more
23,186	-	361	238	4,880	4,983	267	2 adults (1 male and 1 female)	0
14,451	991	210	87	2,333	2,381	112		1 or more
2,440	-	47	33	574	587	58	2 adults (same sex)	0
466	19	2	2	110	111	2		1 or more
8,148	71	28	24	1,803	1,809	32	3 or more adults (male(s) and female(s))	0
3,905	471	63	14	810	817	13		1 or more
576	2	10	2	114	116	8	3 or more adults (same sex)	0
75	7	2	-	19	19	1		1 or more
41,919	4,617	909	245	8,187	8,340	373	TOTAL DEPENDENT CHILDREN AGED 0 - 18	
13,886	1,721	489	150	2,612	2,710	246	Dependent children aged 0 - 4	
25,372	2,729	389	86	5,145	5,194	107	Dependent children aged 5 - 15	
2,151	143	26	6	364	368	12	Dependent children aged 16 - 17	

Tenure							No car	2 or more cars
Owner occupied		Rented privately		Rented with a job or business	Rented from a housing association	Rented from a local authority or new town		
Owned outright	Buying	Furnished	Unfurnished					
j	k	l	m	n	o	p	q	r
17,981	30,752	4,910	3,064	1,571	2,247	12,065	29,067	11,712
6,059	783	269	883	68	997	3,173	10,413	42
1,127	4,162	2,070	492	162	428	1,315	4,623	403
113	1,098	268	149	61	144	1,356	2,137	49
7,385	8,556	1,055	845	386	414	2,503	6,164	3,336
394	9,098	373	315	659	126	1,751	2,345	3,019
619	910	316	121	29	36	378	1,029	451
37	168	28	13	9	12	131	184	36
1,869	3,626	286	173	112	59	863	1,380	2,974
322	2,167	63	59	83	26	529	616	1,232
49	160	157	11	2	3	42	131	161
5	22	9	2	-	1	19	28	9
1,358	22,146	1,114	856	1,555	572	7,602	9,760	7,503
268	7,502	638	422	623	203	2,610	3,640	2,165
867	13,295	404	402	875	343	4,726	5,726	4,661
166	1,078	37	28	45	20	228	328	505
4,835	15,614	1,396	874	2,206	590	5,008	6,659	9,587
1,359	205	50	219	29	263	1,226	2,622	12
357	1,677	512	122	113	64	357	958	195
38	359	59	10	53	35	593	601	36
2,047	4,523	295	263	593	122	1,113	1,222	2,707
133	4,881	167	154	1,195	51	886	619	2,847
161	463	107	25	26	8	144	206	336
15	73	5	5	9	2	48	45	39
605	2,221	117	55	87	27	403	253	2,329
101	1,110	26	17	96	15	220	91	973
17	90	51	2	5	2	13	31	102
1	10	4	2	-	1	5	5	11
445	11,494	392	328	2,312	191	3,407	2,464	6,832
76	3,656	191	127	1,146	59	1,333	1,115	2,018
284	6,915	182	182	1,085	123	1,963	1,268	4,148
55	724	14	15	63	8	92	66	494
17,846	31,547	5,371	3,501	838	2,752	19,285	28,650	16,011
5,273	554	203	1,018	97	1,159	4,363	10,551	34
1,156	4,495	2,495	613	178	403	2,144	5,092	482
120	869	279	118	17	179	2,127	2,407	61
7,649	8,588	987	1,053	261	532	4,116	5,756	4,379
490	9,482	361	278	123	254	3,463	1,971	4,192
562	871	326	137	23	43	478	856	566
36	175	27	14	4	17	193	215	65
2,103	3,865	366	198	78	88	1,450	1,111	4,149
384	2,448	73	50	41	53	856	483	1,800
66	172	219	17	13	19	70	150	264
7	25	13	4	3	3	20	31	18
1,716	23,715	1,195	747	322	965	13,259	9,555	10,869
281	7,329	676	348	81	400	4,771	3,655	3,079
1,127	14,703	457	369	208	535	7,973	5,430	6,747
228	1,351	33	28	27	26	458	390	796

Table 42 Household composition and housing – **continued**

Note: * May include a small number of households with no resident adults

42. Households with residents; dependent children in households

TOTAL HOUSE-HOLDS	Over 1 and up to 1.5 persons per room	Over 1.5 persons per room	Lacking or sharing use of bath/shower and/or inside WC	No central heating	Lacking or sharing use of bath/shower and/or inside WC and/or no central heating	Not self-contained accomm-odation	Household composition		
							Adults		Dependent children
a	b	c	d	e	f	g	h		i

Test Valley

38,391	321	76	183	3,186	3,264	98	ALL HOUSEHOLDS*		
4,757	-	-	52	659	683	16	1 adult of pensionable age		0
3,331	-	-	49	429	454	48	1 adult under pensionable age		0
1,138	7	3	3	57	58	1	1 adult any age		1 or more
12,011	-	35	41	1,056	1,068	14	2 adults (1 male and 1 female)		0
9,010	167	19	14	358	363	12			1 or more
916	-	1	5	127	129	1	2 adults (same sex)		0
192	4	-	1	12	12	-			1 or more
							3 or more adults (male(s) and female(s))		
4,663	25	7	13	373	379	4			0
2,207	112	11	4	102	105	2			1 or more
131	-	-	1	11	11	-	3 or more adults (same sex)		0
26	6	-	-	2	2	-			1 or more
22,563	908	96	38	888	905	28	TOTAL DEPENDENT CHILDREN AGED 0 - 18		
6,518	288	37	14	284	290	11	Dependent children aged 0 - 4		
14,128	588	52	21	527	537	16	Dependent children aged 5 - 15		
1,482	30	7	2	63	64	1	Dependent children aged 16 - 17		

Winchester

37,553	263	99	303	3,608	3,748	202	ALL HOUSEHOLDS*		
5,895	-	-	92	723	763	16	1 adult of pensionable age		0
3,466	-	-	96	422	481	124	1 adult under pensionable age		0
850	8	12	10	90	95	11	1 adult any age		1 or more
11,890	-	34	62	1,131	1,152	23	2 adults (1 male and 1 female)		0
7,888	148	33	23	433	441	11			1 or more
888	-	3	6	142	144	3	2 adults (same sex)		0
165	2	2	1	20	20	1			1 or more
							3 or more adults (male(s) and female(s))		
4,317	17	3	9	470	472	5			0
2,030	88	12	3	161	164	7			1 or more
144	-	-	1	15	15	1	3 or more adults (same sex)		0
16	-	-	-	1	1	-			1 or more
20,072	723	125	52	1,313	1,334	36	TOTAL DEPENDENT CHILDREN AGED 0 - 18		
5,374	233	73	25	383	391	21	Dependent children aged 0 - 4		
12,653	454	48	24	843	854	11	Dependent children aged 5 - 15		
1,557	33	4	3	72	74	3	Dependent children aged 16 - 17		

	Tenure						No car	2 or more cars
Owner occupied		Rented privately		Rented with a job or business	Rented from a housing association	Rented from a local authority or new town		
Owned outright	Buying	Furnished	Unfurnished					
j	k	l	m	n	o	p	q	r
8,454	**18,558**	**846**	**1,561**	**2,053**	**589**	**6,330**	**7,072**	**14,603**
2,246	252	66	332	98	228	1,535	3,295	47
499	1,748	237	165	184	35	463	682	253
92	362	32	48	37	26	541	506	69
3,798	5,193	224	537	615	142	1,502	1,399	4,311
340	6,382	133	224	750	71	1,110	514	4,744
262	302	54	60	34	15	189	233	294
23	91	4	4	6	7	57	48	65
989	2,648	55	127	191	42	611	251	3,244
176	1,513	21	51	132	15	299	109	1,496
24	51	20	11	6	6	13	24	70
5	11	-	-	-	2	8	6	9
1,057	**14,831**	**324**	**575**	**1,688**	**214**	**3,874**	**2,173**	**11,326**
182	4,092	133	197	497	63	1,354	775	2,848
693	9,379	173	336	1,055	138	2,354	1,288	7,220
136	1,036	17	34	104	10	145	93	937
9,488	**16,621**	**1,143**	**1,431**	**2,007**	**896**	**5,967**	**7,299**	**14,686**
2,760	303	82	338	87	447	1,878	3,959	59
592	1,646	341	187	267	76	357	762	261
106	322	37	34	23	25	303	304	48
4,136	4,610	286	479	600	223	1,556	1,402	4,518
393	5,574	150	184	626	67	894	297	4,725
293	270	82	45	49	17	132	205	296
30	76	2	11	10	3	33	41	64
934	2,359	96	116	216	28	568	224	3,149
212	1,411	19	26	124	8	230	85	1,474
25	44	47	9	4	2	13	18	82
6	4	-	2	1	-	3	2	10
1,248	**13,607**	**349**	**443**	**1,444**	**152**	**2,829**	**1,324**	**11,608**
212	3,386	152	153	453	83	935	456	2,755
789	8,722	173	261	893	65	1,750	799	7,402
174	1,138	14	24	80	4	123	56	1,085

Table 43 Household composition and ethnic group

43. Households with residents; residents in households

Note: * May include a small number of households with no resident adults

HAMPSHIRE

Household composition		TOTAL HOUSE-HOLDS	Ethnic group of head of household								Other groups		Household head born in Ireland
Adults	Dependent children		White	Black Caribbean	Black African	Black other	Indian	Pakistani	Bangladeshi	Chinese	Asian	Other	
a	b	c	d	e	f	g	h	i	j	k	l	m	n
ALL HOUSEHOLDS*		603,257	595,071	1,085	391	511	2,219	390	440	1,060	697	1,393	9,566
1 adult of pensionable age	0	83,475	83,238	50	12	9	49	5	2	41	10	59	1,635
1 adult under pensionable age	0	61,769	60,534	219	100	101	226	35	28	148	109	269	1,135
1 adult any age	1 or more	20,396	19,969	83	26	54	60	16	15	54	44	75	236
2 adults (1 male and 1 female)	0	188,932	187,575	196	60	108	336	46	23	169	109	310	2,880
	1 or more	128,863	126,236	251	121	138	804	154	177	344	240	398	1,534
2 adults (same sex)	0	15,320	15,084	44	9	16	32	12	17	31	19	56	268
	1 or more	3,078	3,005	16	3	9	11	4	4	11	5	10	32
3 or more adults (male(s) and female(s))	0	66,348	65,508	145	27	48	289	42	14	107	53	115	1,191
	1 or more	31,977	30,943	63	26	23	392	72	141	142	91	84	561
3 or more adults (same sex)	0	2,604	2,511	9	6	4	14	3	17	12	14	14	8
	1 or more	380	366	7	1	1	2	1	1	-	1	-	
Households containing persons of pensionable age only (any number)		144,528	144,173	76	18	15	74	9	4	51	18	90	2,633
TOTAL PERSONS IN HOUSEHOLDS		1,512,038	1,485,388	2,849	1,094	1,386	8,060	1,637	2,305	3,345	2,204	3,770	23,064
All dependent children 0 - 18		334,808	325,782	731	363	428	2,765	692	1,147	1,056	744	1,100	4,351
Dependent children aged 0 - 4		103,087	100,364	251	113	163	740	188	350	272	250	396	1,074
Dependent children aged 5 - 15		205,709	200,228	415	228	243	1,751	432	725	625	430	632	2,808
Dependent children 0 - 17 included above		329,138	320,326	717	355	424	2,691	667	1,133	1,014	724	1,087	4,240
Persons pensionable age - 74		168,857	168,030	155	33	34	235	31	29	114	43	153	3,213
Persons aged 75 - 84		78,049	77,861	25	8	4	68	5	2	24	19	33	1,273
Persons aged 85 and over		17,543	17,495	1	-	3	24	2	3	8	2	5	253

Table 43 Household composition and ethnic group – continued

Note: * May include a small number of households with no resident adults

43. Households with residents; residents in households

Basingstoke & Deane

Household composition		TOTAL HOUSE-HOLDS	Ethnic group of head of household								Other groups		Household head born in Ireland
Adults	Dependent children		White	Black Caribbean	Black African	Black other	Indian	Pakistani	Bangladeshi	Chinese	Asian	Other	
a	b	c	d	e	f	g	h	i	j	k	l	m	n
ALL HOUSEHOLDS*		54,323	53,346	214	53	69	263	27	26	87	92	146	1,141
1 adult of pensionable age	0	5,659	5,639	9	-	-	2	-	-	3	1	5	145
1 adult under pensionable age	0	5,340	5,180	30	13	15	35	1	4	14	21	27	109
1 adult any age	1 or more	1,568	1,509	16	4	6	10	3	1	3	5	11	30
2 adults (1 male and 1 female)	0	16,916	16,734	40	12	14	54	6	3	13	13	27	330
	1 or more	12,855	12,530	51	18	26	92	13	11	32	42	40	196
2 adults (same sex)	0	1,245	1,224	14	-	-	3	-	1	3	-	1	32
	1 or more	266	258	5	-	1	-	-	-	-	-	1	2
3 or more adults (male(s) and female(s))	0	6,777	6,663	35	2	3	34	3	1	9	4	23	197
	1 or more	3,429	3,347	13	4	4	32	1	5	10	5	8	93
3 or more adults (same sex)	0	224	218	1	-	-	1	-	-	-	1	3	7
	1 or more	39	39	-	-	-	-	-	-	-	-	-	-
Households containing persons of pensionable age only (any number)		9,931	9,903	12	1	-	4	-	-	3	1	7	238
TOTAL PERSONS IN HOUSEHOLDS		143,278	140,332	605	149	194	828	87	114	274	272	423	2,987
All dependent children 0 - 18		32,967	32,027	158	52	70	249	30	59	92	101	129	571
Dependent children aged 0 - 4		9,952	9,655	55	20	27	67	6	17	25	42	38	134
Dependent children aged 5 - 15		20,407	19,842	94	29	39	155	22	38	55	53	80	371
Dependent children 0 - 17 included above		*32,407*	*31,488*	*155*	*51*	*68*	*242*	*29*	*58*	*89*	*99*	*128*	*549*
Persons pensionable age - 74		12,505	12,427	29	2	4	19	-	2	10	3	9	343
Persons aged 75 - 84		5,343	5,333	1	-	-	5	-	-	1	1	3	108
Persons aged 85 and over		1,155	1,153	1	-	-	1	-	-	-	-	-	15

Table 43 Household composition and ethnic group – continued

Note: * May include a small number of households with no resident adults

43. Households with residents; residents in households

East Hampshire

Household composition		TOTAL HOUSE-HOLDS	Ethnic group of head of household								Other groups		Household head born in Ireland
Adults	Dependent children		White	Black Caribbean	Black African	Black other	Indian	Pakistani	Bangladeshi	Chinese	Asian	Other	
a	b	c	d	e	f	g	h	i	j	k	l	m	n
ALL HOUSEHOLDS*		**39,158**	**38,891**	**24**	**13**	**28**	**41**	**3**	**16**	**38**	**39**	**65**	**490**
1 adult of pensionable age	0	5,103	5,093	1	-	1	1	-	-	-	2	5	76
1 adult under pensionable age	0	3,338	3,302	3	1	4	11	-	-	5	5	7	49
1 adult any age	1 or more	1,084	1,076	2	2	2	-	-	1	1	-	-	15
2 adults (1 male and 1 female)	0	12,622	12,572	3	2	6	7	-	-	9	5	18	145
	1 or more	9,371	9,268	9	7	7	12	2	8	11	20	27	108
2 adults (same sex)	0	810	805	-	1	2	-	-	1	1	-	1	15
	1 or more	189	188	-	-	-	-	-	-	1	-	-	3
3 or more adults (male(s) and female(s))	0	4,311	4,285	5	-	5	3	1	-	4	4	4	44
	1 or more	2,179	2,159	1	-	1	7	-	1	7	1	2	33
3 or more adults (same sex)	0	119	111	-	-	-	-	-	5	-	2	1	2
	1 or more	24	24	-	-	-	-	-	-	-	-	-	-
Households containing persons of pensionable age only (any number)		9,017	9,001	1	2	2	1	-	-	1	2	7	127
TOTAL PERSONS IN HOUSEHOLDS		**101,335**	**100,507**	**68**	**43**	**72**	**112**	**13**	**76**	**126**	**127**	**191**	**1,257**
All dependent children 0 - 18		23,613	23,340	20	20	17	25	6	32	40	47	66	307
Dependent children aged 0 - 4		6,821	6,737	6	8	9	10	1	8	10	20	12	71
Dependent children aged 5 - 15		14,596	14,426	14	12	8	11	5	23	22	26	49	206
Dependent children 0 - 17 included above		*23,075*	*22,808*	*20*	*20*	*17*	*23*	*6*	*32*	*38*	*46*	*65*	*296*
Persons pensionable age - 74		10,436	10,410	3	3	3	1	-	-	5	4	7	140
Persons aged 75 - 84		5,058	5,052	-	1	1	-	-	-	2	-	2	69
Persons aged 85 and over		1,190	1,188	-	-	1	-	-	-	-	-	1	16

Table 43 Household composition and ethnic group – **continued**

43. Households with residents; residents in households

Note: * May include a small number of households with no resident adults

Eastleigh

Household composition		TOTAL HOUSE-HOLDS	Ethnic group of head of household								Other groups		Household head born in Ireland
			White	Black Caribbean	Black African	Black other	Indian	Pakistani	Bangladeshi	Chinese	Asian	Other	
Adults	Dependent children												
a	b	c	d	e	f	g	h	i	j	k	l	m	n
ALL HOUSEHOLDS*		**41,219**	**40,736**	**36**	**18**	**19**	**197**	**9**	**18**	**87**	**34**	**65**	**540**
1 adult of pensionable age	0	4,874	4,864	1	-	3	1	-	-	4	-	1	87
1 adult under pensionable age	0	4,010	3,967	7	4	1	8	1	-	10	4	8	61
1 adult any age	1 or more	1,208	1,193	3	2	1	4	-	-	3	1	1	10
2 adults (1 male and 1 female)	0	13,426	13,336	6	2	5	36	1	1	16	5	18	155
	1 or more	9,863	9,688	13	6	8	72	3	3	31	15	24	106
2 adults (same sex)	0	902	894	1	-	-	2	-	2	3	-	-	8
	1 or more	193	190	-	-	-	1	-	-	-	-	2	4
3 or more adults (male(s) and female(s))	0	4,491	4,437	3	2	1	33	2	-	9	1	3	73
	1 or more	2,096	2,015	2	2	-	40	2	9	11	8	7	34
3 or more adults (same sex)	0	134	130	-	-	-	-	-	3	-	-	1	2
	1 or more	19	19	-	-	-	-	-	-	-	-	-	-
Households containing persons of pensionable age only (any number)		8,768	8,755	1	-	4	2	-	-	4	-	2	148
TOTAL PERSONS IN HOUSEHOLDS		**105,298**	**103,609**	**99**	**55**	**54**	**748**	**32**	**108**	**276**	**121**	**196**	**1,360**
All dependent children 0 - 18		24,064	23,486	32	21	19	250	8	52	93	42	61	291
Dependent children aged 0 - 4		7,318	7,153	13	5	7	58	1	17	26	17	21	75
Dependent children aged 5 - 15		14,919	14,569	18	15	10	161	3	32	58	18	35	192
Dependent children 0 - 17 included above		*23,657*	*23,093*	*32*	*20*	*19*	*243*	*7*	*51*	*92*	*40*	*60*	*286*
Persons pensionable age - 74		10,801	10,751	1	1	5	18	2	-	11	6	6	177
Persons aged 75 - 84		4,516	4,506	-	-	-	5	-	-	2	2	1	80
Persons aged 85 and over		1,058	1,055	-	-	-	2	-	1	-	-	-	10

Table 43 Household composition and ethnic group – **continued**

43. Households with residents; residents in households

Note: * May include a small number of households with no resident adults

Fareham

Household composition — Adults	Dependent children	TOTAL HOUSE-HOLDS	White	Black Caribbean	Black African	Black other	Indian	Pakistani	Bangladeshi	Chinese	Other groups — Asian	Other groups — Other	Household head born in Ireland
		c	d	e	f	g	h	i	j	k	l	m	n
ALL HOUSEHOLDS*		38,369	38,114	29	29	9	51	5	10	59	28	56	491
1 adult of pensionable age	0	4,723	4,716	-	-	-	1	1	-	4	-	2	81
1 adult under pensionable age	0	3,099	3,061	3	3	1	5	3	-	8	3	12	35
1 adult any age	1 or more	989	979	1	-	-	1	-	-	4	2	2	16
2 adults (1 male and 1 female)	0	13,212	13,176	4	2	2	8	-	-	8	1	11	172
2 adults (1 male and 1 female)	1 or more	8,583	8,490	11	3	5	20	1	7	19	15	12	91
2 adults (same sex)	0	849	837	1	-	-	-	-	2	2	2	5	7
2 adults (same sex)	1 or more	174	171	1	-	1	-	-	-	-	-	1	1
3 or more adults (male(s) and female(s))	0	4,542	4,515	5	-	-	7	-	1	4	3	7	60
3 or more adults (male(s) and female(s))	1 or more	2,069	2,041	2	-	-	9	1	-	10	2	4	26
3 or more adults (same sex)	0	111	110	1	-	-	-	-	-	-	-	-	2
3 or more adults (same sex)	1 or more	15	15	-	-	-	-	-	-	-	-	-	-
Households containing persons of pensionable age only (any number)		8,961	8,949	1	-	-	2	-	-	4	-	5	140
TOTAL PERSONS IN HOUSEHOLDS		97,607	96,813	92	19	29	185	11	38	186	95	139	1,210
All dependent children 0 - 18		20,878	20,629	29	6	12	54	3	17	61	36	31	243
Dependent children aged 0 - 4		6,351	6,280	11	2	3	19	-	3	16	8	9	65
Dependent children aged 5 - 15		12,808	12,650	15	4	9	31	3	14	38	25	19	159
Dependent children 0 - 17 included above		*20,493*	*20,251*	*27*	*6*	*12*	*53*	*3*	*17*	*60*	*34*	*30*	*240*
Persons pensionable age - 74		11,224	11,200	1	-	-	5	1	-	5	1	11	159
Persons aged 75 - 84		4,793	4,787	1	-	-	1	-	-	3	-	1	75
Persons aged 85 and over		945	945	-	-	-	-	-	-	-	-	-	21

Table 43 Household composition and ethnic group – continued

County, districts

Note: * May include a small number of households with no resident adults

43. Households with residents; residents in households

Gosport

Household composition — Adults	Dependent children	TOTAL HOUSE-HOLDS	White	Black Caribbean	Black African	Black other	Indian	Pakistani	Bangladeshi	Chinese	Other groups Asian	Other groups Other	Household head born in Ireland
	a / b	c	d	e	f	g	h	i	j	k	l	m	n
ALL HOUSEHOLDS*		**29,356**	**29,147**	**25**	**14**	**23**	**35**	**4**	**9**	**39**	**21**	**39**	**501**
1 adult of pensionable age	0	4,161	4,153	-	-	-	3	-	1	2	1	1	80
1 adult under pensionable age	0	2,704	2,687	1	3	4	3	-	1	1	1	3	37
1 adult any age	1 or more	1,232	1,219	1	1	3	-	1	-	3	1	3	13
2 adults (1 male and 1 female)	0	9,075	9,038	5	2	4	4	-	-	4	3	15	161
	1 or more	6,705	6,629	15	4	7	15	2	4	15	6	8	102
2 adults (same sex)	0	746	740	-	-	1	1	-	2	1	1	-	17
	1 or more	165	160	-	1	2	1	-	-	-	-	1	-
3 or more adults (male(s) and female(s))	0	2,941	2,921	2	2	1	3	1	-	5	2	4	54
	1 or more	1,487	1,463	1	1	-	5	-	1	8	6	2	31
3 or more adults (same sex)	0	123	121	-	-	1	-	-	-	-	-	1	5
	1 or more	14	14	-	-	-	-	-	-	-	-	-	1
Households containing persons of pensionable age only (any number)		6,957	6,947	-	-	-	4	-	1	2	1	2	134
TOTAL PERSONS IN HOUSEHOLDS		**73,704**	**73,027**	**89**	**40**	**66**	**115**	**14**	**34**	**143**	**72**	**104**	**1,259**
All dependent children 0 - 18		17,134	16,893	38	13	25	43	6	17	49	24	26	263
Dependent children aged 0 - 4		5,529	5,455	11	6	14	13	2	7	10	4	7	54
Dependent children aged 5 - 15		10,455	10,307	25	7	11	26	4	10	34	16	15	185
Dependent children 0 - 17 included above		*16,935*	*16,698*	*38*	*13*	*25*	*41*	*6*	*17*	*48*	*23*	*26*	*259*
Persons pensionable age - 74		7,820	7,800	-	1	-	5	-	-	9	2	3	151
Persons aged 75 - 84		3,729	3,725	-	-	-	2	-	-	-	2	-	63
Persons aged 85 and over		813	811	-	-	-	-	-	1	-	-	1	16

513

Note: * May include a small number of households with no resident adults

43. Households with residents; residents in households

Hart

| Household composition | | TOTAL HOUSE-HOLDS | Ethnic group of head of household | | | | | | | | | | Household head born in Ireland |
| Adults | Dependent children | | White | Black Caribbean | Black African | Black other | Indian | Pakistani | Bangladeshi | Chinese | Other groups Asian | Other groups Other | |
a	b	c	d	e	f	g	h	i	j	k	l	m	n
ALL HOUSEHOLDS*		**29,073**	**28,798**	**24**	**9**	**19**	**61**	**13**	**13**	**44**	**35**	**57**	**469**
1 adult of pensionable age	0	2,876	2,868	1	1	-	-	-	-	1	1	4	68
1 adult under pensionable age	0	2,556	2,533	3	1	-	5	1	3	4	2	4	44
1 adult any age	1 or more	661	650	-	-	1	1	-	2	1	2	4	11
2 adults (1 male and 1 female)	0	8,702	8,655	3	1	8	12	1	-	5	7	10	134
	1 or more	7,696	7,579	9	4	8	29	8	5	18	14	22	122
2 adults (same sex)	0	680	671	-	-	1	1	1	-	2	2	2	9
	1 or more	143	140	-	-	-	-	-	-	1	2	-	1
3 or more adults (male(s) and female(s))	0	3,697	3,669	6	1	1	7	2	-	3	2	6	47
	1 or more	1,927	1,901	2	1	-	6	1	1	9	2	5	30
3 or more adults (same sex)	0	116	113	-	-	-	-	-	2	-	1	-	2
	1 or more	18	18	-	-	-	-	-	-	-	-	-	1
Households containing persons of pensionable age only (any number)		5,080	5,070	2	1	-	1	-	-	1	1	4	115
TOTAL PERSONS IN HOUSEHOLDS		**79,014**	**78,115**	**69**	**28**	**55**	**201**	**46**	**51**	**165**	**108**	**176**	**1,239**
All dependent children 0 - 18		19,051	18,755	16	9	17	65	17	17	57	37	61	314
Dependent children aged 0 - 4		5,211	5,120	6	4	8	22	7	7	16	12	16	67
Dependent children aged 5 - 15		12,006	11,831	7	4	8	42	9	9	29	22	40	216
Dependent children 0 - 17 included above		*18,610*	*18,324*	*15*	*9*	*16*	*65*	*16*	*17*	*54*	*36*	*58*	*304*
Persons pensionable age - 74		6,213	6,191	3	1	1	7	-	-	3	2	5	130
Persons aged 75 - 84		2,888	2,882	3	-	1	1	-	-	1	-	1	59
Persons aged 85 and over		675	673	-	-	-	1	-	-	1	-	-	10

Table 43 Household composition and ethnic group – continued

43. Households with residents; residents in households

Note: * May include a small number of households with no resident adults

Havant

Household composition		TOTAL HOUSE-HOLDS	Ethnic group of head of household								Other groups		Household head born in Ireland
Adults	Dependent children		White	Black Caribbean	Black African	Black other	Indian	Pakistani	Bangladeshi	Chinese	Asian	Other	
a	b	c	d	e	f	g	h	i	j	k	l	m	n
ALL HOUSEHOLDS*		**46,151**	**45,833**	**29**	**23**	**36**	**71**	**7**	**16**	**50**	**22**	**64**	**606**
1 adult of pensionable age	0	6,321	6,305	1	2	-	4	1	-	2	-	6	141
1 adult under pensionable age	0	4,109	4,065	7	4	6	8	-	1	4	4	10	67
1 adult any age	1 or more	1,951	1,936	3	1	2	3	-	-	4	1	1	13
2 adults (1 male and 1 female)	0	14,576	14,512	7	2	8	11	2	-	8	5	21	163
	1 or more	9,653	9,547	6	9	8	26	2	5	24	9	17	96
2 adults (same sex)	0	960	953	1	-	1	2	-	-	-	-	3	14
	1 or more	313	312	-	-	-	-	-	-	-	-	1	2
3 or more adults (male(s) and female(s))	0	5,329	5,302	1	5	6	7	1	1	3	1	2	69
	1 or more	2,759	2,725	3	-	4	9	1	7	5	2	3	33
3 or more adults (same sex)	0	144	142	-	-	-	-	-	2	-	-	-	7
	1 or more	31	30	-	-	1	-	-	-	-	-	-	1
Households containing persons of pensionable age only (any number)		11,384	11,365	1	2	1	5	1	-	2	1	6	206
TOTAL PERSONS IN HOUSEHOLDS		**118,297**	**117,326**	**77**	**66**	**113**	**217**	**24**	**77**	**171**	**63**	**163**	**1,402**
All dependent children 0 - 18		27,194	26,877	23	16	33	70	7	34	70	20	44	260
Dependent children aged 0 - 4		8,103	8,005	10	3	9	20	2	19	21	2	12	62
Dependent children aged 5 - 15		17,017	16,830	12	11	23	43	3	12	38	15	30	165
Dependent children 0 - 17 included above		*26,770*	*26,459*	*23*	*15*	*32*	*68*	*7*	*33*	*69*	*20*	*44*	*253*
Persons pensionable age - 74		14,423	14,391	2	3	4	5	1	2	7	2	6	222
Persons aged 75 - 84		5,696	5,688	1	-	-	4	-	-	-	-	3	87
Persons aged 85 and over		1,277	1,275	-	-	-	-	-	-	1	-	1	22

Table 43 Household composition and ethnic group – **continued**

43. Households with residents; residents in households

Note: * May include a small number of households with no resident adults

New Forest

| Household composition | | TOTAL HOUSE-HOLDS | Ethnic group of head of household | | | | | | | | | | Household head born in Ireland |
| Adults | Dependent children | | White | Black Caribbean | Black African | Black other | Indian | Pakistani | Bangladeshi | Chinese | Other groups: Asian | Other groups: Other | |
a	b	c	d	e	f	g	h	i	j	k	l	m	n
ALL HOUSEHOLDS*		**65,411**	**65,116**	**26**	**15**	**22**	**55**	**9**	**18**	**56**	**21**	**73**	**756**
1 adult of pensionable age	0	10,856	10,839	1	1	-	3	-	-	4	2	6	164
1 adult under pensionable age	0	5,374	5,336	3	2	4	5	1	3	10	2	8	62
1 adult any age	1 or more	1,670	1,651	1	3	4	-	-	-	1	2	8	11
2 adults (1 male and 1 female)	0	23,216	23,160	5	4	7	7	3	1	11	2	16	273
	1 or more	12,605	12,506	8	3	4	24	5	4	20	8	23	101
2 adults (same sex)	0	1,541	1,532	-	-	-	-	-	4	1	-	4	17
	1 or more	257	253	-	-	1	-	-	1	1	-	1	1
3 or more adults (male(s) and female(s))	0	6,629	6,606	6	1	1	8	-	-	2	1	4	85
	1 or more	3,055	3,031	1	1	1	5	-	3	6	4	3	35
3 or more adults (same sex)	0	178	175	-	-	-	1	-	2	-	-	-	7
	1 or more	22	20	1	-	-	1	-	1	1	-	1	-
Households containing persons of pensionable age only (any number)		20,701	20,674	1	2	1	5	-	-	5	2	11	285
TOTAL PERSONS IN HOUSEHOLDS		**157,604**	**156,723**	**76**	**41**	**55**	**184**	**26**	**78**	**158**	**69**	**194**	**1,719**
All dependent children 0 - 18		31,581	31,290	20	15	17	59	9	35	51	25	60	281
Dependent children aged 0 - 4		9,170	9,089	3	3	7	12	4	11	17	7	17	67
Dependent children aged 5 - 15		19,702	19,522	16	12	8	41	5	21	29	13	35	176
Dependent children 0 - 17 included above		*30,997*	*30,713*	*20*	*15*	*17*	*57*	*9*	*33*	*51*	*24*	*58*	*272*
Persons pensionable age - 74		23,396	23,358	2	4	1	8	1	-	6	2	14	347
Persons aged 75 - 84		11,684	11,669	-	1	1	4	-	1	2	-	6	136
Persons aged 85 and over		2,703	2,702	-	-	-	1	-	-	-	-	-	27

Table 43 Household composition and ethnic group – continued

County, districts

Note: * May include a small number of households with no resident adults

43. Households with residents; residents in households

Portsmouth

Household composition				Ethnic group of head of household											Household head born in Ireland
Adults	Dependent children	TOTAL HOUSE-HOLDS	White	Black Caribbean	Black African	Black other	Indian	Pakistani	Bangladeshi	Chinese	Other groups		
											Asian	Other	
a	b	c	d	e	f	g	h	i	j	k	l	m	n
ALL HOUSEHOLDS*		**72,590**	**71,342**	**87**	**72**	**108**	**207**	**18**	**180**	**219**	**102**	**255**	**1,056**
1 adult of pensionable age	0	12,232	12,205	4	1	3	3	-	-	8	3	5	212
1 adult under pensionable age	0	9,756	9,502	23	31	30	29	2	5	36	32	66	167
1 adult any age	1 or more	3,189	3,123	4	2	11	6	-	6	15	8	14	24
2 adults (1 male and 1 female)	0	21,144	20,935	22	11	18	29	4	9	38	18	60	296
	1 or more	12,716	12,370	17	20	20	75	8	69	53	14	70	135
2 adults (same sex)	0	2,409	2,365	2	2	5	6	3	2	9	4	11	40
	1 or more	398	391	1	-	-	1	-	1	3	1	-	5
3 or more adults (male(s) and female(s))	0	6,988	6,895	6	2	13	24	1	6	24	3	14	108
	1 or more	3,249	3,073	5	2	6	30	-	80	29	14	10	51
3 or more adults (same sex)	0	424	403	1	1	2	4	-	1	3	4	5	16
	1 or more	58	57	1	-	-	-	-	-	-	-	-	2
Households containing persons of pensionable age only (any number)		19,397	19,352	9	1	4	5	-	1	14	3	8	324
TOTAL PERSONS IN HOUSEHOLDS		**169,730**	**165,670**	**200**	**169**	**279**	**716**	**55**	**1,055**	**664**	**261**	**661**	**2,349**
All dependent children 0 - 18		35,203	33,770	42	50	78	249	18	536	195	68	197	401
Dependent children aged 0 - 4		12,266	11,811	21	17	28	68	5	154	41	29	92	111
Dependent children aged 5 - 15		20,912	20,032	21	30	48	163	12	351	124	34	97	244
Dependent children 0 - 17 included above		*34,780*	*33,378*	*42*	*48*	*78*	*241*	*18*	*528*	*186*	*66*	*195*	*392*
Persons pensionable age - 74		20,890	20,769	16	4	8	23	-	17	33	4	16	370
Persons aged 75 - 84		10,554	10,530	5	1	1	5	-	-	6	2	4	157
Persons aged 85 and over		2,393	2,388	-	-	-	1	-	1	3	-	-	42

517

Table 43 Household composition and ethnic group – continued

Note: * May include a small number of households with no resident adults

43. Households with residents; residents in households

Rushmoor

Household composition		TOTAL HOUSE-HOLDS	Ethnic group of head of household								Other groups		Household head born in Ireland
Adults	Dependent children		White	Black Caribbean	Black African	Black other	Indian	Pakistani	Bangladeshi	Chinese	Asian	Other	
a	b	c	d	e	f	g	h	i	j	k	l	m	n
ALL HOUSEHOLDS*		**30,523**	**29,903**	**151**	**31**	**34**	**114**	**52**	**10**	**69**	**70**	**89**	**717**
1 adult of pensionable age	0	3,351	3,332	4	-	-	5	1	-	3	-	6	108
1 adult under pensionable age	0	3,202	3,121	27	5	6	13	3	3	8	7	9	81
1 adult any age	1 or more	1,147	1,120	10	2	3	1	-	1	3	5	2	23
2 adults (1 male and 1 female)	0	8,956	8,862	29	3	8	16	4	-	5	11	18	207
	1 or more	7,467	7,269	30	10	12	45	21	2	26	23	29	128
2 adults (same sex)	0	934	902	9	-	1	4	2	1	5	2	8	19
	1 or more	157	153	3	-	-	-	-	-	1	-	-	3
3 or more adults (male(s) and female(s))	0	3,515	3,437	28	3	4	9	5	1	8	8	12	99
	1 or more	1,585	1,509	7	5	-	20	15	2	8	14	5	42
3 or more adults (same sex)	0	180	172	3	2	-	1	-	-	2	-	-	6
	1 or more	23	20	1	1	-	-	1	-	-	-	-	1
Households containing persons of pensionable age only (any number)		5,508	5,482	6	-	-	6	1	-	3	1	9	166
TOTAL PERSONS IN HOUSEHOLDS		**79,121**	**77,139**	**397**	**111**	**90**	**394**	**251**	**36**	**224**	**226**	**253**	**1,794**
All dependent children 0 - 18		18,569	17,951	81	42	25	140	105	16	74	71	64	354
Dependent children aged 0 - 4		6,588	6,407	30	9	12	27	33	7	9	20	34	99
Dependent children aged 5 - 15		10,734	10,373	40	27	12	99	58	9	51	40	25	219
Dependent children 0 - 17 included above		*18,293*	*17,698*	*81*	*39*	*25*	*135*	*99*	*16*	*68*	*68*	*64*	*347*
Persons pensionable age - 74		6,632	6,564	18	1	-	19	1	-	7	4	18	209
Persons aged 75 - 84		3,011	3,003	1	-	-	2	1	-	-	3	1	89
Persons aged 85 and over		626	619	-	-	-	4	-	-	2	-	1	14

Table 43 Household composition and ethnic group – continued

Note: * May include a small number of households with no resident adults

43. Households with residents; residents in households

Southampton

	Dependent children	TOTAL HOUSE-HOLDS	White	Black Caribbean	Black African	Black other	Indian	Pakistani	Bangladeshi	Chinese	Other groups Asian	Other groups Other	Household head born in Ireland
a	b	c	d	e	f	g	h	i	j	k	l	m	n
ALL HOUSEHOLDS*		**81,140**	**78,455**	**386**	**112**	**107**	**995**	**221**	**101**	**223**	**171**	**369**	**1,809**
1 adult of pensionable age	0	12,667	12,583	24	7	1	25	2	1	10	-	14	283
1 adult under pensionable age	0	11,484	11,046	107	29	22	91	20	8	39	23	99	323
1 adult any age	1 or more	3,709	3,558	40	6	15	33	11	3	9	12	22	51
2 adults (1 male and 1 female)	0	23,186	22,795	58	15	22	129	20	9	38	29	71	530
	1 or more	14,451	13,658	66	32	25	341	82	48	61	50	88	207
2 adults (same sex)	0	2,440	2,372	16	4	3	11	6	2	4	6	16	64
	1 or more	466	436	6	2	4	8	4	1	1	2	2	6
3 or more adults (male(s) and female(s))	0	8,148	7,856	42	7	10	141	23	2	25	18	24	224
	1 or more	3,905	3,504	20	7	5	210	50	26	29	26	28	95
3 or more adults (same sex)	0	576	548	3	3	-	4	3	-	7	5	3	24
	1 or more	75	69	4	-	-	1	-	1	-	-	-	2
Households containing persons of pensionable age only (any number)		20,364	20,234	37	9	2	38	5	2	12	3	22	451
TOTAL PERSONS IN HOUSEHOLDS		**193,866**	**184,710**	**923**	**304**	**287**	**3,915**	**1,013**	**513**	**661**	**588**	**952**	**4,127**
All dependent children 0 - 18		41,919	38,711	226	96	90	1,419	462	274	169	201	271	657
Dependent children aged 0 - 4		13,886	12,910	76	32	33	382	129	87	55	78	104	181
Dependent children aged 5 - 15		25,372	23,427	127	62	50	895	287	165	88	114	157	398
Dependent children 0 - 17 included above		*41,409*	*38,263*	*222*	*96*	*90*	*1,390*	*446*	*273*	*162*	*197*	*270*	*644*
Persons pensionable age - 74		23,020	22,711	68	13	7	121	20	7	17	9	47	626
Persons aged 75 - 84		10,666	10,588	12	5	1	38	3	1	6	5	7	188
Persons aged 85 and over		2,416	2,396	-	-	2	13	2	-	1	1	1	28

Table 43 Household composition and ethnic group – continued

Note: * May include a small number of households with no resident adults

43. Households with residents; residents in households

Test Valley

Household composition – Adults (a)	Dependent children (b)	TOTAL HOUSE-HOLDS (c)	White (d)	Black Caribbean (e)	Black African (f)	Black other (g)	Indian (h)	Pakistani (i)	Bangladeshi (j)	Chinese (k)	Other groups Asian (l)	Other groups Other (m)	Household head born in Ireland (n)
ALL HOUSEHOLDS*		**38,391**	**38,080**	**46**	**13**	**21**	**85**	**10**	**7**	**52**	**25**	**52**	**507**
1 adult of pensionable age	0	4,757	4,751	3	-	-	1	-	-	-	-	2	70
1 adult under pensionable age	0	3,331	3,300	5	2	4	6	1	-	5	2	6	57
1 adult any age	1 or more	1,138	1,119	1	3	4	1	-	-	5	1	4	9
2 adults (1 male and 1 female)	0	12,011	11,950	11	1	4	14	3	-	9	8	11	161
	1 or more	9,010	8,907	14	3	3	34	3	3	19	7	17	75
2 adults (same sex)	0	916	909	-	-	1	2	-	-	3	2	2	12
	1 or more	192	189	-	-	-	-	-	-	3	-	-	4
3 or more adults (male(s) and female(s))	0	4,663	4,630	6	2	2	8	3	-	3	2	7	75
	1 or more	2,207	2,166	5	2	2	16	-	3	8	2	3	41
3 or more adults (same sex)	0	131	127	-	-	1	2	-	1	-	1	-	3
	1 or more	26	25	-	-	-	-	-	-	-	-	-	-
Households containing persons of pensionable age only (any number)		8,418	8,410	3	-	-	1	-	-	-	2	2	123
TOTAL PERSONS IN HOUSEHOLDS		**99,463**	**98,443**	**133**	**42**	**56**	**311**	**28**	**45**	**180**	**75**	**150**	**1,275**
All dependent children 0 - 18		22,563	22,234	40	16	15	99	6	21	68	21	43	228
Dependent children aged 0 - 4		6,518	6,433	6	4	2	31	1	5	16	2	18	52
Dependent children aged 5 - 15		14,128	13,929	24	8	11	56	5	15	41	16	23	157
Dependent children 0 - 17 included above		*22,128*	*21,817*	*36*	*16*	*15*	*91*	*6*	*21*	*63*	*20*	*43*	*225*
Persons pensionable age - 74		10,165	10,141	9	-	-	3	2	1	1	3	5	161
Persons aged 75 - 84		4,649	4,644	1	-	-	1	-	1	1	2	-	75
Persons aged 85 and over		987	985	-	-	-	1	-	-	-	1	-	8

Table 43 Household composition and ethnic group – **continued**

Note: * May include a small number of households with no resident adults

43. Households with residents; residents in households

Winchester

Household composition — Adults	Dependent children	TOTAL HOUSE-HOLDS	White	Black Caribbean	Black African	Black other	Indian	Pakistani	Bangladeshi	Chinese	Other groups Asian	Other groups Other	Household head born in Ireland
a	b	c	d	e	f	g	h	i	j	k	l	m	n
ALL HOUSEHOLDS*		**37,553**	**37,310**	**8**	**10**	**16**	**44**	**12**	**16**	**37**	**37**	**63**	**483**
1 adult of pensionable age	0	5,895	5,890	1	-	1	-	1	-	-	-	2	120
1 adult under pensionable age	0	3,466	3,434	-	2	4	7	2	-	4	3	10	43
1 adult any age	1 or more	850	836	1	-	2	-	1	1	2	4	3	10
2 adults (1 male and 1 female)	0	11,890	11,850	3	3	2	9	2	-	5	2	14	153
	1 or more	7,888	7,795	2	2	5	19	4	8	15	17	21	67
2 adults (same sex)	0	888	880	-	2	1	-	-	1	1	-	3	14
	1 or more	165	164	-	-	-	-	-	-	-	-	1	-
3 or more adults (male(s) and female(s))	0	4,317	4,292	-	-	1	5	-	2	8	4	5	56
	1 or more	2,030	2,009	1	1	-	3	2	3	2	5	4	17
3 or more adults (same sex)	0	144	141	-	-	-	1	-	1	-	1	-	3
	1 or more	16	16	-	-	-	-	-	-	-	-	-	-
Households containing persons of pensionable age only (any number)		10,042	10,031	2	-	1	-	2	-	-	1	5	176
TOTAL PERSONS IN HOUSEHOLDS		**93,721**	**92,974**	**21**	**27**	**36**	**134**	**37**	**80**	**117**	**127**	**168**	**1,086**
All dependent children 0 - 18		20,072	19,819	6	7	10	43	15	37	37	51	47	181
Dependent children aged 0 - 4		5,374	5,309	3	-	4	11	4	8	10	9	16	36
Dependent children aged 5 - 15		12,653	12,490	2	7	6	28	11	26	18	38	27	120
Dependent children 0 - 17 included above		*19,584*	*19,336*	*6*	*7*	*10*	*42*	*15*	*37*	*34*	*51*	*46*	*173*
Persons pensionable age - 74		11,332	11,317	3	-	1	1	3	-	-	1	6	178
Persons aged 75 - 84		5,462	5,454	-	-	-	1	1	-	1	2	4	87
Persons aged 85 and over		1,305	1,305	-	-	-	-	-	-	-	-	-	24

Table 44 Household composition and long-term illness

Note: * May include a small number of households with no resident adults

44. Households containing persons with limiting long-term illness; residents in such households

TOTAL HOUSE-HOLDS	TOTAL PERSONS		Total with limiting long-term illness		Persons with limiting long-term illness aged:				Household composition	
					0 - 4		5 - 15		Adults	Dependent children
	Males	Females	Males	Females	Males	Females	Males	Females		
a	b	c	d	e	f	g	h	i	j	k

HAMPSHIRE

a	b	c	d	e	f	g	h	i	j	k
124,419	127,751	144,405	69,467	82,752	948	743	2,494	1,869	ALL HOUSEHOLDS*	
39,039	11,107	27,932	11,107	27,932					1 adult	0
1,896	1,978	3,423	788	1,541	203	171	419	331		1 or more
46,465	46,465	46,465	32,859	29,603					2 adults (1 male and 1 female)	0
10,319	21,071	20,241	7,131	5,607	647	490	1,632	1,185		1 or more
4,048	2,694	5,402	1,648	3,376					2 adults (same sex)	0
451	539	1,097	160	419	24	10	67	45		1 or more
16,178	29,154	25,365	11,589	10,361					3 or more adults (male(s) and female(s))	0
5,405	13,637	13,440	3,686	3,446	74	69	371	303		1 or more
535	977	807	474	384					3 or more adults (same sex)	0
76	124	228	22	78	-	1	3	5		1 or more
									Households with:	
70,150	44,970	66,251	35,462	50,331	215	163	362	248	0 persons economically active	
28,526	36,522	35,849	16,859	17,583	464	377	960	696	1 person economically active	
24,389	30,757	30,786	14,100	15,211	372	302	794	596	- in employment	
4,137	5,765	5,063	2,759	2,372	92	75	166	100	- unemployed	
25,743	46,259	42,305	17,146	14,838	269	203	1,172	925	2 or more persons economically active	
25,166	45,125	41,416	16,712	14,479	261	197	1,154	912	- 1 or more in employment	
577	1,134	889	434	359	8	6	18	13	- all unemployed	
	54,137	35,545	18,840	10,962					Persons economically active	
	46,441	32,856	15,611	9,798					Persons in employment	

Basingstoke & Deane

a	b	c	d	e	f	g	h	i	j	k
9,455	10,402	11,650	5,228	6,351	69	80	216	182	ALL HOUSEHOLDS*	
2,659	751	1,908	751	1,908					1 adult	0
119	116	223	41	94	9	14	23	16		1 or more
3,434	3,434	3,434	2,353	2,213					2 adults (1 male and 1 female)	0
912	1,824	1,867	577	565	51	59	151	128		1 or more
255	158	352	89	218					2 adults (same sex)	0
32	34	84	10	28	2	1	4	1		1 or more
1,456	2,659	2,328	1,013	949					3 or more adults (male(s) and female(s))	0
539	1,341	1,366	358	333	7	6	38	37		1 or more
40	74	61	35	33					3 or more adults (same sex)	0
9	11	27	1	10	-	-	-	-		1 or more
									Households with:	
4,667	2,925	4,430	2,282	3,431	11	12	20	9	0 persons economically active	
2,242	2,878	2,929	1,294	1,405	29	44	73	66	1 person economically active	
1,976	2,503	2,574	1,118	1,247	24	35	66	57	- in employment	
266	375	355	176	158	5	9	7	9	- unemployed	
2,546	4,599	4,291	1,652	1,515	29	24	123	107	2 or more persons economically active	
2,501	4,514	4,216	1,615	1,486	29	23	122	106	- 1 or more in employment	
45	85	75	37	29	-	1	1	1	- all unemployed	
	5,068	3,411	1,711	1,058					Persons economically active	
	4,472	3,185	1,457	962					Persons in employment	

Persons with limiting long-term illness aged:															
16 - 29		30 - 44		45 - 54		55 - 59		60 - 64		65 - 74		75 - 84		85 and over	
Males	Females	Males	Females	Males	Females	Males	Females	Males	Females	Males	Females	Males	Females	Males	Females
l	m	n	o	p	q	r	s	t	u	v	w	x	y	z	aa
4,864	**4,412**	**7,546**	**7,260**	**7,498**	**7,981**	**5,858**	**5,554**	**8,308**	**7,003**	**16,881**	**19,587**	**12,197**	**20,827**	**2,873**	**7,516**
439	266	1,091	617	1,023	1,118	849	1,105	1,180	1,670	2,638	7,012	2,825	11,499	1,062	4,645
49	337	60	517	33	144	11	16	9	12	3	7	1	5	-	1
743	799	1,412	1,247	2,314	3,055	2,811	2,918	4,927	3,963	11,458	10,030	7,821	6,538	1,373	1,053
811	924	2,573	2,354	949	517	221	65	160	32	118	28	18	9	2	3
177	193	254	325	226	297	129	218	168	222	372	523	256	875	66	723
12	82	25	102	17	56	8	21	3	23	1	46	3	25	-	9
1,817	1,141	1,277	1,189	2,034	2,175	1,508	1,023	1,596	927	1,979	1,565	1,062	1,423	316	918
706	587	719	840	824	556	274	159	215	134	269	324	188	352	46	122
104	55	133	56	71	53	45	23	49	18	41	45	23	93	8	41
5	25	2	13	7	10	2	6	1	2	2	7	-	8	-	1
515	654	1,622	1,311	1,409	1,661	1,608	1,965	3,724	4,094	12,960	15,885	10,580	17,978	2,467	6,372
1,368	1,379	2,642	2,756	2,374	2,824	2,045	2,116	2,769	2,070	2,861	2,762	1,109	1,853	267	750
1,032	1,114	2,055	2,361	1,894	2,399	1,701	1,819	2,352	1,837	2,639	2,459	1,021	1,644	240	680
336	265	587	395	480	425	344	297	417	233	222	303	88	209	27	70
2,981	2,379	3,282	3,193	3,715	3,496	2,205	1,473	1,815	839	1,060	940	508	996	139	394
2,898	2,304	3,176	3,112	3,617	3,404	2,155	1,433	1,771	818	1,042	924	499	987	139	388
83	75	106	81	98	92	50	40	44	21	18	16	9	9	-	6
3,065	2,035	4,842	3,132	4,441	2,967	2,709	1,369	2,434	766	1,016	505	294	156	39	32
2,353	1,694	3,987	2,825	3,724	2,632	2,219	1,231	1,993	740	1,003	493	293	154	39	29
439	**410**	**616**	**633**	**619**	**708**	**459**	**471**	**627**	**533**	**1,170**	**1,386**	**822**	**1,451**	**191**	**497**
34	23	82	39	74	75	54	78	74	98	171	495	192	812	70	288
1	21	3	32	3	6	1	2	1	2	-	1	-	-	-	-
69	74	128	107	172	268	222	247	368	313	790	697	511	434	93	73
70	84	198	235	79	50	16	5	8	1	3	2	1	1	-	-
10	19	12	32	12	18	10	13	9	9	20	35	10	53	6	39
1	3	1	7	1	3	1	4	-	1	-	4	-	3	-	1
176	118	112	105	186	215	128	97	144	97	158	121	89	110	20	86
66	58	72	70	85	62	25	23	20	10	25	30	18	27	2	10
12	6	8	5	6	9	2	2	3	2	3	1	1	8	-	-
-	4	-	1	1	2	-	-	-	-	-	-	-	3	-	-
38	51	101	92	88	116	94	140	220	268	861	1,091	689	1,243	160	409
113	108	207	214	177	220	158	183	222	171	206	221	89	127	20	51
94	96	173	188	147	197	132	160	188	152	192	199	82	118	20	45
19	12	34	26	30	23	26	23	34	19	14	22	7	9	-	6
288	251	308	327	354	372	207	148	185	94	103	74	44	81	11	37
282	246	296	316	347	366	202	146	182	93	101	73	43	81	11	36
6	5	12	11	7	6	5	2	3	1	2	1	1	-	-	1
282	207	425	314	415	302	250	121	219	70	92	31	26	11	2	2
231	180	365	286	358	278	207	109	176	66	92	30	26	11	2	2

Table 44 Household composition and long-term illness – **continued**

Note: * May include a small number of households with no resident adults

44. Households containing persons with limiting long-term illness; residents in such households

TOTAL HOUSE-HOLDS	TOTAL PERSONS		Total with limiting long-term illness		Persons with limiting long-term illness aged:				Household composition	
					0 - 4		5 - 15			
	Males	Females	Males	Females	Males	Females	Males	Females	Adults	Dependent children
a	b	c	d	e	f	g	h	i	j	k
					East Hampshire					
7,134	**7,539**	**8,417**	**3,959**	**4,740**	**61**	**26**	**148**	**82**	**ALL HOUSEHOLDS***	
2,072	549	1,523	549	1,523					1 adult	0
87	93	154	41	63	13	3	21	12		1 or more
2,753	2,753	2,753	1,935	1,695					2 adults (1 male and 1 female)	0
652	1,318	1,223	443	339	44	19	91	50		1 or more
202	116	288	73	180					2 adults (same sex)	0
20	24	53	5	25	-	2	5	3		1 or more
959	1,732	1,513	653	660					3 or more adults (male(s) and female(s))	0
362	913	857	245	233	4	2	30	17		1 or more
24	31	47	13	20					3 or more adults (same sex)	0
3	10	6	2	2	-	-	1	-		1 or more
									Households with:	
3,834	2,427	3,633	1,906	2,760	10	4	12	3	0 persons economically active	
1,617	2,088	2,029	964	976	35	16	53	25	1 person economically active	
1,446	1,841	1,816	846	880	30	15	45	23	- in employment	
171	247	213	118	96	5	1	8	2	- unemployed	
1,683	3,024	2,755	1,089	1,004	16	6	83	54	2 or more persons economically active	
1,665	2,992	2,727	1,077	991	16	6	83	54	- 1 or more in employment	
18	32	28	12	13	-	-	-	-	- all unemployed	
	3,382	2,245	1,180	725					Persons economically active	
	3,060	2,116	1,046	666					Persons in employment	
					Eastleigh					
7,552	**7,763**	**8,809**	**4,193**	**5,058**	**55**	**43**	**152**	**115**	**ALL HOUSEHOLDS***	
2,200	595	1,605	595	1,605					1 adult	0
99	107	186	43	88	7	9	25	22		1 or more
3,010	3,010	3,010	2,103	1,928					2 adults (1 male and 1 female)	0
668	1,341	1,278	441	356	42	30	105	71		1 or more
232	150	314	93	193					2 adults (same sex)	0
23	31	55	7	23	1	1	2	4		1 or more
991	1,751	1,542	701	636					3 or more adults (male(s) and female(s))	0
304	738	777	188	213	5	3	20	18		1 or more
22	40	30	22	13					3 or more adults (same sex)	0
3	-	12	-	3	-	-	-	-		1 or more
									Households with:	
4,165	2,708	3,940	2,141	2,997	10	7	13	11	0 persons economically active	
1,773	2,270	2,241	1,021	1,117	33	24	68	49	1 person economically active	
1,595	2,030	2,031	897	1,013	27	23	64	45	- in employment	
178	240	210	124	104	6	1	4	4	- unemployed	
1,614	2,785	2,628	1,031	944	12	12	71	55	2 or more persons economically active	
1,597	2,744	2,609	1,013	936	12	12	70	55	- 1 or more in employment	
17	41	19	18	8	-	-	1	-	- all unemployed	
	3,320	2,228	1,148	707					Persons economically active	
	2,976	2,117	987	662					Persons in employment	

						Persons with limiting long-term illness aged:									
16 - 29		30 - 44		45 - 54		55 - 59		60 - 64		65 - 74		75 - 84		85 and over	
Males	Females	Males	Females	Males	Females	Males	Females	Males	Females	Males	Females	Males	Females	Males	Females
l	m	n	o	p	q	r	s	t	u	v	w	x	y	z	aa
279	259	412	450	412	476	317	299	460	371	981	1,072	718	1,220	171	485
18	7	47	35	33	49	26	50	61	67	147	369	160	659	57	287
2	11	2	24	1	11	1	-	-	1	1	-	-	1	-	-
40	53	100	84	140	175	160	154	281	222	655	533	465	403	94	71
58	56	147	160	69	41	14	4	10	5	9	3	1	1	-	-
4	7	8	17	15	19	5	7	6	4	17	34	13	41	5	51
-	2	-	5	-	2	-	3	-	1	-	6	-	1	-	-
105	63	57	71	103	143	91	73	86	59	129	104	68	86	14	61
49	51	47	51	49	32	20	7	15	10	20	21	10	28	1	14
2	8	4	3	2	3	-	1	1	2	3	2	1	-	-	1
1	1	-	-	-	1	-	-	-	-	-	-	-	-	-	-
16	13	66	63	58	89	67	95	178	197	731	840	618	1,054	150	402
83	75	155	180	116	146	105	109	166	118	171	154	64	97	16	56
70	67	133	163	98	126	94	96	140	108	160	144	61	87	15	51
13	8	22	17	18	20	11	13	26	10	11	10	3	10	1	5
180	171	191	207	238	241	145	95	116	56	79	78	36	69	5	27
178	169	188	202	235	239	143	92	115	56	79	78	35	68	5	27
2	2	3	5	3	2	2	3	1	-	-	-	1	1	-	-
159	133	288	202	285	200	179	84	174	44	71	46	20	12	4	4
129	119	256	184	258	181	161	78	147	44	71	44	20	12	4	4
261	269	465	475	439	476	346	337	562	456	1,048	1,217	689	1,203	176	467
25	13	59	39	56	46	40	68	56	97	147	441	145	636	67	265
3	13	5	34	-	9	2	1	1	-	-	-	-	-	-	-
38	74	96	74	140	203	183	193	357	263	739	629	461	411	89	81
37	52	165	166	54	30	22	5	12	1	2	1	2	-	-	-
14	6	17	21	8	16	9	11	9	14	26	29	7	46	3	50
-	6	2	4	-	1	1	1	1	1	-	3	-	1	-	1
101	60	84	77	125	146	79	48	111	70	124	93	63	79	14	63
37	42	30	60	54	23	8	7	11	10	10	17	10	29	3	4
6	1	7	-	2	1	2	3	4	-	-	4	1	1	-	3
-	2	-	-	-	1	-	-	-	-	-	-	-	-	-	-
32	29	87	74	64	79	94	127	258	258	820	996	604	1,025	159	391
64	99	161	182	144	156	132	124	179	137	176	167	52	121	12	58
53	90	140	166	129	142	112	108	149	125	164	152	49	110	10	52
11	9	21	16	15	14	20	16	30	12	12	15	3	11	2	6
165	141	217	219	231	241	120	86	125	61	52	54	33	57	5	18
164	141	210	219	226	236	119	85	122	59	52	54	33	57	5	18
1	-	7	-	5	5	1	1	3	2	-	-	-	-	-	-
179	125	304	220	274	199	161	81	168	47	48	27	13	7	1	1
145	115	271	210	244	183	132	74	135	47	46	25	13	7	1	1

Table 44 Household composition and long-term illness – **continued**

Note: * May include a small number of households with no resident adults

44. Households containing persons with limiting long-term illness; residents in such households

TOTAL HOUSE-HOLDS	TOTAL PERSONS		Total with limiting long-term illness		Persons with limiting long-term illness aged:				Household composition	
					0 - 4		5 - 15		Adults	Dependent children
	Males	Females	Males	Females	Males	Females	Males	Females		
a	b	c	d	e	f	g	h	i	j	k

Fareham

7,357	7,540	8,537	4,147	4,868	47	31	147	91	ALL HOUSEHOLDS*	
2,006	508	1,498	508	1,498					1 adult	0
67	70	114	33	49	5	4	20	13		1 or more
3,153	3,153	3,153	2,210	2,000					2 adults (1 male and 1 female)	0
593	1,206	1,132	410	304	37	23	106	66		1 or more
207	124	290	72	173					2 adults (same sex)	0
12	15	27	7	9	3	1	3	-		1 or more
1,019	1,773	1,589	715	635					3 or more adults (male(s) and female(s))	0
281	662	701	181	189	2	3	18	12		1 or more
17	28	25	11	9					3 or more adults (same sex)	0
2	1	8	-	2	-	-	-	-		1 or more
									Households with:	
4,195	2,797	4,002	2,194	2,976	6	4	16	2	0 persons economically active	
1,605	2,077	2,017	933	1,009	31	13	53	41	1 person economically active	
1,443	1,857	1,819	821	910	27	11	43	38	- in employment	
162	220	198	112	99	4	2	10	3	- unemployed	
1,557	2,666	2,518	1,020	883	10	14	78	48	2 or more persons economically active	
1,533	2,617	2,486	1,004	868	10	14	78	47	- 1 or more in employment	
24	49	32	16	15	-	-	-	1	- all unemployed	
	3,185	2,054	1,091	614					Persons economically active	
	2,826	1,923	930	566					Persons in employment	

Gosport

6,313	6,430	7,374	3,427	4,320	71	45	167	120	ALL HOUSEHOLDS*	
2,004	510	1,494	510	1,494					1 adult	0
127	125	224	52	111	12	6	29	30		1 or more
2,285	2,285	2,285	1,604	1,483					2 adults (1 male and 1 female)	0
624	1,295	1,211	413	354	50	34	98	69		1 or more
189	104	274	60	174					2 adults (same sex)	0
32	38	87	16	29	1	1	9	4		1 or more
765	1,369	1,179	536	504					3 or more adults (male(s) and female(s))	0
257	646	583	201	155	8	4	30	17		1 or more
28	56	33	33	15					3 or more adults (same sex)	0
1	-	4	-	1	-	-	-	-		1 or more
									Households with:	
3,568	2,185	3,410	1,729	2,650	15	7	26	21	0 persons economically active	
1,421	1,897	1,834	808	891	28	24	60	48	1 person economically active	
1,206	1,566	1,560	661	772	18	20	45	41	- in employment	
215	331	274	147	119	10	4	15	7	- unemployed	
1,324	2,348	2,130	890	779	28	14	81	51	2 or more persons economically active	
1,286	2,273	2,069	861	752	26	13	81	51	- 1 or more in employment	
38	75	61	29	27	2	1	-	-	- all unemployed	
	2,743	1,740	944	559					Persons economically active	
	2,323	1,584	767	488					Persons in employment	

Persons with limiting long-term illness aged:															
16 - 29		30 - 44		45 - 54		55 - 59		60 - 64		65 - 74		75 - 84		85 and over	
Males	Females	Males	Females	Males	Females	Males	Females	Males	Females	Males	Females	Males	Females	Males	Females
l	m	n	o	p	q	r	s	t	u	v	w	x	y	z	aa
246	**200**	**397**	**386**	**390**	**459**	**364**	**375**	**532**	**474**	**1,087**	**1,170**	**781**	**1,259**	**156**	**423**
12	5	38	19	27	57	29	58	50	99	143	347	159	650	50	263
2	13	1	14	5	5	-	-	-	-	-	-	-	-	-	-
44	33	85	90	129	191	201	231	358	297	794	683	521	423	78	52
31	39	159	143	49	27	9	2	10	2	8	2	1	-	-	-
5	9	10	14	11	18	12	11	10	17	14	18	8	46	2	40
-	2	-	1	1	3	-	1	-	1	-	-	-	-	-	-
114	68	83	58	125	123	94	61	90	52	112	92	76	120	21	61
36	29	21	46	43	33	16	10	11	6	14	27	15	18	5	5
2	2	-	1	-	1	3	-	3	-	2	1	1	2	-	2
-	-	-	-	-	1	-	1	-	-	-	-	-	-	-	-
22	22	73	45	50	83	97	121	258	281	872	968	670	1,087	130	363
53	54	135	139	116	165	119	159	176	139	155	155	78	99	17	45
44	51	111	128	99	149	107	140	157	123	150	139	68	90	15	41
9	3	24	11	17	16	12	19	19	16	5	16	10	9	2	4
171	124	189	202	224	211	148	95	98	54	60	47	33	73	9	15
168	123	185	198	222	205	144	92	96	54	59	47	33	73	9	15
3	1	4	4	2	6	4	3	2	-	1	-	-	-	-	-
166	99	270	186	256	158	179	89	151	51	55	24	14	7	-	-
128	93	235	175	228	140	150	79	124	48	51	24	14	7	-	-
255	**270**	**418**	**387**	**334**	**382**	**303**	**297**	**367**	**361**	**796**	**1,017**	**574**	**1,066**	**142**	**375**
15	9	48	19	50	54	42	72	56	101	117	366	122	623	60	250
4	32	5	33	-	9	2	-	-	-	-	-	-	1	-	-
45	46	73	72	103	144	154	144	221	185	564	528	385	310	59	54
42	76	161	129	46	33	9	7	4	2	3	4	-	-	-	-
6	10	2	12	11	15	6	8	9	21	14	30	7	51	5	27
2	7	1	8	1	4	1	1	-	-	-	2	1	2	-	-
91	61	64	61	78	95	78	58	66	47	93	81	52	62	14	39
42	26	52	50	39	26	8	4	8	4	4	6	6	13	4	5
7	2	12	3	6	2	3	3	3	1	1	-	1	4	-	-
-	1	-	-	-	-	-	-	-	-	-	-	-	-	-	-
29	33	74	56	64	89	86	109	160	217	645	843	510	947	120	328
58	94	145	145	108	131	109	105	128	108	117	131	41	76	14	29
46	75	111	129	85	117	86	90	110	94	109	114	39	65	12	27
12	19	34	16	23	14	23	15	18	14	8	17	2	11	2	2
168	143	199	186	162	162	108	83	79	36	34	43	23	43	8	18
163	137	191	181	155	154	105	82	78	34	33	42	21	41	8	17
5	6	8	5	7	8	3	1	1	2	1	1	2	2	-	1
164	136	278	164	193	131	140	69	122	36	34	15	9	3	4	5
128	109	224	147	156	114	112	61	102	34	33	15	8	3	4	5

Table 44 Household composition and long-term illness – **continued**

Note: * May include a small number of households with no resident adults

44. Households containing persons with limiting long-term illness; residents in such households

TOTAL HOUSE-HOLDS	TOTAL PERSONS		Total with limiting long-term illness		Persons with limiting long-term illness aged:				Household composition	
					0 - 4		5 - 15		Adults	Dependent children
	Males	Females	Males	Females	Males	Females	Males	Females		
a	b	c	d	e	f	g	h	i	j	k

Hart

TOTAL HOUSE-HOLDS	Males	Females	Males	Females	Males	Females	Males	Females	Adults	Dependent children
4,522	4,947	5,555	2,456	3,012	23	22	115	95	ALL HOUSEHOLDS*	
1,244	322	922	322	922					1 adult	0
44	44	75	16	39	2	4	11	7		1 or more
1,661	1,661	1,661	1,142	1,049					2 adults (1 male and 1 female)	0
455	905	886	282	271	17	16	86	73		1 or more
129	88	170	57	105					2 adults (same sex)	0
12	16	30	4	11	2	-	-	1		1 or more
683	1,197	1,133	453	420					3 or more adults (male(s) and female(s))	0
272	689	629	166	166	2	2	18	14		1 or more
20	24	39	14	27					3 or more adults (same sex)	0
2	1	10	-	2	-	-	-	-		1 or more
									Households with:	
2,183	1,321	2,094	1,049	1,603	2	4	8	5	0 persons economically active	
1,119	1,439	1,396	581	716	10	10	39	36	1 person economically active	
1,007	1,276	1,243	524	645	9	9	33	29	- in employment	
112	163	153	57	71	1	1	6	7	- unemployed	
1,220	2,187	2,065	826	693	11	8	68	54	2 or more persons economically active	
1,211	2,169	2,045	821	687	11	8	68	53	- 1 or more in employment	
9	18	20	5	6	-	-	-	1	- all unemployed	
	2,431	1,609	846	483					Persons economically active	
	2,204	1,523	747	451					Persons in employment	

Havant

TOTAL HOUSE-HOLDS	Males	Females	Males	Females	Males	Females	Males	Females	Adults	Dependent children
10,998	11,659	13,184	6,316	7,468	100	89	275	198	ALL HOUSEHOLDS*	
3,187	850	2,337	850	2,337					1 adult	0
212	243	365	93	167	22	21	52	37		1 or more
4,218	4,218	4,218	3,039	2,750					2 adults (1 male and 1 female)	0
968	2,022	1,962	714	525	63	57	171	121		1 or more
308	212	404	133	257					2 adults (same sex)	0
64	77	143	21	53	4	-	6	5		1 or more
1,458	2,629	2,276	1,060	964					3 or more adults (male(s) and female(s))	0
542	1,351	1,397	383	376	11	11	46	34		1 or more
37	51	66	22	34					3 or more adults (same sex)	0
4	6	16	1	5	-	-	-	1		1 or more
									Households with:	
6,183	4,168	6,004	3,243	4,491	26	20	55	37	0 persons economically active	
2,613	3,445	3,401	1,563	1,629	43	38	109	56	1 person economically active	
2,125	2,761	2,748	1,255	1,328	31	30	87	44	- in employment	
488	684	653	308	301	12	8	22	12	- unemployed	
2,202	4,046	3,779	1,510	1,348	31	31	111	105	2 or more persons economically active	
2,129	3,889	3,651	1,448	1,295	29	30	103	98	- 1 or more in employment	
73	157	128	62	53	2	1	8	7	- all unemployed	
	4,737	3,134	1,600	935					Persons economically active	
	3,880	2,851	1,250	806					Persons in employment	

Persons with limiting long-term illness aged:															
16 - 29		30 - 44		45 - 54		55 - 59		60 - 64		65 - 74		75 - 84		85 and over	
Males	Females	Males	Females	Males	Females	Males	Females	Males	Females	Males	Females	Males	Females	Males	Females
l	m	n	o	p	q	r	s	t	u	v	w	x	y	z	aa
215	197	296	296	283	304	179	183	274	221	553	632	433	771	85	291
16	4	34	16	30	31	14	27	32	32	69	204	99	437	28	171
-	9	2	17	1	1	-	-	-	-	-	1	-	-	-	-
32	46	61	59	83	118	102	102	166	144	396	332	264	215	38	33
24	39	105	111	37	29	5	2	2	-	5	1	1	-	-	-
6	4	12	4	7	11	2	6	3	4	11	18	13	31	3	27
-	2	1	2	1	3	-	1	-	-	-	1	-	1	-	-
95	60	45	43	89	82	51	40	61	35	60	55	40	57	12	48
37	24	29	38	34	26	5	3	10	6	12	18	15	25	4	10
5	9	7	6	1	3	-	1	-	-	-	1	1	5	-	2
-	-	-	-	-	-	-	1	-	-	-	1	-	-	-	-
9	15	33	33	32	30	42	57	105	92	394	494	360	644	64	229
38	50	89	119	92	125	53	75	90	92	113	93	44	79	13	37
33	45	72	105	79	117	49	67	83	83	109	84	44	71	13	35
5	5	17	14	13	8	4	8	7	9	4	9	-	8	-	2
168	132	174	144	159	149	84	51	79	37	46	45	29	48	8	25
168	131	172	143	158	146	83	51	78	37	46	45	29	48	8	25
-	1	2	1	1	3	1	-	1	-	-	-	-	-	-	-
144	110	232	139	197	135	98	44	102	36	56	11	12	7	5	1
118	99	202	128	179	129	89	42	87	34	55	11	12	7	5	1
424	385	659	633	705	831	542	609	843	714	1,621	1,821	936	1,636	211	552
27	23	80	56	89	108	58	115	95	156	215	658	201	883	85	338
6	30	6	60	3	15	3	-	1	1	-	1	-	1	-	1
55	39	103	114	220	320	280	312	529	420	1,146	939	616	543	90	63
90	97	248	177	87	54	21	9	16	5	15	2	2	2	1	1
14	20	20	20	13	27	8	28	21	15	37	39	17	53	3	55
3	12	4	15	2	3	1	3	-	4	-	6	1	2	-	3
158	96	108	103	198	231	143	115	159	95	177	136	90	109	27	79
64	64	86	82	89	70	27	23	18	18	29	36	9	31	4	7
7	2	3	5	4	3	1	3	4	-	2	4	-	12	1	5
-	2	1	1	-	-	-	1	-	-	-	-	-	-	-	-
47	68	158	150	138	179	154	232	401	427	1,268	1,498	810	1,410	186	470
127	128	240	240	220	302	185	222	279	210	268	241	78	141	14	51
87	89	172	189	169	234	154	189	234	180	240	209	69	118	12	46
40	39	68	51	51	68	31	33	45	30	28	32	9	23	2	5
250	189	261	243	347	350	203	155	163	77	85	82	48	85	11	31
240	181	246	234	337	334	198	149	155	74	82	80	47	85	11	30
10	8	15	9	10	16	5	6	8	3	3	2	1	-	-	1
276	165	389	232	400	285	236	131	205	61	71	45	23	14	-	2
196	123	291	200	319	247	195	118	155	59	71	43	23	14	-	2

Table 44 Household composition and long-term illness – **continued**

Note: * May include a small number of households with no resident adults

44. Households containing persons with limiting long-term illness; residents in such households

TOTAL HOUSE-HOLDS	TOTAL PERSONS		Total with limiting long-term illness		Persons with limiting long-term illness aged:				Household composition	
					0 - 4		5 - 15		Adults	Dependent children
	Males	Females	Males	Females	Males	Females	Males	Females		
a	b	c	d	e	f	g	h	i	j	k

New Forest

14,458	13,994	16,498	8,015	9,582	74	55	222	159	ALL HOUSEHOLDS*	
4,439	1,109	3,330	1,109	3,330					1 adult	0
142	134	244	54	105	14	10	26	17		1 or more
6,059	6,059	6,059	4,384	3,711					2 adults (1 male and 1 female)	0
1,008	2,005	1,974	692	503	54	41	157	116		1 or more
495	278	712	168	457					2 adults (same sex)	0
35	36	91	13	30	-	-	6	1		1 or more
1,722	3,056	2,734	1,229	1,091					3 or more adults (male(s) and female(s))	0
507	1,251	1,248	343	307	6	3	33	25		1 or more
45	54	94	21	42					3 or more adults (same sex)	0
5	11	11	2	5	-	-	-	-		1 or more
									Households with:	
9,018	5,871	8,610	4,613	6,407	16	10	22	17	0 persons economically active	
2,913	3,672	3,736	1,715	1,763	34	33	83	55	1 person economically active	
2,518	3,121	3,244	1,457	1,532	27	28	74	55	- in employment	
395	551	492	258	231	7	5	9	-	- unemployed	
2,527	4,451	4,152	1,687	1,412	24	12	117	87	2 or more persons economically active	
2,480	4,361	4,085	1,654	1,385	23	12	114	87	- 1 or more in employment	
47	90	67	33	27	1	-	3	-	- all unemployed	
	5,274	3,562	1,842	1,056					Persons economically active	
	4,567	3,329	1,554	953					Persons in employment	

Portsmouth

17,758	17,261	19,816	9,818	11,961	141	110	300	220	ALL HOUSEHOLDS*	
6,494	1,955	4,539	1,955	4,539					1 adult	0
322	331	592	128	269	33	33	70	56		1 or more
6,097	6,097	6,097	4,339	4,039					2 adults (1 male and 1 female)	0
1,149	2,355	2,250	862	614	95	67	177	126		1 or more
696	510	882	316	566					2 adults (same sex)	0
65	82	160	22	61	2	1	11	4		1 or more
2,114	3,846	3,284	1,559	1,386					3 or more adults (male(s) and female(s))	0
717	1,879	1,843	553	417	11	8	41	32		1 or more
82	173	107	79	41					3 or more adults (same sex)	0
20	33	60	5	27	-	1	1	2		1 or more
									Households with:	
10,657	6,599	9,884	5,240	7,727	33	24	54	38	0 persons economically active	
4,075	5,133	4,954	2,533	2,502	80	61	135	98	1 person economically active	
3,342	4,111	4,113	2,002	2,104	60	37	102	76	- in employment	
733	1,022	841	531	398	20	24	33	22	- unemployed	
3,026	5,529	4,978	2,045	1,732	28	25	111	84	2 or more persons economically active	
2,929	5,345	4,822	1,978	1,672	28	23	108	84	- 1 or more in employment	
97	184	156	67	60	-	2	3	-	- all unemployed	
	6,916	4,385	2,436	1,368					Persons economically active	
	5,632	3,950	1,914	1,182					Persons in employment	

	Persons with limiting long-term illness aged:														
16 - 29		30 - 44		45 - 54		55 - 59		60 - 64		65 - 74		75 - 84		85 and over	
Males	Females	Males	Females	Males	Females	Males	Females	Males	Females	Males	Females	Males	Females	Males	Females
l	m	n	o	p	q	r	s	t	u	v	w	x	y	z	aa
421	**391**	**673**	**661**	**694**	**741**	**624**	**518**	**944**	**781**	**2,172**	**2,342**	**1,741**	**2,841**	**450**	**1,093**
30	17	67	61	62	85	77	87	100	187	264	760	366	1,483	143	650
3	26	2	35	6	13	-	2	2	1	1	-	-	1	-	-
56	67	136	108	250	312	313	313	602	467	1,599	1,288	1,177	1,002	251	154
70	74	245	215	103	48	24	4	19	-	15	3	5	2	-	-
10	17	30	36	13	32	14	20	18	31	37	59	40	140	6	122
1	4	3	9	2	5	-	-	1	-	-	5	-	4	-	2
185	124	126	113	188	196	164	81	183	88	227	191	118	155	38	143
64	57	59	78	68	46	28	10	17	5	25	27	33	41	10	15
2	4	5	5	1	4	3	1	2	1	4	7	2	13	2	7
-	1	-	1	1	-	1	-	-	1	-	2	-	-	-	-
33	45	145	112	111	145	174	192	452	524	1,706	1,930	1,556	2,506	398	926
122	116	216	265	238	276	226	197	302	194	337	309	122	219	35	99
99	91	174	231	195	240	184	156	255	176	311	269	106	196	32	90
23	25	42	34	43	36	42	41	47	18	26	40	16	23	3	9
266	230	312	284	345	320	224	129	190	63	129	103	63	116	17	68
261	225	304	279	340	312	220	127	184	61	128	101	63	113	17	68
5	5	8	5	5	8	4	2	6	2	1	2	-	3	-	-
266	187	439	287	430	281	283	139	242	74	141	63	33	18	8	7
207	161	363	262	376	250	225	123	203	71	139	62	33	17	8	7
680	**555**	**1,070**	**948**	**1,125**	**1,146**	**803**	**799**	**1,180**	**979**	**2,375**	**2,989**	**1,749**	**3,131**	**395**	**1,084**
90	60	196	107	209	214	169	204	224	283	481	1,169	440	1,801	146	701
7	46	13	99	2	24	-	6	3	4	-	-	-	1	-	-
109	96	190	156	339	403	346	376	609	502	1,482	1,425	1,075	927	189	154
118	108	306	240	97	56	23	7	25	2	20	7	-	1	1	-
38	35	52	53	50	56	21	41	28	41	71	88	48	140	8	112
-	15	5	17	3	6	1	4	-	6	-	4	-	3	-	1
205	119	178	173	287	301	180	138	238	116	264	239	162	206	45	94
95	66	109	88	133	78	55	19	38	20	47	50	20	42	4	14
18	2	21	9	2	5	8	2	14	5	10	3	4	8	2	7
-	6	-	6	3	3	-	2	1	-	-	4	-	2	-	1
97	121	277	240	253	297	254	314	554	616	1,846	2,436	1,530	2,689	342	952
212	179	428	361	387	416	295	312	393	259	402	409	160	309	41	98
140	139	293	295	296	341	236	260	335	226	355	364	150	274	35	92
72	40	135	66	91	75	59	52	58	33	47	45	10	35	6	6
371	255	365	347	485	433	254	173	233	104	127	144	59	133	12	34
361	242	348	335	463	415	245	164	229	103	125	141	59	131	12	34
10	13	17	12	22	18	9	9	4	1	2	3	-	2	-	-
430	246	625	370	606	370	324	178	290	104	116	76	40	22	5	2
321	187	470	326	470	311	255	156	238	103	115	75	40	22	5	2

Table 44 Household composition and long-term illness – **continued**

Note: * May include a small number of households with no resident adults

44. Households containing persons with limiting long-term illness; residents in such households

TOTAL HOUSE-HOLDS	TOTAL PERSONS		Total with limiting long-term illness		Persons with limiting long-term illness aged:				Household composition	
					0 - 4		5 - 15			
	Males	Females	Males	Females	Males	Females	Males	Females	Adults	Dependent children
a	b	c	d	e	f	g	h	i	j	k

Rushmoor

5,486	5,976	6,537	3,060	3,588	64	34	124	118	**ALL HOUSEHOLDS***	
1,632	506	1,126	506	1,126					1 adult	0
102	95	188	37	82	12	9	14	20		1 or more
1,874	1,874	1,874	1,275	1,207					2 adults (1 male and 1 female)	0
619	1,266	1,210	421	340	49	19	93	77		1 or more
207	154	260	88	155					2 adults (same sex)	0
22	37	45	14	15	1	-	5	1		1 or more
747	1,347	1,148	532	467					3 or more adults (male(s) and female(s))	0
249	630	637	160	171	2	5	12	20		1 or more
30	59	44	24	23					3 or more adults (same sex)	0
3	8	4	3	1	-	-	-	-		1 or more
									Households with:	
2,766	1,769	2,595	1,392	1,967	11	9	14	19	0 persons economically active	
1,367	1,758	1,737	786	851	37	15	48	38	1 person economically active	
1,224	1,551	1,554	694	768	31	14	45	30	- in employment	
143	207	183	92	83	6	1	3	8	- unemployed	
1,353	2,449	2,205	882	770	16	10	62	61	2 or more persons economically active	
1,332	2,409	2,175	868	758	15	10	62	61	- 1 or more in employment	
21	40	30	14	12	1	-	-	-	- all unemployed	
	2,740	1,832	940	568					Persons economically active	
	2,453	1,720	823	514					Persons in employment	

Southampton

18,898	19,543	21,300	10,917	12,209	163	137	381	283	**ALL HOUSEHOLDS***	
6,528	2,246	4,282	2,246	4,282					1 adult	0
418	468	763	193	348	64	40	98	74		1 or more
6,445	6,445	6,445	4,584	4,142					2 adults (1 male and 1 female)	0
1,526	3,182	3,038	1,107	805	84	81	214	150		1 or more
660	522	798	324	488					2 adults (same sex)	0
87	96	209	30	91	4	3	14	11		1 or more
2,297	4,224	3,567	1,743	1,431					3 or more adults (male(s) and female(s))	0
776	2,022	1,959	528	517	11	13	54	48		1 or more
143	307	188	155	91					3 or more adults (same sex)	0
17	30	51	6	14	-	-	-	-		1 or more
									Households with:	
10,863	7,258	10,058	5,736	7,530	62	44	98	67	0 persons economically active	
4,534	5,789	5,568	2,763	2,730	68	68	143	111	1 person economically active	
3,575	4,473	4,449	2,120	2,225	55	51	99	86	- in employment	
959	1,316	1,119	643	505	13	17	44	25	- unemployed	
3,501	6,496	5,674	2,418	1,949	33	25	140	105	2 or more persons economically active	
3,354	6,208	5,461	2,306	1,867	32	24	138	103	- 1 or more in employment	
147	288	213	112	82	1	1	2	2	- all unemployed	
	7,855	5,043	2,789	1,545					Persons economically active	
	6,203	4,490	2,082	1,301					Persons in employment	

Persons with limiting long-term illness aged:															
16 - 29		30 - 44		45 - 54		55 - 59		60 - 64		65 - 74		75 - 84		85 and over	
Males	Females	Males	Females	Males	Females	Males	Females	Males	Females	Males	Females	Males	Females	Males	Females
l	m	n	o	p	q	r	s	t	u	v	w	x	y	z	aa
275	**266**	**426**	**375**	**339**	**382**	**243**	**256**	**281**	**258**	**700**	**783**	**503**	**837**	**105**	**279**
26	16	67	32	40	52	33	52	49	63	118	261	135	477	38	173
3	20	4	23	2	8	1	-	-	-	-	2	1	-	-	-
47	50	69	50	100	150	114	124	156	137	439	420	302	232	48	44
53	65	148	150	52	24	11	3	7	1	8	1	-	-	-	-
12	9	20	15	10	18	6	17	7	7	21	25	8	43	4	21
2	3	3	4	1	3	1	-	1	2	-	-	-	2	-	-
92	65	74	60	97	99	68	50	54	37	92	60	43	66	12	30
33	36	35	39	34	23	8	7	4	8	20	11	10	12	2	10
5	2	6	2	2	5	1	2	3	3	2	3	4	5	1	1
2	-	-	-	1	-	-	1	-	-	-	-	-	-	-	-
21	33	65	57	57	69	62	84	125	147	519	626	429	695	89	228
78	86	151	149	100	142	85	94	91	81	130	119	57	94	9	33
63	62	131	133	80	130	74	90	83	78	125	114	54	87	8	30
15	24	20	16	20	12	11	4	8	3	5	5	3	7	1	3
176	147	210	169	182	171	96	78	65	30	51	38	17	48	7	18
175	146	205	162	180	171	95	76	64	30	49	37	16	48	7	17
1	1	5	7	2	-	1	2	1	-	2	1	1	-	-	1
185	120	304	162	209	152	105	73	81	30	45	24	11	6	-	1
158	107	268	144	179	139	89	65	73	30	45	24	11	5	-	-
863	**772**	**1,324**	**1,162**	**1,315**	**1,213**	**1,012**	**852**	**1,319**	**1,079**	**2,486**	**2,853**	**1,677**	**2,836**	**377**	**1,022**
107	71	272	135	270	228	233	200	276	307	489	1,102	441	1,581	158	658
12	97	11	100	6	28	-	5	1	2	1	2	-	-	-	-
136	144	215	178	352	434	408	413	726	575	1,562	1,378	1,020	878	165	142
141	154	413	324	162	74	42	12	29	6	18	1	4	1	-	2
43	39	53	59	53	40	26	38	29	24	63	75	47	118	10	95
3	17	4	23	2	17	2	2	-	5	1	9	-	3	-	1
286	163	202	191	315	296	237	143	214	125	310	219	139	188	40	106
100	70	109	136	113	81	48	34	36	30	33	55	22	40	2	10
33	11	44	12	41	13	16	5	8	4	7	12	4	26	2	8
2	6	1	4	1	2	-	-	-	1	2	-	-	1	-	-
132	181	386	271	365	335	338	318	656	650	1,917	2,332	1,454	2,454	328	878
266	268	459	427	413	433	360	340	429	315	427	402	166	266	32	100
175	207	322	331	291	332	275	289	343	267	385	344	148	230	27	88
91	61	137	96	122	101	85	51	86	48	42	58	18	36	5	12
465	323	479	464	537	445	314	194	234	114	142	119	57	116	17	44
431	296	461	447	508	429	300	186	225	108	137	117	57	115	17	42
34	27	18	17	29	16	14	8	9	6	5	2	-	1	-	2
518	309	748	459	636	375	389	200	341	108	119	67	38	23	-	4
352	225	565	401	474	313	277	170	259	101	117	64	38	23	-	4

Table 44 Household composition and long-term illness – **continued**

Note: * May include a small number of households with no resident adults

44. Households containing persons with limiting long-term illness; residents in such households

TOTAL HOUSE-HOLDS	TOTAL PERSONS Males	TOTAL PERSONS Females	Total with limiting long-term illness Males	Total with limiting long-term illness Females	Persons with limiting long-term illness aged: 0 - 4 Males	0 - 4 Females	5 - 15 Males	5 - 15 Females	Household composition Adults	Dependent children
a	b	c	d	e	f	g	h	i	j	k
									Test Valley	
7,184	**7,559**	**8,339**	**4,032**	**4,720**	**41**	**38**	**137**	**101**	**ALL HOUSEHOLDS***	
2,125	575	1,550	575	1,550					1 adult	0
93	100	171	35	78	6	13	20	16		1 or more
2,747	2,747	2,747	1,957	1,702					2 adults (1 male and 1 female)	0
575	1,201	1,084	396	313	32	21	94	63		1 or more
231	142	320	89	198					2 adults (same sex)	0
20	25	46	6	19	2	-	1	3		1 or more
1,056	1,943	1,649	746	656					3 or more adults (male(s) and female(s))	0
306	759	733	196	184	1	4	21	17		1 or more
26	55	29	30	16					3 or more adults (same sex)	0
4	11	9	2	3	-	-	1	2		1 or more
									Households with:	
3,829	2,425	3,654	1,923	2,745	7	13	18	10	0 persons economically active	
1,607	2,048	1,936	948	981	19	14	49	31	1 person economically active	
1,432	1,817	1,728	841	869	17	14	47	30	- in employment	
175	231	208	107	112	2	-	2	1	- unemployed	
1,748	3,086	2,749	1,161	994	15	11	70	60	2 or more persons economically active	
1,726	3,048	2,722	1,142	980	15	11	70	60	- 1 or more in employment	
22	38	27	19	14	-	-	-	-	- all unemployed	
	3,503	2,293	1,265	717					Persons economically active	
	3,143	2,170	1,111	669					Persons in employment	
									Winchester	
7,304	**7,138**	**8,389**	**3,899**	**4,875**	**39**	**33**	**110**	**105**	**ALL HOUSEHOLDS***	
2,449	631	1,818	631	1,818					1 adult	0
64	52	124	22	48	4	5	10	11		1 or more
2,729	2,729	2,729	1,934	1,684					2 adults (1 male and 1 female)	0
570	1,151	1,126	373	318	29	23	89	75		1 or more
237	136	338	86	212					2 adults (same sex)	0
27	28	67	5	25	2	-	1	7		1 or more
911	1,628	1,423	649	562					3 or more adults (male(s) and female(s))	0
293	756	710	184	185	4	5	10	12		1 or more
21	25	44	15	20					3 or more adults (same sex)	0
3	2	10	-	3	-	-	-	-		1 or more
									Households with:	
4,222	2,517	3,937	2,014	3,047	6	5	6	9	0 persons economically active	
1,640	2,028	2,071	950	1,013	17	17	47	42	1 person economically active	
1,500	1,850	1,907	864	918	16	15	44	42	- in employment	
140	178	164	86	95	1	2	3	-	- unemployed	
1,442	2,593	2,381	935	815	16	11	57	54	2 or more persons economically active	
1,423	2,556	2,348	925	802	15	11	57	53	- 1 or more in employment	
19	37	33	10	13	1	-	-	1	- all unemployed	
	2,983	2,009	1,048	627					Persons economically active	
	2,702	1,898	943	578					Persons in employment	

Persons with limiting long-term illness aged:															
16 - 29		30 - 44		45 - 54		55 - 59		60 - 64		65 - 74		75 - 84		85 and over	
Males	Females	Males	Females	Males	Females	Males	Females	Males	Females	Males	Females	Males	Females	Males	Females
l	m	n	o	p	q	r	s	t	u	v	w	x	y	z	aa
287	**266**	**432**	**436**	**479**	**448**	**361**	**290**	**451**	**373**	**925**	**1,111**	**764**	**1,243**	**155**	**414**
25	8	55	26	44	60	40	45	46	81	124	390	181	701	60	239
2	13	4	29	3	6	-	-	-	1	-	-	-	-	-	-
47	51	89	82	170	175	173	166	275	212	640	589	497	358	66	69
39	46	148	147	52	27	17	3	5	5	8	-	1	1	-	-
9	13	10	23	12	11	5	6	11	13	19	28	17	61	6	43
-	6	1	4	1	1	-	-	-	2	-	2	1	1	-	-
125	83	71	74	144	140	110	64	102	59	117	88	55	95	22	53
36	41	41	49	50	25	11	6	10	-	15	11	10	24	1	7
4	3	13	2	3	3	4	-	2	-	2	3	2	2	-	3
-	1	-	-	-	-	1	-	-	-	-	-	-	-	-	-
22	28	83	68	78	73	73	79	179	195	679	883	657	1,057	127	339
91	68	125	159	150	151	115	107	137	116	172	170	74	121	16	44
73	55	114	144	126	132	103	95	113	105	163	153	70	104	15	37
18	13	11	15	24	19	12	12	24	11	9	17	4	17	1	7
174	170	224	209	251	224	173	104	135	62	74	58	33	65	12	31
169	167	219	207	249	221	172	101	132	60	73	57	31	65	12	31
5	3	5	2	2	3	1	3	3	2	1	1	2	-	-	-
174	119	300	201	304	204	208	91	173	53	79	32	22	15	5	2
142	108	266	185	270	187	183	88	144	53	79	32	22	15	5	1
219	**172**	**358**	**418**	**364**	**415**	**305**	**268**	**468**	**403**	**967**	**1,194**	**810**	**1,333**	**259**	**534**
14	10	46	33	39	59	34	49	61	99	153	450	184	756	100	362
4	6	2	17	1	9	1	-	-	-	-	-	-	-	-	-
25	26	67	73	116	162	155	143	279	226	652	589	527	402	113	63
38	34	130	157	62	24	8	2	13	2	4	1	-	-	-	-
6	5	8	19	11	16	5	12	8	22	22	45	21	52	5	41
-	3	-	3	2	5	-	1	-	-	-	4	-	2	-	-
84	61	73	60	99	108	85	55	88	47	116	86	67	90	37	55
47	23	29	53	33	31	15	6	17	7	15	15	10	22	4	11
1	3	3	3	1	1	2	-	2	-	5	4	1	7	-	2
-	1	-	-	-	-	-	-	-	-	-	-	-	2	-	-
17	15	74	50	51	77	73	97	178	222	702	948	693	1,167	214	457
63	54	131	176	113	161	103	89	177	130	187	191	84	104	28	49
55	47	109	159	100	142	95	79	162	120	176	174	81	94	26	46
8	7	22	17	13	19	8	10	15	10	11	17	3	10	2	3
139	103	153	192	200	177	129	82	113	51	78	55	33	62	17	28
138	100	151	189	197	176	129	82	111	49	78	52	32	62	17	28
1	3	2	3	3	1	-	-	2	2	-	3	1	-	-	-
122	79	240	196	236	175	157	69	166	52	89	44	33	11	5	1
98	68	211	177	213	160	144	68	150	50	89	44	33	11	5	-

Table 45 Migrant household heads

Note: * May include a small number of heads aged under 16

45. Households with residents

Tenure of household and economic activity of head	Households with head with different address one year before census: age and sex of head									
	Total migrant heads*		16 - 29*		30 - 44		45 up to pensionable age		Pensionable age and over	
	Males	Females	Males	Females	Males	Females	Males	Females	Males	Females
a	b	c	d	e	f	g	h	i	j	k
HAMPSHIRE										
TOTAL HEADS	43,302	17,888	18,343	8,981	15,903	4,423	6,575	1,631	2,481	2,853
Owner occupied	**23,936**	**6,761**	**9,177**	**2,744**	**9,624**	**2,167**	**3,961**	**849**	**1,174**	**1,001**
Economically active	22,222	5,143	9,110	2,532	9,556	1,854	3,442	678	114	79
Unemployed	896	219	284	78	325	73	283	64	4	4
Economically active students (included above)	*14*	*8*	*9*	*4*	*4*	*2*	*1*	*2*	-	-
Economically inactive	1,714	1,618	67	212	68	313	519	171	1,060	922
Rented privately or with a job or business	**13,737**	**5,634**	**7,189**	**3,815**	**4,716**	**1,243**	**1,606**	**371**	**226**	**205**
Economically active	12,750	4,314	6,693	2,990	4,558	990	1,446	306	53	28
Unemployed	1,428	487	802	322	425	120	197	43	4	2
Economically active students (included above)	*67*	*68*	*53*	*64*	*12*	*2*	*1*	*2*	*1*	-
Economically inactive	987	1,320	496	825	158	253	160	65	173	177
Rented from a housing association	**879**	**819**	**327**	**278**	**197**	**120**	**130**	**77**	**225**	**344**
Economically active	540	250	295	125	159	67	79	46	7	12
Unemployed	153	45	85	29	38	10	30	6	-	-
Economically active students (included above)	*3*	-	*1*	-	*2*	-	-	-	-	-
Economically inactive	339	569	32	153	38	53	51	31	218	332
Rented from a local authority or new town	**4,750**	**4,674**	**1,650**	**2,144**	**1,366**	**893**	**878**	**334**	**856**	**1,303**
Economically active	3,416	1,163	1,572	529	1,210	407	584	174	50	53
Unemployed	992	238	506	133	348	75	138	28	-	2
Economically active students (included above)	*3*	*4*	*1*	*4*	*2*	-	-	-	-	-
Economically inactive	1,334	3,511	78	1,615	156	486	294	160	806	1,250
Basingstoke & Deane										
TOTAL HEADS	3,841	1,412	1,736	719	1,402	367	547	128	156	198
Owner occupied	**2,456**	**611**	**1,053**	**297**	**1,002**	**201**	**339**	**57**	**62**	**56**
Economically active	2,358	501	1,049	274	1,000	177	306	45	3	5
Unemployed	65	17	20	5	26	8	19	4	-	-
Economically active students (included above)	-	-	-	-	-	-	-	-	-	-
Economically inactive	98	110	4	23	2	24	33	12	59	51
Rented privately or with a job or business	**887**	**354**	**472**	**226**	**285**	**80**	**118**	**24**	**12**	**24**
Economically active	866	313	468	214	281	71	109	23	8	5
Unemployed	65	14	29	11	26	1	10	2	-	-
Economically active students (included above)	-	*1*	-	*1*	-	-	-	-	-	-
Economically inactive	21	41	4	12	4	9	9	1	4	19
Rented from a housing association	**73**	**84**	**30**	**26**	**12**	**11**	**8**	**5**	**23**	**42**
Economically active	45	23	30	12	10	7	5	3	-	1
Unemployed	7	4	3	3	3	-	1	1	-	-
Economically active students (included above)	-	-	-	-	-	-	-	-	-	-
Economically inactive	28	61	-	14	2	4	3	2	23	41
Rented from a local authority or new town	**425**	**363**	**181**	**170**	**103**	**75**	**82**	**42**	**59**	**76**
Economically active	336	115	174	54	99	37	59	22	4	2
Unemployed	77	13	44	8	24	3	9	2	-	-
Economically active students (included above)	-	*1*	-	*1*	-	-	-	-	-	-
Economically inactive	89	248	7	116	4	38	23	20	55	74

Males	Females	Males	Females	Males	Females	Males	Females	Males	Females	Tenure of household and economic activity of head
		16 - 29*		30 - 44		45 up to pensionable age		Pensionable age and over		
TOTAL HOUSEHOLD HEADS*										All households: age and sex of head
l	m	n	o	p	q	r	s	t	u	a

l	m	n	o	p	q	r	s	t	u	a
434,882	168,375	56,858	25,077	140,212	34,697	150,959	26,974	86,853	81,627	TOTAL HEADS
337,855	100,124	37,637	10,627	113,914	22,446	124,683	18,660	61,621	48,391	Owner occupied
266,137	45,558	37,259	9,012	112,789	18,622	110,158	14,346	5,931	3,578	Economically active
10,807	1,769	1,500	334	3,825	657	5,445	723	37	55	Unemployed
										Economically active students
93	*76*	*20*	*21*	*46*	*43*	*26*	*11*	*1*	*1*	*(included above)*
71,718	54,566	378	1,615	1,125	3,824	14,525	4,314	55,690	44,813	Economically inactive
										Rented privately or with a job
41,163	18,031	12,885	6,576	13,171	3,273	9,223	1,832	5,884	6,350	**or business**
33,901	9,480	12,079	5,001	12,773	2,583	8,244	1,390	805	506	Economically active
3,219	922	1,338	514	1,015	250	854	143	12	15	Unemployed
										Economically active students
102	*98*	*80*	*91*	*20*	*3*	*1*	*4*	*1*	*-*	*(included above)*
7,262	8,551	806	1,575	398	690	979	442	5,079	5,844	Economically inactive
										Rented from a housing
5,330	6,621	686	638	1,035	661	1,106	535	2,503	4,787	**association**
2,440	1,166	619	295	902	401	790	328	129	142	Economically active
466	159	170	58	159	52	136	48	1	1	Unemployed
										Economically active students
5	*5*	*2*	*3*	*3*	*1*	*-*	*1*	*-*	*-*	*(included above)*
2,890	5,455	67	343	133	260	316	207	2,374	4,645	Economically inactive
										Rented from a local authority
50,534	43,599	5,650	7,236	12,092	8,317	15,947	5,947	16,845	22,099	**or new town**
29,587	10,914	5,375	2,071	11,066	4,389	11,971	3,565	1,175	889	Economically active
6,450	1,480	1,652	396	2,415	500	2,369	562	14	22	Unemployed
										Economically active students
15	*23*	*5*	*9*	*8*	*10*	*2*	*4*	*-*	*-*	*(included above)*
20,947	32,685	275	5,165	1,026	3,928	3,976	2,382	15,670	21,210	Economically inactive
41,021	13,302	5,934	2,261	14,425	3,192	14,417	2,248	6,245	5,601	TOTAL HEADS
31,225	7,384	4,395	1,181	11,783	2,059	11,339	1,450	3,708	2,694	Owner occupied
26,882	4,252	4,375	1,053	11,704	1,778	10,344	1,160	459	261	Economically active
869	135	121	24	317	63	428	47	3	1	Unemployed
										Economically active students
5	*1*	*-*	*-*	*4*	*-*	*1*	*1*	*-*	*-*	*(included above)*
4,343	3,132	20	128	79	281	995	290	3,249	2,433	Economically inactive
										Rented privately or with a job
3,484	1,187	846	395	1,138	228	954	129	546	435	**or business**
2,967	718	839	357	1,122	199	891	106	115	56	Economically active
136	31	45	19	49	5	42	6	-	1	Unemployed
										Economically active students
1	*2*	*1*	*2*	*-*	*-*	*-*	*-*	*-*	*-*	*(included above)*
517	469	7	38	16	29	63	23	431	379	Economically inactive
										Rented from a housing
586	642	78	69	150	94	149	64	209	415	**association**
346	145	73	34	142	59	120	41	11	11	Economically active
46	11	9	4	23	4	14	3	-	-	Unemployed
										Economically active students
-	*-*	*-*	*-*	*-*	*-*	*-*	*-*	*-*	*-*	*(included above)*
240	497	5	35	8	35	29	23	198	404	Economically inactive
										Rented from a local authority
5,726	4,089	615	616	1,354	811	1,975	605	1,782	2,057	**or new town**
3,698	1,265	590	252	1,285	506	1,646	412	177	95	Economically active
558	118	131	33	186	39	241	43	-	3	Unemployed
										Economically active students
-	*2*	*-*	*1*	*-*	*1*	*-*	*-*	*-*	*-*	*(included above)*
2,028	2,824	25	364	69	305	329	193	1,605	1,962	Economically inactive

Table 45 Migrant household heads – **continued**

Note: * May include a small number of heads aged under 16

45. Households with residents

Tenure of household and economic activity of head	Households with head with different address one year before census: age and sex of head									
	Total migrant heads*		16 - 29*		30 - 44		45 up to pensionable age		Pensionable age and over	
	Males	Females	Males	Females	Males	Females	Males	Females	Males	Females
a	b	c	d	e	f	g	h	i	j	k
East Hampshire										
TOTAL HEADS	2,846	1,038	967	434	1,220	311	495	120	164	173
Owner occupied	1,758	491	515	155	803	174	347	80	93	82
Economically active	1,631	361	514	145	800	139	305	68	12	9
Unemployed	53	15	9	3	22	5	22	7	-	-
Economically active students (included above)	*1*	-	-	-	-	-	*1*	-	-	-
Economically inactive	127	130	1	10	3	35	42	12	81	73
Rented privately or with a job or business	824	272	341	153	357	88	108	21	18	10
Economically active	790	219	335	131	350	70	104	16	1	2
Unemployed	33	17	13	7	13	8	7	2	-	-
Economically active students (included above)	*3*	*1*	*1*	*1*	*2*	-	-	-	-	-
Economically inactive	34	53	6	22	7	18	4	5	17	8
Rented from a housing association	41	37	22	16	7	4	5	4	7	13
Economically active	33	17	22	13	6	2	5	2	-	-
Unemployed	8	4	5	4	1	-	2	-	-	-
Economically active students (included above)	-	-	-	-	-	-	-	-	-	-
Economically inactive	8	20	-	3	1	2	-	2	7	13
Rented from a local authority or new town	223	238	89	110	53	45	35	15	46	68
Economically active	161	66	85	37	47	18	26	7	3	4
Unemployed	42	13	23	8	11	3	8	2	-	-
Economically active students (included above)	-	-	-	-	-	-	-	-	-	-
Economically inactive	62	172	4	73	6	27	9	8	43	64
Eastleigh										
TOTAL HEADS	2,875	1,026	1,268	489	1,072	274	394	100	141	163
Owner occupied	2,119	551	913	239	841	167	289	66	76	79
Economically active	2,012	425	909	232	837	134	259	56	7	3
Unemployed	79	18	29	6	30	8	19	4	1	-
Economically active students (included above)	-	*2*	-	*1*	-	*1*	-	-	-	-
Economically inactive	107	126	4	7	4	33	30	10	69	76
Rented privately or with a job or business	533	219	274	128	181	64	71	19	7	8
Economically active	510	169	266	104	175	45	68	18	1	2
Unemployed	69	21	36	14	22	2	11	4	-	1
Economically active students (included above)	*2*	*1*	*2*	*1*	-	-	-	-	-	-
Economically inactive	23	50	8	24	6	19	3	1	6	6
Rented from a housing association	39	63	17	27	4	3	5	5	13	28
Economically active	17	18	13	15	3	1	1	1	-	1
Unemployed	2	4	-	4	1	-	1	-	-	-
Economically active students (included above)	-	-	-	-	-	-	-	-	-	-
Economically inactive	22	45	4	12	1	2	4	4	13	27
Rented from a local authority or new town	184	193	64	95	46	40	29	10	45	48
Economically active	123	51	63	20	45	24	14	5	1	2
Unemployed	27	6	14	3	8	2	5	1	-	-
Economically active students (included above)	-	-	-	-	-	-	-	-	-	-
Economically inactive	61	142	1	75	1	16	15	5	44	46

All households: age and sex of head										Tenure of household and economic activity of head
TOTAL HOUSEHOLD HEADS*		16 - 29*		30 - 44		45 up to pensionable age		Pensionable age and over		
Males	Females	Males	Females	Males	Females	Males	Females	Males	Females	
l	m	n	o	p	q	r	s	t	u	a
29,150	10,008	3,060	1,146	9,934	2,068	10,620	1,809	5,536	4,985	**TOTAL HEADS**
23,776	6,712	2,116	553	8,298	1,516	9,144	1,390	4,218	3,253	**Owner occupied**
19,099	3,075	2,094	475	8,230	1,225	8,254	1,100	521	275	Economically active
588	96	57	16	219	34	311	44	1	2	Unemployed
										Economically active students
12	*1*	*2*	-	*5*	*1*	*5*	-	-	-	*(included above)*
4,677	3,637	22	78	68	291	890	290	3,697	2,978	Economically inactive
										Rented privately or with a job
2,814	1,074	637	274	1,060	214	715	142	402	444	**or business**
2,402	568	630	231	1,047	175	673	107	52	55	Economically active
93	30	23	14	31	12	39	4	-	-	Unemployed
										Economically active students
3	*2*	*1*	*2*	*2*	-	-	-	-	-	*(included above)*
412	506	7	43	13	39	42	35	350	389	Economically inactive
										Rented from a housing
181	254	36	26	33	21	31	18	81	189	**association**
92	52	34	20	27	9	26	13	5	10	Economically active
13	6	8	5	1	-	4	1	-	-	Unemployed
										Economically active students
-	-	-	-	-	-	-	-	-	-	*(included above)*
89	202	2	6	6	12	5	5	76	179	Economically inactive
										Rented from a local authority
2,379	1,968	271	293	543	317	730	259	835	1,099	**or new town**
1,412	509	258	104	499	182	578	163	77	60	Economically active
210	53	67	19	76	12	67	20	-	2	Unemployed
										Economically active students
-	-	-	-	-	-	-	-	-	-	*(included above)*
967	1,459	13	189	44	135	152	96	758	1,039	Economically inactive
31,186	10,033	4,170	1,459	10,974	2,229	10,623	1,587	5,419	4,758	**TOTAL HEADS**
26,825	6,728	3,420	889	9,977	1,734	9,563	1,265	3,865	2,840	**Owner occupied**
22,135	3,422	3,391	791	9,887	1,421	8,522	1,002	335	208	Economically active
825	121	133	24	289	48	399	42	4	7	Unemployed
										Economically active students
4	*6*	*1*	*1*	-	*5*	*2*	-	*1*	-	*(included above)*
4,690	3,306	29	98	90	313	1,041	263	3,530	2,632	Economically inactive
										Rented privately or with a job
1,425	746	436	222	394	125	323	70	272	329	**or business**
1,108	350	421	177	379	98	285	52	23	23	Economically active
118	31	59	20	31	4	28	6	-	1	Unemployed
										Economically active students
3	*2*	*2*	*2*	*1*	-	-	-	-	-	*(included above)*
317	396	15	45	15	27	38	18	249	306	Economically inactive
										Rented from a housing
343	427	43	52	44	21	59	22	197	332	**association**
130	62	36	29	43	10	43	11	8	12	Economically active
17	8	7	7	7	1	3	-	-	-	Unemployed
										Economically active students
1	*1*	-	*1*	*1*	-	-	-	-	-	*(included above)*
213	365	7	23	1	11	16	11	189	320	Economically inactive
										Rented from a local authority
2,593	2,132	271	296	559	349	678	230	1,085	1,257	**or new town**
1,332	462	261	89	522	193	485	140	64	40	Economically active
251	42	69	12	98	10	83	19	1	1	Unemployed
										Economically active students
-	*1*	-	-	-	*1*	-	-	-	-	*(included above)*
1,261	1,670	10	207	37	156	193	90	1,021	1,217	Economically inactive

Table 45 Migrant household heads – **continued**

Note: * May include a small number of heads aged under 16

45. Households with residents

Tenure of household and economic activity of head	Households with head with different address one year before census: age and sex of head									
	Total migrant heads*		16 - 29*		30 - 44		45 up to pensionable age		Pensionable age and over	
	Males	Females	Males	Females	Males	Females	Males	Females	Males	Females
a	b	c	d	e	f	g	h	i	j	k
Fareham										
TOTAL HEADS	2,544	868	876	325	1,044	239	456	108	168	196
Owner occupied	1,849	511	605	172	784	174	349	78	111	87
Economically active	1,686	369	602	157	775	148	297	63	12	1
Unemployed	58	18	14	8	20	5	23	5	1	-
Economically active students (included above)	3	-	2	-	1	-	-	-	-	-
Economically inactive	163	142	3	15	9	26	52	15	99	86
Rented privately or with a job or business	529	167	234	101	216	36	71	20	8	10
Economically active	507	134	232	84	215	34	60	16	-	-
Unemployed	36	9	15	7	15	1	6	1	-	-
Economically active students (included above)	4	-	3	-	-	-	1	-	-	-
Economically inactive	22	33	2	17	1	2	11	4	8	10
Rented from a housing association	14	20	5	6	1	2	4	2	4	10
Economically active	9	6	5	4	1	1	3	-	-	1
Unemployed	3	1	1	1	-	-	2	-	-	-
Economically active students (included above)	-	-	-	-	-	-	-	-	-	-
Economically inactive	5	14	-	2	-	1	1	2	4	9
Rented from a local authority or new town	152	170	32	46	43	27	32	8	45	89
Economically active	92	37	30	16	41	14	19	4	2	3
Unemployed	24	7	11	4	8	1	5	2	-	-
Economically active students (included above)	-	-	-	-	-	-	-	-	-	-
Economically inactive	60	133	2	30	2	13	13	4	43	86
Gosport										
TOTAL HEADS	2,343	938	1,143	486	844	236	240	85	116	131
Owner occupied	1,061	294	504	138	390	84	131	39	36	33
Economically active	1,003	230	502	123	387	74	113	31	1	2
Unemployed	34	13	14	3	13	7	7	3	-	-
Economically active students (included above)	2	-	1	-	1	-	-	-	-	-
Economically inactive	58	64	2	15	3	10	18	8	35	31
Rented privately or with a job or business	932	275	538	190	331	70	55	9	8	6
Economically active	910	200	534	140	327	51	49	9	-	-
Unemployed	52	16	29	9	18	7	5	-	-	-
Economically active students (included above)	4	-	3	-	1	-	-	-	-	-
Economically inactive	22	75	4	50	4	19	6	-	8	6
Rented from a housing association	50	45	12	10	5	3	2	2	31	30
Economically active	18	5	12	3	5	-	1	1	-	1
Unemployed	2	1	1	1	1	-	-	-	-	-
Economically active students (included above)	-	-	-	-	-	-	-	-	-	-
Economically inactive	32	40	-	7	-	3	1	1	31	29
Rented from a local authority or new town	300	324	89	148	118	79	52	35	41	62
Economically active	219	89	85	34	101	34	32	20	1	1
Unemployed	63	20	26	9	32	10	5	-	-	1
Economically active students (included above)	-	-	-	-	-	-	-	-	-	-
Economically inactive	81	235	4	114	17	45	20	15	40	61

TOTAL HOUSEHOLD HEADS*		16 - 29*		30 - 44		45 up to pensionable age		Pensionable age and over		Tenure of household and economic activity of head
Males	Females	Males	Females	Males	Females	Males	Females	Males	Females	
l	m	n	o	p	q	r	s	t	u	a
29,130	9,239	2,975	984	9,595	1,948	10,859	1,675	5,701	4,632	**TOTAL HEADS**
26,005	6,994	2,354	597	8,737	1,580	10,084	1,396	4,830	3,421	Owner occupied
20,286	3,112	2,336	509	8,649	1,324	8,940	1,067	361	212	Economically active
713	103	74	17	250	33	385	52	4	1	Unemployed
										Economically active students (included above)
10	6	2	1	6	5	2	-	-	-	
5,719	3,882	18	88	88	256	1,144	329	4,469	3,209	Economically inactive
1,419	628	440	187	496	121	286	67	197	253	Rented privately or with a job or business
1,207	298	435	151	493	89	260	43	19	15	Economically active
89	19	31	11	31	4	26	3	1	1	Unemployed
										Economically active students (included above)
4	1	3	1	-	-	1	-	-	-	
212	330	5	36	3	32	26	24	178	238	Economically inactive
95	159	13	9	9	7	8	8	65	135	Rented from a housing association
29	12	13	5	8	4	6	2	2	1	Economically active
8	4	4	1	2	2	2	1	-	-	Unemployed
										Economically active students (included above)
-	-	-	-	-	-	-	-	-	-	
66	147	-	4	1	3	2	6	63	134	Economically inactive
1,611	1,458	168	191	353	240	481	204	609	823	Rented from a local authority or new town
860	328	157	57	325	134	347	117	31	20	Economically active
194	33	50	8	64	7	79	18	1	-	Unemployed
										Economically active students (included above)
1	-	1	-	-	-	-	-	-	-	
751	1,130	11	134	28	106	134	87	578	803	Economically inactive
20,732	8,624	3,556	1,464	6,858	1,826	6,402	1,266	3,916	4,068	**TOTAL HEADS**
15,694	4,887	2,282	627	5,340	1,072	5,297	844	2,775	2,344	Owner occupied
12,379	2,192	2,272	518	5,286	894	4,656	648	165	132	Economically active
520	114	101	19	174	47	245	47	-	1	Unemployed
										Economically active students (included above)
6	3	1	-	3	3	2	-	-	-	
3,315	2,695	10	109	54	178	641	196	2,610	2,212	Economically inactive
2,196	836	946	344	811	202	270	52	169	238	Rented privately or with a job or business
1,991	447	934	239	799	145	242	45	16	18	Economically active
108	32	48	15	42	14	18	2	-	1	Unemployed
										Economically active students (included above)
6	-	5	-	1	-	-	-	-	-	
205	389	12	105	12	57	28	7	153	220	Economically inactive
258	373	24	21	27	14	16	13	191	325	Rented from a housing association
56	27	23	10	22	7	7	8	4	2	Economically active
6	2	2	2	2	-	1	-	1	-	Unemployed
										Economically active students (included above)
-	-	-	-	-	-	-	-	-	-	
202	346	1	11	5	7	9	5	187	323	Economically inactive
2,584	2,528	304	472	680	538	819	357	781	1,161	Rented from a local authority or new town
1,578	657	286	112	626	285	610	213	56	47	Economically active
377	99	90	23	154	42	131	31	2	3	Unemployed
										Economically active students (included above)
-	-	-	-	-	-	-	-	-	-	
1,006	1,871	18	360	54	253	209	144	725	1,114	Economically inactive

Table 45 Migrant household heads – **continued**

Note: * May include a small number of heads aged under 16

45. Households with residents

Tenure of household and economic activity of head	Households with head with different address one year before census: age and sex of head									
	Total migrant heads*		16 - 29*		30 - 44		45 up to pensionable age		Pensionable age and over	
	Males	Females	Males	Females	Males	Females	Males	Females	Males	Females
a	b	c	d	e	f	g	h	i	j	k

Hart

TOTAL HEADS	2,379	668	848	279	1,058	208	379	73	94	108
Owner occupied	1,547	360	470	121	747	129	266	47	64	63
Economically active	1,471	254	469	112	746	106	250	33	6	3
Unemployed	52	11	13	4	21	4	18	3	-	-
Economically active students (included above)	1	-	-	-	1	-	-	-	-	-
Economically inactive	76	106	1	9	1	23	16	14	58	60
Rented privately or with a job or business	720	204	331	114	286	61	94	22	9	7
Economically active	707	174	330	105	283	50	92	19	2	-
Unemployed	35	13	21	8	11	5	3	-	-	-
Economically active students (included above)	3	-	3	-	-	-	-	-	-	-
Economically inactive	13	30	1	9	3	11	2	3	7	7
Rented from a housing association	16	19	8	9	1	1	2	1	5	8
Economically active	9	3	8	1	1	1	-	1	-	-
Unemployed	-	-	-	-	-	-	-	-	-	-
Economically active students (included above)	-	-	-	-	-	-	-	-	-	-
Economically inactive	7	16	-	8	-	-	2	-	5	8
Rented from a local authority or new town	96	85	39	35	24	17	17	3	16	30
Economically active	81	24	39	10	24	12	13	-	5	2
Unemployed	14	6	9	1	4	4	1	-	-	1
Economically active students (included above)	1	-	-	-	1	-	-	-	-	-
Economically inactive	15	61	-	25	-	5	4	3	11	28

Havant

TOTAL HEADS	2,643	1,201	922	560	1,019	297	508	112	194	232
Owner occupied	1,544	418	486	148	635	125	324	62	99	83
Economically active	1,404	293	484	137	632	95	274	51	14	10
Unemployed	83	12	18	5	32	3	33	2	-	2
Economically active students (included above)	-	-	-	-	-	-	-	-	-	-
Economically inactive	140	125	2	11	3	30	50	11	85	73
Rented privately or with a job or business	554	298	241	187	211	76	94	24	8	11
Economically active	529	219	239	135	209	66	81	17	-	1
Unemployed	72	24	35	9	26	14	11	1	-	-
Economically active students (included above)	2	4	2	4	-	-	-	-	-	-
Economically inactive	25	79	2	52	2	10	13	7	8	10
Rented from a housing association	37	18	19	8	8	2	3	2	7	6
Economically active	26	8	17	6	8	2	1	-	-	-
Unemployed	14	4	11	3	2	1	1	-	-	-
Economically active students (included above)	-	-	-	-	-	-	-	-	-	-
Economically inactive	11	10	2	2	-	-	2	2	7	6
Rented from a local authority or new town	508	467	176	217	165	94	87	24	80	132
Economically active	369	107	164	51	146	42	52	10	7	4
Unemployed	147	30	72	18	54	9	21	3	-	-
Economically active students (included above)	-	1	-	1	-	-	-	-	-	-
Economically inactive	139	360	12	166	19	52	35	14	73	128

	All households: age and sex of head									Tenure of household and economic activity of head
TOTAL HOUSEHOLD HEADS*		16 - 29*		30 - 44		45 up to pensionable age		Pensionable age and over		
Males	Females	Males	Females	Males	Females	Males	Females	Males	Females	
l	m	n	o	p	q	r	s	t	u	a
22,770	6,303	2,511	779	8,318	1,431	8,803	1,235	3,138	2,858	**TOTAL HEADS**
19,142	4,414	1,722	440	7,160	1,100	7,895	980	2,365	1,894	**Owner occupied**
16,412	2,207	1,713	392	7,124	917	7,239	746	336	152	Economically active
480	75	57	11	170	25	250	36	3	3	Unemployed
										Economically active students (included above)
2	6	-	3	1	3	1	-	-	-	
2,730	2,207	9	48	36	183	656	234	2,029	1,742	Economically inactive
2,198	688	656	226	867	157	446	84	229	221	**Rented privately or with a job or business**
1,980	423	653	197	859	131	417	73	51	22	Economically active
81	20	36	8	26	8	19	4	-	-	Unemployed
										Economically active students (included above)
4	1	4	-	-	-	-	1	-	-	
218	265	3	29	8	26	29	11	178	199	Economically inactive
105	196	16	13	12	11	18	12	59	160	**Rented from a housing association**
38	28	14	3	10	10	11	9	3	6	Economically active
2	4	1	1	1	1	-	2	-	-	Unemployed
										Economically active students (included above)
-	-	-	-	-	-	-	-	-	-	
67	168	2	10	2	1	7	3	56	154	Economically inactive
1,325	1,005	117	100	279	163	444	159	485	583	**Rented from a local authority or new town**
789	286	115	28	266	109	359	109	49	40	Economically active
125	36	24	2	54	19	47	14	-	1	Unemployed
										Economically active students (included above)
1	2	-	-	1	-	-	2	-	-	
536	719	2	72	13	54	85	50	436	543	Economically inactive
32,958	13,193	3,332	1,823	10,146	2,837	12,418	2,321	7,062	6,212	**TOTAL HEADS**
25,980	7,529	2,216	609	8,137	1,590	10,362	1,549	5,265	3,781	**Owner occupied**
19,690	3,138	2,200	477	8,041	1,253	9,005	1,148	444	260	Economically active
988	132	106	20	337	48	544	57	1	7	Unemployed
										Economically active students (included above)
11	5	2	-	4	3	5	2	-	-	
6,290	4,391	16	132	96	337	1,357	401	4,821	3,521	Economically inactive
1,527	871	427	311	502	183	369	100	229	277	**Rented privately or with a job or business**
1,246	464	422	220	492	151	312	73	20	20	Economically active
155	40	53	13	57	20	43	7	2	-	Unemployed
										Economically active students (included above)
4	5	4	5	-	-	-	-	-	-	
281	407	5	91	10	32	57	27	209	257	Economically inactive
194	206	38	19	35	15	29	26	92	146	**Rented from a housing association**
90	33	35	11	32	9	20	11	3	2	Economically active
36	11	19	5	12	3	5	3	-	-	Unemployed
										Economically active students (included above)
-	2	-	1	-	-	-	1	-	-	
104	173	3	8	3	6	9	15	89	144	Economically inactive
5,257	4,587	651	884	1,472	1,049	1,658	646	1,476	2,008	**Rented from a local authority or new town**
3,178	1,146	616	245	1,319	491	1,173	352	70	58	Economically active
909	210	233	58	362	75	312	72	2	5	Unemployed
										Economically active students (included above)
2	5	-	2	2	2	-	1	-	-	
2,079	3,441	35	639	153	558	485	294	1,406	1,950	Economically inactive

Table 45 Migrant household heads – **continued**

Note: * May include a small number of heads aged under 16

45. Households with residents

Tenure of household and economic activity of head	Households with head with different address one year before census: age and sex of head									
	Total migrant heads*		16 - 29*		30 - 44		45 up to pensionable age		Pensionable age and over	
	Males	Females	Males	Females	Males	Females	Males	Females	Males	Females
a	b	c	d	e	f	g	h	i	j	k
New Forest										
TOTAL HEADS	4,087	1,576	1,397	641	1,446	420	817	166	427	349
Owner occupied	2,645	678	872	209	932	207	562	101	279	161
Economically active	2,257	450	867	189	925	172	443	75	22	14
Unemployed	114	18	26	4	28	5	59	9	1	-
Economically active students (included above)	1	1	-	-	1	-	-	1	-	-
Economically inactive	388	228	5	20	7	35	119	26	257	147
Rented privately or with a job or business	970	400	352	213	395	112	180	43	43	32
Economically active	899	295	346	169	382	89	161	33	10	4
Unemployed	76	29	27	14	30	10	18	5	1	-
Economically active students (included above)	2	2	-	2	2	-	-	-	-	-
Economically inactive	71	105	6	44	13	23	19	10	33	28
Rented from a housing association	75	57	28	19	19	11	8	3	20	24
Economically active	51	14	27	6	19	5	5	2	-	1
Unemployed	12	-	10	-	1	-	1	-	-	-
Economically active students (included above)	-	-	-	-	-	-	-	-	-	-
Economically inactive	24	43	1	13	-	6	3	1	20	23
Rented from a local authority or new town	397	441	145	200	100	90	67	19	85	132
Economically active	269	82	142	35	85	35	41	9	1	3
Unemployed	91	20	54	13	26	6	11	1	-	-
Economically active students (included above)	-	-	-	-	-	-	-	-	-	-
Economically inactive	128	359	3	165	15	55	26	10	84	129
Portsmouth										
TOTAL HEADS	5,189	2,798	2,713	1,629	1,603	611	647	207	226	351
Owner occupied	2,337	879	1,139	438	830	251	292	81	76	109
Economically active	2,204	693	1,122	393	821	222	255	68	6	10
Unemployed	140	30	67	9	48	7	25	13	-	1
Economically active students (included above)	4	1	4	1	-	-	-	-	-	-
Economically inactive	133	186	17	45	9	29	37	13	70	99
Rented privately or with a job or business	2,219	1,208	1,372	888	591	230	223	57	33	33
Economically active	1,970	889	1,208	674	558	166	195	47	9	2
Unemployed	325	129	206	92	78	28	40	9	1	-
Economically active students (included above)	13	19	10	18	2	1	-	-	1	-
Economically inactive	249	319	164	214	33	64	28	10	24	31
Rented from a housing association	138	170	50	55	30	31	24	21	34	63
Economically active	82	59	40	30	24	15	16	11	2	3
Unemployed	35	17	17	10	11	5	7	2	-	-
Economically active students (included above)	3	-	1	-	2	-	-	-	-	-
Economically inactive	56	111	10	25	6	16	8	10	32	60
Rented from a local authority or new town	495	541	152	248	152	99	108	48	83	146
Economically active	323	119	141	53	115	43	63	21	4	2
Unemployed	128	45	61	22	50	14	17	9	-	-
Economically active students (included above)	1	-	1	-	-	-	-	-	-	-
Economically inactive	172	422	11	195	37	56	45	27	79	144

l	m	n	o	p	q	r	s	t	u	a
TOTAL HOUSEHOLD HEADS*		**16 - 29***		**30 - 44**		**45 up to pensionable age**		**Pensionable age and over**		**Tenure of household and economic activity of head**
Males	Females	Males	Females	Males	Females	Males	Females	Males	Females	
47,478	**17,933**	**4,456**	**1,646**	**13,523**	**3,009**	**16,403**	**2,705**	**13,096**	**10,573**	**TOTAL HEADS**
40,130	**12,858**	**3,348**	**821**	**11,601**	**2,150**	**14,369**	**2,106**	**10,812**	**7,781**	**Owner occupied**
27,903	4,392	3,315	682	11,479	1,732	12,186	1,515	923	463	Economically active
1,238	167	127	22	391	57	710	81	10	7	Unemployed
										Economically active students (included above)
5	*9*	*-*	*3*	*4*	*3*	*1*	*2*	*-*	*1*	
12,227	8,466	33	139	122	418	2,183	591	9,889	7,318	Economically inactive
3,655	**1,674**	**713**	**387**	**1,116**	**292**	**1,031**	**221**	**795**	**774**	**Rented privately or with a job or business**
2,807	777	697	304	1,084	233	922	169	104	71	Economically active
219	58	60	25	82	18	74	14	3	1	Unemployed
										Economically active students (included above)
3	*3*	*1*	*3*	*2*	*-*	*-*	*-*	*-*	*-*	
848	897	16	83	32	59	109	52	691	703	Economically inactive
407	**451**	**49**	**33**	**56**	**40**	**73**	**24**	**229**	**354**	**Rented from a housing association**
158	62	47	11	53	25	53	15	5	11	Economically active
29	2	17	1	5	1	7	-	-	-	Unemployed
										Economically active students (included above)
-	*-*	*-*	*-*	*-*	*-*	*-*	*-*	*-*	*-*	
249	389	2	22	3	15	20	9	224	343	Economically inactive
3,286	**2,950**	**346**	**405**	**750**	**527**	**930**	**354**	**1,260**	**1,664**	**Rented from a local authority or new town**
1,770	618	332	87	681	269	675	213	82	49	Economically active
402	85	119	21	134	29	146	33	3	2	Unemployed
										Economically active students (included above)
1	*3*	*1*	*1*	*-*	*2*	*-*	*-*	*-*	*-*	
1,516	2,332	14	318	69	258	255	141	1,178	1,615	Economically inactive
47,435	**25,155**	**8,268**	**4,544**	**14,017**	**4,880**	**14,567**	**3,622**	**10,583**	**12,109**	**TOTAL HEADS**
34,562	**14,171**	**5,156**	**1,857**	**10,910**	**2,948**	**11,210**	**2,277**	**7,286**	**7,089**	**Owner occupied**
25,951	6,121	5,079	1,503	10,744	2,423	9,591	1,725	537	470	Economically active
1,522	301	320	65	573	114	625	116	4	6	Unemployed
										Economically active students (included above)
17	*15*	*8*	*4*	*7*	*10*	*2*	*1*	*-*	*-*	
8,611	8,050	77	354	166	525	1,619	552	6,749	6,619	Economically inactive
6,049	**3,496**	**2,402**	**1,504**	**1,618**	**593**	**1,195**	**328**	**834**	**1,071**	**Rented privately or with a job or business**
4,751	1,791	2,138	1,079	1,532	423	988	238	93	51	Economically active
791	237	359	141	232	57	197	35	3	4	Unemployed
										Economically active students (included above)
21	*27*	*17*	*26*	*3*	*1*	*-*	*-*	*1*	*-*	
1,298	1,705	264	425	86	170	207	90	741	1,020	Economically inactive
916	**1,331**	**111**	**153**	**182**	**162**	**227**	**130**	**396**	**886**	**Rented from a housing association**
418	273	96	72	146	94	151	79	25	28	Economically active
109	69	30	21	43	23	36	24	-	1	Unemployed
										Economically active students (included above)
3	*2*	*1*	*1*	*2*	*1*	*-*	*-*	*-*	*-*	
498	1,058	15	81	36	68	76	51	371	858	Economically inactive
5,908	**6,157**	**599**	**1,030**	**1,307**	**1,177**	**1,935**	**887**	**2,067**	**3,063**	**Rented from a local authority or new town**
3,187	1,463	563	284	1,150	583	1,362	494	112	102	Economically active
958	276	228	64	375	100	354	111	1	1	Unemployed
										Economically active students (included above)
4	*7*	*1*	*3*	*3*	*3*	*-*	*1*	*-*	*-*	
2,721	4,694	36	746	157	594	573	393	1,955	2,961	Economically inactive

545

Table 45 Migrant household heads – **continued**

Note: * May include a small number of heads aged under 16

45. Households with residents

Tenure of household and economic activity of head	Households with head with different address one year before census: age and sex of head									
	Total migrant heads*		16 - 29*		30 - 44		45 up to pensionable age		Pensionable age and over	
	Males	Females	Males	Females	Males	Females	Males	Females	Males	Females
a	b	c	d	e	f	g	h	i	j	k

Rushmoor

TOTAL HEADS	**3,063**	**1,052**	**1,554**	**619**	**1,132**	**238**	**301**	**76**	**76**	**119**
Owner occupied	**1,339**	**291**	**627**	**141**	**530**	**97**	**159**	**32**	**23**	**21**
Economically active	1,293	254	621	135	522	88	147	29	3	2
Unemployed	37	7	13	5	16	1	8	1	-	-
Economically active students (included above)	-	-	-	-	-	-	-	-	-	-
Economically inactive	46	37	6	6	8	9	12	3	20	19
Rented privately or with a job or business	**1,369**	**369**	**790**	**286**	**501**	**67**	**73**	**12**	**5**	**4**
Economically active	1,337	311	775	242	495	55	66	12	1	2
Unemployed	73	31	44	25	23	5	6	1	-	-
Economically active students (included above)	2	3	2	3	-	-	-	-	-	-
Economically inactive	32	58	15	44	6	12	7	-	4	2
Rented from a housing association	**32**	**26**	**8**	**7**	**8**	**4**	**5**	**3**	**11**	**12**
Economically active	18	10	8	3	6	4	4	3	-	-
Unemployed	1	2	-	-	1	2	-	-	-	-
Economically active students (included above)	-	-	-	-	-	-	-	-	-	-
Economically inactive	14	16	-	4	2	-	1	-	11	12
Rented from a local authority or new town	**323**	**366**	**129**	**185**	**93**	**70**	**64**	**29**	**37**	**82**
Economically active	248	98	121	40	81	33	42	20	4	5
Unemployed	67	16	33	9	21	3	13	4	-	-
Economically active students (included above)	-	-	-	-	-	-	-	-	-	-
Economically inactive	75	268	8	145	12	37	22	9	33	77

Southampton

TOTAL HEADS	**5,781**	**3,136**	**2,998**	**1,857**	**1,672**	**673**	**771**	**236**	**340**	**370**
Owner occupied	**2,297**	**882**	**1,126**	**435**	**783**	**273**	**294**	**84**	**94**	**90**
Economically active	2,140	727	1,109	404	770	248	253	67	8	8
Unemployed	112	37	43	20	39	8	29	9	1	-
Economically active students (included above)	-	3	-	2	-	1	-	-	-	-
Economically inactive	157	155	17	31	13	25	41	17	86	82
Rented privately or with a job or business	**2,334**	**1,257**	**1,465**	**946**	**576**	**208**	**255**	**73**	**38**	**30**
Economically active	1,926	888	1,199	667	508	162	211	55	8	4
Unemployed	507	146	311	107	128	26	66	13	2	-
Economically active students (included above)	21	25	18	23	3	1	-	1	-	-
Economically inactive	408	369	266	279	68	46	44	18	30	26
Rented from a housing association	**229**	**174**	**85**	**66**	**58**	**31**	**44**	**17**	**42**	**60**
Economically active	139	49	71	20	39	16	25	11	4	2
Unemployed	51	6	29	3	11	2	11	1	-	-
Economically active students (included above)	-	-	-	-	-	-	-	-	-	-
Economically inactive	90	125	14	46	19	15	19	6	38	58
Rented from a local authority or new town	**921**	**823**	**322**	**410**	**255**	**161**	**178**	**62**	**166**	**190**
Economically active	664	199	309	97	226	64	122	28	7	10
Unemployed	212	33	106	20	75	11	31	2	-	-
Economically active students (included above)	1	1	-	1	1	-	-	-	-	-
Economically inactive	257	624	13	313	29	97	56	34	159	180

All households: age and sex of head										Tenure of household and economic activity of head
TOTAL HOUSEHOLD HEADS*		16 - 29*		30 - 44		45 up to pensionable age		Pensionable age and over		
Males	Females	Males	Females	Males	Females	Males	Females	Males	Females	
l	m	n	o	p	q	r	s	t	u	a
22,577	7,946	4,474	1,624	7,998	1,717	6,837	1,276	3,268	3,329	**TOTAL HEADS**
16,311	**4,138**	**2,614**	**651**	**6,042**	**1,050**	**5,602**	**815**	**2,053**	**1,622**	**Owner occupied**
13,870	2,336	2,595	571	5,978	899	5,079	689	218	177	Economically active
452	88	75	30	189	23	187	31	1	4	Unemployed
										Economically active students
3	*2*	*1*	*1*	*2*	*1*	-	-	-	-	*(included above)*
2,441	1,802	19	80	64	151	523	126	1,835	1,445	Economically inactive
3,508	**968**	**1,502**	**470**	**1,329**	**171**	**441**	**56**	**236**	**271**	**Rented privately or with a job or business**
3,208	599	1,479	381	1,310	143	393	48	26	27	Economically active
168	65	72	41	54	15	42	6	-	3	Unemployed
										Economically active students
2	*5*	*2*	*5*	-	-	-	-	-	-	*(included above)*
300	369	23	89	19	28	48	8	210	244	Economically inactive
280	**310**	**30**	**20**	**60**	**39**	**46**	**33**	**144**	**218**	**Rented from a housing association**
128	58	28	9	54	27	36	16	10	6	Economically active
15	3	4	-	6	2	5	1	-	-	Unemployed
										Economically active students
-	-	-	-	-	-	-	-	-	-	*(included above)*
152	252	2	11	6	12	10	17	134	212	Economically inactive
2,478	**2,530**	**328**	**483**	**567**	**457**	**748**	**372**	**835**	**1,218**	**Rented from a local authority or new town**
1,481	701	307	124	519	259	573	242	82	76	Economically active
261	66	86	16	90	18	85	32	-	-	Unemployed
										Economically active students
-	-	-	-	-	-	-	-	-	-	*(included above)*
997	1,829	21	359	48	198	175	130	753	1,142	Economically inactive
54,646	26,494	8,752	5,057	16,297	5,492	17,792	3,887	11,805	12,058	**TOTAL HEADS**
36,747	**12,646**	**4,923**	**1,554**	**11,867**	**2,935**	**12,764**	**2,218**	**7,193**	**5,939**	**Owner occupied**
28,207	5,893	4,822	1,305	11,692	2,460	11,046	1,672	647	456	Economically active
1,640	268	244	63	591	93	802	102	3	10	Unemployed
										Economically active students
11	*11*	*1*	*4*	*8*	*6*	*2*	*1*	-	-	*(included above)*
8,540	6,753	101	249	175	475	1,718	546	6,546	5,483	Economically inactive
6,165	**3,545**	**2,373**	**1,552**	**1,463**	**537**	**1,309**	**330**	**1,020**	**1,126**	**Rented privately or with a job or business**
4,446	1,788	1,959	1,076	1,311	417	1,098	236	78	59	Economically active
1,048	291	487	174	298	72	260	43	3	2	Unemployed
										Economically active students
36	*36*	*29*	*32*	*7*	*2*	-	*2*	-	-	*(included above)*
1,719	1,757	414	476	152	120	211	94	942	1,067	Economically inactive
1,260	**1,492**	**173**	**176**	**280**	**184**	**294**	**125**	**513**	**1,007**	**Rented from a housing association**
605	285	147	71	231	106	195	77	32	31	Economically active
140	34	57	10	41	14	42	10	-	-	Unemployed
										Economically active students
1	-	*1*	-	-	-	-	-	-	-	*(included above)*
655	1,207	26	105	49	78	99	48	481	976	Economically inactive
10,474	**8,811**	**1,283**	**1,775**	**2,687**	**1,836**	**3,425**	**1,214**	**3,079**	**3,986**	**Rented from a local authority or new town**
6,263	2,158	1,227	470	2,439	887	2,442	656	155	145	Economically active
1,645	348	413	101	620	116	608	128	4	3	Unemployed
										Economically active students
4	*2*	*1*	*1*	*2*	*1*	*1*	-	-	-	*(included above)*
4,211	6,653	56	1,305	248	949	983	558	2,924	3,841	Economically inactive

Table 45 Migrant household heads – **continued**

Note: * May include a small number of heads aged under 16

45. Households with residents

Tenure of household and economic activity of head	Households with head with different address one year before census: age and sex of head									
	Total migrant heads*		16 - 29*		30 - 44		45 up to pensionable age		Pensionable age and over	
	Males	Females	Males	Females	Males	Females	Males	Females	Males	Females
a	b	c	d	e	f	g	h	i	j	k

Test Valley

TOTAL HEADS	3,136	1,045	1,143	492	1,293	287	541	104	159	162
Owner occupied	1,706	398	568	127	759	154	309	60	70	57
Economically active	1,610	306	565	121	756	134	279	45	10	6
Unemployed	41	11	14	3	18	5	9	3	-	-
Economically active students (included above)	-	-	-	-	-	-	-	-	-	-
Economically inactive	96	92	3	6	3	20	30	15	60	51
Rented privately or with a job or business	968	260	410	158	399	66	144	24	15	12
Economically active	941	223	403	141	397	59	138	21	3	2
Unemployed	27	21	11	11	11	6	5	4	-	-
Economically active students (included above)	2	1	2	1	-	-	-	-	-	-
Economically inactive	27	37	7	17	2	7	6	3	12	10
Rented from a housing association	30	33	9	9	12	4	4	4	5	16
Economically active	23	11	9	3	10	3	4	4	-	1
Unemployed	4	-	2	-	1	-	1	-	-	-
Economically active students (included above)	-	-	-	-	-	-	-	-	-	-
Economically inactive	7	22	-	6	2	1	-	-	5	15
Rented from a local authority or new town	432	354	156	198	123	63	84	16	69	77
Economically active	338	109	147	61	116	28	71	14	4	6
Unemployed	68	19	37	12	22	6	9	1	-	-
Economically active students (included above)	-	-	-	-	-	-	-	-	-	-
Economically inactive	94	245	9	137	7	35	13	2	65	71

Winchester

TOTAL HEADS	2,575	1,130	778	451	1,098	262	479	116	220	301
Owner occupied	1,278	397	299	124	588	131	300	62	91	80
Economically active	1,153	280	297	110	585	117	261	47	10	6
Unemployed	28	12	4	3	12	7	12	1	-	1
Economically active students (included above)	2	1	2	-	-	-	-	1	-	-
Economically inactive	125	117	2	14	3	14	39	15	81	74
Rented privately or with a job or business	898	351	369	225	387	85	120	23	22	18
Economically active	858	280	358	184	378	72	112	20	10	4
Unemployed	58	17	25	8	24	7	9	1	-	1
Economically active students (included above)	9	11	7	10	2	-	-	1	-	-
Economically inactive	40	71	11	41	9	13	8	3	12	14
Rented from a housing association	105	73	34	20	32	13	16	8	23	32
Economically active	70	27	33	9	27	10	9	7	1	1
Unemployed	14	2	6	-	5	-	3	2	-	-
Economically active students (included above)	-	-	-	-	-	-	-	-	-	-
Economically inactive	35	46	1	11	5	3	7	1	22	31
Rented from a local authority or new town	294	309	76	82	91	33	43	23	84	171
Economically active	193	67	72	21	84	23	30	14	7	9
Unemployed	32	10	16	6	13	3	3	1	-	-
Economically active students (included above)	-	1	-	1	-	-	-	-	-	-
Economically inactive	101	242	4	61	7	10	13	9	77	162

TOTAL HOUSEHOLD HEADS*		**16 - 29***		**30 - 44**		**45 up to pensionable age**		**Pensionable age and over**		**Tenure of household and economic activity of head**
Males	Females	Males	Females	Males	Females	Males	Females	Males	Females	
l	m	n	o	p	q	r	s	t	u	a
28,755	9,636	3,193	1,257	9,606	2,093	10,712	1,598	5,244	4,688	**TOTAL HEADS**
21,515	5,497	1,960	469	7,483	1,337	8,618	1,101	3,454	2,590	**Owner occupied**
17,626	2,660	1,948	414	7,434	1,133	7,805	882	439	231	Economically active
540	75	54	13	182	32	304	27	-	3	Unemployed
										Economically active students
1	3	-	1	-	1	1	1	-	-	*(included above)*
3,889	2,837	12	55	49	204	813	219	3,015	2,359	Economically inactive
3,372	1,088	773	299	1,221	211	914	123	464	455	**Rented privately or with a job or business**
2,915	582	759	258	1,210	182	857	98	89	44	Economically active
87	33	22	14	32	12	33	7	-	-	Unemployed
										Economically active students
2	1	2	1	-	-	-	-	-	-	*(included above)*
457	506	14	41	11	29	57	25	375	411	Economically inactive
291	298	25	19	79	29	79	34	108	216	**Rented from a housing association**
173	67	24	9	74	21	68	26	7	11	Economically active
16	2	2	-	6	1	8	1	-	-	Unemployed
										Economically active students
-	-	-	-	-	-	-	-	-	-	*(included above)*
118	231	1	10	5	8	11	8	101	205	Economically inactive
3,577	2,753	435	470	823	516	1,101	340	1,218	1,427	**Rented from a local authority or new town**
2,180	747	415	154	760	285	905	240	100	68	Economically active
346	71	93	27	118	22	135	22	-	-	Unemployed
										Economically active students
-	-	-	-	-	-	-	-	-	-	*(included above)*
1,397	2,006	20	316	63	231	196	100	1,118	1,359	Economically inactive
27,044	10,509	2,177	1,033	8,521	1,975	10,506	1,745	5,840	5,756	**TOTAL HEADS**
19,943	6,166	1,131	379	6,579	1,375	8,436	1,269	3,797	3,143	**Owner occupied**
15,697	2,758	1,119	322	6,541	1,163	7,491	992	546	281	Economically active
432	94	31	10	143	40	255	41	3	3	Unemployed
										Economically active students
6	8	2	3	2	2	2	3	-	-	*(included above)*
4,246	3,408	12	57	38	212	945	277	3,251	2,862	Economically inactive
3,351	1,230	734	405	1,156	239	970	130	491	456	**Rented privately or with a job or business**
2,873	675	713	331	1,135	197	906	102	119	45	Economically active
126	35	43	19	50	9	33	6	-	1	Unemployed
										Economically active students
13	13	9	12	4	-	-	1	-	-	*(included above)*
478	555	21	74	21	42	64	28	372	411	Economically inactive
414	482	50	28	68	24	77	26	219	404	**Rented from a housing association**
177	62	49	11	60	20	54	20	14	11	Economically active
29	3	10	1	10	-	9	2	-	-	Unemployed
										Economically active students
-	-	-	-	-	-	-	-	-	-	*(included above)*
237	420	1	17	8	4	23	6	205	393	Economically inactive
3,336	2,631	262	221	718	337	1,023	320	1,333	1,753	**Rented from a local authority or new town**
1,859	574	248	65	675	206	816	214	120	89	Economically active
214	43	49	12	84	11	81	19	-	1	Unemployed
										Economically active students
2	1	1	1	-	-	1	-	-	-	*(included above)*
1,477	2,057	14	156	43	131	207	106	1,213	1,664	Economically inactive

46. Households with dependent children; residents in such households

HAMPSHIRE

Household composition	TOTAL HOUSE-HOLDS	Over 1 and up to 1.5 persons per room	Over 1.5 persons per room	Lacking or sharing use of bath/shower and/or inside WC	No central heating	Not self-contained accomm-odation	Tenure				No car	TOTAL PERSONS IN HOUSE-HOLDS
							Owner occupied	Rented privately	Rented from a housing association	Rented from a local authority or new town		
a	b	c	d	e	f	g	h	i	j	k	l	m
ALL HOUSEHOLDS WITH DEPENDENT CHILDREN	**184,809**	**6,806**	**1,346**	**814**	**21,259**	**884**	**136,034**	**7,838**	**1,947**	**30,910**	**24,089**	**725,670**
Households of 1 adult with 1 or more dependent children	**20,396**	**257**	**325**	**315**	**3,999**	**391**	**8,469**	**1,782**	**644**	**9,083**	**10,441**	**56,096**
Dependent child(ren) aged 0 - 4 only	4,718	41	241	198	1,008	258	1,174	752	204	2,490	3,069	10,835
Dependent child(ren) aged 5 and over only	12,074	44	62	95	2,186	114	6,242	808	329	4,437	5,035	31,953
Dependent children aged 0 - 4 and 5 and over	3,604	172	22	22	805	19	1,053	222	111	2,156	2,337	13,308
Dependent children in households of 1 adult with 1 or more dependent children												
All dependent children	35,700	978	443	411	7,125	500	14,517	2,682	1,072	16,701	18,779	
Dependent children aged 0 - 4	10,423	389	310	255	2,336	335	2,658	1,145	394	6,021	6,908	
Dependent children aged 5 - 15	22,908	570	123	139	4,433	150	10,303	1,392	634	10,102	11,127	
Dependent children aged 0 - 17	35,177	976	438	404	7,060	492	14,135	2,648	1,061	16,620	18,660	
Other households with dependent children	**164,413**	**6,549**	**1,021**	**499**	**17,260**	**493**	**127,565**	**6,056**	**1,303**	**21,827**	**13,648**	**669,574**
Dependent child(ren) aged 0 - 4 only	40,524	1,274	425	277	4,911	303	29,978	2,665	396	5,099	4,011	143,752
Dependent child(ren) aged 5 and over only	94,076	2,144	201	177	8,795	149	76,524	2,368	595	10,857	6,451	383,011
Dependent children aged 0 - 4 and 5 and over	29,813	3,131	395	45	3,554	41	21,063	1,023	312	5,871	3,186	142,811
Persons in other households with dependent children												
All adults	370,466	17,302	2,671	1,078	39,843	1,017	287,952	13,195	2,890	49,876	30,572	
All dependent children	299,108	19,524	2,869	753	31,850	718	228,104	10,169	2,451	44,307	25,942	
Dependent children aged 0 - 4	92,664	6,831	1,305	395	11,073	417	66,574	4,693	949	15,232	9,724	
Dependent children aged 5 - 15	182,801	11,984	1,462	327	19,056	256	141,173	4,939	1,400	27,191	14,936	
Dependent children aged 0 - 17	293,961	19,428	2,850	747	31,576	707	223,487	10,031	2,439	44,083	25,729	
Households with 3 or more dependent children	30,956	4,325	532	66	4,223	60	20,381	1,032	388	7,790	4,999	164,090
Households with 3 or more persons aged 0 - 15	27,894	4,146	512	63	3,949	55	17,908	966	370	7,398	4,733	148,227
Households with 4 or more dependent children	6,907	2,560	299	14	1,236	20	3,856	240	102	2,418	1,561	43,678
Households with 4 or more persons aged 0 - 15	6,070	2,348	286	14	1,125	17	3,257	216	89	2,249	1,429	38,508

Table 46 Households with dependent children: housing – continued

County, districts

46. Households with dependent children; residents in such households

Basingstoke & Deane

| Household composition | TOTAL HOUSE-HOLDS | Over 1 and up to 1.5 persons per room | Over 1.5 persons per room | Lacking or sharing use of bath/shower and/or inside WC | No central heating | Not self-contained accommodation | Tenure | | | | No car | TOTAL PERSONS IN HOUSE-HOLDS |
| | | | | | | | Owner occupied | Rented privately | Rented from a housing association | Rented from a local authority or new town | | |
a	b	c	d	e	f	g	h	i	j	k	l	m
ALL HOUSEHOLDS WITH DEPENDENT CHILDREN	18,162	570	94	43	915	27	13,414	535	328	3,160	1,863	72,220
Households of 1 adult with 1 or more dependent children	1,568	24	18	19	136	13	644	64	87	742	768	4,394
Dependent child(ren) aged 0 - 4 only	298	5	14	10	38	8	84	20	13	172	174	689
Dependent child(ren) aged 5 and over only	945	6	3	6	63	5	467	34	49	376	385	2,495
Dependent children aged 0 - 4 and 5 and over	325	13	1	3	35	-	93	10	25	194	209	1,210
Dependent children in households of 1 adult with 1 or more dependent children												
All dependent children	2,826	91	24	29	251	18	1,111	105	153	1,409	1,464	
Dependent children aged 0 - 4	777	37	19	17	97	11	206	33	46	475	493	
Dependent children aged 5 - 15	1,833	51	4	11	143	6	784	62	100	863	893	
Dependent children aged 0 - 17	2,778	90	24	29	249	18	1,077	104	152	1,399	1,453	
Other households with dependent children	16,594	546	76	24	779	14	12,770	471	241	2,418	1,095	67,826
Dependent child(ren) aged 0 - 4 only	4,069	101	22	10	219	7	3,167	199	45	502	261	14,501
Dependent child(ren) aged 5 and over only	9,624	174	20	12	397	6	7,553	193	131	1,324	575	39,398
Dependent children aged 0 - 4 and 5 and over	2,901	271	34	2	163	1	2,050	79	65	592	259	13,927
Persons in other households with dependent children												
All adults	37,685	1,532	217	52	1,789	28	28,823	1,043	539	5,696	2,507	
All dependent children	30,141	1,628	250	41	1,412	25	22,834	797	470	4,773	2,122	
Dependent children aged 0 - 4	9,175	564	88	17	495	10	6,819	353	142	1,506	712	
Dependent children aged 5 - 15	18,574	1,009	152	24	837	14	13,998	398	307	3,047	1,304	
Dependent children aged 0 - 17	29,629	1,620	247	41	1,394	24	22,382	788	469	4,745	2,106	
Households with 3 or more dependent children	3,085	360	47	7	184	2	2,022	81	80	775	446	16,377
Households with 3 or more persons aged 0 - 15	2,774	348	46	7	169	2	1,781	72	76	729	414	14,773
Households with 4 or more dependent children	671	226	29	1	49	1	363	19	17	243	156	4,219
Households with 4 or more persons aged 0 - 15	589	214	27	1	43	1	302	19	14	228	142	3,719

Table 46 Households with dependent children: housing – **continued**

46. Households with dependent children; residents in such households

Household composition	TOTAL HOUSE-HOLDS	Over 1 and up to 1.5 persons per room	Over 1.5 persons per room	Lacking or sharing use of bath/shower and/or inside WC	No central heating	Not self-contained accommodation	Tenure				No car	TOTAL PERSONS IN HOUSE-HOLDS
							Owner occupied	Rented privately	Rented from a housing association	Rented from a local authority or new town		
a	b	c	d	e	f	g	h	i	j	k	l	m
East Hampshire												
ALL HOUSEHOLDS WITH DEPENDENT CHILDREN	12,855	392	88	37	881	46	10,123	520	67	1,463	741	51,075
Households of 1 adult with 1 or more dependent children	1,084	14	13	9	140	11	565	104	10	375	350	3,028
Dependent child(ren) aged 0 - 4 only	209	-	11	3	43	4	70	28	2	105	103	456
Dependent child(ren) aged 5 and over only	702	4	2	5	74	5	418	61	4	196	167	1,924
Dependent children aged 0 - 4 and 5 and over	173	10	-	1	23	2	77	15	4	74	80	648
Dependent children in households of 1 adult with 1 or more dependent children												
All dependent children	1,944	60	13	10	225	13	1,024	173	20	668	642	
Dependent children aged 0 - 4	449	16	11	4	81	6	169	48	6	217	213	
Dependent children aged 5 - 15	1,333	43	2	4	139	6	722	118	13	435	412	
Dependent children aged 0 - 17	1,907	60	13	10	224	13	993	172	20	666	638	
Other households with dependent children	11,771	378	75	28	741	35	9,558	416	57	1,088	391	48,047
Dependent child(ren) aged 0 - 4 only	2,695	77	41	17	174	17	2,087	158	20	267	109	9,569
Dependent child(ren) aged 5 and over only	6,953	141	11	8	407	15	5,869	174	30	539	199	28,381
Dependent children aged 0 - 4 and 5 and over	2,123	160	23	3	160	3	1,602	84	7	282	83	10,097
Persons in other households with dependent children												
All adults	26,378	982	183	58	1,716	78	21,440	916	124	2,483	869	
All dependent children	21,669	1,101	179	43	1,379	51	17,399	737	99	2,209	751	
Dependent children aged 0 - 4	6,372	364	87	24	436	22	4,870	308	36	756	269	
Dependent children aged 5 - 15	13,263	691	87	16	856	22	10,692	389	58	1,368	438	
Dependent children aged 0 - 17	21,168	1,094	178	42	1,360	49	16,931	727	98	2,200	744	
Households with 3 or more dependent children	2,208	227	27	3	159	3	1,631	77	13	361	159	11,689
Households with 3 or more persons aged 0 - 15	1,927	211	26	3	149	1	1,386	72	10	345	150	10,224
Households with 4 or more dependent children	482	147	14	-	45	-	312	18	1	118	57	3,026
Households with 4 or more persons aged 0 - 15	404	135	14	-	44	-	247	16	1	111	53	2,548

Table 46 Households with dependent children: housing – continued

46. Households with dependent children; residents in such households

Eastleigh

| Household composition | TOTAL HOUSE-HOLDS | Over 1 and up to 1.5 persons per room | Over 1.5 persons per room | Lacking or sharing use of bath/shower and/or inside WC | No central heating | Not self-contained accomm-odation | Tenure | | | | No car | TOTAL PERSONS IN HOUSE-HOLDS |
| | | | | | | | Owner occupied | Rented privately | Rented from a housing association | Rented from a local authority or new town | | |
a	b	c	d	e	f	g	h	i	j	k	l	m
ALL HOUSEHOLDS WITH DEPENDENT CHILDREN	13,382	344	48	25	1,065	21	11,441	342	102	1,407	946	52,212
Households of 1 adult with 1 or more dependent children	1,208	5	7	9	196	11	720	75	38	371	421	3,312
Dependent child(ren) aged 0 - 4 only	260	1	4	4	68	5	90	32	19	119	130	603
Dependent child(ren) aged 5 and over only	765	1	3	5	99	6	535	31	16	179	210	2,043
Dependent children aged 0 - 4 and 5 and over	183	3	-	-	29	-	95	12	3	73	81	666
Dependent children in households of 1 adult with 1 or more dependent children												
All dependent children	2,104	19	10	12	325	15	1,270	113	53	661	731	
Dependent children aged 0 - 4	552	6	4	5	129	6	222	51	28	251	275	
Dependent children aged 5 - 15	1,388	12	6	7	175	9	914	55	24	390	419	
Dependent children aged 0 - 17	2,067	19	10	12	322	15	1,237	111	52	660	725	
Other households with dependent children	12,174	339	41	16	869	10	10,721	267	64	1,036	525	48,900
Dependent child(ren) aged 0 - 4 only	3,039	60	21	10	307	7	2,600	129	25	266	159	10,616
Dependent child(ren) aged 5 and over only	7,022	117	5	6	408	2	6,354	94	27	500	237	28,377
Dependent children aged 0 - 4 and 5 and over	2,113	162	15	-	154	1	1,767	44	12	270	129	9,907
Persons in other households with dependent children												
All adults	26,940	841	109	33	1,935	23	23,734	571	140	2,300	1,141	
All dependent children	21,960	1,018	99	19	1,537	13	19,205	436	108	2,055	1,043	
Dependent children aged 0 - 4	6,766	356	51	10	613	8	5,695	225	48	748	399	
Dependent children aged 5 - 15	13,531	619	45	7	847	4	11,972	186	60	1,221	597	
Dependent children aged 0 - 17	21,590	1,012	98	18	1,527	12	18,852	430	108	2,046	1,032	
Households with 3 or more dependent children	2,088	222	16	1	173	2	1,689	39	12	330	193	10,919
Households with 3 or more persons aged 0 - 15	1,876	212	16	1	161	2	1,497	35	12	316	182	9,816
Households with 4 or more dependent children	383	130	9	-	33	-	275	7	2	95	54	2,379
Households with 4 or more persons aged 0 - 15	332	116	9	-	32	-	234	5	2	87	50	2,070

Table 46 Households with dependent children: housing – continued

46. Households with dependent children; residents in such households

Fareham

Household composition	TOTAL HOUSE-HOLDS	Over 1 and up to 1.5 persons per room	Over 1.5 persons per room	Lacking or sharing use of bath/shower and/or inside WC	No central heating	Not self-contained accomm-odation	Tenure				No car	TOTAL PERSONS IN HOUSE-HOLDS
							Owner occupied	Rented privately	Rented from a housing association	Rented from a local authority or new town		
a	b	c	d	e	f	g	h	i	j	k	l	m
ALL HOUSEHOLDS WITH DEPENDENT CHILDREN	11,833	268	23	17	938	8	10,247	371	12	907	790	46,179
Households of 1 adult with 1 or more dependent children	989	5	1	6	157	5	622	70	4	271	330	2,626
Dependent child(ren) aged 0 - 4 only	186	-	1	4	31	4	92	23	2	62	83	425
Dependent child(ren) aged 5 and over only	664	1	-	2	90	1	456	36	2	156	184	1,714
Dependent children aged 0 - 4 and 5 and over	139	4	-	-	36	-	74	11	-	53	63	487
Dependent children in households of 1 adult with 1 or more dependent children												
All dependent children	1,637	18	1	6	271	5	1,030	111	5	454	563	
Dependent children aged 0 - 4	397	7	1	4	84	4	200	39	2	146	186	
Dependent children aged 5 - 15	1,088	11	-	2	165	1	711	65	3	285	356	
Dependent children aged 0 - 17	1,603	18	1	6	267	5	1,000	111	5	451	559	
Other households with dependent children	10,844	263	22	11	781	3	9,625	301	8	636	460	43,553
Dependent child(ren) aged 0 - 4 only	2,617	46	6	3	206	1	2,234	134	5	142	109	9,247
Dependent child(ren) aged 5 and over only	6,298	81	7	5	406	-	5,765	113	3	309	237	25,243
Dependent children aged 0 - 4 and 5 and over	1,929	136	9	3	169	2	1,626	54	-	185	114	9,063
Persons in other households with dependent children												
All adults	24,312	735	79	25	1,827	6	21,592	651	17	1,481	1,038	
All dependent children	19,241	790	63	19	1,435	7	16,877	533	10	1,309	882	
Dependent children aged 0 - 4	5,954	283	29	9	502	4	5,007	246	6	469	299	
Dependent children aged 5 - 15	11,720	486	32	9	841	3	10,410	264	1	773	518	
Dependent children aged 0 - 17	18,890	788	62	19	1,425	7	16,543	529	10	1,301	871	
Households with 3 or more dependent children	1,718	171	12	2	177	1	1,387	55	-	217	156	9,016
Households with 3 or more persons aged 0 - 15	1,538	166	11	2	158	1	1,229	52	-	199	142	8,108
Households with 4 or more dependent children	308	108	5	-	44	-	226	6	-	66	43	1,928
Households with 4 or more persons aged 0 - 15	277	103	5	-	40	-	201	5	-	63	41	1,733

Table 46 Households with dependent children: housing – continued

46. Households with dependent children; residents in such households

Gosport

Household composition	TOTAL HOUSE-HOLDS	Over 1 and up to 1.5 persons per room	Over 1.5 persons per room	Lacking or sharing use of bath/shower and/or inside WC	No central heating	Not self-contained accomm-odation	Owner occupied	Rented privately	Rented from a housing association	Rented from a local authority or new town	No car	TOTAL PERSONS IN HOUSE-HOLDS
a	b	c	d	e	f	g	h	i	j	k	l	m
ALL HOUSEHOLDS WITH DEPENDENT CHILDREN	9,606	291	46	30	1,227	12	6,396	478	49	1,857	1,910	36,986
Households of 1 adult with 1 or more dependent children	1,232	1	16	17	202	4	465	86	16	587	716	3,344
Dependent child(ren) aged 0 - 4 only	304	1	14	14	56	1	64	23	7	193	220	688
Dependent child(ren) aged 5 and over only	715	-	2	2	120	2	340	47	6	285	352	1,872
Dependent children aged 0 - 4 and 5 and over	213	-	-	1	26	1	61	16	3	109	144	784
Dependent children in households of 1 adult with 1 or more dependent children												
All dependent children	2,112	2	16	20	348	7	784	135	22	1,018	1,245	
Dependent children aged 0 - 4	633	2	14	15	102	2	143	42	11	382	452	
Dependent children aged 5 - 15	1,337	-	1	4	222	4	561	85	10	586	733	
Dependent children aged 0 - 17	2,080	2	15	19	344	6	764	134	22	1,008	1,232	
Other households with dependent children	8,374	290	30	13	1,025	8	5,931	392	33	1,270	1,194	33,642
Dependent child(ren) aged 0 - 4 only	2,156	53	6	5	358	4	1,423	165	9	288	362	7,492
Dependent child(ren) aged 5 and over only	4,591	90	9	7	485	3	3,530	139	15	614	535	18,410
Dependent children aged 0 - 4 and 5 and over	1,627	147	15	1	182	1	978	88	9	368	297	7,740
Persons in other households with dependent children												
All adults	18,620	749	70	26	2,253	15	13,307	829	77	2,833	2,580	
All dependent children	15,022	908	100	16	1,753	9	10,275	718	70	2,552	2,274	
Dependent children aged 0 - 4	4,896	322	33	6	697	5	3,058	329	27	879	879	
Dependent children aged 5 - 15	9,118	559	65	8	979	2	6,374	371	39	1,570	1,306	
Dependent children aged 0 - 17	14,855	903	99	16	1,741	9	10,128	717	68	2,540	2,261	
Households with 3 or more dependent children	1,550	193	18	1	185	1	857	88	9	441	379	8,153
Households with 3 or more persons aged 0 - 15	1,434	188	18	1	176	1	770	86	9	421	362	7,566
Households with 4 or more dependent children	337	126	11	1	43	1	149	22	4	125	107	2,121
Households with 4 or more persons aged 0 - 15	303	116	9	1	37	1	132	19	3	115	99	1,912

Table 46 Households with dependent children: housing – **continued**

46. Households with dependent children; residents in such households

Hart

Household composition	TOTAL HOUSE-HOLDS	Over 1 and up to 1.5 persons per room	Over 1.5 persons per room	Lacking or sharing use of bath/shower and/or inside WC	No central heating	Not self-contained accomm-odation	Tenure				No car	TOTAL PERSONS IN HOUSE-HOLDS
							Owner occupied	Rented privately	Rented from a housing association	Rented from a local authority or new town		
a	b	c	d	e	f	g	h	i	j	k	l	m
ALL HOUSEHOLDS WITH DEPENDENT CHILDREN	10,446	206	31	24	406	9	8,735	370	26	636	311	41,748
Households of 1 adult with 1 or more dependent children	661	7	4	6	65	5	414	65	12	151	155	1,814
Dependent child(ren) aged 0 - 4 only	112	1	2	2	12	2	47	22	6	30	43	252
Dependent child(ren) aged 5 and over only	469	3	2	4	43	3	328	36	5	90	85	1,261
Dependent children aged 0 - 4 and 5 and over	80	3	-	-	10	-	39	7	1	31	27	301
Dependent children in households of 1 adult with 1 or more dependent children												
All dependent children	1,153	30	4	12	103	6	726	97	19	278	284	
Dependent children aged 0 - 4	235	8	2	3	26	2	103	32	10	79	90	
Dependent children aged 5 - 15	818	20	1	8	71	3	536	62	9	190	187	
Dependent children aged 0 - 17	1,130	30	3	11	103	5	707	95	19	277	283	
Other households with dependent children	9,785	199	27	18	341	4	8,321	305	14	485	156	39,934
Dependent child(ren) aged 0 - 4 only	2,147	46	10	4	98	2	1,708	121	7	115	44	7,668
Dependent child(ren) aged 5 and over only	6,042	76	6	9	181	2	5,323	140	4	261	79	24,771
Dependent children aged 0 - 4 and 5 and over	1,596	77	11	5	62	-	1,290	44	3	109	33	7,495
Persons in other households with dependent children												
All adults	22,036	543	72	38	769	10	18,806	663	29	1,136	343	
All dependent children	17,898	566	70	34	637	4	15,107	550	24	942	271	
Dependent children aged 0 - 4	4,976	190	31	11	220	2	3,964	226	12	314	97	
Dependent children aged 5 - 15	11,188	362	39	22	383	1	9,527	290	11	598	160	
Dependent children aged 0 - 17	17,480	562	70	34	634	4	14,708	542	24	939	267	
Households with 3 or more dependent children	1,675	126	12	6	83	-	1,345	47	5	147	55	8,795
Households with 3 or more persons aged 0 - 15	1,464	120	12	6	79	-	1,151	41	4	144	54	7,707
Households with 4 or more dependent children	311	73	4	2	18	-	231	12	1	44	14	1,938
Households with 4 or more persons aged 0 - 15	265	69	4	2	17	-	188	12	1	42	13	1,657

Table 46 Households with dependent children: housing – continued

46. Households with dependent children; residents in such households

Havant

Household composition	TOTAL HOUSE-HOLDS	Over 1 and up to 1.5 persons per room	Over 1.5 persons per room	Lacking or sharing use of bath/shower and/or inside WC	No central heating	Not self-contained accomm-odation	Tenure				No car	TOTAL PERSONS IN HOUSE-HOLDS
							Owner occupied	Rented privately	Rented from a housing association	Rented from a local authority or new town		
a	b	c	d	e	f	g	h	i	j	k	l	m
ALL HOUSEHOLDS WITH DEPENDENT CHILDREN	**14,712**	**798**	**137**	**89**	**2,916**	**89**	**10,232**	**503**	**72**	**3,722**	**2,550**	**58,324**
Households of 1 adult with 1 or more dependent children	**1,951**	**36**	**34**	**45**	**613**	**42**	**695**	**132**	**17**	**1,089**	**1,156**	**5,493**
Dependent child(ren) aged 0 - 4 only	407	5	27	34	136	33	94	53	2	254	282	948
Dependent child(ren) aged 5 and over only	1,147	5	4	8	332	6	512	61	11	552	579	3,077
Dependent children aged 0 - 4 and 5 and over	397	26	3	3	145	3	89	18	4	283	295	1,468
Dependent children in households of 1 adult with 1 or more dependent children												
All dependent children	3,542	141	46	61	1,119	55	1,190	200	32	2,085	2,188	
Dependent children aged 0 - 4	1,010	60	32	45	368	43	215	81	7	699	739	
Dependent children aged 5 - 15	2,319	79	14	16	706	12	844	112	23	1,315	1,366	
Dependent children aged 0 - 17	3,498	141	46	61	1,113	55	1,156	197	32	2,078	2,176	
Other households with dependent children	**12,761**	**762**	**103**	**44**	**2,303**	**47**	**9,537**	**371**	**55**	**2,633**	**1,394**	**52,831**
Dependent child(ren) aged 0 - 4 only	2,864	113	47	33	572	36	2,048	191	17	568	371	10,391
Dependent child(ren) aged 5 and over only	7,386	264	15	8	1,189	6	5,890	129	22	1,262	639	30,260
Dependent children aged 0 - 4 and 5 and over	2,511	385	41	3	542	5	1,599	51	16	803	384	12,180
Persons in other households with dependent children												
All adults	29,179	2,000	266	91	5,335	94	21,859	805	126	6,027	3,177	
All dependent children	23,652	2,382	291	71	4,497	76	17,056	577	113	5,598	2,806	
Dependent children aged 0 - 4	7,093	763	139	52	1,481	58	4,734	300	46	1,898	1,036	
Dependent children aged 5 - 15	14,698	1,526	145	19	2,803	17	10,737	255	63	3,474	1,640	
Dependent children aged 0 - 17	23,272	2,371	291	71	4,473	76	16,710	572	113	5,574	2,791	
Households with 3 or more dependent children	2,735	561	54	6	675	8	1,574	47	15	1,061	611	14,556
Households with 3 or more persons aged 0 - 15	2,503	544	52	6	638	8	1,395	47	15	1,014	582	13,348
Households with 4 or more dependent children	692	328	33	-	210	2	306	12	8	361	203	4,350
Households with 4 or more persons aged 0 - 15	608	286	32	-	184	2	260	9	6	328	181	3,836

Table 46 Households with dependent children: housing – continued

46. Households with dependent children; residents in such households

New Forest

Household composition	TOTAL HOUSE-HOLDS	Over 1 and up to 1.5 persons per room	Over 1.5 persons per room	Lacking or sharing use of bath/shower and/or inside WC	No central heating	Not self-contained accomm-odation	Tenure				No car	TOTAL PERSONS IN HOUSE-HOLDS
							Owner occupied	Rented privately	Rented from a housing association	Rented from a local authority or new town		
a	b	c	d	e	f	g	h	i	j	k	l	m
ALL HOUSEHOLDS WITH DEPENDENT CHILDREN	17,617	503	89	80	1,438	70	14,118	746	145	2,071	1,233	69,020
Households of 1 adult with 1 or more dependent children	**1,670**	**9**	**19**	**30**	**247**	**29**	**865**	**152**	**51**	**577**	**590**	**4,488**
Dependent child(ren) aged 0 - 4 only	374	1	11	18	69	18	106	50	21	192	207	854
Dependent child(ren) aged 5 and over only	1,082	2	6	12	148	11	672	84	25	283	285	2,867
Dependent children aged 0 - 4 and 5 and over	214	6	2	-	30	-	87	18	5	102	98	767
Dependent children in households of 1 adult with 1 or more dependent children												
All dependent children	2,818	35	27	33	395	31	1,485	232	74	993	991	
Dependent children aged 0 - 4	742	15	15	19	124	19	239	80	32	384	401	
Dependent children aged 5 - 15	1,869	19	12	12	249	11	1,099	136	38	575	548	
Dependent children aged 0 - 17	2,777	35	27	32	391	31	1,456	230	73	987	987	
Other households with dependent children	**15,947**	**494**	**70**	**50**	**1,191**	**41**	**13,253**	**594**	**94**	**1,494**	**643**	**64,532**
Dependent child(ren) aged 0 - 4 only	3,668	92	25	25	358	26	2,932	212	39	344	200	12,968
Dependent child(ren) aged 5 and over only	9,552	158	18	20	606	12	8,199	274	35	754	315	38,745
Dependent children aged 0 - 4 and 5 and over	2,727	244	27	5	227	3	2,122	108	20	396	128	12,819
Persons in other households with dependent children												
All adults	35,769	1,270	190	116	2,747	88	29,714	1,320	202	3,420	1,462	
All dependent children	28,763	1,444	208	76	2,121	57	23,631	1,014	157	3,033	1,188	
Dependent children aged 0 - 4	8,428	516	80	33	770	32	6,604	408	76	1,047	451	
Dependent children aged 5 - 15	17,833	866	119	39	1,231	24	14,821	544	71	1,837	675	
Dependent children aged 0 - 17	28,220	1,437	207	76	2,098	57	23,134	1,000	155	3,017	1,179	
Households with 3 or more dependent children	2,731	311	39	5	251	1	2,041	97	21	494	208	14,355
Households with 3 or more persons aged 0 - 15	2,416	291	37	4	234	-	1,769	90	20	470	200	12,720
Households with 4 or more dependent children	511	183	21	-	63	-	329	20	2	144	57	3,237
Households with 4 or more persons aged 0 - 15	442	163	21	-	56	-	271	20	2	136	55	2,802

46. Households with dependent children; residents in such households

Portsmouth

Household composition	TOTAL HOUSE-HOLDS	Over 1 and up to 1.5 persons per room	Over 1.5 persons per room	Lacking or sharing use of bath/ shower and/or inside WC	No central heating	Not self-contained accomm-odation	Tenure				No car	TOTAL PERSONS IN HOUSE-HOLDS
							Owner occupied	Rented privately	Rented from a housing association	Rented from a local authority or new town		
a	b	c	d	e	f	g	h	i	j	k	l	m
ALL HOUSEHOLDS WITH DEPENDENT CHILDREN	19,637	918	211	161	5,655	181	13,428	1,296	310	3,791	5,327	75,674
Households of 1 adult with 1 or more dependent children	3,189	48	56	63	1,129	87	1,211	417	144	1,356	2,137	8,700
Dependent child(ren) aged 0 - 4 only	812	9	37	38	300	52	216	210	41	332	592	1,861
Dependent child(ren) aged 5 and over only	1,757	9	11	19	625	32	817	159	74	671	1,064	4,566
Dependent children aged 0 - 4 and 5 and over	620	30	8	6	204	3	178	48	29	353	481	2,273
Dependent children in households of 1 adult with 1 or more dependent children												
All dependent children	5,511	174	83	86	1,916	104	2,038	596	251	2,518	3,778	
Dependent children aged 0 - 4	1,797	65	56	56	640	63	483	302	86	895	1,355	
Dependent children aged 5 - 15	3,421	104	23	25	1,174	37	1,389	264	152	1,541	2,272	
Dependent children aged 0 - 17	5,440	173	81	84	1,889	102	1,998	586	246	2,503	3,751	
Other households with dependent children	16,448	870	155	98	4,526	94	12,217	879	166	2,435	3,190	66,974
Dependent child(ren) aged 0 - 4 only	4,716	166	56	58	1,409	60	3,432	476	42	524	989	16,749
Dependent child(ren) aged 5 and over only	8,422	259	28	33	2,180	28	6,566	266	78	1,199	1,462	34,133
Dependent children aged 0 - 4 and 5 and over	3,310	445	71	7	937	6	2,219	137	46	712	739	16,092
Persons in other households with dependent children												
All adults	37,282	2,336	427	216	10,466	201	27,763	1,917	368	5,630	7,223	
All dependent children	29,692	2,653	481	147	8,240	132	21,466	1,374	321	5,084	5,982	
Dependent children aged 0 - 4	10,469	949	197	81	3,031	80	7,287	758	117	1,715	2,285	
Dependent children aged 5 - 15	17,491	1,623	266	61	4,813	47	12,773	542	191	3,185	3,454	
Dependent children aged 0 - 17	29,340	2,643	477	146	8,174	132	21,178	1,345	320	5,061	5,943	
Households with 3 or more dependent children	3,323	603	95	10	1,023	7	1,932	141	72	1,010	1,063	17,695
Households with 3 or more persons aged 0 - 15	3,078	582	91	10	971	7	1,759	133	67	962	1,007	16,409
Households with 4 or more dependent children	830	365	61	6	300	2	402	35	19	338	322	5,314
Households with 4 or more persons aged 0 - 15	754	342	60	6	278	2	349	31	16	323	298	4,838

Table 46 Households with dependent children: housing – continued

46. Households with dependent children; residents in such households

Rushmoor

Household composition	TOTAL HOUSE-HOLDS	Over 1 and up to 1.5 persons per room	Over 1.5 persons per room	Lacking or sharing use of bath/shower and/or inside WC	No central heating	Not self-contained accomm-odation	Tenure				No car	TOTAL PERSONS IN HOUSE-HOLDS
							Owner occupied	Rented privately	Rented from a housing association	Rented from a local authority or new town		
a	b	c	d	e	f	g	h	i	j	k	l	m
ALL HOUSEHOLDS WITH DEPENDENT CHILDREN	10,385	403	113	67	378	114	6,724	452	104	1,752	1,367	40,286
Households of 1 adult with 1 or more dependent children	1,147	10	46	24	46	57	397	69	35	593	601	3,098
Dependent child(ren) aged 0 - 4 only	316	1	31	14	11	35	67	33	3	197	208	733
Dependent child(ren) aged 5 and over only	644	-	15	8	29	20	280	31	27	277	280	1,696
Dependent children aged 0 - 4 and 5 and over	187	9	-	2	6	2	50	5	5	119	113	669
Dependent children in households of 1 adult with 1 or more dependent children												
All dependent children	1,951	38	58	29	77	72	672	98	54	1,037	1,021	
Dependent children aged 0 - 4	636	14	39	18	19	46	138	42	9	415	413	
Dependent children aged 5 - 15	1,201	23	19	10	48	25	460	49	39	598	572	
Dependent children aged 0 - 17	1,921	38	58	28	77	71	650	96	53	1,032	1,014	
Other households with dependent children	9,238	393	67	43	332	57	6,327	383	69	1,159	766	37,188
Dependent child(ren) aged 0 - 4 only	2,784	87	41	24	127	37	1,690	167	19	317	306	9,826
Dependent child(ren) aged 5 and over only	4,784	118	16	17	161	17	3,586	161	35	540	284	19,407
Dependent children aged 0 - 4 and 5 and over	1,670	188	10	2	44	3	1,051	55	15	302	176	7,955
Persons in other households with dependent children												
All adults	20,570	1,036	187	92	733	116	14,222	824	159	2,654	1,661	
All dependent children	16,618	1,156	159	65	546	81	11,267	622	137	2,370	1,443	
Dependent children aged 0 - 4	5,952	441	88	32	215	51	3,594	276	50	918	702	
Dependent children aged 5 - 15	9,533	680	64	31	292	24	6,739	315	84	1,365	696	
Dependent children aged 0 - 17	16,372	1,149	156	65	538	80	11,060	615	137	2,356	1,435	
Households with 3 or more dependent children	1,611	241	25	4	50	7	986	61	22	397	241	8,598
Households with 3 or more persons aged 0 - 15	1,468	240	24	3	45	6	873	58	21	381	226	7,872
Households with 4 or more dependent children	376	143	13	-	14	1	207	8	5	128	69	2,408
Households with 4 or more persons aged 0 - 15	340	132	12	-	13	1	184	4	4	121	61	2,186

Table 46 Households with dependent children: housing – continued

46. Households with dependent children; residents in such households

Southampton

Household composition	TOTAL HOUSE-HOLDS	Over 1 and up to 1.5 persons per room	Over 1.5 persons per room	Lacking or sharing use of bath/shower and/or inside WC	No central heating	Not self-contained accommodation	Tenure: Owner occupied	Tenure: Rented privately	Tenure: Rented from a housing association	Tenure: Rented from a local authority or new town	No car	TOTAL PERSONS IN HOUSE-HOLDS
a	b	c	d	e	f	g	h	i	j	k	l	m
ALL HOUSEHOLDS WITH DEPENDENT CHILDREN	22,639	1,571	374	182	4,204	262	14,039	1,240	508	6,664	5,134	88,821
Households of 1 adult with 1 or more dependent children	3,709	83	96	74	921	115	989	397	179	2,127	2,407	10,345
Dependent child(ren) aged 0 - 4 only	1,051	16	77	52	215	88	155	223	68	602	780	2,451
Dependent child(ren) aged 5 and over only	1,900	10	12	18	467	19	709	130	84	964	1,058	5,022
Dependent children aged 0 - 4 and 5 and over	758	57	7	4	239	8	125	44	27	561	569	2,872
Dependent children in households of 1 adult with 1 or more dependent children												
All dependent children	6,636	309	139	91	1,854	160	1,672	589	309	4,042	4,406	
Dependent children aged 0 - 4	2,348	140	102	61	609	124	343	334	126	1,540	1,767	
Dependent children aged 5 - 15	3,998	167	35	29	1,178	34	1,183	239	176	2,384	2,490	
Dependent children aged 0 - 17	6,587	309	138	90	1,844	158	1,642	585	307	4,030	4,386	
Other households with dependent children	18,930	1,488	278	108	3,283	147	13,050	843	329	4,537	2,727	78,476
Dependent child(ren) aged 0 - 4 only	4,947	355	122	65	804	90	3,260	421	105	1,125	808	17,714
Dependent child(ren) aged 5 and over only	10,227	464	43	32	1,756	44	7,485	296	129	2,207	1,315	42,088
Dependent children aged 0 - 4 and 5 and over	3,756	669	113	11	723	13	2,305	126	95	1,205	604	18,674
Persons in other households with dependent children												
All adults	43,193	3,870	672	228	7,732	278	29,978	1,843	731	10,240	6,103	
All dependent children	35,283	4,308	770	154	6,333	213	23,759	1,353	656	9,217	5,149	
Dependent children aged 0 - 4	11,538	1,581	387	89	2,003	122	7,267	690	274	3,231	1,888	
Dependent children aged 5 - 15	21,374	2,562	354	57	3,967	73	14,647	587	359	5,589	2,940	
Dependent children aged 0 - 17	34,822	4,284	766	152	6,277	207	23,377	1,326	654	9,172	5,089	
Households with 3 or more dependent children	4,372	949	152	14	1,056	24	2,348	149	113	1,734	1,099	23,555
Households with 3 or more persons aged 0 - 15	4,020	907	147	13	983	23	2,104	142	110	1,640	1,048	21,705
Households with 4 or more dependent children	1,228	537	82	3	358	13	602	53	36	527	356	7,897
Households with 4 or more persons aged 0 - 15	1,104	495	77	3	330	10	523	50	33	489	326	7,119

Table 46 Households with dependent children: housing – **continued**

46. Households with dependent children; residents in such households

Test Valley

Household composition	TOTAL HOUSE-HOLDS	Over 1 and up to 1.5 persons per room	Over 1.5 persons per room	Lacking or sharing use of bath/shower and/or inside WC	No central heating	Not self-contained accommodation	Tenure: Owner occupied	Rented privately	Rented from a housing association	Rented from a local authority or new town	No car	TOTAL PERSONS IN HOUSE-HOLDS
a	b	c	d	e	f	g	h	i	j	k	l	m
ALL HOUSEHOLDS WITH DEPENDENT CHILDREN	12,582	296	33	22	531	15	9,000	519	121	2,017	1,188	49,386
Households of 1 adult with 1 or more dependent children	1,138	7	3	3	57	1	454	80	26	541	506	3,111
Dependent child(ren) aged 0 - 4 only	238	-	2	-	10	1	52	14	7	156	161	536
Dependent child(ren) aged 5 and over only	708	1	1	2	39	-	360	56	17	249	232	1,864
Dependent children aged 0 - 4 and 5 and over	192	6	-	1	8	-	42	10	2	136	113	711
Dependent children in households of 1 adult with 1 or more dependent children												
All dependent children	1,973	30	5	7	85	1	767	125	43	979	908	
Dependent children aged 0 - 4	523	10	2	2	21	1	112	27	12	360	339	
Dependent children aged 5 - 15	1,305	19	3	4	55	-	564	85	30	583	534	
Dependent children aged 0 - 17	1,939	30	5	7	83	1	743	122	43	973	903	
Other households with dependent children	11,444	289	30	19	474	14	8,546	439	95	1,476	682	46,275
Dependent child(ren) aged 0 - 4 only	2,660	43	8	7	135	5	1,889	153	22	370	176	9,353
Dependent child(ren) aged 5 and over only	6,899	113	12	10	268	6	5,371	203	57	741	352	27,968
Dependent children aged 0 - 4 and 5 and over	1,885	133	10	2	71	3	1,286	83	16	365	154	8,954
Persons in other households with dependent children												
All adults	25,685	778	83	43	1,091	30	19,217	962	213	3,354	1,509	
All dependent children	20,590	878	91	31	803	27	15,121	774	171	2,895	1,265	
Dependent children aged 0 - 4	5,995	278	35	12	263	10	4,162	303	51	994	436	
Dependent children aged 5 - 15	12,823	569	49	17	472	16	9,508	424	108	1,771	754	
Dependent children aged 0 - 17	20,189	876	91	30	791	27	14,775	768	168	2,880	1,253	
Households with 3 or more dependent children	1,950	203	17	4	67	4	1,215	84	19	468	243	10,287
Households with 3 or more persons aged 0 - 15	1,742	192	15	4	61	4	1,058	76	19	444	231	9,212
Households with 4 or more dependent children	401	110	9	-	15	-	203	13	5	140	76	2,520
Households with 4 or more persons aged 0 - 15	342	102	8	-	13	-	165	13	5	128	69	2,158

Table 46 Households with dependent children: housing – continued

46. Households with dependent children; residents in such households

Winchester

Household composition	TOTAL HOUSE-HOLDS	Over 1 and up to 1.5 persons per room	Over 1.5 persons per room	Lacking or sharing use of bath/ shower and/or inside WC	No central heating	Not self-contained accomm-odation	Tenure: Owner occupied	Rented privately	Rented from a housing association	Rented from a local authority or new town	No car	TOTAL PERSONS IN HOUSE-HOLDS
a	b	c	d	e	f	g	h	i	j	k	l	m
ALL HOUSEHOLDS WITH DEPENDENT CHILDREN	10,953	246	59	37	705	30	8,137	466	103	1,463	729	43,739
Households of 1 adult with 1 or more dependent children	850	8	12	10	90	11	428	71	25	303	304	2,343
Dependent child(ren) aged 0 - 4 only	151	1	10	5	19	7	37	21	13	76	86	339
Dependent child(ren) aged 5 and over only	576	2	1	4	57	4	348	42	9	159	154	1,552
Dependent children aged 0 - 4 and 5 and over	123	5	1	1	14	-	43	8	3	68	64	452
Dependent children in households of 1 adult with 1 or more dependent children												
All dependent children	1,493	31	17	15	156	13	748	108	37	559	558	7,658
Dependent children aged 0 - 4	324	9	13	6	36	8	85	34	19	178	185	25,830
Dependent children aged 5 - 15	998	22	3	7	108	2	536	60	17	357	345	7,908
Dependent children aged 0 - 17	1,450	31	17	15	154	12	712	105	37	556	553	
Other households with dependent children	10,103	238	47	27	615	19	7,709	395	78	1,160	425	41,396
Dependent child(ren) aged 0 - 4 only	2,162	35	20	16	144	11	1,508	139	41	271	117	
Dependent child(ren) aged 5 and over only	6,276	89	11	10	351	8	5,033	186	29	607	222	
Dependent children aged 0 - 4 and 5 and over	1,665	114	16	1	120	-	1,168	70	8	282	86	
Persons in other households with dependent children												
All adults	22,817	630	116	60	1,450	50	17,497	851	165	2,622	959	
All dependent children	18,579	692	108	37	1,157	23	14,107	684	115	2,270	766	
Dependent children aged 0 - 4	5,050	224	60	19	347	13	3,513	271	64	757	271	
Dependent children aged 5 - 15	11,655	432	45	17	735	9	8,975	374	48	1,393	454	
Dependent children aged 0 - 17	18,134	689	108	37	1,144	23	13,709	672	115	2,252	758	
Households with 3 or more dependent children	1,910	158	18	3	140	-	1,354	66	7	355	146	10,095
Households with 3 or more persons aged 0 - 15	1,654	145	17	3	125	-	1,136	62	7	333	135	8,767
Households with 4 or more dependent children	377	84	8	1	44	-	251	15	2	89	47	2,341
Households with 4 or more persons aged 0 - 15	310	75	8	1	38	-	201	13	2	78	41	1,930

Table 47 Households with pensioners: housing

47. Households with one or more residents of pensionable age; residents in such households

Household composition	TOTAL HOUSE-HOLDS	Up to 0.5 persons per room	Lacking or sharing use of bath/shower and/or inside WC	No central heating	Lacking or sharing use of bath/shower and/or inside WC and/or no central heating	Not self-contained accommodation
a	b	c	d	e	f	g

HAMPSHIRE

TOTAL HOUSEHOLDS WITH 1 OR MORE PENSIONER(S)	194,381	170,101	2,793	39,182	40,381	746
Lone male 65 - 74	7,849	7,439	311	2,188	2,329	163
Lone male 75 - 84	6,816	6,529	228	1,736	1,837	51
Lone male 85 and over	1,938	1,856	91	519	557	10
Lone female 60 - 74	32,102	31,575	420	6,363	6,567	137
Lone female 75 - 84	26,845	25,905	709	5,644	6,021	130
Lone female 85 and over	7,925	7,533	314	1,900	2,059	52
2 or more, all pensioners, under 75	35,255	32,208	137	5,547	5,580	48
2 or more, all pensioners, any aged 75 and over	25,798	21,845	278	5,132	5,214	72
1 or more pensioner(s) with 1 non-pensioner	34,836	30,014	226	7,243	7,284	57
1 or more pensioner(s) with 2 or more non-pensioners	15,017	5,197	79	2,910	2,933	26
TOTAL PERSONS IN HOUSEHOLDS WITH PENSIONERS	340,273	269,431	3,703	66,781	68,220	1,014
Total persons of pensionable age	264,449	227,848	3,276	51,973	53,307	878
Pensionable age - 74	168,857	145,614	1,365	31,126	31,636	494
75 - 84	78,049	67,141	1,424	16,685	17,293	294
85 and over	17,543	15,093	487	4,162	4,378	90
Persons with limiting long-term illness						
Pensionable age - 74	43,471	36,186	463	8,950	9,173	154
75 - 84	33,024	27,760	674	6,983	7,302	118
85 and over	10,389	8,846	310	2,405	2,549	54

Basingstoke & Deane

TOTAL HOUSEHOLDS WITH 1 OR MORE PENSIONER(S)	14,021	12,188	90	1,542	1,571	21
Lone male 65 - 74	556	546	3	96	98	1
Lone male 75 - 84	437	426	11	79	82	3
Lone male 85 and over	122	118	4	24	24	-
Lone female 60 - 74	2,180	2,152	13	208	212	2
Lone female 75 - 84	1,872	1,824	16	199	209	5
Lone female 85 and over	492	479	9	70	74	2
2 or more, all pensioners, under 75	2,517	2,310	4	208	208	5
2 or more, all pensioners, any aged 75 and over	1,755	1,473	15	213	216	1
1 or more pensioner(s) with 1 non-pensioner	2,787	2,392	12	338	338	1
1 or more pensioner(s) with 2 or more non-pensioners	1,303	468	3	107	110	1
TOTAL PERSONS IN HOUSEHOLDS WITH PENSIONERS	25,322	19,691	135	2,678	2,721	31
Total persons of pensionable age	19,003	16,252	115	2,059	2,094	28
Pensionable age - 74	12,505	10,705	41	1,241	1,252	16
75 - 84	5,343	4,573	58	641	659	10
85 and over	1,155	974	16	177	183	2
Persons with limiting long-term illness						
Pensionable age - 74	3,089	2,549	10	314	318	1
75 - 84	2,273	1,913	23	245	254	3
85 and over	688	568	12	94	98	1

Owner occupied	Rented privately		Rented with a job or business	Rented from a housing association	Rented from a local authority or new town	No car	Persons with limiting long-term illness	Household composition
	Furnished	Unfurnished						
h	i	j	k	l	m	n	o	a
131,363	1,968	9,057	2,473	7,506	42,014	88,776	96,689	**TOTAL HOUSEHOLDS WITH 1 OR MORE PENSIONER(S)**
4,263	275	430	139	365	2,377	3,619	2,638	Lone male 65 - 74
3,789	128	475	99	399	1,926	4,070	2,825	Lone male 75 - 84
1,111	47	139	28	135	478	1,538	1,062	Lone male 85 and over
19,656	353	1,486	294	1,669	8,644	22,150	8,682	Lone female 60 - 74
14,855	350	1,825	237	2,163	7,415	23,013	11,499	Lone female 75 - 84
4,083	140	577	50	707	2,368	7,499	4,645	Lone female 85 and over
27,181	139	1,125	416	681	5,713	6,972	18,010	2 or more, all pensioners, under 75
18,485	202	1,452	281	912	4,466	10,931	20,736	2 or more, all pensioners, any aged 75 and over
26,164	192	1,213	653	360	6,254	7,100	17,613	1 or more pensioner(s) with 1 non-pensioner
11,776	142	335	276	115	2,373	1,884	8,979	1 or more pensioner(s) with 2 or more non-pensioners
242,633	2,970	14,001	4,677	9,837	66,155	120,257	96,689	**TOTAL PERSONS IN HOUSEHOLDS WITH PENSIONERS**
183,987	2,350	11,946	3,307	9,166	53,693	108,312	86,884	Total persons of pensionable age
121,902	1,256	6,104	2,286	4,256	33,053	51,847		Pensionable age - 74
50,996	824	4,719	839	3,892	16,779	43,974		75 - 84
11,089	270	1,123	182	1,018	3,861	12,491		85 and over
								Persons with limiting long-term illness
27,618	365	1,616	575	1,569	11,728	17,395		Pensionable age - 74
20,210	354	1,890	351	1,876	8,343	20,565		75 - 84
6,464	158	631	111	622	2,403	7,513		85 and over
8,037	117	579	421	656	4,211	6,316	6,794	**TOTAL HOUSEHOLDS WITH 1 OR MORE PENSIONER(S)**
277	4	25	22	28	200	226	171	Lone male 65 - 74
197	10	28	15	28	159	276	192	Lone male 75 - 84
53	2	9	6	10	42	106	70	Lone male 85 and over
1,122	25	97	37	143	756	1,588	593	Lone female 60 - 74
801	27	92	44	198	710	1,654	812	Lone female 75 - 84
190	6	27	6	51	212	470	288	Lone female 85 and over
1,655	9	87	80	65	621	518	1,234	2 or more, all pensioners, under 75
1,010	19	95	52	72	507	800	1,376	2 or more, all pensioners, any aged 75 and over
1,805	8	95	110	41	728	538	1,342	1 or more pensioner(s) with 1 non-pensioner
927	7	24	49	20	276	140	716	1 or more pensioner(s) with 2 or more non-pensioners
15,491	177	946	823	902	6,983	8,634	6,794	**TOTAL PERSONS IN HOUSEHOLDS WITH PENSIONERS**
11,150	149	796	584	803	5,521	7,748	6,050	Total persons of pensionable age
7,720	64	453	413	394	3,461	3,791		Pensionable age - 74
2,834	68	270	143	335	1,693	3,146		75 - 84
596	17	73	28	74	367	811		85 and over
								Persons with limiting long-term illness
1,650	13	102	86	141	1,097	1,193		Pensionable age - 74
1,127	31	100	66	154	795	1,467		75 - 84
361	8	35	17	47	220	482		85 and over

Table 47 Households with pensioners: housing – **continued**

47. Households with one or more residents of pensionable age; residents in such households

Household composition	TOTAL HOUSE-HOLDS	Up to 0.5 persons per room	Lacking or sharing use of bath/shower and/or inside WC	No central heating	Lacking or sharing use of bath/shower and/or inside WC and/or no central heating	Not self-contained accommodation
a	b	c	d	e	f	g

East Hampshire

TOTAL HOUSEHOLDS WITH 1 OR MORE PENSIONER(S)	**12,192**	**10,755**	**183**	**1,772**	**1,884**	**28**
Lone male 65 - 74	452	434	18	104	117	4
Lone male 75 - 84	440	423	9	80	87	-
Lone male 85 and over	123	114	7	24	29	-
Lone female 60 - 74	1,851	1,824	32	272	287	7
Lone female 75 - 84	1,731	1,661	56	260	301	4
Lone female 85 and over	506	468	26	85	104	4
2 or more, all pensioners, under 75	2,197	2,073	6	237	239	1
2 or more, all pensioners, any aged 75 and over	1,717	1,493	13	201	207	5
1 or more pensioner(s) with 1 non-pensioner	2,134	1,862	10	351	353	1
1 or more pensioner(s) with 2 or more non-pensioners	1,041	403	6	158	160	2
TOTAL PERSONS IN HOUSEHOLDS WITH PENSIONERS	**21,711**	**17,360**	**236**	**3,070**	**3,200**	**42**
Total persons of pensionable age	**16,684**	**14,572**	**207**	**2,310**	**2,432**	**34**
Pensionable age - 74	10,436	9,173	80	1,403	1,439	16
75 - 84	5,058	4,392	86	707	764	10
85 and over	1,190	1,007	41	200	229	8
Persons with limiting long-term illness						
Pensionable age - 74	2,424	2,043	31	365	384	6
75 - 84	1,938	1,640	36	263	292	3
85 and over	656	554	26	107	126	2

Eastleigh

TOTAL HOUSEHOLDS WITH 1 OR MORE PENSIONER(S)	**11,943**	**10,458**	**122**	**1,871**	**1,936**	**15**
Lone male 65 - 74	473	456	19	92	100	2
Lone male 75 - 84	384	363	4	80	84	-
Lone male 85 and over	115	105	6	19	22	-
Lone female 60 - 74	1,976	1,945	16	282	289	4
Lone female 75 - 84	1,475	1,397	31	244	265	3
Lone female 85 and over	451	414	21	74	87	2
2 or more, all pensioners, under 75	2,344	2,168	4	308	309	1
2 or more, all pensioners, any aged 75 and over	1,550	1,307	12	266	271	1
1 or more pensioner(s) with 1 non-pensioner	2,293	2,008	8	388	390	1
1 or more pensioner(s) with 2 or more non-pensioners	882	295	1	118	119	1
TOTAL PERSONS IN HOUSEHOLDS WITH PENSIONERS	**21,084**	**16,803**	**151**	**3,258**	**3,335**	**22**
Total persons of pensionable age	**16,375**	**14,144**	**141**	**2,551**	**2,624**	**17**
Pensionable age - 74	10,801	9,416	56	1,581	1,606	9
75 - 84	4,516	3,842	53	782	813	6
85 and over	1,058	886	32	188	205	2
Persons with limiting long-term illness						
Pensionable age - 74	2,721	2,300	19	432	443	2
75 - 84	1,892	1,552	27	310	328	2
85 and over	643	531	21	109	121	2

Owner occupied	Tenure					No car	Persons with limiting long-term illness	Household composition
	Rented privately		Rented with a job or business	Rented from a housing association	Rented from a local authority or new town			
	Furnished	Unfurnished						
h	i	j	k	l	m	n	o	a
8,902	138	576	239	275	2,062	4,383	5,546	**TOTAL HOUSEHOLDS WITH 1 OR MORE PENSIONER(S)**
284	10	21	15	9	113	153	147	Lone male 65 - 74
267	10	29	11	18	105	212	160	Lone male 75 - 84
70	3	13	6	5	26	87	57	Lone male 85 and over
1,289	35	94	26	59	348	1,023	436	Lone female 60 - 74
1,080	20	112	24	83	412	1,331	659	Lone female 75 - 84
265	11	42	2	37	149	465	287	Lone female 85 and over
1,798	14	71	41	15	258	252	994	2 or more, all pensioners, under 75
1,331	18	81	28	34	225	519	1,300	2 or more, all pensioners, any aged 75 and over
1,666	11	83	55	10	309	274	930	1 or more pensioner(s) with 1 non-pensioner
852	6	30	31	5	117	67	576	1 or more pensioner(s) with 2 or more non-pensioners
16,549	201	911	444	348	3,258	5,664	5,546	**TOTAL PERSONS IN HOUSEHOLDS WITH PENSIONERS**
12,489	173	749	315	324	2,634	5,224	5,018	**Total persons of pensionable age**
8,087	95	384	213	128	1,529	2,151		Pensionable age - 74
3,620	58	276	81	144	879	2,304		75 - 84
782	20	89	21	52	226	769		85 and over
								Persons with limiting long-term illness
1,681	25	106	48	47	517	689		Pensionable age - 74
1,321	28	107	31	59	392	1,002		75 - 84
429	9	42	15	25	136	435		85 and over
8,283	81	486	73	539	2,481	5,122	5,848	**TOTAL HOUSEHOLDS WITH 1 OR MORE PENSIONER(S)**
289	7	22	7	22	126	190	147	Lone male 65 - 74
211	4	20	3	35	111	225	145	Lone male 75 - 84
60	1	4	1	12	37	95	67	Lone male 85 and over
1,268	14	88	10	118	478	1,348	538	Lone female 60 - 74
790	21	106	7	143	408	1,297	636	Lone female 75 - 84
202	2	30	4	56	157	432	265	Lone female 85 and over
1,812	7	57	12	56	400	399	1,157	2 or more, all pensioners, under 75
1,034	8	84	11	77	336	682	1,260	2 or more, all pensioners, any aged 75 and over
1,857	11	67	11	15	332	388	1,149	1 or more pensioner(s) with 1 non-pensioner
760	6	8	7	5	96	66	484	1 or more pensioner(s) with 2 or more non-pensioners
15,525	124	726	128	706	3,875	6,854	5,848	**TOTAL PERSONS IN HOUSEHOLDS WITH PENSIONERS**
11,554	96	642	98	678	3,307	6,294	5,256	**Total persons of pensionable age**
8,060	53	323	62	310	1,993	3,013		Pensionable age - 74
2,869	39	265	26	288	1,029	2,526		75 - 84
625	4	54	10	80	285	755		85 and over
								Persons with limiting long-term illness
1,798	12	74	20	108	709	1,015		Pensionable age - 74
1,117	17	94	11	146	507	1,175		75 - 84
368	3	31	5	46	190	461		85 and over

Table 47 Households with pensioners: housing – **continued**

47. Households with one or more residents of pensionable age; residents in such households

Household composition	TOTAL HOUSE-HOLDS	Up to 0.5 persons per room	Lacking or sharing use of bath/shower and/or inside WC	No central heating	Lacking or sharing use of bath/shower and/or inside WC and/or no central heating	Not self-contained accommodation
a	b	c	d	e	f	g

Fareham

TOTAL HOUSEHOLDS WITH 1 OR MORE PENSIONER(S)	**12,172**	**10,740**	**163**	**2,061**	**2,169**	**19**
Lone male 65 - 74	408	387	23	87	102	2
Lone male 75 - 84	393	372	20	93	110	1
Lone male 85 and over	99	92	9	29	37	1
Lone female 60 - 74	1,902	1,887	18	338	349	3
Lone female 75 - 84	1,512	1,460	41	289	321	5
Lone female 85 and over	409	388	16	97	109	1
2 or more, all pensioners, under 75	2,583	2,410	5	317	320	1
2 or more, all pensioners, any aged 75 and over	1,655	1,415	16	286	294	2
1 or more pensioner(s) with 1 non-pensioner	2,275	1,988	9	387	389	3
1 or more pensioner(s) with 2 or more non-pensioners	936	341	6	138	138	-
TOTAL PERSONS IN HOUSEHOLDS WITH PENSIONERS	**21,724**	**17,494**	**208**	**3,513**	**3,635**	**25**
Total persons of pensionable age	16,962	14,767	186	2,779	2,899	22
Pensionable age - 74	11,224	9,872	68	1,637	1,675	10
75 - 84	4,793	4,098	87	927	986	9
85 and over	945	797	31	215	238	3
Persons with limiting long-term illness						
Pensionable age - 74	2,731	2,339	29	429	448	3
75 - 84	2,040	1,696	50	389	426	6
85 and over	579	474	23	124	143	3

Gosport

TOTAL HOUSEHOLDS WITH 1 OR MORE PENSIONER(S)	**9,175**	**7,802**	**123**	**2,019**	**2,090**	**11**
Lone male 65 - 74	367	355	15	113	118	2
Lone male 75 - 84	305	288	12	87	96	1
Lone male 85 and over	96	91	1	30	31	-
Lone female 60 - 74	1,598	1,563	26	348	363	-
Lone female 75 - 84	1,391	1,310	32	357	383	1
Lone female 85 and over	404	364	24	112	123	2
2 or more, all pensioners, under 75	1,621	1,379	2	271	272	2
2 or more, all pensioners, any aged 75 and over	1,175	889	5	287	288	-
1 or more pensioner(s) with 1 non-pensioner	1,599	1,357	6	316	318	3
1 or more pensioner(s) with 2 or more non-pensioners	619	206	-	98	98	-
TOTAL PERSONS IN HOUSEHOLDS WITH PENSIONERS	**15,572**	**12,019**	**137**	**3,212**	**3,287**	**16**
Total persons of pensionable age	12,362	10,230	131	2,662	2,735	13
Pensionable age - 74	7,820	6,503	54	1,487	1,512	9
75 - 84	3,729	3,063	52	950	986	2
85 and over	813	664	25	225	237	2
Persons with limiting long-term illness						
Pensionable age - 74	2,174	1,729	22	442	458	5
75 - 84	1,640	1,300	27	406	425	-
85 and over	517	419	19	136	146	1

h	i	j	k	l	m	n	o	a
Owner occupied	Rented privately — Furnished	Rented privately — Unfurnished	Rented with a job or business	Rented from a housing association	Rented from a local authority or new town	No car	Persons with limiting long-term illness	Household composition
9,948	90	318	79	203	1,534	4,860	5,930	**TOTAL HOUSEHOLDS WITH 1 OR MORE PENSIONER(S)**
291	2	17	3	9	86	142	143	Lone male 65 - 74
281	6	14	4	9	79	219	159	Lone male 75 - 84
66	2	5	-	2	24	79	50	Lone male 85 and over
1,466	14	39	7	41	335	1,263	446	Lone female 60 - 74
1,056	26	67	9	63	291	1,314	650	Lone female 75 - 84
276	6	21	2	25	79	391	263	Lone female 85 and over
2,323	4	33	13	20	190	384	1,288	2 or more, all pensioners, under 75
1,365	17	52	11	27	183	685	1,318	2 or more, all pensioners, any aged 75 and over
1,995	8	54	19	5	194	311	1,096	1 or more pensioner(s) with 1 non-pensioner
829	5	16	11	2	73	72	517	1 or more pensioner(s) with 2 or more non-pensioners
18,328	134	510	149	259	2,344	6,517	5,930	**TOTAL PERSONS IN HOUSEHOLDS WITH PENSIONERS**
14,126	113	419	107	250	1,947	6,018	5,350	**Total persons of pensionable age**
9,667	41	194	69	108	1,145	2,767		Pensionable age - 74
3,751	56	180	33	113	660	2,592		75 - 84
708	16	45	5	29	142	659		85 and over
								Persons with limiting long-term illness
2,213	12	51	11	42	402	849		Pensionable age - 74
1,518	25	85	19	62	331	1,204		75 - 84
425	8	26	4	22	94	412		85 and over
6,104	78	274	91	520	2,108	4,761	4,807	**TOTAL HOUSEHOLDS WITH 1 OR MORE PENSIONER(S)**
201	7	18	4	28	109	170	117	Lone male 65 - 74
186	5	10	3	23	78	195	122	Lone male 75 - 84
52	1	9	1	14	19	78	60	Lone male 85 and over
931	23	61	13	85	485	1,208	467	Lone female 60 - 74
763	11	57	6	177	377	1,242	623	Lone female 75 - 84
213	12	17	2	55	105	395	250	Lone female 85 and over
1,229	4	32	9	45	302	421	932	2 or more, all pensioners, under 75
828	10	39	10	81	207	547	991	2 or more, all pensioners, any aged 75 and over
1,225	3	26	31	9	305	408	844	1 or more pensioner(s) with 1 non-pensioner
476	2	5	12	3	121	97	401	1 or more pensioner(s) with 2 or more non-pensioners
10,944	101	391	175	663	3,298	6,461	4,807	**TOTAL PERSONS IN HOUSEHOLDS WITH PENSIONERS**
8,470	93	355	114	647	2,683	5,814	4,331	**Total persons of pensionable age**
5,554	44	183	75	248	1,716	2,860		Pensionable age - 74
2,423	33	136	31	309	797	2,327		75 - 84
493	16	36	8	90	170	627		85 and over
								Persons with limiting long-term illness
1,369	13	60	26	99	607	970		Pensionable age - 74
1,011	10	61	16	143	399	1,096		75 - 84
311	12	23	4	59	108	391		85 and over

Table 47 Households with pensioners: housing – **continued**

47. Households with one or more residents of pensionable age; residents in such households

Household composition	TOTAL HOUSE-HOLDS	Up to 0.5 persons per room	Lacking or sharing use of bath/shower and/or inside WC	No central heating	Lacking or sharing use of bath/shower and/or inside WC and/or no central heating	Not self-contained accommodation
a	b	c	d	e	f	g

Hart

TOTAL HOUSEHOLDS WITH 1 OR MORE PENSIONER(S)	7,237	6,283	53	868	882	11
Lone male 65 - 74	223	214	1	38	38	-
Lone male 75 - 84	231	222	1	39	39	-
Lone male 85 and over	62	59	2	16	16	-
Lone female 60 - 74	1,021	1,005	10	112	116	2
Lone female 75 - 84	1,040	990	17	123	126	-
Lone female 85 and over	299	279	3	53	53	3
2 or more, all pensioners, under 75	1,316	1,203	1	130	130	-
2 or more, all pensioners, any aged 75 and over	888	760	5	114	118	4
1 or more pensioner(s) with 1 non-pensioner	1,412	1,246	9	167	169	2
1 or more pensioner(s) with 2 or more non-pensioners	745	305	4	76	77	-
TOTAL PERSONS IN HOUSEHOLDS WITH PENSIONERS	13,297	10,358	78	1,515	1,537	18
Total persons of pensionable age	9,776	8,396	61	1,155	1,173	16
Pensionable age - 74	6,213	5,360	19	665	671	4
75 - 84	2,888	2,465	35	388	400	7
85 and over	675	571	7	102	102	5
Persons with limiting long-term illness						
Pensionable age - 74	1,406	1,127	8	184	187	4
75 - 84	1,204	1,007	12	172	175	3
85 and over	376	313	4	53	53	3

Havant

TOTAL HOUSEHOLDS WITH 1 OR MORE PENSIONER(S)	15,618	13,611	206	3,361	3,528	17
Lone male 65 - 74	586	569	25	170	190	3
Lone male 75 - 84	478	465	13	96	107	1
Lone male 85 and over	133	129	4	26	30	-
Lone female 60 - 74	2,610	2,570	39	599	630	1
Lone female 75 - 84	1,920	1,852	81	375	445	2
Lone female 85 and over	594	567	27	125	148	1
2 or more, all pensioners, under 75	3,154	2,916	7	540	542	2
2 or more, all pensioners, any aged 75 and over	1,909	1,625	4	358	359	5
1 or more pensioner(s) with 1 non-pensioner	2,922	2,518	5	726	731	2
1 or more pensioner(s) with 2 or more non-pensioners	1,312	400	1	346	346	-
TOTAL PERSONS IN HOUSEHOLDS WITH PENSIONERS	27,890	21,805	225	6,068	6,244	26
Total persons of pensionable age	21,396	18,406	218	4,445	4,616	24
Pensionable age - 74	14,423	12,461	85	3,050	3,110	12
75 - 84	5,696	4,876	102	1,145	1,229	11
85 and over	1,277	1,069	31	250	277	1
Persons with limiting long-term illness						
Pensionable age - 74	4,156	3,494	35	1,020	1,049	5
75 - 84	2,572	2,145	63	528	584	4
85 and over	763	631	21	155	174	1

Owner occupied	Rented privately Furnished	Rented privately Unfurnished	Rented with a job or business	Rented from a housing association	Rented from a local authority or new town	No car	Persons with limiting long-term illness	Household composition
h	i	j	k	l	m	n	o	a
5,363	90	319	93	225	1,147	2,442	3,307	**TOTAL HOUSEHOLDS WITH 1 OR MORE PENSIONER(S)**
143	8	11	4	8	49	53	69	Lone male 65 - 74
155	3	10	4	12	47	114	99	Lone male 75 - 84
29	1	6	1	3	22	44	28	Lone male 85 and over
728	15	45	8	44	181	551	236	Lone female 60 - 74
660	19	65	5	76	215	816	437	Lone female 75 - 84
151	10	18	4	29	87	278	171	Lone female 85 and over
1,045	5	60	17	20	169	145	604	2 or more, all pensioners, under 75
676	10	50	9	21	122	271	685	2 or more, all pensioners, any aged 75 and over
1,150	8	45	24	12	173	136	598	1 or more pensioner(s) with 1 non-pensioner
626	11	9	17	-	82	34	380	1 or more pensioner(s) with 2 or more non-pensioners
10,297	147	505	193	280	1,875	3,108	3,307	**TOTAL PERSONS IN HOUSEHOLDS WITH PENSIONERS**
7,343	109	440	125	268	1,491	2,888	2,986	**Total persons of pensionable age**
4,843	58	242	86	113	871	1,128		Pensionable age - 74
2,076	36	158	28	121	469	1,346		75 - 84
424	15	40	11	34	151	414		85 and over
								Persons with limiting long-term illness
986	20	46	18	41	295	369		Pensionable age - 74
803	20	64	11	58	248	642		75 - 84
231	10	23	6	19	87	245		85 and over
10,998	121	335	101	245	3,818	6,753	8,444	**TOTAL HOUSEHOLDS WITH 1 OR MORE PENSIONER(S)**
317	19	20	4	8	218	260	215	Lone male 65 - 74
266	6	19	8	15	164	286	201	Lone male 75 - 84
88	4	2	-	6	33	99	85	Lone male 85 and over
1,628	16	51	18	65	832	1,784	814	Lone female 60 - 74
1,124	25	71	9	58	633	1,645	883	Lone female 75 - 84
309	10	29	5	14	227	562	338	Lone female 85 and over
2,541	6	44	19	33	511	608	1,812	2 or more, all pensioners, under 75
1,448	11	51	5	32	362	771	1,624	2 or more, all pensioners, any aged 75 and over
2,271	15	32	23	9	572	564	1,607	1 or more pensioner(s) with 1 non-pensioner
1,006	9	16	10	5	266	174	865	1 or more pensioner(s) with 2 or more non-pensioners
20,591	181	510	184	331	6,093	9,264	8,444	**TOTAL PERSONS IN HOUSEHOLDS WITH PENSIONERS**
15,567	140	437	131	312	4,809	8,241	7,491	**Total persons of pensionable age**
10,817	68	218	92	165	3,063	4,237		Pensionable age - 74
3,897	54	172	31	124	1,418	3,118		75 - 84
853	18	47	8	23	328	886		85 and over
								Persons with limiting long-term illness
2,705	20	73	34	55	1,269	1,603		Pensionable age - 74
1,602	32	84	9	59	786	1,582		75 - 84
498	12	27	4	15	207	545		85 and over

Table 47 Households with pensioners: housing – **continued**

47. Households with one or more residents of pensionable age; residents in such households

Household composition	TOTAL HOUSE-HOLDS	Up to 0.5 persons per room	Lacking or sharing use of bath/shower and/or inside WC	No central heating	Lacking or sharing use of bath/shower and/or inside WC and/or no central heating	Not self-contained accommodation
a	b	c	d	e	f	g

New Forest

TOTAL HOUSEHOLDS WITH 1 OR MORE PENSIONER(S)	**26,773**	**24,205**	**338**	**3,258**	**3,450**	**54**
Lone male 65 - 74	922	884	33	181	204	9
Lone male 75 - 84	934	900	27	160	175	4
Lone male 85 and over	289	282	17	54	62	2
Lone female 60 - 74	3,976	3,908	52	466	500	5
Lone female 75 - 84	3,592	3,480	82	485	543	11
Lone female 85 and over	1,143	1,095	48	168	205	4
2 or more, all pensioners, under 75	5,439	5,188	11	462	463	2
2 or more, all pensioners, any aged 75 and over	4,406	4,009	31	488	496	13
1 or more pensioner(s) with 1 non-pensioner	4,370	3,835	20	550	551	2
1 or more pensioner(s) with 2 or more non-pensioners	1,702	624	17	244	251	2
TOTAL PERSONS IN HOUSEHOLDS WITH PENSIONERS	**46,792**	**39,127**	**449**	**5,551**	**5,773**	**78**
Total persons of pensionable age	**37,783**	**33,880**	**390**	**4,375**	**4,580**	**71**
Pensionable age - 74	23,396	21,011	145	2,468	2,538	25
75 - 84	11,684	10,476	167	1,511	1,601	36
85 and over	2,703	2,393	78	396	441	10
Persons with limiting long-term illness						
Pensionable age - 74	5,295	4,618	57	663	705	11
75 - 84	4,582	4,021	78	579	627	14
85 and over	1,543	1,355	48	215	244	8

Portsmouth

TOTAL HOUSEHOLDS WITH 1 OR MORE PENSIONER(S)	**25,502**	**22,276**	**818**	**11,133**	**11,310**	**277**
Lone male 65 - 74	1,279	1,202	69	636	648	54
Lone male 75 - 84	936	898	57	494	505	21
Lone male 85 and over	264	253	21	138	141	4
Lone female 60 - 74	4,728	4,619	130	1,959	2,000	54
Lone female 75 - 84	3,904	3,755	198	1,718	1,766	56
Lone female 85 and over	1,121	1,077	84	552	568	19
2 or more, all pensioners, under 75	3,894	3,453	53	1,548	1,557	20
2 or more, all pensioners, any aged 75 and over	3,271	2,759	108	1,448	1,471	19
1 or more pensioner(s) with 1 non-pensioner	4,277	3,665	77	1,881	1,894	23
1 or more pensioner(s) with 2 or more non-pensioners	1,828	595	21	759	760	7
TOTAL PERSONS IN HOUSEHOLDS WITH PENSIONERS	**43,104**	**33,944**	**1,129**	**18,563**	**18,791**	**361**
Total persons of pensionable age	**33,837**	**29,010**	**1,000**	**14,675**	**14,888**	**320**
Pensionable age - 74	20,890	17,803	438	8,671	8,769	186
75 - 84	10,554	9,098	432	4,819	4,912	106
85 and over	2,393	2,109	130	1,185	1,207	28
Persons with limiting long-term illness						
Pensionable age - 74	6,343	5,299	134	2,707	2,736	55
75 - 84	4,880	4,154	206	2,227	2,272	45
85 and over	1,479	1,297	85	720	736	19

Owner occupied	Tenure		Rented with a job or business	Rented from a housing association	Rented from a local authority or new town	No car	Persons with limiting long-term illness	Household composition
	Rented privately							
	Furnished	Unfurnished						
h	i	j	k	l	m	n	o	a

21,308	279	1,174	290	598	3,124	8,997	12,550	**TOTAL HOUSEHOLDS WITH 1 OR MORE PENSIONER(S)**
619	29	52	13	26	183	314	264	Lone male 65 - 74
669	19	58	10	42	136	405	366	Lone male 75 - 84
232	9	11	1	9	27	195	143	Lone male 85 and over
2,980	39	170	46	100	641	2,091	947	Lone female 60 - 74
2,576	44	239	23	188	522	2,650	1,483	Lone female 75 - 84
792	20	71	5	55	200	1,028	650	Lone female 85 and over
4,710	35	152	47	52	443	538	2,467	2 or more, all pensioners, under 75
3,693	32	226	34	87	334	1,172	3,200	2 or more, all pensioners, any aged 75 and over
3,649	33	154	76	29	429	490	2,051	1 or more pensioner(s) with 1 non-pensioner
1,388	19	41	35	10	209	114	979	1 or more pensioner(s) with 2 or more non-pensioners
38,146	434	1,841	560	797	5,014	11,583	12,550	**TOTAL PERSONS IN HOUSEHOLDS WITH PENSIONERS**
30,690	352	1,587	392	744	4,018	10,810	11,420	**Total persons of pensionable age**
19,385	192	774	272	304	2,469	4,384		Pensionable age - 74
9,195	112	670	96	360	1,251	4,774		75 - 84
2,110	48	143	24	80	298	1,652		85 and over
								Persons with limiting long-term illness
3,987	57	192	69	123	867	1,417		Pensionable age - 74
3,418	48	248	40	182	646	2,271		75 - 84
1,189	33	85	16	44	176	978		85 and over
16,652	370	1,499	183	1,317	5,481	15,832	14,165	**TOTAL HOUSEHOLDS WITH 1 OR MORE PENSIONER(S)**
658	76	81	14	83	367	798	481	Lone male 65 - 74
523	27	75	7	61	243	688	440	Lone male 75 - 84
158	11	22	2	18	53	230	146	Lone male 85 and over
2,777	69	283	21	345	1,233	3,950	1,452	Lone female 60 - 74
2,128	64	313	19	370	1,010	3,651	1,801	Lone female 75 - 84
598	22	109	5	120	267	1,096	701	Lone female 85 and over
2,919	17	165	22	113	658	1,404	2,363	2 or more, all pensioners, under 75
2,354	22	214	20	123	538	1,982	2,919	2 or more, all pensioners, any aged 75 and over
3,112	41	184	53	70	817	1,571	2,555	1 or more pensioner(s) with 1 non-pensioner
1,425	21	53	20	14	295	462	1,307	1 or more pensioner(s) with 2 or more non-pensioners
29,861	523	2,245	348	1,674	8,453	22,394	14,165	**TOTAL PERSONS IN HOUSEHOLDS WITH PENSIONERS**
22,834	415	1,928	241	1,565	6,854	19,607	12,702	**Total persons of pensionable age**
14,499	242	987	159	798	4,205	10,143		Pensionable age - 74
6,795	132	754	68	606	2,199	7,509		75 - 84
1,540	41	187	14	161	450	1,955		85 and over
								Persons with limiting long-term illness
3,891	69	309	54	310	1,710	3,549		Pensionable age - 74
2,970	54	348	34	306	1,168	3,630		75 - 84
936	21	110	9	103	300	1,210		85 and over

Table 47 Households with pensioners: housing – **continued**

47. Households with one or more residents of pensionable age; residents in such households

Household composition	TOTAL HOUSE-HOLDS	Up to 0.5 persons per room	Lacking or sharing use of bath/shower and/or inside WC	No central heating	Lacking or sharing use of bath/shower and/or inside WC and/or no central heating	Not self-contained accommodation
a	b	c	d	e	f	g

Rushmoor

TOTAL HOUSEHOLDS WITH 1 OR MORE PENSIONER(S)	**7,707**	**6,520**	**103**	**907**	**949**	**34**
Lone male 65 - 74	316	281	15	54	60	16
Lone male 75 - 84	294	271	10	49	51	-
Lone male 85 and over	71	65	-	13	13	-
Lone female 60 - 74	1,276	1,239	16	128	135	5
Lone female 75 - 84	1,096	1,030	25	155	168	2
Lone female 85 and over	298	268	10	54	56	4
2 or more, all pensioners, under 75	1,284	1,144	4	107	110	1
2 or more, all pensioners, any aged 75 and over	873	718	11	126	130	1
1 or more pensioner(s) with 1 non-pensioner	1,530	1,294	8	155	158	2
1 or more pensioner(s) with 2 or more non-pensioners	669	210	4	66	68	3
TOTAL PERSONS IN HOUSEHOLDS WITH PENSIONERS	**13,604**	**10,278**	**140**	**1,488**	**1,550**	**48**
Total persons of pensionable age	**10,269**	**8,541**	**119**	**1,180**	**1,230**	**36**
Pensionable age - 74	6,632	5,509	54	624	650	27
75 - 84	3,011	2,516	49	440	462	4
85 and over	626	516	16	116	118	5
Persons with limiting long-term illness						
Pensionable age - 74	1,741	1,373	13	160	166	11
75 - 84	1,340	1,086	17	178	188	2
85 and over	384	314	8	64	65	1

Southampton

TOTAL HOUSEHOLDS WITH 1 OR MORE PENSIONER(S)	**27,089**	**23,088**	**369**	**7,218**	**7,355**	**205**
Lone male 65 - 74	1,369	1,234	76	456	489	68
Lone male 75 - 84	1,098	1,027	38	324	337	19
Lone male 85 and over	297	285	10	95	99	3
Lone female 60 - 74	4,864	4,769	42	1,186	1,209	39
Lone female 75 - 84	3,865	3,748	83	1,036	1,066	29
Lone female 85 and over	1,174	1,124	25	363	373	8
2 or more, all pensioners, under 75	4,445	3,838	20	969	975	9
2 or more, all pensioners, any aged 75 and over	3,252	2,564	34	897	909	15
1 or more pensioner(s) with 1 non-pensioner	4,729	3,911	35	1,330	1,335	11
1 or more pensioner(s) with 2 or more non-pensioners	1,996	588	6	562	563	4
TOTAL PERSONS IN HOUSEHOLDS WITH PENSIONERS	**46,352**	**35,208**	**483**	**12,344**	**12,507**	**251**
Total persons of pensionable age	**36,102**	**30,037**	**432**	**9,524**	**9,680**	**231**
Pensionable age - 74	23,020	18,993	203	5,765	5,845	141
75 - 84	10,666	8,964	185	3,008	3,066	72
85 and over	2,416	2,080	44	751	769	18
Persons with limiting long-term illness						
Pensionable age - 74	6,418	5,107	66	1,623	1,655	43
75 - 84	4,513	3,700	82	1,169	1,194	28
85 and over	1,399	1,194	22	418	424	9

Owner occupied	Rented privately Furnished	Unfurnished	Rented with a job or business	Rented from a housing association	Rented from a local authority or new town	No car	Persons with limiting long-term illness	Household composition
h	i	j	k	l	m	n	o	a
4,561	76	406	73	375	2,216	3,706	3,840	**TOTAL HOUSEHOLDS WITH 1 OR MORE PENSIONER(S)**
150	18	13	7	21	107	154	118	Lone male 65 - 74
131	2	26	4	27	104	181	135	Lone male 75 - 84
32	3	7	1	9	19	60	38	Lone male 85 and over
664	11	63	8	72	458	955	324	Lone female 60 - 74
473	10	80	6	102	425	984	477	Lone female 75 - 84
114	6	30	3	32	113	288	173	Lone female 85 and over
897	5	43	9	33	297	264	710	2 or more, all pensioners, under 75
519	4	67	6	50	227	416	753	2 or more, all pensioners, any aged 75 and over
1,075	6	62	23	26	338	315	725	1 or more pensioner(s) with 1 non-pensioner
506	11	15	6	3	128	89	387	1 or more pensioner(s) with 2 or more non-pensioners
8,751	129	627	128	502	3,467	4,996	3,840	**TOTAL PERSONS IN HOUSEHOLDS WITH PENSIONERS**
6,286	87	531	89	466	2,810	4,456	3,465	Total persons of pensionable age
4,320	53	256	60	210	1,733	2,171		Pensionable age - 74
1,639	24	219	25	203	901	1,814		75 - 84
327	10	56	4	53	176	471		85 and over
								Persons with limiting long-term illness
974	19	70	14	88	576	726		Pensionable age - 74
690	10	95	10	108	427	864		75 - 84
202	5	30	1	32	114	288		85 and over
15,573	296	1,786	216	1,569	7,649	15,627	13,875	**TOTAL HOUSEHOLDS WITH 1 OR MORE PENSIONER(S)**
558	75	97	19	89	531	827	489	Lone male 65 - 74
487	29	110	12	88	372	786	441	Lone male 75 - 84
150	6	22	-	27	92	259	158	Lone male 85 and over
2,408	48	308	34	377	1,689	3,946	1,409	Lone female 60 - 74
1,731	34	362	27	441	1,270	3,595	1,581	Lone female 75 - 84
493	11	119	5	137	409	1,138	658	Lone female 85 and over
3,032	15	214	34	128	1,022	1,409	2,424	2 or more, all pensioners, under 75
2,029	26	293	15	179	710	1,832	2,704	2 or more, all pensioners, any aged 75 and over
3,220	24	206	52	76	1,151	1,424	2,683	1 or more pensioner(s) with 1 non-pensioner
1,465	28	55	18	27	403	411	1,328	1 or more pensioner(s) with 2 or more non-pensioners
28,913	463	2,715	377	2,040	11,844	21,717	13,875	**TOTAL PERSONS IN HOUSEHOLDS WITH PENSIONERS**
21,592	343	2,355	270	1,886	9,656	19,214	12,330	Total persons of pensionable age
14,397	202	1,179	187	891	6,164	9,993		Pensionable age - 74
5,887	114	972	77	793	2,823	7,281		75 - 84
1,308	27	204	6	202	669	1,940		85 and over
								Persons with limiting long-term illness
3,458	67	339	52	329	2,173	3,339		Pensionable age - 74
2,358	39	355	36	377	1,348	3,208		75 - 84
733	14	112	4	119	417	1,130		85 and over

Table 47 Households with pensioners: housing – **continued**

47. Households with one or more residents of pensionable age; residents in such households

Household composition	TOTAL HOUSE-HOLDS	Up to 0.5 persons per room	Lacking or sharing use of bath/shower and/or inside WC	No central heating	Lacking or sharing use of bath/shower and/or inside WC and/or no central heating	Not self-contained accommodation
a	b	c	d	e	f	g
Test Valley						
TOTAL HOUSEHOLDS WITH 1 OR MORE PENSIONER(S)	**11,575**	**10,225**	**91**	**1,491**	**1,524**	**22**
Lone male 65 - 74	437	428	6	84	86	2
Lone male 75 - 84	413	411	5	74	76	1
Lone male 85 and over	111	109	2	26	26	-
Lone female 60 - 74	1,847	1,840	14	206	213	6
Lone female 75 - 84	1,540	1,525	16	204	212	5
Lone female 85 and over	409	400	9	65	70	2
2 or more, all pensioners, under 75	2,104	1,964	10	213	216	1
2 or more, all pensioners, any aged 75 and over	1,557	1,326	10	220	223	3
1 or more pensioner(s) with 1 non-pensioner	2,174	1,883	13	291	292	2
1 or more pensioner(s) with 2 or more non-pensioners	983	339	6	108	110	-
TOTAL PERSONS IN HOUSEHOLDS WITH PENSIONERS	**20,639**	**16,407**	**143**	**2,547**	**2,593**	**29**
Total persons of pensionable age	15,801	13,736	115	1,998	2,038	27
Pensionable age - 74	10,165	8,879	60	1,164	1,182	13
75 - 84	4,649	3,993	43	668	685	10
85 and over	987	864	12	166	171	4
Persons with limiting long-term illness						
Pensionable age - 74	2,409	2,038	23	301	308	4
75 - 84	2,007	1,694	20	259	265	1
85 and over	569	497	4	96	98	2
Winchester						
TOTAL HOUSEHOLDS WITH 1 OR MORE PENSIONER(S)	**13,377**	**11,950**	**134**	**1,681**	**1,733**	**32**
Lone male 65 - 74	461	449	8	77	79	-
Lone male 75 - 84	473	463	21	81	88	-
Lone male 85 and over	156	154	8	25	27	-
Lone female 60 - 74	2,273	2,254	12	259	264	9
Lone female 75 - 84	1,907	1,873	31	199	216	7
Lone female 85 and over	625	610	12	82	89	-
2 or more, all pensioners, under 75	2,357	2,162	10	237	239	3
2 or more, all pensioners, any aged 75 and over	1,790	1,507	14	228	232	3
1 or more pensioner(s) with 1 non-pensioner	2,334	2,055	14	363	366	4
1 or more pensioner(s) with 2 or more non-pensioners	1,001	423	4	130	133	6
TOTAL PERSONS IN HOUSEHOLDS WITH PENSIONERS	**23,182**	**18,937**	**189**	**2,974**	**3,047**	**67**
Total persons of pensionable age	18,099	15,877	161	2,260	2,318	39
Pensionable age - 74	11,332	9,929	62	1,370	1,387	26
75 - 84	5,462	4,785	75	699	730	11
85 and over	1,305	1,163	24	191	201	2
Persons with limiting long-term illness						
Pensionable age - 74	2,564	2,170	16	310	316	4
75 - 84	2,143	1,852	33	258	272	7
85 and over	793	699	17	114	121	2

Owner occupied	Rented privately		Rented with a job or business	Rented from a housing association	Rented from a local authority or new town	No car	Persons with limiting long-term illness	Household composition
	Furnished	Unfurnished						
h	i	j	k	l	m	n	o	a
7,317	98	662	296	341	2,861	4,656	5,535	**TOTAL HOUSEHOLDS WITH 1 OR MORE PENSIONER(S)**
237	10	24	13	4	149	171	124	Lone male 65 - 74
192	3	38	10	15	155	232	181	Lone male 75 - 84
54	1	8	5	7	36	87	60	Lone male 85 and over
1,084	19	94	37	71	542	1,128	471	Lone female 60 - 74
731	24	140	29	95	521	1,303	701	Lone female 75 - 84
200	9	28	4	36	132	374	239	Lone female 85 and over
1,514	8	87	59	40	396	312	977	2 or more, all pensioners, under 75
1,032	9	102	38	38	338	608	1,235	2 or more, all pensioners, any aged 75 and over
1,533	10	102	70	20	439	350	1,015	1 or more pensioner(s) with 1 non-pensioner
740	5	39	31	15	153	91	532	1 or more pensioner(s) with 2 or more non-pensioners
13,853	143	1,073	552	480	4,538	6,215	5,535	**TOTAL PERSONS IN HOUSEHOLDS WITH PENSIONERS**
10,285	118	867	405	421	3,705	5,645	4,985	**Total persons of pensionable age**
6,900	63	470	290	206	2,236	2,540		Pensionable age - 74
2,784	41	337	92	163	1,232	2,456		75 - 84
601	14	60	23	52	237	649		85 and over
								Persons with limiting long-term illness
1,396	18	102	74	73	746	835		Pensionable age - 74
1,102	20	133	32	76	644	1,207		75 - 84
338	5	38	11	36	141	382		85 and over
8,317	134	643	318	643	3,322	5,321	6,048	**TOTAL HOUSEHOLDS WITH 1 OR MORE PENSIONER(S)**
239	10	29	14	30	139	161	153	Lone male 65 - 74
224	4	38	8	26	173	251	184	Lone male 75 - 84
67	3	21	4	13	48	119	100	Lone male 85 and over
1,311	25	93	29	149	666	1,315	549	Lone female 60 - 74
942	25	121	29	169	621	1,531	756	Lone female 75 - 84
280	15	36	3	60	231	582	362	Lone female 85 and over
1,706	10	80	54	61	446	318	1,048	2 or more, all pensioners, under 75
1,166	16	98	42	91	377	646	1,371	2 or more, all pensioners, any aged 75 and over
1,606	14	103	106	38	467	331	1,018	1 or more pensioner(s) with 1 non-pensioner
776	12	24	29	6	154	67	507	1 or more pensioner(s) with 2 or more non-pensioners
15,384	213	1,001	616	855	5,113	6,850	6,048	**TOTAL PERSONS IN HOUSEHOLDS WITH PENSIONERS**
11,601	162	840	436	802	4,258	6,353	5,500	**Total persons of pensionable age**
7,653	81	441	308	381	2,468	2,669		Pensionable age - 74
3,226	57	310	108	333	1,428	2,781		75 - 84
722	24	89	20	88	362	903		85 and over
								Persons with limiting long-term illness
1,510	20	92	69	113	760	841		Pensionable age - 74
1,173	20	116	36	146	652	1,217		75 - 84
443	18	49	15	55	213	554		85 and over

Table 48   Households with dependants: housing   County, districts

48. Households with residents

Non-dependants, dependants and age of youngest or only dependant	Age of oldest dependant	ALL HOUSE-HOLDS	Over 1 person per room	Lacking or sharing use of bath/ shower and/or inside WC	No central heating	Not self-contained accomm-odation	No car
a	b	c	d	e	f	g	h

HAMPSHIRE

a	b	c	d	e	f	g	h
TOTAL HOUSEHOLDS		603,257	9,792	7,073	95,028	6,318	144,615
1 or more non-dependants, no dependants		340,397	1,461	4,788	56,701	4,842	80,977
1 dependent male living alone							
0 up to pensionable age		2,328		182	736	237	1,545
Pensionable age - 74		2,485		123	662	65	1,419
75 - 84		2,749		106	681	18	1,920
85 and over		1,033		53	269	5	877
1 dependent female living alone							
0 up to pensionable age		1,770		58	452	73	1,288
Pensionable age - 74		6,947		128	1,453	30	5,652
75 - 84		8,921		300	1,766	40	8,185
85 and over		3,434		169	800	23	3,327
2 or more persons dependant, no non-dependants							
0 up to pensionable age	0 up to pensionable age	1,005	23	20	241	17	445
	Pensionable age - 74	718	2	1	153	2	280
	75 - 84	238	1	4	86	-	151
	85 and over	81	-	1	37	-	48
Pensionable age - 74	Pensionable age - 74	3,508	1	15	645	5	1,135
	75 - 84	1,692	4	24	355	5	879
	85 and over	347	-	3	65	-	142
75 - 84	75 - 84	2,002	6	26	422	4	1,149
	85 and over	518	-	13	122	6	367
85 and over	85 and over	201	-	3	49	1	160
1 male non-dependant with 1 or more dependant(s)							
0 - 4	0 - 4	208	11	5	41	9	76
	5 - 15	151	13	2	21	2	57
	16 up to pensionable age	260	19	-	37	1	36
	Pensionable age and over	7	-	-	2	-	1
5 - 15	5 - 15	1,220	17	12	225	17	317
	16 up to pensionable age	620	13	1	94	-	87
	Pensionable age and over	31	1	-	9	-	7
16 up to pensionable age	16 up to pensionable age	3,225	28	34	640	23	719
	Pensionable age and over	153	1	2	47	-	51
Pensionable age and over	Pensionable age and over	7,164	5	68	1,695	11	2,056
1 female non-dependant with 1 or more dependant(s)							
0 - 4	0 - 4	4,474	270	191	963	247	2,973
	5 - 15	3,337	170	20	760	16	2,208
	16 up to pensionable age	571	103	12	162	7	215
	Pensionable age and over	38	1	-	12	-	24
5 - 15	5 - 15	8,611	74	65	1,603	80	3,983
	16 up to pensionable age	1,580	44	9	280	4	497
	Pensionable age and over	150	5	2	33	-	48
16 up to pensionable age	16 up to pensionable age	6,525	24	41	1,327	28	1,809
	Pensionable age and over	267	1	2	58	1	95
Pensionable age and over	Pensionable age and over	13,292	13	79	2,534	30	4,989
2 or more non-dependants with 1 or more dependant(s)							
0 - 4	0 - 4	39,632	1,623	262	4,685	290	3,799
	5 - 15	28,243	3,106	40	3,279	37	2,904
	16 up to pensionable age	1,364	340	2	246	4	235
	Pensionable age and over	290	42	2	54	1	34
5 - 15	5 - 15	70,259	1,688	129	6,772	103	4,845
	16 up to pensionable age	10,461	469	11	824	9	593
	Pensionable age and over	682	49	4	87	1	56
16 up to pensionable age	16 up to pensionable age	15,533	126	39	1,879	20	1,276
	Pensionable age and over	286	7	-	53	-	36
Pensionable age and over	Pensionable age and over	4,249	31	22	911	4	643

48. Households with residents

Non-dependants, dependants and age of youngest or only dependant	Age of oldest dependant	ALL HOUSE-HOLDS	Over 1 person per room	Lacking or sharing use of bath/ shower and/or inside WC	No central heating	Not self-contained accomm-odation	No car
a	b	c	d	e	f	g	h

Basingstoke & Deane

TOTAL HOUSEHOLDS		**54,323**	**775**	**293**	**4,187**	**203**	**10,361**
1 or more non-dependants, no dependants		30,576	98	213	2,685	172	5,701
1 dependent male living alone							
0 up to pensionable age		133		4	22	-	77
Pensionable age - 74		163		1	22	-	75
75 - 84		187		4	28	1	133
85 and over		69		3	16	-	63
1 dependent female living alone							
0 up to pensionable age		123		2	17	-	84
Pensionable age - 74		473		2	46	-	397
75 - 84		680		8	63	1	646
85 and over		239		5	27	-	230
2 or more persons dependant, no non-dependants							
0 up to pensionable age	0 up to pensionable age	68	1	1	6	-	31
	Pensionable age - 74	63	-	-	6	-	33
	75 - 84	10	-	-	3	-	8
	85 and over	4	-	-	-	-	4
Pensionable age - 74	Pensionable age - 74	257	-	-	17	-	75
	75 - 84	116	-	-	14	-	55
	85 and over	25	-	-	-	-	11
75 - 84	75 - 84	143	1	-	12	-	101
	85 and over	39	-	-	8	-	25
85 and over	85 and over	15	-	-	3	-	12
1 male non-dependant with 1 or more dependant(s)							
0 - 4	0 - 4	15	-	-	1	-	3
	5 - 15	11	2	-	1	-	1
	16 up to pensionable age	23	-	-	1	-	6
	Pensionable age and over	-	-	-	-	-	-
5 - 15	5 - 15	86	1	-	8	-	20
	16 up to pensionable age	56	1	-	7	-	7
	Pensionable age and over	3	-	-	1	-	1
16 up to pensionable age	16 up to pensionable age	263	2	-	17	-	46
	Pensionable age and over	13	-	1	1	-	2
Pensionable age and over	Pensionable age and over	549	-	1	71	-	170
1 female non-dependant with 1 or more dependant(s)							
0 - 4	0 - 4	282	19	10	37	8	171
	5 - 15	297	10	3	32	-	196
	16 up to pensionable age	43	6	1	5	-	20
	Pensionable age and over	2	-	-	-	-	1
5 - 15	5 - 15	664	7	5	47	4	296
	16 up to pensionable age	122	5	2	6	1	42
	Pensionable age and over	8	1	-	1	-	4
16 up to pensionable age	16 up to pensionable age	465	2	-	35	1	129
	Pensionable age and over	21	-	-	1	-	6
Pensionable age and over	Pensionable age and over	829	-	5	79	1	324
2 or more non-dependants with 1 or more dependant(s)							
0 - 4	0 - 4	3,996	119	9	214	7	245
	5 - 15	2,773	269	2	158	1	239
	16 up to pensionable age	125	34	-	5	-	19
	Pensionable age and over	23	2	-	1	-	2
5 - 15	5 - 15	7,233	144	10	306	5	437
	16 up to pensionable age	1,088	32	-	41	-	62
	Pensionable age and over	71	3	-	2	-	2
16 up to pensionable age	16 up to pensionable age	1,501	13	-	77	1	101
	Pensionable age and over	19	-	-	2	-	1
Pensionable age and over	Pensionable age and over	359	3	1	35	-	47

48. Households with residents

East Hampshire

Non-dependants, dependants and age of youngest or only dependant	Age of oldest dependant	ALL HOUSE-HOLDS	Over 1 person per room	Lacking or sharing use of bath/ shower and/or inside WC	No central heating	Not self-contained accomm-odation	No car
a	b	c	d	e	f	g	h
TOTAL HOUSEHOLDS		39,158	570	344	4,030	158	6,087
1 or more non-dependants, no dependants		22,141	85	227	2,505	101	3,625
1 dependent male living alone							
0 up to pensionable age		83		6	14	1	33
Pensionable age - 74		137		7	31	2	65
75 - 84		155		3	28	-	92
85 and over		55		4	10	-	43
1 dependent female living alone							
0 up to pensionable age		76		3	20	1	43
Pensionable age - 74		339		8	50	1	239
75 - 84		485		21	64	2	418
85 and over		201		15	33	1	193
2 or more persons dependant, no non-dependants							
0 up to pensionable age	0 up to pensionable age	38	-	2	6	1	9
	Pensionable age - 74	35	1	-	9	-	11
	75 - 84	9	-	-	3	-	3
	85 and over	3	-	-	1	-	-
Pensionable age - 74	Pensionable age - 74	167	-	1	20	-	32
	75 - 84	94	1	2	10	-	39
	85 and over	16	-	-	1	-	4
75 - 84	75 - 84	87	-	-	13	-	43
	85 and over	30	-	1	5	-	19
85 and over	85 and over	14	-	-	2	-	14
1 male non-dependant with 1 or more dependant(s)							
0 - 4	0 - 4	16	-	-	2	-	3
	5 - 15	9	1	-	-	-	2
	16 up to pensionable age	18	1	-	1	-	-
	Pensionable age and over	1	-	-	-	-	-
5 - 15	5 - 15	86	1	1	18	-	14
	16 up to pensionable age	45	-	-	4	-	4
	Pensionable age and over	3	1	-	2	-	-
16 up to pensionable age	16 up to pensionable age	151	-	1	21	-	24
	Pensionable age and over	8	1	-	2	-	3
Pensionable age and over	Pensionable age and over	382	-	5	67	1	73
1 female non-dependant with 1 or more dependant(s)							
0 - 4	0 - 4	193	11	3	41	4	100
	5 - 15	159	8	1	23	2	77
	16 up to pensionable age	23	5	1	5	1	5
	Pensionable age and over	3	-	-	1	-	3
5 - 15	5 - 15	466	5	2	51	3	135
	16 up to pensionable age	102	-	-	5	-	15
	Pensionable age and over	9	2	-	2	-	5
16 up to pensionable age	16 up to pensionable age	350	-	1	49	1	55
	Pensionable age and over	11	-	-	1	-	2
Pensionable age and over	Pensionable age and over	849	1	-	93	2	223
2 or more non-dependants with 1 or more dependant(s)							
0 - 4	0 - 4	2,646	115	16	163	16	102
	5 - 15	2,023	173	2	151	1	76
	16 up to pensionable age	87	7	-	9	1	6
	Pensionable age and over	20	1	1	4	1	1
5 - 15	5 - 15	5,005	104	4	309	10	143
	16 up to pensionable age	879	34	1	40	3	19
	Pensionable age and over	49	6	-	2	-	1
16 up to pensionable age	16 up to pensionable age	1,121	6	5	87	2	46
	Pensionable age and over	26	-	-	5	-	2
Pensionable age and over	Pensionable age and over	253	-	-	47	-	23

48. Households with residents

Non-dependants, dependants and age of youngest or only dependant	Age of oldest dependant	ALL HOUSE-HOLDS	Over 1 person per room	Lacking or sharing use of bath/ shower and/or inside WC	No central heating	Not self-contained accomm-odation	No car
a	b	c	d	e	f	g	h

Eastleigh

TOTAL HOUSEHOLDS		41,219	464	278	4,746	167	7,366
1 or more non-dependants, no dependants		23,144	57	182	2,919	137	4,215
1 dependent male living alone							
0 up to pensionable age		111		3	18	4	64
Pensionable age - 74		140		7	22	1	67
75 - 84		143		2	26	-	100
85 and over		66		4	10	-	58
1 dependent female living alone							
0 up to pensionable age		93		4	19	2	58
Pensionable age - 74		426		4	62	-	343
75 - 84		485		19	66	1	443
85 and over		190		13	29	-	182
2 or more persons dependant, no non-dependants							
0 up to pensionable age	0 up to pensionable age	61	2	2	14	2	23
	Pensionable age - 74	43	-	-	9	-	18
	75 - 84	13	1	-	4	-	8
	85 and over	6	-	1	2	-	2
Pensionable age - 74	Pensionable age - 74	232	-	1	30	-	69
	75 - 84	97	1	1	17	-	50
	85 and over	21	-	-	3	-	10
75 - 84	75 - 84	130	2	-	17	-	78
	85 and over	28	-	-	9	-	23
85 and over	85 and over	10	-	-	1	-	8
1 male non-dependant with 1 or more dependant(s)							
0 - 4	0 - 4	13	-	-	2	-	3
	5 - 15	6	1	-	1	-	-
	16 up to pensionable age	13	3	-	1	-	-
	Pensionable age and over	1	-	-	-	-	-
5 - 15	5 - 15	83	3	2	7	-	15
	16 up to pensionable age	45	1	-	5	-	2
	Pensionable age and over	2	-	-	1	-	-
16 up to pensionable age	16 up to pensionable age	225	1	2	34	-	30
	Pensionable age and over	6	-	-	1	-	-
Pensionable age and over	Pensionable age and over	453	2	4	104	-	114
1 female non-dependant with 1 or more dependant(s)							
0 - 4	0 - 4	247	5	4	66	5	127
	5 - 15	171	1	-	26	-	79
	16 up to pensionable age	32	3	2	10	1	5
	Pensionable age and over	-	-	-	-	-	-
5 - 15	5 - 15	527	1	2	70	5	155
	16 up to pensionable age	102	-	-	10	-	19
	Pensionable age and over	6	-	-	-	-	-
16 up to pensionable age	16 up to pensionable age	434	-	3	68	-	97
	Pensionable age and over	17	-	-	6	-	7
Pensionable age and over	Pensionable age and over	827	-	1	122	-	310
2 or more non-dependants with 1 or more dependant(s)							
0 - 4	0 - 4	2,996	77	8	297	6	157
	5 - 15	2,028	160	-	150	1	123
	16 up to pensionable age	72	13	-	2	-	4
	Pensionable age and over	15	3	-	3	-	1
5 - 15	5 - 15	5,381	88	4	322	1	184
	16 up to pensionable age	710	26	-	37	-	25
	Pensionable age and over	39	1	-	3	-	2
16 up to pensionable age	16 up to pensionable age	1,038	11	2	76	1	50
	Pensionable age and over	19	-	-	3	-	3
Pensionable age and over	Pensionable age and over	272	1	1	42	-	35

48. Households with residents

Non-dependants, dependants and age of youngest or only dependant	Age of oldest dependant	ALL HOUSE-HOLDS	Over 1 person per room	Lacking or sharing use of bath/ shower and/or inside WC	No central heating	Not self-contained accomm-odation	No car
a	b	c	d	e	f	g	h

Fareham

TOTAL HOUSEHOLDS		38,369	337	229	4,621	77	6,683
1 or more non-dependants, no dependants		21,864	33	129	2,831	56	3,915
1 dependent male living alone							
0 up to pensionable age		80		2	25	2	39
Pensionable age - 74		138		11	29	1	58
75 - 84		155		12	35	-	101
85 and over		50		7	12	1	43
1 dependent female living alone							
0 up to pensionable age		80		1	19	1	50
Pensionable age - 74		341		6	67	-	259
75 - 84		479		18	82	4	441
85 and over		188		8	43	1	183
2 or more persons dependant, no non-dependants							
0 up to pensionable age	0 up to pensionable age	53	-	-	7	-	9
	Pensionable age - 74	47	-	-	6	-	14
	75 - 84	13	-	-	6	-	8
	85 and over	3	-	-	-	-	1
Pensionable age - 74	Pensionable age - 74	252	-	1	34	-	51
	75 - 84	88	-	3	11	-	38
	85 and over	25	-	-	2	-	9
75 - 84	75 - 84	132	-	-	26	-	71
	85 and over	30	-	2	4	1	22
85 and over	85 and over	12	-	-	1	-	10
1 male non-dependant with 1 or more dependant(s)							
0 - 4	0 - 4	13	-	-	2	-	4
	5 - 15	10	-	-	-	-	2
	16 up to pensionable age	16	-	-	2	-	1
	Pensionable age and over	-	-	-	-	-	-
5 - 15	5 - 15	68	1	1	11	1	10
	16 up to pensionable age	29	-	-	-	-	1
	Pensionable age and over	1	-	-	-	-	-
16 up to pensionable age	16 up to pensionable age	228	4	-	40	-	35
	Pensionable age and over	4	-	-	2	-	3
Pensionable age and over	Pensionable age and over	458	2	4	86	-	99
1 female non-dependant with 1 or more dependant(s)							
0 - 4	0 - 4	172	1	4	29	4	79
	5 - 15	126	4	-	34	-	59
	16 up to pensionable age	31	4	-	8	-	6
	Pensionable age and over	2	-	-	-	-	-
5 - 15	5 - 15	448	-	1	57	-	152
	16 up to pensionable age	88	-	-	19	-	16
	Pensionable age and over	6	-	-	1	-	2
16 up to pensionable age	16 up to pensionable age	425	1	2	68	2	66
	Pensionable age and over	16	-	-	3	-	8
Pensionable age and over	Pensionable age and over	924	2	5	141	-	319
2 or more non-dependants with 1 or more dependant(s)							
0 - 4	0 - 4	2,566	50	3	198	1	106
	5 - 15	1,850	132	3	154	2	104
	16 up to pensionable age	67	10	-	13	-	6
	Pensionable age and over	15	1	-	2	-	2
5 - 15	5 - 15	4,725	67	4	302	-	160
	16 up to pensionable age	647	15	1	55	-	35
	Pensionable age and over	46	3	-	2	-	3
16 up to pensionable age	16 up to pensionable age	1,070	5	-	105	-	55
	Pensionable age and over	17	-	-	3	-	2
Pensionable age and over	Pensionable age and over	271	2	1	44	-	26

48. Households with residents

Non-dependants, dependants and age of youngest or only dependant	Age of oldest dependant	ALL HOUSE-HOLDS	Over 1 person per room	Lacking or sharing use of bath/ shower and/or inside WC	No central heating	Not self-contained accomm-odation	No car
a	b	c	d	e	f	g	h

Gosport

TOTAL HOUSEHOLDS		29,356	374	217	5,193	89	8,600
1 or more non-dependants, no dependants		15,890	32	127	3,088	71	4,627
1 dependent male living alone							
0 up to pensionable age		99		1	34	1	66
Pensionable age - 74		110		7	29	1	58
75 - 84		121		5	32	-	83
85 and over		58		1	16	-	48
1 dependent female living alone							
0 up to pensionable age		90		1	20	1	59
Pensionable age - 74		362		9	79	-	293
75 - 84		484		16	118	-	452
85 and over		172		14	44	1	169
2 or more persons dependant, no non-dependants							
0 up to pensionable age	0 up to pensionable age	48	1	1	9	-	23
	Pensionable age - 74	37	-	-	7	-	7
	75 - 84	8	-	-	3	-	7
	85 and over	1	-	-	-	-	1
Pensionable age - 74	Pensionable age - 74	199	-	-	34	2	73
	75 - 84	92	-	1	18	-	57
	85 and over	14	-	-	4	-	7
75 - 84	75 - 84	122	-	-	33	-	68
	85 and over	19	-	-	2	-	13
85 and over	85 and over	10	-	-	2	-	9
1 male non-dependant with 1 or more dependant(s)							
0 - 4	0 - 4	10	1	-	-	-	4
	5 - 15	14	-	-	1	-	5
	16 up to pensionable age	20	3	-	4	-	3
	Pensionable age and over	1	-	-	-	-	-
5 - 15	5 - 15	65	-	-	8	-	16
	16 up to pensionable age	44	-	-	9	-	6
	Pensionable age and over	3	-	-	1	-	2
16 up to pensionable age	16 up to pensionable age	177	1	1	33		52
	Pensionable age and over	2	-	-	-	-	1
Pensionable age and over	Pensionable age and over	341	-	3	82	-	99
1 female non-dependant with 1 or more dependant(s)							
0 - 4	0 - 4	292	13	13	56	1	214
	5 - 15	194	-	1	25	1	135
	16 up to pensionable age	29	4	2	5	1	17
	Pensionable age and over	-	-	-	-	-	-
5 - 15	5 - 15	513	1	1	88	1	276
	16 up to pensionable age	89	2	-	18	-	46
	Pensionable age and over	3	-	-	1	-	2
16 up to pensionable age	16 up to pensionable age	310	1	1	64	2	99
	Pensionable age and over	13	-	-	3	-	5
Pensionable age and over	Pensionable age and over	622	1	2	128	-	265
2 or more non-dependants with 1 or more dependant(s)							
0 - 4	0 - 4	2,120	56	4	353	3	354
	5 - 15	1,558	144	-	171	1	283
	16 up to pensionable age	51	13	-	7	-	6
	Pensionable age and over	8	1	-	-	-	-
5 - 15	5 - 15	3,518	75	5	398	1	417
	16 up to pensionable age	457	18	-	33	-	45
	Pensionable age and over	24	1	-	2	-	2
16 up to pensionable age	16 up to pensionable age	725	6	1	88	1	77
	Pensionable age and over	11	-	-	1	-	1
Pensionable age and over	Pensionable age and over	206	-	-	42	-	48

48. Households with residents

Non-dependants, dependants and age of youngest or only dependant	Age of oldest dependant	ALL HOUSE-HOLDS	Over 1 person per room	Lacking or sharing use of bath/ shower and/or inside WC	No central heating	Not self-contained accomm-odation	No car
a	b	c	d	e	f	g	h

Hart

TOTAL HOUSEHOLDS		**29,073**	**266**	**150**	**1,922**	**70**	**3,287**
1 or more non-dependants, no dependants		16,092	26	100	1,166	53	1,931
1 dependent male living alone							
0 up to pensionable age		42		2	8	-	18
Pensionable age - 74		60		-	9	-	20
75 - 84		95		1	16	-	59
85 and over		26		-	6	-	22
1 dependent female living alone							
0 up to pensionable age		32		-	3	-	22
Pensionable age - 74		180		4	26	2	131
75 - 84		349		4	45	-	310
85 and over		130		2	20	1	126
2 or more persons dependant, no non-dependants							
0 up to pensionable age	0 up to pensionable age	22	1	1	2	-	10
	Pensionable age - 74	18	-	-	2	-	8
	75 - 84	12	-	1	3	-	5
	85 and over	2	-	-	2	-	2
Pensionable age - 74	Pensionable age - 74	97	-	-	11	-	22
	75 - 84	51	-	1	12	1	25
	85 and over	6	-	-	1	-	1
75 - 84	75 - 84	63	-	-	10	-	29
	85 and over	17	-	1	6	-	10
85 and over	85 and over	5	-	-	1	-	4
1 male non-dependant with 1 or more dependant(s)							
0 - 4	0 - 4	3	-	-	-	-	-
	5 - 15	5	-	-	1	-	1
	16 up to pensionable age	8	-	-	1	-	-
	Pensionable age and over	-	-	-	-	-	-
5 - 15	5 - 15	54	-	-	3	-	6
	16 up to pensionable age	33	-	-	4	-	2
	Pensionable age and over	-	-	-	-	-	-
16 up to pensionable age	16 up to pensionable age	122	2	3	18	3	11
	Pensionable age and over	4	-	-	-	-	-
Pensionable age and over	Pensionable age and over	238	-	4	35	-	46
1 female non-dependant with 1 or more dependant(s)							
0 - 4	0 - 4	109	3	2	12	2	43
	5 - 15	74	3	-	9	-	26
	16 up to pensionable age	6	-	-	1	-	-
	Pensionable age and over	-	-	-	-	-	-
5 - 15	5 - 15	319	3	3	32	2	71
	16 up to pensionable age	58	2	-	6	-	5
	Pensionable age and over	8	-	-	-	-	1
16 up to pensionable age	16 up to pensionable age	200	1	3	23	-	26
	Pensionable age and over	11	-	-	2	1	-
Pensionable age and over	Pensionable age and over	485	-	-	61	1	122
2 or more non-dependants with 1 or more dependant(s)							
0 - 4	0 - 4	2,121	53	4	94	2	44
	5 - 15	1,535	82	5	60	-	33
	16 up to pensionable age	59	8	-	3	-	-
	Pensionable age and over	15	1	-	1	-	-
5 - 15	5 - 15	4,363	70	7	140	1	58
	16 up to pensionable age	771	8	-	13	-	5
	Pensionable age and over	36	2	-	-	-	1
16 up to pensionable age	16 up to pensionable age	945	-	1	33	1	23
	Pensionable age and over	17	-	-	-	-	-
Pensionable age and over	Pensionable age and over	175	1	1	21	-	8

48. Households with residents

Non-dependants, dependants and age of youngest or only dependant	Age of oldest dependant	ALL HOUSE-HOLDS	Over 1 person per room	Lacking or sharing use of bath/ shower and/or inside WC	No central heating	Not self-contained accomm-odation	No car
a	b	c	d	e	f	g	h

Havant

TOTAL HOUSEHOLDS		46,151	1,032	389	9,594	197	11,636
1 or more non-dependants, no dependants		24,555	81	181	4,948	97	5,832
1 dependent male living alone							
0 up to pensionable age		193		7	86	3	122
Pensionable age - 74		205		13	61	1	119
75 - 84		199		9	39	1	147
85 and over		83		3	17	-	67
1 dependent female living alone							
0 up to pensionable age		175		-	56	2	118
Pensionable age - 74		634		15	152	-	523
75 - 84		666		46	130	1	605
85 and over		253		16	53	-	244
2 or more persons dependant, no non-dependants							
0 up to pensionable age	0 up to pensionable age	118	1	1	40	1	54
	Pensionable age - 74	62	-	-	18	-	24
	75 - 84	23	-	-	9	-	14
	85 and over	9	-	-	5	-	4
Pensionable age - 74	Pensionable age - 74	379	-	1	75	1	111
	75 - 84	149	-	-	39	1	74
	85 and over	46	-	-	16	-	22
75 - 84	75 - 84	162	1	1	30	-	85
	85 and over	41	-	-	12	-	29
85 and over	85 and over	16	-	-	5	-	12
1 male non-dependant with 1 or more dependant(s)							
0 - 4	0 - 4	16	1	-	7	-	9
	5 - 15	15	2	1	-	1	5
	16 up to pensionable age	25	1	-	7	-	5
	Pensionable age and over	1	-	-	-	-	-
5 - 15	5 - 15	115	-	-	26	-	28
	16 up to pensionable age	60	3	1	20	-	13
	Pensionable age and over	6	-	-	3	-	-
16 up to pensionable age	16 up to pensionable age	327	1	1	83	-	67
	Pensionable age and over	21	-	-	6	-	6
Pensionable age and over	Pensionable age and over	617	-	1	156	-	154
1 female non-dependant with 1 or more dependant(s)							
0 - 4	0 - 4	385	31	34	127	33	269
	5 - 15	367	25	2	142	2	278
	16 up to pensionable age	61	10	-	22	-	31
	Pensionable age and over	5	-	-	1	-	2
5 - 15	5 - 15	835	9	8	257	6	475
	16 up to pensionable age	163	10	1	39	-	59
	Pensionable age and over	20	1	-	8	-	5
16 up to pensionable age	16 up to pensionable age	676	2	3	204	1	182
	Pensionable age and over	26	-	-	8	-	6
Pensionable age and over	Pensionable age and over	1,126	-	-	248	-	406
2 or more non-dependants with 1 or more dependant(s)							
0 - 4	0 - 4	2,764	152	33	535	36	344
	5 - 15	2,361	375	3	498	5	350
	16 up to pensionable age	138	42	-	45	-	31
	Pensionable age and over	29	8	-	6	-	2
5 - 15	5 - 15	5,442	199	5	918	5	464
	16 up to pensionable age	803	57	1	105	-	60
	Pensionable age and over	55	3	-	11	-	6
16 up to pensionable age	16 up to pensionable age	1,332	12	1	223	-	112
	Pensionable age and over	28	1	-	3	-	3
Pensionable age and over	Pensionable age and over	364	4	1	95	-	58

48. Households with residents

Non-dependants, dependants and age of youngest or only dependant	Age of oldest dependant	ALL HOUSE-HOLDS	Over 1 person per room	Lacking or sharing use of bath/ shower and/or inside WC	No central heating	Not self-contained accomm-odation	No car
a	b	c	d	e	f	g	h

New Forest

		c	d	e	f	g	h
TOTAL HOUSEHOLDS		65,411	706	590	7,182	234	11,848
1 or more non-dependants, no dependants		38,245	103	326	4,471	128	6,857
1 dependent male living alone							
0 up to pensionable age		161		12	28	7	73
Pensionable age - 74		244		13	35	4	111
75 - 84		355		15	52	2	200
85 and over		140		8	23	1	108
1 dependent female living alone							
0 up to pensionable age		124		6	20	3	81
Pensionable age - 74		743		25	97	1	515
75 - 84		1,095		40	140	4	930
85 and over		459		31	72	4	433
2 or more persons dependant, no non-dependants							
0 up to pensionable age	0 up to pensionable age	87	-	1	11	-	17
	Pensionable age - 74	71	-	-	11	-	15
	75 - 84	20	-	-	3	-	11
	85 and over	6	-	-	2	-	2
Pensionable age - 74	Pensionable age - 74	437	-	1	54	-	92
	75 - 84	198	-	2	25	-	77
	85 and over	34	-	-	4	-	11
75 - 84	75 - 84	295	-	5	39	1	123
	85 and over	89	-	1	15	-	45
85 and over	85 and over	41	-	1	8	1	31
1 male non-dependant with 1 or more dependant(s)							
0 - 4	0 - 4	14	-	-	4	1	3
	5 - 15	13	1	-	3	-	7
	16 up to pensionable age	17	1	-	1	-	-
	Pensionable age and over	-	-	-	-	-	-
5 - 15	5 - 15	113	1	1	16	1	11
	16 up to pensionable age	42	-	-	1	-	1
	Pensionable age and over	3	-	-	-	-	-
16 up to pensionable age	16 up to pensionable age	292	-	3	36	-	41
	Pensionable age and over	18	-	1	3	-	5
Pensionable age and over	Pensionable age and over	897	-	6	130	2	150
1 female non-dependant with 1 or more dependant(s)							
0 - 4	0 - 4	355	12	18	65	17	200
	5 - 15	196	7	-	27	-	90
	16 up to pensionable age	41	7	1	16	-	8
	Pensionable age and over	2	-	-	-	-	2
5 - 15	5 - 15	770	6	9	107	9	231
	16 up to pensionable age	173	3	1	22	-	29
	Pensionable age and over	22	-	1	1	-	2
16 up to pensionable age	16 up to pensionable age	760	2	4	90	1	128
	Pensionable age and over	30	-	-	2	-	4
Pensionable age and over	Pensionable age and over	2,042	2	3	223	5	496
2 or more non-dependants with 1 or more dependant(s)							
0 - 4	0 - 4	3,601	111	24	345	26	184
	5 - 15	2,584	237	4	204	3	116
	16 up to pensionable age	122	27	-	13	-	13
	Pensionable age and over	28	5	1	6	-	5
5 - 15	5 - 15	7,047	119	12	469	11	235
	16 up to pensionable age	1,108	42	5	54	1	28
	Pensionable age and over	70	7	-	5	-	4
16 up to pensionable age	16 up to pensionable age	1,642	10	6	157	1	84
	Pensionable age and over	30	-	-	3	-	2
Pensionable age and over	Pensionable age and over	535	3	3	69	-	37

48. Households with residents

Non-dependants, dependants and age of youngest or only dependant	Age of oldest dependant	ALL HOUSE-HOLDS	Over 1 person per room	Lacking or sharing use of bath/ shower and/or inside WC	No central heating	Not self-contained accomm-odation	No car
a	b	c	d	e	f	g	h

Portsmouth

TOTAL HOUSEHOLDS		72,590	1,422	1,905	26,293	1,905	29,067
1 or more non-dependants, no dependants		41,098	268	1,339	15,369	1,513	16,154
1 dependent male living alone							
0 up to pensionable age		483		44	260	69	362
Pensionable age - 74		457		22	204	22	320
75 - 84		427		27	239	9	345
85 and over		140		11	74	2	126
1 dependent female living alone							
0 up to pensionable age		344		19	153	26	288
Pensionable age - 74		1,213		39	493	15	1,082
75 - 84		1,454		73	595	18	1,388
85 and over		531		42	246	12	524
2 or more persons dependant, no non-dependants							
0 up to pensionable age	0 up to pensionable age	177	3	5	75	5	103
	Pensionable age - 74	113	-	-	43	2	52
	75 - 84	46	-	2	28	-	35
	85 and over	22	-	-	13	-	16
Pensionable age - 74	Pensionable age - 74	499	1	5	213	1	248
	75 - 84	292	2	9	119	2	183
	85 and over	46	-	1	14	-	24
75 - 84	75 - 84	280	1	12	134	-	195
	85 and over	71	-	5	29	4	59
85 and over	85 and over	31	-	2	16	-	27
1 male non-dependant with 1 or more dependant(s)							
0 - 4	0 - 4	35	3	3	14	3	11
	5 - 15	20	2	-	6	-	13
	16 up to pensionable age	39	3	-	11	-	14
	Pensionable age and over	2	-	-	1	-	-
5 - 15	5 - 15	172	6	4	68	9	84
	16 up to pensionable age	73	2	-	20	-	17
	Pensionable age and over	3	-	-	-	-	2
16 up to pensionable age	16 up to pensionable age	460	4	8	197	10	166
	Pensionable age and over	28	-	-	16	-	17
Pensionable age and over	Pensionable age and over	1,068	-	21	508	3	457
1 female non-dependant with 1 or more dependant(s)							
0 - 4	0 - 4	768	43	34	284	48	576
	5 - 15	584	33	6	190	3	455
	16 up to pensionable age	93	19	1	38	1	39
	Pensionable age and over	10	1	-	5	-	8
5 - 15	5 - 15	1,304	9	11	457	19	831
	16 up to pensionable age	186	7	1	65	1	86
	Pensionable age and over	23	-	-	5	-	9
16 up to pensionable age	16 up to pensionable age	904	3	9	364	7	394
	Pensionable age and over	31	-	1	14	-	12
Pensionable age and over	Pensionable age and over	1,699	4	40	752	9	928
2 or more non-dependants with 1 or more dependant(s)							
0 - 4	0 - 4	4,563	212	54	1,339	58	933
	5 - 15	3,073	435	6	861	5	663
	16 up to pensionable age	208	63	1	77	-	68
	Pensionable age and over	45	7	-	17	-	9
5 - 15	5 - 15	6,528	201	26	1,702	21	1,147
	16 up to pensionable age	805	57	1	191	2	128
	Pensionable age and over	92	11	1	31	-	18
16 up to pensionable age	16 up to pensionable age	1,447	14	13	473	4	278
	Pensionable age and over	50	4	-	22	-	11
Pensionable age and over	Pensionable age and over	553	4	7	248	2	162

48. Households with residents

Non-dependants, dependants and age of youngest or only dependant	Age of oldest dependant	ALL HOUSE-HOLDS	Over 1 person per room	Lacking or sharing use of bath/shower and/or inside WC	No central heating	Not self-contained accomm-odation	No car
a	b	c	d	e	f	g	h
Rushmoor							
TOTAL HOUSEHOLDS		30,523	623	492	2,341	581	6,659
1 or more non-dependants, no dependants		16,878	98	364	1,580	430	3,576
1 dependent male living alone							
0 up to pensionable age		100		15	16	17	60
Pensionable age - 74		112		6	20	9	66
75 - 84		131		3	19	-	97
85 and over		37		-	7	-	34
1 dependent female living alone							
0 up to pensionable age		84		4	6	7	64
Pensionable age - 74		275		3	29	1	240
75 - 84		403		10	50	-	377
85 and over		136		3	20	-	133
2 or more persons dependant, no non-dependants							
0 up to pensionable age	0 up to pensionable age	43	-	-	3	-	16
	Pensionable age - 74	29	-	-	1	-	14
	75 - 84	18	-	-	5	-	11
	85 and over	1	-	-	1	-	1
Pensionable age - 74	Pensionable age - 74	154	-	-	16	-	48
	75 - 84	71	-	1	9	1	37
	85 and over	10	-	-	-	-	5
75 - 84	75 - 84	82	-	-	8	-	50
	85 and over	14	-	-	2	-	11
85 and over	85 and over	9	-	-	3	-	6
1 male non-dependant with 1 or more dependant(s)							
0 - 4	0 - 4	17	-	-	-	-	8
	5 - 15	12	-	-	1	-	5
	16 up to pensionable age	23	1	-	-	-	1
	Pensionable age and over	-	-	-	-	-	-
5 - 15	5 - 15	52	3	-	2	3	11
	16 up to pensionable age	35	-	-	2	-	4
	Pensionable age and over	1	-	-	-	-	-
16 up to pensionable age	16 up to pensionable age	167	1	3	17	3	48
	Pensionable age and over	3	-	-	-	-	-
Pensionable age and over	Pensionable age and over	309	-	5	37	-	90
1 female non-dependant with 1 or more dependant(s)							
0 - 4	0 - 4	296	32	14	11	35	199
	5 - 15	171	8	2	5	2	107
	16 up to pensionable age	25	4	-	1	-	9
	Pensionable age and over	4	-	-	-	-	1
5 - 15	5 - 15	480	12	7	18	16	230
	16 up to pensionable age	82	3	-	5	-	30
	Pensionable age and over	6	-	-	-	-	1
16 up to pensionable age	16 up to pensionable age	257	3	5	27	3	67
	Pensionable age and over	14	-	-	-	-	6
Pensionable age and over	Pensionable age and over	487	-	3	54	-	195
2 or more non-dependants with 1 or more dependant(s)							
0 - 4	0 - 4	2,735	127	24	126	37	297
	5 - 15	1,589	182	2	41	3	161
	16 up to pensionable age	63	13	-	3	-	9
	Pensionable age and over	14	-	-	-	-	2
5 - 15	5 - 15	3,635	99	15	120	11	227
	16 up to pensionable age	531	25	-	17	1	19
	Pensionable age and over	37	4	1	4	1	2
16 up to pensionable age	16 up to pensionable age	693	5	2	32	1	48
	Pensionable age and over	8	-	-	1	-	-
Pensionable age and over	Pensionable age and over	190	3	-	22	-	36

48. Households with residents

Non-dependants, dependants and age of youngest or only dependant	Age of oldest dependant	ALL HOUSE-HOLDS	Over 1 person per room	Lacking or sharing use of bath/ shower and/or inside WC	No central heating	Not self-contained accomm-odation	No car
a	b	c	d	e	f	g	h

Southampton

Non-dependants, dependants and age of youngest or only dependant	Age of oldest dependant	ALL HOUSE-HOLDS	Over 1 person per room	Lacking or sharing use of bath/ shower and/or inside WC	No central heating	Not self-contained accomm-odation	No car
TOTAL HOUSEHOLDS		81,140	2,464	1,700	18,125	2,337	28,650
1 or more non-dependants, no dependants		46,428	465	1,268	10,723	1,851	16,223
1 dependent male living alone							
0 up to pensionable age		662		80	197	128	528
Pensionable age - 74		468		32	156	23	336
75 - 84		433		13	111	5	346
85 and over		155		5	47	1	139
1 dependent female living alone							
0 up to pensionable age		397		17	101	30	324
Pensionable age - 74		1,171		8	269	8	1,023
75 - 84		1,261		27	300	6	1,208
85 and over		497		11	146	3	491
2 or more persons dependant, no non-dependants							
0 up to pensionable age	0 up to pensionable age	202	11	5	58	7	112
	Pensionable age - 74	139	1	1	34	-	67
	75 - 84	41	-	1	12	-	27
	85 and over	15	-	-	6	-	10
Pensionable age - 74	Pensionable age - 74	497	-	1	103	1	237
	75 - 84	242	-	2	57	-	149
	85 and over	54	-	1	14	-	25
75 - 84	75 - 84	287	1	6	73	3	193
	85 and over	60	-	2	14	1	49
85 and over	85 and over	22	-	-	5	-	17
1 male non-dependant with 1 or more dependant(s)							
0 - 4	0 - 4	37	5	-	8	4	21
	5 - 15	23	4	1	7	1	14
	16 up to pensionable age	34	5	-	7	1	6
	Pensionable age and over	1	-	-	1	-	1
5 - 15	5 - 15	172	-	2	46	3	73
	16 up to pensionable age	88	5	-	17	-	22
	Pensionable age and over	3	-	-	1	-	1
16 up to pensionable age	16 up to pensionable age	486	10	10	115	6	149
	Pensionable age and over	27	-	-	11	-	10
Pensionable age and over	Pensionable age and over	1,025	1	7	292	4	388
1 female non-dependant with 1 or more dependant(s)							
0 - 4	0 - 4	1,008	88	52	207	84	757
	5 - 15	712	59	3	225	6	539
	16 up to pensionable age	136	34	3	44	3	57
	Pensionable age and over	7	-	-	4	-	5
5 - 15	5 - 15	1,441	19	14	356	14	832
	16 up to pensionable age	256	10	2	77	1	111
	Pensionable age and over	24	1	-	10	-	8
16 up to pensionable age	16 up to pensionable age	1,037	7	5	258	7	418
	Pensionable age and over	41	1	-	12	-	22
Pensionable age and over	Pensionable age and over	1,715	3	15	448	5	858
2 or more non-dependants with 1 or more dependant(s)							
0 - 4	0 - 4	4,784	454	62	753	84	750
	5 - 15	3,483	677	10	657	12	542
	16 up to pensionable age	223	78	-	53	1	52
	Pensionable age and over	50	11	-	11	-	9
5 - 15	5 - 15	7,727	361	23	1,320	25	939
	16 up to pensionable age	1,049	106	-	167	2	122
	Pensionable age and over	88	7	1	22	-	14
16 up to pensionable age	16 up to pensionable age	1,841	33	8	383	6	295
	Pensionable age and over	35	1	-	10	-	10
Pensionable age and over	Pensionable age and over	556	6	2	177	1	121

48. Households with residents

Non-dependants, dependants and age of youngest or only dependant	Age of oldest dependant	ALL HOUSE-HOLDS	Over 1 person per room	Lacking or sharing use of bath/ shower and/or inside WC	No central heating	Not self-contained accomm-odation	No car
a	b	c	d	e	f	g	h
Test Valley							
TOTAL HOUSEHOLDS		38,391	397	183	3,186	98	7,072
1 or more non-dependants, no dependants		21,504	61	124	2,101	76	3,902
1 dependent male living alone							
0 up to pensionable age		90		2	13	1	49
Pensionable age - 74		110		1	19	1	65
75 - 84		174		5	30	-	113
85 and over		54		1	16	-	47
1 dependent female living alone							
0 up to pensionable age		67		1	10	-	49
Pensionable age - 74		376		3	38	1	297
75 - 84		503		6	58	-	456
85 and over		174		3	31	-	167
2 or more persons dependant, no non-dependants							
0 up to pensionable age	0 up to pensionable age	57	2	1	5	-	26
	Pensionable age - 74	30	-	-	3	-	12
	75 - 84	13	-	-	3	-	8
	85 and over	4	-	-	2	-	2
Pensionable age - 74	Pensionable age - 74	177	-	3	24	-	42
	75 - 84	100	-	2	11	-	51
	85 and over	25	-	-	2	-	5
75 - 84	75 - 84	110	-	1	14	-	62
	85 and over	30	-	-	7	-	25
85 and over	85 and over	8	-	-	2	-	5
1 male non-dependant with 1 or more dependant(s)							
0 - 4	0 - 4	9	-	-	-	-	3
	5 - 15	9	-	-	-	-	2
	16 up to pensionable age	13	1	-	-	-	-
	Pensionable age and over	-	-	-	-	-	-
5 - 15	5 - 15	92	1	1	6	-	18
	16 up to pensionable age	34	-	-	2	-	6
	Pensionable age and over	3	-	-	-	-	1
16 up to pensionable age	16 up to pensionable age	168	1	-	15	-	26
	Pensionable age and over	8	-	-	-	-	-
Pensionable age and over	Pensionable age and over	414	-	4	67	1	112
1 female non-dependant with 1 or more dependant(s)							
0 - 4	0 - 4	227	2	-	10	1	157
	5 - 15	173	6	1	8	-	107
	16 up to pensionable age	29	4	1	2	-	11
	Pensionable age and over	3	-	-	1	-	2
5 - 15	5 - 15	484	-	-	24	-	180
	16 up to pensionable age	77	1	-	4	-	21
	Pensionable age and over	6	-	1	1	-	4
16 up to pensionable age	16 up to pensionable age	343	-	1	33	-	75
	Pensionable age and over	17	-	1	3	-	7
Pensionable age and over	Pensionable age and over	804	-	1	93	2	260
2 or more non-dependants with 1 or more dependant(s)							
0 - 4	0 - 4	2,616	48	5	131	5	170
	5 - 15	1,804	129	2	67	3	141
	16 up to pensionable age	72	11	1	5	-	8
	Pensionable age and over	12	1	-	-	-	-
5 - 15	5 - 15	5,175	93	6	195	5	258
	16 up to pensionable age	785	26	1	30	-	32
	Pensionable age and over	36	-	1	-	-	1
16 up to pensionable age	16 up to pensionable age	1,103	6	-	73	1	65
	Pensionable age and over	12	-	-	-	-	1
Pensionable age and over	Pensionable age and over	257	4	3	27	1	21

48. Households with residents

Non-dependants, dependants and age of youngest or only dependant	Age of oldest dependant	ALL HOUSE-HOLDS	Over 1 person per room	Lacking or sharing use of bath/ shower and/or inside WC	No central heating	Not self-contained accomm- odation	No car
a	b	c	d	e	f	g	h

Winchester

TOTAL HOUSEHOLDS		37,553	362	303	3,608	202	7,299
1 or more non-dependants, no dependants		21,982	54	208	2,315	157	4,419
1 dependent male living alone							
0 up to pensionable age		91		4	15	4	54
Pensionable age - 74		141		3	25	-	59
75 - 84		174		7	26	-	104
85 and over		100		6	15	-	79
1 dependent female living alone							
0 up to pensionable age		85		-	8	-	48
Pensionable age - 74		414		2	45	1	310
75 - 84		577		12	55	3	511
85 and over		264		6	36	-	252
2 or more persons dependant, no non-dependants							
0 up to pensionable age	0 up to pensionable age	31	1	-	5	1	12
	Pensionable age - 74	31	-	-	4	-	5
	75 - 84	12	-	-	4	-	6
	85 and over	5	-	-	3	-	3
Pensionable age - 74	Pensionable age - 74	161	-	1	14	-	35
	75 - 84	102	-	-	13	-	44
	85 and over	25	-	1	4	-	8
75 - 84	75 - 84	109	-	1	13	-	51
	85 and over	50	-	1	9	-	37
85 and over	85 and over	8	-	-	-	-	5
1 male non-dependant with 1 or more dependant(s)							
0 - 4	0 - 4	10	1	2	1	1	4
	5 - 15	4	-	-	-	-	-
	16 up to pensionable age	11	-	-	1	-	-
	Pensionable age and over	-	-	-	-	-	-
5 - 15	5 - 15	62	-	-	6	-	11
	16 up to pensionable age	36	1	-	3	-	2
	Pensionable age and over	-	-	-	-	-	-
16 up to pensionable age	16 up to pensionable age	159	1	2	14	1	24
	Pensionable age and over	11	-	-	5	-	4
Pensionable age and over	Pensionable age and over	413	-	3	60	-	104
1 female non-dependant with 1 or more dependant(s)							
0 - 4	0 - 4	140	10	3	18	5	81
	5 - 15	113	6	1	14	-	60
	16 up to pensionable age	22	3	-	5	-	7
	Pensionable age and over	-	-	-	-	-	-
5 - 15	5 - 15	360	2	2	39	1	119
	16 up to pensionable age	82	1	2	4	1	18
	Pensionable age and over	9	-	-	3	-	5
16 up to pensionable age	16 up to pensionable age	364	2	4	44	3	73
	Pensionable age and over	19	-	-	3	-	10
Pensionable age and over	Pensionable age and over	883	-	4	92	5	283
2 or more non-dependants with 1 or more dependant(s)							
0 - 4	0 - 4	2,124	49	16	137	9	113
	5 - 15	1,582	111	1	107	-	73
	16 up to pensionable age	77	21	-	11	2	13
	Pensionable age and over	16	1	-	3	-	1
5 - 15	5 - 15	4,480	68	8	271	7	176
	16 up to pensionable age	828	23	1	41	-	13
	Pensionable age and over	39	1	-	3	-	-
16 up to pensionable age	16 up to pensionable age	1,075	5	-	72	1	42
	Pensionable age and over	14	1	-	-	-	-
Pensionable age and over	Pensionable age and over	258	-	2	42	-	21

Table 49 Ethnic group: housing

49. Households with residents; residents in households

HAMPSHIRE

a	TOTAL HOUSE-HOLDS	Ethnic group of household head								Other groups		Household head born in:	
		White	Black Caribbean	Black African	Black other	Indian	Pakistani	Bangladeshi	Chinese	Asian	Other	New Common-wealth	Ireland
	b	c	d	e	f	g	h	i	j	k	l	m	n
ALL HOUSEHOLDS	**603,257**	**595,071**	**1,085**	**391**	**511**	**2,219**	**390**	**440**	**1,060**	**697**	**1,393**	**13,305**	**9,566**
Over 1 and up to 1.5 persons per room	7,174	6,628	28	21	14	168	56	112	71	34	42	505	123
Over 1.5 persons per room	2,618	2,410	7	9	7	43	16	64	21	24	17	187	55
Owner occupied - owned outright	146,621	145,779	108	25	29	268	59	20	159	39	135	2,502	2,229
- buying	291,358	286,602	586	175	241	1,506	237	250	579	390	792	7,561	4,074
Rented privately	41,360	40,406	86	89	56	163	35	64	117	132	212	1,083	829
Rented from a housing association	11,951	11,753	31	15	16	52	13	8	13	25	25	231	253
Rented from local authority or new town	94,133	93,050	253	69	125	168	39	60	130	81	158	1,450	1,854
Lacking or sharing use of bath/shower and/or inside WC	7,073	6,900	16	23	16	28	4	17	27	15	27	168	172
No central heating	95,028	93,780	158	81	110	221	65	143	166	89	215	1,804	1,526
Not self-contained accommodation	6,318	6,104	22	26	12	32	10	16	24	29	43	208	182
No car	144,615	142,602	349	137	170	385	77	225	228	151	291	2,726	3,141
Containing person(s) with limiting long-term illness	124,419	123,044	194	83	82	424	97	98	94	97	206	2,307	2,316
ALL RESIDENTS IN HOUSEHOLDS	**1,512,038**	**1,485,388**	**2,849**	**1,094**	**1,386**	**8,060**	**1,637**	**2,305**	**3,345**	**2,204**	**3,770**	**38,676**	**23,064**
Over 1 and up to 1.5 persons per room	39,854	36,500	147	104	70	1,077	381	789	371	178	237	3,135	708
Over 1.5 persons per room	9,118	7,862	29	32	21	251	133	510	104	100	76	1,165	187
Lacking or sharing use of bath/shower and/or inside WC	10,635	10,301	16	34	27	61	14	51	58	27	46	306	219
No central heating	212,255	208,409	375	180	257	778	277	718	522	213	526	5,007	3,139
Not self-contained accommodation	9,371	9,028	25	31	14	67	34	36	43	41	52	341	243
No car	254,030	248,521	779	324	369	1,168	246	1,133	541	352	597	6,454	5,368

Table 49 Ethnic group: housing – continued

49. Households with residents; residents in households

Basingstoke & Deane

	TOTAL HOUSE-HOLDS	Ethnic group of household head								Other groups		Household head born in:	
		White	Black Caribbean	Black African	Black other	Indian	Pakistani	Bangladeshi	Chinese	Asian	Other	New Common-wealth	Ireland
a	b	c	d	e	f	g	h	i	j	k	l	m	n
ALL HOUSEHOLDS	54,323	53,346	214	53	69	263	27	26	87	92	146	1,260	1,141
Over 1 and up to 1.5 persons per room	594	549	9	3	1	9	3	7	5	4	4	44	13
Over 1.5 persons per room	181	174	-	-	-	2	-	2	2	-	1	6	4
Owner occupied - owned outright	9,010	8,968	8	5	-	10	-	-	9	4	6	121	184
- buying	29,599	28,940	139	24	25	212	23	12	58	63	103	861	553
Rented privately	2,639	2,580	5	7	4	9	3	6	4	13	8	63	45
Rented from a housing association	1,228	1,212	3	1	3	3	-	-	-	-	6	17	39
Rented from local authority or new town	9,815	9,665	58	11	20	19	1	2	13	8	18	164	288
Lacking or sharing use of bath/shower and/or inside WC	293	284	-	1	-	1	-	3	-	1	3	8	10
No central heating	4,187	4,142	12	7	4	10	-	1	3	2	6	58	83
Not self-contained accommodation	203	198	-	-	-	-	-	3	-	1	1	3	5
No car	10,361	10,190	55	8	18	20	-	14	14	14	28	185	332
Containing person(s) with limiting long-term illness	9,455	9,336	30	13	5	30	3	3	3	12	20	169	264
ALL RESIDENTS IN HOUSEHOLDS	143,278	140,332	605	149	194	828	87	114	274	272	423	3,663	2,987
Over 1 and up to 1.5 persons per room	3,402	3,145	51	16	5	50	14	45	29	22	25	251	82
Over 1.5 persons per room	702	658	-	-	-	14	-	16	12	-	2	47	12
Lacking or sharing use of bath/shower and/or inside WC	482	470	-	1	-	3	-	3	-	1	4	11	19
No central heating	9,443	9,341	31	11	5	26	-	1	11	2	15	146	172
Not self-contained accommodation	312	306	-	-	-	-	-	3	-	1	2	3	12
No car	18,920	18,496	129	15	37	50	-	64	28	33	68	407	596

Table 49 Ethnic group: housing – **continued**

49. Households with residents; residents in households

East Hampshire

	TOTAL HOUSE-HOLDS	Ethnic group of household head								Other groups		Household head born in:	
		White	Black Caribbean	Black African	Black other	Indian	Pakistani	Bangladeshi	Chinese	Asian	Other	New Common-wealth	Ireland
a	b	c	d	e	f	g	h	i	j	k	l	m	n
ALL HOUSEHOLDS	**39,158**	**38,891**	**24**	**13**	**28**	**41**	**3**	**16**	**38**	**39**	**65**	**813**	**490**
Over 1 and up to 1.5 persons per room	418	403	-	-	-	1	-	4	4	5	1	16	7
Over 1.5 persons per room	152	150	-	1	1	-	-	-	-	-	-	3	1
Owner occupied - owned outright	10,192	10,163	2	2	1	6	-	-	9	2	7	231	129
- buying	20,296	20,120	17	8	18	28	3	13	18	22	49	459	230
Rented privately	2,259	2,238	-	-	3	4	-	1	2	9	2	51	29
Rented from a housing association	435	433	-	-	-	-	-	-	-	1	1	5	7
Rented from local authority or new town	4,347	4,333	4	1	2	-	-	-	6	1	-	33	63
Lacking or sharing use of bath/shower and/or inside WC	344	343	-	-	-	-	-	-	1	-	-	1	2
No central heating	4,030	4,011	4	-	3	2	-	2	4	1	3	41	38
Not self-contained accommodation	158	158	-	-	-	-	-	-	-	-	-	4	3
No car	6,087	6,050	2	4	6	3	-	3	11	4	4	85	104
Containing person(s) with limiting long-term illness	7,134	7,099	2	7	8	5	-	1	3	2	7	121	89
ALL RESIDENTS IN HOUSEHOLDS	**101,335**	**100,507**	**68**	**43**	**72**	**112**	**13**	**76**	**126**	**127**	**191**	**2,182**	**1,257**
Over 1 and up to 1.5 persons per room	2,288	2,205	-	-	-	4	-	24	22	27	6	87	38
Over 1.5 persons per room	529	518	-	8	3	-	-	-	-	-	-	12	12
Lacking or sharing use of bath/shower and/or inside WC	526	521	-	-	-	-	-	-	5	-	-	5	2
No central heating	9,187	9,128	10	-	7	7	-	12	15	1	7	114	72
Not self-contained accommodation	310	310	-	-	-	-	-	-	-	-	-	9	5
No car	9,766	9,683	4	14	9	4	-	11	31	6	4	141	159

Table 49 Ethnic group: housing – continued

49. Households with residents; residents in households

Eastleigh

	TOTAL HOUSE-HOLDS	Ethnic group of household head								Other groups		Household head born in:	
		White	Black Caribbean	Black African	Black other	Indian	Pakistani	Bangladeshi	Chinese	Asian	Other	New Common-wealth	Ireland
a	b	c	d	e	f	g	h	i	j	k	l	m	n
ALL HOUSEHOLDS	41,219	40,736	36	18	19	197	9	18	87	34	65	756	540
Over 1 and up to 1.5 persons per room	362	340	2	1	-	11	1	4	2	-	1	26	14
Over 1.5 persons per room	102	95	-	1	-	-	-	3	2	1	-	6	1
Owner occupied - owned outright	9,538	9,494	1	-	2	24	1	-	11	-	5	105	129
- buying	24,015	23,645	29	12	11	162	7	12	59	28	50	541	271
Rented privately	1,839	1,814	1	4	2	3	1	1	5	4	4	33	37
Rented from a housing association	770	766	1	-	-	1	-	1	-	4	1	7	14
Rented from local authority or new town	4,725	4,696	4	2	4	6	-	1	6	1	5	54	86
Lacking or sharing use of bath/shower and/or inside WC	278	277	-	-	-	1	-	-	-	-	-	5	7
No central heating	4,746	4,711	1	2	4	11	-	2	8	2	5	59	62
Not self-contained accommodation	167	167	-	-	-	-	-	-	-	-	-	5	1
No car	7,366	7,309	5	2	5	15	-	11	13	2	4	98	144
Containing person(s) with limiting long-term illness	7,552	7,466	6	2	3	44	3	5	7	7	9	120	130
ALL RESIDENTS IN HOUSEHOLDS	105,298	103,609	99	55	54	748	32	108	276	121	196	2,385	1,360
Over 1 and up to 1.5 persons per room	1,965	1,830	9	5	-	67	7	32	11	-	4	156	73
Over 1.5 persons per room	349	297	-	6	-	-	-	33	9	4	-	44	2
Lacking or sharing use of bath/shower and/or inside WC	412	411	-	-	-	1	-	-	-	-	-	7	7
No central heating	10,554	10,466	3	4	8	30	-	8	17	3	15	126	139
Not self-contained accommodation	239	239	-	-	-	-	-	-	-	-	-	6	1
No car	12,129	11,940	13	4	10	44	-	78	25	9	6	268	250

Table 49 Ethnic group: housing – **continued**

49. Households with residents; residents in households

Fareham

a	TOTAL HOUSE-HOLDS	Ethnic group of household head								Other groups		Household head born in:	
		White	Black Caribbean	Black African	Black other	Indian	Pakistani	Bangladeshi	Chinese	Asian	Other	New Common-wealth	Ireland
	b	c	d	e	f	g	h	i	j	k	l	m	n
ALL HOUSEHOLDS	**38,369**	**38,114**	**29**	**8**	**9**	**51**	**5**	**10**	**59**	**28**	**56**	**684**	**491**
Over 1 and up to 1.5 persons per room	282	276	-	-	-	1	-	2	2	1	-	9	7
Over 1.5 persons per room	55	52	-	-	-	-	-	-	2	-	1	2	1
Owner occupied - owned outright	11,328	11,300	2	-	-	8	2	-	8	-	8	134	138
- buying	21,671	21,485	25	5	7	40	3	4	42	24	36	449	271
Rented privately	1,501	1,480	2	2	-	1	-	3	3	3	7	38	24
Rented from a housing association	254	253	-	1	-	-	-	-	-	-	-	4	3
Rented from local authority or new town	3,069	3,060	-	-	1	1	-	1	3	-	3	36	43
Lacking or sharing use of bath/shower and/or inside WC	229	228	-	-	-	-	-	-	1	-	-	7	2
No central heating	4,621	4,594	2	2	-	4	-	4	7	1	7	65	46
Not self-contained accommodation	77	76	-	-	-	-	-	-	1	-	-	1	1
No car	6,683	6,652	4	3	-	3	-	4	10	2	5	82	95
Containing person(s) with limiting long-term illness	7,357	7,332	1	2	1	5	1	-	6	3	6	82	103
ALL RESIDENTS IN HOUSEHOLDS	**97,607**	**96,813**	**92**	**19**	**29**	**185**	**11**	**38**	**186**	**95**	**139**	**1,865**	**1,210**
Over 1 and up to 1.5 persons per room	1,613	1,578	-	-	-	14	-	8	8	5	-	49	38
Over 1.5 persons per room	210	191	-	-	-	-	-	-	14	-	5	14	2
Lacking or sharing use of bath/shower and/or inside WC	347	343	-	-	-	-	-	-	4	-	-	11	2
No central heating	10,254	10,186	6	3	-	6	-	15	23	2	13	147	87
Not self-contained accommodation	121	120	-	-	-	-	-	-	1	-	-	1	2
No car	10,940	10,869	15	4	-	4	-	13	19	7	9	151	138

Table 49 Ethnic group: housing – **continued**

49. Households with residents; residents in households

Gosport

a	TOTAL HOUSE-HOLDS	Ethnic group of household head										Household head born in:	
		White	Black Caribbean	Black African	Black other	Indian	Pakistani	Bangladeshi	Chinese	Other groups Asian	Other groups Other	New Common-wealth	Ireland
	b	c	d	e	f	g	h	i	j	k	l	m	n
ALL HOUSEHOLDS	**29,356**	**29,147**	**25**	**14**	**23**	**35**	**4**	**9**	**39**	**21**	**39**	**564**	**501**
Over 1 and up to 1.5 persons per room	306	291	3	1	2	2	-	3	3	-	1	18	4
Over 1.5 persons per room	68	65	-	-	-	1	-	-	2	-	-	4	1
Owner occupied - owned outright	6,491	6,476	-	-	-	2	-	-	8	2	3	86	120
- buying	14,090	13,965	16	9	18	21	3	3	18	11	26	309	234
Rented privately	1,649	1,632	2	1	-	3	-	2	3	2	4	31	35
Rented from a housing association	631	629	1	1	-	-	-	-	-	-	-	11	16
Rented from local authority or new town	5,112	5,083	4	1	3	4	1	-	7	5	4	83	71
Lacking or sharing use of bath/shower and/or inside WC	217	214	-	-	-	1	1	-	1	-	-	7	5
No central heating	5,193	5,141	3	2	7	7	1	5	13	4	10	99	81
Not self-contained accommodation	89	89	-	-	-	-	-	-	-	-	-	1	-
No car	8,600	8,556	8	2	3	6	1	4	6	4	10	142	155
Containing person(s) with limiting long-term illness	6,313	6,272	4	2	3	7	-	1	4	7	13	115	111
ALL RESIDENTS IN HOUSEHOLDS	**73,704**	**73,027**	**89**	**40**	**66**	**115**	**14**	**34**	**143**	**72**	**104**	**1,561**	**1,259**
Over 1 and up to 1.5 persons per room	1,734	1,648	17	4	9	12	-	20	17	-	7	108	22
Over 1.5 persons per room	249	233	-	-	-	6	-	-	10	-	-	18	6
Lacking or sharing use of bath/shower and/or inside WC	307	299	-	-	-	3	3	-	2	-	-	13	6
No central heating	11,396	11,231	11	7	20	26	2	17	45	11	26	265	176
Not self-contained accommodation	136	136	-	-	-	-	-	-	-	-	-	2	-
No car	16,451	16,333	29	5	5	14	2	12	19	10	22	322	291

Table 49 Ethnic group: housing – **continued**

49. Households with residents; residents in households

Hart

	TOTAL HOUSE-HOLDS	Ethnic group of household head								Other groups		Household head born in:	
		White	Black Caribbean	Black African	Black other	Indian	Pakistani	Bangladeshi	Chinese	Asian	Other	New Common-wealth	Ireland
a	b	c	d	e	f	g	h	i	j	k	l	m	n
ALL HOUSEHOLDS	**29,073**	**28,798**	**24**	**9**	**19**	**61**	**13**	**13**	**44**	**35**	**57**	**670**	**469**
Over 1 and up to 1.5 persons per room	220	211	-	-	-	1	1	2	4	-	2	9	3
Over 1.5 persons per room	46	44	-	-	-	1	-	-	1	-	-	3	1
Owner occupied - owned outright	6,072	6,043	4	-	2	2	1	2	7	4	7	136	118
- buying	17,484	17,305	14	5	10	47	10	10	30	14	39	423	244
Rented privately	1,634	1,603	2	-	1	6	1	1	5	9	6	48	36
Rented from a housing association	301	300	-	1	-	-	-	-	-	-	-	11	7
Rented from local authority or new town	2,330	2,319	1	2	3	2	-	-	-	-	3	18	36
Lacking or sharing use of bath/shower and/or inside WC	150	148	-	-	-	-	-	1	-	-	1	3	4
No central heating	1,922	1,908	1	1	2	3	1	2	2	1	1	28	29
Not self-contained accommodation	70	70	-	-	-	-	-	-	-	-	-	2	1
No car	3,287	3,267	1	2	2	4	1	2	2	4	2	46	77
Containing person(s) with limiting long-term illness	4,522	4,490	6	3	1	9	-	2	2	2	7	95	79
ALL RESIDENTS IN HOUSEHOLDS	**79,014**	**78,115**	**69**	**28**	**55**	**201**	**46**	**51**	**165**	**108**	**176**	**1,884**	**1,239**
Over 1 and up to 1.5 persons per room	1,219	1,167	-	-	-	-	6	14	24	-	8	56	18
Over 1.5 persons per room	180	165	-	-	-	9	-	-	6	-	-	17	5
Lacking or sharing use of bath/shower and/or inside WC	267	262	-	-	-	-	-	1	-	-	4	3	8
No central heating	4,385	4,348	1	4	7	4	2	7	8	3	1	65	47
Not self-contained accommodation	108	108	-	-	-	-	-	-	-	-	-	3	2
No car	4,939	4,901	1	5	4	7	2	4	4	9	2	67	114

Table 49   Ethnic group: housing – continued

49. Households with residents; residents in households

Havant

a	TOTAL HOUSE-HOLDS	Ethnic group of household head White	Black Caribbean	Black African	Black other	Indian	Pakistani	Bangladeshi	Chinese	Other groups Asian	Other	Household head born in: New Common-wealth	Ireland
	b	c	d	e	f	g	h	i	j	k	l	m	n
ALL HOUSEHOLDS	**46,151**	**45,833**	**29**	**23**	**36**	**71**	**7**	**16**	**50**	**22**	**64**	**872**	**606**
Over 1 and up to 1.5 persons per room	834	814	-	-	3	6	1	3	3	1	3	27	12
Over 1.5 persons per room	198	193	1	-	-	1	-	2	1	-	-	5	1
Owner occupied - owned outright	11,465	11,436	2	1	2	6	-	-	11	1	6	176	154
- buying	22,044	21,859	16	10	20	38	6	9	27	17	42	473	248
Rented privately	1,912	1,896	1	3	1	6	-	2	2	-	1	49	36
Rented from a housing association	400	395	1	1	1	-	-	-	-	1	1	7	12
Rented from local authority or new town	9,844	9,777	9	7	12	15	1	1	7	2	13	140	144
Lacking or sharing use of bath/shower and/or inside WC	389	382	-	2	4	-	-	-	1	-	-	6	9
No central heating	9,594	9,523	7	5	14	14	1	6	6	2	16	175	132
Not self-contained accommodation	197	197	-	-	-	-	-	-	-	-	-	5	2
No car	11,636	11,564	6	6	9	16	1	7	3	5	19	176	197
Containing person(s) with limiting long-term illness	10,998	10,950	8	5	5	12	-	1	4	2	11	156	175
ALL RESIDENTS IN HOUSEHOLDS	**118,297**	**117,326**	**77**	**66**	**113**	**217**	**24**	**77**	**171**	**63**	**163**	**2,389**	**1,402**
Over 1 and up to 1.5 persons per room	4,749	4,628	-	-	17	35	6	24	18	3	18	166	74
Over 1.5 persons per room	768	733	7	-	-	5	-	17	6	-	-	35	5
Lacking or sharing use of bath/shower and/or inside WC	620	606	-	2	9	-	-	-	3	-	-	11	9
No central heating	24,041	23,844	18	12	41	44	1	18	20	3	40	482	270
Not self-contained accommodation	415	415	-	-	-	-	-	-	-	-	-	10	3
No car	22,139	21,974	17	10	24	38	1	25	8	7	35	344	322

Table 49 Ethnic group: housing – **continued**

49. Households with residents; residents in households

New Forest

a	TOTAL HOUSE-HOLDS	Ethnic group of household head								Other groups		Household head born in:	
		White	Black Caribbean	Black African	Black other	Indian	Pakistani	Bangladeshi	Chinese	Asian	Other	New Common-wealth	Ireland
	b	c	d	e	f	g	h	i	j	k	l	m	n
ALL HOUSEHOLDS	**65,411**	**65,116**	**26**	**15**	**22**	**55**	**9**	**18**	**56**	**21**	**73**	**947**	**756**
Over 1 and up to 1.5 persons per room	526	514	-	-	-	5	-	2	2	2	1	13	8
Over 1.5 persons per room	180	176	-	-	-	1	-	2	-	1	-	8	1
Owner occupied - owned outright	23,921	23,880	-	7	1	7	2	-	12	1	11	350	271
- buying	29,067	28,895	21	6	11	32	4	6	36	12	44	452	300
Rented privately	3,830	3,798	3	-	3	8	2	2	2	2	10	51	55
Rented from a housing association	858	856	-	-	1	-	-	-	-	-	1	5	14
Rented from local authority or new town	6,236	6,211	1	2	4	4	1	2	2	4	5	55	94
Lacking or sharing use of bath/shower and/or inside WC	590	588	-	-	1	-	-	1	-	-	-	4	8
No central heating	7,182	7,145	1	1	4	3	1	6	8	2	11	74	77
Not self-contained accommodation	234	234	-	-	-	-	-	-	-	-	-	-	3
No car	11,848	11,792	1	7	7	8	-	9	8	5	11	122	194
Containing person(s) with limiting long-term illness	14,458	14,416	2	6	5	7	1	2	-	2	17	163	195
ALL RESIDENTS IN HOUSEHOLDS	**157,604**	**156,723**	**76**	**41**	**55**	**184**	**26**	**78**	**158**	**69**	**194**	**2,355**	**1,719**
Over 1 and up to 1.5 persons per room	2,886	2,823	-	-	-	25	-	15	8	10	5	65	42
Over 1.5 persons per room	658	621	-	-	-	9	-	18	-	10	-	67	5
Lacking or sharing use of bath/shower and/or inside WC	931	925	-	-	1	-	-	5	-	-	-	11	10
No central heating	15,554	15,451	2	4	8	14	1	22	17	7	28	181	174
Not self-contained accommodation	416	416	-	-	-	-	-	-	-	-	-	-	3
No car	18,227	18,102	3	20	15	20	-	23	10	8	26	236	302

Table 49 Ethnic group: housing – continued

49. Households with residents; residents in households

Portsmouth

	TOTAL HOUSE-HOLDS	Ethnic group of household head										Household head born in:	
		White	Black Caribbean	Black African	Black other	Indian	Pakistani	Bangladeshi	Chinese	Other groups Asian	Other groups Other	New Common-wealth	Ireland
a	b	c	d	e	f	g	h	i	j	k	l	m	n
ALL HOUSEHOLDS	**72,590**	**71,342**	**87**	**72**	**108**	**207**	**18**	**180**	**219**	**102**	**255**	**1,738**	**1,056**
Over 1 and up to 1.5 persons per room	980	871	-	3	4	19	-	46	23	6	8	96	13
Over 1.5 persons per room	442	380	1	2	1	8	-	36	3	7	4	55	5
Owner occupied - owned outright	17,981	17,867	11	3	9	19	1	11	40	3	17	274	263
- buying	30,752	30,121	44	26	49	130	10	112	101	31	128	903	401
Rented privately	7,974	7,753	15	25	16	25	4	23	30	31	52	233	147
Rented from a housing association	2,247	2,204	6	3	4	5	1	1	3	14	6	42	41
Rented from local authority or new town	12,065	11,887	9	12	30	17	-	30	39	22	19	248	171
Lacking or sharing use of bath/shower and/or inside WC	1,905	1,865	1	6	2	6	-	1	10	8	6	36	37
No central heating	26,293	25,915	26	30	42	40	2	79	54	39	66	570	385
Not self-contained accommodation	1,905	1,840	3	9	3	7	1	2	9	19	12	56	47
No car	29,067	28,606	28	36	52	53	2	107	62	48	73	648	521
Containing person(s) with limiting long-term illness	17,758	17,547	21	11	16	33	6	50	29	18	27	342	285
ALL RESIDENTS IN HOUSEHOLDS	**169,730**	**165,670**	**200**	**169**	**279**	**716**	**55**	**1,055**	**664**	**261**	**661**	**5,060**	**2,349**
Over 1 and up to 1.5 persons per room	5,497	4,804	-	13	21	114	-	340	119	33	53	611	80
Over 1.5 persons per room	1,563	1,162	2	8	2	34	-	301	12	18	24	376	21
Lacking or sharing use of bath/shower and/or inside WC	2,814	2,740	1	11	3	15	-	6	17	14	7	59	48
No central heating	56,978	55,714	58	68	103	154	4	465	181	83	148	1,657	789
Not self-contained accommodation	2,675	2,580	4	9	3	19	2	3	13	29	13	73	62
No car	53,606	52,196	54	78	113	158	6	613	146	99	143	1,746	909

Table 49 Ethnic group: housing – continued

49. Households with residents; residents in households

Rushmoor

a	TOTAL HOUSE-HOLDS	White	Black Caribbean	Black African	Black other	Indian	Pakistani	Bangladeshi	Chinese	Other groups Asian	Other groups Other	New Common-wealth	Ireland
	b	c	d	e	f	g	h	i	j	k	l	m	n
ALL HOUSEHOLDS	**30,523**	**29,903**	**151**	**31**	**34**	**114**	**52**	**10**	**69**	**70**	**89**	**900**	**717**
Over 1 and up to 1.5 persons per room	424	391	3	2	-	9	10	4	2	2	1	32	10
Over 1.5 persons per room	199	181	2	1	1	5	4	-	-	5	-	12	11
Owner occupied - owned outright	4,835	4,777	17	-	3	12	3	1	9	3	10	134	99
- buying	15,614	15,236	83	23	10	76	39	6	43	48	50	507	308
Rented privately	2,270	2,223	15	3	4	6	4	-	4	4	7	55	69
Rented from a housing association	590	581	3	-	1	1	-	-	2	1	1	11	18
Rented from local authority or new town	5,008	4,921	29	4	9	9	4	1	7	12	12	122	176
Lacking or sharing use of bath/shower and/or inside WC	492	473	3	1	3	6	-	-	1	3	2	14	15
No central heating	2,341	2,301	8	3	1	6	3	3	5	6	5	68	64
Not self-contained accommodation	581	562	4	1	3	3	-	-	-	4	4	11	29
No car	6,659	6,552	33	7	10	9	7	4	11	9	17	162	261
Containing person(s) with limiting long-term illness	5,486	5,402	24	1	5	16	12	2	2	9	13	137	182
ALL RESIDENTS IN HOUSEHOLDS	**79,121**	**77,139**	**397**	**111**	**90**	**394**	**251**	**36**	**224**	**226**	**253**	**2,619**	**1,794**
Over 1 and up to 1.5 persons per room	2,328	2,141	15	14	-	49	59	23	12	12	3	178	62
Over 1.5 persons per room	647	547	9	2	2	24	46	-	-	17	-	81	32
Lacking or sharing use of bath/shower and/or inside WC	726	687	3	2	4	21	-	-	2	5	2	37	19
No central heating	4,723	4,634	16	6	1	15	14	3	12	11	11	155	118
Not self-contained accommodation	893	866	4	2	4	7	-	-	-	6	4	22	42
No car	12,093	11,833	75	29	21	19	23	13	25	20	35	325	489

Column groups: columns c–l = Ethnic group of household head (with Asian/Other under "Other groups"); columns m–n = Household head born in.

Table 49 Ethnic group: housing – continued

49. Households with residents; residents in households

Southampton

a	b TOTAL HOUSE-HOLDS	Ethnic group of household head								Other groups		Household head born in:	
		White	Black Caribbean	Black African	Black other	Indian	Pakistani	Bangladeshi	Chinese	Asian	Other	New Common-wealth	Ireland
	b	c	d	e	f	g	h	i	j	k	l	m	n
ALL HOUSEHOLDS	**81,140**	**78,455**	**386**	**112**	**107**	**995**	**221**	**101**	**223**	**171**	**369**	**2,732**	**1,809**
Over 1 and up to 1.5 persons per room	1,644	1,403	11	10	3	103	39	29	17	10	19	195	29
Over 1.5 persons per room	820	733	3	3	4	23	12	18	7	9	8	78	26
Owner occupied - owned outright	17,846	17,478	58	6	7	165	46	6	25	17	38	459	387
- buying	31,547	30,208	151	36	43	614	114	49	94	82	156	1,431	592
Rented privately	8,872	8,456	36	41	18	84	20	22	54	44	97	325	252
Rented from a housing association	2,752	2,644	15	7	6	41	12	6	8	6	7	92	64
Rented from local authority or new town	19,285	18,862	124	22	29	85	29	15	33	21	65	392	487
Lacking or sharing use of bath/shower and/or inside WC	1,700	1,623	12	11	4	13	3	11	11	2	10	72	64
No central heating	18,125	17,633	89	25	26	117	55	29	53	25	73	485	453
Not self-contained accommodation	2,337	2,217	15	15	6	21	9	11	13	5	25	109	86
No car	28,650	27,783	192	55	47	238	63	50	73	45	104	800	802
Containing person(s) with limiting long-term illness	18,898	18,309	81	25	25	246	68	29	26	27	62	622	487
ALL RESIDENTS IN HOUSEHOLDS	**193,866**	**184,710**	**923**	**304**	**287**	**3,915**	**1,013**	**513**	**661**	**588**	**952**	**8,948**	**4,127**
Over 1 and up to 1.5 persons per room	8,913	7,380	55	44	14	694	285	201	85	52	103	1,288	163
Over 1.5 persons per room	2,640	2,147	11	6	14	145	87	115	33	47	35	431	75
Lacking or sharing use of bath/shower and/or inside WC	2,399	2,267	12	13	7	18	11	36	20	2	13	128	79
No central heating	40,770	39,201	211	55	51	441	249	127	162	77	196	1,477	957
Not self-contained accommodation	3,268	3,060	17	18	7	40	32	30	27	5	32	198	106
No car	51,159	48,789	406	127	108	784	207	218	180	121	219	2,062	1,384

Table 49 Ethnic group: housing – continued

49. Households with residents; residents in households

Test Valley

a	TOTAL HOUSE-HOLDS	Ethnic group of household head								Other groups		Household head born in:	
		White	Black Caribbean	Black African	Black other	Indian	Pakistani	Bangladeshi	Chinese	Asian	Other	New Common-wealth	Ireland
	b	c	d	e	f	g	h	i	j	k	l	m	n
ALL HOUSEHOLDS	**38,391**	**38,080**	**46**	**13**	**21**	**85**	**10**	**7**	**52**	**25**	**52**	**658**	**507**
Over 1 and up to 1.5 persons per room	321	315	-	-	-	1	-	2	3	-	-	6	3
Over 1.5 persons per room	76	73	-	-	-	1	-	1	1	-	-	3	2
Owner occupied - owned outright	8,454	8,436	3	1	-	4	1	-	6	1	2	111	107
- buying	18,558	18,341	27	4	15	72	8	5	34	19	33	392	230
Rented privately	2,407	2,385	3	1	2	4	-	1	1	3	7	50	27
Rented from a housing association	589	588	1	-	-	-	-	-	-	-	-	4	15
Rented from local authority or new town	6,330	6,294	8	5	2	5	1	1	3	2	9	54	104
Lacking or sharing use of bath/shower and/or inside WC	183	180	-	1	1	-	-	-	1	-	-	4	3
No central heating	3,186	3,173	3	2	-	2	-	1	2	1	2	36	37
Not self-contained accommodation	98	97	-	-	-	-	-	-	1	-	-	7	-
No car	7,072	7,030	11	3	4	6	-	3	7	2	6	80	120
Containing person(s) with limiting long-term illness	7,184	7,150	8	4	1	7	1	1	5	2	5	86	105
ALL RESIDENTS IN HOUSEHOLDS	**99,463**	**98,443**	**133**	**42**	**56**	**311**	**28**	**45**	**180**	**75**	**150**	**1,890**	**1,275**
Over 1 and up to 1.5 persons per room	1,811	1,774	-	-	-	7	-	16	14	-	-	42	16
Over 1.5 persons per room	282	265	-	-	-	5	-	10	2	-	-	17	10
Lacking or sharing use of bath/shower and/or inside WC	323	314	-	3	1	-	-	-	5	-	-	9	3
No central heating	6,775	6,737	6	4	-	6	-	10	7	1	4	71	71
Not self-contained accommodation	166	164	-	-	-	-	-	-	2	-	-	8	-
No car	12,339	12,217	28	9	10	15	-	21	24	4	11	186	213

Table 49 Ethnic group: housing – continued

49. Households with residents; residents in households

Winchester

| | TOTAL HOUSE-HOLDS | Ethnic group of household head | | | | | | | | Other groups | | Household head born in: | |
| | | White | Black Caribbean | Black African | Black other | Indian | Pakistani | Bangladeshi | Chinese | Asian | Other | New Commonwealth | Ireland |
a	b	c	d	e	f	g	h	i	j	k	l	m	n
ALL HOUSEHOLDS	37,553	37,310	8	10	16	44	12	16	37	37	63	711	483
Over 1 and up to 1.5 persons per room	263	250	-	1	1	1	1	4	1	3	1	14	-
Over 1.5 persons per room	99	94	-	1	-	-	-	-	-	1	3	2	-
Owner occupied - owned outright	9,488	9,461	-	-	2	3	2	-	4	1	15	185	130
- buying	16,621	16,482	4	7	4	34	7	9	19	19	36	361	192
Rented privately	2,574	2,548	1	2	2	4	-	-	2	8	7	56	37
Rented from a housing association	896	892	-	-	-	1	-	-	-	2	1	15	3
Rented from local authority or new town	5,967	5,942	2	-	6	1	1	6	4	3	2	51	91
Lacking or sharing use of bath/shower and/or inside WC	303	295	-	1	1	-	-	-	-	1	5	1	6
No central heating	3,608	3,583	1	1	3	2	1	3	1	3	10	46	39
Not self-contained accommodation	202	199	-	1	-	1	-	-	-	-	1	4	4
No car	7,299	7,251	3	2	7	4	2	7	8	7	8	100	139
Containing person(s) with limiting long-term illness	7,304	7,275	1	2	4	3	2	1	3	4	9	99	111
ALL RESIDENTS IN HOUSEHOLDS	93,721	92,974	21	27	36	134	37	80	117	127	168	1,875	1,086
Over 1 and up to 1.5 persons per room	1,449	1,377	-	8	4	6	4	27	4	14	5	78	-
Over 1.5 persons per room	341	325	-	2	-	-	-	-	-	4	10	6	-
Lacking or sharing use of bath/shower and/or inside WC	481	456	-	2	2	-	-	-	-	5	16	1	7
No central heating	8,195	8,128	2	2	6	5	4	13	4	9	22	121	67
Not self-contained accommodation	312	308	-	2	-	1	-	-	-	-	1	6	5
No car	11,322	11,188	5	4	13	11	5	38	22	19	17	199	201

Table 50 Country of birth: household heads and residents

Notes: (1) * Includes Channel Islands, the Isle of Man and United Kingdom (part not stated)
(2) ** Includes Ireland (part not stated)

50. Residents in households; household heads

Country of birth of household head	TOTAL PERSONS	Age and birthplace of persons							
		Total born		0 - 4		5 - 15		16 - 29	
		Inside UK	Outside UK	Inside UK	Outside UK	Inside UK	Outside UK	Inside UK	Outside UK
a	b	c	d	e	f	g	h	i	j

HAMPSHIRE

ALL COUNTRIES OF BIRTH	1,512,038	1,431,798	80,240	101,204	1,883	198,308	7,401	295,771	16,534
United Kingdom*	1,424,596	1,391,179	33,417	95,218	1,316	187,114	5,247	285,110	8,603
England	1,342,618	1,313,235	29,383	90,436	1,146	176,593	4,623	270,051	7,765
Scotland	41,371	39,873	1,498	2,491	89	5,572	348	7,821	379
Wales	28,535	27,697	838	1,606	54	3,430	150	5,022	213
Northern Ireland	9,538	9,126	412	545	20	1,280	86	1,894	104
Irish Republic**	13,526	6,072	7,454	481	28	1,185	257	1,880	584
Old Commonwealth	5,315	2,496	2,819	351	61	554	130	549	569
New Commonwealth	38,676	18,568	20,108	3,182	183	6,059	887	4,787	3,942
Eastern Africa	4,504	2,065	2,439	401	20	779	85	435	579
Other Africa	1,665	801	864	175	21	245	76	193	186
Caribbean	3,098	1,495	1,603	161	13	430	40	540	166
Bangladesh	2,286	806	1,480	308	41	402	309	74	472
India	10,032	4,723	5,309	524	12	1,529	92	1,341	580
Pakistan	2,295	1,133	1,162	193	12	442	54	275	222
South East Asia	6,283	3,019	3,264	701	35	968	127	741	1,063
Cyprus	1,316	745	571	172	7	200	17	206	162
Other New Commonwealth	7,197	3,781	3,416	547	22	1,064	87	982	512
Other European Community	12,980	6,452	6,528	966	67	1,676	241	1,794	1,348
Other Europe	3,348	1,346	2,002	91	12	244	70	314	115
United States of America	2,292	879	1,413	173	65	183	163	202	251
China	833	246	587	17	6	81	15	70	94
Vietnam	415	70	345	30	4	31	36	4	149
Rest of the world	10,057	4,490	5,567	695	141	1,181	355	1,061	879

Basingstoke & Deane

ALL COUNTRIES OF BIRTH	143,278	135,232	8,046	9,802	150	19,768	639	30,938	1,587
United Kingdom*	133,681	130,724	2,957	9,153	80	18,543	394	29,636	818
England	125,580	122,939	2,641	8,723	77	17,443	348	28,035	743
Scotland	4,209	4,078	131	223	2	602	34	852	35
Wales	2,797	2,724	73	150	1	341	7	530	23
Northern Ireland	933	894	39	53	-	136	5	196	9
Irish Republic**	2,054	979	1,075	76	5	199	31	366	63
Old Commonwealth	561	260	301	41	12	66	8	48	76
New Commonwealth	3,663	1,759	1,904	305	11	573	79	465	312
Eastern Africa	483	219	264	49	1	81	9	51	48
Other Africa	222	115	107	30	3	39	5	22	21
Caribbean	581	289	292	36	-	78	6	116	18
Bangladesh	127	42	85	18	1	14	24	4	29
India	967	426	541	44	2	132	15	117	74
Pakistan	121	50	71	6	-	19	7	10	11
South East Asia	448	229	219	57	2	75	9	54	57
Cyprus	124	72	52	19	-	21	1	15	19
Other New Commonwealth	590	317	273	46	2	114	3	76	35
Other European Community	1,426	733	693	101	4	197	28	225	125
Other Europe	379	153	226	7	4	26	7	46	12
United States of America	509	162	347	40	23	37	58	37	83
China	34	13	21	-	-	5	-	5	4
Vietnam	26	6	20	5	-	1	1	-	11
Rest of the world	945	443	502	74	11	121	33	110	83

Age and birthplace of persons								TOTAL HOUSEHOLD HEADS	Country of birth of household head
30 - 44		45 up to pensionable age		Pensionable age - 74		75 and over			
Inside UK	Outside UK	Inside UK	Outside UK	Inside UK	Outside UK	Inside UK	Outside UK		
k	l	m	n	o	p	q	r	s	a
310,905	21,995	276,335	17,253	157,997	10,860	91,278	4,314	603,257	**ALL COUNTRIES OF BIRTH**
304,831	8,032	272,543	5,344	155,737	3,895	90,626	980	569,832	**United Kingdom***
287,229	7,136	256,705	4,595	146,041	3,365	86,180	753	536,900	England
9,416	312	8,021	181	4,693	161	1,859	28	16,332	Scotland
5,930	191	5,687	116	3,897	93	2,125	21	11,756	Wales
2,045	87	1,944	56	994	48	424	11	3,759	Northern Ireland
903	1,359	942	2,645	514	1,657	167	924	5,807	Irish Republic**
458	869	235	468	281	450	68	272	2,235	Old Commonwealth
2,352	6,984	1,363	5,225	610	1,896	215	991	13,305	**New Commonwealth**
315	1,115	90	482	28	119	17	39	1,490	Eastern Africa
138	432	35	106	12	29	3	14	599	Other Africa
211	492	96	637	39	187	18	68	1,181	Caribbean
13	381	5	242	4	30	-	5	443	Bangladesh
434	1,442	530	1,854	271	858	94	471	3,509	India
67	342	92	346	51	123	13	63	676	Pakistan
427	1,357	119	444	44	147	19	91	2,215	South East Asia
129	238	27	111	10	26	1	10	462	Cyprus
618	1,185	369	1,003	151	377	50	230	2,730	Other New Commonwealth
1,171	2,002	486	1,398	301	1,148	58	324	5,189	Other European Community
235	313	186	459	232	778	44	255	1,595	Other Europe
178	483	82	252	50	120	11	79	905	United States of America
18	131	28	165	25	118	7	58	336	China
5	81	-	62	-	11	-	2	120	Vietnam
754	1,741	470	1,235	247	787	82	429	3,933	Rest of the world
31,245	2,415	25,687	2,044	11,599	906	6,193	305	54,323	**ALL COUNTRIES OF BIRTH**
30,559	775	25,273	546	11,421	286	6,139	58	50,768	**United Kingdom***
28,752	701	23,518	474	10,641	252	5,827	46	47,649	England
1,019	30	873	24	367	6	142	-	1,604	Scotland
576	19	669	11	320	9	138	3	1,111	Wales
193	11	199	7	88	5	29	2	337	Northern Ireland
137	226	139	470	48	202	14	78	804	Irish Republic**
49	95	28	50	21	41	7	19	229	Old Commonwealth
246	721	117	595	32	133	21	53	1,260	**New Commonwealth**
32	140	4	57	1	8	1	1	164	Eastern Africa
20	62	3	13	1	1	-	2	77	Other Africa
35	86	15	145	6	31	3	6	206	Caribbean
4	18	-	10	2	2	-	1	32	Bangladesh
57	147	57	220	13	59	6	24	341	India
4	20	8	28	1	3	2	2	44	Pakistan
32	110	8	28	2	10	1	3	156	South East Asia
13	24	2	6	2	1	-	1	44	Cyprus
49	114	20	88	4	18	8	13	196	Other New Commonwealth
123	225	51	184	33	103	3	24	537	Other European Community
27	42	22	57	23	71	2	33	178	Other Europe
34	141	7	22	4	11	3	9	173	United States of America
-	6	3	9	-	1	-	1	14	China
-	5	-	3	-	-	-	-	9	Vietnam
70	179	47	108	17	58	4	30	351	Rest of the world

Table 50 Country of birth: household heads and residents – **continued**

Notes: (1) * Includes Channel Islands, the Isle of Man and United Kingdom (part not stated)
(2) ** Includes Ireland (part not stated)

50. Residents in households; household heads

Country of birth of household head	TOTAL PERSONS	Total born Inside UK	Outside UK	0 - 4 Inside UK	Outside UK	5 - 15 Inside UK	Outside UK	16 - 29 Inside UK	Outside UK
a	b	c	d	e	f	g	h	i	j

East Hampshire

ALL COUNTRIES OF BIRTH	101,335	95,437	5,898	6,610	211	13,897	699	18,039	1,083
United Kingdom*	95,477	92,673	2,804	6,208	162	13,165	525	17,425	659
England	90,289	87,791	2,498	5,886	141	12,424	452	16,572	599
Scotland	2,869	2,716	153	179	11	409	46	480	35
Wales	1,626	1,561	65	86	8	225	13	261	14
Northern Ireland	559	526	33	49	2	93	12	89	6
Irish Republic**	698	326	372	20	-	85	16	91	23
Old Commonwealth	509	243	266	38	7	66	19	41	37
New Commonwealth	2,182	1,065	1,117	182	17	294	53	232	189
Eastern Africa	305	151	154	37	2	43	9	26	39
Other Africa	125	59	66	19	-	14	6	9	18
Caribbean	153	72	81	8	1	20	3	18	12
Bangladesh	82	36	46	8	-	22	2	5	23
India	498	226	272	5	-	49	6	54	13
Pakistan	110	52	58	2	-	13	-	15	1
South East Asia	408	221	187	59	1	64	9	42	38
Cyprus	75	43	32	9	2	13	2	13	8
Other New Commonwealth	426	205	221	35	11	56	16	50	37
Other European Community	1,096	542	554	91	7	138	31	126	101
Other Europe	262	103	159	9	3	22	8	20	10
United States of America	184	78	106	19	5	13	7	18	13
China	63	18	45	1	-	2	-	7	6
Vietnam	11	1	10	-	-	-	-	1	3
Rest of the world	853	388	465	42	10	112	40	78	42

Eastleigh

ALL COUNTRIES OF BIRTH	105,298	100,641	4,657	7,262	56	14,590	329	20,512	916
United Kingdom*	99,843	97,949	1,894	6,826	38	13,803	234	19,873	497
England	95,251	93,565	1,686	6,609	34	13,166	211	19,075	458
Scotland	2,128	2,060	68	94	4	340	14	365	17
Wales	1,767	1,729	38	86	-	221	7	298	10
Northern Ireland	522	510	12	28	-	73	1	102	2
Irish Republic**	838	420	418	47	-	99	19	108	28
Old Commonwealth	332	165	167	25	4	38	3	26	30
New Commonwealth	2,385	1,199	1,186	231	6	396	40	298	204
Eastern Africa	276	128	148	25	2	47	1	29	33
Other Africa	110	51	59	10	3	18	6	8	10
Caribbean	109	62	47	11	1	20	-	13	6
Bangladesh	114	38	76	19	-	14	18	3	24
India	823	410	413	59	-	152	3	127	37
Pakistan	57	28	29	2	-	4	-	9	3
South East Asia	417	211	206	58	-	68	6	41	56
Cyprus	101	65	36	16	-	15	-	21	15
Other New Commonwealth	378	206	172	31	-	58	6	47	20
Other European Community	865	451	414	59	1	122	13	116	79
Other Europe	330	114	216	10	-	21	5	29	6
United States of America	90	43	47	3	2	8	3	18	11
China	48	14	34	3	-	4	-	1	7
Vietnam	19	2	17	-	-	2	2	-	7
Rest of the world	548	284	264	58	5	97	10	43	47

Age and birthplace of persons								TOTAL HOUSEHOLD HEADS	Country of birth of household head
30 - 44		45 up to pensionable age		Pensionable age - 74		75 and over			
Inside UK	Outside UK	Inside UK	Outside UK	Inside UK	Outside UK	Inside UK	Outside UK		
k	l	m	n	o	p	q	r	s	a
21,748	1,621	19,546	1,197	9,683	753	5,914	334	39,158	ALL COUNTRIES OF BIRTH
21,282	684	19,244	447	9,494	268	5,855	59	36,888	United Kingdom*
20,108	619	18,205	402	9,002	235	5,594	50	34,928	England
671	31	578	15	263	14	136	1	1,066	Scotland
357	14	347	9	181	5	104	2	647	Wales
137	7	104	4	36	1	18	1	195	Northern Ireland
48	69	44	133	31	72	7	59	295	Irish Republic**
44	97	26	51	22	32	6	23	197	Old Commonwealth
172	386	108	244	55	138	22	90	813	New Commonwealth
30	72	8	26	3	5	4	1	101	Eastern Africa
12	30	3	4	1	6	1	2	46	Other Africa
14	26	6	22	5	12	1	5	60	Caribbean
1	20	-	1	-	-	-	-	18	Bangladesh
27	33	49	105	30	67	12	48	224	India
3	6	11	24	6	17	2	10	52	Pakistan
45	100	9	20	-	12	2	7	137	South East Asia
8	17	-	1	-	1	-	1	25	Cyprus
32	82	22	41	10	18	-	16	150	Other New Commonwealth
100	171	56	113	25	100	6	31	415	Other European Community
12	27	14	49	18	46	8	16	118	Other Europe
17	42	9	24	1	7	1	8	73	United States of America
2	2	3	14	2	15	1	8	29	China
-	3	-	4	-	-	-	-	4	Vietnam
71	140	42	118	35	75	8	40	326	Rest of the world
23,593	1,477	19,192	996	10,144	657	5,348	226	41,219	ALL COUNTRIES OF BIRTH
23,142	535	18,976	329	10,018	213	5,311	48	39,224	United Kingdom*
22,098	481	18,065	288	9,483	184	5,069	30	37,383	England
528	19	416	2	216	9	101	3	834	Scotland
379	10	372	7	255	3	118	1	724	Wales
125	4	108	1	53	4	21	-	204	Northern Ireland
67	81	56	144	27	93	16	53	336	Irish Republic**
32	60	18	24	22	32	4	14	141	Old Commonwealth
164	525	65	279	35	98	10	34	756	New Commonwealth
20	76	6	28	1	7	-	1	90	Eastern Africa
11	35	4	4	-	1	-	-	38	Other Africa
10	24	4	13	2	-	2	3	37	Caribbean
1	19	-	14	1	-	-	1	20	Bangladesh
28	178	24	126	15	50	5	19	244	India
7	7	3	10	3	7	-	2	19	Pakistan
33	99	7	32	4	12	-	1	141	South East Asia
9	13	3	7	-	1	1	-	32	Cyprus
45	74	14	45	9	20	2	7	135	Other New Commonwealth
104	137	31	93	17	71	2	20	337	Other European Community
23	28	15	36	14	108	2	33	161	Other Europe
6	12	6	10	1	6	1	3	38	United States of America
1	6	2	13	3	4	-	4	19	China
-	6	-	2	-	-	-	-	5	Vietnam
54	87	23	66	7	32	2	17	202	Rest of the world

Table 50 Country of birth: household heads and residents – **continued**

Notes: (1) * Includes Channel Islands, the Isle of Man and United Kingdom (part not stated)
(2) ** Includes Ireland (part not stated)

50. Residents in households; household heads

Country of birth of household head	TOTAL PERSONS	Age and birthplace of persons							
		Total born		0 - 4		5 - 15		16 - 29	
		Inside UK	Outside UK	Inside UK	Outside UK	Inside UK	Outside UK	Inside UK	Outside UK
a	b	c	d	e	f	g	h	i	j
Fareham									
ALL COUNTRIES OF BIRTH	97,607	93,527	4,080	6,259	92	12,434	374	17,345	816
United Kingdom*	93,525	91,481	2,044	5,988	67	11,897	306	16,855	504
England	87,848	86,004	1,844	5,604	61	11,124	274	15,869	459
Scotland	2,843	2,780	63	198	1	389	12	523	23
Wales	2,030	1,986	44	130	4	269	11	329	10
Northern Ireland	626	612	14	42	1	99	4	104	3
Irish Republic**	584	268	316	20	2	51	5	69	17
Old Commonwealth	267	129	138	18	2	32	9	27	23
New Commonwealth	1,865	968	897	156	6	269	26	236	178
Eastern Africa	197	93	104	17	1	34	3	21	18
Other Africa	69	38	31	12	-	10	3	5	2
Caribbean	119	64	55	4	1	25	1	19	3
Bangladesh	41	14	27	3	-	10	2	-	10
India	308	162	146	10	1	33	1	45	7
Pakistan	54	25	29	-	-	6	1	5	1
South East Asia	429	212	217	47	3	66	6	47	79
Cyprus	45	28	17	9	-	2	-	10	9
Other New Commonwealth	603	332	271	54	-	83	9	84	49
Other European Community	608	319	289	44	9	88	9	86	49
Other Europe	154	67	87	2	-	13	-	12	7
United States of America	82	29	53	3	1	5	6	5	6
China	28	12	16	2	-	3	1	3	-
Vietnam	1	-	1	-	-	-	-	-	-
Rest of the world	493	254	239	26	5	76	12	52	32
Gosport									
ALL COUNTRIES OF BIRTH	73,704	70,552	3,152	5,456	73	10,168	287	15,872	826
United Kingdom*	70,488	68,908	1,580	5,186	53	9,707	233	15,434	504
England	64,900	63,530	1,370	4,809	43	8,875	211	14,221	443
Scotland	2,987	2,906	81	216	3	445	11	659	28
Wales	1,736	1,691	45	117	6	247	5	355	16
Northern Ireland	761	731	30	37	1	129	6	186	10
Irish Republic**	498	235	263	16	-	45	5	58	24
Old Commonwealth	207	93	114	18	5	20	9	26	21
New Commonwealth	1,561	843	718	159	10	257	27	227	161
Eastern Africa	119	61	58	14	1	22	2	13	17
Other Africa	21	11	10	-	2	4	1	2	1
Caribbean	111	58	53	10	3	22	8	13	11
Bangladesh	32	16	16	6	1	9	1	-	4
India	237	115	122	12	-	20	-	35	5
Pakistan	26	10	16	3	-	4	-	2	3
South East Asia	407	223	184	55	1	72	7	66	74
Cyprus	50	26	24	6	-	9	1	6	4
Other New Commonwealth	558	323	235	53	2	95	7	90	42
Other European Community	468	262	206	59	4	82	2	67	68
Other Europe	62	28	34	3	-	-	-	7	-
United States of America	50	17	33	-	1	4	4	5	4
China	41	14	27	-	-	6	-	6	6
Vietnam	36	5	31	2	-	2	2	-	13
Rest of the world	293	147	146	13	-	45	5	42	25

Age and birthplace of persons								TOTAL HOUSEHOLD HEADS	Country of birth of household head
30 - 44		45 up to pensionable age		Pensionable age - 74		75 and over			
Inside UK	Outside UK	Inside UK	Outside UK	Inside UK	Outside UK	Inside UK	Outside UK		
k	l	m	n	o	p	q	r	s	a
21,113	1,209	20,196	807	10,659	565	5,521	217	38,369	ALL COUNTRIES OF BIRTH
20,760	549	19,981	330	10,514	243	5,486	45	36,769	United Kingdom*
19,462	502	18,888	289	9,851	218	5,206	41	34,590	England
676	13	555	10	330	4	109	-	1,083	Scotland
449	8	398	6	270	4	141	1	797	Wales
158	2	129	2	52	2	28	-	232	Northern Ireland
45	59	42	101	31	74	10	58	259	Irish Republic**
22	40	11	28	16	28	3	8	111	Old Commonwealth
153	340	99	211	44	79	11	57	684	New Commonwealth
16	55	4	20	1	4	-	3	56	Eastern Africa
9	19	2	6	-	1	-	-	24	Other Africa
11	19	3	19	1	8	1	4	41	Caribbean
-	8	1	4	-	3	-	-	12	Bangladesh
20	33	29	55	20	31	5	18	124	India
1	5	6	12	6	5	1	5	23	Pakistan
36	85	11	30	4	4	1	10	157	South East Asia
3	5	3	3	1	-	-	-	17	Cyprus
57	111	40	62	11	23	3	17	230	Other New Commonwealth
56	101	24	46	18	58	3	17	238	Other European Community
17	11	9	25	12	38	2	6	76	Other Europe
6	17	4	12	6	7	-	4	37	United States of America
1	6	1	3	1	3	1	3	11	China
-	1	-	-	-	-	-	-	1	Vietnam
53	85	25	51	17	35	5	19	183	Rest of the world
15,202	866	12,082	510	7,407	413	4,365	177	29,356	ALL COUNTRIES OF BIRTH
14,972	370	11,942	206	7,323	172	4,344	42	28,105	United Kingdom*
13,627	319	11,107	177	6,785	146	4,106	31	25,958	England
726	21	469	6	285	10	106	2	1,140	Scotland
420	9	245	4	202	3	105	2	682	Wales
191	7	113	3	49	2	26	1	279	Northern Ireland
34	44	45	75	28	72	9	43	222	Irish Republic**
15	45	4	6	8	15	2	13	85	Old Commonwealth
111	269	58	133	21	70	10	48	564	New Commonwealth
8	29	4	7	-	2	-	-	39	Eastern Africa
4	5	-	-	1	-	-	1	7	Other Africa
9	21	3	7	1	3	-	-	33	Caribbean
1	6	-	3	-	-	-	1	8	Bangladesh
14	22	22	43	6	27	6	25	104	India
-	5	-	4	1	3	-	1	10	Pakistan
23	74	5	16	-	7	2	5	142	South East Asia
5	15	-	4	-	-	-	-	20	Cyprus
47	92	24	49	12	28	2	15	201	Other New Commonwealth
38	63	9	24	7	35	-	10	184	Other European Community
4	7	5	10	9	13	-	4	31	Other Europe
3	14	2	5	3	3	-	2	22	United States of America
1	7	1	6	-	7	-	1	14	China
1	6	-	8	-	2	-	-	12	Vietnam
23	41	16	37	8	24	-	14	117	Rest of the world

Table 50 Country of birth: household heads and residents – **continued**

Notes: (1) * Includes Channel Islands, the Isle of Man and United Kingdom (part not stated)
(2) ** Includes Ireland (part not stated)

50. Residents in households; household heads

Country of birth of household head	TOTAL PERSONS	Total born		0 - 4		5 - 15		16 - 29	
		Inside UK	Outside UK	Inside UK	Outside UK	Inside UK	Outside UK	Inside UK	Outside UK
a	b	c	d	e	f	g	h	i	j
Hart									
ALL COUNTRIES OF BIRTH	79,014	74,043	4,971	5,030	181	11,331	675	15,091	1,007
United Kingdom*	74,243	71,790	2,453	4,713	137	10,733	523	14,532	603
England	68,969	66,823	2,146	4,397	114	9,852	453	13,667	539
Scotland	2,611	2,471	140	149	14	453	41	435	35
Wales	2,014	1,943	71	130	2	318	12	327	14
Northern Ireland	550	505	45	31	5	99	11	90	10
Irish Republic**	689	296	393	30	1	70	36	83	36
Old Commonwealth	296	136	160	18	1	29	8	33	35
New Commonwealth	1,884	939	945	144	11	263	32	233	164
Eastern Africa	278	142	136	20	1	49	7	28	21
Other Africa	124	59	65	14	5	14	4	18	13
Caribbean	135	65	70	8	-	18	1	19	16
Bangladesh	61	26	35	11	-	6	3	8	15
India	501	239	262	12	1	61	5	61	15
Pakistan	115	61	54	1	-	21	1	21	4
South East Asia	312	145	167	35	3	42	9	34	53
Cyprus	86	50	36	14	1	13	1	8	13
Other New Commonwealth	272	152	120	29	-	39	1	36	14
Other European Community	794	382	412	46	7	114	21	94	94
Other Europe	175	76	99	4	1	18	7	19	4
United States of America	188	68	120	17	18	10	15	17	18
China	46	19	27	-	-	2	-	10	1
Vietnam	4	-	4	-	-	-	-	-	3
Rest of the world	695	337	358	58	5	92	33	70	49
Havant									
ALL COUNTRIES OF BIRTH	118,297	113,606	4,691	8,033	70	16,641	376	21,859	821
United Kingdom*	113,197	110,998	2,199	7,697	53	15,911	306	21,231	528
England	107,404	105,447	1,957	7,378	50	15,165	285	20,266	485
Scotland	3,061	2,981	80	168	1	420	12	528	19
Wales	1,933	1,889	44	104	-	227	5	311	6
Northern Ireland	601	583	18	33	2	75	1	105	5
Irish Republic**	801	365	436	24	3	84	5	107	23
Old Commonwealth	293	159	134	16	-	41	3	30	14
New Commonwealth	2,389	1,285	1,104	197	5	397	24	302	163
Eastern Africa	244	143	101	18	-	58	2	31	18
Other Africa	74	40	34	5	-	14	2	9	4
Caribbean	131	70	61	6	-	24	1	15	5
Bangladesh	81	32	49	15	3	11	4	4	14
India	493	238	255	25	1	47	1	66	17
Pakistan	64	30	34	2	-	7	-	8	7
South East Asia	447	230	217	52	1	75	6	52	61
Cyprus	104	71	33	20	-	21	1	17	10
Other New Commonwealth	751	431	320	54	-	140	7	100	27
Other European Community	771	399	372	53	2	109	15	100	55
Other Europe	192	83	109	2	1	17	1	19	6
United States of America	83	38	45	11	-	5	7	7	5
China	37	14	23	-	-	6	1	2	2
Vietnam	14	1	13	1	2	-	1	-	2
Rest of the world	520	264	256	32	4	71	13	61	23

Age and birthplace of persons								TOTAL HOUSEHOLD HEADS	Country of birth of household head
30 - 44		45 up to pensionable age		Pensionable age - 74		75 and over			
Inside UK	Outside UK	Inside UK	Outside UK	Inside UK	Outside UK	Inside UK	Outside UK		
k	l	m	n	o	p	q	r	s	a
17,826	1,353	15,766	978	5,673	540	3,326	237	29,073	ALL COUNTRIES OF BIRTH
17,430	563	15,528	361	5,556	205	3,298	61	27,297	United Kingdom*
16,113	495	14,469	318	5,197	178	3,128	49	25,411	England
683	26	510	14	165	7	76	3	923	Scotland
487	17	447	9	155	12	79	5	734	Wales
137	11	94	3	39	4	15	1	196	Northern Ireland
41	79	45	128	19	68	8	45	273	Irish Republic**
21	56	16	20	18	25	1	15	119	Old Commonwealth
161	330	93	250	32	103	13	55	670	New Commonwealth
36	76	6	19	1	9	2	3	96	Eastern Africa
9	29	4	10	-	4	-	-	42	Other Africa
10	20	8	23	-	4	2	6	53	Caribbean
-	11	-	6	1	-	-	-	15	Bangladesh
35	54	41	96	21	62	8	29	197	India
6	11	10	25	2	8	-	5	42	Pakistan
26	67	5	24	2	7	1	4	99	South East Asia
11	15	2	4	2	2	-	-	31	Cyprus
28	47	17	43	3	7	-	8	95	Other New Commonwealth
86	135	29	90	12	50	1	15	308	Other European Community
15	19	4	26	15	34	1	8	75	Other Europe
10	33	9	16	5	10	-	10	63	United States of America
-	3	5	11	1	6	1	6	20	China
-	1	-	-	-	-	-	-	1	Vietnam
62	134	37	76	15	39	3	22	247	Rest of the world
23,474	1,251	23,297	1,079	13,608	815	6,694	279	46,151	ALL COUNTRIES OF BIRTH
23,051	521	23,020	408	13,446	313	6,642	70	44,148	United Kingdom*
21,942	458	21,777	348	12,604	276	6,315	55	41,837	England
631	20	646	14	462	14	126	-	1,195	Scotland
339	12	436	13	300	7	172	1	782	Wales
122	5	144	2	76	3	28	-	251	Northern Ireland
58	90	43	140	35	108	14	67	355	Irish Republic**
34	42	10	29	19	33	9	13	118	Old Commonwealth
195	384	131	321	49	142	14	65	872	New Commonwealth
28	56	6	15	2	8	-	2	77	Eastern Africa
5	18	4	8	3	1	-	1	25	Other Africa
12	21	9	22	3	8	1	4	50	Caribbean
1	17	1	8	-	3	-	-	18	Bangladesh
22	40	52	104	19	60	7	32	210	India
4	9	5	10	3	6	1	2	24	Pakistan
34	88	12	41	5	15	-	5	161	South East Asia
10	15	3	5	-	2	-	-	31	Cyprus
79	120	39	108	14	39	5	19	276	Other New Commonwealth
71	107	41	68	21	100	4	25	314	Other European Community
9	16	14	26	20	49	2	10	92	Other Europe
7	15	3	10	2	7	3	1	33	United States of America
3	5	2	9	1	5	-	1	11	China
-	4	-	-	-	4	-	-	5	Vietnam
46	67	33	68	15	54	6	27	203	Rest of the world

Table 50 Country of birth: household heads and residents – **continued**

Notes: (1) * Includes Channel Islands, the Isle of Man and United Kingdom (part not stated)
     (2) ** Includes Ireland (part not stated)

50. Residents in households; household heads

Country of birth of household head	TOTAL PERSONS	Total born		0 - 4		5 - 15		16 - 29	
		Inside UK	Outside UK	Inside UK	Outside UK	Inside UK	Outside UK	Inside UK	Outside UK
a	b	c	d	e	f	g	h	i	j
New Forest									
ALL COUNTRIES OF BIRTH	157,604	150,797	6,807	9,071	99	19,119	583	25,756	1,083
United Kingdom*	150,731	147,684	3,047	8,724	70	18,375	440	25,080	647
England	142,876	140,174	2,702	8,325	56	17,514	397	23,923	594
Scotland	3,369	3,257	112	179	6	375	18	513	17
Wales	3,524	3,446	78	171	5	381	16	523	21
Northern Ireland	702	672	30	34	3	74	5	98	4
Irish Republic**	1,017	470	547	27	3	84	13	122	41
Old Commonwealth	637	277	360	28	4	54	22	45	54
New Commonwealth	2,355	1,098	1,257	157	8	315	41	205	180
Eastern Africa	323	152	171	30	2	53	10	21	32
Other Africa	141	61	80	11	2	16	9	14	15
Caribbean	130	57	73	2	1	18	1	11	11
Bangladesh	57	17	40	7	-	9	6	1	19
India	632	270	362	21	-	68	1	44	14
Pakistan	139	55	84	10	1	12	4	4	11
South East Asia	408	206	202	37	2	71	5	47	48
Cyprus	97	58	39	11	-	16	-	15	7
Other New Commonwealth	428	222	206	28	-	52	5	48	23
Other European Community	1,308	629	679	71	2	162	22	171	78
Other Europe	332	129	203	7	-	23	5	19	13
United States of America	212	79	133	11	5	12	10	20	18
China	43	12	31	-	-	1	-	1	2
Vietnam	22	8	14	3	-	4	-	-	9
Rest of the world	947	411	536	43	7	89	30	93	41
Portsmouth									
ALL COUNTRIES OF BIRTH	169,730	161,224	8,506	12,100	166	20,282	630	36,738	2,197
United Kingdom*	160,228	157,175	3,053	11,403	82	19,181	304	35,646	929
England	151,503	148,819	2,684	10,838	79	18,269	271	33,868	845
Scotland	4,551	4,455	96	319	-	486	12	924	34
Wales	2,800	2,731	69	157	3	265	5	586	20
Northern Ireland	1,037	1,004	33	69	-	124	5	233	12
Irish Republic**	1,312	546	766	40	2	93	22	166	76
Old Commonwealth	450	205	245	31	3	35	9	68	73
New Commonwealth	5,060	2,223	2,837	432	33	738	224	558	746
Eastern Africa	450	193	257	32	2	69	8	59	67
Other Africa	156	80	76	12	-	29	5	24	14
Caribbean	185	87	98	8	1	18	2	27	20
Bangladesh	1,006	330	676	126	22	171	164	31	195
India	743	314	429	34	2	94	18	82	59
Pakistan	71	28	43	4	-	10	6	6	9
South East Asia	1,002	444	558	111	-	138	14	133	258
Cyprus	95	51	44	9	2	16	-	9	20
Other New Commonwealth	1,352	696	656	96	4	193	7	187	104
Other European Community	1,046	487	559	78	1	106	9	155	132
Other Europe	224	97	127	11	-	12	2	22	11
United States of America	88	25	63	7	2	1	2	7	21
China	155	42	113	1	-	22	1	15	19
Vietnam	94	15	79	5	1	7	11	1	42
Rest of the world	1,073	409	664	92	42	87	46	100	148

30 - 44 Inside UK	30 - 44 Outside UK	45 up to pensionable age Inside UK	45 up to pensionable age Outside UK	Pensionable age - 74 Inside UK	Pensionable age - 74 Outside UK	75 and over Inside UK	75 and over Outside UK	TOTAL HOUSEHOLD HEADS	Country of birth of household head
k	l	m	n	o	p	q	r	s	a
30,710	1,607	30,377	1,416	22,023	1,373	13,741	646	65,411	**ALL COUNTRIES OF BIRTH**
30,201	715	29,987	478	21,700	547	13,617	150	62,482	**United Kingdom***
28,739	640	28,435	411	20,299	475	12,939	129	59,180	England
659	19	671	17	601	28	259	7	1,412	Scotland
639	17	709	10	657	8	366	1	1,486	Wales
129	4	158	5	131	9	48	-	294	Northern Ireland
62	76	92	175	57	150	26	89	462	Irish Republic**
57	79	32	61	46	81	15	59	285	Old Commonwealth
180	369	117	298	86	200	38	161	947	**New Commonwealth**
25	62	12	41	6	15	5	9	115	Eastern Africa
17	37	1	10	1	4	1	3	55	Other Africa
12	20	8	21	4	9	2	10	55	Caribbean
-	9	-	5	-	-	-	1	14	Bangladesh
39	54	43	103	40	107	15	83	289	India
6	12	11	24	10	18	2	14	61	Pakistan
29	86	12	31	6	16	4	14	151	South East Asia
10	24	5	5	1	2	-	1	35	Cyprus
42	65	25	58	18	29	9	26	172	Other New Commonwealth
108	184	56	198	46	142	15	53	520	Other European Community
17	21	24	47	32	85	7	32	173	Other Europe
17	35	14	33	4	16	1	16	97	United States of America
1	4	2	4	6	13	1	8	28	China
1	3	-	2	-	-	-	-	6	Vietnam
66	121	53	120	46	139	21	78	411	Rest of the world

30 - 44 Inside UK	30 - 44 Outside UK	45 up to pensionable age Inside UK	45 up to pensionable age Outside UK	Pensionable age - 74 Inside UK	Pensionable age - 74 Outside UK	75 and over Inside UK	75 and over Outside UK	TOTAL HOUSEHOLD HEADS	Country of birth of household head
32,093	2,221	27,728	1,738	19,805	1,085	12,478	469	72,590	**ALL COUNTRIES OF BIRTH**
31,569	729	27,365	478	19,586	407	12,425	124	68,842	**United Kingdom***
29,827	637	25,805	411	18,400	349	11,812	92	64,990	England
946	18	883	12	629	16	268	4	1,993	Scotland
551	21	479	8	419	12	274	-	1,286	Wales
219	9	172	3	121	2	66	2	433	Northern Ireland
81	121	88	245	64	183	14	117	623	Irish Republic**
30	71	14	44	26	26	1	19	208	Old Commonwealth
245	830	155	672	73	215	22	117	1,738	**New Commonwealth**
21	111	8	58	4	9	-	2	167	Eastern Africa
10	38	3	16	2	2	-	1	59	Other Africa
17	28	10	24	3	14	4	9	87	Caribbean
1	163	1	117	-	15	-	-	170	Bangladesh
30	97	45	162	22	50	7	41	267	India
1	11	4	10	2	4	1	3	26	Pakistan
44	177	13	74	3	22	2	13	371	South East Asia
14	16	-	1	3	3	-	2	40	Cyprus
107	189	71	210	34	96	8	46	551	Other New Commonwealth
81	170	40	104	22	111	5	32	484	Other European Community
17	22	17	23	15	50	3	19	115	Other Europe
5	15	3	11	2	9	-	3	52	United States of America
1	25	1	40	2	23	-	5	60	China
2	14	-	8	-	2	-	1	27	Vietnam
62	224	45	113	15	59	8	32	441	Rest of the world

Table 50 Country of birth: household heads and residents – **continued**

Notes: (1) * Includes Channel Islands, the Isle of Man and United Kingdom (part not stated)
(2) ** Includes Ireland (part not stated)

50. Residents in households; household heads

Country of birth of household head	TOTAL PERSONS	Age and birthplace of persons							
		Total born		0 - 4		5 - 15		16 - 29	
		Inside UK	Outside UK	Inside UK	Outside UK	Inside UK	Outside UK	Inside UK	Outside UK
a	b	c	d	e	f	g	h	i	j

Rushmoor

ALL COUNTRIES OF BIRTH	79,121	73,246	5,875	6,344	244	10,026	708	18,753	1,324
United Kingdom*	72,975	70,362	2,613	5,879	202	9,257	554	17,864	710
England	67,285	65,062	2,223	5,420	162	8,588	444	16,530	618
Scotland	3,234	3,027	207	255	28	403	66	808	49
Wales	1,704	1,604	100	149	10	167	32	367	27
Northern Ireland	668	624	44	50	1	85	12	151	14
Irish Republic**	1,126	508	618	46	2	97	25	186	48
Old Commonwealth	334	168	166	22	4	33	9	50	44
New Commonwealth	2,619	1,234	1,385	208	17	391	64	363	250
Eastern Africa	275	119	156	28	3	49	5	24	46
Other Africa	136	69	67	15	2	21	7	23	17
Caribbean	350	149	201	13	3	34	4	78	27
Bangladesh	47	19	28	9	-	9	3	-	12
India	601	278	323	24	2	79	8	80	15
Pakistan	274	131	143	30	4	48	9	35	37
South East Asia	484	242	242	51	3	90	15	56	55
Cyprus	111	60	51	14	-	15	4	15	13
Other New Commonwealth	341	167	174	24	-	46	9	52	28
Other European Community	1,135	621	514	127	8	173	13	192	152
Other Europe	186	72	114	7	-	14	2	23	9
United States of America	84	29	55	9	1	1	10	9	11
China	49	16	33	1	1	6	3	3	6
Vietnam	80	6	74	4	1	2	11	-	25
Rest of the world	533	230	303	41	8	52	17	63	69

Southampton

ALL COUNTRIES OF BIRTH	193,866	180,744	13,122	13,706	180	24,650	722	40,723	2,879
United Kingdom*	176,847	173,392	3,455	12,528	69	22,322	315	38,561	926
England	167,402	164,499	2,903	12,059	60	21,313	280	36,662	823
Scotland	4,625	4,493	132	246	2	553	15	949	35
Wales	2,819	2,750	69	135	2	273	8	556	21
Northern Ireland	1,512	1,455	57	70	3	156	8	332	14
Irish Republic**	2,615	1,052	1,563	103	5	171	63	341	174
Old Commonwealth	640	291	349	40	4	54	11	80	93
New Commonwealth	8,948	4,090	4,858	751	50	1,630	185	1,197	1,082
Eastern Africa	1,041	398	643	76	2	181	15	88	203
Other Africa	276	105	171	26	4	28	23	36	55
Caribbean	815	373	442	40	1	117	9	158	23
Bangladesh	522	196	326	75	14	106	65	12	98
India	3,266	1,592	1,674	249	3	703	23	495	281
Pakistan	1,063	568	495	127	6	267	21	141	122
South East Asia	824	316	508	73	17	99	21	85	189
Cyprus	283	138	145	25	1	36	2	56	23
Other New Commonwealth	858	404	454	60	2	93	6	126	88
Other European Community	1,718	747	971	99	6	170	25	245	253
Other Europe	614	232	382	15	3	37	22	59	25
United States of America	266	128	138	15	2	39	8	32	27
China	203	45	158	5	5	16	4	13	36
Vietnam	78	20	58	9	-	11	5	-	26
Rest of the world	1,937	747	1,190	141	36	200	84	195	237

30 - 44 Inside UK	30 - 44 Outside UK	45 up to pensionable age Inside UK	45 up to pensionable age Outside UK	Pensionable age - 74 Inside UK	Pensionable age - 74 Outside UK	75 and over Inside UK	75 and over Outside UK	TOTAL HOUSEHOLD HEADS	Country of birth of household head
k	l	m	n	o	p	q	r	s	a
16,659	1,535	12,088	1,171	5,976	656	3,400	237	30,523	ALL COUNTRIES OF BIRTH
16,251	526	11,882	334	5,862	237	3,367	50	28,251	United Kingdom*
14,991	469	10,989	280	5,381	205	3,163	45	26,069	England
729	28	521	21	231	15	80	-	1,199	Scotland
383	15	249	8	192	8	97	-	686	Wales
140	5	119	7	52	3	27	2	264	Northern Ireland
77	116	65	236	27	127	10	64	453	Irish Republic**
32	52	12	31	18	18	1	8	126	Old Commonwealth
151	513	75	373	35	125	11	43	900	New Commonwealth
13	72	3	25	1	4	1	1	92	Eastern Africa
8	35	-	6	1	-	1	-	44	Other Africa
18	65	5	82	1	17	-	3	133	Caribbean
1	12	-	1	-	-	-	-	13	Bangladesh
33	78	42	129	17	72	3	19	227	India
5	48	9	41	4	3	-	1	63	Pakistan
35	128	4	27	5	9	1	5	161	South East Asia
13	23	3	8	-	2	-	1	41	Cyprus
25	52	9	54	6	18	5	13	126	Other New Commonwealth
99	196	18	81	10	53	2	11	424	Other European Community
6	13	7	25	11	42	4	23	90	Other Europe
6	17	4	14	-	-	-	2	31	United States of America
2	10	1	5	2	6	1	2	15	China
-	19	-	14	-	3	-	1	23	Vietnam
35	73	24	58	11	45	4	33	210	Rest of the world
36,374	3,750	31,616	3,164	21,240	1,780	12,435	647	81,140	ALL COUNTRIES OF BIRTH
35,551	855	31,104	639	20,953	498	12,373	153	74,955	United Kingdom*
33,809	740	29,204	514	19,648	397	11,804	89	70,728	England
940	38	955	19	615	19	235	4	2,022	Scotland
513	14	524	12	479	11	270	1	1,305	Wales
269	13	382	10	192	8	54	1	652	Northern Ireland
165	302	171	533	83	343	18	143	1,157	Irish Republic**
48	95	29	47	33	67	7	32	290	Old Commonwealth
292	1,686	150	1,329	57	385	13	141	2,732	New Commonwealth
36	249	13	131	3	33	1	10	321	Eastern Africa
12	69	1	13	2	6	-	1	107	Other Africa
39	117	13	217	6	65	-	10	329	Caribbean
1	85	2	57	-	6	-	1	100	Bangladesh
75	608	42	515	22	169	6	75	894	India
18	189	8	116	6	33	1	8	237	Pakistan
38	188	15	68	4	13	2	12	293	South East Asia
16	44	4	60	1	12	-	3	97	Cyprus
57	137	52	152	13	48	3	21	354	Other New Commonwealth
124	246	62	225	40	160	7	56	750	Other European Community
45	59	34	82	31	152	11	39	288	Other Europe
22	42	12	34	7	16	1	9	111	United States of America
3	45	5	39	3	19	-	10	74	China
-	12	-	15	-	-	-	-	18	Vietnam
124	408	49	221	33	140	5	64	765	Rest of the world

Table 50 Country of birth: household heads and residents – **continued**

Notes: (1) * Includes Channel Islands, the Isle of Man and United Kingdom (part not stated)
(2) ** Includes Ireland (part not stated)

50. Residents in households; household heads

Country of birth of household head	TOTAL PERSONS	Total born		0 - 4		5 - 15		16 - 29	
		Inside UK	Outside UK	Inside UK	Outside UK	Inside UK	Outside UK	Inside UK	Outside UK
a	b	c	d	e	f	g	h	i	j
Test Valley									
ALL COUNTRIES OF BIRTH	99,463	94,155	5,308	6,310	208	13,356	772	18,414	1,121
United Kingdom*	94,503	91,751	2,752	5,975	181	12,751	635	17,807	714
England	89,282	86,825	2,457	5,679	157	12,025	569	16,971	647
Scotland	2,537	2,420	117	148	11	364	37	441	29
Wales	1,996	1,918	78	112	11	277	17	272	16
Northern Ireland	542	515	27	27	-	73	9	107	10
Irish Republic**	733	356	377	21	4	64	11	109	20
Old Commonwealth	334	162	172	25	4	30	6	41	32
New Commonwealth	1,890	929	961	141	4	279	46	238	188
Eastern Africa	277	143	134	33	1	61	6	15	20
Other Africa	89	48	41	9	-	17	2	8	9
Caribbean	186	99	87	10	1	26	3	36	8
Bangladesh	36	10	26	4	-	6	6	-	11
India	483	232	251	20	-	44	2	75	32
Pakistan	88	36	52	3	1	10	5	7	9
South East Asia	379	189	190	34	1	69	13	45	58
Cyprus	82	41	41	14	-	6	4	12	17
Other New Commonwealth	270	131	139	14	-	40	5	40	24
Other European Community	983	501	482	82	11	129	34	110	105
Other Europe	223	97	126	6	-	19	6	22	6
United States of America	190	79	111	13	2	23	18	10	18
China	56	22	34	4	-	7	3	4	2
Vietnam	7	-	7	-	-	-	2	-	2
Rest of the world	544	258	286	43	2	54	11	73	34
Winchester									
ALL COUNTRIES OF BIRTH	93,721	88,594	5,127	5,221	153	12,046	607	15,731	874
United Kingdom*	88,858	86,292	2,566	4,938	122	11,469	478	15,166	564
England	84,029	81,757	2,272	4,709	112	10,835	428	14,392	512
Scotland	2,347	2,229	118	117	6	333	30	344	23
Wales	1,789	1,725	64	79	2	219	12	307	15
Northern Ireland	525	495	30	22	2	64	7	101	5
Irish Republic**	561	251	310	11	1	43	6	74	11
Old Commonwealth	455	208	247	31	11	56	14	34	37
New Commonwealth	1,875	936	939	119	5	257	46	233	125
Eastern Africa	236	123	113	22	2	32	8	29	17
Other Africa	122	65	57	12	-	21	3	15	7
Caribbean	93	50	43	5	-	10	1	17	6
Bangladesh	80	30	50	7	-	15	11	6	18
India	480	221	259	9	-	47	9	60	11
Pakistan	113	59	54	3	-	21	-	12	4
South East Asia	318	151	167	32	1	39	7	39	37
Cyprus	63	42	21	6	1	17	1	9	4
Other New Commonwealth	370	195	175	23	1	55	6	46	21
Other European Community	762	379	383	56	5	86	19	107	57
Other Europe	215	95	120	8	-	22	5	17	6
United States of America	266	104	162	25	3	25	15	17	16
China	30	5	25	-	-	1	2	-	3
Vietnam	23	6	17	1	-	2	1	2	6
Rest of the world	676	318	358	32	6	85	21	81	49

Age and birthplace of persons								TOTAL HOUSEHOLD HEADS	Country of birth of household head
30 - 44		45 up to pensionable age		Pensionable age - 74		75 and over			
Inside UK	Outside UK	Inside UK	Outside UK	Inside UK	Outside UK	Inside UK	Outside UK		
k	l	m	n	o	p	q	r	s	a
21,578	1,344	19,504	1,055	9,581	584	5,412	224	38,391	**ALL COUNTRIES OF BIRTH**
21,162	584	19,243	375	9,442	217	5,371	46	36,521	**United Kingdom***
19,889	527	18,201	325	8,942	196	5,118	36	34,527	England
670	21	480	12	225	7	92	-	945	Scotland
464	14	440	12	221	5	132	3	781	Wales
122	3	113	4	50	1	23	-	211	Northern Ireland
54	55	65	160	33	77	10	50	296	Irish Republic**
29	55	18	35	14	19	5	21	135	Old Commonwealth
144	334	90	262	26	74	11	53	658	**New Commonwealth**
25	75	7	25	1	4	1	3	87	Eastern Africa
9	22	5	8	-	-	-	-	32	Other Africa
19	35	3	26	3	10	2	4	62	Caribbean
-	5	-	4	-	-	-	-	6	Bangladesh
33	47	44	108	12	37	4	25	181	India
5	8	8	21	2	3	1	5	33	Pakistan
28	83	8	26	4	6	1	3	122	South East Asia
8	16	1	4	-	-	-	-	32	Cyprus
17	43	14	40	4	14	2	13	103	Other New Commonwealth
109	158	38	81	26	81	7	12	375	Other European Community
21	20	9	26	19	54	1	14	103	Other Europe
21	35	4	18	7	14	1	6	67	United States of America
1	8	1	8	3	8	2	5	22	China
-	3	-	-	-	-	-	-	2	Vietnam
37	92	36	90	11	40	4	17	212	Rest of the world
19,290	1,346	19,256	1,098	10,599	733	6,451	316	37,553	**ALL COUNTRIES OF BIRTH**
18,901	626	18,998	413	10,422	289	6,398	74	35,582	**United Kingdom***
17,872	548	18,042	358	9,808	254	6,099	60	33,650	England
538	28	464	15	304	12	129	4	916	Scotland
373	21	372	7	246	6	129	1	735	Wales
103	6	109	5	55	4	41	1	211	Northern Ireland
34	41	47	105	31	88	11	58	272	Irish Republic**
45	82	17	42	18	33	7	28	191	Old Commonwealth
138	297	105	258	65	134	19	74	711	**New Commonwealth**
25	42	9	30	4	11	2	3	85	Eastern Africa
12	33	5	8	-	3	-	3	43	Other Africa
5	10	9	16	4	6	-	4	35	Caribbean
2	8	-	12	-	1	-	-	17	Bangladesh
21	51	40	88	34	67	10	33	207	India
7	11	9	21	5	13	2	5	42	Pakistan
24	72	10	27	5	14	2	9	124	South East Asia
9	11	1	3	-	-	-	1	17	Cyprus
33	59	22	53	13	19	3	16	141	Other New Commonwealth
72	109	31	91	24	84	3	18	303	Other European Community
22	28	12	27	13	36	1	18	95	Other Europe
24	65	5	43	8	14	-	6	108	United States of America
2	4	1	4	1	8	-	4	19	China
1	4	-	6	-	-	-	-	7	Vietnam
51	90	40	109	17	47	12	36	265	Rest of the world

Table 51   Country of birth and ethnic group

County, districts

Notes: (1) * Includes Channel Islands, the Isle of Man and United Kingdom (part not stated)
(2) ** Includes Ireland (part not stated)

51. Residents in households; household heads

Country of birth	TOTAL PERSONS	Ethnic group								Other groups	
		White	Black Caribbean	Black African	Black other	Indian	Pakistani	Bangla-deshi	Chinese	Asian	Other
a	b	c	d	e	f	g	h	i	j	k	l

HAMPSHIRE

	b	c	d	e	f	g	h	i	j	k	l
TOTAL PERSONS	1,512,038	1,483,557	2,547	1,220	2,292	7,667	1,554	2,281	3,509	2,476	4,935
United Kingdom*	1,433,847	1,421,044	1,267	548	1,786	3,369	745	795	962	484	2,847
England	1,370,271	1,357,721	1,250	528	1,750	3,323	739	790	941	479	2,750
Scotland	31,810	31,681	10	12	11	38	6	-	10	1	41
Wales	22,112	22,038	5	3	10	5	-	5	5	2	39
Northern Ireland	7,537	7,516	1	5	5	2	-	-	-	1	7
Irish Republic**	10,667	10,651	1	3	2	3	-	-	1	-	6
Old Commonwealth	5,681	5,612	1	16	3	1	1	-	10	7	30
New Commonwealth	29,047	16,855	1,231	467	323	4,166	804	1,486	1,875	970	870
Eastern Africa	3,286	1,678	1	125	31	1,132	34	-	1	167	117
Other Africa	1,443	1,080	3	304	22	11	2	-	-	1	20
Caribbean	2,284	832	1,198	5	61	49	1	1	29	18	90
Bangladesh	1,514	33	5	-	2	17	4	1,426	2	16	9
India	6,479	3,175	5	6	32	2,739	73	9	12	80	348
Pakistan	1,338	506	-	2	4	52	685	47	-	13	29
South East Asia	5,836	3,538	5	2	21	89	1	1	1,783	235	161
Cyprus	1,165	1,144	-	-	6	-	-	-	6	1	8
Other New Commonwealth	5,702	4,869	14	23	144	77	4	2	42	439	88
Other European Community	16,381	16,199	20	6	41	9	1	-	8	24	73
Other Europe	3,349	3,320	1	8	5	4	-	-	-	-	11
United States of America	2,597	2,493	6	7	56	1	-	-	3	8	23
China	669	243	1	-	-	-	-	-	407	6	12
Vietnam	375	15	-	-	-	-	-	-	156	191	13
Rest of the world	9,425	7,125	19	165	76	114	3	-	87	786	1,050
Total household heads	603,257	595,071	1,085	391	511	2,219	390	440	1,060	697	1,393
United Kingdom*	569,832	568,276	350	85	295	217	33	21	51	41	463
England	536,900	535,417	348	77	283	208	30	21	50	41	425
Scotland	16,332	16,296	1	6	5	8	3	-	-	-	13
Wales	11,756	11,730	1	1	4	1	-	-	1	-	18
Northern Ireland	3,759	3,756	-	1	-	-	-	-	-	-	2
Irish Republic**	5,807	5,804	-	-	2	1	-	-	-	-	-
Old Commonwealth	2,235	2,220	-	5	-	-	-	-	2	1	7
New Commonwealth	13,305	7,947	721	230	150	1,936	356	419	752	399	395
Eastern Africa	1,490	750	1	58	12	523	18	-	-	75	53
Other Africa	599	432	1	149	7	3	1	-	-	1	5
Caribbean	1,181	371	705	2	33	19	-	-	12	10	29
Bangladesh	443	18	1	-	-	8	2	402	1	5	6
India	3,509	1,923	2	3	15	1,282	36	3	6	41	198
Pakistan	676	312	-	1	1	29	298	12	-	7	16
South East Asia	2,215	1,336	-	2	5	36	1	-	708	79	48
Cyprus	462	454	-	-	2	-	-	-	3	-	3
Other New Commonwealth	2,730	2,351	11	15	75	36	-	2	22	181	37
Other European Community	5,189	5,154	6	1	7	-	-	-	1	5	15
Other Europe	1,595	1,584	-	2	3	2	-	-	-	-	4
United States of America	905	872	1	3	24	-	-	-	-	1	4
China	336	147	-	-	-	-	-	-	179	2	8
Vietnam	120	7	-	-	-	-	-	-	48	63	2
Rest of the world	3,933	3,060	7	65	30	63	1	-	27	185	495

Notes: (1) * Includes Channel Islands, the Isle of Man and United Kingdom (part not stated)
(2) ** Includes Ireland (part not stated)

51. Residents in households; household heads

Country of birth	TOTAL PERSONS	White	Black Caribbean	Black African	Black other	Indian	Pakistani	Bangla-deshi	Chinese	Other groups Asian	Other groups Other
a	b	c	d	e	f	g	h	i	j	k	l

HAMPSHIRE – *continued*

TOTAL PERSONS	1,512,038	1,483,557	2,547	1,220	2,292	7,667	1,554	2,281	3,509	2,476	4,935
Country of birth of household head											
United Kingdom*	1,424,596	1,416,437	1,115	575	1,456	978	134	95	592	719	2,495
England	1,342,618	1,334,935	1,077	552	1,383	904	123	95	540	686	2,323
Scotland	41,371	41,104	20	16	33	62	10	-	25	15	86
Wales	28,535	28,399	11	4	18	9	1	-	19	12	62
Northern Ireland	9,538	9,486	6	3	12	3	-	-	7	5	16
Irish Republic**	13,526	13,470	12	6	7	9	-	-	-	4	18
Old Commonwealth	5,315	5,271	3	5	-	1	-	-	8	10	17
New Commonwealth	38,676	21,633	1,372	474	643	6,513	1,404	2,185	2,152	1,087	1,213
Eastern Africa	4,504	2,231	4	111	55	1,659	55	-	4	206	179
Other Africa	1,665	1,237	13	298	66	13	4	5	-	3	26
Caribbean	3,098	1,234	1,311	8	274	37	1	1	19	22	191
Bangladesh	2,286	56	6	4	15	38	14	2,093	2	34	24
India	10,032	4,849	11	10	38	4,440	132	13	19	140	380
Pakistan	2,295	781	1	2	11	137	1,192	69	4	38	60
South East Asia	6,283	3,743	2	4	10	91	6	-	2,044	187	196
Cyprus	1,316	1,289	-	3	5	-	-	-	7	3	9
Other New Commonwealth	7,197	6,213	24	34	169	98	-	4	53	454	148
Other European Community	12,980	12,816	18	5	33	6	1	-	7	20	74
Other Europe	3,348	3,313	-	6	5	7	-	-	1	1	15
United States of America	2,292	2,172	4	6	75	-	-	-	2	17	16
China	833	289	2	1	-	-	-	-	511	5	25
Vietnam	415	27	-	-	-	2	-	-	167	201	18
Rest of the world	10,057	8,129	21	142	73	151	15	1	69	412	1,044

Basingstoke & Deane

TOTAL PERSONS	143,278	140,156	545	151	381	750	91	114	259	278	553
United Kingdom*	135,355	133,871	291	76	310	257	34	38	79	51	348
England	129,100	127,635	288	74	308	253	34	36	79	51	342
Scotland	3,194	3,183	2	1	-	3	-	-	-	-	5
Wales	2,251	2,244	1	1	2	-	-	2	-	-	1
Northern Ireland	684	684	-	-	-	-	-	-	-	-	-
Irish Republic**	1,521	1,518	1	-	-	-	-	-	-	-	2
Old Commonwealth	567	557	-	1	-	-	-	-	-	1	8
New Commonwealth	2,587	1,291	245	53	27	479	56	76	135	110	115
Eastern Africa	336	141	-	8	2	152	4	-	-	21	8
Other Africa	168	124	1	41	1	1	-	-	-	-	-
Caribbean	375	84	240	-	9	10	-	-	6	5	21
Bangladesh	84	5	-	-	-	1	1	76	-	-	1
India	617	285	-	1	3	269	6	-	-	6	47
Pakistan	96	40	-	1	1	5	45	-	-	1	3
South East Asia	413	252	1	-	-	11	-	-	116	15	18
Cyprus	104	100	-	-	2	-	-	-	-	1	1
Other New Commonwealth	394	260	3	2	9	30	-	-	13	61	16
Other European Community	1,519	1,501	2	-	5	1	-	-	-	2	8
Other Europe	361	360	-	1	-	-	-	-	-	2	-
United States of America	475	426	3	2	37	-	-	-	-	2	5
China	28	11	-	-	-	-	-	-	15	1	1
Vietnam	17	4	-	-	-	-	-	-	13	-	-
Rest of the world	848	617	3	18	2	13	1	-	17	111	66

Notes: (1) * Includes Channel Islands, the Isle of Man and United Kingdom (part not stated)
(2) ** Includes Ireland (part not stated)

51. Residents in households; household heads

Country of birth	TOTAL PERSONS	White	Black Caribbean	Black African	Black other	Indian	Pakistani	Bangla-deshi	Chinese	Other groups Asian	Other
a	b	c	d	e	f	g	h	i	j	k	l
Basingstoke & Deane – *continued*											
Total household heads	54,323	53,346	214	53	69	263	27	26	87	92	146
United Kingdom*	50,768	50,574	67	16	35	16	-	2	4	3	51
England	47,649	47,459	67	15	35	16	-	2	4	3	48
Scotland	1,604	1,601	-	1	-	-	-	-	-	-	2
Wales	1,111	1,110	-	-	-	-	-	-	-	-	1
Northern Ireland	337	337	-	-	-	-	-	-	-	-	-
Irish Republic**	804	804	-	-	-	-	-	-	-	-	-
Old Commonwealth	229	229	-	-	-	-	-	-	-	-	-
New Commonwealth	1,260	606	145	29	14	241	26	24	63	54	58
Eastern Africa	164	68	-	1	1	75	3	-	-	12	4
Other Africa	77	49	-	27	-	1	-	-	-	-	-
Caribbean	206	38	143	-	5	4	-	-	3	4	9
Bangladesh	32	5	-	-	-	1	1	24	-	-	1
India	341	168	-	-	2	137	4	-	-	2	28
Pakistan	44	21	-	-	-	3	18	-	-	-	2
South East Asia	156	87	-	-	-	5	-	-	51	7	6
Cyprus	44	42	-	-	2	-	-	-	-	-	-
Other New Commonwealth	196	128	2	1	4	15	-	-	9	29	8
Other European Community	537	536	-	-	-	-	-	-	-	-	1
Other Europe	178	178	-	-	-	-	-	-	-	-	-
United States of America	173	151	-	1	19	-	-	-	-	1	1
China	14	6	-	-	-	-	-	-	7	-	1
Vietnam	9	2	-	-	-	-	-	-	7	-	-
Rest of the world	351	260	2	7	1	6	1	-	6	34	34
TOTAL PERSONS	143,278	140,156	545	151	381	750	91	114	259	278	553
Country of birth of household head											
United Kingdom*	133,681	132,688	240	68	217	70	8	6	29	73	282
England	125,580	124,627	233	65	211	67	8	6	24	70	269
Scotland	4,209	4,183	6	3	3	2	-	-	3	1	8
Wales	2,797	2,788	1	-	1	1	-	-	-	2	4
Northern Ireland	933	928	-	-	2	-	-	-	2	-	1
Irish Republic**	2,054	2,043	1	1	-	-	-	-	-	2	7
Old Commonwealth	561	559	-	-	-	-	-	-	-	-	2
New Commonwealth	3,663	1,878	296	62	99	665	81	108	172	122	180
Eastern Africa	483	211	-	5	1	221	10	-	-	23	12
Other Africa	222	152	1	52	15	1	-	-	-	1	-
Caribbean	581	170	289	1	54	8	1	-	5	9	44
Bangladesh	127	10	-	-	-	2	4	108	-	-	3
India	967	494	1	3	12	372	17	-	-	11	57
Pakistan	121	52	-	-	-	10	49	-	-	2	8
South East Asia	448	261	-	-	-	11	-	-	145	9	22
Cyprus	124	122	-	-	2	-	-	-	-	-	-
Other New Commonwealth	590	406	5	1	15	40	-	-	22	67	34
Other European Community	1,426	1,410	1	1	6	1	-	-	-	4	3
Other Europe	379	378	-	-	1	-	-	-	-	-	-
United States of America	509	438	3	1	53	-	-	-	1	6	7
China	34	12	-	-	-	-	-	-	19	-	3
Vietnam	26	6	-	-	-	1	-	-	18	-	1
Rest of the world	945	744	4	18	5	13	2	-	20	71	68

Notes: (1) * Includes Channel Islands, the Isle of Man and United Kingdom (part not stated)
(2) ** Includes Ireland (part not stated)

51. Residents in households; household heads

Country of birth	TOTAL PERSONS	Ethnic group								Other groups	
		White	Black Caribbean	Black African	Black other	Indian	Pakistani	Bangla-deshi	Chinese	Asian	Other
a	b	c	d	e	f	g	h	i	j	k	l

East Hampshire

TOTAL PERSONS	101,335	100,371	75	49	98	112	11	71	144	152	252
United Kingdom*	95,540	95,142	34	32	68	32	6	29	30	10	157
England	91,593	91,208	33	32	64	32	6	29	30	10	149
Scotland	2,091	2,090	1	-	-	-	-	-	-	-	-
Wales	1,317	1,306	-	-	3	-	-	-	-	-	8
Northern Ireland	434	434	-	-	-	-	-	-	-	-	-
Irish Republic**	585	584	-	-	-	-	-	-	-	-	1
Old Commonwealth	535	532	-	3	-	-	-	-	-	-	-
New Commonwealth	1,814	1,414	38	11	22	80	5	42	90	71	41
Eastern Africa	221	174	-	2	1	34	-	-	-	4	6
Other Africa	127	116	-	8	3	-	-	-	-	-	-
Caribbean	142	89	36	1	5	2	-	-	2	-	7
Bangladesh	45	4	-	-	-	-	-	41	-	-	-
India	382	324	-	-	2	39	-	1	-	3	13
Pakistan	75	68	-	-	-	-	5	-	-	-	2
South East Asia	385	271	2	-	3	4	-	-	86	9	10
Cyprus	95	92	-	-	-	-	-	-	2	-	1
Other New Commonwealth	342	276	-	-	8	1	-	-	-	55	2
Other European Community	1,465	1,452	-	1	2	-	-	-	-	3	7
Other Europe	286	283	-	-	-	-	-	-	-	-	3
United States of America	223	222	-	-	-	-	-	-	-	-	1
China	47	34	-	-	-	-	-	-	12	-	1
Vietnam	21	2	-	-	-	-	-	-	11	7	1
Rest of the world	819	706	3	2	6	-	-	-	1	61	40
Total household heads	39,158	38,891	24	13	28	41	3	16	38	39	65
United Kingdom*	36,888	36,825	8	5	19	3	-	-	2	-	26
England	34,928	34,869	8	5	17	3	-	-	2	-	24
Scotland	1,066	1,066	-	-	-	-	-	-	-	-	-
Wales	647	644	-	-	1	-	-	-	-	-	2
Northern Ireland	195	195	-	-	-	-	-	-	-	-	-
Irish Republic**	295	295	-	-	-	-	-	-	-	-	-
Old Commonwealth	197	196	-	1	-	-	-	-	-	-	-
New Commonwealth	813	660	14	6	8	38	3	16	30	26	12
Eastern Africa	101	79	-	-	1	17	-	-	-	3	1
Other Africa	46	41	-	5	-	-	-	-	-	-	-
Caribbean	60	40	14	1	1	2	-	-	-	-	2
Bangladesh	18	2	-	-	-	-	-	16	-	-	-
India	224	197	-	-	1	17	-	-	-	3	6
Pakistan	52	48	-	-	-	-	3	-	-	-	1
South East Asia	137	101	-	-	2	2	-	-	29	1	2
Cyprus	25	24	-	-	-	-	-	-	1	-	-
Other New Commonwealth	150	128	-	-	3	-	-	-	-	19	-
Other European Community	415	413	-	1	-	-	-	-	-	-	1
Other Europe	118	117	-	-	-	-	-	-	-	-	1
United States of America	73	72	-	-	-	-	-	-	-	-	1
China	29	24	-	-	-	-	-	-	4	-	1
Vietnam	4	1	-	-	-	-	-	-	2	1	-
Rest of the world	326	288	2	-	1	-	-	-	-	12	23

Notes: (1) * Includes Channel Islands, the Isle of Man and United Kingdom (part not stated)
(2) ** Includes Ireland (part not stated)

51. Residents in households; household heads

Country of birth	TOTAL PERSONS	Ethnic group									
		White	Black Caribbean	Black African	Black other	Indian	Pakistani	Bangla-deshi	Chinese	Other groups	
										Asian	Other
a	b	c	d	e	f	g	h	i	j	k	l

East Hampshire – continued

TOTAL PERSONS	101,335	100,371	75	49	98	112	11	71	144	152	252
Country of birth of household head											
United Kingdom*	95,477	95,090	43	27	70	17	4	-	44	37	145
England	90,289	89,935	40	27	66	17	4	-	39	36	125
Scotland	2,869	2,852	3	-	-	-	-	-	2	1	11
Wales	1,626	1,612	-	-	2	-	-	-	3	-	9
Northern Ireland	559	558	-	-	1	-	-	-	-	-	-
Irish Republic**	698	697	-	-	-	1	-	-	-	-	-
Old Commonwealth	509	508	-	1	-	-	-	-	-	-	-
New Commonwealth	2,182	1,736	28	18	26	93	7	71	81	75	47
Eastern Africa	305	249	-	-	3	46	-	-	-	6	1
Other Africa	125	109	-	14	2	-	-	-	-	-	-
Caribbean	153	103	28	3	6	2	-	-	-	-	11
Bangladesh	82	10	-	-	-	1	-	71	-	-	-
India	498	442	-	-	2	40	-	-	-	3	11
Pakistan	110	98	-	-	1	-	7	-	-	-	4
South East Asia	408	302	-	1	2	4	-	-	80	4	15
Cyprus	75	74	-	-	-	-	-	-	1	-	-
Other New Commonwealth	426	349	-	-	10	-	-	-	-	62	5
Other European Community	1,096	1,089	-	1	-	1	-	-	-	-	5
Other Europe	262	254	-	2	-	-	-	-	-	-	6
United States of America	184	182	-	-	-	-	-	-	1	-	1
China	63	45	-	-	-	-	-	-	12	3	3
Vietnam	11	2	-	-	-	-	-	-	6	3	-
Rest of the world	853	768	4	-	2	-	-	-	-	34	45

Eastleigh

TOTAL PERSONS	105,298	103,565	86	50	101	718	31	107	278	125	237
United Kingdom*	100,795	100,036	42	18	85	319	8	34	94	26	133
England	97,117	96,366	42	17	83	318	8	34	93	26	130
Scotland	1,693	1,691	-	1	-	1	-	-	-	-	-
Wales	1,416	1,412	-	-	1	-	-	-	1	-	2
Northern Ireland	413	412	-	-	1	-	-	-	-	-	-
Irish Republic**	571	571	-	-	-	-	-	-	-	-	-
Old Commonwealth	340	333	-	1	-	-	-	-	2	-	4
New Commonwealth	1,649	868	44	22	9	386	22	73	139	52	34
Eastern Africa	208	99	-	3	-	86	2	-	-	6	12
Other Africa	96	76	-	16	-	3	-	-	-	-	1
Caribbean	84	38	41	-	1	2	-	-	-	2	-
Bangladesh	76	3	-	-	-	-	-	73	-	-	-
India	489	168	2	-	2	288	7	-	-	9	13
Pakistan	41	26	-	-	1	-	13	-	-	-	1
South East Asia	319	155	-	-	2	6	-	-	139	11	6
Cyprus	64	64	-	-	-	-	-	-	-	-	-
Other New Commonwealth	272	239	1	3	3	1	-	-	-	24	1
Other European Community	899	893	-	-	-	-	1	-	1	-	4
Other Europe	308	307	-	-	-	1	-	-	-	-	-
United States of America	148	148	-	-	-	-	-	-	-	-	-
China	36	9	-	-	-	-	-	-	22	-	5
Vietnam	17	-	-	-	-	-	-	-	14	2	1
Rest of the world	535	400	-	9	7	12	-	-	6	45	56

Table 51 Country of birth and ethnic group – **continued**

Notes: (1) * Includes Channel Islands, the Isle of Man and United Kingdom (part not stated)
(2) ** Includes Ireland (part not stated)

51. Residents in households; household heads

Country of birth	TOTAL PERSONS	Ethnic group								Other groups	
		White	Black Caribbean	Black African	Black other	Indian	Pakistani	Bangla-deshi	Chinese	Asian	Other
a	b	c	d	e	f	g	h	i	j	k	l
Eastleigh – *continued*											
Total household heads	41,219	40,736	36	18	19	197	9	18	87	34	65
United Kingdom*	39,224	39,145	18	4	13	12	-	-	8	-	24
England	37,383	37,307	18	3	13	12	-	-	8	-	22
Scotland	834	833	-	1	-	-	-	-	-	-	-
Wales	724	723	-	-	-	-	-	-	-	-	1
Northern Ireland	204	204	-	-	-	-	-	-	-	-	-
Irish Republic**	336	336	-	-	-	-	-	-	-	-	-
Old Commonwealth	141	138	-	-	-	-	-	-	1	-	2
New Commonwealth	756	420	18	10	4	178	9	18	61	25	13
Eastern Africa	90	40	-	1	-	40	2	-	-	4	3
Other Africa	38	31	-	7	-	-	-	-	-	-	-
Caribbean	37	18	17	-	-	-	-	-	-	2	-
Bangladesh	20	2	-	-	-	-	-	18	-	-	-
India	244	91	1	-	2	134	2	-	-	5	9
Pakistan	19	14	-	-	-	-	5	-	-	-	-
South East Asia	141	72	-	-	1	3	-	-	61	4	-
Cyprus	32	32	-	-	-	-	-	-	-	-	-
Other New Commonwealth	135	120	-	2	1	1	-	-	-	10	1
Other European Community	337	336	-	-	-	-	-	-	1	-	-
Other Europe	161	161	-	-	-	-	-	-	-	-	-
United States of America	38	38	-	-	-	-	-	-	-	-	-
China	19	7	-	-	-	-	-	-	9	-	3
Vietnam	5	-	-	-	-	-	-	-	4	1	-
Rest of the world	202	155	-	4	2	7	-	-	3	8	23
TOTAL PERSONS	105,298	103,565	86	50	101	718	31	107	278	125	237
Country of birth of household head											
United Kingdom*	99,843	99,425	52	26	72	50	6	-	43	42	127
England	95,251	94,851	51	25	70	49	4	-	42	40	119
Scotland	2,128	2,122	1	1	-	1	2	-	-	-	1
Wales	1,767	1,756	-	-	2	-	-	-	1	2	6
Northern Ireland	522	522	-	-	-	-	-	-	-	-	-
Irish Republic**	838	837	-	-	1	-	-	-	-	-	-
Old Commonwealth	332	321	1	-	-	-	-	-	5	1	4
New Commonwealth	2,385	1,231	32	18	17	655	25	107	181	63	56
Eastern Africa	276	114	-	1	-	138	2	-	-	7	14
Other Africa	110	88	-	13	1	3	-	-	-	-	5
Caribbean	109	62	30	-	10	-	-	-	-	2	5
Bangladesh	114	6	-	-	-	1	-	107	-	-	-
India	823	272	2	1	3	503	7	-	1	16	18
Pakistan	57	38	-	-	-	-	16	-	-	-	3
South East Asia	417	217	-	-	1	7	-	-	180	4	8
Cyprus	101	101	-	-	-	-	-	-	-	-	-
Other New Commonwealth	378	333	-	3	2	3	-	-	-	34	3
Other European Community	865	861	1	-	-	-	-	-	2	-	1
Other Europe	330	330	-	-	-	-	-	-	-	-	-
United States of America	90	90	-	-	-	-	-	-	-	-	-
China	48	17	-	-	-	-	-	-	24	-	7
Vietnam	19	-	-	-	-	-	-	-	16	2	1
Rest of the world	548	453	-	6	11	13	-	-	7	17	41

Notes: (1) * Includes Channel Islands, the Isle of Man and United Kingdom (part not stated)
(2) ** Includes Ireland (part not stated)

51. Residents in households; household heads

Country of birth	TOTAL PERSONS	Ethnic group									
		White	Black Caribbean	Black African	Black other	Indian	Pakistani	Bangla-deshi	Chinese	Other groups	
										Asian	Other
a	b	c	d	e	f	g	h	i	j	k	l
Fareham											
TOTAL PERSONS	97,607	96,691	76	37	71	181	10	38	196	121	186
United Kingdom*	93,671	93,271	43	24	55	68	3	14	58	25	110
England	89,237	88,841	43	24	55	67	3	14	56	25	109
Scotland	2,334	2,331	-	-	-	1	-	-	2	-	-
Wales	1,488	1,487	-	-	-	-	-	-	-	-	1
Northern Ireland	462	462	-	-	-	-	-	-	-	-	-
Irish Republic**	472	472	-	-	-	-	-	-	-	-	-
Old Commonwealth	306	305	-	1	-	-	-	-	-	-	-
New Commonwealth	1,618	1,223	30	5	6	106	7	24	119	60	38
Eastern Africa	146	74	-	-	1	55	-	-	-	13	3
Other Africa	62	55	-	4	-	2	-	-	-	-	1
Caribbean	98	55	30	-	-	3	-	-	-	-	10
Bangladesh	25	2	-	-	-	-	-	21	-	1	1
India	210	154	-	-	-	42	1	-	-	1	12
Pakistan	42	32	-	-	-	1	6	3	-	-	-
South East Asia	425	286	-	-	-	-	-	-	116	13	10
Cyprus	48	47	-	-	1	-	-	-	-	-	-
Other New Commonwealth	562	518	-	1	4	3	-	-	3	32	1
Other European Community	725	719	2	-	2	-	-	-	-	1	1
Other Europe	169	164	-	3	1	-	-	-	-	-	1
United States of America	120	118	-	-	2	-	-	-	-	-	-
China	24	10	-	-	-	-	-	-	14	-	-
Vietnam	1	-	-	-	-	-	-	-	1	-	-
Rest of the world	501	409	1	4	5	7	-	-	4	35	36
Total household heads	38,369	38,114	29	8	9	51	5	10	59	28	56
United Kingdom*	36,769	36,720	11	3	6	4	-	-	2	2	21
England	34,590	34,542	11	3	6	4	-	-	2	2	20
Scotland	1,083	1,083	-	-	-	-	-	-	-	-	-
Wales	797	796	-	-	-	-	-	-	-	-	1
Northern Ireland	232	232	-	-	-	-	-	-	-	-	-
Irish Republic**	259	259	-	-	-	-	-	-	-	-	-
Old Commonwealth	111	111	-	-	-	-	-	-	-	-	-
New Commonwealth	684	514	18	3	1	44	5	10	47	24	18
Eastern Africa	56	26	-	-	-	23	-	-	-	7	-
Other Africa	24	22	-	2	-	-	-	-	-	-	-
Caribbean	41	18	18	-	-	-	-	-	-	-	5
Bangladesh	12	1	-	-	-	-	-	9	-	1	1
India	124	95	-	-	-	20	1	-	-	-	8
Pakistan	23	18	-	-	-	-	4	1	-	-	-
South East Asia	157	106	-	-	-	-	-	-	45	3	3
Cyprus	17	17	-	-	-	-	-	-	-	-	-
Other New Commonwealth	230	211	-	1	1	1	-	-	2	13	1
Other European Community	238	238	-	-	-	-	-	-	-	-	-
Other Europe	76	75	-	-	1	-	-	-	-	-	-
United States of America	37	36	-	-	1	-	-	-	-	-	-
China	11	3	-	-	-	-	-	-	8	-	-
Vietnam	1	-	-	-	-	-	-	-	1	-	-
Rest of the world	183	158	-	2	-	3	-	-	1	2	17

Notes: (1) * Includes Channel Islands, the Isle of Man and United Kingdom (part not stated)
　　　　(2) ** Includes Ireland (part not stated)

51. Residents in households; household heads

Country of birth	TOTAL PERSONS	White	Black Caribbean	Black African	Black other	Indian	Pakistani	Bangla-deshi	Chinese	Other groups Asian	Other groups Other
a	b	c	d	e	f	g	h	i	j	k	l
Fareham – continued											
TOTAL PERSONS	97,607	96,691	76	37	71	181	10	38	196	121	186
Country of birth of household head											
United Kingdom*	93,525	93,206	39	26	52	26	1	-	30	50	95
England	87,848	87,536	39	24	52	26	1	-	29	49	92
Scotland	2,843	2,839	-	2	-	-	-	-	1	1	-
Wales	2,030	2,027	-	-	-	-	-	-	-	-	3
Northern Ireland	626	626	-	-	-	-	-	-	-	-	-
Irish Republic**	584	579	-	-	-	3	-	-	-	-	2
Old Commonwealth	267	267	-	-	-	-	-	-	-	-	-
New Commonwealth	1,865	1,351	35	9	11	147	9	38	145	65	55
Eastern Africa	197	82	-	-	3	90	1	-	1	19	1
Other Africa	69	59	2	8	-	-	-	-	-	-	-
Caribbean	119	56	33	-	5	-	-	-	-	1	24
Bangladesh	41	2	-	-	-	-	-	34	-	2	3
India	308	242	-	-	-	55	1	-	1	-	9
Pakistan	54	41	-	-	-	1	7	4	-	-	1
South East Asia	429	272	-	-	-	-	-	-	137	9	11
Cyprus	45	45	-	-	-	-	-	-	-	-	-
Other New Commonwealth	603	552	-	1	3	1	-	-	6	34	6
Other European Community	608	606	2	-	-	-	-	-	-	-	-
Other Europe	154	153	-	-	1	-	-	-	-	-	-
United States of America	82	76	-	-	5	-	-	-	-	1	-
China	28	9	-	-	-	-	-	-	19	-	-
Vietnam	1	-	-	-	-	-	-	-	1	-	-
Rest of the world	493	444	-	2	2	5	-	-	1	5	34
Gosport											
TOTAL PERSONS	73,704	72,939	70	47	82	91	16	34	172	72	181
United Kingdom*	70,649	70,286	33	19	67	34	8	16	56	8	122
England	66,215	65,866	33	19	62	34	8	16	54	8	115
Scotland	2,592	2,584	-	-	2	-	-	-	2	-	4
Wales	1,224	1,221	-	-	1	-	-	-	-	-	2
Northern Ireland	518	517	-	-	-	-	-	-	-	-	1
Irish Republic**	376	376	-	-	-	-	-	-	-	-	-
Old Commonwealth	218	218	-	-	-	-	-	-	-	-	-
New Commonwealth	1,450	1,164	34	17	12	56	8	18	83	24	34
Eastern Africa	75	46	-	9	-	16	2	-	-	-	2
Other Africa	38	32	-	4	-	-	-	-	-	-	2
Caribbean	78	32	33	-	4	3	-	-	1	-	5
Bangladesh	19	1	-	-	-	-	-	16	1	1	-
India	168	124	-	1	3	30	2	-	-	-	8
Pakistan	19	9	-	-	-	4	4	2	-	-	-
South East Asia	432	323	-	1	3	3	-	-	81	9	12
Cyprus	46	46	-	-	-	-	-	-	-	-	-
Other New Commonwealth	575	551	1	2	2	-	-	-	-	14	5
Other European Community	556	548	3	2	1	-	-	-	-	-	2
Other Europe	73	72	-	1	-	-	-	-	-	-	-
United States of America	74	71	-	-	-	-	-	-	1	1	1
China	24	5	-	-	-	-	-	-	19	-	-
Vietnam	32	-	-	-	-	-	-	-	13	19	-
Rest of the world	252	199	-	8	2	1	-	-	-	20	22

Table 51   Country of birth and ethnic group – **continued**

Notes: (1) * Includes Channel Islands, the Isle of Man and United Kingdom (part not stated)
(2) ** Includes Ireland (part not stated)

51. Residents in households; household heads

Country of birth	TOTAL PERSONS	Ethnic group								Other groups	
		White	Black Caribbean	Black African	Black other	Indian	Pakistani	Bangla-deshi	Chinese	Asian	Other
a	b	c	d	e	f	g	h	i	j	k	l
Gosport – *continued*											
Total household heads	29,356	29,147	25	14	23	35	4	9	39	21	39
United Kingdom*	28,105	28,057	8	3	16	5	-	-	1	-	15
England	25,958	25,915	8	3	14	5	-	-	1	-	12
Scotland	1,140	1,138	-	-	1	-	-	-	-	-	1
Wales	682	679	-	-	1	-	-	-	-	-	2
Northern Ireland	279	279	-	-	-	-	-	-	-	-	-
Irish Republic**	222	222	-	-	-	-	-	-	-	-	-
Old Commonwealth	85	85	-	-	-	-	-	-	-	-	-
New Commonwealth	564	448	17	8	5	30	4	9	23	6	14
Eastern Africa	39	24	-	3	-	9	1	-	-	-	2
Other Africa	7	4	-	3	-	-	-	-	-	-	-
Caribbean	33	12	16	-	2	1	-	-	-	-	2
Bangladesh	8	-	-	-	-	-	-	8	-	-	-
India	104	81	-	-	2	17	1	-	-	-	3
Pakistan	10	5	-	-	-	2	2	1	-	-	-
South East Asia	142	110	-	1	-	1	-	-	23	2	5
Cyprus	20	20	-	-	-	-	-	-	-	-	-
Other New Commonwealth	201	192	1	1	1	-	-	-	-	4	2
Other European Community	184	184	-	-	-	-	-	-	-	-	-
Other Europe	31	31	-	-	-	-	-	-	-	-	-
United States of America	22	21	-	-	-	-	-	-	-	-	1
China	14	4	-	-	-	-	-	-	10	-	-
Vietnam	12	-	-	-	-	-	-	-	5	7	-
Rest of the world	117	95	-	3	2	-	-	-	-	8	9
TOTAL PERSONS	73,704	72,939	70	47	82	91	16	34	172	72	181
Country of birth of household head											
United Kingdom*	70,488	70,182	30	26	54	13	2	-	36	21	124
England	64,900	64,624	28	26	50	12	2	-	32	20	106
Scotland	2,987	2,966	2	-	1	1	-	-	4	1	12
Wales	1,736	1,732	-	-	1	-	-	-	-	-	3
Northern Ireland	761	756	-	-	2	-	-	-	-	-	3
Irish Republic**	498	495	-	2	-	1	-	-	-	-	-
Old Commonwealth	207	204	1	-	-	-	-	-	-	-	2
New Commonwealth	1,561	1,221	39	15	25	77	14	34	87	14	35
Eastern Africa	119	74	-	6	2	30	4	-	-	-	3
Other Africa	21	14	1	6	-	-	-	-	-	-	-
Caribbean	111	49	35	-	18	1	-	-	-	-	8
Bangladesh	32	-	-	-	-	-	-	32	-	-	-
India	237	190	-	1	2	36	3	-	-	-	5
Pakistan	26	8	-	-	-	9	7	2	-	-	-
South East Asia	407	309	-	1	-	1	-	-	87	2	7
Cyprus	50	46	-	-	-	-	-	-	-	-	4
Other New Commonwealth	558	531	3	1	3	-	-	-	-	12	8
Other European Community	468	468	-	-	-	-	-	-	-	-	-
Other Europe	62	62	-	-	-	-	-	-	-	-	-
United States of America	50	47	-	-	-	-	-	-	-	2	1
China	41	5	-	-	-	-	-	-	36	-	-
Vietnam	36	1	-	-	-	-	-	-	13	22	-
Rest of the world	293	254	-	4	3	-	-	-	-	13	19

Table 51 Country of birth and ethnic group – **continued**

Notes: (1) * Includes Channel Islands, the Isle of Man and United Kingdom (part not stated)
(2) ** Includes Ireland (part not stated)

51. Residents in households; household heads

Country of birth	TOTAL PERSONS	Ethnic group								Other groups	
		White	Black Caribbean	Black African	Black other	Indian	Pakistani	Bangla-deshi	Chinese	Asian	Other
a	b	c	d	e	f	g	h	i	j	k	l
Hart											
TOTAL PERSONS	79,014	78,036	77	41	66	183	26	49	179	124	233
United Kingdom*	74,110	73,739	33	23	41	59	11	16	53	12	123
England	70,075	69,721	33	21	39	59	10	16	52	11	113
Scotland	1,975	1,966	-	2	1	-	1	-	1	-	4
Wales	1,519	1,514	-	-	1	-	-	-	-	1	3
Northern Ireland	473	470	-	-	-	-	-	-	-	-	3
Irish Republic**	618	618	-	-	-	-	-	-	-	-	-
Old Commonwealth	375	372	-	1	-	-	-	-	-	-	2
New Commonwealth	1,542	1,115	42	12	16	116	15	33	112	30	51
Eastern Africa	216	145	1	4	2	53	1	-	-	7	3
Other Africa	106	93	1	8	1	-	1	-	-	-	2
Caribbean	147	91	40	-	2	2	-	-	4	-	8
Bangladesh	38	5	-	-	-	-	-	32	-	-	1
India	338	249	-	-	4	59	2	1	-	2	21
Pakistan	67	51	-	-	-	-	11	-	-	2	3
South East Asia	354	229	-	-	2	2	-	-	102	10	9
Cyprus	93	91	-	-	1	-	-	-	-	-	1
Other New Commonwealth	183	161	-	-	4	-	-	-	6	9	3
Other European Community	1,236	1,221	1	-	1	4	-	-	2	-	7
Other Europe	229	227	-	1	-	-	-	-	-	-	1
United States of America	215	206	-	-	4	-	-	-	1	-	4
China	29	18	-	-	-	-	-	-	10	1	-
Vietnam	5	1	-	-	-	-	-	-	-	4	-
Rest of the world	655	519	1	4	4	4	-	-	1	77	45
Total household heads	29,073	28,798	24	9	19	61	13	13	44	35	57
United Kingdom*	27,297	27,257	6	3	8	5	2	-	2	1	13
England	25,411	25,374	6	2	8	5	1	-	2	1	12
Scotland	923	920	-	1	-	-	1	-	-	-	1
Wales	734	734	-	-	-	-	-	-	-	-	-
Northern Ireland	196	196	-	-	-	-	-	-	-	-	-
Irish Republic**	273	273	-	-	-	-	-	-	-	-	-
Old Commonwealth	119	119	-	-	-	-	-	-	-	-	-
New Commonwealth	670	495	18	4	10	54	11	13	36	11	18
Eastern Africa	96	64	1	1	-	26	1	-	-	3	-
Other Africa	42	36	1	3	1	-	1	-	-	-	-
Caribbean	53	33	16	-	2	1	-	-	-	-	1
Bangladesh	15	2	-	-	-	-	-	12	-	-	1
India	197	149	-	-	4	27	1	1	-	2	13
Pakistan	42	32	-	-	-	-	8	-	-	1	1
South East Asia	99	63	-	-	1	-	-	-	34	-	1
Cyprus	31	31	-	-	-	-	-	-	-	-	-
Other New Commonwealth	95	85	-	-	2	-	-	-	2	5	1
Other European Community	308	306	-	-	-	-	-	-	-	-	2
Other Europe	75	75	-	-	-	-	-	-	-	-	-
United States of America	63	61	-	-	1	-	-	-	-	-	1
China	20	13	-	-	-	-	-	-	6	1	-
Vietnam	1	-	-	-	-	-	-	-	-	1	-
Rest of the world	247	199	-	2	-	2	-	-	-	21	23

Notes: (1) * Includes Channel Islands, the Isle of Man and United Kingdom (part not stated)
(2) ** Includes Ireland (part not stated)

51. Residents in households; household heads

Country of birth	TOTAL PERSONS	Ethnic group								Other groups	
		White	Black Caribbean	Black African	Black other	Indian	Pakistani	Bangla-deshi	Chinese	Asian	Other
a	b	c	d	e	f	g	h	i	j	k	l

Hart – continued

TOTAL PERSONS	79,014	78,036	77	41	66	183	26	49	179	124	233
Country of birth of household head											
United Kingdom*	74,243	73,896	41	30	36	37	3	1	33	40	126
England	68,969	68,648	40	26	34	33	2	1	30	36	119
Scotland	2,611	2,591	1	4	2	2	1	-	1	3	6
Wales	2,014	2,009	-	-	-	2	-	-	2	1	-
Northern Ireland	550	549	-	-	-	-	-	-	-	-	1
Irish Republic**	689	685	2	2	-	-	-	-	-	-	-
Old Commonwealth	296	295	-	-	-	1	-	-	-	-	-
New Commonwealth	1,884	1,409	34	7	23	141	23	48	126	22	51
Eastern Africa	278	192	2	1	-	67	1	-	-	5	10
Other Africa	124	106	5	6	4	-	3	-	-	-	-
Caribbean	135	93	26	-	10	2	-	-	-	-	4
Bangladesh	61	9	1	-	-	-	-	46	-	-	5
India	501	400	-	-	4	71	5	1	-	3	17
Pakistan	115	91	-	-	-	1	14	1	-	5	3
South East Asia	312	183	-	-	2	-	-	-	119	1	7
Cyprus	86	86	-	-	-	-	-	-	-	-	-
Other New Commonwealth	272	249	-	-	3	-	-	-	7	8	5
Other European Community	794	789	-	-	-	-	-	-	1	1	3
Other Europe	175	175	-	-	-	-	-	-	-	-	-
United States of America	188	180	-	-	5	-	-	-	-	-	3
China	46	26	-	-	-	-	-	-	17	1	2
Vietnam	4	-	-	-	-	-	-	-	2	2	-
Rest of the world	695	581	-	2	2	4	-	-	-	58	48

Havant

TOTAL PERSONS	118,297	117,212	68	104	140	180	28	74	183	88	220
United Kingdom*	113,753	113,228	34	70	104	59	11	28	61	24	134
England	109,388	108,878	33	69	100	59	11	28	54	24	132
Scotland	2,353	2,346	-	1	3	-	-	-	2	-	1
Wales	1,396	1,392	1	-	-	-	-	-	2	-	1
Northern Ireland	464	463	-	-	1	-	-	-	-	-	-
Irish Republic**	657	656	-	-	-	1	-	-	-	-	-
Old Commonwealth	317	316	-	-	1	-	-	-	-	-	-
New Commonwealth	1,793	1,343	34	24	31	117	17	46	100	28	53
Eastern Africa	145	93	-	4	1	37	3	-	-	3	4
Other Africa	73	53	-	17	-	-	1	-	-	-	2
Caribbean	98	53	31	1	2	3	-	-	2	1	5
Bangladesh	46	4	-	-	-	-	-	40	-	1	1
India	343	241	2	-	2	71	4	2	-	4	17
Pakistan	47	33	-	-	-	1	9	4	-	-	-
South East Asia	397	281	-	-	1	2	-	-	96	8	9
Cyprus	81	79	-	-	-	-	-	-	1	-	1
Other New Commonwealth	563	506	1	2	25	3	-	-	1	11	14
Other European Community	963	955	-	-	3	-	-	-	-	-	5
Other Europe	180	179	-	-	-	-	-	-	-	-	1
United States of America	114	109	-	4	-	-	-	-	-	1	-
China	26	12	-	-	-	-	-	-	13	-	1
Vietnam	13	1	-	-	-	-	-	-	4	8	-
Rest of the world	481	413	-	6	1	3	-	-	5	27	26

Notes: (1) * Includes Channel Islands, the Isle of Man and United Kingdom (part not stated)
(2) ** Includes Ireland (part not stated)

51. Residents in households; household heads

Country of birth	TOTAL PERSONS	Ethnic group									
		White	Black Caribbean	Black African	Black other	Indian	Pakistani	Bangla-deshi	Chinese	Other groups	
										Asian	Other
a	b	c	d	e	f	g	h	i	j	k	l

Havant – continued

Total household heads	46,151	45,833	29	23	36	71	7	16	50	22	64
United Kingdom*	44,148	44,081	9	7	18	5	1	1	1	4	21
England	41,837	41,771	9	7	17	5	1	1	1	4	21
Scotland	1,195	1,194	-	-	1	-	-	-	-	-	-
Wales	782	782	-	-	-	-	-	-	-	-	-
Northern Ireland	251	251	-	-	-	-	-	-	-	-	-
Irish Republic**	355	355	-	-	-	-	-	-	-	-	-
Old Commonwealth	118	118	-	-	-	-	-	-	-	-	-
New Commonwealth	872	657	20	14	17	65	6	15	39	11	28
Eastern Africa	77	50	-	4	-	18	1	-	-	1	3
Other Africa	25	17	-	8	-	-	-	-	-	-	-
Caribbean	50	24	18	-	2	2	-	-	1	-	3
Bangladesh	18	3	-	-	-	-	-	13	-	1	1
India	210	153	1	-	-	41	2	-	-	3	10
Pakistan	24	18	-	-	-	1	3	2	-	-	-
South East Asia	161	116	-	-	-	1	-	-	37	1	6
Cyprus	31	31	-	-	-	-	-	-	-	-	-
Other New Commonwealth	276	245	1	2	15	2	-	-	1	5	5
Other European Community	314	311	-	-	1	-	-	-	-	-	2
Other Europe	92	91	-	-	-	-	-	-	-	-	1
United States of America	33	32	-	1	-	-	-	-	-	-	-
China	11	5	-	-	-	-	-	-	6	-	-
Vietnam	5	1	-	-	-	-	-	-	1	3	-
Rest of the world	203	182	-	1	-	1	-	-	3	4	12
TOTAL PERSONS	118,297	117,212	68	104	140	180	28	74	183	88	220
Country of birth of household head											
United Kingdom*	113,197	112,784	33	70	90	17	7	4	32	38	122
England	107,404	107,009	32	67	85	13	7	4	31	37	119
Scotland	3,061	3,049	1	2	3	4	-	-	-	-	2
Wales	1,933	1,927	-	1	2	-	-	-	1	1	1
Northern Ireland	601	601	-	-	-	-	-	-	-	-	-
Irish Republic**	801	799	-	-	-	1	-	-	-	-	1
Old Commonwealth	293	293	-	-	-	-	-	-	-	-	-
New Commonwealth	2,389	1,811	35	29	46	161	21	70	116	31	69
Eastern Africa	244	159	-	12	-	61	1	-	-	5	6
Other Africa	74	53	2	12	4	-	-	-	-	-	3
Caribbean	131	81	27	-	8	5	-	-	2	-	8
Bangladesh	81	6	-	-	-	-	-	66	-	5	4
India	493	365	5	-	-	86	8	-	-	6	23
Pakistan	64	47	-	-	-	1	12	4	-	-	-
South East Asia	447	314	-	-	-	1	-	-	113	4	15
Cyprus	104	101	-	3	-	-	-	-	-	-	-
Other New Commonwealth	751	685	1	2	34	7	-	-	1	11	10
Other European Community	771	760	-	-	2	-	-	-	1	1	7
Other Europe	192	191	-	-	-	-	-	-	-	-	1
United States of America	83	75	-	4	-	-	-	-	-	4	-
China	37	12	-	-	-	-	-	-	24	-	1
Vietnam	14	2	-	-	-	-	-	-	5	7	-
Rest of the world	520	485	-	1	2	1	-	-	5	7	19

Notes: (1) * Includes Channel Islands, the Isle of Man and United Kingdom (part not stated)
(2) ** Includes Ireland (part not stated)

51. Residents in households; household heads

Country of birth	TOTAL PERSONS	Ethnic group								Other groups	
		White	Black Caribbean	Black African	Black other	Indian	Pakistani	Bangla-deshi	Chinese	Asian	Other
a	b	c	d	e	f	g	h	i	j	k	l
New Forest											
TOTAL PERSONS	157,604	156,565	75	56	91	169	11	77	165	111	284
United Kingdom*	151,006	150,569	42	25	63	47	-	22	44	20	174
England	144,814	144,384	41	25	62	47	-	22	44	20	169
Scotland	2,631	2,627	1	-	1	-	-	-	-	-	2
Wales	2,779	2,777	-	-	-	-	-	-	-	-	2
Northern Ireland	567	567	-	-	-	-	-	-	-	-	-
Irish Republic**	839	839	-	-	-	-	-	-	-	-	-
Old Commonwealth	645	639	-	2	-	-	-	-	4	-	-
New Commonwealth	2,005	1,564	32	21	13	117	11	55	91	42	59
Eastern Africa	281	217	-	3	1	44	-	-	-	4	12
Other Africa	132	111	-	17	3	-	-	-	-	-	1
Caribbean	131	84	30	-	4	2	1	-	2	2	6
Bangladesh	44	3	-	-	-	-	-	40	-	-	1
India	477	400	-	-	1	54	2	-	-	4	16
Pakistan	111	86	-	-	-	-	8	15	-	-	2
South East Asia	417	285	1	-	3	10	-	-	87	13	18
Cyprus	76	76	-	-	-	-	-	-	-	-	-
Other New Commonwealth	336	302	1	1	1	7	-	-	2	19	3
Other European Community	1,503	1,494	-	-	4	-	-	-	-	1	4
Other Europe	353	351	-	1	-	-	-	-	-	-	1
United States of America	220	210	-	-	7	-	-	-	-	-	3
China	49	33	-	-	-	-	-	-	15	-	1
Vietnam	19	-	-	-	-	-	-	-	7	8	4
Rest of the world	965	866	1	7	4	5	-	-	4	40	38
Total household heads	65,411	65,116	26	15	22	55	9	18	56	21	73
United Kingdom*	62,482	62,412	11	3	11	4	-	1	4	-	36
England	59,180	59,113	11	3	10	4	-	1	4	-	34
Scotland	1,412	1,410	-	-	1	-	-	-	-	-	1
Wales	1,486	1,485	-	-	-	-	-	-	-	-	1
Northern Ireland	294	294	-	-	-	-	-	-	-	-	-
Irish Republic**	462	462	-	-	-	-	-	-	-	-	-
Old Commonwealth	285	282	-	2	-	-	-	-	1	-	-
New Commonwealth	947	779	15	5	5	49	9	17	38	13	17
Eastern Africa	115	97	-	-	-	13	-	-	-	1	4
Other Africa	55	51	-	4	-	-	-	-	-	-	-
Caribbean	55	35	14	-	3	-	-	-	2	-	1
Bangladesh	14	-	-	-	-	-	-	14	-	-	-
India	289	251	-	-	1	28	2	-	-	2	5
Pakistan	61	50	-	-	-	-	7	3	-	-	1
South East Asia	151	108	-	-	-	2	-	-	35	3	3
Cyprus	35	35	-	-	-	-	-	-	-	-	-
Other New Commonwealth	172	152	1	1	1	6	-	-	1	7	3
Other European Community	520	518	-	-	2	-	-	-	-	-	-
Other Europe	173	172	-	1	-	-	-	-	-	-	-
United States of America	97	96	-	-	1	-	-	-	-	-	-
China	28	18	-	-	-	-	-	-	9	-	1
Vietnam	6	-	-	-	-	-	-	-	3	2	1
Rest of the world	411	377	-	4	3	2	-	-	1	6	18

Table 51 Country of birth and ethnic group – **continued**

Notes: (1) * Includes Channel Islands, the Isle of Man and United Kingdom (part not stated)
(2) ** Includes Ireland (part not stated)

51. Residents in households; household heads

Country of birth	TOTAL PERSONS	Ethnic group								Other groups	
		White	Black Caribbean	Black African	Black other	Indian	Pakistani	Bangla-deshi	Chinese	Asian	Other
a	b	c	d	e	f	g	h	i	j	k	l
New Forest – *continued*											
TOTAL PERSONS	157,604	156,565	75	56	91	169	11	77	165	111	284
Country of birth of household head											
United Kingdom*	150,731	150,270	46	38	63	23	1	1	44	64	181
England	142,876	142,430	44	38	60	22	1	1	44	61	175
Scotland	3,369	3,360	2	-	2	1	-	-	-	1	3
Wales	3,524	3,518	-	-	1	-	-	-	-	2	3
Northern Ireland	702	702	-	-	-	-	-	-	-	-	-
Irish Republic**	1,017	1,017	-	-	-	-	-	-	-	-	-
Old Commonwealth	637	634	-	2	-	-	-	-	1	-	-
New Commonwealth	2,355	1,886	29	11	13	143	10	76	101	31	55
Eastern Africa	323	253	-	-	-	54	-	-	-	1	15
Other Africa	141	130	-	8	3	-	-	-	-	-	-
Caribbean	130	93	27	-	6	-	-	-	2	-	2
Bangladesh	57	-	-	-	1	-	-	56	-	-	-
India	632	531	-	-	2	70	2	-	1	10	16
Pakistan	139	110	-	-	-	-	8	20	-	-	1
South East Asia	408	287	-	-	-	4	-	-	97	5	15
Cyprus	97	97	-	-	-	-	-	-	-	-	-
Other New Commonwealth	428	385	2	3	1	15	-	-	1	15	6
Other European Community	1,308	1,294	-	-	5	-	-	-	-	1	8
Other Europe	332	330	-	1	1	-	-	-	-	-	-
United States of America	212	206	-	-	6	-	-	-	-	-	1
China	43	31	-	-	-	-	-	-	11	-	1
Vietnam	22	4	-	-	-	1	-	-	7	6	4
Rest of the world	947	893	-	4	3	2	-	-	1	9	35
Portsmouth											
TOTAL PERSONS	169,730	165,400	164	225	354	668	58	1,041	694	325	801
United Kingdom*	161,462	159,720	91	90	242	293	24	339	195	64	404
England	154,616	152,910	89	87	234	290	23	339	193	64	387
Scotland	3,591	3,576	2	2	2	1	1	-	-	-	7
Wales	2,238	2,229	-	1	-	1	-	-	1	-	6
Northern Ireland	761	760	-	-	-	1	-	-	-	-	-
Irish Republic**	1,068	1,065	-	3	-	-	-	-	3	-	4
Old Commonwealth	505	496	-	1	1	-	-	-	-	-	-
New Commonwealth	3,898	1,940	67	94	91	370	34	702	353	122	125
Eastern Africa	321	121	-	30	5	109	3	-	-	14	39
Other Africa	134	68	-	56	5	2	-	-	-	1	2
Caribbean	155	73	60	1	8	7	-	-	1	1	4
Bangladesh	693	1	-	-	2	-	-	687	-	3	-
India	509	226	-	2	5	229	7	5	1	3	31
Pakistan	55	18	-	-	-	3	23	8	-	-	3
South East Asia	882	433	1	1	2	13	-	1	346	61	24
Cyprus	87	85	-	-	-	-	-	-	1	-	1
Other New Commonwealth	1,062	915	6	4	64	7	1	1	4	39	21
Other European Community	1,212	1,191	2	1	4	-	-	-	2	3	9
Other Europe	214	214	-	-	-	-	-	-	-	-	-
United States of America	153	142	2	1	3	1	-	-	-	-	4
China	125	20	1	-	-	-	-	-	102	1	1
Vietnam	78	5	-	-	-	-	-	-	28	39	6
Rest of the world	1,015	607	1	35	13	4	-	-	11	96	248

Notes: (1) * Includes Channel Islands, the Isle of Man and United Kingdom (part not stated)
(2) ** Includes Ireland (part not stated)

51. Residents in households; household heads

Country of birth	TOTAL PERSONS	Ethnic group								Other groups	
		White	Black Caribbean	Black African	Black other	Indian	Pakistani	Bangla-deshi	Chinese	Asian	Other
a	b	c	d	e	f	g	h	i	j	k	l
Portsmouth – *continued*											
Total household heads	72,590	71,342	87	72	108	207	18	180	219	102	255
United Kingdom*	68,842	68,599	43	15	51	32	3	7	10	7	75
England	64,990	64,763	43	13	48	32	3	7	9	7	65
Scotland	1,993	1,988	-	1	2	-	-	-	-	-	2
Wales	1,286	1,279	-	1	-	-	-	-	1	-	5
Northern Ireland	433	433	-	-	-	-	-	-	-	-	-
Irish Republic**	623	623	-	-	-	-	-	-	-	-	-
Old Commonwealth	208	207	-	-	-	-	-	-	-	-	1
New Commonwealth	1,738	971	41	47	50	173	15	173	149	56	63
Eastern Africa	167	58	-	17	5	52	2	-	-	8	25
Other Africa	59	28	-	26	2	1	-	-	-	1	1
Caribbean	87	41	36	-	5	4	-	-	-	1	-
Bangladesh	170	1	-	-	-	-	-	168	-	1	-
India	267	134	-	1	2	106	3	2	-	2	17
Pakistan	26	10	-	-	-	2	10	2	-	-	2
South East Asia	371	180	-	1	-	6	-	-	148	27	9
Cyprus	40	39	-	-	-	-	-	-	-	-	1
Other New Commonwealth	551	480	5	2	36	2	-	1	1	16	8
Other European Community	484	476	2	-	1	-	-	-	-	1	4
Other Europe	115	115	-	-	-	-	-	-	-	-	-
United States of America	52	49	1	1	1	-	-	-	-	-	-
China	60	12	-	-	-	-	-	-	47	1	-
Vietnam	27	3	-	-	-	-	-	-	9	14	1
Rest of the world	441	287	-	9	5	2	-	-	4	23	111
TOTAL PERSONS	169,730	165,400	164	225	354	668	58	1,041	694	325	801
Country of birth of household head											
United Kingdom*	160,228	159,062	107	105	215	149	16	40	93	89	352
England	151,503	150,403	103	103	200	149	16	40	82	85	322
Scotland	4,551	4,536	-	1	6	-	-	-	3	2	3
Wales	2,800	2,767	4	1	1	-	-	-	6	2	19
Northern Ireland	1,037	1,029	-	-	2	-	-	-	2	-	4
Irish Republic**	1,312	1,306	-	1	1	-	-	-	-	-	4
Old Commonwealth	450	447	-	-	-	-	-	-	-	2	1
New Commonwealth	5,060	2,517	53	87	125	513	41	1,001	418	140	165
Eastern Africa	450	178	-	29	14	145	2	-	1	22	59
Other Africa	156	77	1	46	17	5	-	5	-	2	3
Caribbean	185	109	44	1	13	7	-	-	1	1	9
Bangladesh	1,006	6	-	3	7	2	1	969	1	17	-
India	743	346	-	2	2	330	12	12	2	8	29
Pakistan	71	23	-	-	-	3	26	14	1	-	4
South East Asia	1,002	485	1	1	-	16	-	-	408	58	33
Cyprus	95	94	-	-	-	-	-	-	-	-	1
Other New Commonwealth	1,352	1,199	7	5	72	5	-	1	4	32	27
Other European Community	1,046	1,022	2	3	4	1	-	-	-	2	12
Other Europe	224	223	-	1	-	-	-	-	-	-	-
United States of America	88	83	1	1	1	-	-	-	-	1	1
China	155	19	1	-	-	-	-	-	132	1	2
Vietnam	94	9	-	-	-	-	-	-	40	39	6
Rest of the world	1,073	712	-	27	8	5	1	-	11	51	258

Notes: (1) * Includes Channel Islands, the Isle of Man and United Kingdom (part not stated)
(2) ** Includes Ireland (part not stated)

51. Residents in households; household heads

Country of birth	TOTAL PERSONS	Ethnic group								Other groups	
		White	Black Caribbean	Black African	Black other	Indian	Pakistani	Bangla-deshi	Chinese	Asian	Other
a	b	c	d	e	f	g	h	i	j	k	l
Rushmoor											
TOTAL PERSONS	79,121	77,046	346	92	180	363	238	37	249	236	334
United Kingdom*	73,323	72,401	166	40	147	141	111	14	61	34	208
England	69,035	68,132	165	39	144	137	111	14	61	34	198
Scotland	2,223	2,211	-	1	-	4	-	-	-	-	7
Wales	1,310	1,307	1	-	1	-	-	-	-	-	1
Northern Ireland	671	667	-	-	2	-	-	-	-	-	2
Irish Republic**	872	869	-	-	1	-	-	-	-	-	2
Old Commonwealth	309	304	-	-	1	-	-	-	1	-	3
New Commonwealth	1,913	1,027	175	44	14	220	125	23	137	80	68
Eastern Africa	178	86	-	13	-	66	2	-	-	8	3
Other Africa	91	61	1	25	1	1	-	-	-	-	2
Caribbean	244	46	174	1	4	2	-	-	6	3	8
Bangladesh	28	1	-	-	-	2	-	23	-	-	2
India	405	225	-	-	-	136	8	-	4	3	29
Pakistan	148	24	-	1	1	-	115	-	-	-	7
South East Asia	425	260	-	-	2	9	-	-	122	22	10
Cyprus	124	122	-	-	1	-	-	-	-	-	1
Other New Commonwealth	270	202	-	4	5	4	-	-	5	44	6
Other European Community	1,785	1,756	4	1	7	-	-	-	-	7	10
Other Europe	189	186	-	-	3	-	-	-	-	-	-
United States of America	101	101	-	-	-	-	-	-	-	-	-
China	33	7	-	-	-	-	-	-	24	2	-
Vietnam	83	-	-	-	-	-	-	-	22	61	-
Rest of the world	513	395	1	7	7	2	2	-	4	52	43
Total household heads	30,523	29,903	151	31	34	114	52	10	69	70	89
United Kingdom*	28,251	28,122	49	3	24	8	5	-	2	5	33
England	26,069	25,946	48	3	23	8	5	-	2	5	29
Scotland	1,199	1,197	-	-	-	-	-	-	-	-	2
Wales	686	683	1	-	1	-	-	-	-	-	1
Northern Ireland	264	263	-	-	-	-	-	-	-	-	1
Irish Republic**	453	452	-	-	1	-	-	-	-	-	-
Old Commonwealth	126	124	-	-	-	-	-	-	-	-	2
New Commonwealth	900	486	101	24	5	104	47	10	53	35	35
Eastern Africa	92	47	-	5	-	35	2	-	-	2	1
Other Africa	44	26	-	16	-	-	-	-	-	-	2
Caribbean	133	22	101	-	3	1	-	-	2	3	1
Bangladesh	13	-	-	-	-	1	-	10	-	-	2
India	227	142	-	-	-	60	4	-	2	1	18
Pakistan	63	16	-	1	1	-	41	-	-	-	4
South East Asia	161	95	-	-	-	5	-	-	46	11	4
Cyprus	41	41	-	-	-	-	-	-	-	-	-
Other New Commonwealth	126	97	-	2	1	2	-	-	3	18	3
Other European Community	424	420	1	-	-	-	-	-	-	1	2
Other Europe	90	89	-	-	1	-	-	-	-	-	-
United States of America	31	31	-	-	-	-	-	-	-	-	-
China	15	5	-	-	-	-	-	-	10	-	-
Vietnam	23	-	-	-	-	-	-	-	4	19	-
Rest of the world	210	174	-	4	3	2	-	-	-	10	17

Notes: (1) * Includes Channel Islands, the Isle of Man and United Kingdom (part not stated)
　　　　(2) ** Includes Ireland (part not stated)

51. Residents in households; household heads

Country of birth	TOTAL PERSONS	Ethnic group									
		White	Black Caribbean	Black African	Black other	Indian	Pakistani	Bangla-deshi	Chinese	Other groups	
										Asian	Other
a	b	c	d	e	f	g	h	i	j	k	l

Rushmoor – *continued*

TOTAL PERSONS	79,121	77,046	346	92	180	363	238	37	249	236	334
Country of birth of household head											
United Kingdom*	72,975	72,360	124	30	122	38	17	1	46	65	172
England	67,285	66,720	119	29	113	35	17	1	38	64	149
Scotland	3,234	3,203	1	-	4	2	-	-	6	1	17
Wales	1,704	1,689	4	1	3	1	-	-	2	-	4
Northern Ireland	668	664	-	-	2	-	-	-	-	-	2
Irish Republic**	1,126	1,123	-	-	1	-	-	-	-	-	2
Old Commonwealth	334	331	1	-	-	-	-	-	-	-	2
New Commonwealth	2,619	1,373	217	52	48	321	221	36	155	86	110
Eastern Africa	275	127	-	15	-	114	6	-	-	7	6
Other Africa	136	92	-	29	6	1	-	-	-	-	8
Caribbean	350	80	214	-	29	2	-	-	5	6	14
Bangladesh	47	1	-	-	-	6	-	36	-	-	4
India	601	366	1	-	-	186	9	-	3	5	31
Pakistan	274	49	1	1	5	1	206	-	-	-	11
South East Asia	484	296	-	-	2	7	-	-	139	22	18
Cyprus	111	111	-	-	-	-	-	-	-	-	-
Other New Commonwealth	341	251	1	7	6	4	-	-	8	46	18
Other European Community	1,135	1,110	4	-	5	1	-	-	1	4	10
Other Europe	186	184	-	-	1	-	-	-	-	1	-
United States of America	84	84	-	-	-	-	-	-	-	-	-
China	49	15	-	-	-	-	-	-	32	-	2
Vietnam	80	1	-	-	-	-	-	-	15	63	1
Rest of the world	533	465	-	10	3	3	-	-	-	17	35

Southampton

TOTAL PERSONS	193,866	184,356	818	289	576	3,834	984	514	657	627	1,211
United Kingdom*	181,162	176,596	397	92	488	1,907	515	204	140	171	652
England	173,909	169,428	391	84	485	1,876	511	201	137	167	629
Scotland	3,405	3,358	2	2	1	26	4	-	2	1	9
Wales	2,278	2,256	2	1	1	4	-	3	1	1	9
Northern Ireland	1,138	1,129	1	5	-	1	-	-	-	1	1
Irish Republic**	2,034	2,030	-	-	1	2	-	-	-	-	1
Old Commonwealth	629	616	-	1	-	1	1	-	-	5	5
New Commonwealth	5,663	1,621	412	148	59	1,865	468	310	338	266	176
Eastern Africa	760	178	-	47	18	405	12	-	1	80	19
Other Africa	232	126	-	95	6	1	-	-	-	-	4
Caribbean	526	77	405	1	15	12	-	1	3	2	10
Bangladesh	331	2	5	-	-	14	3	300	1	5	1
India	1,840	285	1	2	8	1,360	29	-	7	40	108
Pakistan	519	40	-	-	-	36	420	8	-	9	6
South East Asia	657	244	-	-	1	20	1	-	319	55	17
Cyprus	186	182	-	-	1	-	-	-	1	-	2
Other New Commonwealth	612	487	1	3	10	17	3	1	6	75	9
Other European Community	1,748	1,728	2	1	7	2	-	-	-	4	4
Other Europe	516	507	-	1	1	3	-	-	-	-	4
United States of America	256	244	1	-	3	-	-	-	1	4	3
China	167	36	-	-	-	-	-	-	130	-	1
Vietnam	60	2	-	-	-	-	-	-	25	33	-
Rest of the world	1,631	976	6	46	17	54	-	-	23	144	365

Table 51 Country of birth and ethnic group – **continued**

Notes: (1) * Includes Channel Islands, the Isle of Man and United Kingdom (part not stated)
(2) ** Includes Ireland (part not stated)

51. Residents in households; household heads

Country of birth	TOTAL PERSONS	Ethnic group									
		White	Black Caribbean	Black African	Black other	Indian	Pakistani	Bangla-deshi	Chinese	Other groups Asian	Other groups Other
a	b	c	d	e	f	g	h	i	j	k	l

Southampton – *continued*

Total household heads	81,140	78,455	386	112	107	995	221	101	223	171	369
United Kingdom*	74,955	74,498	108	16	66	112	20	10	11	15	99
England	70,728	70,295	107	15	64	103	18	10	11	15	90
Scotland	2,022	2,007	1	-	-	8	2	-	-	-	4
Wales	1,305	1,300	-	-	1	1	-	-	-	-	3
Northern Ireland	652	650	-	1	-	-	-	-	-	-	1
Irish Republic**	1,157	1,155	-	-	1	1	-	-	-	-	-
Old Commonwealth	290	286	-	1	-	-	-	-	-	1	2
New Commonwealth	2,732	891	274	71	24	845	201	91	145	103	87
Eastern Africa	321	74	-	24	5	180	2	-	-	30	6
Other Africa	107	61	-	42	3	-	-	-	-	-	1
Caribbean	329	40	272	1	7	4	-	-	2	-	3
Bangladesh	100	1	1	-	-	6	1	89	1	1	-
India	894	172	-	2	-	622	14	-	4	18	62
Pakistan	237	25	-	-	-	19	183	1	-	5	4
South East Asia	293	125	-	-	1	9	1	-	135	16	6
Cyprus	97	94	-	-	-	-	-	-	1	-	2
Other New Commonwealth	354	299	1	2	8	5	-	1	2	33	3
Other European Community	750	741	2	-	3	-	-	-	-	2	2
Other Europe	288	282	-	1	1	2	-	-	-	-	2
United States of America	111	110	-	-	1	-	-	-	-	-	-
China	74	20	-	-	-	-	-	-	53	-	1
Vietnam	18	-	-	-	-	-	-	-	6	12	-
Rest of the world	765	472	2	23	11	35	-	-	8	38	176
TOTAL PERSONS	193,866	184,356	818	289	576	3,834	984	514	657	627	1,211

Country of birth of household head

United Kingdom*	176,847	174,842	296	85	358	460	59	42	74	122	509
England	167,402	165,527	287	81	342	407	51	42	72	114	479
Scotland	4,625	4,538	2	1	8	48	7	-	1	3	17
Wales	2,819	2,801	1	-	4	3	1	-	1	-	8
Northern Ireland	1,512	1,495	5	3	1	2	-	-	-	4	2
Irish Republic**	2,615	2,596	9	-	3	3	-	-	-	2	2
Old Commonwealth	640	626	-	1	-	-	-	-	1	6	6
New Commonwealth	8,948	2,468	501	152	178	3,264	912	471	378	341	283
Eastern Africa	1,041	228	2	40	29	590	14	-	2	98	38
Other Africa	276	163	1	94	12	-	1	-	-	-	5
Caribbean	815	173	487	3	93	10	-	1	2	2	44
Bangladesh	522	4	5	-	7	26	9	460	1	5	5
India	3,266	495	2	3	10	2,483	63	-	11	69	130
Pakistan	1,063	76	-	1	5	105	819	9	2	25	21
South East Asia	824	340	-	1	3	30	6	-	354	65	25
Cyprus	283	272	-	-	3	-	-	-	3	3	2
Other New Commonwealth	858	717	4	10	16	20	-	1	3	74	13
Other European Community	1,718	1,676	3	-	10	1	1	-	1	6	20
Other Europe	614	597	-	1	1	7	-	-	1	-	7
United States of America	266	262	-	-	3	-	-	-	-	-	1
China	203	46	1	1	-	-	-	-	152	-	3
Vietnam	78	1	-	-	-	-	-	1	27	50	-
Rest of the world	1,937	1,242	8	49	23	99	12	1	23	100	380

Notes: (1) * Includes Channel Islands, the Isle of Man and United Kingdom (part not stated)
(2) ** Includes Ireland (part not stated)

51. Residents in households; household heads

Country of birth	TOTAL PERSONS	Ethnic group								Other groups	
		White	Black Caribbean	Black African	Black other	Indian	Pakistani	Bangla-deshi	Chinese	Asian	Other
a	b	c	d	e	f	g	h	i	j	k	l

Test Valley

TOTAL PERSONS	99,463	98,352	109	45	107	291	21	45	200	87	206
United Kingdom*	94,284	93,809	40	23	80	118	7	10	59	13	125
England	90,220	89,751	39	21	79	117	7	10	59	13	124
Scotland	1,935	1,931	1	2	-	1	-	-	-	-	-
Wales	1,490	1,489	-	-	-	-	-	-	-	-	1
Northern Ireland	509	508	-	-	1	-	-	-	-	-	-
Irish Republic**	561	561	-	-	-	-	-	-	-	-	-
Old Commonwealth	404	398	1	4	-	-	-	-	-	-	1
New Commonwealth	1,520	1,035	64	7	18	166	14	35	111	33	37
Eastern Africa	198	135	-	2	-	55	-	-	-	5	1
Other Africa	80	70	-	5	2	1	-	-	-	-	2
Caribbean	121	45	64	-	6	1	-	-	-	1	4
Bangladesh	32	1	-	-	-	-	-	31	-	-	-
India	337	215	-	-	2	99	3	-	-	1	17
Pakistan	51	33	-	-	-	2	11	4	-	-	1
South East Asia	387	259	-	-	1	7	-	-	109	3	8
Cyprus	95	94	-	-	-	-	-	-	1	-	-
Other New Commonwealth	219	183	-	-	7	1	-	-	1	23	4
Other European Community	1,676	1,660	3	-	3	1	-	-	-	-	9
Other Europe	235	235	-	-	-	-	-	-	-	-	-
United States of America	200	199	-	-	-	-	-	-	-	-	1
China	45	23	-	-	-	-	-	-	22	-	-
Vietnam	8	-	-	-	-	-	-	-	3	4	1
Rest of the world	530	432	1	11	6	6	-	-	5	37	32
Total household heads	38,391	38,080	46	13	21	85	10	7	52	25	52
United Kingdom*	36,521	36,462	8	5	14	9	2	-	2	3	16
England	34,527	34,470	8	3	14	9	2	-	2	3	16
Scotland	945	943	-	2	-	-	-	-	-	-	-
Wales	781	781	-	-	-	-	-	-	-	-	-
Northern Ireland	211	211	-	-	-	-	-	-	-	-	-
Irish Republic**	296	296	-	-	-	-	-	-	-	-	-
Old Commonwealth	135	134	-	1	-	-	-	-	-	-	-
New Commonwealth	658	451	36	4	6	74	8	7	43	13	16
Eastern Africa	87	55	-	2	-	27	-	-	-	2	1
Other Africa	32	28	-	2	1	1	-	-	-	-	-
Caribbean	62	23	36	-	3	-	-	-	-	-	-
Bangladesh	6	-	-	-	-	-	-	6	-	-	-
India	181	124	-	-	1	42	2	-	-	1	11
Pakistan	33	24	-	-	-	2	6	1	-	-	-
South East Asia	122	76	-	-	-	1	-	-	41	2	2
Cyprus	32	31	-	-	-	-	-	-	1	-	-
Other New Commonwealth	103	90	-	-	1	1	-	-	1	8	2
Other European Community	375	373	1	-	-	-	-	-	-	-	1
Other Europe	103	103	-	-	-	-	-	-	-	-	-
United States of America	67	67	-	-	-	-	-	-	-	-	-
China	22	16	-	-	-	-	-	-	6	-	-
Vietnam	2	-	-	-	-	-	-	-	1	1	-
Rest of the world	212	178	1	3	1	2	-	-	-	8	19

Table 51 Country of birth and ethnic group – **continued**

Notes: (1) * Includes Channel Islands, the Isle of Man and United Kingdom (part not stated)
(2) ** Includes Ireland (part not stated)

51. Residents in households; household heads

Country of birth	TOTAL PERSONS	Ethnic group								Other groups	
		White	Black Caribbean	Black African	Black other	Indian	Pakistani	Bangla-deshi	Chinese	Asian	Other
a	b	c	d	e	f	g	h	i	j	k	l
Test Valley – *continued*											
TOTAL PERSONS	99,463	98,352	109	45	107	291	21	45	200	87	206
Country of birth of household head											
United Kingdom*	94,503	94,108	33	28	68	53	9	-	51	43	110
England	89,282	88,908	31	26	64	50	9	-	48	41	105
Scotland	2,537	2,525	1	2	4	1	-	-	1	1	2
Wales	1,996	1,992	1	-	-	1	-	-	-	1	1
Northern Ireland	542	537	-	-	-	1	-	-	2	-	2
Irish Republic**	733	732	-	-	1	-	-	-	-	-	-
Old Commonwealth	334	332	-	1	-	-	-	-	1	-	-
New Commonwealth	1,890	1,293	67	6	27	233	12	45	123	30	54
Eastern Africa	277	174	-	2	1	86	-	-	-	9	5
Other Africa	89	79	-	4	2	3	-	-	-	-	1
Caribbean	186	86	66	-	20	-	-	36	-	1	13
Bangladesh	36	-	-	-	-	-	-	36	-	-	-
India	483	335	-	-	1	129	5	-	-	1	12
Pakistan	88	62	-	-	-	6	7	9	1	-	3
South East Asia	379	239	-	-	-	7	-	-	118	2	13
Cyprus	82	77	-	-	-	-	-	-	3	-	2
Other New Commonwealth	270	241	1	-	3	2	-	-	1	17	5
Other European Community	983	973	5	-	1	-	-	-	-	-	4
Other Europe	223	221	-	1	-	-	-	-	-	-	1
United States of America	190	188	-	-	2	-	-	-	-	-	-
China	56	34	-	-	-	-	-	-	22	-	-
Vietnam	7	-	-	-	-	-	-	-	3	3	1
Rest of the world	544	471	4	9	8	5	-	-	-	11	36
Winchester											
TOTAL PERSONS	93,721	92,868	38	34	45	127	29	80	133	130	237
United Kingdom*	88,737	88,376	21	16	36	35	7	31	32	26	157
England	84,952	84,601	20	16	35	34	7	31	29	26	153
Scotland	1,793	1,787	1	-	1	1	-	-	1	-	2
Wales	1,406	1,404	-	-	-	-	-	-	-	-	2
Northern Ireland	443	443	-	-	-	-	-	-	-	-	-
Irish Republic**	493	492	-	-	-	-	-	-	1	-	-
Old Commonwealth	531	526	-	1	-	-	-	-	-	1	3
New Commonwealth	1,595	1,250	14	9	5	88	22	49	67	52	39
Eastern Africa	201	169	-	-	-	20	5	-	-	2	5
Other Africa	104	95	-	8	-	-	-	-	-	-	1
Caribbean	85	65	14	-	1	-	-	-	2	1	2
Bangladesh	53	1	-	-	-	-	-	46	-	5	1
India	364	279	-	-	-	63	2	-	-	4	16
Pakistan	67	46	-	-	1	-	15	3	-	1	1
South East Asia	343	260	-	-	1	2	-	-	64	6	10
Cyprus	66	66	-	-	-	-	-	-	-	-	-
Other New Commonwealth	312	269	-	1	2	3	-	-	1	33	3
Other European Community	1,094	1,081	1	-	2	1	-	-	3	3	3
Other Europe	236	235	1	-	-	-	-	-	-	-	-
United States of America	298	297	-	-	-	-	-	-	-	-	1
China	36	25	-	-	-	-	-	-	9	1	1
Vietnam	21	-	-	-	-	-	-	-	15	6	-
Rest of the world	680	586	1	8	2	3	-	-	6	41	33

Notes: (1) * Includes Channel Islands, the Isle of Man and United Kingdom (part not stated)
(2) ** Includes Ireland (part not stated)

51. Residents in households; household heads

Country of birth	TOTAL PERSONS	Ethnic group								Other groups	
		White	Black Caribbean	Black African	Black other	Indian	Pakistani	Bangla-deshi	Chinese	Asian	Other
a	b	c	d	e	f	g	h	i	j	k	l

Winchester – *continued*

Total household heads	37,553	37,310	8	10	16	44	12	16	37	37	63
United Kingdom*	35,582	35,524	4	2	14	2	-	-	2	1	33
England	33,650	33,593	4	2	14	2	-	-	2	1	32
Scotland	916	916	-	-	-	-	-	-	-	-	-
Wales	735	734	-	-	-	-	-	-	-	-	1
Northern Ireland	211	211	-	-	-	-	-	-	-	-	-
Irish Republic**	272	272	-	-	-	-	-	-	-	-	-
Old Commonwealth	191	191	-	-	-	-	-	-	-	-	-
New Commonwealth	711	569	4	5	1	41	12	16	25	22	16
Eastern Africa	85	68	-	-	-	8	4	-	-	2	3
Other Africa	43	38	-	4	-	-	-	-	-	-	1
Caribbean	35	27	4	-	-	-	-	-	2	-	2
Bangladesh	17	1	-	-	-	-	-	15	-	1	-
India	207	166	-	-	-	31	-	-	-	2	8
Pakistan	42	31	-	-	-	-	8	1	-	1	1
South East Asia	124	97	-	-	-	1	-	-	23	2	1
Cyprus	17	17	-	-	-	-	-	-	-	-	-
Other New Commonwealth	141	124	-	1	1	1	-	-	-	14	-
Other European Community	303	302	-	-	-	-	-	-	-	1	-
Other Europe	95	95	-	-	-	-	-	-	-	-	-
United States of America	108	108	-	-	-	-	-	-	-	-	-
China	19	14	-	-	-	-	-	-	4	-	1
Vietnam	7	-	-	-	-	-	-	-	5	2	-
Rest of the world	265	235	-	3	1	1	-	-	1	11	13
TOTAL PERSONS	93,721	92,868	38	34	45	127	29	80	133	130	237

Country of birth of household head

United Kingdom*	88,858	88,524	31	16	39	25	1	-	37	35	150
England	84,029	83,717	30	15	36	24	1	-	29	33	144
Scotland	2,347	2,340	-	-	-	-	-	-	3	-	4
Wales	1,789	1,781	-	1	1	1	-	-	3	1	1
Northern Ireland	525	519	1	-	2	-	-	-	1	1	1
Irish Republic**	561	561	-	-	-	-	-	-	-	-	-
Old Commonwealth	455	454	-	-	-	-	-	-	-	1	-
New Commonwealth	1,875	1,459	6	8	5	100	28	80	69	67	53
Eastern Africa	236	190	-	-	2	17	14	-	-	4	9
Other Africa	122	115	-	6	-	-	-	-	-	-	1
Caribbean	93	79	5	-	2	-	-	-	2	-	5
Bangladesh	80	2	-	1	-	-	-	72	-	5	-
India	480	371	-	-	-	79	-	-	-	8	22
Pakistan	113	86	-	-	-	-	14	6	-	6	1
South East Asia	318	238	1	-	-	3	-	-	67	2	7
Cyprus	63	63	-	-	-	-	-	-	-	-	-
Other New Commonwealth	370	315	-	1	1	1	-	2	-	42	8
Other European Community	762	758	-	-	-	1	-	-	1	1	1
Other Europe	215	215	-	-	-	-	-	-	-	-	-
United States of America	266	261	-	-	-	-	-	-	-	3	2
China	30	18	-	-	-	-	-	-	11	-	1
Vietnam	23	1	-	-	-	-	-	-	14	4	4
Rest of the world	676	617	1	10	1	1	-	-	1	19	26

Table 52 Language indicators

County, districts

52. Residents

Age	Country of birth		Age	Country of birth	
	New Commonwealth	Outside of United Kingdom, Ireland, Old Commonwealth and United States of America		New Commonwealth	Outside of United Kingdom, Ireland, Old Commonwealth and United States of America
a	b	c	a	b	c
HAMPSHIRE			**East Hampshire**		
TOTAL PERSONS	29,658	61,473	**TOTAL PERSONS**	1,858	4,586
0 - 17	2,652	8,647	0 - 17	184	845
18 - 44	16,380	30,779	18 - 44	980	2,077
45 up to pensionable age	6,715	11,975	45 up to pensionable age	380	859
Pensionable age and over	3,911	10,072	Pensionable age and over	314	805
Persons in households	29,047	59,246	**Persons in households**	1,814	4,452
0 - 17	2,624	8,583	0 - 17	183	843
18 - 44	15,970	29,098	18 - 44	955	2,000
45 up to pensionable age	6,660	11,848	45 up to pensionable age	375	846
Pensionable age and over	3,793	9,717	Pensionable age and over	301	763
Persons in households by country of birth of head	38,676	66,309	**Persons in households by country of birth of head**	2,182	4,467
0 - 17	11,399	18,000	0 - 17	593	1,155
18 - 44	16,977	28,614	18 - 44	932	1,808
45 up to pensionable age	6,588	11,077	45 up to pensionable age	352	765
Pensionable age and over	3,712	8,618	Pensionable age and over	305	739
Basingstoke & Deane			**Eastleigh**		
TOTAL PERSONS	2,634	5,460	**TOTAL PERSONS**	1,655	3,467
0 - 17	194	646	0 - 17	115	330
18 - 44	1,460	2,833	18 - 44	1,011	1,861
45 up to pensionable age	726	1,256	45 up to pensionable age	360	683
Pensionable age and over	254	725	Pensionable age and over	169	593
Persons in households	2,587	5,360	**Persons in households**	1,649	3,444
0 - 17	190	639	0 - 17	115	330
18 - 44	1,427	2,774	18 - 44	1,008	1,854
45 up to pensionable age	726	1,248	45 up to pensionable age	359	680
Pensionable age and over	244	699	Pensionable age and over	167	580
Persons in households by country of birth of head	3,663	6,473	**Persons in households by country of birth of head**	2,385	4,195
0 - 17	1,073	1,771	0 - 17	740	1,184
18 - 44	1,639	2,864	18 - 44	1,124	1,873
45 up to pensionable age	712	1,196	45 up to pensionable age	344	625
Pensionable age and over	239	642	Pensionable age and over	177	513

Table 52 Language indicators – **continued**

County, districts

52. Residents

Age	Country of birth		Age	Country of birth	
	New Commonwealth	Outside of United Kingdom, Ireland, Old Commonwealth and United States of America		New Commonwealth	Outside of United Kingdom, Ireland, Old Commonwealth and United States of America
a	b	c	a	b	c
Fareham			**Hart**		
TOTAL PERSONS	**1,639**	**3,082**	**TOTAL PERSONS**	**1,581**	**4,468**
0 - 17	169	417	0 - 17	176	772
18 - 44	942	1,576	18 - 44	838	2,470
45 up to pensionable age	322	569	45 up to pensionable age	345	706
Pensionable age and over	206	520	Pensionable age and over	222	520
Persons in households	**1,618**	**3,038**	**Persons in households**	**1,542**	**3,696**
0 - 17	166	411	0 - 17	175	765
18 - 44	934	1,556	18 - 44	815	1,736
45 up to pensionable age	320	567	45 up to pensionable age	340	697
Pensionable age and over	198	504	Pensionable age and over	212	498
Persons in households by country of birth of head	**1,865**	**3,149**	**Persons in households by country of birth of head**	**1,884**	**3,598**
0 - 17	492	814	0 - 17	496	942
18 - 44	872	1,412	18 - 44	842	1,603
45 up to pensionable age	310	494	45 up to pensionable age	343	621
Pensionable age and over	191	429	Pensionable age and over	203	432
Gosport			**Havant**		
TOTAL PERSONS	**1,492**	**2,460**	**TOTAL PERSONS**	**1,802**	**3,483**
0 - 17	204	383	0 - 17	136	412
18 - 44	917	1,377	18 - 44	948	1,589
45 up to pensionable age	203	345	45 up to pensionable age	426	746
Pensionable age and over	168	355	Pensionable age and over	292	736
Persons in households	**1,450**	**2,387**	**Persons in households**	**1,793**	**3,456**
0 - 17	203	381	0 - 17	136	412
18 - 44	879	1,310	18 - 44	944	1,577
45 up to pensionable age	203	345	45 up to pensionable age	425	744
Pensionable age and over	165	351	Pensionable age and over	288	723
Persons in households by country of birth of head	**1,561**	**2,461**	**Persons in households by country of birth of head**	**2,389**	**3,923**
0 - 17	493	748	0 - 17	687	1,066
18 - 44	728	1,123	18 - 44	980	1,530
45 up to pensionable age	191	307	45 up to pensionable age	452	713
Pensionable age and over	149	283	Pensionable age and over	270	614

Table 52 Language indicators – **continued**

County, districts

52. Residents

Age	Country of birth		Age	Country of birth	
	New Commonwealth	Outside of United Kingdom, Ireland, Old Commonwealth and United States of America		New Commonwealth	Outside of United Kingdom, Ireland, Old Commonwealth and United States of America
a	b	c	a	b	c
New Forest			**Rushmoor**		
TOTAL PERSONS	2,028	5,029	**TOTAL PERSONS**	1,959	4,629
0 - 17	166	646	0 - 17	137	934
18 - 44	909	1,978	18 - 44	1,153	2,349
45 up to pensionable age	422	981	45 up to pensionable age	451	765
Pensionable age and over	531	1,424	Pensionable age and over	218	581
Persons in households	2,005	4,894	**Persons in households**	1,913	4,516
0 - 17	165	643	0 - 17	137	934
18 - 44	902	1,927	18 - 44	1,110	2,251
45 up to pensionable age	421	975	45 up to pensionable age	450	762
Pensionable age and over	517	1,349	Pensionable age and over	216	569
Persons in households by country of birth of head	2,355	5,007	**Persons in households by country of birth of head**	2,619	4,602
0 - 17	585	1,123	0 - 17	748	1,284
18 - 44	870	1,754	18 - 44	1,209	2,159
45 up to pensionable age	415	921	45 up to pensionable age	448	681
Pensionable age and over	485	1,209	Pensionable age and over	214	478
Portsmouth			**Southampton**		
TOTAL PERSONS	4,018	6,794	**TOTAL PERSONS**	5,781	10,066
0 - 17	432	816	0 - 17	382	821
18 - 44	2,269	3,641	18 - 44	3,307	5,426
45 up to pensionable age	844	1,296	45 up to pensionable age	1,473	2,262
Pensionable age and over	473	1,041	Pensionable age and over	619	1,557
Persons in households	3,898	6,542	**Persons in households**	5,663	9,785
0 - 17	422	802	0 - 17	378	812
18 - 44	2,204	3,502	18 - 44	3,213	5,212
45 up to pensionable age	822	1,254	45 up to pensionable age	1,468	2,245
Pensionable age and over	450	984	Pensionable age and over	604	1,516
Persons in households by country of birth of head	5,060	7,652	**Persons in households by country of birth of head**	8,948	13,498
0 - 17	1,551	2,139	0 - 17	2,922	3,904
18 - 44	2,255	3,464	18 - 44	3,951	6,017
45 up to pensionable age	827	1,218	45 up to pensionable age	1,479	2,211
Pensionable age and over	427	831	Pensionable age and over	596	1,366

Table 52 Language indicators – **continued**

County, districts

52. Residents

Age	Country of birth		Age	Country of birth	
	New Commonwealth	Outside of United Kingdom, Ireland, Old Commonwealth and United States of America		New Commonwealth	Outside of United Kingdom, Ireland, Old Commonwealth and United States of America
a	b	c	a	b	c
Test Valley			**Winchester**		
TOTAL PERSONS	**1,551**	**4,106**	**TOTAL PERSONS**	**1,660**	**3,843**
0 - 17	159	948	0 - 17	198	677
18 - 44	848	1,921	18 - 44	798	1,681
45 up to pensionable age	373	714	45 up to pensionable age	390	793
Pensionable age and over	171	523	Pensionable age and over	274	692
Persons in households	**1,520**	**4,014**	**Persons in households**	**1,595**	**3,662**
0 - 17	159	945	0 - 17	195	666
18 - 44	823	1,843	18 - 44	756	1,556
45 up to pensionable age	371	712	45 up to pensionable age	380	773
Pensionable age and over	167	514	Pensionable age and over	264	667
Persons in households by country of birth of head	**1,890**	**3,703**	**Persons in households by country of birth of head**	**1,875**	**3,581**
0 - 17	536	991	0 - 17	483	879
18 - 44	838	1,603	18 - 44	737	1,404
45 up to pensionable age	352	641	45 up to pensionable age	363	684
Pensionable age and over	164	468	Pensionable age and over	292	614

Table 53 'Lifestages'

County, districts

53. Residents aged 16 and over in households

Lifestage category		ALL PERSONS		All household heads	
		In a 'couple' household	Not in a 'couple' household	In a 'couple' household	Not in a 'couple' household
a		b	c	d	e

HAMPSHIRE

		b	c	d	e
Aged 16 - 24	No children aged 0 - 15 in household	29,247	102,127	9,971	9,635
	Child(ren) aged 0 - 15 in household	14,259	45,350	4,587	3,369
Aged 25 - 34	No children aged 0 - 15 in household	58,815	51,368	29,435	23,835
	Child(ren) aged 0 - 4 in household	79,915	11,054	37,453	6,518
	Child(ren) in household, youngest aged 5 - 10	22,767	6,285	8,958	4,371
	Child(ren) in household, youngest aged 11 - 15	2,405	2,050	882	828
Aged 35 - 54	No children 0 - 15 in household	86,527	135,317	41,417	75,827
	Child(ren) aged 0 - 4 in household	32,474	9,485	20,388	5,192
	Child(ren) in household, youngest aged 5 - 10	50,655	18,544	27,768	10,686
	Child(ren) in household, youngest aged 11 - 15	27,529	39,797	14,272	21,476
Aged 55 - pensionable age	Working or retired	50,468	35,012	36,151	27,643
	Unemployed or economically inactive (but not retired)	14,891	12,452	6,598	7,463
Pensionable age - 74		102,700	66,157	44,566	51,763
Aged 75 and over		38,886	56,706	23,323	48,828

Basingstoke & Deane

		b	c	d	e
Aged 16 - 24	No children aged 0 - 15 in household	3,285	10,471	1,159	752
	Child(ren) aged 0 - 15 in household	1,242	4,724	388	197
Aged 25 - 34	No children aged 0 - 15 in household	6,660	5,268	3,376	2,472
	Child(ren) aged 0 - 4 in household	7,921	1,119	3,702	603
	Child(ren) in household, youngest aged 5 - 10	2,185	508	837	339
	Child(ren) in household, youngest aged 11 - 15	236	204	72	83
Aged 35 - 54	No children 0 - 15 in household	8,347	13,407	4,042	7,365
	Child(ren) aged 0 - 4 in household	3,323	945	2,071	517
	Child(ren) in household, youngest aged 5 - 10	5,220	1,797	2,864	1,011
	Child(ren) in household, youngest aged 11 - 15	2,857	4,234	1,498	2,239
Aged 55 - pensionable age	Working or retired	4,535	3,371	3,224	2,625
	Unemployed or economically inactive (but not retired)	1,087	970	470	569
Pensionable age - 74		7,626	4,879	3,292	3,716
Aged 75 and over		2,604	3,894	1,569	3,269

East Hampshire

		b	c	d	e
Aged 16 - 24	No children aged 0 - 15 in household	1,678	6,568	559	370
	Child(ren) aged 0 - 15 in household	717	3,085	214	118
Aged 25 - 34	No children aged 0 - 15 in household	4,015	2,859	1,963	1,181
	Child(ren) aged 0 - 4 in household	5,281	559	2,409	319
	Child(ren) in household, youngest aged 5 - 10	1,310	316	488	209
	Child(ren) in household, youngest aged 11 - 15	125	121	49	39
Aged 35 - 54	No children 0 - 15 in household	6,437	8,885	3,079	4,861
	Child(ren) aged 0 - 4 in household	2,801	614	1,716	329
	Child(ren) in household, youngest aged 5 - 10	3,979	1,325	2,143	735
	Child(ren) in household, youngest aged 11 - 15	2,070	2,985	1,055	1,602
Aged 55 - pensionable age	Working or retired	3,477	2,469	2,545	1,971
	Unemployed or economically inactive (but not retired)	880	678	323	353
Pensionable age - 74		6,434	4,002	2,815	3,058
Aged 75 and over		2,588	3,660	1,538	3,110

Table 53 'Lifestages' – **continued**

County, districts

53. Residents aged 16 and over in households

Lifestage category	ALL PERSONS		All household heads	
	In a 'couple' household	Not in a 'couple' household	In a 'couple' household	Not in a 'couple' household
a	b	c	d	e

Eastleigh

		b	c	d	e
Aged 16 - 24	No children aged 0 - 15 in household	2,185	6,922	755	555
	Child(ren) aged 0 - 15 in household	841	2,826	255	148
Aged 25 - 34	No children aged 0 - 15 in household	4,861	3,249	2,457	1,633
	Child(ren) aged 0 - 4 in household	6,214	567	2,864	341
	Child(ren) in household, youngest aged 5 - 10	1,645	378	634	262
	Child(ren) in household, youngest aged 11 - 15	136	89	48	39
Aged 35 - 54	No children 0 - 15 in household	6,233	9,517	2,995	5,321
	Child(ren) aged 0 - 4 in household	2,516	533	1,614	301
	Child(ren) in household, youngest aged 5 - 10	4,284	1,252	2,327	728
	Child(ren) in household, youngest aged 11 - 15	2,147	2,828	1,109	1,522
Aged 55 - pensionable age	Working or retired	3,622	2,116	2,587	1,691
	Unemployed or economically inactive (but not retired)	1,040	685	466	388
Pensionable age - 74		6,782	4,019	2,915	3,124
Aged 75 and over		2,384	3,190	1,419	2,719

Fareham

		b	c	d	e
Aged 16 - 24	No children aged 0 - 15 in household	1,462	6,596	444	340
	Child(ren) aged 0 - 15 in household	573	2,629	148	110
Aged 25 - 34	No children aged 0 - 15 in household	3,765	2,669	1,839	1,165
	Child(ren) aged 0 - 4 in household	5,428	529	2,511	274
	Child(ren) in household, youngest aged 5 - 10	1,332	322	516	212
	Child(ren) in household, youngest aged 11 - 15	124	97	47	37
Aged 35 - 54	No children 0 - 15 in household	6,444	9,206	3,122	5,021
	Child(ren) aged 0 - 4 in household	2,309	559	1,445	298
	Child(ren) in household, youngest aged 5 - 10	3,577	1,087	1,936	629
	Child(ren) in household, youngest aged 11 - 15	1,998	2,648	1,032	1,403
Aged 55 - pensionable age	Working or retired	3,962	2,286	2,855	1,791
	Unemployed or economically inactive (but not retired)	1,141	743	444	414
Pensionable age - 74		7,368	3,856	3,160	2,961
Aged 75 and over		2,503	3,235	1,494	2,718

Gosport

		b	c	d	e
Aged 16 - 24	No children aged 0 - 15 in household	1,998	4,524	764	414
	Child(ren) aged 0 - 15 in household	1,141	2,174	393	222
Aged 25 - 34	No children aged 0 - 15 in household	2,901	2,278	1,494	1,052
	Child(ren) aged 0 - 4 in household	4,725	592	2,326	414
	Child(ren) in household, youngest aged 5 - 10	1,701	426	728	312
	Child(ren) in household, youngest aged 11 - 15	184	141	66	63
Aged 35 - 54	No children 0 - 15 in household	3,894	6,072	1,869	3,479
	Child(ren) aged 0 - 4 in household	1,137	368	723	203
	Child(ren) in household, youngest aged 5 - 10	2,023	869	1,147	506
	Child(ren) in household, youngest aged 11 - 15	1,252	1,871	669	1,032
Aged 55 - pensionable age	Working or retired	2,320	1,459	1,674	1,159
	Unemployed or economically inactive (but not retired)	713	595	315	347
Pensionable age - 74		4,705	3,115	2,001	2,482
Aged 75 and over		1,804	2,738	1,080	2,421

Table 53 'Lifestages' – **continued**

County, districts

53. Residents aged 16 and over in households

Lifestage category		ALL PERSONS		All household heads	
		In a 'couple' household	Not in a 'couple' household	In a 'couple' household	Not in a 'couple' household
a		b	c	d	e
Hart					
Aged 16 - 24	No children aged 0 - 15 in household	1,166	6,177	363	371
	Child(ren) aged 0 - 15 in household	428	2,580	116	59
Aged 25 - 34	No children aged 0 - 15 in household	3,301	2,546	1,620	1,087
	Child(ren) aged 0 - 4 in household	4,063	386	1,808	187
	Child(ren) in household, youngest aged 5 - 10	969	187	353	111
	Child(ren) in household, youngest aged 11 - 15	104	80	40	25
Aged 35 - 54	No children 0 - 15 in household	4,682	7,747	2,271	4,237
	Child(ren) aged 0 - 4 in household	2,383	439	1,474	238
	Child(ren) in household, youngest aged 5 - 10	3,688	1,136	1,966	648
	Child(ren) in household, youngest aged 11 - 15	1,744	2,669	890	1,389
Aged 55 - pensionable age	Working or retired	2,623	1,918	1,922	1,520
	Unemployed or economically inactive (but not retired)	542	463	172	210
Pensionable age - 74		3,914	2,299	1,664	1,693
Aged 75 and over		1,347	2,216	818	1,821
Havant					
Aged 16 - 24	No children aged 0 - 15 in household	1,633	7,602	503	438
	Child(ren) aged 0 - 15 in household	1,235	4,026	403	332
Aged 25 - 34	No children aged 0 - 15 in household	3,175	3,300	1,542	1,274
	Child(ren) aged 0 - 4 in household	5,928	1,001	2,821	607
	Child(ren) in household, youngest aged 5 - 10	1,980	658	786	467
	Child(ren) in household, youngest aged 11 - 15	194	206	73	92
Aged 35 - 54	No children 0 - 15 in household	6,646	10,624	3,146	5,871
	Child(ren) aged 0 - 4 in household	2,219	953	1,393	531
	Child(ren) in household, youngest aged 5 - 10	3,543	1,589	1,979	923
	Child(ren) in household, youngest aged 11 - 15	2,037	3,160	1,061	1,728
Aged 55 - pensionable age	Working or retired	4,533	2,842	3,206	2,215
	Unemployed or economically inactive (but not retired)	1,537	1,160	754	729
Pensionable age - 74		9,062	5,361	3,927	4,159
Aged 75 and over		2,868	4,105	1,701	3,487
New Forest					
Aged 16 - 24	No children aged 0 - 15 in household	2,320	9,203	722	605
	Child(ren) aged 0 - 15 in household	1,087	4,126	341	237
Aged 25 - 34	No children aged 0 - 15 in household	5,204	4,278	2,571	1,756
	Child(ren) aged 0 - 4 in household	7,227	797	3,293	459
	Child(ren) in household, youngest aged 5 - 10	1,902	444	704	302
	Child(ren) in household, youngest aged 11 - 15	191	155	67	56
Aged 35 - 54	No children 0 - 15 in household	9,357	13,051	4,318	7,059
	Child(ren) aged 0 - 4 in household	3,400	757	2,143	390
	Child(ren) in household, youngest aged 5 - 10	5,440	1,868	2,954	1,073
	Child(ren) in household, youngest aged 11 - 15	2,984	4,063	1,523	2,179
Aged 55 - pensionable age	Working or retired	6,147	3,728	4,465	2,961
	Unemployed or economically inactive (but not retired)	1,889	1,331	805	757
Pensionable age - 74		15,344	8,052	6,751	6,335
Aged 75 and over		6,564	7,823	3,871	6,712

Table 53 'Lifestages' – **continued**

County, districts

53. Residents aged 16 and over in households

Lifestage category	ALL PERSONS		All household heads	
	In a 'couple' household	Not in a 'couple' household	In a 'couple' household	Not in a 'couple' household
a	b	c	d	e

Portsmouth

Aged 16 - 24	No children aged 0 - 15 in household	4,342	11,297	1,574	2,000
	Child(ren) aged 0 - 15 in household	2,174	4,840	725	584
Aged 25 - 34	No children aged 0 - 15 in household	6,982	7,090	3,537	3,747
	Child(ren) aged 0 - 4 in household	9,194	1,794	4,466	1,103
	Child(ren) in household, youngest aged 5 - 10	2,731	993	1,170	714
	Child(ren) in household, youngest aged 11 - 15	327	281	138	125
Aged 35 - 54	No children 0 - 15 in household	8,726	14,476	4,246	8,633
	Child(ren) aged 0 - 4 in household	2,634	1,312	1,682	720
	Child(ren) in household, youngest aged 5 - 10	3,974	1,914	2,217	1,151
	Child(ren) in household, youngest aged 11 - 15	2,340	3,485	1,226	1,961
Aged 55 - pensionable age	Working or retired	4,557	3,743	3,147	2,957
	Unemployed or economically inactive (but not retired)	1,705	1,804	863	1,200
Pensionable age - 74		11,482	9,408	5,097	7,586
Aged 75 and over		4,894	8,053	2,943	7,066

Rushmoor

Aged 16 - 24	No children aged 0 - 15 in household	2,157	5,583	749	624
	Child(ren) aged 0 - 15 in household	1,103	2,434	383	249
Aged 25 - 34	No children aged 0 - 15 in household	4,294	3,344	2,217	1,566
	Child(ren) aged 0 - 4 in household	5,443	650	2,629	381
	Child(ren) in household, youngest aged 5 - 10	1,494	385	609	271
	Child(ren) in household, youngest aged 11 - 15	157	124	63	60
Aged 35 - 54	No children 0 - 15 in household	3,907	6,937	1,936	3,946
	Child(ren) aged 0 - 4 in household	1,613	462	1,025	250
	Child(ren) in household, youngest aged 5 - 10	2,492	932	1,390	531
	Child(ren) in household, youngest aged 11 - 15	1,267	1,970	655	1,061
Aged 55 - pensionable age	Working or retired	2,040	1,748	1,451	1,366
	Unemployed or economically inactive (but not retired)	506	488	234	277
Pensionable age - 74		3,834	2,798	1,656	2,145
Aged 75 and over		1,341	2,296	827	1,969

Southampton

Aged 16 - 24	No children aged 0 - 15 in household	4,314	13,684	1,536	2,329
	Child(ren) aged 0 - 15 in household	2,290	6,100	777	836
Aged 25 - 34	No children aged 0 - 15 in household	6,956	8,562	3,517	4,493
	Child(ren) aged 0 - 4 in household	9,527	2,001	4,551	1,261
	Child(ren) in household, youngest aged 5 - 10	2,977	1,101	1,177	812
	Child(ren) in household, youngest aged 11 - 15	352	330	126	138
Aged 35 - 54	No children 0 - 15 in household	9,920	17,138	4,732	10,087
	Child(ren) aged 0 - 4 in household	3,331	1,455	2,122	819
	Child(ren) in household, youngest aged 5 - 10	4,974	2,283	2,817	1,340
	Child(ren) in household, youngest aged 11 - 15	2,798	4,258	1,480	2,361
Aged 55 - pensionable age	Working or retired	5,591	4,278	3,928	3,406
	Unemployed or economically inactive (but not retired)	2,069	2,217	1,090	1,532
Pensionable age - 74		13,014	10,006	5,685	7,993
Aged 75 and over		4,963	8,119	3,000	7,185

Table 53 'Lifestages' – **continued**　　　　　　　　　　　　　　　　　　　　County, districts

53. Residents aged 16 and over in households

		ALL PERSONS		All household heads	
Lifestage category		In a 'couple' household	Not in a 'couple' household	In a 'couple' household	Not in a 'couple' household
a		b	c	d	e

Test Valley

Aged 16 - 24	No children aged 0 - 15 in household	1,657	6,807	551	405
	Child(ren) aged 0 - 15 in household	897	3,042	288	178
Aged 25 - 34	No children aged 0 - 15 in household	3,589	3,040	1,799	1,225
	Child(ren) aged 0 - 4 in household	5,041	594	2,337	334
	Child(ren) in household, youngest aged 5 - 10	1,493	348	574	229
	Child(ren) in household, youngest aged 11 - 15	172	143	54	44
Aged 35 - 54	No children 0 - 15 in household	6,261	9,438	2,980	5,112
	Child(ren) aged 0 - 4 in household	2,344	571	1,464	313
	Child(ren) in household, youngest aged 5 - 10	3,759	1,269	2,044	720
	Child(ren) in household, youngest aged 11 - 15	2,194	2,934	1,136	1,569
Aged 55 - pensionable age	Working or retired	3,353	2,500	2,436	1,970
	Unemployed or economically inactive (but not retired)	892	678	346	345
Pensionable age - 74		6,225	3,940	2,655	3,023
Aged 75 and over		2,313	3,323	1,431	2,823

Winchester

Aged 16 - 24	No children aged 0 - 15 in household	1,050	6,693	292	432
	Child(ren) aged 0 - 15 in household	531	2,764	156	99
Aged 25 - 34	No children aged 0 - 15 in household	3,112	2,885	1,503	1,184
	Child(ren) aged 0 - 4 in household	3,923	465	1,736	235
	Child(ren) in household, youngest aged 5 - 10	1,048	219	382	131
	Child(ren) in household, youngest aged 11 - 15	103	79	39	27
Aged 35 - 54	No children 0 - 15 in household	5,673	8,819	2,681	4,835
	Child(ren) aged 0 - 4 in household	2,464	517	1,516	283
	Child(ren) in household, youngest aged 5 - 10	3,702	1,223	1,984	691
	Child(ren) in household, youngest aged 11 - 15	1,841	2,692	938	1,430
Aged 55 - pensionable age	Working or retired	3,708	2,554	2,711	2,011
	Unemployed or economically inactive (but not retired)	890	640	316	342
Pensionable age - 74		6,910	4,422	2,948	3,488
Aged 75 and over		2,713	4,054	1,632	3,528

54. Household spaces; rooms in household spaces; rooms in hotels and boarding houses

Occupancy type	TOTAL HOUSEHOLD SPACES	TOTAL ROOMS	Occupancy type	TOTAL HOUSEHOLD SPACES	TOTAL ROOMS
a	b	c	a	b	c
HAMPSHIRE			**East Hampshire**		
ALL TYPES OF OCCUPANCY	**637,765**	**3,339,464**	**ALL TYPES OF OCCUPANCY**	**41,093**	**229,249**
Households with residents	**603,257**	**3,177,356**	**Households with residents**	**39,158**	**219,547**
Enumerated with person(s) present	582,749	3,078,349	Enumerated with person(s) present	37,889	212,867
Absent households (enumerated)	11,875	59,452	Absent households (enumerated)	796	4,306
Absent households (imputed)	8,633	39,555	Absent households (imputed)	473	2,374
Vacant accommodation	**27,357**	**128,328**	**Vacant accommodation**	**1,624**	**8,087**
New, never occupied	4,384	21,257	New, never occupied	394	2,114
Under improvement	3,011	14,960	Under improvement	152	829
Other	19,962	92,111	Other	1,078	5,144
Accommodation not used as main residence	**7,151**	**33,780**	**Accommodation not used as main residence**	**311**	**1,615**
No persons present	3,418	16,748	No persons present	154	860
Second residences	2,495	12,912	Second residences	142	801
Holiday accommodation	700	2,952	Holiday accommodation	12	59
Student accommodation	223	884	Student accommodation	-	-
Persons enumerated but no residents	3,733	17,032	Persons enumerated but no residents	157	755
Owner occupied	1,380	6,420	Owner occupied	100	500
Not owner occupied	2,353	10,612	Not owner occupied	57	255
Hotels and boarding houses		12,639	Hotels and boarding houses		494
Basingstoke & Deane			**Eastleigh**		
ALL TYPES OF OCCUPANCY	**56,462**	**309,047**	**ALL TYPES OF OCCUPANCY**	**43,169**	**227,148**
Households with residents	**54,323**	**298,029**	**Households with residents**	**41,219**	**217,822**
Enumerated with person(s) present	52,626	289,315	Enumerated with person(s) present	39,905	211,330
Absent households (enumerated)	1,052	5,482	Absent households (enumerated)	785	3,833
Absent households (imputed)	645	3,232	Absent households (imputed)	529	2,659
Vacant accommodation	**1,857**	**9,366**	**Vacant accommodation**	**1,757**	**8,360**
New, never occupied	391	2,200	New, never occupied	562	2,811
Under improvement	149	810	Under improvement	156	726
Other	1,317	6,356	Other	1,039	4,823
Accommodation not used as main residence	**282**	**1,652**	**Accommodation not used as main residence**	**193**	**966**
No persons present	125	809	No persons present	94	503
Second residences	108	731	Second residences	91	487
Holiday accommodation	15	72	Holiday accommodation	3	16
Student accommodation	2	6	Student accommodation	-	-
Persons enumerated but no residents	157	843	Persons enumerated but no residents	99	463
Owner occupied	65	403	Owner occupied	51	254
Not owner occupied	92	440	Not owner occupied	48	209
Hotels and boarding houses		1,073	Hotels and boarding houses		418

54. Household spaces; rooms in household spaces; rooms in hotels and boarding houses

Occupancy type	TOTAL HOUSEHOLD SPACES	TOTAL ROOMS	Occupancy type	TOTAL HOUSEHOLD SPACES	TOTAL ROOMS
a	b	c	a	b	c
Fareham			**Hart**		
ALL TYPES OF OCCUPANCY	39,992	215,327	**ALL TYPES OF OCCUPANCY**	30,291	178,200
Households with residents	38,369	207,336	**Households with residents**	29,073	172,142
Enumerated with person(s) present	37,258	201,696	Enumerated with person(s) present	28,138	167,016
Absent households (enumerated)	832	4,277	Absent households (enumerated)	593	3,313
Absent households (imputed)	279	1,363	Absent households (imputed)	342	1,813
Vacant accommodation	1,403	6,911	**Vacant accommodation**	1,064	5,283
New, never occupied	301	1,586	New, never occupied	257	1,208
Under improvement	79	395	Under improvement	82	467
Other	1,023	4,930	Other	725	3,608
Accommodation not used as main residence	220	1,080	**Accommodation not used as main residence**	154	775
No persons present	111	551	No persons present	55	322
Second residences	107	528	Second residences	53	311
Holiday accommodation	3	13	Holiday accommodation	2	11
Student accommodation	1	10	Student accommodation	-	-
Persons enumerated but no residents	109	529	Persons enumerated but no residents	99	453
Owner occupied	68	338	Owner occupied	49	275
Not owner occupied	41	191	Not owner occupied	50	178
Hotels and boarding houses		127	Hotels and boarding houses		422
Gosport			**Havant**		
ALL TYPES OF OCCUPANCY	31,425	157,997	**ALL TYPES OF OCCUPANCY**	48,339	246,510
Households with residents	29,356	148,121	**Households with residents**	46,151	236,878
Enumerated with person(s) present	28,364	143,406	Enumerated with person(s) present	44,850	230,713
Absent households (enumerated)	641	3,085	Absent households (enumerated)	787	3,818
Absent households (imputed)	351	1,630	Absent households (imputed)	514	2,347
Vacant accommodation	1,892	8,988	**Vacant accommodation**	1,585	7,210
New, never occupied	110	467	New, never occupied	198	912
Under improvement	117	576	Under improvement	171	769
Other	1,665	7,945	Other	1,216	5,529
Accommodation not used as main residence	177	888	**Accommodation not used as main residence**	603	2,422
No persons present	94	487	No persons present	456	1,834
Second residences	75	393	Second residences	273	1,191
Holiday accommodation	19	94	Holiday accommodation	181	633
Student accommodation	-	-	Student accommodation	2	10
Persons enumerated but no residents	83	401	Persons enumerated but no residents	147	588
Owner occupied	47	227	Owner occupied	100	409
Not owner occupied	36	174	Not owner occupied	47	179
Hotels and boarding houses		239	Hotels and boarding houses		998

54. Household spaces; rooms in household spaces; rooms in hotels and boarding houses

Occupancy type	TOTAL HOUSEHOLD SPACES	TOTAL ROOMS	Occupancy type	TOTAL HOUSEHOLD SPACES	TOTAL ROOMS
a	b	c	a	b	c
New Forest			**Rushmoor**		
ALL TYPES OF OCCUPANCY	70,492	373,926	**ALL TYPES OF OCCUPANCY**	31,977	160,815
Households with residents	65,411	349,572	**Households with residents**	30,523	154,294
Enumerated with person(s) present	63,033	337,500	Enumerated with person(s) present	29,465	149,492
Absent households (enumerated)	1,378	7,280	Absent households (enumerated)	613	2,858
Absent households (imputed)	1,000	4,792	Absent households (imputed)	445	1,944
Vacant accommodation	3,111	15,181	**Vacant accommodation**	1,328	5,991
New, never occupied	611	2,977	New, never occupied	62	265
Under improvement	349	1,817	Under improvement	204	945
Other	2,151	10,387	Other	1,062	4,781
Accommodation not used as main residence	1,970	9,173	**Accommodation not used as main residence**	126	530
No persons present	1,269	6,439	No persons present	28	134
Second residences	928	4,883	Second residences	26	127
Holiday accommodation	341	1,556	Holiday accommodation	1	5
Student accommodation	-	-	Student accommodation	1	2
Persons enumerated but no residents	701	2,734	Persons enumerated but no residents	98	396
Owner occupied	478	1,909	Owner occupied	28	113
Not owner occupied	223	825	Not owner occupied	70	283
Hotels and boarding houses		1,674	Hotels and boarding houses		719
Portsmouth			**Southampton**		
ALL TYPES OF OCCUPANCY	78,134	387,313	**ALL TYPES OF OCCUPANCY**	86,576	405,428
Households with residents	72,590	362,219	**Households with residents**	81,140	382,726
Enumerated with person(s) present	69,795	349,727	Enumerated with person(s) present	77,939	369,790
Absent households (enumerated)	1,247	5,773	Absent households (enumerated)	1,566	6,733
Absent households (imputed)	1,548	6,719	Absent households (imputed)	1,635	6,203
Vacant accommodation	4,272	19,262	**Vacant accommodation**	4,336	17,837
New, never occupied	343	1,515	New, never occupied	565	2,054
Under improvement	544	2,587	Under improvement	550	2,609
Other	3,385	15,160	Other	3,221	13,174
Accommodation not used as main residence	1,272	5,832	**Accommodation not used as main residence**	1,100	4,865
No persons present	341	1,390	No persons present	327	1,337
Second residences	219	966	Second residences	162	704
Holiday accommodation	57	186	Holiday accommodation	21	58
Student accommodation	65	238	Student accommodation	144	575
Persons enumerated but no residents	931	4,442	Persons enumerated but no residents	773	3,528
Owner occupied	135	634	Owner occupied	86	388
Not owner occupied	796	3,808	Not owner occupied	687	3,140
Hotels and boarding houses		2,535	Hotels and boarding houses		1,760

54. Household spaces; rooms in household spaces; rooms in hotels and boarding houses

Occupancy type	TOTAL HOUSEHOLD SPACES	TOTAL ROOMS	Occupancy type	TOTAL HOUSEHOLD SPACES	TOTAL ROOMS
a	b	c	a	b	c
Test Valley			**Winchester**		
ALL TYPES OF OCCUPANCY	40,292	223,718	ALL TYPES OF OCCUPANCY	39,523	224,786
Households with residents	**38,391**	**213,730**	**Households with residents**	**37,553**	**214,940**
Enumerated with person(s) present	37,167	207,176	Enumerated with person(s) present	36,320	208,321
Absent households (enumerated)	696	3,845	Absent households (enumerated)	889	4,849
Absent households (imputed)	528	2,709	Absent households (imputed)	344	1,770
Vacant accommodation	**1,586**	**8,199**	**Vacant accommodation**	**1,542**	**7,653**
New, never occupied	296	1,584	New, never occupied	294	1,564
Under improvement	232	1,263	Under improvement	226	1,167
Other	1,058	5,352	Other	1,022	4,922
Accommodation not used as main residence	**315**	**1,789**	**Accommodation not used as main residence**	**428**	**2,193**
No persons present	187	1,065	No persons present	177	1,017
Second residences	158	897	Second residences	153	893
Holiday accommodation	28	163	Holiday accommodation	17	86
Student accommodation	1	5	Student accommodation	7	38
Persons enumerated but no residents	128	724	Persons enumerated but no residents	251	1,176
Owner occupied	76	460	Owner occupied	97	510
Not owner occupied	52	264	Not owner occupied	154	666
Hotels and boarding houses		795	Hotels and boarding houses		1,385

Table 55 Household spaces and occupancy

County, districts

55. Household spaces in permanent buildings: dwellings

Occupancy type	TOTAL HOUSEHOLD SPACES	Household spaces in dwellings with the following number of household spaces			Unattached household spaces (not in a dwelling)
		1	2	3 or more	
a	b	c	d	e	f

HAMPSHIRE

ALL TYPES OF OCCUPANCY	**632,843**	**625,752**	**1,472**	**5,079**	**540**
Households with residents	**598,749**	**592,839**	**1,309**	**4,149**	**452**
Enumerated with person(s) present	578,506	573,274	1,198	3,611	423
Absent households (enumerated)	11,774	11,554	46	159	15
Absent households (imputed)	8,469	8,011	65	379	14
Vacant accommodation	**27,357**	**26,611**	**95**	**595**	**56**
New, never occupied	4,384	4,376	2	6	-
Under improvement	3,011	2,962	9	34	6
Other	19,962	19,273	84	555	50
Accommodation not used as main residence	**6,737**	**6,302**	**68**	**335**	**32**
No persons present	3,418	3,337	10	68	3
Second residences	2,495	2,476	2	14	3
Holiday accommodation	700	690	1	9	-
Student accommodation	223	171	7	45	-
Persons enumerated but no residents	3,319	2,965	58	267	29
Owner occupied	1,084	1,078	-	4	2
Not owner occupied	2,235	1,887	58	263	27
TOTAL DWELLINGS	**627,550**	**625,752**	**736**	**1,062**	

Basingstoke & Deane

ALL TYPES OF OCCUPANCY	**56,197**	**56,000**	**56**	**135**	**6**
Households with residents	**54,063**	**53,879**	**53**	**126**	**5**
Enumerated with person(s) present	52,389	52,233	47	105	4
Absent households (enumerated)	1,045	1,031	4	10	-
Absent households (imputed)	629	615	2	11	1
Vacant accommodation	**1,857**	**1,849**	**2**	**6**	**-**
New, never occupied	391	391	-	-	-
Under improvement	149	149	-	-	-
Other	1,317	1,309	2	6	-
Accommodation not used as main residence	**277**	**272**	**1**	**3**	**1**
No persons present	125	125	-	-	-
Second residences	108	108	-	-	-
Holiday accommodation	15	15	-	-	-
Student accommodation	2	2	-	-	-
Persons enumerated but no residents	152	147	1	3	1
Owner occupied	60	60	-	-	-
Not owner occupied	92	87	1	3	1
TOTAL DWELLINGS	**56,055**	**56,000**	**28**	**27**	

Table 55 Household spaces and occupancy – **continued**

County, districts

55. Household spaces in permanent buildings: dwellings

Occupancy type	TOTAL HOUSEHOLD SPACES	Household spaces in dwellings with the following number of household spaces			Unattached household spaces (not in a dwelling)
		1	2	3 or more	
a	b	c	d	e	f

East Hampshire

Occupancy type	b	c	d	e	f
ALL TYPES OF OCCUPANCY	40,582	40,436	50	82	14
Households with residents	38,670	38,533	49	74	14
Enumerated with person(s) present	37,427	37,294	49	72	12
Absent households (enumerated)	782	781	-	-	1
Absent households (imputed)	461	458	-	2	1
Vacant accommodation	1,624	1,617	-	7	-
New, never occupied	394	394	-	-	-
Under improvement	152	152	-	-	-
Other	1,078	1,071	-	7	-
Accommodation not used as main residence	288	286	1	1	-
No persons present	154	154	-	-	-
Second residences	142	142	-	-	-
Holiday accommodation	12	12	-	-	-
Student accommodation	-	-	-	-	-
Persons enumerated but no residents	134	132	1	1	-
Owner occupied	79	79	-	-	-
Not owner occupied	55	53	1	1	-
TOTAL DWELLINGS	40,479	40,436	25	18	

Eastleigh

Occupancy type	b	c	d	e	f
ALL TYPES OF OCCUPANCY	42,710	42,525	44	129	12
Households with residents	40,764	40,605	38	110	11
Enumerated with person(s) present	39,497	39,354	35	97	11
Absent households (enumerated)	776	766	2	8	-
Absent households (imputed)	491	485	1	5	-
Vacant accommodation	1,757	1,737	6	13	1
New, never occupied	562	562	-	-	-
Under improvement	156	153	2	-	1
Other	1,039	1,022	4	13	-
Accommodation not used as main residence	189	183	-	6	-
No persons present	94	94	-	-	-
Second residences	91	91	-	-	-
Holiday accommodation	3	3	-	-	-
Student accommodation	-	-	-	-	-
Persons enumerated but no residents	95	89	-	6	-
Owner occupied	48	48	-	-	-
Not owner occupied	47	41	-	6	-
TOTAL DWELLINGS	42,578	42,525	22	31	

Table 55 Household spaces and occupancy – **continued**County, districts

55. Household spaces in permanent buildings: dwellings

Occupancy type	TOTAL HOUSEHOLD SPACES	Household spaces in dwellings with the following number of household spaces			Unattached household spaces (not in a dwelling)
		1	2	3 or more	
a	b	c	d	e	f

Fareham

ALL TYPES OF OCCUPANCY	39,701	39,628	36	32	5
Households with residents	38,082	38,012	35	31	4
Enumerated with person(s) present	36,979	36,910	34	31	4
Absent households (enumerated)	828	827	1	-	-
Absent households (imputed)	275	275	-	-	-
Vacant accommodation	1,403	1,401	1	-	1
New, never occupied	301	301	-	-	-
Under improvement	79	79	-	-	-
Other	1,023	1,021	1	-	1
Accommodation not used as main residence	216	215	-	1	-
No persons present	111	111	-	-	-
Second residences	107	107	-	-	-
Holiday accommodation	3	3	-	-	-
Student accommodation	1	1	-	-	-
Persons enumerated but no residents	105	104	-	1	-
Owner occupied	65	65	-	-	-
Not owner occupied	40	39	-	1	-
TOTAL DWELLINGS	39,654	39,628	18	8	

Gosport

ALL TYPES OF OCCUPANCY	31,331	31,234	24	57	16
Households with residents	29,268	29,185	23	46	14
Enumerated with person(s) present	28,278	28,200	21	44	13
Absent households (enumerated)	639	635	2	2	-
Absent households (imputed)	351	350	-	-	1
Vacant accommodation	1,892	1,879	1	10	2
New, never occupied	110	110	-	-	-
Under improvement	117	117	-	-	-
Other	1,665	1,652	1	10	2
Accommodation not used as main residence	171	170	-	1	-
No persons present	94	94	-	-	-
Second residences	75	75	-	-	-
Holiday accommodation	19	19	-	-	-
Student accommodation	-	-	-	-	-
Persons enumerated but no residents	77	76	-	1	-
Owner occupied	41	41	-	-	-
Not owner occupied	36	35	-	1	-
TOTAL DWELLINGS	31,258	31,234	12	12	

Table 55 Household spaces and occupancy – **continued**

County, districts

55. Household spaces in permanent buildings: dwellings

Occupancy type	TOTAL HOUSEHOLD SPACES	Household spaces in dwellings with the following number of household spaces			Unattached household spaces (not in a dwelling)
		1	2	3 or more	
a	b	c	d	e	f

Hart

Occupancy type	b	c	d	e	f
ALL TYPES OF OCCUPANCY	29,953	29,883	30	32	8
Households with residents	28,743	28,682	30	24	7
Enumerated with person(s) present	27,828	27,772	30	19	7
Absent households (enumerated)	587	586	-	1	-
Absent households (imputed)	328	324	-	4	-
Vacant accommodation	1,064	1,059	-	5	-
New, never occupied	257	257	-	-	-
Under improvement	82	82	-	-	-
Other	725	720	-	5	-
Accommodation not used as main residence	146	142	-	3	1
No persons present	55	55	-	-	-
Second residences	53	53	-	-	-
Holiday accommodation	2	2	-	-	-
Student accommodation	-	-	-	-	-
Persons enumerated but no residents	91	87	-	3	1
Owner occupied	47	47	-	-	-
Not owner occupied	44	40	-	3	1
TOTAL DWELLINGS	29,903	29,883	15	5	

Havant

Occupancy type	b	c	d	e	f
ALL TYPES OF OCCUPANCY	48,183	47,983	74	115	11
Households with residents	46,037	45,854	70	104	9
Enumerated with person(s) present	44,740	44,566	68	97	9
Absent households (enumerated)	786	783	1	2	-
Absent households (imputed)	511	505	1	5	-
Vacant accommodation	1,585	1,568	4	11	2
New, never occupied	198	198	-	-	-
Under improvement	171	164	-	7	-
Other	1,216	1,206	4	4	2
Accommodation not used as main residence	561	561	-	-	-
No persons present	456	456	-	-	-
Second residences	273	273	-	-	-
Holiday accommodation	181	181	-	-	-
Student accommodation	2	2	-	-	-
Persons enumerated but no residents	105	105	-	-	-
Owner occupied	69	69	-	-	-
Not owner occupied	36	36	-	-	-
TOTAL DWELLINGS	48,043	47,983	37	23	

Table 55 Household spaces and occupancy – **continued**

County, districts

55. Household spaces in permanent buildings: dwellings

Occupancy type	TOTAL HOUSEHOLD SPACES	Household spaces in dwellings with the following number of household spaces			Unattached household spaces (not in a dwelling)
		1	2	3 or more	
a	b	c	d	e	f

New Forest					
ALL TYPES OF OCCUPANCY	69,032	68,810	66	133	23
Households with residents	64,225	64,032	64	111	18
Enumerated with person(s) present	61,916	61,737	58	104	17
Absent households (enumerated)	1,354	1,348	3	2	1
Absent households (imputed)	955	947	3	5	-
Vacant accommodation	3,111	3,088	2	18	3
New, never occupied	611	611	-	-	-
Under improvement	349	343	-	6	-
Other	2,151	2,134	2	12	3
Accommodation not used as main residence	1,696	1,690	-	4	2
No persons present	1,269	1,268	-	1	-
Second residences	928	927	-	1	-
Holiday accommodation	341	341	-	-	-
Student accommodation	-	-	-	-	-
Persons enumerated but no residents	427	422	-	3	2
Owner occupied	288	285	-	2	1
Not owner occupied	139	137	-	1	1
TOTAL DWELLINGS	68,872	68,810	33	29	
Portsmouth					
ALL TYPES OF OCCUPANCY	77,998	75,841	430	1,484	243
Households with residents	72,462	70,653	383	1,224	202
Enumerated with person(s) present	69,670	68,034	366	1,084	186
Absent households (enumerated)	1,244	1,189	8	36	11
Absent households (imputed)	1,548	1,430	9	104	5
Vacant accommodation	4,272	4,079	25	146	22
New, never occupied	343	341	2	-	-
Under improvement	544	536	-	5	3
Other	3,385	3,202	23	141	19
Accommodation not used as main residence	1,264	1,109	22	114	19
No persons present	341	315	2	22	2
Second residences	219	214	-	3	2
Holiday accommodation	57	47	1	9	-
Student accommodation	65	54	1	10	-
Persons enumerated but no residents	923	794	20	92	17
Owner occupied	130	127	-	2	1
Not owner occupied	793	667	20	90	16
TOTAL DWELLINGS	76,360	75,841	215	304	

Table 55 Household spaces and occupancy – **continued**

County, districts

55. Household spaces in permanent buildings: dwellings

Occupancy type	TOTAL HOUSEHOLD SPACES	Household spaces in dwellings with the following number of household spaces			Unattached household spaces (not in a dwelling)
		1	2	3 or more	
a	b	c	d	e	f

Rushmoor

ALL TYPES OF OCCUPANCY	31,765	31,120	82	538	25
Households with residents	30,318	29,757	67	472	22
Enumerated with person(s) present	29,273	28,777	58	417	21
Absent households (enumerated)	605	582	3	20	-
Absent households (imputed)	440	398	6	35	1
Vacant accommodation	1,328	1,261	13	52	2
New, never occupied	62	62	-	-	-
Under improvement	204	203	-	1	-
Other	1,062	996	13	51	2
Accommodation not used as main residence	119	102	2	14	1
No persons present	28	24	-	4	-
Second residences	26	22	-	4	-
Holiday accommodation	1	1	-	-	-
Student accommodation	1	1	-	-	-
Persons enumerated but no residents	91	78	2	10	1
Owner occupied	23	23	-	-	-
Not owner occupied	68	55	2	10	1
TOTAL DWELLINGS	31,276	31,120	41	115	

Southampton

ALL TYPES OF OCCUPANCY	86,504	83,745	498	2,120	141
Households with residents	81,071	78,858	425	1,675	113
Enumerated with person(s) present	77,877	75,994	368	1,407	108
Absent households (enumerated)	1,563	1,477	16	69	1
Absent households (imputed)	1,631	1,387	41	199	4
Vacant accommodation	4,336	4,008	39	267	22
New, never occupied	565	565	-	-	-
Under improvement	550	526	7	15	2
Other	3,221	2,917	32	252	20
Accommodation not used as main residence	1,097	879	34	178	6
No persons present	327	277	8	41	1
Second residences	162	153	2	6	1
Holiday accommodation	21	21	-	-	-
Student accommodation	144	103	6	35	-
Persons enumerated but no residents	770	602	26	137	5
Owner occupied	83	83	-	-	-
Not owner occupied	687	519	26	137	5
TOTAL DWELLINGS	84,446	83,745	249	452	

Table 55 Household spaces and occupancy – **continued**

County, districts

55. Household spaces in permanent buildings: dwellings

Occupancy type	TOTAL HOUSEHOLD SPACES	Household spaces in dwellings with the following number of household spaces			Unattached household spaces (not in a dwelling)
		1	2	3 or more	
a	b	c	d	e	f

Test Valley

ALL TYPES OF OCCUPANCY	39,905	39,821	26	49	9
Households with residents	38,011	37,938	25	39	9
Enumerated with person(s) present	36,805	36,741	24	31	9
Absent households (enumerated)	689	686	1	2	-
Absent households (imputed)	517	511	-	6	-
Vacant accommodation	1,586	1,576	-	10	-
New, never occupied	296	296	-	-	-
Under improvement	232	232	-	-	-
Other	1,058	1,048	-	10	-
Accommodation not used as main residence	308	307	1	-	-
No persons present	187	187	-	-	-
Second residences	158	158	-	-	-
Holiday accommodation	28	28	-	-	-
Student accommodation	1	1	-	-	-
Persons enumerated but no residents	121	120	1	-	-
Owner occupied	71	71	-	-	-
Not owner occupied	50	49	1	-	-
TOTAL DWELLINGS	39,845	39,821	13	11	

Winchester

ALL TYPES OF OCCUPANCY	38,982	38,726	56	173	27
Households with residents	37,035	36,851	47	113	24
Enumerated with person(s) present	35,827	35,662	40	103	22
Absent households (enumerated)	876	863	5	7	1
Absent households (imputed)	332	326	2	3	1
Vacant accommodation	1,542	1,489	2	50	1
New, never occupied	294	288	-	6	-
Under improvement	226	226	-	-	-
Other	1,022	975	2	44	1
Accommodation not used as main residence	405	386	7	10	2
No persons present	177	177	-	-	-
Second residences	153	153	-	-	-
Holiday accommodation	17	17	-	-	-
Student accommodation	7	7	-	-	-
Persons enumerated but no residents	228	209	7	10	2
Owner occupied	80	80	-	-	-
Not owner occupied	148	129	7	10	2
TOTAL DWELLINGS	38,781	38,726	28	27	

Table 56 Household space type and occupancy

County, districts

661

56. Household spaces

HAMPSHIRE

Occupancy type (a)	Total household spaces (b)	Detached (c)	Semi-detached (d)	Terraced (e)	Purpose-built flat: Residential building (f)	Purpose-built flat: Commercial building (g)	Converted flat (h)	Converted flatlet (i)	Unshared – not self-contained flat (j)	Unshared – not self-contained 'rooms' (k)	Unshared – Bedsit (l)	Other – not self-contained flat (m)	Other – not self-contained 'rooms' (n)	Other – Bedsit (o)	Non-permanent accommodation (p)
ALL TYPES OF OCCUPANCY	637,765	178,240	153,193	180,680	89,447	7,915	14,695	1,123	213	69	151	1,066	810	4,971	4,922
Households with residents	603,257	170,620	148,119	171,521	81,983	6,611	12,626	951	213	69	126	1,066	810	4,034	4,508
Enumerated with person(s) present	582,749	165,233	144,446	166,448	77,943	6,248	11,724	857	196	65	114	994	746	3,492	4,243
Absent households	20,508	5,387	3,673	5,073	4,040	363	902	94	17	4	12	72	64	542	265
Vacant accommodation	27,357	5,889	4,181	7,348	6,368	1,101	1,562	127	16		19			604	
New, never occupied	4,384	1,447	204	809	1,766	46	95	9			-	6		2	-
Other	22,973	4,442	3,977	6,539	4,602	1,055	1,467	118	16		19	136		602	-
Accommodation not used as main residence	7,151	1,731	893	1,811	1,096	203	507	45	10		6	102		333	
No persons present	3,418	1,155	440	758	644	96	224	17	1		2	11		70	-
Persons enumerated but no residents	3,733	576	453	1,053	452	107	283	28	7	2	4	62	29	263	414

Unshared dwellings – not self-contained subtotal (ALL TYPES): 308 · Other household spaces – not self-contained subtotal (ALL TYPES): 2,120

Basingstoke & Deane

Occupancy type	Total household spaces	Detached	Semi-detached	Terraced	Purpose-built flat: Residential building	Purpose-built flat: Commercial building	Converted flat	Converted flatlet	Unshared – not self-contained flat	Unshared – not self-contained 'rooms'	Unshared – Bedsit	Other – not self-contained flat	Other – not self-contained 'rooms'	Other – Bedsit	Non-permanent accommodation
ALL TYPES OF OCCUPANCY	56,462	17,685	12,943	19,072	5,416	379	407	79	11	6	2	37	23	135	265
Households with residents	54,323	16,947	12,602	18,498	5,051	330	368	64	11	6	2	37	23	124	260
Enumerated with person(s) present	52,626	16,444	12,304	17,966	4,775	314	350	61	11	6	2	34	18	104	237
Absent households	1,697	503	298	532	276	16	18	3	-	-	-	3	5	20	23
Vacant accommodation	1,857	616	296	516	334	41	31	15						8	
New, never occupied	391	211	11	41	120	1	-	7						-	-
Other	1,466	405	285	475	214	40	31	8						8	8
Accommodation not used as main residence	282	122	45	58	31	8	8	-					2	3	
No persons present	125	72	17	21	9	3	3	-					1	-	-
Persons enumerated but no residents	157	50	28	37	22	5	5	-				1	1	3	5

Unshared dwellings – not self-contained subtotal (ALL TYPES): 17 · Other household spaces – not self-contained subtotal (ALL TYPES): 62

Table 56 Household space type and occupancy – continued

56. Household spaces

Column groups — Household space type in permanent buildings:
Unshared dwellings - purpose-built (c Detached, d Semi-detached, e Terraced, Purpose-built flat in: f Residential building, g Commercial building); Unshared dwellings - converted (h Converted flat, i Converted flatlet); Unshared dwellings - not self-contained (j Not self-contained flat, k Not self-contained 'rooms', l Bedsit); Other household spaces - not self-contained (m Not self-contained flat, n Not self-contained 'rooms', o Bedsit); p Non-permanent accommodation.

Occupancy type	Total household spaces	Detached	Semi-detached	Terraced	Res. building	Comm. building	Converted flat	Converted flatlet	NSC flat	NSC 'rooms'	Bedsit	NSC flat (other)	NSC 'rooms' (other)	Bedsit (other)	Non-permanent accomm.
a	b	c	d	e	f	g	h	i	j	k	l	m	n	o	p
East Hampshire															
ALL TYPES OF OCCUPANCY	**41,093**	**17,567**	**9,700**	**8,181**	**3,765**	**437**	**724**	**39**	**17**	**5**	**1**	**41**	**17**	**88**	**511**
Households with residents	**39,158**	**16,833**	**9,402**	**7,791**	**3,433**	**375**	**643**	**35**	**17**	**4**	**–**	**38**	**17**	**82**	**488**
Enumerated with person(s) present	37,889	16,288	9,149	7,556	3,281	360	607	33	17	3	–	37	17	79	462
Absent households	1,269	545	253	235	152	15	36	2	–	1	–	1	–	3	26
Vacant accommodation	**1,624**	**596**	**245**	**349**	**309**	**56**	**61**	**1**	**–**	**–**	**–**	**2**	**–**	**5**	**–**
New, never occupied	394	189	20	42	133	5	5	–	–	–	–	–	–	–	–
Other	1,230	407	225	307	176	51	56	1	–	–	–	2	–	5	–
Accommodation not used as main residence	**311**	**138**	**53**	**41**	**23**	**6**	**20**	**3**	**–**	**1**	**1**	**1**	**–**	**1**	**23**
No persons present	154	81	30	18	11	4	8	2	–	–	–	–	–	–	–
Persons enumerated but no residents	157	57	23	23	12	2	12	1	–	1	1	1	–	1	23
Eastleigh															
ALL TYPES OF OCCUPANCY	**43,169**	**14,874**	**12,429**	**10,037**	**4,433**	**348**	**383**	**8**	**3**	**6**	**7**	**30**	**24**	**128**	**459**
Households with residents	**41,219**	**14,306**	**12,119**	**9,558**	**3,998**	**311**	**297**	**8**	**3**	**2**	**3**	**23**	**24**	**112**	**455**
Enumerated with person(s) present	39,905	13,854	11,820	9,287	3,805	299	273	8	3	2	3	21	21	101	408
Absent households	1,314	452	299	271	193	12	24	–	–	–	–	2	3	11	47
Vacant accommodation	**1,757**	**501**	**288**	**437**	**397**	**32**	**77**	**–**	**–**	**4**	**4**	**4**	**–**	**13**	**–**
New, never occupied	562	211	28	114	177	2	30	–	–	–	–	–	–	–	–
Other	1,195	290	260	323	220	30	47	–	–	4	4	4	–	13	–
Accommodation not used as main residence	**193**	**67**	**22**	**42**	**38**	**5**	**9**	**–**	**–**	**–**	**–**	**3**	**–**	**3**	**4**
No persons present	94	39	11	17	20	1	6	–	–	–	–	–	–	–	–
Persons enumerated but no residents	99	28	11	25	18	4	3	–	–	–	–	3	–	3	4

Table 56 Household space type and occupancy – **continued**

56. Household spaces

| Occupancy type (a) | TOTAL HOUSEHOLD SPACES (b) | Unshared dwellings - purpose-built | | | Purpose-built flat in: | | Unshared dwellings - converted | | Unshared dwellings - not self-contained | | | Other household spaces - not self-contained | | | Non-permanent accommodation (p) |
		Detached (c)	Semi-detached (d)	Terraced (e)	Residential building (f)	Commercial building (g)	Converted flat (h)	Converted flatlet (i)	Not self-contained flat (j)	Not self-contained 'rooms' (k)	Bedsit (l)	Not self-contained flat (m)	Not self-contained 'rooms' (n)	Bedsit (o)	
Fareham															
ALL TYPES OF OCCUPANCY	39,992	13,653	13,485	8,506	3,474	291	196	15	3	7	1	18	14	38	291
Households with residents	38,369	13,157	13,104	8,118	3,206	231	176	13	3	5	-	18	14	37	287
Enumerated with person(s) present	37,258	12,770	12,787	7,888	3,053	225	167	13	3	5	-	18	13	37	279
Absent households	1,111	387	317	230	153	6	9	-	-	-	-	-	1	-	8
Vacant accommodation	1,403	426	331	327	248	52	14	2	-	1	1	-	-	1	-
New, never occupied	301	132	15	68	85	1	-	-	-	-	-	-	-	-	-
Other	1,102	294	316	259	163	51	14	2	-	1	1	-	-	1	-
Accommodation not used as main residence	220	70	50	61	20	8	6	-	-	1	-	-	-	-	4
No persons present	111	40	18	35	8	4	6	-	-	-	-	-	-	-	-
Persons enumerated but no residents	109	30	32	26	12	4	-	-	-	1	-	-	-	-	4
Gosport															
ALL TYPES OF OCCUPANCY	31,425	3,574	8,008	12,896	5,968	427	346	9	3	4	2	26	9	59	94
Households with residents	29,356	3,442	7,739	12,067	5,259	360	304	8	3	1	2	26	9	48	88
Enumerated with person(s) present	28,364	3,321	7,557	11,723	4,961	347	278	8	2	1	2	25	9	44	86
Absent households	992	121	182	344	298	13	26	-	1	-	-	1	-	4	2
Vacant accommodation	1,892	104	236	799	639	63	37	1	-	3	-	-	-	10	-
New, never occupied	110	16	2	30	62	-	-	-	-	-	-	-	-	-	-
Other	1,782	88	234	769	577	63	37	1	-	3	-	-	-	10	-
Accommodation not used as main residence	177	28	33	30	70	4	5	-	-	-	-	-	-	1	6
No persons present	94	16	21	17	34	3	3	-	-	-	-	-	-	-	-
Persons enumerated but no residents	83	12	12	13	36	1	2	-	-	-	-	-	-	1	6

Table 56 Household space type and occupancy – continued

56. Household spaces

Occupancy type	TOTAL HOUSEHOLD SPACES	Household space type in permanent buildings													Non-permanent accommodation
		Unshared dwellings - purpose-built			Purpose-built flat in:		Unshared dwellings - converted		Unshared dwellings - not self-contained			Other household spaces - not self-contained			
		Detached	Semi-detached	Terraced	Residential building	Commercial building	Converted flat	Converted flatlet	Not self-contained flat	Not self-contained 'rooms'	Bedsit	Not self-contained flat	Not self-contained 'rooms'	Bedsit	
a	b	c	d	e	f	g	h	i	j	k	l	m	n	o	p
Hart															
ALL TYPES OF OCCUPANCY	30,291	13,774	7,621	5,772	2,133	278	276	20	5	1	3	20	14	36	338
Households with residents	29,073	13,378	7,455	5,479	1,868	222	256	15	5	1	3	20	14	27	330
Enumerated with person(s) present	28,138	12,993	7,254	5,293	1,763	208	239	13	5	1	3	20	14	22	310
Absent households	935	385	201	186	105	14	17	2	-	-	-	-	-	5	20
Vacant accommodation	1,064	337	147	260	243	51	16	5	-	-	-	-	-	5	-
New, never occupied	257	86	7	22	141	-	1	-	-	-	-	-	-	-	-
Other	807	251	140	238	102	51	15	5	-	-	-	-	-	5	-
Accommodation not used as main residence	154	59	19	33	22	5	4	-	-	-	-	-	-	4	8
No persons present	55	29	4	15	5	2	-	-	-	-	-	-	-	-	-
Persons enumerated but no residents	99	30	15	18	17	3	4	-	-	-	-	-	-	4	8
Havant															
ALL TYPES OF OCCUPANCY	48,339	13,897	11,963	13,895	7,068	638	440	68	11	4	3	33	45	118	156
Households with residents	46,151	13,268	11,629	13,483	6,512	503	386	59	7	4	3	33	43	107	114
Enumerated with person(s) present	44,850	12,864	11,380	13,205	6,198	487	366	52	7	4	3	32	41	101	110
Absent households	1,301	404	249	278	314	16	20	7	-	-	-	1	2	6	4
Vacant accommodation	1,585	401	261	319	425	112	45	5	4	-	-	-	2	11	-
New, never occupied	198	68	8	25	80	15	2	-	-	-	-	-	-	-	-
Other	1,387	333	253	294	345	97	43	5	4	-	-	-	2	11	-
Accommodation not used as main residence	603	228	73	93	131	23	9	4	-	-	-	-	-	-	42
No persons present	456	190	56	81	102	18	7	2	-	-	-	-	-	-	-
Persons enumerated but no residents	147	38	17	12	29	5	2	2	-	-	-	-	-	-	42

Table 56 Household space type and occupancy – continued

56. Household spaces

Occupancy type	TOTAL HOUSEHOLD SPACES	Household space type in permanent buildings													Non-permanent accommodation
		Unshared dwellings - purpose-built					Unshared dwellings - converted		Unshared dwellings - not self-contained			Other household spaces - not self-contained			
		Detached	Semi-detached	Terraced	Purpose-built flat in:		Converted flat	Converted flatlet	Not self-contained flat	Not self-contained 'rooms'	Bedsit	Not self-contained flat	Not self-contained 'rooms'	Bedsit	
					Residential building	Commercial building									
a	b	c	d	e	f	g	h	i	j	k	l	m	n	o	p

New Forest

a	b	c	d	e	f	g	h	i	j	k	l	m	n	o	p
ALL TYPES OF OCCUPANCY	**70,492**	**33,207**	**15,217**	**11,907**	**6,296**	**1,013**	**1,066**	**60**	**35**	**6**	**9**	**106**	**44**	**116**	**1,460**
Households with residents	**65,411**	**31,330**	**14,479**	**11,028**	**5,375**	**872**	**863**	**44**	**28**	**6**	**7**	**49**	**44**	**100**	**1,186**
Enumerated with person(s) present	63,033	30,273	14,079	10,623	5,074	820	790	38	27	6	7	47	42	90	1,117
Absent households	2,378	1,057	400	405	301	52	73	6	1	-	-	2	2	10	69
Vacant accommodation	**3,111**	**1,241**	**508**	**509**	**617**	**108**	**91**	**11**	**1**	-	**2**	**9**	**9**	**14**	
New, never occupied	611	228	36	116	217	9	5	-	-		-	-	-	-	
Other	2,500	1,013	472	393	400	99	86	11	1		2	9	9	14	
Accommodation not used as main residence	**1,970**	**636**	**230**	**370**	**304**	**33**	**112**	**5**	-		-	**4**		**2**	**274**
No persons present	1,269	476	159	286	246	23	77	1	-		-	-	-	1	1
Persons enumerated but no residents	701	160	71	84	58	10	35	4	-		-	3	1	1	274

Portsmouth

a	b	c	d	e	f	g	h	i	j	k	l	m	n	o	p
ALL TYPES OF OCCUPANCY	**78,134**	**2,543**	**9,696**	**40,307**	**15,755**	**1,640**	**5,505**	**278**	**69**	**12**	**48**	**789**	**254**	**1,368**	**136**
Households with residents	**72,590**	**2,408**	**9,398**	**38,064**	**14,457**	**1,354**	**4,637**	**239**	**44**	**12**	**40**	**432**	**254**	**1,123**	**128**
Enumerated with person(s) present	69,795	2,318	9,156	36,932	13,790	1,256	4,276	215	42	12	37	405	238	993	125
Absent households	2,795	90	242	1,132	667	98	361	24	2	-	3	27	16	130	3
Vacant accommodation	**4,272**	**120**	**253**	**1,658**	**1,135**	**237**	**644**	**21**	**7**	-	**4**	**56**	**56**	**137**	
New, never occupied	343	22	9	108	180	-	21	1	-		-	-	-	2	
Other	3,929	98	244	1,550	955	237	623	20	7		4	56	56	135	
Accommodation not used as main residence	**1,272**	**15**	**45**	**585**	**163**	**49**	**224**	**18**	**6**		**4**	**47**		**108**	**8**
No persons present	341	3	15	118	88	11	69	9	5		2	30	8	18	
Persons enumerated but no residents	931	12	30	467	75	38	155	9	1		2	9	9	90	8

Table 56 Household space type and occupancy – continued

56. Household spaces

Column key: a = Occupancy type; b = Total household spaces. Household space type in permanent buildings: Unshared dwellings – purpose-built [c = Detached, d = Semi-detached, e = Terraced, Purpose-built flat in: f = Residential building, g = Commercial building]; Unshared dwellings – converted [h = Converted flat, i = Converted flatlet]; Unshared dwellings – not self-contained [j = Not self-contained flat, k = Not self-contained 'rooms', l = Bedsit]; Other household spaces – not self-contained [m = Not self-contained flat, n = Not self-contained 'rooms', o = Bedsit]. p = Non-permanent accommodation.

Rushmoor

a	b	c	d	e	f	g	h	i	j	k	l	m	n	o	p
ALL TYPES OF OCCUPANCY	**31,977**	**5,213**	**9,898**	**9,494**	**5,251**	**503**	**691**	**45**	**19**	**6**	**6**	**106**	**55**	**539**	**212**
Households with residents	**30,523**	**5,052**	**9,620**	**9,028**	**4,965**	**414**	**621**	**37**	**11**	**6**	**3**	**51**	**45**	**465**	**205**
Enumerated with person(s) present	29,465	4,920	9,381	8,741	4,714	390	581	31	11	5	3	46	39	411	192
Absent households	1,058	132	239	287	251	24	40	6	–	1	–	5	6	54	13
Vacant accommodation	**1,328**	**144**	**257**	**437**	**259**	**83**	**70**	**7**	**8**	–	**2**	**55**	**8**	**59**	–
New, never occupied	62	13	1	–	44	–	4	–	–	–	–	–	–	–	–
Other	1,266	131	256	437	215	83	66	7	8	–	2	55	8	59	–
Accommodation not used as main residence	**126**	**17**	**21**	**29**	**27**	**6**	–	**1**	–	–	**1**	–	**2**	**15**	**7**
No persons present	28	8	7	3	2	3	–	1	–	–	–	–	–	4	–
Persons enumerated but no residents	98	9	14	26	25	3	–	–	–	–	1	–	2	11	7

Southampton

a	b	c	d	e	f	g	h	i	j	k	l	m	n	o	p
ALL TYPES OF OCCUPANCY	**86,576**	**12,162**	**22,709**	**21,386**	**22,521**	**1,252**	**3,143**	**434**	**80**	**18**	**58**	**642**	**292**	**2,117**	**72**
Households with residents	**81,140**	**11,665**	**21,757**	**20,196**	**21,014**	**1,022**	**2,711**	**369**	**54**	**18**	**52**	**274**	**292**	**1,647**	**69**
Enumerated with person(s) present	77,939	11,283	21,222	19,599	20,001	957	2,498	331	41	18	44	250	264	1,369	62
Absent households	3,201	382	535	597	1,013	65	213	38	13	–	8	24	28	278	7
Vacant accommodation	**4,336**	**441**	**752**	**874**	**1,308**	**200**	**366**	**56**	**18**	–	**6**	**274**	–	**287**	–
New, never occupied	565	22	27	122	375	8	11	–	–	–	–	–	–	–	–
Other	3,771	419	725	752	933	192	355	56	18	–	6	274	–	287	–
Accommodation not used as main residence	**1,100**	**56**	**200**	**316**	**199**	**30**	**66**	**9**	**3**	**1**	–	**20**	**3**	**183**	**3**
No persons present	327	26	44	77	91	9	28	1	1	–	–	–	3	47	–
Persons enumerated but no residents	773	30	156	239	108	21	38	8	1	1	–	20	12	136	3

Table 56 Household space type and occupancy – continued

56. Household spaces

Column groupings (under "Household space type in permanent buildings" except column p):
- c–g: Unshared dwellings - purpose-built (f, g = Purpose-built flat in: Residential building / Commercial building)
- h–i: Unshared dwellings - converted (Converted flat / Converted flatlet)
- j–l: Unshared dwellings - not self-contained (Not self-contained flat / 'rooms' / Bedsit)
- m–o: Other household spaces - not self-contained (Not self-contained flat / 'rooms' / Bedsit)
- p: Non-permanent accommodation

Occupancy type	TOTAL HOUSEHOLD SPACES	Detached	Semi-detached	Terraced	Residential building	Commercial building	Converted flat	Converted flatlet	Not self-contained flat	Not self-contained 'rooms'	Bedsit	Not self-contained flat	Not self-contained 'rooms'	Bedsit	Non-permanent accommodation
a	b	c	d	e	f	g	h	i	j	k	l	m	n	o	p
Test Valley															
ALL TYPES OF OCCUPANCY	**40,292**	**15,033**	**9,927**	**10,511**	**3,440**	**274**	**590**	**21**	**15**	**2**	**8**	**18**	**10**	**56**	**387**
Households with residents	**38,391**	**14,385**	**9,524**	**9,954**	**3,244**	**247**	**539**	**20**	**15**	**2**	**8**	**18**	**10**	**45**	**380**
Enumerated with person(s) present	37,167	13,903	9,287	9,665	3,088	239	516	19	15	2	7	18	10	36	362
Absent households	1,224	482	237	289	156	8	23	1	-	-	1	-	-	9	18
Vacant accommodation	**1,586**	**492**	**347**	**498**	**180**	**22**	**37**	-	-	-	-	-	-	**10**	-
New, never occupied	296	130	30	63	67	5	1	-	-	-	-	-	-	-	-
Other	1,290	362	317	435	113	17	36	-	-	-	-	-	-	10	-
Accommodation not used as main residence	**315**	**156**	**56**	**59**	**16**	**5**	**14**	**1**	-	-	-	-	-	**1**	**7**
No persons present	187	96	37	34	8	3	8	1	-	-	-	-	-	-	-
Persons enumerated but no residents	128	60	19	25	8	2	6	-	-	-	-	-	-	1	7
Winchester															
ALL TYPES OF OCCUPANCY	**39,523**	**15,058**	**9,597**	**8,716**	**3,927**	**435**	**928**	**47**	**12**	**3**	**3**	**63**	**20**	**173**	**541**
Households with residents	**37,553**	**14,449**	**9,291**	**8,257**	**3,601**	**370**	**825**	**40**	**12**	**3**	**3**	**47**	**20**	**117**	**518**
Enumerated with person(s) present	36,320	14,002	9,070	7,970	3,440	346	783	35	12	1	3	41	19	105	493
Absent households	1,233	447	221	287	161	24	42	5	-	2	-	6	1	12	25
Vacant accommodation	**1,542**	**470**	**260**	**365**	**274**	**44**	**73**	**3**	-	-	-	**9**	-	**44**	-
New, never occupied	294	119	10	58	85	-	15	1	-	-	-	6	-	-	-
Other	1,248	351	250	307	189	44	58	2	-	-	-	3	-	44	-
Accommodation not used as main residence	**428**	**139**	**46**	**94**	**52**	**21**	**30**	**4**	-	-	-	**7**	-	**12**	**23**
No persons present	177	79	21	36	20	12	9	-	-	-	-	7	-	-	-
Persons enumerated but no residents	251	60	25	58	32	9	21	4	-	-	-	-	-	12	23

Table 57 Household space type: rooms and household size

Note: Maximum number of rooms in non-permanent accommodation is 5

57. Households with residents; residents in households; rooms in household spaces

HAMPSHIRE

a	TOTAL HOUSE-HOLDS	Unshared dwellings - purpose-built			Purpose-built flat in:		Unshared dwellings - converted		Unshared dwellings - not self-contained			Other household spaces - not self-contained			Non-permanent accomm-odation	With migrant head
		Detached	Semi-detached	Terraced	Residential building	Commercial building	Converted flat	Converted flatlet	Not self-contained flat	Not self-contained 'rooms'	Bedsit	Not self-contained flat	Not self-contained 'rooms'	Bedsit		
	b	c	d	e	f	g	h	i	j	k	l	m	n	o	p	q
Households with the following rooms																
TOTAL	**603,257**	**170,620**	**148,119**	**171,521**	**81,983**	**6,611**	**12,626**	**951**	**213**	**69**	**126**	**1,066**	**810**	**4,034**	**4,508**	**61,190**
1	9,899	75	92	169	4,078	150	-	951	-	-	126	-	-	4,034	224	3,429
2	21,487	235	802	2,279	14,304	535	2,099		23	32		235	421		522	4,270
3	44,952	1,436	3,791	7,874	24,096	1,347	4,313		49	24		308	208		1,506	7,295
4	104,709	15,472	20,818	31,807	29,007	1,852	3,625		60	8		222	84		1,754	12,790
5	174,101	37,234	53,897	70,499	8,909	1,604	1,285		20	2		106	43		502	14,819
6	137,471	40,131	49,506	45,238	1,196	700	566		18	-		89	27			9,925
7 or more	110,638	76,037	19,213	13,655	393	423	738		43	3		106	27			8,662
TOTAL ROOMS	**3,177,356**	**1,105,899**	**808,072**	**882,674**	**276,185**	**28,250**	**47,999**	**951**	**1,042**	**204**	**126**	**4,214**	**2,394**	**4,034**	**15,312**	**286,789**
Households with the following persons																
TOTAL	**603,257**	**170,620**	**148,119**	**171,521**	**81,983**	**6,611**	**12,626**	**951**	**213**	**69**	**126**	**1,066**	**810**	**4,034**	**4,508**	**61,190**
1	145,320	24,995	26,383	35,261	44,074	2,047	5,575	668	70	33	84	500	418	3,229	1,983	15,102
2	213,595	65,281	52,760	58,433	26,173	2,387	5,080	232	86	29	23	355	233	580	1,943	23,152
3	98,661	29,121	27,147	32,359	6,953	1,058	1,198	36	19	4	13	115	109	176	353	10,254
4	100,509	36,326	29,080	30,114	3,388	743	535	13	25	1	2	54	31	32	165	8,758
5	33,666	11,609	9,501	10,941	1,037	280	183	1	9	2	1	27	14	12	49	2,886
6	8,819	2,656	2,497	3,251	273	68	42	1	3	-	1	11	3	3	10	769
7 or more	2,687	632	751	1,162	85	28	13	-	1	-	2	4	2	2	5	269
TOTAL PERSONS	**1,512,038**	**466,972**	**397,755**	**452,672**	**138,301**	**15,000**	**22,734**	**1,303**	**471**	**117**	**204**	**2,004**	**1,437**	**5,138**	**7,930**	**148,291**
Households with the following persons per room																
TOTAL	**603,257**	**170,620**	**148,119**	**171,521**	**81,983**	**6,611**	**12,626**	**951**	**213**	**69**	**126**	**1,066**	**810**	**4,034**	**4,508**	**61,190**
Over 1.5	2,618	67	148	317	688	78	40	283	-	1	42	16	17	805	116	1,029
Over 1 and up to 1.5	7,174	491	1,671	3,242	1,169	205	202	-	2	3	-	27	67	-	95	884
Over 0.5 and up to 1	200,870	44,585	53,920	66,101	23,934	2,473	3,879	668	70	26	84	304	242	3,229	1,355	23,726
Up to 0.5	392,595	125,477	92,380	101,861	56,192	3,855	8,505	-	141	39	-	719	484	-	2,942	35,551

Table 57 Household space type: rooms and household size – continued

Note: Maximum number of rooms in non-permanent accommodation is 5

57. Households with residents; residents in households; rooms in household spaces

Basingstoke & Deane

a	TOTAL HOUSE-HOLDS	Unshared dwellings - purpose-built			Purpose-built flat in:		Unshared dwellings - converted		Unshared dwellings - not self-contained			Other household spaces - not self-contained			Non-permanent accommodation	With migrant head
		Detached	Semi-detached	Terraced	Residential building	Commercial building	Converted flat	Converted flatlet	Not self-contained flat	Not self-contained 'rooms'	Bedsit	Not self-contained flat	Not self-contained 'rooms'	Bedsit		
	b	c	d	e	f	g	h	i	j	k	l	m	n	o	p	q
Households with the following rooms																
TOTAL	**54,323**	**16,947**	**12,602**	**18,498**	**5,051**	**330**	**368**	**64**	**11**	**6**	**2**	**37**	**23**	**124**	**260**	**5,253**
1	466	10	10	19	228	1	-	64	1	1	2	12	6	124	8	167
2	1,483	26	100	424	786	33	50		1	5		5	6		44	280
3	3,636	125	446	1,177	1,606	71	107		2	-		5	1		87	573
4	7,990	994	1,749	3,142	1,832	100	73		-	-		6	5		92	1,015
5	16,691	3,373	4,771	7,992	401	67	47		4	-		4	3		29	1,428
6	12,148	3,553	3,911	4,442	167	38	26		3	-		5	2			850
7 or more	11,909	8,866	1,615	1,302	31	20	65									940
TOTAL ROOMS	**298,029**	**114,998**	**68,185**	**93,108**	**17,223**	**1,403**	**1,715**	**64**	**73**	**17**	**2**	**156**	**91**	**124**	**870**	**26,285**
Households with the following persons																
TOTAL	**54,323**	**16,947**	**12,602**	**18,498**	**5,051**	**330**	**368**	**64**	**11**	**6**	**2**	**37**	**23**	**124**	**260**	**5,253**
1	11,001	1,957	2,170	3,442	2,886	90	140	56	3	4	2	19	14	94	124	1,222
2	18,847	5,952	4,560	6,259	1,654	133	148	5	5	2	-	10	4	22	93	2,073
3	9,555	3,167	2,363	3,566	351	45	28	1	-	-	-	5	4	4	21	861
4	10,254	4,189	2,528	3,326	114	39	36	-	2	-	-	2	1	3	13	760
5	3,479	1,314	749	1,347	33	18	9	1	1	-	-	-	-	1	7	271
6	930	305	183	419	10	5	6	-	-	-	-	1	-	-	1	51
7 or more	257	63	49	139	3	-	1	-	-	-	-	-	-	-	1	15
TOTAL PERSONS	**143,278**	**48,985**	**33,700**	**50,257**	**7,952**	**767**	**753**	**79**	**26**	**8**	**2**	**71**	**38**	**167**	**473**	**12,763**
Households with the following persons per room																
TOTAL	**54,323**	**16,947**	**12,602**	**18,498**	**5,051**	**330**	**368**	**64**	**11**	**6**	**2**	**37**	**23**	**124**	**260**	**5,253**
Over 1.5	181	6	12	45	68	2	2	8	-	-	-	1	-	30	7	50
Over 1 and up to 1.5	594	43	112	371	38	10	6	-	-	-	-	-	-	-	14	50
Over 0.5 and up to 1	18,910	4,752	4,693	7,736	1,254	122	108	56	4	2	2	10	7	94	70	1,805
Up to 0.5	34,638	12,146	7,785	10,346	3,691	196	252	-	7	4	-	26	16	-	169	3,348

Table 57 Household space type: rooms and household size – **continued**

Note: Maximum number of rooms in non-permanent accommodation is 5

57. Households with residents; residents in households; rooms in household spaces

East Hampshire

a	TOTAL HOUSE-HOLDS	Unshared dwellings - purpose-built			Purpose-built flat in:		Unshared dwellings - converted		Unshared dwellings - not self-contained			Other household spaces - not self-contained			Non-permanent accomm-odation	With migrant head
		Detached	Semi-detached	Terraced	Residential building	Commercial building	Converted flat	Converted flatlet	Not self-contained flat	Not self-contained 'rooms'	Bedsit	Not self-contained flat	Not self-contained 'rooms'	Bedsit		
	b	c	d	e	f	g	h	i	j	k	l	m	n	o	p	q
Households with the following rooms																
TOTAL	39,158	16,833	9,402	7,791	3,433	375	643	35	17	4	-	38	17	82	488	3,884
1	429	9	6	4	265	11	-	35	2	2	-	9	7	82	17	127
2	1,212	29	110	155	701	30	103		4	-	-	8	6		64	225
3	2,539	141	348	521	1,085	75	173		3	1	-	5	1		178	412
4	6,261	1,292	1,538	1,911	1,109	95	136		-	-	-	6	2		170	791
5	10,587	3,300	3,511	3,317	238	77	77		-	-	-	4	-		59	906
6	7,699	3,554	2,609	1,408	20	43	61		-	-	-	6	1			574
7 or more	10,431	8,508	1,280	475	15	44	93		8	1	-					849
TOTAL ROOMS	219,547	113,492	50,406	38,188	10,791	1,672	2,880	35	112	18	-	164	53	82	1,654	19,809
Households with the following persons																
TOTAL	39,158	16,833	9,402	7,791	3,433	375	643	35	17	4	-	38	17	82	488	3,884
1	8,443	2,419	1,762	1,621	1,945	125	276	26	4	2	-	14	5	49	195	763
2	13,899	6,241	3,318	2,586	1,120	124	235	5	6	1	-	12	7	19	225	1,465
3	6,474	2,827	1,703	1,499	262	63	60	2	3	-	-	4	4	10	37	725
4	7,105	3,662	1,809	1,431	85	46	38	2	3	-	-	6	1	2	21	635
5	2,422	1,289	597	473	18	8	25	-	-	1	-	2	-	1	7	212
6	640	323	163	133	2	8	8	-	1	-	-	-	-	-	2	62
7 or more	175	72	50	48	1	1	1	-	-	-	-	-	-	1	1	22
TOTAL PERSONS	101,335	46,950	25,075	20,529	5,421	848	1,258	50	43	9	-	84	36	138	894	9,998
Households with the following persons per room																
TOTAL	39,158	16,833	9,402	7,791	3,433	375	643	35	17	4	-	38	17	82	488	3,884
Over 1.5	152	7	14	11	59	2	3	9	-	-	-	-	-	33	14	65
Over 1 and up to 1.5	418	56	115	168	40	15	7	-	-	-	-	1	2	-	14	67
Over 0.5 and up to 1	12,519	4,198	3,428	3,295	1,032	133	175	26	5	-	-	17	9	49	152	1,464
Up to 0.5	26,069	12,572	5,845	4,317	2,302	225	458	-	12	4	-	20	6	-	308	2,288

Table 57 Household space type: rooms and household size – continued

Note: Maximum number of rooms in non-permanent accommodation is 5

57. Households with residents; residents in households; rooms in household spaces

Eastleigh

a	TOTAL HOUSE-HOLDS	Detached	Semi-detached	Terraced	Purpose-built flat in: Residential building	Purpose-built flat in: Commercial building	Converted flat	Converted flatlet	Not self-contained flat	Not self-contained 'rooms'	Bedsit	Other: Not self-contained flat	Other: Not self-contained 'rooms'	Other: Bedsit	Non-permanent accommodation	With migrant head
	b	c	d	e	f	g	h	i	j	k	l	m	n	o	p	q
Households with the following rooms																
TOTAL	**41,219**	**14,306**	**12,119**	**9,558**	**3,998**	**311**	**297**	**8**	**3**	**2**	**3**	**23**	**24**	**112**	**455**	**3,901**
1	475	6	2	4	290	5	-	8	1	-	3	4	9	112	45	134
2	1,014	8	124	136	597	32	51		1	2		7	11		52	222
3	2,807	89	427	627	1,291	79	107		-	-		5	3		166	489
4	7,229	1,343	1,533	2,571	1,459	89	71		-	-		3	-		155	873
5	12,679	3,838	4,810	3,580	317	68	26		-	-		3	-		37	950
6	9,768	3,468	4,024	2,205	26	22	20		1	-		1	1		-	631
7 or more	7,247	5,554	1,199	435	18	16	22		-	-		-	-		-	602
TOTAL ROOMS	**217,822**	**88,778**	**64,699**	**47,114**	**13,078**	**1,265**	**1,134**	**8**	**13**	**6**	**3**	**90**	**70**	**112**	**1,452**	**18,663**
Households with the following persons																
TOTAL	**41,219**	**14,306**	**12,119**	**9,558**	**3,998**	**311**	**297**	**8**	**3**	**2**	**3**	**23**	**24**	**112**	**455**	**3,901**
1	8,887	1,824	2,015	2,121	2,340	106	127	4	2	1	3	7	13	96	228	915
2	14,857	5,332	4,176	3,597	1,333	99	123	1	-	-	-	10	7	10	169	1,631
3	6,923	2,579	2,257	1,704	251	51	27	2	-	-	-	3	3	6	39	619
4	7,627	3,382	2,582	1,534	63	39	11	-	1	1	-	-	1	-	14	532
5	2,303	962	847	457	9	13	8	1	-	-	-	2	-	-	4	163
6	502	185	198	113	2	2	1	-	-	-	-	1	-	-	-	27
7 or more	120	42	44	32	-	1	-	-	-	-	-	-	-	-	1	14
TOTAL PERSONS	**105,298**	**39,982**	**33,211**	**23,772**	**6,068**	**697**	**544**	**17**	**6**	**4**	**3**	**52**	**40**	**134**	**768**	**9,241**
Households with the following persons per room																
TOTAL	**41,219**	**14,306**	**12,119**	**9,558**	**3,998**	**311**	**297**	**8**	**3**	**2**	**3**	**23**	**24**	**112**	**455**	**3,901**
Over 1.5	102	1	10	12	41	5	-	4	-	-	-	-	-	16	13	32
Over 1 and up to 1.5	362	40	126	135	30	18	5	-	-	-	-	-	1	-	7	33
Over 0.5 and up to 1	14,332	4,365	4,900	3,478	1,092	116	102	4	-	1	3	10	9	96	156	1,352
Up to 0.5	26,423	9,900	7,083	5,933	2,835	172	190	-	3	1	-	13	14	-	279	2,484

Table 57 Household space type: rooms and household size – **continued**

Note: Maximum number of rooms in non-permanent accommodation is 5

57. Households with residents; residents in households; rooms in household spaces

Fareham

a	b	c	d	e	f	g	h	i	j	k	l	m	n	o	p	q
			Unshared dwellings - purpose-built		Purpose-built flat in:		Unshared dwellings - converted		Unshared dwellings - not self-contained			Other household spaces - not self-contained				
	TOTAL HOUSE-HOLDS	Detached	Semi-detached	Terraced	Residential building	Commercial building	Converted flat	Converted flatlet	Not self-contained flat	Not self-contained 'rooms'	Bedsit	Not self-contained flat	Not self-contained 'rooms'	Bedsit	Non-permanent accommodation	With migrant head
Households with the following rooms																
TOTAL	**38,369**	**13,157**	**13,104**	**8,118**	**3,206**	**231**	**176**	**13**	**3**	**4**	**-**	**18**	**15**	**37**	**287**	**3,412**
1	275	3	3	3	201	7	-	13	1	2	-	5	5	37	8	49
2	900	16	60	69	665	21	31		-	1		5	4		25	168
3	2,025	65	331	479	976	36	48		-	1		4	5		80	353
4	6,406	1,088	2,541	1,417	1,099	72	41		-	-		2	1		138	660
5	12,039	3,131	5,088	3,474	236	55	16		-	-		2	-		36	941
6	9,053	3,119	3,711	2,151	26	26	18		2	-		-				630
7 or more	7,671	5,735	1,370	525	3	14	22			-						611
TOTAL ROOMS	**207,336**	**83,468**	**69,230**	**41,457**	**10,243**	**982**	**736**	**13**	**19**	**11**	**-**	**63**	**47**	**37**	**1,030**	**17,267**
Households with the following persons																
TOTAL	**38,369**	**13,157**	**13,104**	**8,118**	**3,206**	**231**	**176**	**13**	**3**	**4**	**-**	**18**	**15**	**37**	**287**	**3,412**
1	7,823	1,677	2,428	1,570	1,852	66	70	9	-	3	-	6	7	30	105	713
2	14,535	5,179	5,122	2,851	1,036	99	67	3	2	1	-	9	6	7	153	1,369
3	6,649	2,463	2,362	1,572	188	34	13	-	1	-	-	3	1	-	17	583
4	6,761	2,811	2,366	1,431	101	20	17	1	-	-	-	3	1	-	9	523
5	2,050	834	643	530	20	11	8	-	-	-	-	-	1	-	3	177
6	448	153	151	133	9	1	1	-	-	-	-	-	-	-	-	42
7 or more	103	40	32	31	-	-	-	-	-	-	-	-	-	-	-	5
TOTAL PERSONS	**97,607**	**36,072**	**33,580**	**21,392**	**5,046**	**507**	**357**	**19**	**8**	**5**	**-**	**36**	**28**	**44**	**513**	**8,472**
Households with the following persons per room																
TOTAL	**38,369**	**13,157**	**13,104**	**8,118**	**3,206**	**231**	**176**	**13**	**3**	**4**	**-**	**18**	**15**	**37**	**287**	**3,412**
Over 1.5	55	1	7	10	14	5	1	4	-	-	-	1	-	7	5	18
Over 1 and up to 1.5	282	33	86	118	38	3	-	-	-	-	-	-	-	-	4	32
Over 0.5 and up to 1	12,470	3,562	4,489	3,239	917	82	55	9	1	1	-	6	4	30	75	1,177
Up to 0.5	25,562	9,561	8,522	4,751	2,237	141	120	-	2	3	-	11	11	-	203	2,185

Table 57 Household space type: rooms and household size – continued

Note: Maximum number of rooms in non-permanent accommodation is 5

57. Households with residents; residents in households; rooms in household spaces

Gosport

Column groupings (Household space type in permanent buildings):
Unshared dwellings – purpose-built: c Detached, d Semi-detached, e Terraced, f Purpose-built flat in Residential building, g Purpose-built flat in Commercial building. Unshared dwellings – converted: h Converted flat, i Converted flatlet. Unshared dwellings – not self-contained: j Not self-contained flat, k Not self-contained 'rooms', l Bedsit. Other household spaces – not self-contained: m Not self-contained flat, n Not self-contained 'rooms', o Bedsit. p Non-permanent accommodation. q With migrant head.

a	b	c	d	e	f	g	h	i	j	k	l	m	n	o	p	q
Households with the following rooms																
TOTAL	29,356	3,442	7,739	12,067	5,259	360	304	8	3	1	2	26	9	48	88	3,281
1	327	1	-	20	234	2	-	8	-	-	2	6	3	48	12	79
2	1,067	3	17	125	843	22	37	-	-	1	-	9	3	-	11	149
3	2,413	27	126	583	1,457	68	108	-	1	-	-	4	-	-	31	343
4	5,718	329	1,016	2,145	2,001	98	98	-	2	-	-	1	1	-	26	878
5	9,005	837	2,491	4,889	638	104	34	-	-	-	-	2	2	-	8	911
6	7,593	862	3,141	3,466	63	44	13	-	-	-	-	4	-	-	-	657
7 or more	3,233	1,383	948	839	23	22	14	-	-	-	-	-	-	-	-	264
TOTAL ROOMS	148,121	21,537	43,115	62,207	18,038	1,599	1,144	8	14	3	2	103	32	48	271	15,393
Households with the following persons																
TOTAL	29,356	3,442	7,739	12,067	5,259	360	304	8	3	1	2	26	9	48	88	3,281
1	6,866	540	1,182	2,284	2,532	78	146	2	-	1	-	13	2	40	46	582
2	10,407	1,487	2,654	3,996	1,944	153	114	5	2	-	1	10	3	7	31	1,270
3	5,097	557	1,462	2,430	535	67	32	-	-	-	1	3	2	1	7	622
4	4,886	621	1,663	2,339	202	44	11	1	1	-	-	-	1	-	3	546
5	1,571	190	574	754	35	15	1	-	-	-	-	-	1	-	1	182
6	415	43	155	205	9	3	-	-	-	-	-	-	-	-	-	61
7 or more	114	4	49	59	2	-	-	-	-	-	-	-	-	-	-	18
TOTAL PERSONS	73,704	8,906	21,690	32,361	9,076	854	519	16	8	1	5	42	23	57	146	8,583
Households with the following persons per room																
TOTAL	29,356	3,442	7,739	12,067	5,259	360	304	8	3	1	2	26	9	48	88	3,281
Over 1.5	68	1	7	8	28	4	-	6	-	-	2	-	-	8	4	30
Over 1 and up to 1.5	306	7	85	161	42	5	4	-	-	-	-	1	-	-	1	43
Over 0.5 and up to 1	10,691	819	2,968	4,976	1,607	143	87	2	1	-	-	7	6	40	35	1,455
Up to 0.5	18,291	2,615	4,679	6,922	3,582	208	213	-	2	1	-	18	3	-	48	1,753

Table 57 Household space type: rooms and household size – continued

Note: Maximum number of rooms in non-permanent accommodation is 5

57. Households with residents; residents in households; rooms in household spaces

Hart

a	b	c	d	e	f	g	h	i	j	k	l	m	n	o	p	q
		Unshared dwellings - purpose-built			Purpose-built flat in:		Unshared dwellings - converted		Unshared dwellings - not self-contained			Other household spaces - not self-contained				
	TOTAL HOUSE-HOLDS	Detached	Semi-detached	Terraced	Residential building	Commercial building	Converted flat	Converted flatlet	Not self-contained flat	Not self-contained 'rooms'	Bedsit	Not self-contained flat	Not self-contained 'rooms'	Bedsit	Non-permanent accommodation	With migrant head
Households with the following rooms																
TOTAL	**29,073**	**13,378**	**7,455**	**5,479**	**1,868**	**222**	**256**	**15**	**5**	**1**	**3**	**20**	**14**	**27**	**330**	**3,047**
1	212	9	5	3	131	2	-	15	5	1	3	3	7	27	17	45
2	671	15	42	112	400	3	35		1	-		3	1		54	129
3	1,465	64	288	383	525	39	43		1	-		4	1		117	241
4	3,715	561	1,096	1,184	615	64	68		1	-		5	4		120	497
5	7,302	1,648	2,802	2,536	178	78	32		-	-		1	1		22	743
6	5,581	2,495	2,165	861	15	21	20		-	-		3	-			493
7 or more	10,127	8,586	1,057	400	4	15	58		2	1		4	-			899
TOTAL ROOMS	**172,142**	**95,419**	**40,215**	**26,953**	**5,976**	**1,033**	**1,252**	**15**	**30**	**9**	**3**	**97**	**47**	**27**	**1,066**	**16,933**
Households with the following persons																
TOTAL	**29,073**	**13,378**	**7,455**	**5,479**	**1,868**	**222**	**256**	**15**	**5**	**1**	**3**	**20**	**14**	**27**	**330**	**3,047**
1	5,433	1,394	1,294	1,230	1,150	55	98	8	-	1	2	8	7	26	160	568
2	9,665	4,296	2,646	1,813	562	90	101	7	2	-	1	7	5	1	134	1,158
3	4,970	2,434	1,372	981	101	35	20	-	3	-	-	4	2	-	18	495
4	6,380	3,711	1,523	1,034	44	32	25	-	-	-	-	4	-	-	11	592
5	2,068	1,237	484	318	8	7	8	-	-	-	-	1	-	-	5	178
6	455	251	111	86	2	1	3	-	-	-	-	-	-	-	1	48
7 or more	102	55	25	17	1	2	1	-	-	-	-	-	-	-	1	8
TOTAL PERSONS	**79,014**	**40,229**	**20,060**	**14,171**	**2,812**	**523**	**525**	**22**	**13**	**1**	**4**	**39**	**23**	**28**	**564**	**7,972**
Households with the following persons per room																
TOTAL	**29,073**	**13,378**	**7,455**	**5,479**	**1,868**	**222**	**256**	**15**	**5**	**1**	**3**	**20**	**14**	**27**	**330**	**3,047**
Over 1.5	46	5	2	6	13	-	-	7	-	-	1	-	-	1	11	9
Over 1 and up to 1.5	220	29	74	80	24	5	-	-	-	-	-	-	1	-	7	29
Over 0.5 and up to 1	9,419	3,537	2,847	2,247	506	83	66	8	1	-	2	4	3	26	89	1,021
Up to 0.5	19,388	9,807	4,532	3,146	1,325	134	190	-	4	1	-	16	10	-	223	1,988

Table 57 Household space type: rooms and household size – continued

57. Households with residents; residents in households; rooms in household spaces

Note: Maximum number of rooms in non-permanent accommodation is 5

Havant

a	b	c	d	e	f	g	h	i	j	k	l	m	n	o	p	q
	TOTAL HOUSE-HOLDS	Unshared dwellings – purpose-built: Detached	Semi-detached	Terraced	Purpose-built flat in: Residential building	Commercial building	Unshared dwellings – converted: Converted flat	Converted flatlet	Unshared dwellings – not self-contained: Not self-contained flat	Not self-contained 'rooms'	Bedsit	Other household spaces not self-contained: Not self-contained flat	Not self-contained 'rooms'	Bedsit	Non-permanent accomm-odation	With migrant head
Households with the following rooms																
TOTAL	**46,151**	**13,268**	**11,629**	**13,483**	**6,512**	**503**	**386**	**59**	**7**	**4**	**3**	**33**	**43**	**107**	**114**	**3,844**
1	509	5	4	16	299	12	-	59	-	-	3	-	-	107	4	144
2	1,844	22	35	167	1,459	35	74	-	2	3	-	3	23	-	21	327
3	3,129	178	236	511	1,907	101	124	-	2	-	-	8	14	-	48	446
4	9,269	1,580	2,243	2,998	2,173	131	101	-	1	1	-	7	2	-	32	894
5	14,512	3,454	4,091	6,173	581	149	46	-	-	-	-	6	3	-	9	1,006
6	9,606	3,037	3,548	2,870	68	56	19	-	1	-	-	7	-	-	-	578
7 or more	7,282	4,992	1,472	748	25	19	22	-	1	-	-	2	1	-	-	449
TOTAL ROOMS	**236,878**	**81,235**	**62,478**	**67,552**	**21,161**	**2,147**	**1,467**	**59**	**27**	**10**	**3**	**151**	**118**	**107**	**363**	**17,661**
Households with the following persons																
TOTAL	**46,151**	**13,268**	**11,629**	**13,483**	**6,512**	**503**	**386**	**59**	**7**	**4**	**3**	**33**	**43**	**107**	**114**	**3,844**
1	10,432	2,298	1,980	1,960	3,726	139	164	49	1	1	2	10	7	49	46	890
2	16,370	5,486	4,264	4,302	1,870	167	152	9	4	3	1	14	10	38	50	1,338
3	7,703	2,164	2,146	2,719	487	103	41	1	-	-	-	3	11	17	11	702
4	7,719	2,382	2,239	2,711	273	65	22	-	1	-	-	3	13	3	7	604
5	2,828	727	736	1,226	104	25	6	-	1	-	-	1	2	-	-	212
6	831	175	192	422	36	4	-	-	-	-	-	2	-	-	-	79
7 or more	268	36	72	143	16	-	1	-	-	-	-	-	-	-	-	19
TOTAL PERSONS	**118,297**	**34,251**	**31,277**	**39,299**	**10,871**	**1,191**	**716**	**70**	**18**	**7**	**4**	**76**	**122**	**188**	**207**	**9,771**
Households with the following persons per room																
TOTAL	**46,151**	**13,268**	**11,629**	**13,483**	**6,512**	**503**	**386**	**59**	**7**	**4**	**3**	**33**	**43**	**107**	**114**	**3,844**
Over 1.5	198	9	9	37	53	9	-	10	-	-	1	1	9	58	2	64
Over 1 and up to 1.5	834	44	147	486	121	15	7	-	-	-	-	1	10	-	3	91
Over 0.5 and up to 1	16,010	3,250	4,221	6,192	1,827	210	128	49	5	2	2	10	16	49	49	1,560
Up to 0.5	29,109	9,965	7,252	6,768	4,511	269	251	-	2	2	-	21	8	-	60	2,129

Table 57 Household space type: rooms and household size – **continued**

Note: Maximum number of rooms in non-permanent accommodation is 5

57. Households with residents; residents in households; rooms in household spaces

New Forest

a	TOTAL HOUSE-HOLDS	Unshared dwellings - purpose-built — Detached	Unshared dwellings - purpose-built — Semi-detached	Unshared dwellings - purpose-built — Terraced	Purpose-built flat in: Residential building	Purpose-built flat in: Commercial building	Unshared dwellings - converted — Converted flat	Unshared dwellings - converted — Converted flatlet	Unshared dwellings - not self-contained — Not self-contained flat	Unshared dwellings - not self-contained — Not self-contained 'rooms'	Unshared dwellings - not self-contained — Bedsit	Other household spaces - not self-contained — Not self-contained flat	Other household spaces - not self-contained — Not self-contained 'rooms'	Other household spaces - not self-contained — Bedsit	Non-permanent accommodation	With migrant head
	b	c	d	e	f	g	h	i	j	k	l	m	n	o	p	q
Households with the following rooms																
TOTAL	**65,411**	**31,330**	**14,479**	**11,028**	**5,375**	**872**	**863**	**44**	**28**	**6**	**7**	**49**	**44**	**100**	**1,186**	**5,663**
1	675	15	4	9	450	12	-	44	3	4	7	-	29	100	34	159
2	1,681	51	98	215	977	60	118		4	1		6	10		120	333
3	3,699	322	488	748	1,422	131	205		8	1		14	1		354	575
4	12,906	4,387	2,663	2,806	1,963	285	262		-	-		10	-		520	1,394
5	20,004	8,418	5,709	4,901	486	210	116		6	-		6	1		158	1,473
6	14,005	7,782	4,197	1,786	50	107	73		7	-		3	3		-	907
7 or more	12,441	10,355	1,320	563	27	67	89			-		10			-	822
TOTAL ROOMS	**349,572**	**190,170**	**75,978**	**53,428**	**17,451**	**3,893**	**3,762**	**44**	**163**	**15**	**7**	**224**	**131**	**100**	**4,206**	**27,443**
Households with the following persons																
TOTAL	**65,411**	**31,330**	**14,479**	**11,028**	**5,375**	**872**	**863**	**44**	**28**	**6**	**7**	**49**	**44**	**100**	**1,186**	**5,663**
1	16,235	5,777	2,998	2,767	3,357	268	411	35	6	1	3	22	12	77	501	1,292
2	25,541	13,377	5,346	3,897	1,663	325	314	8	13	5	2	16	17	13	545	2,310
3	9,570	4,605	2,525	1,867	239	143	67	1	4	-	2	4	13	7	93	914
4	9,978	5,404	2,554	1,719	107	96	45	-	4	-	-	6	1	2	40	801
5	3,164	1,703	819	574	8	29	21	-	1	-	-	1	1	1	7	258
6	718	372	179	154	1	7	4	-	-	-	-	-	-	-	-	62
7 or more	205	92	58	50	-	4	1	-	-	-	-	-	-	-	-	26
TOTAL PERSONS	**157,604**	**79,396**	**37,087**	**27,202**	**7,874**	**1,953**	**1,557**	**54**	**65**	**11**	**13**	**95**	**95**	**137**	**2,065**	**13,713**
Households with the following persons per room																
TOTAL	**65,411**	**31,330**	**14,479**	**11,028**	**5,375**	**872**	**863**	**44**	**28**	**6**	**7**	**49**	**44**	**100**	**1,186**	**5,663**
Over 1.5	180	18	16	19	65	4	1	9	-	-	4	-	1	23	20	56
Over 1 and up to 1.5	526	84	154	210	22	18	11	-	-	-	-	-	10	-	17	100
Over 0.5 and up to 1	19,017	7,645	5,029	4,085	1,294	291	185	35	10	4	3	19	19	77	321	1,961
Up to 0.5	45,688	23,583	9,280	6,714	3,994	559	666	-	18	2	-	30	14	-	828	3,546

Table 57 Household space type: rooms and household size – continued

Note: Maximum number of rooms in non-permanent accommodation is 5

57. Households with residents; residents in households; rooms in household spaces

Portsmouth

| a | TOTAL HOUSE-HOLDS | Unshared dwellings - purpose-built | | | Purpose-built flat in: | | Unshared dwellings - converted | | Unshared dwellings - not self-contained | | | Other household spaces - not self-contained | | | Non-permanent accomm-odation | With migrant head |
| | | Detached | Semi-detached | Terraced | Residential building | Commercial building | Converted flat | Converted flatlet | Not self-contained flat | Not self-contained 'rooms' | Bedsit | Not self-contained flat | Not self-contained 'rooms' | Bedsit | | |
a	b	c	d	e	f	g	h	i	j	k	l	m	n	o	p	q
Households with the following rooms																
TOTAL	**72,590**	**2,408**	**9,398**	**38,064**	**14,457**	**1,354**	**4,637**	**239**	**44**	**12**	**40**	**432**	**254**	**1,123**	**128**	**7,987**
1	1,946	3	17	37	446	41	-	239	9	4	40	100	137	1,123	-	701
2	3,168	5	52	200	1,779	115	749		14	6		131	60		18	681
3	6,927	27	132	720	3,667	324	1,769		13	2		108	30		77	1,212
4	11,918	257	640	3,901	5,124	356	1,462		1			31	12		25	1,618
5	19,863	482	2,464	13,215	2,920	295	435		1			32	5		8	1,828
6	20,759	531	4,156	15,368	397	137	132		6			30	10			1,350
7 or more	8,009	1,103	1,937	4,623	124	86	90									597
TOTAL ROOMS	**362,219**	**15,608**	**55,444**	**211,277**	**53,513**	**5,643**	**16,357**	**239**	**166**	**34**	**40**	**1,627**	**741**	**1,123**	**407**	**34,003**
Households with the following persons																
TOTAL	**72,590**	**2,408**	**9,398**	**38,064**	**14,457**	**1,354**	**4,637**	**239**	**44**	**12**	**40**	**432**	**254**	**1,123**	**128**	**7,987**
1	22,009	417	1,668	8,781	7,078	469	2,021	162	19	7	27	217	143	939	61	2,499
2	25,105	925	3,339	13,483	4,401	488	1,946	60	16	5	7	150	74	153	58	2,962
3	11,093	429	1,610	6,807	1,471	177	475	14	3	-	5	43	27	26	6	1,227
4	9,669	434	1,879	6,113	926	145	141	3	3	-	-	12	5	5	3	870
5	3,359	156	625	2,069	398	52	45	-	3	-	-	8	3	-	-	307
6	970	36	193	584	136	12	5	-	-	-	1	2	1	-	-	79
7 or more	385	11	84	227	47	11	4	-	-	-	-	-	1	-	-	43
TOTAL PERSONS	**169,730**	**6,368**	**25,602**	**96,207**	**27,171**	**2,976**	**8,188**	**336**	**87**	**17**	**62**	**746**	**420**	**1,343**	**207**	**17,932**
Households with the following persons per room																
TOTAL	**72,590**	**2,408**	**9,398**	**38,064**	**14,457**	**1,354**	**4,637**	**239**	**44**	**12**	**40**	**432**	**254**	**1,123**	**128**	**7,987**
Over 1.5	442	1	7	51	69	22	15	77	-	-	13	-	3	184	-	179
Over 1 and up to 1.5	980	10	113	446	264	46	70	-	1	-	-	12	15	-	3	112
Over 0.5 and up to 1	23,102	582	3,087	11,715	4,289	497	1,545	162	17	4	27	120	69	939	49	3,189
Up to 0.5	48,066	1,815	6,191	25,852	9,835	789	3,007	-	26	8	-	300	167	-	76	4,507

Table 57 Household space type: rooms and household size – **continued**

Note: Maximum number of rooms in non-permanent accommodation is 5

57. Households with residents; residents in households; rooms in household spaces

Rushmoor

| | TOTAL HOUSE-HOLDS | Unshared dwellings - purpose-built | | | | | Unshared dwellings - converted | | Unshared dwellings - not self-contained | | | Other household spaces - not self-contained | | | Non-permanent accomm-odation | With migrant head |
| | | Detached | Semi-detached | Terraced | Purpose-built flat in: Residential building | Commercial building | Converted flat | Converted flatlet | Not self-contained flat | Not self-contained 'rooms' | Bedsit | Not self-contained flat | Not self-contained 'rooms' | Bedsit | | |
a	b	c	d	e	f	g	h	i	j	k	l	m	n	o	p	q
Households with the following rooms																
TOTAL	**30,523**	**5,052**	**9,620**	**9,028**	**4,965**	**414**	**621**	**37**	**11**	**6**	**3**	**51**	**45**	**465**	**205**	**4,115**
1	779	1	7	5	235	18	114	37	-	5	3	11	20	465	8	331
2	1,073	5	19	141	703	33	189		3	1		15	14		22	216
3	2,367	41	140	412	1,370	122	199		2	-		9	7		60	440
4	5,606	275	812	2,095	2,002	120	67		3	-		8	1		85	952
5	9,082	925	3,721	3,682	580	65	28		2	-		5	2		30	1,055
6	7,362	1,448	3,579	2,205	58	35	24		1	-		3	1			724
7 or more	4,254	2,357	1,342	488	17	21										397
TOTAL ROOMS	**154,294**	**32,711**	**53,677**	**45,200**	**17,174**	**1,629**	**2,282**	**37**	**52**	**13**	**3**	**195**	**134**	**465**	**722**	**18,473**
Households with the following persons																
TOTAL	**30,523**	**5,052**	**9,620**	**9,028**	**4,965**	**414**	**621**	**37**	**11**	**6**	**3**	**51**	**45**	**465**	**205**	**4,115**
1	6,558	636	1,393	1,439	2,231	134	213	26	4	2	1	17	20	337	105	805
2	10,440	1,684	3,120	3,179	1,809	149	291	9	1	3	1	20	12	87	75	1,526
3	5,590	966	1,963	1,873	558	75	79	2	1	1	-	9	9	35	19	818
4	5,626	1,231	2,241	1,791	279	39	29	-	3	-	-	2	1	5	5	709
5	1,696	404	674	517	73	12	7	-	1	-	1	3	2	1	1	182
6	468	106	171	173	12	4	1	-	-	-	-	-	1	-	-	54
7 or more	145	25	58	56	3	1	1	-	1	-	-	-	-	-	-	21
TOTAL PERSONS	**79,121**	**14,678**	**27,336**	**24,629**	**9,097**	**904**	**1,197**	**50**	**35**	**11**	**8**	**107**	**91**	**641**	**337**	**10,554**
Households with the following persons per room																
TOTAL	**30,523**	**5,052**	**9,620**	**9,028**	**4,965**	**414**	**621**	**37**	**11**	**6**	**3**	**51**	**45**	**465**	**205**	**4,115**
Over 1.5	199	1	16	10	20	4	2	11	-	-	2	2	2	128	1	110
Over 1 and up to 1.5	424	19	105	192	79	13	7	-	1	1	-	4	3	-	-	68
Over 0.5 and up to 1	12,056	1,622	3,951	3,893	1,704	175	247	26	6	3	1	16	17	337	58	1,910
Up to 0.5	17,844	3,410	5,548	4,933	3,162	222	365	-	4	2	-	29	23	-	146	2,027

Table 57 Household space type: rooms and household size – continued

57. Households with residents; residents in households; rooms in household spaces

Note: Maximum number of rooms in non-permanent accommodation is 5

Southampton

Column groupings — Household space type in permanent buildings: columns c–e *Unshared dwellings – purpose-built* (Detached, Semi-detached, Terraced); f–g *Purpose-built flat in:* (Residential building, Commercial building); h–i *Unshared dwellings – converted* (Converted flat, Converted flatlet); j–l *Unshared dwellings – not self-contained* (Not self-contained flat, Not self-contained 'rooms', Bedsit); m–o *Other household spaces – not self-contained* (Not self-contained flat, Not self-contained 'rooms', Bedsit).

	Total house-holds	Detached	Semi-detached	Terraced	Resid. building	Comm. building	Converted flat	Converted flatlet	Not self-cont. flat	Not self-cont. 'rooms'	Bedsit	Not self-cont. flat	Not self-cont. 'rooms'	Bedsit	Non-permanent accomm.	With migrant head
	b	c	d	e	f	g	h	i	j	k	l	m	n	o	p	q
Households with the following rooms																
TOTAL	**81,140**	**11,665**	**21,757**	**20,196**	**21,014**	**1,022**	**2,711**	**369**	**54**	**18**	**52**	**274**	**292**	**1,647**	**69**	**8,917**
1	3,224	8	29	38	1,036	30	-	369		9	52		164	1,647	15	1,291
2	5,424	18	31	212	4,234	108	566		3	6		67	74		12	1,132
3	8,734	173	236	675	6,232	203	1,018		12	1		83	26		22	1,386
4	16,130	1,615	2,106	3,931	7,302	276	789		23	2		50	10		11	1,713
5	21,528	2,776	7,417	8,929	1,877	263	214		6	-		25	11		9	1,610
6	17,777	3,753	8,870	4,717	247	99	61		2	-		17	7			1,120
7 or more	8,323	3,322	3,068	1,694	86	43	63		8			32				665
TOTAL ROOMS	**382,726**	**69,417**	**122,382**	**103,847**	**69,136**	**4,204**	**9,304**	**369**	**244**	**50**	**52**	**1,054**	**826**	**1,647**	**194**	**34,468**
Households with the following persons																
TOTAL	**81,140**	**11,665**	**21,757**	**20,196**	**21,014**	**1,022**	**2,711**	**369**	**54**	**18**	**52**	**274**	**292**	**1,647**	**69**	**8,917**
1	24,178	2,158	3,945	3,680	10,803	338	1,258	248	18	8	37	134	165	1,366	20	3,142
2	27,326	4,566	7,506	6,573	6,677	358	1,102	104	27	7	7	82	86	202	29	3,135
3	12,427	1,954	3,935	3,887	2,100	155	245	13	2	2	5	31	30	60	8	1,266
4	11,058	2,022	4,054	3,695	1,064	96	78	4	4	1	1	15	6	10	8	877
5	4,282	696	1,642	1,545	308	54	17	-	2	-	-	6	5	5	3	343
6	1,317	191	506	537	52	16	8	-	1	-	-	3	3	3	-	106
7 or more	552	78	169	279	10	5	3	-	-	-	2	3	1	1	1	48
TOTAL PERSONS	**193,866**	**30,468**	**59,484**	**56,370**	**36,640**	**2,305**	**4,664**	**511**	**110**	**32**	**86**	**522**	**478**	**2,040**	**156**	**19,435**
Households with the following persons per room																
TOTAL	**81,140**	**11,665**	**21,757**	**20,196**	**21,014**	**1,022**	**2,711**	**369**	**54**	**18**	**52**	**274**	**292**	**1,647**	**69**	**8,917**
Over 1.5	820	5	37	87	220	14	15	121	-	1	15	10	2	281	12	350
Over 1 and up to 1.5	1,644	66	368	633	426	38	73	-	-	2	-	8	25	-	5	190
Over 0.5 and up to 1	29,070	3,220	7,618	8,343	6,801	390	855	248	14	6	37	63	80	1,366	29	3,932
Up to 0.5	49,606	8,374	13,734	11,133	13,567	580	1,768	-	40	9	-	193	185	-	23	4,445

Table 57 Household space type: rooms and household size – **continued**

Note: Maximum number of rooms in non-permanent accommodation is 5

57. Households with residents; residents in households; rooms in household spaces

Test Valley

a	TOTAL HOUSE-HOLDS	Unshared dwellings - purpose-built			Purpose-built flat in:		Unshared dwellings - converted		Unshared dwellings - not self-contained			Other household spaces - not self-contained			Non-permanent accomm-odation	With migrant head
		Detached	Semi-detached	Terraced	Residential building	Commercial building	Converted flat	Converted flatlet	Not self-contained flat	Not self-contained 'rooms'	Bedsit	Not self-contained flat	Not self-contained 'rooms'	Bedsit		
	b	c	d	e	f	g	h	i	j	k	l	m	n	o	p	q
Households with the following rooms																
TOTAL	**38,391**	**14,385**	**9,524**	**9,954**	**3,244**	**247**	**539**	**20**	**15**	**2**	**8**	**18**	**10**	**45**	**380**	**4,181**
1	229	4	2	4	116	1	-	20			8			45	29	69
2	976	21	66	135	629	17	67		5			9	1		40	178
3	2,378	94	335	429	1,157	44	183		4	1		1	2		120	381
4	5,686	1,000	1,557	1,704	1,041	74	145		2			3	5		154	778
5	11,903	2,719	4,002	4,755	257	65	63		2			3	-		37	1,193
6	8,153	3,421	2,496	2,137	34	26	33			1		2	1			795
7 or more	9,066	7,126	1,066	790	10	20	48		1							787
TOTAL ROOMS	**213,730**	**96,880**	**50,407**	**51,002**	**10,618**	**1,094**	**2,186**	**20**	**68**	**11**	**8**	**80**	**41**	**45**	**1,270**	**21,658**
Households with the following persons																
TOTAL	**38,391**	**14,385**	**9,524**	**9,954**	**3,244**	**247**	**539**	**20**	**15**	**2**	**8**	**18**	**10**	**45**	**380**	**4,181**
1	8,091	1,875	1,796	1,878	1,937	62	265	14	7	1	5	6	6	39	200	749
2	13,454	5,399	3,456	3,128	1,033	82	189	5	5	-	2	4	1	4	146	1,603
3	6,744	2,536	1,785	2,104	193	57	42	1	2	-	-	2	2	1	20	801
4	7,179	3,308	1,834	1,892	67	29	31	-	-	-	1	4	1	1	10	739
5	2,226	968	517	700	11	15	9	-	1	-	-	2	-	-	3	219
6	559	239	117	197	1	-	3	-	-	1	-	-	-	-	1	54
7 or more	138	60	19	55	2	2	-	-	-	-	-	-	-	-	-	16
TOTAL PERSONS	**99,463**	**40,244**	**24,828**	**27,098**	**4,925**	**605**	**956**	**28**	**29**	**6**	**13**	**46**	**18**	**54**	**613**	**10,849**
Households with the following persons per room																
TOTAL	**38,391**	**14,385**	**9,524**	**9,954**	**3,244**	**247**	**539**	**20**	**15**	**2**	**8**	**18**	**10**	**45**	**380**	**4,181**
Over 1.5	76	8	3	10	26	5	1	6	-	-	3	-	-	6	8	19
Over 1 and up to 1.5	321	43	84	149	24	9	6	-	-	-	-	-	-	-	6	40
Over 0.5 and up to 1	12,670	3,719	3,492	4,270	770	91	146	14	4	1	5	10	2	39	107	1,628
Up to 0.5	25,324	10,615	5,945	5,525	2,424	142	386	-	11	1	-	8	8	-	259	2,494

Table 57 Household space type: rooms and household size – continued

Note: Maximum number of rooms in non-permanent accommodation is 5

57. Households with residents; residents in households; rooms in household spaces

Winchester

	TOTAL HOUSE-HOLDS	Unshared dwellings - purpose-built: Detached	Semi-detached	Terraced	Purpose-built flat in: Residential building	Purpose-built flat in: Commercial building	Unshared dwellings - converted: Converted flat	Converted flatlet	Unshared dwellings - not self-contained: Not self-contained flat	Not self-contained 'rooms'	Bedsit	Other household spaces - not self-contained: Not self-contained flat	Not self-contained 'rooms'	Bedsit	Non-permanent accommodation	With migrant head
a	b	c	d	e	f	g	h	i	j	k	l	m	n	o	p	q
Households with the following rooms																
TOTAL	**37,553**	**14,449**	**9,291**	**8,257**	**3,601**	**370**	**825**	**40**	**12**	**3**	**3**	**47**	**20**	**117**	**518**	**3,705**
1	353	1	3	7	147	8	-	40	1	2	3	-	10	117	27	133
2	974	16	48	188	531	26	104		2	1		9	3		39	230
3	2,833	90	258	609	1,401	54	239		-			10	2		166	444
4	5,875	751	1,324	2,002	1,287	92	180		5			9	1		226	727
5	8,906	2,333	3,020	3,056	200	108	112		-			8	-		60	775
6	7,967	3,108	3,099	1,622	25	46	62		2			4				616
7 or more	10,645	8,150	1,539	773	10	36	128		2			7				780
TOTAL ROOMS	**214,940**	**102,186**	**51,856**	**41,341**	**11,783**	**1,686**	**3,780**	**40**	**61**	**7**	**3**	**210**	**63**	**117**	**1,807**	**18,733**
Households with the following persons																
TOTAL	**37,553**	**14,449**	**9,291**	**8,257**	**3,601**	**370**	**825**	**40**	**12**	**3**	**3**	**47**	**20**	**117**	**518**	**3,705**
1	9,364	2,023	1,752	2,488	2,237	117	386	29	6	1	2	27	17	87	192	962
2	13,149	5,357	3,253	2,769	1,071	120	298	11	3	2	1	11	1	17	235	1,312
3	5,866	2,440	1,664	1,350	217	53	69		1	-	-	4	2	9	57	621
4	6,267	3,169	1,808	1,098	63	53	51		2	-	-	1	-	1	21	570
5	2,218	1,129	594	431	12	21	19		-	-	-	1	-	3	8	182
6	566	277	178	95	1	5	2		-	-	-	3	-	-	5	44
7 or more	123	54	42	26	-	1	-		-	-	-	-	-	-	-	14
TOTAL PERSONS	**93,721**	**40,443**	**24,825**	**19,385**	**5,348**	**870**	**1,500**	**51**	**23**	**5**	**5**	**88**	**25**	**167**	**987**	**9,008**
Households with the following persons per room																
TOTAL	**37,553**	**14,449**	**9,291**	**8,257**	**3,601**	**370**	**825**	**40**	**12**	**3**	**3**	**47**	**20**	**117**	**518**	**3,705**
Over 1.5	99	4	8	11	12	2	-	11	-	-	1	1	-	30	19	47
Over 1 and up to 1.5	263	17	102	93	21	10	6	-	-	-	-	-	-	-	14	29
Over 0.5 and up to 1	10,604	3,314	3,197	2,632	841	140	180	29	2	2	2	12	-	87	165	1,272
Up to 0.5	26,587	11,114	5,984	5,521	2,727	218	639	-	10	1	-	34	19	-	320	2,357

Table 58 Household space type: tenure and amenities

58. Households with residents

HAMPSHIRE

Tenure and amenities	TOTAL HOUSE-HOLDS	Unshared dwellings - purpose-built			Purpose-built flat in:		Unshared dwellings - converted		Unshared dwellings - not self-contained			Other household spaces - not self-contained			Non-permanent accommodation
		Detached	Semi-detached	Terraced	Residential building	Commercial building	Converted flat	Converted flatlet	Not self-contained flat	Not self-contained 'rooms'	Bedsit	Not self-contained flat	Not self-contained 'rooms'	Bedsit	
a	b	c	d	e	f	g	h	i	j	k	l	m	n	o	p
TOTAL HOUSEHOLDS	**603,257**	**170,620**	**148,119**	**171,521**	**81,983**	**6,611**	**12,626**	**951**	**213**	**69**	**126**	**1,066**	**810**	**4,034**	**4,508**
Owner occupied - owned outright	146,621	61,697	37,496	30,481	10,944	640	1,819	31	36	8	2	169	82	19	3,197
- buying	291,358	98,610	77,393	92,376	15,732	1,511	4,475	173	67	4	5	228	68	60	656
Rented privately - furnished	22,247	2,725	2,920	5,056	2,485	1,066	2,912	462	59	41	95	429	447	3,283	267
- unfurnished	19,113	3,152	4,485	5,054	2,487	1,284	1,859	103	25	10	11	160	101	220	162
Rented with a job or business	17,834	3,571	4,740	4,856	2,353	1,699	357	25	12	1	5	22	11	61	121
Rented from a housing association	11,951	223	941	2,587	7,260	56	573	94	2	-	3	20	20	161	11
Rented from a local authority or new town	94,133	642	20,144	31,111	40,722	355	631	63	12	5	5	38	81	230	94
Exclusive use of bath/shower and inside WC	**596,184**	**170,213**	**147,621**	**170,261**	**80,786**	**6,455**	**12,626**	**951**	**213**		**70**	**1,066**	**50**	**1,781**	**4,141**
With central heating - all rooms	422,275	150,588	102,510	100,829	52,528	3,365	7,430	529	144		38	546	11	954	2,814
- some rooms	82,670	12,923	20,716	31,441	14,647	856	1,317	63	18		3	104	4	111	471
No central heating	91,239	6,702	24,395	37,991	13,611	2,234	3,879	359	51		29	416	35	716	856
Exclusive use of bath/shower, shared or no inside WC	**1,410**	**164**	**254**	**642**	**79**	**42**	-	-		**5**	**4**			**62**	**108**
With central heating - all rooms	277	57	46	48	50	23	-	-		1	2			15	24
- some rooms	130	19	28	48	17	3	-	-		1	-			5	5
No central heating	1,003	88	180	546	12	16	-	-		3	2			42	79
Exclusive use of inside WC, shared or no bath/shower	**1,306**	**73**	**88**	**182**	**796**	**13**	-	-		**9**	**1**		**63**	**43**	**38**
With central heating - all rooms	839	9	16	11	744	4	-	-		3	-		26	22	4
- some rooms	63	8	6	11	27	-	-	-		-	-		4	3	4
No central heating	404	56	66	160	25	9	-	-		6	1		33	18	30
Lacking or sharing use of bath/shower and inside WC	**4,357**	**170**	**156**	**436**	**322**	**101**	-	-		**55**	**51**		**697**	**2,148**	**221**
With central heating - all rooms	1,736	21	15	17	236	41	-	-		33	29		302	1,018	24
- some rooms	239	4	8	10	19	11	-	-		6	1		53	123	4
No central heating	2,382	145	133	409	67	49	-	-		16	21		342	1,007	193

Table 58 Household space type: tenure and amenities – **continued**

58. Households with residents

Basingstoke & Deane

Tenure and amenities	TOTAL HOUSE-HOLDS	Detached	Semi-detached	Terraced	Purpose-built flat in: Residential building	Purpose-built flat in: Commercial building	Converted flat	Converted flatlet	Unshared not self-cont: Not self-contained flat	Unshared not self-cont: Not self-contained 'rooms'	Unshared not self-cont: Bedsit	Other spaces: Not self-contained flat	Other spaces: Not self-contained 'rooms'	Other spaces: Bedsit	Non-permanent accommodation
a	b	c	d	e	f	g	h	i	j	k	l	m	n	o	p
TOTAL HOUSEHOLDS	54,323	16,947	12,602	18,498	5,051	330	368	64	11	6	2	37	23	124	260
Owner occupied - owned outright	9,010	4,329	2,374	1,556	509	13	52	1	5	2	-	5	1	2	161
- buying	29,599	11,309	6,533	9,963	1,535	63	119	1	3	-	-	12	8	3	50
Rented privately - furnished	1,254	250	205	406	158	22	65	11	2	3	1	8	8	98	18
- unfurnished	1,385	368	458	349	105	52	29	3	-	1	1	6	-	3	10
Rented with a job or business	2,032	588	774	399	76	116	45	6	1	-	-	3	4	5	14
Rented from a housing association	1,228	22	128	490	537	9	7	33	-	-	-	-	1	1	-
Rented from a local authority or new town	9,815	81	2,130	5,335	2,131	55	51	9	-	-	-	3	1	12	7
Exclusive use of bath/shower and inside WC	**54,030**	**16,905**	**12,570**	**18,465**	**5,017**	**326**	**368**	**64**	**11**	**6**	**1**	**37**		**39**	**227**
With central heating - all rooms	43,204	15,275	9,600	13,481	4,067	225	289	53	9		1	31		23	150
- some rooms	6,767	1,148	1,706	3,336	464	41	32	3	-			3		6	28
No central heating	4,059	482	1,264	1,648	486	60	47	8	2			3		10	49
Exclusive use of bath/shower, shared or no inside WC	**47**	**12**	**10**	**12**	**6**	**4**									**2**
With central heating - all rooms	22	4	6	4	4	4									
- some rooms	3	1	-	1	1										
No central heating	22	7	4	7	1										2
Exclusive use of inside WC, shared or no bath/shower	**24**	**3**	**5**	**12**	**3**										**1**
With central heating - all rooms	6	-	2	2	2										
- some rooms	5	2	1	1	1										
No central heating	13	1	2	9											1
Lacking or sharing use of bath/shower and inside WC	**222**	**27**	**17**	**9**	**25**						**1**		**23**	**85**	**30**
With central heating - all rooms	127	8	-	3	25								16	68	1
- some rooms	2	1	-	-	-								1	-	-
No central heating	93	18	17	6									6	17	29

Table 58 Household space type: tenure and amenities – continued

58. Households with residents

East Hampshire

Tenure and amenities	TOTAL HOUSE-HOLDS	Unshared dwellings - purpose-built			Purpose-built flat in:		Unshared dwellings - converted		Unshared dwellings - not self-contained			Other household spaces - not self-contained			Non-permanent accomm-odation
		Detached	Semi-detached	Terraced	Residential building	Commercial building	Converted flat	Converted flatlet	Not self-contained flat	Not self-contained 'rooms'	Bedsit	Not self-contained flat	Not self-contained 'rooms'	Bedsit	
a	b	c	d	e	f	g	h	i	j	k	l	m	n	o	p
TOTAL HOUSEHOLDS	**39,158**	**16,833**	**9,402**	**7,791**	**3,433**	**375**	**643**	**35**	**17**	**4**	**-**	**38**	**17**	**82**	**488**
Owner occupied - owned outright	10,192	5,827	2,009	1,169	646	42	148	2	4	-	-	10	1	-	334
- buying	20,296	9,812	4,948	4,127	940	106	252	10	5	1	-	12	2	1	80
Rented privately - furnished	1,001	329	178	216	86	30	60	7	-	3	-	9	4	40	39
- unfurnished	1,258	323	361	330	60	77	76	3	3	-	-	3	2	3	17
Rented with a job or business	1,629	475	436	464	64	101	61	3	2	-	-	2	3	1	17
Rented from a housing association	435	27	51	86	225	4	25	8	-	-	-	-	1	8	-
Rented from a local authority or new town	4,347	40	1,419	1,399	1,412	15	21	2	3	-	-	2	4	29	1
Exclusive use of bath/shower and inside WC	**38,814**	**16,796**	**9,363**	**7,751**	**3,319**	**365**	**643**	**35**	**17**	**-**	**-**	**38**	**-**	**39**	**448**
With central heating - all rooms	30,089	14,971	6,428	5,057	2,507	237	493	25	11	-	-	29	-	28	303
- some rooms	4,832	1,196	1,348	1,701	384	39	94	5	2	-	-	5	-	9	49
No central heating	3,893	629	1,587	993	428	89	56	5	4	-	-	4	-	2	96
Exclusive use of bath/shower, shared or no inside WC	**61**	**17**	**13**	**14**	**3**	**5**	**-**	**-**	**-**	**2**	**-**	**-**	**2**	**-**	**5**
With central heating - all rooms	15	4	3	1	3	3	-	-	-	1	-	-	-	-	-
- some rooms	7	1	2	1	-	-	-	-	-	1	-	-	2	-	-
No central heating	39	12	8	12	-	2	-	-	-	-	-	-	-	-	5
Exclusive use of inside WC, shared or no bath/shower	**130**	**7**	**11**	**6**	**92**	**2**	**-**	**-**	**-**	**-**	**-**	**-**	**1**	**4**	**7**
With central heating - all rooms	99	2	2	-	90	-	-	-	-	-	-	-	1	3	1
- some rooms	4	-	-	-	2	-	-	-	-	-	-	-	-	1	1
No central heating	27	5	9	6	-	2	-	-	-	-	-	-	-	-	5
Lacking or sharing use of bath/shower and inside WC	**153**	**13**	**15**	**20**	**19**	**3**	**-**	**-**	**-**	**2**	**-**	**-**	**14**	**39**	**28**
With central heating - all rooms	72	-	1	2	19	3	-	-	-	2	-	-	11	31	3
- some rooms	10	1	2	2	-	-	-	-	-	-	-	-	1	3	-
No central heating	71	12	12	16	-	-	-	-	-	-	-	-	2	5	24

Household space type in permanent buildings

Table 58 Household space type: tenure and amenities – continued

58. Households with residents

Eastleigh

Tenure and amenities	TOTAL HOUSE-HOLDS	Unshared dwellings - purpose-built			Purpose-built flat in:		Unshared dwellings - converted		Unshared dwellings - not self-contained			Other household spaces - not self-contained			Non-permanent accommodation
		Detached	Semi-detached	Terraced	Residential building	Commercial building	Converted flat	Converted flatlet	Not self-contained flat	Not self-contained 'rooms'	Bedsit	Not self-contained flat	Not self-contained 'rooms'	Bedsit	
a	b	c	d	e	f	g	h	i	j	k	l	m	n	o	p
TOTAL HOUSEHOLDS	41,219	14,306	12,119	9,558	3,998	311	297	8	3	2	3	23	24	112	455
Owner occupied - owned outright	9,538	4,648	2,480	1,345	668	23	37	-	1	-	-	6	2	3	325
- buying	24,015	9,240	7,069	6,161	1,245	59	146	4	2	-	-	7	3	1	78
Rented privately - furnished	956	149	162	262	141	45	56	1	-	2	3	6	10	94	25
- unfurnished	883	140	246	303	87	47	46	1	-	-	-	2	1	5	5
Rented with a job or business	332	79	65	45	35	89	7	-	-	-	-	-	-	7	5
Rented from a housing association	770	18	93	189	446	19	1	2	-	-	-	-	-	1	1
Rented from a local authority or new town	4,725	32	2,004	1,253	1,376	29	4	-	-	-	-	2	8	1	16
Exclusive use of bath/shower and inside WC	40,941	14,283	12,085	9,527	3,941	305	297	8	3	2	2	20	-	53	414
With central heating - all rooms	31,168	13,168	8,456	5,892	2,903	173	219	5	2	2	2	16	-	46	286
- some rooms	5,156	798	2,006	1,765	473	36	23	3	1	-	-	4	-	3	48
No central heating	4,617	317	1,623	1,870	565	96	55	-	-	-	-	-	-	4	80
Exclusive use of bath/shower, shared or no inside WC	61	13	19	15	-	3	-	-	-	-	-	-	1	-	10
With central heating - all rooms	22	6	6	4	-	3	-	-	-	-	-	-	-	-	3
- some rooms	6	2	3	-	-	-	-	-	-	-	-	-	1	-	-
No central heating	33	5	10	11	-	-	-	-	-	-	-	-	-	-	7
Exclusive use of inside WC, shared or no bath/shower	70	4	5	3	51	-	-	-	-	-	-	2	2	1	4
With central heating - all rooms	55	-	1	-	51	-	-	-	-	-	-	2	2	1	1
- some rooms	1	-	-	-	-	-	-	-	-	-	-	-	-	-	-
No central heating	14	4	4	3	-	-	-	-	-	-	-	-	-	-	3
Lacking or sharing use of bath/shower and inside WC	147	6	10	13	6	3	-	-	-	-	1	1	21	58	27
With central heating - all rooms	54	1	-	2	5	1	-	-	-	-	1	1	10	30	2
- some rooms	11	-	1	-	1	-	-	-	-	-	-	-	3	6	-
No central heating	82	5	9	11	-	2	-	-	-	-	-	-	8	22	25

Table 58 Household space type: tenure and amenities – **continued**

58. Households with residents

Fareham

a	b	c	d	e	f	g	h	i	j	k	l	m	n	o	p
Tenure and amenities	TOTAL HOUSE-HOLDS	Household space type in permanent buildings — Unshared dwellings - purpose-built — Detached	Semi-detached	Terraced	Purpose-built flat in: Residential building	Commercial building	Unshared dwellings - converted — Converted flat	Converted flatlet	Unshared dwellings - not self-contained — Not self-contained flat	Not self-contained 'rooms'	Bedsit	Other household spaces - not self-contained — Not self-contained flat	Not self-contained 'rooms'	Bedsit	Non-permanent accomm-odation
TOTAL HOUSEHOLDS	**38,369**	**13,157**	**13,104**	**8,118**	**3,206**	**231**	**176**	**13**	**3**	**4**	**-**	**18**	**15**	**37**	**287**
Owner occupied - owned outright	11,328	4,483	4,521	1,412	623	30	48	-	1	-	-	3	4	-	203
- buying	21,671	8,234	7,529	5,054	697	62	48	2	2	1	-	7	1	1	33
Rented privately - furnished	782	181	201	212	68	32	23	-	-	2	-	3	3	27	30
- unfurnished	719	120	213	245	51	41	27	2	-	-	-	4	4	1	11
Rented with a job or business	546	116	104	202	42	62	8	-	-	1	-	-	-	2	9
Rented from a housing association	254	6	16	20	199	-	7	3	-	-	-	-	-	3	-
Rented from a local authority or new town	3,069	17	520	973	1,526	4	15	6	-	-	-	1	3	3	1
Exclusive use of bath/shower and inside WC	**38,140**	**13,141**	**13,079**	**8,076**	**3,113**	**226**	**176**	**13**	**3**	**-**	**-**	**18**	**-**	**25**	**270**
With central heating - all rooms	29,711	11,944	9,722	5,356	2,221	115	127	12	1	-	-	12	-	16	185
- some rooms	3,891	853	1,616	1,054	285	24	17	-	1	-	-	2	-	6	33
No central heating	4,538	344	1,741	1,666	607	87	32	1	1	-	-	4	-	3	52
Exclusive use of bath/shower, shared or no inside WC	**57**	**5**	**15**	**21**	**5**	**3**	**-**	**-**	**-**	**-**	**-**	**-**	**-**	**1**	**5**
With central heating - all rooms	23	2	4	3	4	3	-	-	-	-	-	-	-	1	4
- some rooms	8	3	2	2	1	-	-	-	-	-	-	-	-	-	1
No central heating	26	-	9	16	-	-	-	-	-	-	-	-	-	-	-
Exclusive use of inside WC, shared or no bath/shower	**106**	**7**	**5**	**4**	**85**	**1**	**-**	**-**	**-**	**1**	**-**	**-**	**-**	**-**	**3**
With central heating - all rooms	86	1	1	-	82	1	-	-	-	1	-	-	-	-	-
- some rooms	3	-	-	-	3	-	-	-	-	-	-	-	-	-	-
No central heating	17	6	4	4	-	-	-	-	-	-	-	-	-	-	3
Lacking or sharing use of bath/shower and inside WC	**66**	**4**	**5**	**17**	**3**	**1**	**-**	**-**	**-**	**3**	**-**	**-**	**13**	**11**	**9**
With central heating - all rooms	23	2	3	-	3	1	-	-	-	1	-	-	6	6	1
- some rooms	3	-	-	1	-	-	-	-	-	-	-	-	2	-	-
No central heating	40	2	2	16	-	-	-	-	-	2	-	-	5	5	8

Table 58 Household space type: tenure and amenities – **continued**

58. Households with residents

Gosport

Tenure and amenities	TOTAL HOUSE-HOLDS	Household space type in permanent buildings — Unshared dwellings - purpose-built — Detached	Semi-detached	Terraced	Purpose-built flat in: Residential building	Commercial building	Unshared dwellings - converted — Converted flat	Converted flatlet	Unshared dwellings - not self-contained — Not self-contained flat	Not self-contained 'rooms'	Bedsit	Other household spaces - not self-contained — Not self-contained flat	Not self-contained 'rooms'	Bedsit	Non-permanent accommodation
a	b	c	d	e	f	g	h	i	j	k	l	m	n	o	p
TOTAL HOUSEHOLDS	29,356	3,442	7,739	12,067	5,259	360	304	8	3	1	2	26	9	48	88
Owner occupied - owned outright	6,491	1,441	2,021	2,133	737	34	50	-	1	-	-	3	1	-	70
- buying	14,090	1,858	4,188	6,703	1,115	88	112	5	1	-	1	4	2	2	11
Rented privately - furnished	865	52	113	275	211	66	85	2	-	1	1	10	4	43	2
- unfurnished	784	14	136	346	152	85	37	1	1	-	-	8	1	1	2
Rented with a job or business	1,383	42	217	564	476	79	2	-	-	-	-	-	-	-	3
Rented from a housing association	631	3	82	75	457	1	13	-	-	-	-	1	1	-	-
Rented from a local authority or new town	5,112	32	982	1,971	2,111	7	5	-	-	-	-	1	1	2	-
Exclusive use of bath/shower and inside WC	29,139	3,440	7,722	12,008	5,175	355	304	8	3	-	2	26	-	21	75
With central heating - all rooms	17,286	2,949	4,735	6,301	2,928	151	158	3	2	-	-	12	-	13	34
- some rooms	6,755	351	1,789	3,023	1,491	45	35	1	-	-	-	6	-	1	13
No central heating	5,098	140	1,198	2,684	756	159	111	4	1	-	2	8	-	7	28
Exclusive use of bath/shower, shared or no inside WC	40	-	10	24	2	3	-	-	-	-	-	-	1	-	-
With central heating - all rooms	7	-	2	3	1	1	-	-	-	-	-	-	-	-	-
- some rooms	6	-	2	3	1	-	-	-	-	-	-	-	-	-	-
No central heating	27	-	6	18	-	2	-	-	-	-	-	-	1	-	-
Exclusive use of inside WC, shared or no bath/shower	81	2	6	6	65	-	-	-	-	-	-	-	-	1	1
With central heating - all rooms	64	-	1	-	62	-	-	-	-	-	-	-	-	1	-
- some rooms	3	1	-	-	2	-	-	-	-	-	-	-	-	-	-
No central heating	14	1	5	6	1	-	-	-	-	-	-	-	-	-	1
Lacking or sharing use of bath/shower and inside WC	96	-	1	29	17	2	-	-	-	1	-	-	8	26	12
With central heating - all rooms	33	-	-	1	17	2	-	-	-	-	-	-	3	8	2
- some rooms	9	-	-	-	-	-	-	-	-	1	-	-	2	6	-
No central heating	54	-	1	28	-	-	-	-	-	-	-	-	3	12	10

Table 58 Household space type: tenure and amenities – **continued**

58. Households with residents

Hart

Column group structure — *Household space type in permanent buildings*: **Unshared dwellings - purpose-built** (c Detached, d Semi-detached, e Terraced, and *Purpose-built flat in:* f Residential building, g Commercial building); **Unshared dwellings - converted** (h Converted flat, i Converted flatlet); **Unshared dwellings - not self-contained** (j Not self-contained flat, k Not self-contained 'rooms', l Bedsit). *Other household spaces - not self-contained*: m Not self-contained flat, n Not self-contained 'rooms', o Bedsit. p Non-permanent accommodation.

Tenure and amenities	TOTAL HOUSE-HOLDS	Detached	Semi-detached	Terraced	Residential building	Commercial building	Converted flat	Converted flatlet	Not self-contained flat	Not self-contained 'rooms'	Bedsit	Not self-contained flat	Not self-contained 'rooms'	Bedsit	Non-permanent accommodation
a	b	c	d	e	f	g	h	i	j	k	l	m	n	o	p
TOTAL HOUSEHOLDS	**29,073**	**13,378**	**7,455**	**5,479**	**1,868**	**222**	**256**	**15**	**5**	**1**	**3**	**20**	**14**	**27**	**330**
Owner occupied - owned outright	6,072	3,217	1,530	665	334	14	65	-	1	1	-	5	2	-	238
- buying	17,484	9,418	4,021	3,347	525	39	101	1	2	-	-	8	3	-	19
Rented privately - furnished	915	275	176	244	88	28	37	9	-	-	1	4	8	24	21
- unfurnished	719	184	223	170	46	46	25	2	1	-	-	2	1	1	17
Rented with a job or business	1,252	248	407	456	25	91	12	-	-	-	1	-	-	-	12
Rented from a housing association	301	8	29	81	171	-	9	1	-	-	1	-	-	1	1
Rented from a local authority or new town	2,330	28	1,069	516	679	4	7	2	1	-	-	1	-	1	22
Exclusive use of bath/shower and inside WC	**28,923**	**13,356**	**7,435**	**5,458**	**1,863**	**218**	**256**	**15**	**5**	-	**1**	**20**	-	**5**	**291**
With central heating - all rooms	24,733	12,614	5,699	4,370	1,488	106	205	11	3	-	1	16	-	5	215
- some rooms	2,344	541	713	771	233	37	26	2	1	-	-	2	-	-	18
No central heating	1,846	201	1,023	317	142	75	25	2	1	-	-	2	-	-	58
Exclusive use of bath/shower, shared or no inside WC	**44**	**9**	**4**	**1**	**4**	-	-	-	-	-	-	-	-	-	**26**
With central heating - all rooms	19	7	1	1	4	-	-	-	-	-	-	-	-	-	6
- some rooms	3	-	1	-	-	-	-	-	-	-	-	-	-	-	2
No central heating	22	2	2	-	-	-	-	-	-	-	-	-	-	-	18
Exclusive use of inside WC, shared or no bath/shower	**24**	**4**	**4**	**8**	-	**1**	-	-	-	-	-	-	**5**	-	**2**
With central heating - all rooms	9	2	2	-	-	-	-	-	-	-	-	-	5	-	-
- some rooms	2	1	1	-	-	-	-	-	-	-	-	-	-	-	-
No central heating	13	1	1	8	-	1	-	-	-	-	-	-	-	-	2
Lacking or sharing use of bath/shower and inside WC	**82**	**9**	**12**	**12**	**1**	**3**	-	-	-	**1**	**2**	-	**9**	**22**	**11**
With central heating - all rooms	37	2	1	-	1	3	-	-	-	1	2	-	5	19	3
- some rooms	4	-	2	-	-	-	-	-	-	-	-	-	2	-	-
No central heating	41	7	9	12	-	-	-	-	-	-	-	-	2	3	8

Table 58 Household space type: tenure and amenities – continued

58. Households with residents

Havant

Tenure and amenities	TOTAL HOUSE-HOLDS	Unshared dwellings - purpose-built			Purpose-built flat in:		Unshared dwellings - converted		Unshared dwellings - not self-contained			Other household spaces not self-contained			Non-permanent accomm-odation
		Detached	Semi-detached	Terraced	Residential building	Commercial building	Converted flat	Converted flatlet	Not self-contained flat	Not self-contained 'rooms'	Bedsit	Not self-contained flat	Not self-contained 'rooms'	Bedsit	
a	b	c	d	e	f	g	h	i	j	k	l	m	n	o	p
TOTAL HOUSEHOLDS	**46,151**	**13,268**	**11,629**	**13,483**	**6,512**	**503**	**386**	**59**	**7**	**4**	**3**	**33**	**43**	**107**	**114**
Owner occupied - owned outright	11,465	5,670	3,398	1,479	723	51	63	3	-	1	-	6	2	-	69
- buying	22,044	7,117	6,395	7,415	897	96	85	4	3	-	-	5	5	3	19
Rented privately - furnished	1,195	243	184	197	174	96	153	46	3	3	2	14	10	59	11
- unfurnished	717	96	185	168	91	107	47	6	-	-	1	4	-	3	9
Rented with a job or business	486	72	100	95	87	119	8	-	-	-	-	-	-	-	5
Rented from a housing association	400	11	20	85	270	3	7	-	-	-	-	-	-	3	1
Rented from a local authority or new town	9,844	59	1,347	4,044	4,270	31	23	-	1	-	-	4	26	39	-
Exclusive use of bath/shower and inside WC	**45,762**	**13,252**	**11,614**	**13,455**	**6,307**	**500**	**386**	**59**	**7**	**2**	**2**	**14**	**16**	**43**	**105**
With central heating - all rooms	29,735	11,669	8,144	5,740	3,635	225	202	15	5	1	-	6	10	26	57
- some rooms	6,547	1,054	1,479	2,865	1,020	77	37	1	1	-	-	3	2	1	7
No central heating	9,480	529	1,991	4,850	1,652	198	147	43	1	1	2	5	4	16	41
Exclusive use of bath/shower, shared or no inside WC	**42**	**9**	**8**	**13**	**6**	-	-	-	-	-	**1**	-	**2**	**1**	**2**
With central heating - all rooms	12	4	1	2	3	-	-	-	-	-	-	-	2	-	-
- some rooms	2	-	2	-	-	-	-	-	-	-	-	-	-	-	-
No central heating	28	5	5	11	3	-	-	-	-	-	1	-	-	1	2
Exclusive use of inside WC, shared or no bath/shower	**184**	**5**	**1**	**3**	**166**	**1**	-	-	-	**1**	-	**3**	**4**	-	-
With central heating - all rooms	149	-	-	1	146	-	-	-	-	-	-	1	1	-	-
- some rooms	18	1	-	-	15	-	-	-	-	1	-	-	1	-	-
No central heating	17	4	1	2	5	1	-	-	-	-	-	2	2	-	-
Lacking or sharing use of bath/shower and inside WC	**163**	**2**	**6**	**12**	**33**	**2**	-	-	-	**1**	-	**16**	**21**	**63**	**7**
With central heating - all rooms	88	-	3	1	23	2	-	-	-	-	-	8	8	43	-
- some rooms	6	-	-	-	4	-	-	-	-	-	-	-	1	1	-
No central heating	69	2	3	11	6	-	-	-	-	1	-	8	12	19	7

Table 58 Household space type: tenure and amenities – continued

58. Households with residents

New Forest

Tenure and amenities	TOTAL HOUSE-HOLDS	Unshared dwellings - purpose-built			Purpose-built flat in:		Unshared dwellings - converted		Unshared dwellings - not self-contained			Other household spaces - not self-contained			Non-permanent accomm-odation
		Detached	Semi-detached	Terraced	Residential building	Commercial building	Converted flat	Converted flatlet	Not self-contained flat	Not self-contained 'rooms'	Bedsit	Not self-contained flat	Not self-contained 'rooms'	Bedsit	
a	b	c	d	e	f	g	h	i	j	k	l	m	n	o	p
TOTAL HOUSEHOLDS	65,411	31,330	14,479	11,028	5,375	872	863	44	28	6	7	49	44	100	1,186
Owner occupied - owned outright	23,921	14,945	3,596	2,262	1,821	119	259	4	8	1	-	10	7	-	889
- buying	29,067	14,570	6,904	5,735	1,205	233	255	4	8	-	-	16	2	2	133
Rented privately - furnished	1,613	463	262	318	152	96	147	16	5	2	4	10	7	68	63
- unfurnished	2,217	701	597	339	200	174	115	8	5	1	1	7	1	7	61
Rented with a job or business	1,499	538	390	127	154	220	40	3	2	-	-	2	1	1	21
Rented from a housing association	858	31	160	130	513	4	10	3	-	-	1	-	1	2	3
Rented from a local authority or new town	6,236	82	2,570	2,117	1,330	26	37	6	-	2	1	4	25	20	16
Exclusive use of bath/shower and inside WC	**64,821**	**31,214**	**14,409**	**10,989**	**5,205**	**858**	**863**	**44**	**28**		**3**	**49**		**41**	**1,118**
With central heating - all rooms	51,165	26,650	10,240	8,075	4,210	492	579	31	20		3	32		28	805
- some rooms	6,739	3,001	1,551	1,272	522	143	104	1	4		-	7		5	129
No central heating	6,917	1,563	2,618	1,642	473	223	180	12	4		-	10		8	184
Exclusive use of bath/shower, shared or no inside WC	**128**	**42**	**27**	**15**	**5**	**2**							**2**	**2**	**33**
With central heating - all rooms	30	10	5	1	4	2							1	1	6
- some rooms	14	6	3	2	1	-							-	1	1
No central heating	84	26	19	12	-	-							1	-	26
Exclusive use of inside WC, shared or no bath/shower	**164**	**23**	**15**	**8**	**100**	**1**				**2**			**4**	**3**	**8**
With central heating - all rooms	109	3	2	-	97	-				1			1	3	2
- some rooms	8	1	-	4	1	-				-			2	-	-
No central heating	47	19	13	4	2	1				1			1	-	6
Lacking or sharing use of bath/shower and inside WC	**298**	**51**	**28**	**16**	**65**	**11**				**4**	**4**		**38**	**54**	**27**
With central heating - all rooms	147	3	2	-	65	3				4	2		32	35	1
- some rooms	17	-	3	1	-	3				-	1		1	6	2
No central heating	134	48	23	15	-	5				-	1		5	13	24

Table 58 Household space type: tenure and amenities – continued

58. Households with residents

Portsmouth

Tenure and amenities (a)	TOTAL HOUSE-HOLDS (b)	Unshared dwellings - purpose-built: Detached (c)	Semi-detached (d)	Terraced (e)	Purpose-built flat in: Residential building (f)	Purpose-built flat in: Commercial building (g)	Unshared dwellings - converted: Converted flat (h)	Converted flatlet (i)	Unshared dwellings - not self-contained: Not self-contained flat (j)	Not self-contained 'rooms' (k)	Bedsit (l)	Other household spaces - not self-contained: Not self-contained flat (m)	Not self-contained 'rooms' (n)	Bedsit (o)	Non-permanent accommodation (p)
TOTAL HOUSEHOLDS	**72,590**	**2,408**	**9,398**	**38,064**	**14,457**	**1,354**	**4,637**	**239**	**44**	**12**	**40**	**432**	**254**	**1,123**	**128**
Owner occupied - owned outright	17,981	987	3,202	11,342	1,579	134	526	10	4	1	1	63	21	8	103
- buying	30,752	1,190	4,726	20,865	1,673	360	1,762	39	13	-	3	75	17	15	14
Rented privately - furnished	4,910	45	153	1,286	395	300	1,186	140	17	8	33	204	159	980	4
- unfurnished	3,064	38	136	1,270	534	264	632	23	5	3	2	72	44	41	-
Rented with a job or business	1,571	117	219	398	529	256	37	1	-	-	-	3	1	7	3
Rented from a housing association	2,247	10	51	353	1,395	5	337	21	2	-	1	11	9	52	-
Rented from a local authority or new town	12,065	21	911	2,550	8,352	35	157	5	3	-	-	4	3	20	4
Exclusive use of bath/shower and inside WC	**70,685**	**2,402**	**9,359**	**37,314**	**14,312**	**1,301**	**4,637**	**239**	**44**	-	**23**	**432**	-	**497**	**125**
With central heating - all rooms	35,028	1,957	5,420	17,231	7,160	569	2,208	77	16	-	7	153	-	168	62
- some rooms	10,775	257	1,386	5,574	2,880	135	451	18	1	-	-	38	-	18	17
No central heating	24,882	188	2,553	14,509	4,272	597	1,978	144	27	-	16	241	-	311	46
Exclusive use of bath/shower, shared or no inside WC	**568**	**5**	**34**	**455**	**12**	**10**	-	-	-	-	**4**	-	**20**	**28**	-
With central heating - all rooms	46	2	4	22	6	2	-	-	-	-	2	-	3	5	-
- some rooms	36	1	-	32	2	1	-	-	-	-	-	-	-	-	-
No central heating	486	2	30	401	4	7	-	-	-	-	2	-	17	23	-
Exclusive use of inside WC, shared or no bath/shower	**224**	**1**	**1**	**85**	**94**	**2**	-	-	-	**3**	**1**	-	**18**	**17**	**2**
With central heating - all rooms	100	1	1	4	85	1	-	-	-	-	-	-	4	5	-
- some rooms	5	-	-	3	-	-	-	-	-	-	-	-	1	-	-
No central heating	119	-	-	78	9	1	-	-	-	3	1	-	13	12	2
Lacking or sharing use of bath/shower and inside WC	**1,113**	-	**4**	**210**	**39**	**41**	-	-	-	**9**	**12**	-	**216**	**581**	**1**
With central heating - all rooms	250	-	1	5	19	7	-	-	-	2	4	-	59	152	1
- some rooms	57	-	-	3	3	6	-	-	-	3	-	-	12	30	-
No central heating	806	-	3	202	17	28	-	-	-	4	8	-	145	399	-

Table 58 Household space type: tenure and amenities – **continued**

58. Households with residents

Rushmoor

Tenure and amenities	TOTAL HOUSE-HOLDS	Unshared dwellings - purpose-built			Purpose-built flat in:		Unshared dwellings - converted		Unshared dwellings - not self-contained			Other household spaces - not self-contained			Non-permanent accomm-odation
		Detached	Semi-detached	Terraced	Residential building	Commercial building	Converted flat	Converted flatlet	Not self-contained flat	Not self-contained 'rooms'	Bedsit	Not self-contained flat	Not self-contained 'rooms'	Bedsit	
a	b	c	d	e	f	g	h	i	j	k	l	m	n	o	p
TOTAL HOUSEHOLDS	**30,523**	**5,052**	**9,620**	**9,028**	**4,965**	**414**	**621**	**37**	**11**	**6**	**3**	**51**	**45**	**465**	**205**
Owner occupied - owned outright	4,835	1,437	2,023	780	346	30	55	1	-	-	-	1	2	-	160
- buying	15,614	3,328	5,581	4,972	1,181	99	372	9	8	-	-	13	4	9	38
Rented privately - furnished	1,396	97	247	292	152	81	115	14	1	5	2	19	30	338	3
- unfurnished	874	62	261	291	82	73	44	9	1	-	1	5	3	41	1
Rented with a job or business	2,206	86	607	969	409	120	4	-	-	-	-	4	1	5	1
Rented from a housing association	590	5	34	110	418	1	1	-	-	-	-	-	-	21	-
Rented from a local authority or new town	5,008	37	867	1,614	2,377	10	30	4	1	1	-	9	5	51	2
Exclusive use of bath/shower and inside WC	**30,031**	**5,045**	**9,594**	**8,982**	**4,897**	**405**	**621**	**37**	**11**	**-**	**1**	**51**	**-**	**197**	**190**
With central heating - all rooms	24,168	4,593	7,699	6,711	4,158	228	445	20	8	-	1	33	-	132	140
- some rooms	3,720	327	1,248	1,441	563	42	57	8	1	-	-	4	-	15	14
No central heating	2,143	125	647	830	176	135	119	9	2	-	-	14	-	50	36
Exclusive use of bath/shower, shared or no inside WC	**32**	**4**	**9**	**10**	**2**	**-**	**-**	**-**	**-**	**-**	**-**	**-**	**2**	**3**	**2**
With central heating - all rooms	12	3	2	2	2	-	-	-	-	-	-	-	1	1	1
- some rooms	3	-	2	-	-	-	-	-	-	-	-	-	-	1	-
No central heating	17	1	5	8	-	-	-	-	-	-	-	-	1	1	1
Exclusive use of inside WC, shared or no bath/shower	**54**	**1**	**9**	**10**	**22**	**-**	**-**	**-**	**-**	**-**	**-**	**-**	**4**	**4**	**4**
With central heating - all rooms	27	-	2	-	22	-	-	-	-	-	-	-	-	3	-
- some rooms	3	-	2	-	-	-	-	-	-	-	-	-	-	-	1
No central heating	24	1	5	10	-	-	-	-	-	-	-	-	4	1	3
Lacking or sharing use of bath/shower and inside WC	**406**	**2**	**8**	**26**	**44**	**9**	**-**	**-**	**-**	**6**	**2**	**-**	**39**	**261**	**9**
With central heating - all rooms	238	1	1	1	30	5	-	-	-	4	1	-	26	169	-
- some rooms	11	-	-	1	1	-	-	-	-	-	-	-	-	8	1
No central heating	157	1	7	24	13	4	-	-	-	2	1	-	13	84	8

Household space type in permanent buildings

Table 58 Household space type: tenure and amenities – **continued**

58. Households with residents

Southampton

Tenure and amenities	TOTAL HOUSE-HOLDS	Unshared dwellings - purpose-built			Purpose-built flat in:		Unshared dwellings - converted		Unshared dwellings - not self-contained			Other household spaces - not self-contained			Non-permanent accomm-odation
		Detached	Semi-detached	Terraced	Residential building	Commercial building	Converted flat	Converted flatlet	Not self-contained flat	Not self-contained 'rooms'	Bedsit	Not self-contained flat	Not self-contained 'rooms'	Bedsit	
a	b	c	d	e	f	g	h	i	j	k	l	m	n	o	p
TOTAL HOUSEHOLDS	81,140	11,665	21,757	20,196	21,014	1,022	2,711	369	54	18	52	274	292	1,647	69
Owner occupied - owned outright	17,846	5,035	6,665	3,653	2,013	81	271	9	5	1	1	46	33	5	28
- buying	31,547	5,948	10,738	9,966	3,690	176	834	84	15	2	1	48	17	20	8
Rented privately - furnished	5,371	188	679	791	694	220	779	190	25	9	43	124	194	1,425	10
- unfurnished	3,501	300	753	563	840	218	587	40	8	4	3	38	35	109	3
Rented with a job or business	838	101	112	112	259	215	21	2	1	-	-	4	-	10	1
Rented from a housing association	2,752	15	73	555	1,895	3	114	23	-	-	1	8	8	55	2
Rented from a local authority or new town	19,285	78	2,737	4,556	11,623	109	105	21	-	2	3	6	5	23	17
Exclusive use of bath/shower and inside WC	79,440	11,638	21,638	20,083	20,856	993	2,711	369	54	17	27	274		745	52
With central heating - all rooms	46,603	9,384	12,973	9,778	11,683	446	1,475	228	41	10	17	147		414	17
- some rooms	15,597	1,238	3,235	5,064	5,521	148	286	20	6	1	2	27		42	8
No central heating	17,240	1,016	5,430	5,241	3,652	399	950	121	7	6	8	100		289	27
Exclusive use of bath/shower, shared or no inside WC	212	17	72	41	29	7				1			16	23	6
With central heating - all rooms	39	6	9	4	15	-				-			2	2	1
- some rooms	27	2	5	4	10	2				-			-	4	-
No central heating	146	9	58	33	4	5				1			14	17	5
Exclusive use of inside WC, shared or no bath/shower	158	4	19	25	70	3							23	12	2
With central heating - all rooms	84	-	1	1	61	2							12	6	1
- some rooms	7	-	1	2	3	-							-	1	-
No central heating	67	4	17	22	6	1							11	5	1
Lacking or sharing use of bath/shower and inside WC	1,330	6	28	47	59	19					25		253	867	9
With central heating - all rooms	563	2	2	1	19	9					15		105	399	1
- some rooms	95	-	-	1	10	1					-		25	57	-
No central heating	672	4	26	45	30	9					10		123	411	8

Table 58 Household space type: tenure and amenities – continued

58. Households with residents

Test Valley

Tenure and amenities	TOTAL HOUSE-HOLDS	Unshared dwellings - purpose-built: Detached	Semi-detached	Terraced	Purpose-built flat in: Residential building	Commercial building	Unshared dwellings - converted: Converted flat	Converted flatlet	Unshared dwellings - not self-contained: Not self-contained flat	Not self-contained 'rooms'	Bedsit	Other household spaces - not self-contained: Not self-contained flat	Not self-contained 'rooms'	Bedsit	Non-permanent accommodation
a	**b**	**c**	**d**	**e**	**f**	**g**	**h**	**i**	**j**	**k**	**l**	**m**	**n**	**o**	**p**
TOTAL HOUSEHOLDS	38,391	14,385	9,524	9,954	3,244	247	539	20	15	2	8	18	10	45	380
Owner occupied - owned outright	8,454	4,701	1,806	1,177	382	36	83	-	4	1	-	2	5	-	257
- buying	18,558	8,340	4,784	4,544	597	49	152	5	3	1	-	9	1	1	73
Rented privately - furnished	846	209	172	227	70	11	74	8	4	-	4	5	2	35	24
- unfurnished	1,561	453	505	310	160	39	73	3	-	-	1	2	2	2	11
Rented with a job or business	2,053	555	650	559	112	101	49	2	3	-	3	-	-	4	15
Rented from a housing association	589	47	147	160	228	1	6	-	-	-	-	-	-	-	-
Rented from a local authority or new town	6,330	80	1,460	2,977	1,695	10	102	2	1	-	-	-	-	3	-
Exclusive use of bath/shower and inside WC	38,208	14,343	9,498	9,932	3,221	243	539	20	15	-	7	18	-	27	345
With central heating - all rooms	29,642	12,649	6,861	6,752	2,527	166	391	17	14	-	5	15	-	23	222
- some rooms	5,485	1,095	1,442	2,419	383	35	62	1	1	-	1	1	-	1	44
No central heating	3,081	599	1,195	761	311	42	86	2	-	-	1	2	-	3	79
Exclusive use of bath/shower, shared or no inside WC	54	12	18	11	3	-	-	-	-	-	-	-	1	3	6
With central heating - all rooms	15	6	2	2	2	-	-	-	-	-	-	-	-	2	1
- some rooms	8	1	6	-	1	-	-	-	-	-	-	-	-	-	-
No central heating	31	5	10	9	-	-	-	-	-	-	-	-	1	1	5
Exclusive use of inside WC, shared or no bath/shower	32	5	2	3	17	1	-	-	-	-	-	-	2	-	2
With central heating - all rooms	19	1	-	2	16	-	-	-	-	-	-	-	-	-	-
- some rooms	2	-	1	-	-	-	-	-	-	-	-	-	-	-	1
No central heating	11	4	1	1	1	1	-	-	-	-	-	-	2	-	1
Lacking or sharing use of bath/shower and inside WC	97	25	6	8	3	3	-	-	-	2	1	-	7	15	27
With central heating - all rooms	29	1	-	-	2	1	-	-	-	2	1	-	4	13	5
- some rooms	5	1	-	1	-	1	-	-	-	-	-	-	2	-	-
No central heating	63	23	6	7	1	1	-	-	-	-	-	-	1	2	22

Table 58 Household space type: tenure and amenities – **continued**

58. Households with residents

Winchester

Tenure and amenities	TOTAL HOUSE-HOLDS	Unshared dwellings - purpose-built			Purpose-built flat in:		Unshared dwellings - converted		Unshared dwellings - not self-contained			Other household spaces - not self-contained			Non-permanent accomm-odation
		Detached	Semi-detached	Terraced	Residential building	Commercial building	Converted flat	Converted flatlet	Not self-contained flat	Not self-contained 'rooms'	Bedsit	Not self-contained flat	Not self-contained 'rooms'	Bedsit	
a	b	c	d	e	f	g	h	i	j	k	l	m	n	o	p
TOTAL HOUSEHOLDS	**37,553**	**14,449**	**9,291**	**8,257**	**3,601**	**370**	**825**	**40**	**12**	**3**	**3**	**47**	**20**	**117**	**518**
Owner occupied - owned outright	9,488	4,977	1,871	1,508	563	33	162	1	2	-	-	9	1	1	360
- buying	16,621	8,246	3,977	3,524	432	81	237	5	2	-	-	12	3	2	100
Rented privately - furnished	1,143	244	188	330	96	39	132	18	2	2	2	13	8	52	17
- unfurnished	1,431	353	411	370	79	61	121	2	1	1	-	7	7	3	15
Rented with a job or business	2,007	554	659	466	85	130	63	8	3	-	-	4	1	19	15
Rented from a housing association	896	20	57	253	506	6	36	-	-	-	1	1	-	14	3
Rented from a local authority or new town	5,967	55	2,128	1,806	1,840	20	74	6	2	-	1	1	-	26	8
Exclusive use of bath/shower and inside WC	**37,250**	**14,398**	**9,255**	**8,221**	**3,560**	**360**	**825**	**40**	**12**	-	**1**	**47**	-	**50**	**481**
With central heating - all rooms	29,743	12,765	6,533	6,085	3,041	232	639	32	12	-	1	34	-	31	338
- some rooms	4,062	1,064	1,197	1,156	428	54	93	3	-	-	-	2	-	2	63
No central heating	3,445	569	1,525	980	91	74	93	5	-	-	-	11	-	17	80
Exclusive use of bath/shower, shared or no inside WC	**64**	**19**	**15**	**10**	**2**	**5**	-	-	-	-	-	-	**1**	**1**	**11**
With central heating - all rooms	15	3	1	1	2	5	-	-	-	-	-	-	1	1	2
- some rooms	7	2	1	1	-	-	-	-	-	-	-	-	-	-	2
No central heating	42	14	13	8	-	-	-	-	-	-	-	-	-	-	7
Exclusive use of inside WC, shared or no bath/shower	**55**	**7**	**5**	**9**	**31**	**1**	-	-	-	-	-	-	-	-	**2**
With central heating - all rooms	32	-	1	1	30	-	-	-	-	-	-	-	-	-	-
- some rooms	2	1	-	1	-	-	-	-	-	-	-	-	-	-	-
No central heating	21	6	4	7	1	1	-	-	-	-	-	-	-	-	2
Lacking or sharing use of bath/shower and inside WC	**184**	**25**	**16**	**17**	**8**	**4**	-	-	-	**3**	**2**	-	**19**	**66**	**24**
With central heating - all rooms	75	1	1	1	8	4	-	-	-	-	2	-	9	45	4
- some rooms	9	1	-	-	-	-	-	-	-	1	-	-	1	6	-
No central heating	100	23	15	16	-	-	-	-	-	2	-	-	9	15	20

695

Table 59 Household space type: household composition

Note: * May include a small number of households with no resident adults

59. Households with residents; residents in households

Household composition		TOTAL HOUSE-HOLDS	Household space type in permanent buildings						
			Unshared dwellings - purpose-built					Unshared dwellings - converted	
						Purpose-built flat in:			
Adults	Dependent children		Detached	Semi-detached	Terraced	Residential building	Commercial building	Converted flat	Converted flatlet
a	b	c	d	e	f	g	h	i	j

HAMPSHIRE

Household composition		TOTAL HOUSE-HOLDS	Detached	Semi-detached	Terraced	Residential building	Commercial building	Converted flat	Converted flatlet
All households*		**603,257**	**170,620**	**148,119**	**171,521**	**81,983**	**6,611**	**12,626**	**951**
1 adult of pensionable age	0	83,475	16,497	16,292	17,822	28,641	502	2,108	140
1 adult under pensionable age	0	61,769	8,490	10,083	17,425	15,425	1,542	3,463	525
1 adult any age	1 or more	20,396	2,323	4,181	7,964	4,760	257	418	23
2 adults (1 male and 1 female)	0	188,932	61,249	47,638	49,961	21,056	1,944	4,260	195
	1 or more	128,863	41,924	35,883	41,373	6,739	1,043	1,118	41
2 adults (same sex)	0	15,320	3,138	3,590	5,337	2,193	281	506	16
	1 or more	3,078	658	804	1,233	292	31	40	1
3 or more adults (male(s) and female(s))	0	66,348	23,753	19,919	19,248	2,065	610	484	6
	1 or more	31,977	11,953	8,913	9,879	640	327	167	1
3 or more adults (same sex)	0	2,604	528	699	1,096	139	61	55	-
	1 or more	380	84	107	156	20	9	2	-
Households containing persons of pensionable age only (any number)		144,528	38,720	32,365	30,670	36,749	705	2,874	151
Households containing persons aged 75 and over only (any number)		56,381	12,708	10,964	11,184	19,083	282	1,320	87
All dependent children		334,808	104,148	92,012	111,544	19,773	2,716	2,573	84
Dependent children aged 0 - 4		103,087	23,583	27,785	37,845	10,556	931	1,260	63
Dependent children aged 5 - 15		205,709	68,246	57,812	67,470	8,683	1,567	1,109	17
Persons pensionable age - 74		168,857	55,106	44,462	38,998	24,553	870	2,342	71
Persons aged 75 - 84		78,049	21,645	17,767	16,518	19,260	383	1,450	76
Persons aged 85 and over		17,543	4,967	3,522	3,306	5,100	80	371	18

Basingstoke & Deane

Household composition		TOTAL HOUSE-HOLDS	Detached	Semi-detached	Terraced	Residential building	Commercial building	Converted flat	Converted flatlet
All households*		**54,323**	**16,947**	**12,602**	**18,498**	**5,051**	**330**	**368**	**64**
1 adult of pensionable age	0	5,659	1,087	1,328	1,537	1,545	24	50	35
1 adult under pensionable age	0	5,340	870	841	1,905	1,341	66	90	21
1 adult any age	1 or more	1,568	221	294	883	141	7	3	1
2 adults (1 male and 1 female)	0	16,916	5,594	4,157	5,376	1,419	117	135	5
	1 or more	12,855	4,996	3,120	4,264	320	56	57	1
2 adults (same sex)	0	1,245	272	273	525	141	13	10	-
	1 or more	266	62	57	135	7	2	2	-
3 or more adults (male(s) and female(s))	0	6,777	2,474	1,748	2,406	98	26	10	-
	1 or more	3,429	1,301	730	1,334	31	17	11	1
3 or more adults (same sex)	0	224	56	48	112	8	-	-	-
	1 or more	39	11	5	21	-	2	-	-
Households containing persons of pensionable age only (any number)		9,931	2,517	2,628	2,635	1,916	40	82	36
Households containing persons aged 75 and over only (any number)		3,769	782	847	1,008	1,027	18	35	29
All dependent children		32,967	12,074	7,568	12,201	730	144	135	5
Dependent children aged 0 - 4		9,952	2,951	2,467	3,929	450	48	47	3
Dependent children aged 5 - 15		20,407	7,788	4,599	7,549	265	87	68	2
Persons pensionable age - 74		12,505	3,881	3,747	3,493	1,166	43	78	7
Persons aged 75 - 84		5,343	1,403	1,367	1,426	1,030	22	44	23
Persons aged 85 and over		1,155	327	277	275	251	4	7	7

	Household space type in permanent buildings					Non-perm-anent accomm-odation	Households with migrant head	Persons in households with migrant head	Household composition	
Unshared dwellings - not self-contained			Other household spaces - not self-contained							
Not self-contained flat	Not self-contained 'rooms'	Bedsit	Not self-contained flat	Not self-contained 'rooms'	Bedsit				Adults	Dependent children
k	l	m	n	o	p	q	r	s	a	b
213	69	126	1,066	810	4,034	4,508	61,190	148,291	**All households***	
30	14	4	156	111	228	930	3,120	3,120	1 adult of pensionable age	0
40	19	78	342	306	2,980	1,051	11,939	11,939	1 adult under pensionable age	0
9	10	8	74	94	196	79	3,849	10,042	1 adult any age	1 or more
57	16	11	261	150	362	1,772	19,059	38,118	2 adults (1 male and 1 female)	0
25	3	6	113	95	157	343	15,343	58,373		1 or more
21	4	6	43	21	49	115	1,946	3,892	2 adults (same sex)	0
-	-	1	3	1	5	9	312	1,127		1 or more
12	1	3	48	15	22	162	3,167	10,819	3 or more adults (male(s) and female(s))	0
16	2	3	12	12	10	42	1,755	8,536		1 or more
3	-	4	10	4	3	2	608	2,079	3 or more adults (same sex)	0
-	-	-	2	-	-	-	37	173		1 or more
47	18	4	228	132	234	1,631	4,817	6,527	Households containing persons of pensionable age only (any number)	
25	16	1	115	57	77	462	1,681	1,999	Households containing persons aged 75 and over only (any number)	
80	19	24	345	293	457	740	37,260		All dependent children	
34	8	14	152	182	362	312	17,814		Dependent children aged 0 - 4	
40	8	6	180	101	71	399	17,978		Dependent children aged 5 - 15	
38	2	5	178	105	166	1,961	5,487		Persons pensionable age - 74	
25	16	2	128	54	69	656	2,246		Persons aged 75 - 84	
14	4	-	37	20	15	89	433		Persons aged 85 and over	
11	6	2	37	23	124	260	5,253	12,763	**All households***	
1	4	1	3	1	3	40	215	215	1 adult of pensionable age	0
2	-	1	16	13	91	83	1,006	1,006	1 adult under pensionable age	0
-	-	-	1	1	11	5	256	677	1 adult any age	1 or more
5	2	-	8	3	13	82	1,766	3,532	2 adults (1 male and 1 female)	0
2	-	-	6	3	3	27	1,331	5,019		1 or more
-	-	-	2	-	1	8	164	328	2 adults (same sex)	0
-	-	-	-	-	-	1	19	74		1 or more
1	-	-	1	2	2	9	297	1,023	3 or more adults (male(s) and female(s))	0
-	-	-	-	-	-	4	152	725		1 or more
-	-	-	-	-	-	-	43	151	3 or more adults (same sex)	0
-	-	-	-	-	-	-	3	12		1 or more
4	4	1	5	1	4	58	318	421	Households containing persons of pensionable age only (any number)	
2	3	-	3	1	2	12	131	152	Households containing persons aged 75 and over only (any number)	
4	-	-	16	4	19	67	3,034		All dependent children	
-	-	-	4	2	15	36	1,488		Dependent children aged 0 - 4	
4	-	-	11	2	3	29	1,426		Dependent children aged 5 - 15	
5	1	1	4	2	3	74	347		Persons pensionable age - 74	
2	2	-	3	1	2	18	160		Persons aged 75 - 84	
1	1	-	-	-	-	5	37		Persons aged 85 and over	

Table 59 Household space type: household composition – **continued**

Note: * May include a small number of households with no resident adults

59. Households with residents; residents in households

Household composition		TOTAL HOUSE-HOLDS	Household space type in permanent buildings						
			Unshared dwellings - purpose-built					Unshared dwellings - converted	
			Detached	Semi-detached	Terraced	Purpose-built flat in:		Converted flat	Converted flatlet
Adults	Dependent children					Residential building	Commercial building		
a	b	c	d	e	f	g	h	i	j

East Hampshire

All households*		39,158	16,833	9,402	7,791	3,433	375	643	35
1 adult of pensionable age	0	5,103	1,574	1,032	786	1,389	36	159	5
1 adult under pensionable age	0	3,338	844	730	834	556	89	117	21
1 adult any age	1 or more	1,084	253	266	351	169	17	6	-
2 adults (1 male and 1 female)	0	12,622	5,887	3,003	2,256	909	101	219	5
	1 or more	9,371	4,412	2,353	2,169	241	57	72	3
2 adults (same sex)	0	810	282	211	205	74	13	13	-
	1 or more	189	68	63	47	7	-	1	-
3 or more adults (male(s) and female(s))	0	4,311	2,197	1,196	756	68	40	36	1
	1 or more	2,179	1,260	506	350	15	18	16	-
3 or more adults (same sex)	0	119	47	31	28	5	4	3	-
	1 or more	24	5	10	7	-	-	1	-
Households containing persons of pensionable age only (any number)		9,017	3,652	1,930	1,260	1,705	41	210	5
Households containing persons aged 75 and over only (any number)		3,670	1,235	693	526	1,036	13	114	1
All dependent children		23,613	11,216	5,931	5,409	571	138	181	5
Dependent children aged 0 - 4		6,821	2,467	1,867	1,942	366	49	55	2
Dependent children aged 5 - 15		14,596	7,316	3,640	3,191	195	73	100	3
Persons pensionable age - 74		10,436	5,099	2,605	1,394	877	57	139	5
Persons aged 75 - 84		5,058	2,119	1,066	701	978	12	109	-
Persons aged 85 and over		1,190	464	217	161	288	3	39	1

Eastleigh

All households*		41,219	14,306	12,119	9,558	3,998	311	297	8
1 adult of pensionable age	0	4,874	1,125	1,231	898	1,439	41	45	1
1 adult under pensionable age	0	4,010	699	784	1,222	901	65	81	3
1 adult any age	1 or more	1,208	205	399	418	145	10	9	-
2 adults (1 male and 1 female)	0	13,426	5,026	3,823	3,118	1,104	84	110	1
	1 or more	9,863	3,864	3,314	2,346	213	53	30	2
2 adults (same sex)	0	902	230	222	307	110	9	7	-
	1 or more	193	53	62	63	10	2	1	-
3 or more adults (male(s) and female(s))	0	4,491	2,043	1,567	759	62	30	7	1
	1 or more	2,096	1,013	677	376	8	11	4	-
3 or more adults (same sex)	0	134	40	37	43	6	5	2	-
	1 or more	19	8	3	7	-	1	-	-
Households containing persons of pensionable age only (any number)		8,768	2,671	2,451	1,575	1,835	49	49	1
Households containing persons aged 75 and over only (any number)		3,208	823	794	580	927	24	26	-
All dependent children		24,064	9,240	8,382	5,670	471	129	71	2
Dependent children aged 0 - 4		7,318	2,119	2,547	2,204	322	48	31	2
Dependent children aged 5 - 15		14,919	6,115	5,319	3,202	130	70	33	-
Persons pensionable age - 74		10,801	3,995	3,423	1,944	1,202	37	34	1
Persons aged 75 - 84		4,516	1,458	1,239	823	902	25	27	-
Persons aged 85 and over		1,058	332	261	172	274	7	5	-

	Household space type in permanent buildings					Non-perm-anent accomm-odation	Households with migrant head	Persons in households with migrant head	Household composition		
Unshared dwellings - not self-contained			Other household spaces - not self-contained								
Not self-contained flat	Not self-contained 'rooms'	Bedsit	Not self-contained flat	Not self-contained 'rooms'	Bedsit				Adults		Dependent children
k	l	m	n	o	p	q	r	s	a		b
17	4	-	38	17	82	488	3,884	9,998	**All households***		
3	-	-	6	-	10	103	200	200	1 adult of pensionable age		0
1	2	-	8	5	39	92	563	563	1 adult under pensionable age		0
1	1	-	3	3	3	11	217	574	1 adult any age		1 or more
4	-	-	8	4	15	211	1,277	2,554	2 adults (1 male and 1 female)		0
3	-	-	9	3	12	37	1,184	4,525			1 or more
1	-	-	2	1	1	7	73	146	2 adults (same sex)		0
-	-	-	-	-	1	2	20	68			1 or more
1	-	-	-	-	1	15	196	661	3 or more adults (male(s) and female(s))		0
3	1	-	1	1	-	8	121	590			1 or more
-	-	-	-	-	-	1	29	97	3 or more adults (same sex)		0
-	-	-	1	-	-	-	3	18			1 or more
5	-	-	10	-	10	189	310	420	Households containing persons of pensionable age only (any number)		
3	-	-	5	-	4	40	113	140	Households containing persons aged 75 and over only (any number)		
10	3	-	22	9	20	98	2,748		All dependent children		
3	1	-	3	6	15	45	1,222		Dependent children aged 0 - 4		
4	1	-	16	2	5	50	1,400		Dependent children aged 5 - 15		
3	-	-	6	1	6	244	349		Persons pensionable age - 74		
3	-	-	5	-	2	63	158		Persons aged 75 - 84		
3	-	-	3	-	2	9	23		Persons aged 85 and over		
3	2	3	23	24	112	455	3,901	9,241	**All households***		
1	1	-	2	4	3	83	185	185	1 adult of pensionable age		0
1	-	3	5	9	93	144	728	728	1 adult under pensionable age		0
-	-	-	4	5	2	11	211	560	1 adult any age		1 or more
-	-	-	6	4	8	142	1,405	2,810	2 adults (1 male and 1 female)		0
-	-	-	2	1	5	33	936	3,529			1 or more
-	-	-	1	-	-	16	116	232	2 adults (same sex)		0
-	-	-	-	-	-	2	18	65			1 or more
-	1	-	1	1	1	18	182	609	3 or more adults (male(s) and female(s))		0
1	-	-	1	-	-	5	87	413			1 or more
-	-	-	1	-	-	-	29	99	3 or more adults (same sex)		0
-	-	-	-	-	-	-	2	9			1 or more
1	1	-	4	4	3	124	282	380	Households containing persons of pensionable age only (any number)		
-	1	-	2	1	2	28	115	133	Households containing persons aged 75 and over only (any number)		
1	-	-	11	9	7	71	2,168		All dependent children		
-	-	-	3	4	7	31	1,056		Dependent children aged 0 - 4		
-	-	-	8	5	-	37	1,034		Dependent children aged 5 - 15		
1	-	-	4	3	1	156	302		Persons pensionable age - 74		
-	1	-	3	1	1	36	135		Persons aged 75 - 84		
-	-	-	1	-	1	5	31		Persons aged 85 and over		

Table 59 Household space type: household composition – **continued**

Note: * May include a small number of households with no resident adults

59. Households with residents; residents in households

Household composition		TOTAL HOUSE-HOLDS	Household space type in permanent buildings						
			Unshared dwellings - purpose-built					Unshared dwellings - converted	
Adults	Dependent children		Detached	Semi-detached	Terraced	Purpose-built flat in:		Converted flat	Converted flatlet
						Residential building	Commercial building		
a	b	c	d	e	f	g	h	i	j

Fareham

All households*		38,369	13,157	13,104	8,118	3,206	231	176	13
1 adult of pensionable age	0	4,723	1,063	1,525	668	1,324	15	51	8
1 adult under pensionable age	0	3,099	613	903	902	528	51	19	1
1 adult any age	1 or more	989	186	286	338	156	10	4	-
2 adults (1 male and 1 female)	0	13,212	4,885	4,737	2,434	852	79	59	3
	1 or more	8,583	3,276	2,967	2,101	174	25	21	1
2 adults (same sex)	0	849	215	269	266	75	12	6	-
	1 or more	174	60	54	48	10	2	-	-
3 or more adults (male(s) and female(s))	0	4,542	1,908	1,654	874	62	24	8	-
	1 or more	2,069	902	667	455	22	10	8	-
3 or more adults (same sex)	0	111	39	37	30	2	3	-	-
	1 or more	15	7	5	2	1	-	-	-
Households containing persons of pensionable age only (any number)		8,961	2,627	3,172	1,193	1,723	24	68	9
Households containing persons aged 75 and over only (any number)		3,248	788	1,057	415	901	7	38	6
All dependent children		20,878	7,907	6,989	5,270	532	75	57	2
Dependent children aged 0 - 4		6,351	1,913	2,191	1,907	289	22	12	-
Dependent children aged 5 - 15		12,808	5,119	4,286	3,063	226	48	38	2
Persons pensionable age - 74		11,224	4,057	4,163	1,592	1,128	40	48	4
Persons aged 75 - 84		4,793	1,373	1,722	668	918	10	43	5
Persons aged 85 and over		945	290	296	120	223	3	6	1

Gosport

All households*		29,356	3,442	7,739	12,067	5,259	360	304	8
1 adult of pensionable age	0	4,161	383	784	1,241	1,653	20	56	1
1 adult under pensionable age	0	2,704	157	398	1,043	879	58	90	1
1 adult any age	1 or more	1,232	42	269	610	284	13	10	-
2 adults (1 male and 1 female)	0	9,075	1,393	2,381	3,419	1,593	133	105	5
	1 or more	6,705	620	1,982	3,449	547	70	24	1
2 adults (same sex)	0	746	76	178	332	141	12	2	-
	1 or more	165	11	46	93	15	-	-	-
3 or more adults (male(s) and female(s))	0	2,941	495	1,086	1,209	102	31	13	-
	1 or more	1,487	247	579	599	37	20	3	-
3 or more adults (same sex)	0	123	14	30	66	8	3	1	-
	1 or more	14	3	5	6	-	-	-	-
Households containing persons of pensionable age only (any number)		6,957	941	1,588	2,110	2,179	31	75	1
Households containing persons aged 75 and over only (any number)		2,795	274	531	824	1,105	14	38	-
All dependent children		17,134	1,611	5,414	8,664	1,208	159	49	2
Dependent children aged 0 - 4		5,529	287	1,389	2,985	773	66	19	-
Dependent children aged 5 - 15		10,455	1,086	3,596	5,244	400	88	25	2
Persons pensionable age - 74		7,820	1,416	2,254	2,529	1,488	41	52	1
Persons aged 75 - 84		3,729	487	870	1,185	1,131	15	31	-
Persons aged 85 and over		813	118	166	204	291	10	21	-

Unshared dwellings - not self-contained			Other household spaces - not self-contained			Non-permanent accommodation	Households with migrant head	Persons in households with migrant head	Household composition	
Not self-contained flat	Not self-contained 'rooms'	Bedsit	Not self-contained flat	Not self-contained 'rooms'	Bedsit				Adults	Dependent children
k	l	m	n	o	p	q	r	s	a	b
3	4	-	18	15	37	287	3,412	8,472	**All households***	
-	1	-	4	2	6	56	203	203	1 adult of pensionable age	0
-	2	-	2	5	24	49	510	510	1 adult under pensionable age	0
-	-	-	1	3	1	4	133	348	1 adult any age	1 or more
2	1	-	7	3	6	144	1,199	2,398	2 adults (1 male and 1 female)	0
-	-	-	2	1	-	15	940	3,580		1 or more
-	-	-	1	-	-	5	100	200	2 adults (same sex)	0
-	-	-	-	-	-	-	15	54		1 or more
1	-	-	1	1	-	9	196	658	3 or more adults (male(s) and female(s))	0
-	-	-	-	-	-	5	92	441		1 or more
-	-	-	-	-	-	-	22	71	3 or more adults (same sex)	0
-	-	-	-	-	-	-	2	9		1 or more
-	2	-	6	2	6	129	323	443	Households containing persons of pensionable age only (any number)	
-	2	-	3	1	3	27	118	144	Households containing persons aged 75 and over only (any number)	
-	-	-	5	6	1	34	2,079		All dependent children	
-	-	-	4	3	1	9	943		Dependent children aged 0 - 4	
-	-	-	1	3	-	22	1,052		Dependent children aged 5 - 15	
-	-	-	5	2	3	182	391		Persons pensionable age - 74	
-	2	-	4	-	3	45	148		Persons aged 75 - 84	
-	1	-	1	1	-	3	39		Persons aged 85 and over	
3	1	2	26	9	48	88	3,281	8,583	**All households***	
-	-	-	2	2	2	17	148	148	1 adult of pensionable age	0
-	1	-	11	-	37	29	433	433	1 adult under pensionable age	0
-	-	-	-	1	3	-	256	639	1 adult any age	1 or more
2	-	-	8	3	3	30	1,012	2,024	2 adults (1 male and 1 female)	0
1	-	1	1	2	1	6	1,067	4,102		1 or more
-	-	1	2	-	1	1	97	194	2 adults (same sex)	0
-	-	-	-	-	-	-	18	65		1 or more
-	-	-	1	-	-	4	142	483	3 or more adults (male(s) and female(s))	0
-	-	-	-	1	-	1	87	424		1 or more
-	-	-	1	-	-	-	19	66	3 or more adults (same sex)	0
-	-	-	-	-	-	-	1	4		1 or more
1	-	-	3	2	2	24	224	301	Households containing persons of pensionable age only (any number)	
-	-	-	1	1	2	5	69	74	Households containing persons aged 75 and over only (any number)	
2	-	1	1	7	5	11	2,524		All dependent children	
1	-	1	1	2	2	3	1,218		Dependent children aged 0 - 4	
1	-	-	-	4	1	8	1,237		Dependent children aged 5 - 15	
2	-	-	5	2	-	30	266		Persons pensionable age - 74	
-	-	-	-	-	2	8	95		Persons aged 75 - 84	
-	-	-	1	1	-	1	18		Persons aged 85 and over	

Table 59 Household space type: household composition – **continued**

Note: * May include a small number of households with no resident adults

59. Households with residents; residents in households

			Household space type in permanent buildings						
			Unshared dwellings - purpose-built					Unshared dwellings - converted	
Household composition		TOTAL HOUSE-HOLDS				Purpose-built flat in:			
Adults	Dependent children		Detached	Semi-detached	Terraced	Residential building	Commercial building	Converted flat	Converted flatlet
a	b	c	d	e	f	g	h	i	j

Hart

All households*		29,073	13,378	7,455	5,479	1,868	222	256	15
1 adult of pensionable age	0	2,876	765	725	464	749	3	59	5
1 adult under pensionable age	0	2,556	628	569	766	401	52	39	3
1 adult any age	1 or more	661	204	161	211	66	5	3	1
2 adults (1 male and 1 female)	0	8,702	3,996	2,402	1,557	453	69	89	6
	1 or more	7,696	4,127	1,881	1,489	105	40	26	-
2 adults (same sex)	0	680	226	182	167	62	19	10	-
	1 or more	143	54	43	39	6	1	-	-
3 or more adults (male(s) and female(s))	0	3,697	2,108	1,035	482	19	22	20	-
	1 or more	1,927	1,212	420	269	5	9	10	-
3 or more adults (same sex)	0	116	45	35	31	2	2	-	-
	1 or more	18	12	2	4	-	-	-	-
Households containing persons of pensionable age only (any number)		5,080	1,816	1,396	689	915	7	81	5
Households containing persons aged 75 and over only (any number)		2,090	576	496	313	590	1	38	3
All dependent children		19,051	10,423	4,538	3,597	261	93	68	1
Dependent children aged 0 - 4		5,211	2,197	1,420	1,360	154	37	17	1
Dependent children aged 5 - 15		12,006	6,919	2,788	2,063	102	52	39	-
Persons pensionable age - 74		6,213	2,883	1,949	702	424	21	76	2
Persons aged 75 - 84		2,888	1,037	785	391	538	5	44	3
Persons aged 85 and over		675	236	154	94	163	2	8	-

Havant

All households*		46,151	13,268	11,629	13,483	6,512	503	386	59
1 adult of pensionable age	0	6,321	1,612	1,249	939	2,375	35	62	11
1 adult under pensionable age	0	4,109	686	730	1,021	1,351	104	102	38
1 adult any age	1 or more	1,951	189	407	840	410	32	27	-
2 adults (1 male and 1 female)	0	14,576	5,164	3,884	3,696	1,491	130	125	8
	1 or more	9,653	2,635	2,716	3,586	522	95	42	-
2 adults (same sex)	0	960	244	224	323	138	17	6	1
	1 or more	313	56	81	147	24	4	-	-
3 or more adults (male(s) and female(s))	0	5,329	1,813	1,561	1,758	136	44	12	1
	1 or more	2,759	827	731	1,099	58	33	9	-
3 or more adults (same sex)	0	144	35	36	59	6	7	1	-
	1 or more	31	7	9	13	1	1	-	-
Households containing persons of pensionable age only (any number)		11,384	3,751	2,597	1,824	3,000	52	87	12
Households containing persons aged 75 and over only (any number)		4,066	1,165	849	437	1,529	17	42	5
All dependent children		27,194	6,587	7,237	11,103	1,750	251	109	-
Dependent children aged 0 - 4		8,103	1,469	2,203	3,311	866	93	54	-
Dependent children aged 5 - 15		17,017	4,252	4,509	7,178	843	141	48	-
Persons pensionable age - 74		14,423	5,338	3,697	3,168	2,001	71	73	8
Persons aged 75 - 84		5,696	1,910	1,364	837	1,482	22	48	4
Persons aged 85 and over		1,277	457	275	109	416	3	12	1

Household space type in permanent buildings						Non-perm-anent accomm-odation	Households with migrant head	Persons in households with migrant head	Household composition	
Unshared dwellings - not self-contained			Other household spaces - not self-contained							
Not self-contained flat	Not self-contained 'rooms'	Bedsit	Not self-contained flat	Not self-contained 'rooms'	Bedsit				Adults	Dependent children
k	l	m	n	o	p	q	r	s	a	b
5	1	3	20	14	27	330	3,047	7,972	All households*	
-	-	-	4	1	-	101	112	112	1 adult of pensionable age	0
-	1	2	4	6	26	59	456	456	1 adult under pensionable age	0
1	-	1	2	-	1	5	124	323	1 adult any age	1 or more
1	-	-	6	4	-	119	1,012	2,024	2 adults (1 male and 1 female)	0
1	-	-	1	1	-	25	924	3,600		1 or more
-	-	-	-	1	-	13	85	170	2 adults (same sex)	0
-	-	-	-	-	-	-	8	35		1 or more
2	-	-	2	-	-	7	175	593	3 or more adults (male(s) and female(s))	0
-	-	-	1	-	-	1	116	539		1 or more
-	-	-	-	1	-	-	34	116	3 or more adults (same sex)	0
-	-	-	-	-	-	-	1	4		1 or more
-	-	-	7	2	-	162	186	260	Households containing persons of pensionable age only (any number)	
-	-	-	5	1	-	67	84	98	Households containing persons aged 75 and over only (any number)	
2	-	1	5	1	1	60	2,134		All dependent children	
2	-	-	-	1	1	21	902		Dependent children aged 0 - 4	
-	-	-	4	-	-	39	1,122		Dependent children aged 5 - 15	
1	-	-	2	1	-	152	199		Persons pensionable age - 74	
1	-	-	3	3	-	78	112		Persons aged 75 - 84	
-	-	-	5	-	-	13	13		Persons aged 85 and over	
7	4	3	33	43	107	114	3,844	9,771	All households*	
1	1	1	2	2	1	30	248	248	1 adult of pensionable age	0
-	-	1	7	5	48	16	640	640	1 adult under pensionable age	0
-	-	-	-	16	26	4	313	828	1 adult any age	1 or more
4	3	-	14	4	9	44	1,097	2,194	2 adults (1 male and 1 female)	0
1	-	-	8	16	19	13	1,062	4,098		1 or more
-	-	1	-	-	3	3	76	152	2 adults (same sex)	0
-	-	-	-	-	-	1	22	79		1 or more
-	-	-	-	-	1	3	201	664	3 or more adults (male(s) and female(s))	0
1	-	-	1	-	-	-	163	800		1 or more
-	-	-	-	-	-	-	19	64	3 or more adults (same sex)	0
-	-	-	-	-	-	-	-	-		1 or more
1	2	1	8	2	1	46	381	516	Households containing persons of pensionable age only (any number)	
-	2	1	4	-	-	15	114	141	Households containing persons aged 75 and over only (any number)	
4	-	-	20	59	48	26	2,790		All dependent children	
3	-	-	8	45	45	6	1,309		Dependent children aged 0 - 4	
1	-	-	11	14	3	17	1,372		Dependent children aged 5 - 15	
1	-	-	6	3	2	55	472		Persons pensionable age - 74	
-	3	1	7	-	-	18	167		Persons aged 75 - 84	
-	-	-	1	-	-	3	29		Persons aged 85 and over	

Table 59 Household space type: household composition – **continued**

Note: * May include a small number of households with no resident adults

59. Households with residents; residents in households

Household composition		TOTAL HOUSE-HOLDS	Household space type in permanent buildings						
			Unshared dwellings - purpose-built					Unshared dwellings - converted	
Adults	Dependent children		Detached	Semi-detached	Terraced	Purpose-built flat in:		Converted flat	Converted flatlet
						Residential building	Commercial building		
a	b	c	d	e	f	g	h	i	j

New Forest

All households*		**65,411**	**31,330**	**14,479**	**11,028**	**5,375**	**872**	**863**	**44**
1 adult of pensionable age	0	10,856	4,239	1,887	1,485	2,595	80	236	13
1 adult under pensionable age	0	5,374	1,538	1,110	1,280	762	186	175	22
1 adult any age	1 or more	1,670	362	474	575	174	30	9	-
2 adults (1 male and 1 female)	0	23,216	12,571	4,791	3,324	1,422	276	286	6
	1 or more	12,605	6,274	3,287	2,482	223	146	79	1
2 adults (same sex)	0	1,541	662	368	320	101	32	23	2
	1 or more	257	109	70	68	3	3	2	-
3 or more adults (male(s) and female(s))	0	6,629	3,761	1,661	968	77	78	34	-
	1 or more	3,055	1,730	770	478	10	36	19	-
3 or more adults (same sex)	0	178	75	54	37	8	2	-	-
	1 or more	22	7	6	8	-	1	-	-
Households containing persons of pensionable age only (any number)		20,701	10,161	3,675	2,487	3,306	127	351	13
Households containing persons aged 75 and over only (any number)		8,232	3,533	1,271	967	2,042	53	166	6
All dependent children		31,581	15,444	8,267	6,543	549	355	186	1
Dependent children aged 0 - 4		9,170	3,511	2,675	2,339	367	118	51	1
Dependent children aged 5 - 15		19,702	10,194	5,055	3,850	164	202	117	-
Persons pensionable age - 74		23,396	13,200	4,779	2,690	1,650	153	284	7
Persons aged 75 - 84		11,684	5,846	2,002	1,373	1,927	76	188	5
Persons aged 85 and over		2,703	1,318	399	262	617	16	46	1

Portsmouth

All households*		**72,590**	**2,408**	**9,398**	**38,064**	**14,457**	**1,354**	**4,637**	**239**
1 adult of pensionable age	0	12,232	272	1,133	5,063	4,751	118	638	25
1 adult under pensionable age	0	9,756	143	535	3,712	2,322	350	1,381	135
1 adult any age	1 or more	3,189	45	246	1,398	1,152	60	191	9
2 adults (1 male and 1 female)	0	21,144	862	3,030	11,543	3,391	375	1,562	47
	1 or more	12,716	479	2,067	8,050	1,466	180	380	12
2 adults (same sex)	0	2,409	51	230	1,331	429	72	233	5
	1 or more	398	5	43	227	90	5	21	1
3 or more adults (male(s) and female(s))	0	6,988	366	1,407	4,354	546	109	170	3
	1 or more	3,249	169	661	2,047	251	74	35	-
3 or more adults (same sex)	0	424	12	36	295	40	10	24	-
	1 or more	58	2	10	36	10	-	-	-
Households containing persons of pensionable age only (any number)		19,397	617	2,332	8,784	6,308	156	873	30
Households containing persons aged 75 and over only (any number)		7,825	242	730	3,382	2,942	58	332	19
All dependent children		35,203	1,296	5,781	21,091	5,411	522	826	28
Dependent children aged 0 - 4		12,266	262	1,513	7,418	2,231	178	489	23
Dependent children aged 5 - 15		20,912	876	3,838	12,486	3,022	304	296	3
Persons pensionable age - 74		20,890	844	3,327	10,555	4,914	188	802	12
Persons aged 75 - 84		10,554	392	1,310	4,988	3,245	88	383	21
Persons aged 85 and over		2,393	101	266	1,128	753	14	97	3

Household space type in permanent buildings						Non-perm-anent accomm-odation	Households with migrant head	Persons in households with migrant head	Household composition	
Unshared dwellings - not self-contained			Other household spaces - not self-contained							
Not self-contained flat	Not self-contained 'rooms'	Bedsit	Not self-contained flat	Not self-contained 'rooms'	Bedsit				Adults	Dependent children
k	l	m	n	o	p	q	r	s	a	b
28	6	7	49	44	100	1,186	5,663	13,713	**All households***	
2	1	-	12	4	16	286	376	376	1 adult of pensionable age	0
4	-	3	10	8	61	215	913	913	1 adult under pensionable age	0
-	4	1	4	13	7	17	364	918	1 adult any age	1 or more
12	1	1	11	4	7	504	1,961	3,922	2 adults (1 male and 1 female)	0
5	-	1	8	14	8	77	1,410	5,397		1 or more
1	-	-	2	-	-	30	132	264	2 adults (same sex)	0
-	-	-	-	-	-	2	33	117		1 or more
1	-	-	1	-	-	48	277	924	3 or more adults (male(s) and female(s))	0
2	-	-	1	1	1	7	168	802		1 or more
1	-	1	-	-	-	-	23	71	3 or more adults (same sex)	0
-	-	-	-	-	-	-	-	-		1 or more
9	2	-	17	5	17	531	704	1,036	Households containing persons of pensionable age only (any number)	
5	2	-	12	4	8	163	249	307	Households containing persons aged 75 and over only (any number)	
10	4	2	21	31	20	148	3,449		All dependent children	
6	1	1	9	23	11	57	1,640		Dependent children aged 0 - 4	
4	2	1	12	7	9	85	1,681		Dependent children aged 5 - 15	
8	-	-	6	2	9	608	840		Persons pensionable age - 74	
8	2	1	13	3	9	231	359		Persons aged 75 - 84	
3	1	-	3	2	1	34	58		Persons aged 85 and over	
44	12	40	432	254	1,123	128	7,987	17,932	**All households***	
5	2	1	63	43	94	24	379	379	1 adult of pensionable age	0
14	5	26	154	100	842	37	2,108	2,108	1 adult under pensionable age	0
4	1	3	27	18	34	1	603	1,548	1 adult any age	1 or more
8	3	3	109	53	106	52	2,223	4,446	2 adults (1 male and 1 female)	0
3	-	2	27	21	22	7	1,490	5,611		1 or more
4	1	2	20	9	17	5	387	774	2 adults (same sex)	0
-	-	1	2	1	1	1	54	195		1 or more
2	-	1	23	4	3	-	424	1,487	3 or more adults (male(s) and female(s))	0
3	-	1	3	3	1	1	187	948		1 or more
1	-	-	4	2	-	-	110	387	3 or more adults (same sex)	0
-	-	-	-	-	-	-	7	31		1 or more
6	3	1	88	53	96	50	512	646	Households containing persons of pensionable age only (any number)	
4	3	-	43	23	36	11	179	200	Households containing persons aged 75 and over only (any number)	
11	1	8	85	63	68	12	4,017		All dependent children	
5	1	4	41	35	57	9	2,012		Dependent children aged 0 - 4	
6	-	4	42	26	6	3	1,861		Dependent children aged 5 - 15	
4	-	2	75	42	63	62	549		Persons pensionable age - 74	
2	3	-	50	23	28	21	224		Persons aged 75 - 84	
2	1	-	10	5	10	3	52		Persons aged 85 and over	

Table 59 Household space type: household composition – **continued**

Note: * May include a small number of households with no resident adults

59. Households with residents; residents in households

Household composition			Household space type in permanent buildings							
			Unshared dwellings - purpose-built						Unshared dwellings - converted	
		TOTAL HOUSE-HOLDS	Detached	Semi-detached	Terraced	Purpose-built flat in:		Converted flat	Converted flatlet
Adults	Dependent children					Residential building	Commercial building		
a	b	c	d	e	f	g	h	i	j
Rushmoor									
All households*		30,523	5,052	9,620	9,028	4,965	414	621	37
1 adult of pensionable age	0	3,351	363	794	618	1,431	21	58	4
1 adult under pensionable age	0	3,202	272	598	821	800	113	155	22
1 adult any age	1 or more	1,147	66	238	392	360	13	18	1
2 adults (1 male and 1 female)	0	8,956	1,576	2,794	2,663	1,406	117	252	7
	1 or more	7,467	1,387	2,773	2,546	570	60	66	2
2 adults (same sex)	0	934	85	247	356	184	22	25	1
	1 or more	157	18	52	63	20	2	1	-
3 or more adults (male(s) and female(s))	0	3,515	843	1,430	1,002	146	49	31	-
	1 or more	1,585	403	621	496	39	12	9	-
3 or more adults (same sex)	0	180	35	58	64	9	5	6	-
	1 or more	23	3	14	6	-	-	-	-
Households containing persons of pensionable age only (any number)		5,508	857	1,572	1,102	1,786	25	71	4
Households containing persons aged 75 and over only (any number)		2,166	279	513	363	938	11	39	2
All dependent children		18,569	3,519	6,828	6,251	1,534	134	124	3
Dependent children aged 0 - 4		6,588	810	2,227	2,440	875	50	77	3
Dependent children aged 5 - 15		10,734	2,329	4,142	3,462	628	74	37	-
Persons pensionable age - 74		6,632	1,349	2,286	1,595	1,209	34	47	3
Persons aged 75 - 84		3,011	478	913	575	956	14	45	1
Persons aged 85 and over		626	124	154	105	230	1	5	1
Southampton									
All households*		81,140	11,665	21,757	20,196	21,014	1,022	2,711	369
1 adult of pensionable age	0	12,667	1,491	2,450	1,735	6,358	63	375	28
1 adult under pensionable age	0	11,484	666	1,493	1,942	4,444	275	882	219
1 adult any age	1 or more	3,709	182	667	1,021	1,557	43	112	8
2 adults (1 male and 1 female)	0	23,186	4,213	6,595	5,621	5,193	290	895	91
	1 or more	14,451	2,315	5,015	4,589	2,039	147	204	17
2 adults (same sex)	0	2,440	280	697	664	562	41	129	5
	1 or more	466	49	127	185	88	7	8	-
3 or more adults (male(s) and female(s))	0	8,148	1,672	2,980	2,719	579	93	70	-
	1 or more	3,905	741	1,479	1,457	143	49	19	-
3 or more adults (same sex)	0	576	51	224	226	41	11	15	-
	1 or more	75	4	28	31	8	3	-	-
Households containing persons of pensionable age only (any number)		20,364	3,209	4,839	3,276	8,231	90	492	31
Households containing persons aged 75 and over only (any number)		8,031	1,094	1,772	934	3,887	35	225	14
All dependent children		41,919	6,054	14,035	14,402	6,071	435	487	30
Dependent children aged 0 - 4		13,886	1,428	4,056	4,210	3,451	144	308	25
Dependent children aged 5 - 15		25,372	3,936	9,088	9,335	2,472	259	160	3
Persons pensionable age - 74		23,020	4,394	6,609	5,169	6,157	123	395	19
Persons aged 75 - 84		10,666	1,817	2,813	1,625	4,035	57	232	12
Persons aged 85 and over		2,416	398	638	268	1,010	11	69	3

Household space type in permanent buildings						Non-permanent accomm-odation	Households with migrant head	Persons in households with migrant head	Household composition	
Unshared dwellings - not self-contained			Other household spaces - not self-contained							
Not self-contained flat	Not self-contained 'rooms'	Bedsit	Not self-contained flat	Not self-contained 'rooms'	Bedsit				Adults	Dependent children
k	l	m	n	o	p	q	r	s	a	b
11	6	3	51	45	465	205	4,115	10,554	**All households***	
2	-	-	4	5	16	35	125	125	1 adult of pensionable age	0
2	2	1	13	15	318	70	677	677	1 adult under pensionable age	0
-	3	-	8	3	43	2	272	710	1 adult any age	1 or more
1	1	1	13	9	50	66	1,230	2,460	2 adults (1 male and 1 female)	0
2	-	-	10	8	28	15	1,273	4,773		1 or more
-	-	-	-	1	6	7	147	294	2 adults (same sex)	0
-	-	-	-	-	1	-	19	66		1 or more
1	-	1	1	1	-	10	214	726	3 or more adults (male(s) and female(s))	0
2	-	-	1	2	-	-	116	583		1 or more
1	-	-	1	1	-	-	35	116	3 or more adults (same sex)	0
-	-	-	-	-	-	-	3	16		1 or more
									Households containing persons of pensionable age only (any number)	
2	-	-	6	5	16	62	170	215		
									Households containing persons aged 75 and over only (any number)	
1	-	-	2	2	1	15	65	74		
10	4	-	26	19	94	23	2,889		All dependent children	
5	2	-	14	6	70	9	1,538		Dependent children aged 0 - 4	
4	1	-	11	12	21	13	1,262		Dependent children aged 5 - 15	
1	-	-	5	6	15	82	180		Persons pensionable age - 74	
1	-	-	1	1	1	25	91		Persons aged 75 - 84	
1	-	-	2	2	-	1	11		Persons aged 85 and over	
54	18	52	274	292	1,647	69	8,917	19,435	**All households***	
8	3	-	43	41	71	1	442	442	1 adult of pensionable age	0
10	5	35	90	123	1,281	19	2,683	2,683	1 adult under pensionable age	0
2	1	3	23	29	57	4	698	1,851	1 adult any age	1 or more
10	4	3	60	58	132	21	2,365	4,730	2 adults (1 male and 1 female)	0
4	2	2	31	23	50	13	1,420	5,380		1 or more
15	2	2	10	9	20	4	382	764	2 adults (same sex)	0
-	-	-	1	-	1	-	52	189		1 or more
3	-	1	11	4	13	3	447	1,611	3 or more adults (male(s) and female(s))	0
2	1	1	1	4	4	4	213	1,064		1 or more
-	-	3	2	-	3	-	183	640	3 or more adults (same sex)	0
-	-	-	1	-	-	-	13	60		1 or more
									Households containing persons of pensionable age only (any number)	
8	3	-	56	50	73	6	639	837		
									Households containing persons aged 75 and over only (any number)	
5	2	-	26	20	17	-	190	228		
16	4	11	111	79	152	32	4,165		All dependent children	
3	2	8	59	52	122	18	2,160		Dependent children aged 0 - 4	
13	2	1	49	24	18	12	1,851		Dependent children aged 5 - 15	
5	1	-	42	36	57	13	710		Persons pensionable age - 74	
4	2	-	28	19	19	3	251		Persons aged 75 - 84	
1	-	-	8	9	-	1	54		Persons aged 85 and over	

Table 59 Household space type: household composition – **continued**

Note: * May include a small number of households with no resident adults

59. Households with residents; residents in households

Household composition										
		TOTAL HOUSE-HOLDS	Household space type in permanent buildings							
			Unshared dwellings - purpose-built						Unshared dwellings - converted	
Adults	Dependent children		Detached	Semi-detached	Terraced	Purpose-built flat in:		Converted flat	Converted flatlet
						Residential building	Commercial building		
a	b	c	d	e	f	g	h	i	j

Test Valley

All households*		**38,391**	**14,385**	**9,524**	**9,954**	**3,244**	**247**	**539**	**20**
1 adult of pensionable age	0	4,757	1,187	1,036	971	1,300	17	151	2
1 adult under pensionable age	0	3,331	688	759	906	636	45	114	12
1 adult any age	1 or more	1,138	175	233	641	66	6	13	1
2 adults (1 male and 1 female)	0	12,011	5,044	3,096	2,575	904	71	165	4
	1 or more	9,010	3,836	2,218	2,683	141	52	47	1
2 adults (same sex)	0	916	277	260	267	85	7	12	-
	1 or more	192	54	51	78	6	2	1	-
3 or more adults (male(s) and female(s))	0	4,663	2,025	1,300	1,181	88	28	27	-
	1 or more	2,207	1,048	527	587	15	16	9	-
3 or more adults (same sex)	0	131	40	39	47	2	3	-	-
	1 or more	26	8	4	14	-	-	-	-
Households containing persons of pensionable age only (any number)		8,418	2,832	2,006	1,616	1,620	27	183	2
Households containing persons aged 75 and over only (any number)		3,216	903	667	564	907	14	113	1
All dependent children		22,563	9,352	5,333	7,262	320	118	111	3
Dependent children aged 0 - 4		6,518	2,175	1,630	2,427	177	32	51	1
Dependent children aged 5 - 15		14,128	6,117	3,317	4,419	118	69	50	2
Persons pensionable age - 74		10,165	4,224	2,668	2,010	1,006	24	100	1
Persons aged 75 - 84		4,649	1,573	1,125	846	902	19	123	1
Persons aged 85 and over		987	399	177	157	225	2	18	-

Winchester

All households*		**37,553**	**14,449**	**9,291**	**8,257**	**3,601**	**370**	**825**	**40**
1 adult of pensionable age	0	5,895	1,336	1,118	1,417	1,732	29	168	2
1 adult under pensionable age	0	3,466	686	633	1,071	504	88	218	27
1 adult any age	1 or more	850	193	241	286	80	11	13	2
2 adults (1 male and 1 female)	0	11,890	5,038	2,945	2,379	919	102	258	7
	1 or more	7,888	3,703	2,190	1,619	178	62	70	-
2 adults (same sex)	0	888	238	229	274	91	12	30	2
	1 or more	165	59	55	40	6	1	3	-
3 or more adults (male(s) and female(s))	0	4,317	2,048	1,294	780	82	36	46	-
	1 or more	2,030	1,100	545	332	6	22	15	-
3 or more adults (same sex)	0	144	39	34	58	2	6	3	-
	1 or more	16	7	6	1	-	1	1	-
Households containing persons of pensionable age only (any number)		10,042	3,069	2,179	2,119	2,225	36	252	2
Households containing persons aged 75 and over only (any number)		4,065	1,014	744	871	1,252	17	114	1
All dependent children		20,072	9,425	5,709	4,081	365	163	169	2
Dependent children aged 0 - 4		5,374	1,994	1,600	1,373	235	46	49	2
Dependent children aged 5 - 15		12,653	6,199	3,635	2,428	118	100	98	-
Persons pensionable age - 74		11,332	4,426	2,955	2,157	1,331	38	214	1
Persons aged 75 - 84		5,462	1,752	1,191	1,080	1,216	18	133	1
Persons aged 85 and over		1,305	403	242	251	359	4	38	-

Household space type in permanent buildings						Non-perm-anent accomm-odation	Households with migrant head	Persons in households with migrant head	Household composition	
Unshared dwellings - not self-contained			Other household spaces - not self-contained							
Not self-contained flat	Not self-contained 'rooms'	Bedsit	Not self-contained flat	Not self-contained 'rooms'	Bedsit				Adults	Dependent children
k	l	m	n	o	p	q	r	s	a	b
15	2	8	18	10	45	380	4,181	10,849	All households*	
4	1	1	3	4	3	77	167	167	1 adult of pensionable age	0
3	-	4	3	2	36	123	581	581	1 adult under pensionable age	0
-	-	-	-	-	1	2	244	656	1 adult any age	1 or more
5	-	2	3	1	3	138	1,384	2,768	2 adults (1 male and 1 female)	0
2	1	-	7	1	1	20	1,301	4,928		1 or more
-	-	-	1	-	-	7	89	178	2 adults (same sex)	0
-	-	-	-	-	-	-	18	63		1 or more
-	-	-	1	2	1	10	227	743	3 or more adults (male(s) and female(s))	0
1	-	1	-	-	-	3	145	685		1 or more
-	-	-	-	-	-	-	22	69	3 or more adults (same sex)	0
-	-	-	-	-	-	-	1	5		1 or more
5	1	1	6	4	3	112	290	416	Households containing persons of pensionable age only (any number)	
3	1	-	3	2	1	37	88	112	Households containing persons aged 75 and over only (any number)	
5	3	1	15	2	2	36	2,991		All dependent children	
4	1	-	2	2	2	14	1,307		Dependent children aged 0 - 4	
1	2	-	13	-	-	20	1,537		Dependent children aged 5 - 15	
2	-	1	4	4	2	119	374		Persons pensionable age - 74	
1	1	-	5	2	1	50	135		Persons aged 75 - 84	
3	-	-	-	-	1	5	28		Persons aged 85 and over	
12	3	3	47	20	117	518	3,705	9,008	All households*	
3	-	-	8	2	3	77	320	320	1 adult of pensionable age	0
3	1	2	19	15	84	115	641	641	1 adult under pensionable age	0
1	-	-	1	2	7	13	158	410	1 adult any age	1 or more
3	1	1	8	-	10	219	1,128	2,256	2 adults (1 male and 1 female)	0
1	-	-	1	1	8	55	1,005	3,831		1 or more
-	1	-	2	-	-	9	98	196	2 adults (same sex)	0
-	-	-	-	-	1	-	16	57		1 or more
-	-	-	5	-	-	26	189	637	3 or more adults (male(s) and female(s))	0
1	-	-	2	-	4	3	108	522		1 or more
-	-	-	1	-	-	1	40	132	3 or more adults (same sex)	0
-	-	-	-	-	-	-	1	5		1 or more
5	-	-	12	2	3	138	478	636	Households containing persons of pensionable age only (any number)	
2	-	-	6	1	1	42	166	196	Households containing persons aged 75 and over only (any number)	
5	-	-	7	4	20	122	2,272		All dependent children	
2	-	-	4	1	14	54	1,019		Dependent children aged 0 - 4	
2	-	-	2	2	5	64	1,143		Dependent children aged 5 - 15	
5	-	1	14	1	5	184	508		Persons pensionable age - 74	
3	-	-	6	1	1	60	211		Persons aged 75 - 84	
-	-	-	2	-	-	6	40		Persons aged 85 and over	

Table 60 Dwellings and household spaces

Note: * Includes unshared dwelling(s) plus an unattached household space (not in a dwelling)

60. Converted or shared accommodation; dwellings; household spaces; rooms in such accommodation

Type of dwelling(s) in converted or shared accommodation	TOTAL CONVERTED OR SHARED ACCOMMODATION	TOTAL DWELLINGS	Total shared dwellings	Shared dwellings with the following household spaces 2	3	4	5 or more	Un-attached spaces	TOTAL HOUSE-HOLD SPACES	Household space type Converted flat	Converted flatlet	Not self-contained flat	Not self-contained 'rooms'	Bedsit	Not self-contained unocc-upied	TOTAL ROOMS
a	b	c	d	e	f	g	h	i	j	k	l	m	n	o	p	q
HAMPSHIRE																
TOTAL CONVERTED OR SHARED ACCOMMODATION	7,491	18,075	1,798	736	339	253	470	540	23,368	14,695	1,123	1,348	910	5,122	170	70,530
Unconverted accommodation																
1 shared dwelling	1,202	1,202	1,202	544	204	159	295		4,198			649	557	2,927	65	7,652
Partly converted accommodation																
1 shared, 1 unshared dwelling*	670	1,012	342	105	74	51	112	328	2,393	548	102	298	179	1,216	50	5,152
1 shared, 2 unshared dwellings*	225	591	141	44	34	22	41	84	1,101	323	108	90	65	492	23	2,299
1 shared, 3 or more unshared dwellings*	241	1,217	113	43	27	21	22	128	1,623	827	249	101	49	380	17	3,909
Converted accommodation																
2 unshared dwellings	3,628	7,256							7,256	6,727	257	143	50	67	12	28,260
3 unshared dwellings	586	1,758							1,758	1,615	83	34	7	17	2	6,614
4 or more unshared dwellings	939	5,039							5,039	4,655	324	33	3	23	1	16,644
Basingstoke & Deane																
TOTAL CONVERTED OR SHARED ACCOMMODATION	252	560	55	28	8	4	15	6	702	407	79	49	30	137	-	2,425
Unconverted accommodation																
1 shared dwelling	44	44	44	23	7	3	11		143			28	20	95	-	291
Partly converted accommodation																
1 shared, 1 unshared dwelling*	11	18	7	4	-	1	2	4	45	10	1	4	2	28	-	86
1 shared, 2 unshared dwellings*	4	11	3	1	1	-	1	1	22	2	6	3	-	11	-	35
1 shared, 3 or more unshared dwellings*	2	12	1	-	-	-	1	1	17	7	4	3	2	1	-	63
Converted accommodation																
2 unshared dwellings	150	300							300	238	45	9	6	2	-	1,221
3 unshared dwellings	20	60							60	52	6	2	-	-	-	284
4 or more unshared dwellings	21	115							115	98	17	-	-	-	-	445

Table 60 Dwellings and household spaces – continued

County, districts

Note: * Includes unshared dwelling(s) plus an unattached household space (not in a dwelling)

60. Converted or shared accommodation; dwellings; household spaces; rooms in such accommodation

East Hampshire

Type of dwelling(s) in converted or shared accommodation	TOTAL CONVERTED OR SHARED ACCOMMODATION	TOTAL DWELLINGS	Total shared dwellings	Shared dwellings with the following household spaces				Un-attached spaces	TOTAL HOUSEHOLD SPACES	Household space type						TOTAL ROOMS
				2	3	4	5 or more			Converted flat	Converted flatlet	Not self-contained flat	Not self-contained 'rooms'	Bedsit	Not self-contained unoccupied	
a	b	c	d	e	f	g	h	i	j	k	l	m	n	o	p	q
TOTAL CONVERTED OR SHARED ACCOMMODATION	318	829	43	25	5	5	8	14	932	724	39	57	21	89	2	3,707
Unconverted accommodation																
1 shared dwelling	38	38	38	21	5	5	7	-	117	-	-	24	14	77	2	230
Partly converted accommodation																
1 shared, 1 unshared dwelling*	13	17	4	3	-	-	1	9	35	10	2	11	2	10	-	104
1 shared, 2 unshared dwellings*	3	6	-	-	-	-	-	3	9	5	1	2	-	1	-	22
1 shared, 3 or more unshared dwellings*	3	17	1	1	-	-	-	2	20	15	1	3	1	-	-	66
Converted accommodation																
2 unshared dwellings	169	338								338	302	17	14	4	1	-	1,565
3 unshared dwellings	41	123								123	119	2	2	-	-	-	605
4 or more unshared dwellings	51	290								290	273	16	1	-	-	-	1,115

Eastleigh

Type of dwelling(s) in converted or shared accommodation	TOTAL CONVERTED OR SHARED ACCOMMODATION	TOTAL DWELLINGS	Total shared dwellings	Shared dwellings with the following household spaces				Un-attached spaces	TOTAL HOUSEHOLD SPACES	Household space type						TOTAL ROOMS
				2	3	4	5 or more			Converted flat	Converted flatlet	Not self-contained flat	Not self-contained 'rooms'	Bedsit	Not self-contained unoccupied	
a	b	c	d	e	f	g	h	i	j	k	l	m	n	o	p	q
TOTAL CONVERTED OR SHARED ACCOMMODATION	210	457	53	22	14	5	12	12	589	383	8	26	29	135	8	1,848
Unconverted accommodation																
1 shared dwelling	45	45	45	19	10	4	12	-	151	-	-	18	25	102	6	267
Partly converted accommodation																
1 shared, 1 unshared dwelling*	17	23	6	2	3	1	-	11	45	15	1	5	2	21	1	123
1 shared, 2 unshared dwellings*	1	3	1	-	1	-	-	-	5	2	-	-	-	3	-	11
1 shared, 3 or more unshared dwellings*	2	7	1	1	-	-	-	1	9	6	-	-	-	3	-	19
Converted accommodation																
2 unshared dwellings	121	242								242	233	5	2	1	-	1	885
3 unshared dwellings	10	30								30	29	-	1	-	-	-	106
4 or more unshared dwellings	14	107								107	98	2	-	1	6	-	437

Table 60 Dwellings and household spaces – continued

Note: * Includes unshared dwelling(s) plus an unattached household space (not in a dwelling)

60. Converted or shared accommodation; dwellings; household spaces; rooms in such accommodation

Type of dwelling(s) in converted or shared accommodation	TOTAL CONVERTED OR SHARED ACCOMMODATION	TOTAL DWELLINGS	Total shared dwellings	Shared dwellings with the following household spaces				Un-attached spaces	TOTAL HOUSE-HOLD SPACES	Household space type						TOTAL ROOMS
				2	3	4	5 or more			Converted flat	Converted flatlet	Not self-contained flat	Not self-contained 'rooms'	Bedsit	Not self-contained unoccupied	
a	b	c	d	e	f	g	h	i	j	k	l	m	n	o	p	q
Fareham																
TOTAL CONVERTED OR SHARED ACCOMMODATION	**108**	**245**	**26**	**18**	**6**	**-**	**2**	**5**	**292**	**196**	**15**	**21**	**20**	**39**	**1**	**999**
Unconverted accommodation																
1 shared dwelling	19	19	19	15	3	-	1	1	46			15	13	17	1	112
Partly converted accommodation																
1 shared, 1 unshared dwelling*	8	12	4	1	2	-	1	4	27	7	-	3	3	14	-	62
1 shared, 2 unshared dwellings*	2	6	2	2	-	-	-	-	8	3	1	-	1	3	-	16
1 shared, 3 or more unshared dwellings*	2	12	1	-	1	-	-	1	15	6	5	-	-	4	-	25
Converted accommodation																
2 unshared dwellings	65	130							130	119	4	3	3	1	-	579
3 unshared dwellings	3	9							9	9	-	-	-	-	-	29
4 or more unshared dwellings	9	57							57	52	5	-	-	-	-	176
Gosport																
TOTAL CONVERTED OR SHARED ACCOMMODATION	**165**	**385**	**24**	**12**	**2**	**4**	**6**	**16**	**458**	**346**	**9**	**29**	**10**	**61**	**3**	**1,514**
Unconverted accommodation																
1 shared dwelling	19	19	19	10	2	2	5		62			9	6	46	1	112
Partly converted accommodation																
1 shared, 1 unshared dwelling*	15	20	5	2	-	2	1	10	44	13	2	12	3	13	1	120
1 shared, 2 unshared dwellings*	1	2	-	-	-	-	-	1	3	2	-	1	-	-	-	13
1 shared, 3 or more unshared dwellings*	5	21	-	-	-	-	-	5	26	21	-	4	-	-	1	80
Converted accommodation																
2 unshared dwellings	88	176							176	167	6	2	1	-	-	668
3 unshared dwellings	19	57							57	54	-	1	-	2	-	208
4 or more unshared dwellings	18	90							90	89	1	-	-	-	-	313

Table 60 Dwellings and household spaces – continued

County, districts

60. Converted or shared accommodation; dwellings; household spaces; rooms in such accommodation

Note: * Includes unshared dwelling(s) plus an unattached household space (not in a dwelling)

Type of dwelling(s) in converted or shared accommodation	TOTAL CONVERTED OR SHARED ACCOMM-ODATION	TOTAL DWELLINGS	Total shared dwellings	Shared dwellings with the following household spaces				Un-attached spaces	TOTAL HOUSE-HOLD SPACES	Household space type						TOTAL ROOMS
				2	3	4	5 or more			Converted flat	Converted flatlet	Not self-contained flat	Not self-contained 'rooms'	Bedsit	Not self-contained unocc-upied	
a	b	c	d	e	f	g	h	i	j	k	l	m	n	o	p	q

Hart

	b	c	d	e	f	g	h	i	j	k	l	m	n	o	p	q
TOTAL CONVERTED OR SHARED ACCOMMODATION	133	325	20	15	-	-	3	8	375	276	20	25	15	39	-	1,572
Unconverted accommodation																
1 shared dwelling	19	19	19	14	-	-	3		60			13	13	34	-	141
Partly converted accommodation																
1 shared, 1 unshared dwelling*	6	6	-	-	-	-	-	6	12	6	-	3	1	2	-	50
1 shared, 2 unshared dwellings*	1	2	-	-	-	-	-	1	3	-	2	1	-	-	-	4
1 shared, 3 or more unshared dwellings*	2	10	1	1	-	-	-	1	12	9	-	3	-	-	-	49
Converted accommodation																
2 unshared dwellings	77	154							154	143	5	2	1	3	-	774
3 unshared dwellings	10	30							30	26	1	3	-	-	-	144
4 or more unshared dwellings	18	104							104	92	12	-	-	-	-	410

Havant

	b	c	d	e	f	g	h	i	j	k	l	m	n	o	p	q
TOTAL CONVERTED OR SHARED ACCOMMODATION	237	582	60	37	2	8	13	11	722	440	68	40	47	121	6	2,239
Unconverted accommodation																
1 shared dwelling	52	52	52	33	2	7	10		155			26	36	90	3	402
Partly converted accommodation																
1 shared, 1 unshared dwelling*	9	13	4	1	-	1	2	5	34	8	1	5	6	13	1	75
1 shared, 2 unshared dwellings*	2	5	1	1	-	-	-	1	7	2	1	1	2	1	-	16
1 shared, 3 or more unshared dwellings*	8	60	3	2	-	-	1	5	74	33	23	1	-	15	2	142
Converted accommodation																
2 unshared dwellings	123	246							246	227	10	4	3	2	-	1,000
3 unshared dwellings	15	45							45	35	8	2	-	-	-	148
4 or more unshared dwellings	28	161							161	135	25	1	-	-	-	456

Table 60 Dwellings and household spaces – **continued**

Note: * Includes unshared dwelling(s) plus an unattached household space (not in a dwelling)

60. Converted or shared accommodation; dwellings; household spaces; rooms in such accommodation

Type of dwelling(s) in converted or shared accommodation	TOTAL CONVERTED OR SHARED ACCOMM-ODATION	TOTAL DWELLINGS	Total shared dwellings	Shared dwellings with the following household spaces				Un-attached spaces	TOTAL HOUSE-HOLD SPACES	Household space type						TOTAL ROOMS
				2	3	4	5 or more			Converted flat	Converted flatlet	Not self-contained flat	Not self-contained 'rooms'	Bedsit	Not self-contained unocc-upied	
a	b	c	d	e	f	g	h	i	j	k	l	m	n	o	p	q
New Forest																
TOTAL CONVERTED OR SHARED ACCOMMODATION	**451**	**1,232**	**62**	**33**	**10**	**4**	**15**	**23**	**1,392**	**1,066**	**60**	**80**	**51**	**125**	**10**	**5,298**
Unconverted accommodation																
1 shared dwelling	42	42	42	26	4	2	10		125			36	30	57	2	325
Partly converted accommodation																
1 shared, 1 unshared dwelling*	22	31	9	5	1	1	2	13	68	19	2	6	9	26	6	165
1 shared, 2 unshared dwellings*	9	23	5	2	2	-	1	4	37	9	5	3	5	15	-	130
1 shared, 3 or more unshared dwellings*	12	88	6	-	3	1	2	6	114	62	20	7	3	21	1	318
Converted accommodation																
2 unshared dwellings	262	524							524	483	16	18	3	4	-	2,341
3 unshared dwellings	34	102							102	95	2	4	-	-	1	471
4 or more unshared dwellings	70	422							422	398	15	6	1	2	-	1,548
Portsmouth																
TOTAL CONVERTED OR SHARED ACCOMMODATION	**2,477**	**6,419**	**519**	**215**	**103**	**64**	**137**	**243**	**8,057**	**5,505**	**278**	**511**	**276**	**1,416**	**71**	**24,043**
Unconverted accommodation																
1 shared dwelling	280	280	280	135	46	33	66		968			220	135	597	16	1,957
Partly converted accommodation																
1 shared, 1 unshared dwelling*	273	405	132	44	30	14	44	141	953	233	34	144	79	435	28	2,130
1 shared, 2 unshared dwellings*	106	271	59	20	15	5	19	47	503	178	29	56	30	199	11	1,147
1 shared, 3 or more unshared dwellings*	103	502	48	16	12	12	8	55	672	375	68	47	23	149	10	1,712
Converted accommodation																
2 unshared dwellings	1,070	2,140							2,140	2,043	38	27	7	21	4	7,823
3 unshared dwellings	226	678							678	634	23	10	1	9	1	2,326
4 or more unshared dwellings	419	2,143							2,143	2,042	86	7	1	6	1	6,948

Table 60 Dwellings and household spaces – continued

County, districts

Note: * Includes unshared dwelling(s) plus an unattached household space (not in a dwelling)

60. Converted or shared accommodation; dwellings; household spaces; rooms in such accommodation

Type of dwelling(s) in converted or shared accommodation	TOTAL CONVERTED OR SHARED ACCOMM- ODATION	TOTAL DWELLINGS	Total shared dwellings	Shared dwellings with the following household spaces 2	3	4	5 or more	Un- attached spaces	TOTAL HOUSE- HOLD SPACES	Household space type Converted flat	Converted flatlet	Not self- contained flat	Not self- contained 'rooms'	Bedsit	Not self- contained unocc- upied	TOTAL ROOMS
a	b	c	d	e	f	g	h	i	j	k	l	m	n	o	p	q
Rushmoor																
TOTAL CONVERTED OR SHARED ACCOMMODATION	**441**	**917**	**156**	**41**	**32**	**34**	**49**	**25**	**1,406**	**691**	**45**	**62**	**53**	**545**	**10**	**3,569**
Unconverted accommodation																
1 shared dwelling	121	121	121	32	23	29	37		479			34	33	408	4	658
Partly converted accommodation																
1 shared, 1 unshared dwelling*	34	55	21	3	6	3	9	13	137	27	5	6	9	89	1	232
1 shared, 2 unshared dwellings*	15	41	11	4	3	2	2	4	69	21	7	7	4	26	4	146
1 shared, 3 or more unshared dwellings*	11	44	3	2	-	-	1	8	65	34	7	4	1	19	-	210
Converted accommodation																
2 unshared dwellings	182	364							364	331	17	8	5	2	1	1,338
3 unshared dwellings	36	108							108	102	3	1	1	1	-	416
4 or more unshared dwellings	42	184							184	176	6	2	-	-	-	569
Southampton																
TOTAL CONVERTED OR SHARED ACCOMMODATION	**2,036**	**4,416**	**701**	**249**	**140**	**119**	**193**	**141**	**6,474**	**3,143**	**434**	**349**	**323**	**2,175**	**50**	**15,856**
Unconverted accommodation																
1 shared dwelling	469	469	469	183	91	69	126		1,704			191	208	1,283	22	2,786
Partly converted accommodation																
1 shared, 1 unshared dwelling*	220	355	135	36	28	28	43	85	848	163	50	75	58	491	11	1,595
1 shared, 2 unshared dwellings*	74	203	55	12	12	14	17	19	398	88	53	12	22	215	8	677
1 shared, 3 or more unshared dwellings*	79	374	42	18	9	8	7	37	509	212	106	19	19	150	3	990
Converted accommodation																
2 unshared dwellings	940	1,880							1,880	1,729	73	36	11	25	6	6,652
3 unshared dwellings	95	285							285	245	27	3	5	5	-	867
4 or more unshared dwellings	159	850							850	706	125	13	-	6	-	2,289

Table 60 Dwellings and household spaces – continued

Note: * Includes unshared dwelling(s) plus an unattached household space (not in a dwelling)

60. Converted or shared accommodation; dwellings; household spaces; rooms in such accommodation

Type of dwelling(s) in converted or shared accommodation	TOTAL CONVERTED OR SHARED ACCOMMODATION	TOTAL DWELLINGS	Total shared dwellings	Shared dwellings with the following household spaces				Un-attached spaces	TOTAL HOUSEHOLD SPACES	Household space type						TOTAL ROOMS
				2	3	4	5 or more			Converted flat	Converted flatlet	Not self-contained flat	Not self-contained 'rooms'	Bedsit	Not self-contained unoccupied	
a	b	c	d	e	f	g	h	i	j	k	l	m	n	o	p	q

Test Valley

Type of dwelling(s) in converted or shared accommodation	b	c	d	e	f	g	h	i	j	k	l	m	n	o	p	q
TOTAL CONVERTED OR SHARED ACCOMMODATION	**246**	**660**	**24**	**13**	**2**	**4**	**5**	**9**	**720**	**590**	**21**	**33**	**12**	**64**	**-**	**2,677**
Unconverted accommodation																
1 shared dwelling	14	14	14	10	1	3	-	-	35			8	8	19	-	91
Partly converted accommodation																
1 shared, 1 unshared dwelling*	13	18	5	1	-	-	4	8	45	12	1	7	2	23	-	104
1 shared, 2 unshared dwellings*	3	9	3	2	-	1	-	-	14	6	-	2	-	6	-	32
1 shared, 3 or more unshared dwellings*	3	15	2	-	1	-	1	1	22	9	3	2	-	8	-	48
Converted accommodation																
2 unshared dwellings	149	298							298	271	10	10	2	5	-	1,295
3 unshared dwellings	26	78							78	72	4	2	-	-	-	311
4 or more unshared dwellings	38	228							228	220	3	2	-	3	-	796

Winchester

Type of dwelling(s) in converted or shared accommodation	b	c	d	e	f	g	h	i	j	k	l	m	n	o	p	q
TOTAL CONVERTED OR SHARED ACCOMMODATION	**417**	**1,048**	**55**	**28**	**13**	**2**	**12**	**27**	**1,249**	**928**	**47**	**66**	**23**	**176**	**9**	**4,783**
Unconverted accommodation																
1 shared dwelling	40	40	40	23	8	2	7		153			27	16	102	8	280
Partly converted accommodation																
1 shared, 1 unshared dwelling*	29	39	10	3	4	-	3	19	100	25	3	17	3	51	1	306
1 shared, 2 unshared dwellings*	4	9	1	-	-	-	1	3	23	5	3	2	1	12	-	50
1 shared, 3 or more unshared dwellings*	9	55	4	2	1	-	1	5	68	38	12	8	-	10	-	187
Converted accommodation																
2 unshared dwellings	232	464							464	441	11	8	3	1	-	2,119
3 unshared dwellings	51	153							153	143	7	3	-	-	-	699
4 or more unshared dwellings	52	288							288	276	11	1	-	-	-	1,142

Table 61   Dwelling type and occupancy

61. Dwellings; non-permanent accommodation

Occupancy type	TOTAL DWELLINGS	Unshared dwellings												Shared dwellings	TOTAL NON-PERMANENT ACCOMMODATION
		Total unshared dwellings	Unshared dwellings - purpose-built					Unshared dwellings - converted		Unshared dwellings - not self-contained				
			Detached	Semi-detached	Terraced	Purpose-built flat in: Residential building	Purpose-built flat in: Commercial building	Converted flat	Converted flatlet	Not self-contained flat	Not self-contained 'rooms'	Bedsit		
a	b	c	d	e	f	g	h	i	j	k	l	m	n	o
HAMPSHIRE														
ALL TYPES OF OCCUPANCY	627,550	625,752	178,240	153,193	180,680	89,447	7,915	14,695	1,123	213	308	151	1,798	4,922
Dwellings with residents	594,568	592,839	170,620	148,119	171,521	81,983	6,611	12,626	951	213	69	126	1,729	4,508
Dwellings with person(s) present	574,975	573,274	165,233	144,446	166,448	77,943	6,248	11,724	857	196	65	114	1,701	4,243
Dwellings with no person(s) present	19,593	19,565	5,387	3,673	5,073	4,040	363	902	94	17	4	12	28	265
Vacant accommodation	26,650	26,611	5,889	4,181	7,348	6,368	1,101	1,562	127			19	39	
New, never occupied	4,378	4,376	1,447	204	809	1,766	46	95	9			-	2	
Under improvement	2,968	2,962	622	585	918	418	102	296	17			1	6	
Other	19,304	19,273	3,820	3,392	5,621	4,184	953	1,171	101			18	31	
Accommodation not used as main residence	6,332	6,302	1,731	893	1,811	1,096	203	507	45		10	6	30	414
No persons present	3,340	3,337	1,155	440	758	644	96	224	17		1	2	3	-
Second residences	2,476	2,476	893	321	566	501	62	126	7				-	
Holiday accommodation	690	690	250	85	129	123	26	72	5				-	
Student accommodation	174	171	12	34	63	20	8	26	5		1	2	3	-
Persons enumerated but no residents	2,992	2,965	576	453	1,053	452	107	283	28	7	2	4	27	414
Owner occupied	1,079	1,078	355	182	272	181	27	56	4	1	-	-	1	296
Not owner occupied	1,913	1,887	221	271	781	271	80	227	24	6	2	4	26	118
Basingstoke & Deane														
ALL TYPES OF OCCUPANCY	56,055	56,000	17,685	12,943	19,072	5,416	379	407	79	11	6	2	55	265
Dwellings with residents	53,933	53,879	16,947	12,602	18,498	5,051	330	368	64	11	6	2	54	260
Dwellings with person(s) present	52,286	52,233	16,444	12,304	17,966	4,775	314	350	61	11	6	2	53	237
Dwellings with no person(s) present	1,647	1,646	503	298	532	276	16	18	3	-	-	-	1	23
Vacant accommodation	1,850	1,849	616	296	516	334	41	31	15				1	
New, never occupied	391	391	211	11	41	120	1	-	7				-	
Under improvement	149	149	52	39	38	7	5	8	-				-	
Other	1,310	1,309	353	246	437	207	35	23	8				1	
Accommodation not used as main residence	272	272	122	45	58	31	8	8	-					5
No persons present	125	125	72	17	21	9	3	3						
Second residences	108	108	62	16	17	9	2	2						
Holiday accommodation	15	15	9	1	4	-	-	1						
Student accommodation	2	2	1	-	-	-	-	-						
Persons enumerated but no residents	147	147	50	28	37	22	5	5	-				-	5
Owner occupied	60	60	25	15	11	8	-	1	-				-	5
Not owner occupied	87	87	25	13	26	14	5	4	-				-	-

Table 61 Dwelling type and occupancy – continued

61. Dwellings; non-permanent accommodation

Columns: a = Occupancy type; b = TOTAL DWELLINGS; c = Total unshared dwellings; d–h = Unshared dwellings – purpose-built (d Detached, e Semi-detached, f Terraced, and Purpose-built flat in: g Residential building, h Commercial building); i–m = Unshared dwellings – converted / not self-contained (i Converted flat, j Converted flatlet, and Not self-contained: k Not self-contained flat, l Not self-contained 'rooms', m Bedsit); n = Shared dwellings; o = TOTAL NON-PERMANENT ACCOMMODATION

East Hampshire

a	b	c	d	e	f	g	h	i	j	k	l	m	n	o
ALL TYPES OF OCCUPANCY	40,479	40,436	17,567	9,700	8,181	3,765	437	724	39	17	5	1	43	511
Dwellings with residents	38,576	38,533	16,833	9,402	7,791	3,433	375	643	35	17	4	-	43	488
Dwellings with person(s) present	37,337	37,294	16,288	9,149	7,556	3,281	360	607	33	17	3	-	43	462
Dwellings with no person(s) present	1,239	1,239	545	253	235	152	15	36	2	-	1	-	-	26
Vacant accommodation	1,617	1,617	596	245	349	309	56	61	1	-	-	-	-	
New, never occupied	394	394	189	20	42	133	5	5	-	-	-	-	-	
Under improvement	152	152	53	44	31	3	5	16	-	-	-	-	-	
Other	1,071	1,071	354	181	276	173	46	40	1	-	-	-	-	
Accommodation not used as main residence	286	286	138	53	41	23	6	20	3	-	1	1	-	23
No persons present	154	154	81	30	18	11	4	8	2	-	-	-	-	
Second residences	142	142	73	28	17	11	3	8	2	-	-	-	-	
Holiday accommodation	12	12	8	2	1	-	1	-	-	-	-	-	-	
Student accommodation	-	-	-	-	-	-	-	-	-	-	-	-	-	
Persons enumerated but no residents	132	132	57	23	23	12	2	12	1	-	1	1	-	23
Owner occupied	79	79	44	13	13	5	2	1	-	-	1	-	-	21
Not owner occupied	53	53	13	10	10	7	-	11	1	-	-	1	-	2

Eastleigh

a	b	c	d	e	f	g	h	i	j	k	l	m	n	o
ALL TYPES OF OCCUPANCY	42,578	42,525	14,874	12,429	10,037	4,433	348	383	8	3	3	7	53	459
Dwellings with residents	40,654	40,605	14,306	12,119	9,558	3,998	311	297	8	3	2	3	49	455
Dwellings with person(s) present	39,403	39,354	13,854	11,820	9,287	3,805	299	273	8	3	2	3	49	408
Dwellings with no person(s) present	1,251	1,251	452	299	271	193	12	24	-	-	-	-	-	47
Vacant accommodation	1,740	1,737	501	288	437	397	32	77	-	-	1	4	3	
New, never occupied	562	562	211	28	114	177	2	30	-	-	-	-	-	
Under improvement	154	153	38	24	43	30	1	18	-	-	-	-	1	
Other	1,024	1,022	252	236	280	190	30	29	-	-	1	4	2	
Accommodation not used as main residence	184	183	67	22	42	38	5	9	-	-	-	-	1	4
No persons present	94	94	39	11	17	20	1	6	-	-	-	-	-	
Second residences	91	91	38	11	17	20	1	4	-	-	-	-	-	
Holiday accommodation	3	3	1	-	-	-	-	2	-	-	-	-	-	
Student accommodation	-	-	-	-	-	-	-	-	-	-	-	-	-	
Persons enumerated but no residents	90	89	28	11	25	18	4	3	-	-	-	-	1	4
Owner occupied	48	48	14	7	17	9	1	-	-	-	-	-	-	3
Not owner occupied	42	41	14	4	8	9	3	3	-	-	-	-	1	1

Table 61 Dwelling type and occupancy – continued

61. Dwellings; non-permanent accommodation

| Occupancy type | TOTAL DWELLINGS | Total unshared dwellings | Unshared dwellings - purpose-built | | | | | Unshared dwellings - converted | | Unshared dwellings - not self-contained | | | Shared dwellings | TOTAL NON-PERMANENT ACCOMMODATION |
| | | | Detached | Semi-detached | Terraced | Purpose-built flat in: Residential building | Purpose-built flat in: Commercial building | Converted flat | Converted flatlet | Not self-contained flat | Not self-contained 'rooms' | Bedsit | | |
a	b	c	d	e	f	g	h	i	j	k	l	m	n	o
Fareham														
ALL TYPES OF OCCUPANCY	**39,654**	**39,628**	**13,653**	**13,485**	**8,506**	**3,474**	**291**	**196**	**15**	**3**	**4**	**1**	**26**	**291**
Dwellings with residents	**38,038**	**38,012**	**13,157**	**13,104**	**8,118**	**3,206**	**231**	**176**	**13**	**3**	**4**	**-**	**26**	**287**
Dwellings with person(s) present	36,936	36,910	12,770	12,787	7,888	3,053	225	167	13	3	4	-	26	279
Dwellings with no person(s) present	1,102	1,102	387	317	230	153	6	9	-	-	-	-	-	8
Vacant accommodation	**1,401**	**1,401**	**426**	**331**	**327**	**248**	**52**	**14**	**2**	**-**	**-**	**1**	**-**	**4**
New, never occupied	301	301	132	15	68	85	1	-	-	-	-	-	-	-
Under improvement	79	79	15	28	23	11	1	-	1	-	-	1	-	-
Other	1,021	1,021	279	288	236	152	50	14	1	-	-	-	-	-
Accommodation not used as main residence	**215**	**215**	**70**	**50**	**61**	**20**	**8**	**6**	**-**	**-**	**-**	**-**	**-**	**4**
No persons present	111	111	40	18	35	8	4	6	-	-	-	-	-	-
Second residences	107	107	37	18	34	8	4	6	-	-	-	-	-	-
Holiday accommodation	3	3	2	-	1	-	-	-	-	-	-	-	-	-
Student accommodation	1	1	1	-	-	-	-	-	-	-	-	-	-	-
Persons enumerated but no residents	104	104	30	32	26	12	4	-	-	-	-	-	-	4
Owner occupied	65	65	21	24	15	4	1	-	-	-	-	-	-	3
Not owner occupied	39	39	9	8	11	8	3	-	-	-	-	-	-	1
Gosport														
ALL TYPES OF OCCUPANCY	**31,258**	**31,234**	**3,574**	**8,008**	**12,896**	**5,968**	**427**	**346**	**9**	**3**	**1**	**2**	**24**	**94**
Dwellings with residents	**29,208**	**29,185**	**3,442**	**7,739**	**12,067**	**5,259**	**360**	**304**	**8**	**3**	**1**	**2**	**23**	**88**
Dwellings with person(s) present	28,222	28,200	3,321	7,557	11,723	4,961	347	278	8	2	1	2	22	86
Dwellings with no person(s) present	986	985	121	182	344	298	13	26	-	1	-	-	1	2
Vacant accommodation	**1,880**	**1,879**	**104**	**236**	**799**	**639**	**63**	**37**	**1**	**-**	**-**	**-**	**1**	**-**
New, never occupied	110	110	16	2	30	62	-	-	-	-	-	-	-	-
Under improvement	117	117	12	14	57	18	8	8	-	-	-	-	-	-
Other	1,653	1,652	76	220	712	559	55	29	1	1	-	-	1	-
Accommodation not used as main residence	**170**	**170**	**28**	**33**	**30**	**70**	**4**	**5**	**-**	**-**	**-**	**-**	**-**	**6**
No persons present	94	94	16	21	17	34	3	3	-	-	-	-	-	-
Second residences	75	75	14	16	14	29	2	-	-	-	-	-	-	-
Holiday accommodation	19	19	2	5	3	5	1	3	-	-	-	-	-	-
Student accommodation	-	-	-	-	-	-	-	-	-	-	-	-	-	-
Persons enumerated but no residents	76	76	12	12	13	36	1	2	-	-	-	-	-	6
Owner occupied	41	41	5	9	9	17	-	1	-	-	-	-	-	6
Not owner occupied	35	35	7	3	4	19	1	1	-	-	-	-	-	-

Table 61 Dwelling type and occupancy – continued

61. Dwellings; non-permanent accommodation

Occupancy type	TOTAL DWELLINGS	Total unshared dwellings	Unshared dwellings - purpose-built: Detached	Semi-detached	Terraced	Purpose-built flat in: Residential building	Purpose-built flat in: Commercial building	Unshared dwellings - converted: Converted flat	Converted flatlet	Unshared dwellings - not self-contained: Not self-contained flat	Not self-contained 'rooms'	Bedsit	Shared dwellings	TOTAL NON-PERMANENT ACCOMMODATION
a	b	c	d	e	f	g	h	i	j	k	l	m	n	o
Hart														
ALL TYPES OF OCCUPANCY	**29,903**	**29,883**	**13,774**	**7,621**	**5,772**	**2,133**	**278**	**276**	**20**	**5**	**6**	**3**	**20**	**338**
Dwellings with residents	**28,701**	**28,682**	**13,378**	**7,455**	**5,479**	**1,868**	**222**	**256**	**15**	**5**	**1**	**3**	**19**	**330**
Dwellings with person(s) present	27,791	27,772	12,993	7,254	5,293	1,763	208	239	13	5	1	3	19	310
Dwellings with no person(s) present	910	910	385	201	186	105	14	17	2	-	-	-	-	20
Vacant accommodation	**1,060**	**1,059**	**337**	**147**	**260**	**243**	**51**	**16**	**5**	-	-	-	**1**	
New, never occupied	257	257	86	7	22	141	4	1	-				-	
Under improvement	82	82	34	22	20	1	-	1	-				-	
Other	721	720	217	118	218	101	47	14	5				1	
Accommodation not used as main residence	**142**	**142**	**59**	**19**	**33**	**22**	**5**	**4**	-	-	-	-	-	**8**
No persons present	55	55	29	4	15	5	2	-	-				-	
Second residences	53	53	29	4	13	5	2	-	-				-	
Holiday accommodation	2	2	-	-	2	-	-	-	-				-	
Student accommodation	-	-	-	-	-	-	-	-	-				-	
Persons enumerated but no residents	87	87	30	15	18	17	3	4	-				-	8
Owner occupied	47	47	23	6	12	3	1	2	-				-	2
Not owner occupied	40	40	7	9	6	14	2	2	-				-	6
Havant														
ALL TYPES OF OCCUPANCY	**48,043**	**47,983**	**13,897**	**11,963**	**13,895**	**7,068**	**638**	**440**	**68**	**7**	**11**	**3**	**60**	**156**
Dwellings with residents	**45,913**	**45,854**	**13,268**	**11,629**	**13,483**	**6,512**	**503**	**386**	**59**	**7**	**4**	**3**	**59**	**114**
Dwellings with person(s) present	44,625	44,566	12,864	11,380	13,205	6,198	487	366	52	7	4	3	59	110
Dwellings with no person(s) present	1,288	1,288	404	249	278	314	16	20	7	-	-	-	-	4
Vacant accommodation	**1,569**	**1,568**	**401**	**261**	**319**	**425**	**112**	**45**	**5**	-	-	-	**1**	
New, never occupied	198	198	68	8	25	80	15	2	-				-	
Under improvement	164	164	42	35	23	49	6	7	2				-	
Other	1,207	1,206	291	218	271	296	91	36	3				1	
Accommodation not used as main residence	**561**	**561**	**228**	**73**	**93**	**131**	**23**	**9**	**4**	-	-	-	-	**42**
No persons present	456	456	190	56	81	102	18	7	2				-	
Second residences	273	273	93	43	69	57	6	4	1				-	
Holiday accommodation	181	181	96	13	11	45	12	3	1				-	
Student accommodation	2	2	1	-	1	-	-	-	-				-	
Persons enumerated but no residents	105	105	38	17	12	29	5	2	2				-	42
Owner occupied	69	69	28	10	9	18	3	-	1				-	31
Not owner occupied	36	36	10	7	3	11	2	2	1				-	11

Table 61 Dwelling type and occupancy – continued

61. Dwellings: non-permanent accommodation

Column groupings: columns d–h = **Unshared dwellings – purpose-built** (g, h = Purpose-built flat in: Residential building / Commercial building); columns i–j = **Unshared dwellings – converted**; columns k–m = **Unshared dwellings – not self-contained**.

Occupancy type (a)	TOTAL DWELLINGS (b)	Total unshared dwellings (c)	Detached (d)	Semi-detached (e)	Terraced (f)	Residential building (g)	Commercial building (h)	Converted flat (i)	Converted flatlet (j)	Not self-contained flat (k)	Not self-contained 'rooms' (l)	Bedsit (m)	Shared dwellings (n)	TOTAL NON-PERMANENT ACCOMMODATION (o)
New Forest														
ALL TYPES OF OCCUPANCY	68,872	68,810	33,207	15,217	11,907	6,296	1,013	1,066	60	28	7	9	62	1,460
Dwellings with residents	64,092	64,032	31,330	14,479	11,028	5,375	872	863	44	28	6	7	60	1,186
Dwellings with person(s) present	61,796	61,737	30,273	14,079	10,623	5,074	820	790	38	27	6	7	59	1,117
Dwellings with no person(s) present	2,296	2,295	1,057	400	405	301	52	73	6	1	-	-	1	69
Vacant accommodation	3,089	3,088	1,241	508	509	617	108	91	11	-	1	2	1	
New, never occupied	611	611	228	36	116	217	9	5	-	-	-	-	-	
Under improvement	344	343	152	79	41	23	15	33	-	-	-	-	1	
Other	2,134	2,134	861	393	352	377	84	53	11	-	1	2	-	
Accommodation not used as main residence	1,691	1,690	636	230	370	304	33	112	5	-	-	-	1	274
No persons present	1,268	1,268	476	159	286	246	23	77	1	-	-	-	-	
Second residences	927	927	363	107	201	194	13	49	-	-	-	-	-	
Holiday accommodation	341	341	113	52	85	52	10	28	1	-	-	-	-	
Student accommodation	-	-	-	-	-	-	-	-	-	-	-	-	-	
Persons enumerated but no residents	423	422	160	71	84	58	10	35	4	-	-	-	1	274
Owner occupied	286	285	110	42	58	43	6	25	1	-	-	-	1	190
Not owner occupied	137	137	50	29	26	15	4	10	3	-	-	-	-	84
Portsmouth														
ALL TYPES OF OCCUPANCY	76,360	75,841	2,543	9,696	40,307	15,755	1,640	5,505	278	56	13	48	519	136
Dwellings with residents	71,154	70,653	2,408	9,398	38,064	14,457	1,354	4,637	239	44	12	40	501	128
Dwellings with person(s) present	68,531	68,034	2,318	9,156	36,932	13,790	1,256	4,276	215	42	12	37	497	125
Dwellings with no person(s) present	2,623	2,619	90	242	1,132	667	98	361	24	2	-	3	4	3
Vacant accommodation	4,087	4,079	120	253	1,658	1,135	237	644	21	7	-	4	8	
New, never occupied	342	341	22	9	108	180	-	21	1	-	-	-	1	
Under improvement	537	536	10	24	256	125	19	99	1	1	-	1	1	
Other	3,208	3,202	88	220	1,294	830	218	524	19	6	-	3	6	
Accommodation not used as main residence	1,119	1,109	15	45	585	163	49	224	18	5	1	4	10	8
No persons present	315	315	3	15	118	88	11	69	9	-	-	2	-	
Second residences	214	214	3	13	87	71	8	31	1	-	-	-	-	
Holiday accommodation	47	47	-	1	8	14	1	20	3	-	-	-	-	
Student accommodation	54	54	-	1	23	3	2	18	5	-	-	2	-	
Persons enumerated but no residents	804	794	12	30	467	75	38	155	9	5	1	2	10	8
Owner occupied	127	127	1	7	70	27	6	15	1	-	-	-	-	5
Not owner occupied	677	667	11	23	397	48	32	140	8	5	1	2	10	3

Table 61 Dwelling type and occupancy – continued

61. Dwellings; non-permanent accommodation

Rushmoor

Occupancy type (a)	TOTAL DWELLINGS (b)	Total unshared dwellings (c)	Detached (d)	Semi-detached (e)	Terraced (f)	Purpose-built flat – Residential building (g)	Purpose-built flat – Commercial building (h)	Converted flat (i)	Converted flatlet (j)	Not self-contained flat (k)	Not self-contained 'rooms' (l)	Bedsit (m)	Shared dwellings (n)	TOTAL NON-PERMANENT ACCOMMODATION (o)
ALL TYPES OF OCCUPANCY	**31,276**	**31,120**	**5,213**	**9,898**	**9,494**	**5,251**	**503**	**691**	**45**	**11**	**19**	**6**	**156**	**212**
Dwellings with residents	**29,911**	**29,757**	**5,052**	**9,620**	**9,028**	**4,965**	**414**	**621**	**37**	**11**	**6**	**3**	**154**	**205**
Dwellings with person(s) present	28,927	28,777	4,920	9,381	8,741	4,714	390	581	31	11	5	3	150	192
Dwellings with no person(s) present	984	980	132	239	287	251	24	40	6	-	1	-	4	13
Vacant accommodation	**1,263**	**1,261**	**144**	**257**	**437**	**259**	**83**	**70**	**7**	-	**2**	**2**	**2**	-
New, never occupied	62	62	13	1	-	44	-	4	-	-	-	-	-	-
Under improvement	203	203	12	61	83	23	9	10	4	-	1	1	-	-
Other	998	996	119	195	354	192	74	56	3	-	1	1	2	-
Accommodation not used as main residence	**102**	**102**	**17**	**21**	**29**	**27**	**6**	-	**1**	-	-	**1**	-	**7**
No persons present	24	24	8	7	3	2	3	-	1	-	-	-	-	-
Second residences	22	22	7	6	3	2	3	-	1	-	-	-	-	-
Holiday accommodation	1	1	1	1	-	-	-	-	-	-	-	-	-	-
Student accommodation	1	1	1	-	-	-	-	-	-	-	-	-	-	-
Persons enumerated but no residents	78	78	9	14	26	25	3	-	-	-	-	1	-	7
Owner occupied	23	23	3	8	9	2	1	-	-	-	-	-	-	5
Not owner occupied	55	55	6	6	17	23	2	-	-	-	1	1	-	2

Southampton

Occupancy type (a)	TOTAL DWELLINGS (b)	Total unshared dwellings (c)	Detached (d)	Semi-detached (e)	Terraced (f)	Purpose-built flat – Residential building (g)	Purpose-built flat – Commercial building (h)	Converted flat (i)	Converted flatlet (j)	Not self-contained flat (k)	Not self-contained 'rooms' (l)	Bedsit (m)	Shared dwellings (n)	TOTAL NON-PERMANENT ACCOMMODATION (o)
ALL TYPES OF OCCUPANCY	**84,446**	**83,745**	**12,162**	**22,709**	**21,386**	**22,521**	**1,252**	**3,143**	**434**	**54**	**80**	**58**	**701**	**72**
Dwellings with residents	**79,524**	**78,858**	**11,665**	**21,757**	**20,196**	**21,014**	**1,022**	**2,711**	**369**	**54**	**18**	**52**	**666**	**69**
Dwellings with person(s) present	76,644	75,994	11,283	21,222	19,599	20,001	957	2,498	331	54	18	44	650	62
Dwellings with no person(s) present	2,880	2,864	382	535	597	1,013	65	213	38	13	-	8	16	7
Vacant accommodation	**4,026**	**4,008**	**441**	**752**	**874**	**1,308**	**200**	**366**	**56**	**5**	**3**	**6**	**18**	**3**
New, never occupied	565	565	22	27	122	375	8	11	-	-	-	-	-	-
Under improvement	529	526	75	141	116	89	21	74	9	-	1	1	3	-
Other	2,932	2,917	344	584	636	844	171	281	47	-	4	5	15	-
Accommodation not used as main residence	**896**	**879**	**56**	**200**	**316**	**199**	**30**	**66**	**9**	**1**	**3**	-	**17**	**3**
No persons present	280	277	26	44	77	91	9	28	1	1	1	-	3	-
Second residences	153	153	18	12	38	71	7	6	1	1	-	-	-	-
Holiday accommodation	21	21	1	1	1	4	-	14	-	-	-	-	-	-
Student accommodation	106	103	7	31	38	16	2	8	-	-	1	-	3	-
Persons enumerated but no residents	616	602	30	156	239	108	21	38	8	-	1	-	14	3
Owner occupied	83	83	8	20	18	29	3	4	1	-	-	-	-	3
Not owner occupied	533	519	22	136	221	79	18	34	7	1	1	-	14	-

Table 61 Dwelling type and occupancy – continued

61. Dwellings; non-permanent accommodation

- Unshared dwellings – purpose-built: Detached (d), Semi-detached (e), Terraced (f)
- Purpose-built flat in: Residential building (g), Commercial building (h)
- Unshared dwellings – converted: Converted flat (i), Converted flatlet (j)
- Unshared dwellings – not self-contained: Not self-contained flat (k), Not self-contained 'rooms' (l), Bedsit (m)

Occupancy type (a)	Total dwellings (b)	Total unshared dwellings (c)	Detached (d)	Semi-detached (e)	Terraced (f)	Residential building (g)	Commercial building (h)	Converted flat (i)	Converted flatlet (j)	Not self-contained [total]	Not self-contained flat (k)	Not self-contained 'rooms' (l)	Bedsit (m)	Shared dwellings (n)	Total non-permanent accommodation (o)
Test Valley															
ALL TYPES OF OCCUPANCY	39,845	39,821	15,033	9,927	10,511	3,440	274	590	21	17	15	2	8	24	387
Dwellings with residents	37,961	37,938	14,385	9,524	9,954	3,244	247	539	20	15	15	2	8	23	380
Dwellings with person(s) present	36,764	36,741	13,903	9,287	9,665	3,088	239	516	19		15	2	7	23	362
Dwellings with no person(s) present	1,197	1,197	482	237	289	156	8	23	1		-	-	1	-	18
Vacant accommodation	1,577	1,576	492	347	498	180	22	37	-		-	-	-	1	
New, never occupied	296	296	130	30	63	67	5	1	-		-	-	-	-	-
Under improvement	232	232	66	29	122	4	5	6	-		-	-	-	-	-
Other	1,049	1,048	296	288	313	109	12	30	-		-	-	-	1	-
Accommodation not used as main residence	307	307	156	56	59	16	5	14	1		-	-	-	-	7
No persons present	187	187	96	37	34	8	3	8	1		-	-	-	-	-
Second residences	158	158	83	32	26	6	2	8	1		-	-	-	-	-
Holiday accommodation	28	28	12	5	8	2	1	-	-		-	-	-	-	-
Student accommodation	1	1	1	-	-	-	-	-	-		-	-	-	-	-
Persons enumerated but no residents	120	120	60	19	25	8	2	6	-		-	-	-	-	7
Owner occupied	71	71	38	11	16	3	1	2	-		-	-	-	-	5
Not owner occupied	49	49	22	8	9	5	1	4	-		-	-	-	-	2
Winchester															
ALL TYPES OF OCCUPANCY	38,781	38,726	15,058	9,597	8,716	3,927	435	928	47	15	12	3	3	55	541
Dwellings with residents	36,903	36,851	14,449	9,291	8,257	3,601	370	825	40		12	3	3	52	518
Dwellings with person(s) present	35,713	35,662	14,002	9,070	7,970	3,440	346	783	35		12	1	3	51	493
Dwellings with no person(s) present	1,190	1,189	447	221	287	161	24	42	5		-	2	-	1	25
Vacant accommodation	1,491	1,489	470	260	365	274	44	73	3		-	-	-	2	
New, never occupied	289	288	119	10	58	85	-	15	1		-	-	-	1	-
Under improvement	226	226	61	45	65	35	4	16	-		-	-	-	-	-
Other	976	975	290	205	242	154	40	42	2		-	-	-	1	-
Accommodation not used as main residence	387	386	139	46	94	52	21	30	4		-	-	-	1	23
No persons present	177	177	79	21	36	20	12	9	-		-	-	-	-	-
Second residences	153	153	73	15	30	18	9	8	-		-	-	-	-	-
Holiday accommodation	17	17	6	4	5	1	-	1	-		-	-	-	-	-
Student accommodation	7	7	-	2	1	1	3	-	-		-	-	-	-	-
Persons enumerated but no residents	210	209	60	25	58	32	9	21	4		-	-	-	1	23
Owner occupied	80	80	35	10	15	13	2	5	-		-	-	-	-	17
Not owner occupied	130	129	25	15	43	19	7	16	4		-	-	-	1	6

Table 62 Occupancy and tenure of dwellings

County, districts

62. Dwellings with persons present or resident

Occupancy type	TOTAL DWELLINGS	Owner occupied		Rented privately		Rented with a job or business	Rented from a housing association	Rented from a local authority or new town
		Owned outright	Buying	Furnished	Unfurnished			
a	b	c	d	e	f	g	h	i

HAMPSHIRE

ALL TYPES OF OCCUPANCY	597,560	143,866	291,147	20,216	18,772	17,800	11,841	93,918
Dwellings with residents	594,568	143,347	290,587	18,681	18,692	17,636	11,804	93,821
Dwellings with person(s) present	574,975	137,340	282,082	17,631	18,014	16,997	11,288	91,623
Dwellings with no person(s) present	19,593	6,007	8,505	1,050	678	639	516	2,198
Dwellings with persons enumerated but no residents	2,992	519	560	1,535	80	164	37	97

Basingstoke & Deane

ALL TYPES OF OCCUPANCY	54,080	8,874	29,577	1,189	1,382	2,027	1,229	9,802
Dwellings with residents	53,933	8,846	29,545	1,138	1,370	2,010	1,228	9,796
Dwellings with person(s) present	52,286	8,474	28,730	1,080	1,307	1,945	1,184	9,566
Dwellings with no person(s) present	1,647	372	815	58	63	65	44	230
Dwellings with persons enumerated but no residents	147	28	32	51	12	17	1	6

East Hampshire

ALL TYPES OF OCCUPANCY	38,708	9,898	20,246	943	1,240	1,624	434	4,323
Dwellings with residents	38,576	9,856	20,209	917	1,236	1,608	430	4,320
Dwellings with person(s) present	37,337	9,423	19,622	869	1,208	1,573	415	4,227
Dwellings with no person(s) present	1,239	433	587	48	28	35	15	93
Dwellings with persons enumerated but no residents	132	42	37	26	4	16	4	3

Eastleigh

ALL TYPES OF OCCUPANCY	40,744	9,223	23,968	875	876	325	769	4,708
Dwellings with residents	40,654	9,210	23,933	843	875	321	768	4,704
Dwellings with person(s) present	39,403	8,841	23,241	798	840	312	744	4,627
Dwellings with no person(s) present	1,251	369	692	45	35	9	24	77
Dwellings with persons enumerated but no residents	90	13	35	32	1	4	1	4

Fareham

ALL TYPES OF OCCUPANCY	38,142	11,154	21,667	752	706	542	252	3,069
Dwellings with residents	38,038	11,123	21,633	726	704	535	252	3,065
Dwellings with person(s) present	36,936	10,706	21,098	700	686	515	237	2,994
Dwellings with no person(s) present	1,102	417	535	26	18	20	15	71
Dwellings with persons enumerated but no residents	104	31	34	26	2	7	-	4

Gosport

ALL TYPES OF OCCUPANCY	29,284	6,435	14,099	830	776	1,394	633	5,117
Dwellings with residents	29,208	6,418	14,075	817	776	1,380	631	5,111
Dwellings with person(s) present	28,222	6,169	13,654	766	753	1,304	594	4,982
Dwellings with no person(s) present	986	249	421	51	23	76	37	129
Dwellings with persons enumerated but no residents	76	17	24	13	-	14	2	6

62. Dwellings with persons present or resident

Occupancy type	TOTAL DWELLINGS	Owner occupied		Rented privately		Rented with a job or business	Rented from a housing association	Rented from a local authority or new town
		Owned outright	Buying	Furnished	Unfurnished			
a	b	c	d	e	f	g	h	i

Hart

Occupancy type	TOTAL DWELLINGS	Owned outright	Buying	Furnished	Unfurnished	Rented with a job or business	Rented from a housing association	Rented from a local authority or new town
ALL TYPES OF OCCUPANCY	28,788	5,853	17,488	877	705	1,259	299	2,307
Dwellings with residents	28,701	5,833	17,461	862	699	1,240	299	2,307
Dwellings with person(s) present	27,791	5,559	17,010	823	680	1,183	290	2,246
Dwellings with no person(s) present	910	274	451	39	19	57	9	61
Dwellings with persons enumerated but no residents	87	20	27	15	6	19	-	-

Havant

Occupancy type	TOTAL DWELLINGS	Owned outright	Buying	Furnished	Unfurnished	Rented with a job or business	Rented from a housing association	Rented from a local authority or new town
ALL TYPES OF OCCUPANCY	46,018	11,427	22,056	1,140	705	484	400	9,806
Dwellings with residents	45,913	11,395	22,019	1,117	703	481	398	9,800
Dwellings with person(s) present	44,625	10,963	21,500	1,061	673	464	372	9,592
Dwellings with no person(s) present	1,288	432	519	56	30	17	26	208
Dwellings with persons enumerated but no residents	105	32	37	23	2	3	2	6

New Forest

Occupancy type	TOTAL DWELLINGS	Owned outright	Buying	Furnished	Unfurnished	Rented with a job or business	Rented from a housing association	Rented from a local authority or new town
ALL TYPES OF OCCUPANCY	64,515	23,202	29,036	1,582	2,155	1,489	856	6,195
Dwellings with residents	64,092	23,028	28,924	1,481	2,145	1,474	854	6,186
Dwellings with person(s) present	61,796	21,977	28,023	1,397	2,066	1,438	808	6,087
Dwellings with no person(s) present	2,296	1,051	901	84	79	36	46	99
Dwellings with persons enumerated but no residents	423	174	112	101	10	15	2	9

Portsmouth

Occupancy type	TOTAL DWELLINGS	Owned outright	Buying	Furnished	Unfurnished	Rented with a job or business	Rented from a housing association	Rented from a local authority or new town
ALL TYPES OF OCCUPANCY	71,958	17,903	30,784	4,462	2,970	1,573	2,201	12,065
Dwellings with residents	71,154	17,851	30,709	3,832	2,965	1,558	2,188	12,051
Dwellings with person(s) present	68,531	17,119	29,635	3,618	2,852	1,490	2,095	11,722
Dwellings with no person(s) present	2,623	732	1,074	214	113	68	93	329
Dwellings with persons enumerated but no residents	804	52	75	630	5	15	13	14

Rushmoor

Occupancy type	TOTAL DWELLINGS	Owned outright	Buying	Furnished	Unfurnished	Rented with a job or business	Rented from a housing association	Rented from a local authority or new town
ALL TYPES OF OCCUPANCY	29,989	4,679	15,584	1,113	856	2,205	575	4,977
Dwellings with residents	29,911	4,674	15,566	1,081	855	2,195	574	4,966
Dwellings with person(s) present	28,927	4,498	15,099	1,030	818	2,088	549	4,845
Dwellings with no person(s) present	984	176	467	51	37	107	25	121
Dwellings with persons enumerated but no residents	78	5	18	32	1	10	1	11

Southampton

Occupancy type	TOTAL DWELLINGS	Owned outright	Buying	Furnished	Unfurnished	Rented with a job or business	Rented from a housing association	Rented from a local authority or new town
ALL TYPES OF OCCUPANCY	80,140	17,821	31,575	4,475	3,432	844	2,715	19,278
Dwellings with residents	79,524	17,796	31,517	4,009	3,414	825	2,710	19,253
Dwellings with person(s) present	76,644	17,072	30,456	3,729	3,277	772	2,589	18,749
Dwellings with no person(s) present	2,880	724	1,061	280	137	53	121	504
Dwellings with persons enumerated but no residents	616	25	58	466	18	19	5	25

62. Dwellings with persons present or resident

Occupancy type	TOTAL DWELLINGS	Owner occupied		Rented privately		Rented with a job or business	Rented from a housing association	Rented from a local authority or new town
		Owned outright	Buying	Furnished	Unfurnished			
a	b	c	d	e	f	g	h	i
Test Valley								
ALL TYPES OF OCCUPANCY	38,081	8,238	18,507	814	1,555	2,045	591	6,331
Dwellings with residents	37,961	8,195	18,479	787	1,547	2,036	589	6,328
Dwellings with person(s) present	36,764	7,823	17,968	750	1,491	1,983	571	6,178
Dwellings with no person(s) present	1,197	372	511	37	56	53	18	150
Dwellings with persons enumerated but no residents	120	43	28	27	8	9	2	3
Winchester								
ALL TYPES OF OCCUPANCY	37,113	9,159	16,560	1,164	1,414	1,989	887	5,940
Dwellings with residents	36,903	9,122	16,517	1,071	1,403	1,973	883	5,934
Dwellings with person(s) present	35,713	8,716	16,046	1,010	1,363	1,930	840	5,808
Dwellings with no person(s) present	1,190	406	471	61	40	43	43	126
Dwellings with persons enumerated but no residents	210	37	43	93	11	16	4	6

Table 63 Dwelling type and tenure

63. Dwellings with residents; non-permanent accommodation

HAMPSHIRE

Tenure	TOTAL DWELLINGS	Total unshared dwellings	Unshared dwellings - purpose-built Detached	Semi-detached	Terraced	Purpose-built flat in: Residential building	Commercial building	Unshared dwellings - converted Converted flat	Converted flatlet	Unshared dwellings - not self-contained Not self-contained flat	Not self-contained 'rooms'	Bedsit	Shared dwellings	TOTAL NON-PERMANENT ACCOMMODATION
a	b	c	d	e	f	g	h	i	j	k	l	m	n	o
ALL TENURES	594,568	592,839	170,620	148,119	171,521	81,983	6,611	12,626	951	213	69	126	1,729	4,508
Owner occupied - owned outright	143,347	143,154	61,697	37,496	30,481	10,944	640	1,819	31	36	8	2	193	3,197
- buying	290,587	290,346	98,610	77,390	92,376	15,732	1,511	4,475	173	67	4	5	241	656
Rented privately - furnished	18,681	17,821	2,725	2,920	5,056	2,485	1,066	2,912	462	59	41	95	860	267
- unfurnished	18,692	18,470	3,152	4,485	5,054	2,487	1,284	1,859	103	25	10	11	222	162
Rented with a job or business	17,636	17,619	3,571	4,740	4,856	2,353	1,699	357	25	12	1	5	17	121
Rented from a housing association	11,804	11,739	223	941	2,587	7,260	56	573	94	2	-	3	65	11
Rented from a local authority or new town	93,821	93,690	642	20,144	31,111	40,722	355	631	63	12	5	5	131	94

Basingstoke & Deane

Tenure	TOTAL DWELLINGS	Total unshared dwellings	Detached	Semi-detached	Terraced	Residential building	Commercial building	Converted flat	Converted flatlet	Not self-contained flat	Not self-contained 'rooms'	Bedsit	Shared dwellings	TOTAL NON-PERMANENT ACCOMMODATION
ALL TENURES	53,933	53,879	16,947	12,602	18,498	5,051	330	368	64	11	6	2	54	260
Owner occupied - owned outright	8,846	8,841	4,329	2,374	1,556	509	13	52	1	5	2	-	5	161
- buying	29,545	29,526	11,309	6,533	9,963	1,535	63	119	1	3	-	-	19	50
Rented privately - furnished	1,138	1,122	250	205	406	158	22	65	11	2	3	-	16	18
- unfurnished	1,370	1,366	368	458	349	105	52	29	3	-	1	1	4	10
Rented with a job or business	2,010	2,006	588	774	399	76	116	45	6	1	-	1	4	14
Rented from a housing association	1,228	1,226	22	128	490	537	9	7	33	-	-	-	2	-
Rented from a local authority or new town	9,796	9,792	81	2,130	5,335	2,131	55	51	9	-	-	-	4	7

East Hampshire

Tenure	TOTAL DWELLINGS	Total unshared dwellings	Detached	Semi-detached	Terraced	Residential building	Commercial building	Converted flat	Converted flatlet	Not self-contained flat	Not self-contained 'rooms'	Bedsit	Shared dwellings	TOTAL NON-PERMANENT ACCOMMODATION
ALL TENURES	38,576	38,533	16,833	9,402	7,791	3,433	375	643	35	17	4	-	43	488
Owner occupied - owned outright	9,856	9,847	5,827	2,009	1,169	646	42	148	2	4	-	-	9	334
- buying	20,209	20,201	9,812	4,948	4,127	940	106	252	10	5	1	-	8	80
Rented privately - furnished	917	909	329	178	216	86	30	60	7	-	3	-	8	39
- unfurnished	1,236	1,233	323	361	330	60	77	76	3	3	-	-	3	17
Rented with a job or business	1,608	1,606	475	436	464	64	101	61	3	2	-	-	2	17
Rented from a housing association	430	426	27	51	86	225	4	25	8	-	-	-	4	-
Rented from a local authority or new town	4,320	4,311	40	1,419	1,399	1,412	15	21	2	3	-	-	9	1

Table 63 Dwelling type and tenure – continued

63. Dwellings with residents; non-permanent accommodation

Tenure	TOTAL DWELLINGS	Total unshared dwellings	Unshared dwellings - purpose-built			Purpose-built flat in:		Unshared dwellings - converted		Unshared dwellings - not self-contained			Shared dwellings	TOTAL NON-PERMANENT ACCOMMODATION
			Detached	Semi-detached	Terraced	Residential building	Commercial building	Converted flat	Converted flatlet	Not self-contained flat	Not self-contained 'rooms'	Bedsit		
a	b	c	d	e	f	g	h	i	j	k	l	m	n	o
Eastleigh														
ALL TENURES	**40,654**	**40,605**	**14,306**	**12,119**	**9,558**	**3,998**	**311**	**297**	**8**	**3**	**2**	**3**	**49**	**455**
Owner occupied - owned outright	9,210	9,202	4,648	2,480	1,345	668	23	37	-	1	-	-	8	325
- buying	23,933	23,926	9,240	7,069	6,161	1,245	59	146	4	2	-	-	7	78
Rented privately - furnished	843	821	149	162	262	141	45	56	1	-	2	3	22	25
- unfurnished	875	870	140	246	303	87	47	46	1	-	-	-	5	5
Rented with a job or business	321	320	79	65	45	35	89	7	-	-	-	-	1	5
Rented from a housing association	768	768	18	93	189	446	19	1	2	-	-	-	-	1
Rented from a local authority or new town	4,704	4,698	32	2,004	1,253	1,376	29	4	-	-	-	-	6	16
Fareham														
ALL TENURES	**38,038**	**38,012**	**13,157**	**13,104**	**8,118**	**3,206**	**231**	**176**	**13**	**3**	**4**	**-**	**26**	**287**
Owner occupied - owned outright	11,123	11,118	4,483	4,521	1,412	623	30	48	-	1	-	-	5	203
- buying	21,633	21,629	8,234	7,529	5,054	697	62	48	2	2	1	-	4	33
Rented privately - furnished	726	719	181	201	212	68	32	23	-	-	2	-	7	30
- unfurnished	704	699	120	213	245	51	41	27	2	-	-	-	5	11
Rented with a job or business	535	535	116	104	202	42	62	8	-	-	1	-	-	9
Rented from a housing association	252	251	6	16	20	199	-	7	3	-	-	-	1	-
Rented from a local authority or new town	3,065	3,061	17	520	973	1,526	4	15	6	-	-	-	4	1
Gosport														
ALL TENURES	**29,208**	**29,185**	**3,442**	**7,739**	**12,067**	**5,259**	**360**	**304**	**8**	**3**	**1**	**2**	**23**	**88**
Owner occupied - owned outright	6,418	6,417	1,441	2,021	2,133	737	34	50	-	1	-	1	1	70
- buying	14,075	14,071	1,858	4,188	6,703	1,115	88	112	5	1	-	1	4	11
Rented privately - furnished	817	806	52	113	275	211	66	85	2	-	1	1	11	2
- unfurnished	776	772	14	136	346	152	85	37	1	1	-	-	4	2
Rented with a job or business	1,380	1,380	42	217	564	476	79	2	-	-	-	-	-	-
Rented from a housing association	631	631	3	82	75	457	1	13	-	-	-	-	-	3
Rented from a local authority or new town	5,111	5,108	32	982	1,971	2,111	7	5	-	-	-	-	3	-

Table 63 Dwelling type and tenure – continued

63. Dwellings with residents; non-permanent accommodation

Tenure	TOTAL DWELLINGS	Total unshared dwellings	Detached	Semi-detached	Terraced	Residential building	Commercial building	Converted flat	Converted flatlet	Not self-contained flat	Not self-contained 'rooms'	Bedsit	Shared dwellings	TOTAL NON-PERMANENT ACCOMMODATION
a	b	c	d	e	f	g	h	i	j	k	l	m	n	o
Hart														
ALL TENURES	**28,701**	**28,682**	**13,378**	**7,455**	**5,479**	**1,868**	**222**	**256**	**15**	**5**	**1**	**3**	**19**	**330**
Owner occupied - owned outright	5,833	5,827	3,217	1,530	665	334	14	65	-	1	1	-	6	238
- buying	17,461	17,454	9,418	4,021	3,347	525	39	101	1	2	-	-	7	19
Rented privately - furnished	862	858	275	176	244	88	28	37	9	-	-	1	4	21
- unfurnished	699	698	184	223	170	46	46	25	2	1	-	1	1	17
Rented with a job or business	1,240	1,240	248	407	456	25	91	12	-	-	-	1	-	12
Rented from a housing association	299	299	8	29	81	171	-	9	1	-	-	-	-	1
Rented from a local authority or new town	2,307	2,306	28	1,069	516	679	4	7	2	1	-	-	1	22
Havant														
ALL TENURES	**45,913**	**45,854**	**13,268**	**11,629**	**13,483**	**6,512**	**503**	**386**	**59**	**7**	**4**	**3**	**59**	**114**
Owner occupied - owned outright	11,395	11,388	5,670	3,398	1,479	723	51	63	3	-	1	-	7	69
- buying	22,019	22,012	7,117	6,395	7,415	897	96	85	4	3	-	-	7	19
Rented privately - furnished	1,117	1,101	243	184	197	174	96	153	46	3	3	2	16	11
- unfurnished	703	701	96	185	168	91	107	47	6	-	-	1	2	9
Rented with a job or business	481	481	72	100	95	87	119	8	-	-	-	-	-	5
Rented from a housing association	398	396	11	20	85	270	3	7	-	-	-	-	2	1
Rented from a local authority or new town	9,800	9,775	59	1,347	4,044	4,270	31	23	-	1	-	-	25	-
New Forest														
ALL TENURES	**64,092**	**64,032**	**31,330**	**14,479**	**11,028**	**5,375**	**872**	**863**	**44**	**28**	**6**	**7**	**60**	**1,186**
Owner occupied - owned outright	23,028	23,015	14,945	3,596	2,262	1,821	119	259	4	8	1	-	13	889
- buying	28,924	28,914	14,570	6,904	5,735	1,205	233	255	4	8	-	-	10	133
Rented privately - furnished	1,481	1,465	463	262	318	152	96	147	16	5	2	4	16	63
- unfurnished	2,145	2,141	701	597	339	200	174	115	8	5	1	1	4	61
Rented with a job or business	1,474	1,474	538	390	127	154	220	40	3	2	-	-	-	21
Rented from a housing association	854	852	31	160	130	513	4	10	3	-	-	1	2	3
Rented from a local authority or new town	6,186	6,171	82	2,570	2,117	1,330	26	37	6	-	2	1	15	16

Column group notes: columns d–h are Unshared dwellings - purpose-built (g and h are Purpose-built flat in: Residential building / Commercial building); columns i–j are Unshared dwellings - converted; columns k–m are Unshared dwellings - not self-contained.

Table 63 Dwelling type and tenure – continued

63. Dwellings with residents; non-permanent accommodation

Tenure	TOTAL DWELLINGS	Unshared dwellings: Total unshared dwellings	Unshared dwellings - purpose-built: Detached	Semi-detached	Terraced	Purpose-built flat in: Residential building	Commercial building	Unshared dwellings - converted: Converted flat	Converted flatlet	Unshared dwellings - not self-contained: Not self-contained flat	Not self-contained 'rooms'	Bedsit	Shared dwellings	TOTAL NON-PERMANENT ACCOMMODATION
a	b	c	d	e	f	g	h	i	j	k	l	m	n	o
Portsmouth														
ALL TENURES	**71,154**	**70,653**	**2,408**	**9,398**	**38,064**	**14,457**	**1,354**	**4,637**	**239**	**44**	**12**	**40**	**501**	**128**
Owner occupied - owned outright	17,851	17,786	987	3,202	11,342	1,579	134	526	10	4	1	1	65	103
- buying	30,709	30,631	1,190	4,726	20,865	1,673	360	1,762	39	13	-	3	78	14
Rented privately - furnished	3,832	3,563	45	153	1,286	395	300	1,186	140	17	8	33	269	4
- unfurnished	2,965	2,907	38	136	1,270	534	264	632	23	5	3	2	58	-
Rented with a job or business	1,558	1,557	117	219	398	529	256	37	1	-	-	-	1	3
Rented from a housing association	2,188	2,175	10	51	353	1,395	5	337	21	2	-	-	13	-
Rented from a local authority or new town	12,051	12,034	21	911	2,550	8,352	35	157	5	3	-	-	17	4
Rushmoor														
ALL TENURES	**29,911**	**29,757**	**5,052**	**9,620**	**9,028**	**4,965**	**414**	**621**	**37**	**11**	**6**	**3**	**154**	**205**
Owner occupied - owned outright	4,674	4,672	1,437	2,023	780	346	30	55	1	-	-	-	2	160
- buying	15,566	15,550	3,328	5,581	4,972	1,181	99	372	9	8	-	-	16	38
Rented privately - furnished	1,081	1,006	97	247	292	152	81	115	14	1	5	2	75	3
- unfurnished	855	824	62	261	291	82	73	44	9	1	-	1	31	1
Rented with a job or business	2,195	2,195	86	607	969	409	120	4	-	-	-	-	-	1
Rented from a housing association	574	569	5	34	110	418	1	1	-	-	1	-	5	-
Rented from a local authority or new town	4,966	4,941	37	867	1,614	2,377	10	30	4	1	-	-	25	2
Southampton														
ALL TENURES	**79,524**	**78,858**	**11,665**	**21,757**	**20,196**	**21,014**	**1,022**	**2,711**	**369**	**54**	**18**	**52**	**666**	**69**
Owner occupied - owned outright	17,796	17,734	5,035	6,665	3,653	2,013	81	271	9	5	1	1	62	28
- buying	31,517	31,454	5,948	10,738	9,966	3,690	176	834	84	15	2	1	63	8
Rented privately - furnished	4,009	3,618	188	679	791	694	220	779	190	25	9	43	391	10
- unfurnished	3,414	3,316	300	753	563	840	218	587	40	8	4	3	98	3
Rented with a job or business	825	823	101	112	112	259	215	21	2	1	-	-	2	1
Rented from a housing association	2,710	2,679	15	73	555	1,895	3	114	23	-	-	1	31	2
Rented from a local authority or new town	19,253	19,234	78	2,737	4,556	11,623	109	105	21	-	2	3	19	17

Table 63 Dwelling type and tenure – continued

63. Dwellings with residents; non-permanent accommodation

Tenure	TOTAL DWELLINGS	Total unshared dwellings	Unshared dwellings - purpose-built			Purpose-built flat in:		Unshared dwellings - converted		Unshared dwellings - not self-contained			Shared dwellings	TOTAL NON-PERMANENT ACCOMMODATION
			Detached	Semi-detached	Terraced	Residential building	Commercial building	Converted flat	Converted flatlet	Not self-contained flat	Not self-contained 'rooms'	Bedsit		
a	b	c	d	e	f	g	h	i	j	k	l	m	n	o
Test Valley														
ALL TENURES	37,961	37,938	14,385	9,524	9,954	3,244	247	539	20	15	2	8	23	380
Owner occupied - owned outright	8,195	8,190	4,701	1,806	1,177	382	36	83	-	4	1	-	5	257
- buying	18,479	18,474	8,340	4,784	4,544	597	49	152	5	3	-	-	5	73
Rented privately - furnished	787	780	209	172	227	70	11	74	8	4	1	4	7	24
- unfurnished	1,547	1,544	453	505	310	160	39	73	3	-	-	1	3	11
Rented with a job or business	2,036	2,034	555	650	559	112	101	49	2	3	-	3	2	15
Rented from a housing association	589	589	47	147	160	228	1	6	-	-	-	-	-	-
Rented from a local authority or new town	6,328	6,327	80	1,460	2,977	1,695	10	102	2	1	-	-	1	-
Winchester														
ALL TENURES	36,903	36,851	14,449	9,291	8,257	3,601	370	825	40	12	3	3	52	518
Owner occupied - owned outright	9,122	9,117	4,977	1,871	1,508	563	33	162	1	2	-	-	5	360
- buying	16,517	16,504	8,246	3,977	3,524	432	81	237	5	2	-	-	13	100
Rented privately - furnished	1,071	1,053	244	188	330	96	39	132	18	2	2	2	18	17
- unfurnished	1,403	1,399	353	411	370	79	61	121	2	1	1	-	4	15
Rented with a job or business	1,973	1,968	554	659	466	85	130	63	8	3	-	-	5	15
Rented from a housing association	883	878	20	57	253	506	6	36	-	-	-	-	5	3
Rented from a local authority or new town	5,934	5,932	55	2,128	1,806	1,840	20	74	6	2	-	1	2	8

Table 64 Tenure of dwellings and household spaces

64. Dwellings: household spaces in dwellings

Columns f–p fall under "Tenure or occupancy type of household spaces"; columns n–p under "Accommodation not used as main residence – no persons present".

Tenure or occupancy type of dwelling	TOTAL DWELLINGS	Unshared dwellings	Shared dwellings	TOTAL HOUSEHOLD SPACES	Owner occupied – Owned outright	Owner occupied – Buying	Rented privately – Furnished	Rented privately – Unfurnished	Rented with a job or business	Rented from a housing association	Rented from a local authority or new town	Vacant accommodation	Second residences	Holiday accommodation	Student accommodation
a	b	c	d	e	f	g	h	i	j	k	l	m	n	o	p
HAMPSHIRE															
ALL TENURES OR OCCUPANCY TYPES	**627,550**	**625,752**	**1,798**	**632,303**	**143,889**	**291,200**	**23,576**	**18,946**	**17,875**	**11,972**	**94,129**	**27,301**	**2,492**	**700**	**223**
Dwellings with residents	**594,568**	**592,839**	**1,729**	**599,156**	**143,370**	**290,639**	**21,986**	**18,865**	**17,711**	**11,935**	**94,032**	**559**	**15**	**9**	**35**
Owner occupied - owned outright	143,347	143,154	193	143,632	143,370	15	191	36	4	-	-	15	-	-	-
- buying	290,587	290,346	241	290,976	-	290,624	282	21	2	4	13	26	-	-	4
Rented privately - furnished	18,681	17,821	860	21,279	-	-	20,850	-	26	-	-	363	13	5	22
- unfurnished	18,692	18,470	222	19,315	-	-	455	18,789	6	-	-	63	1	-	1
Rented with a job or business	17,636	17,619	17	17,688	-	-	-	-	17,666	-	-	19	-	-	3
Rented from a housing association	11,804	11,739	65	12,072	-	-	78	8	-	11,931	13	34	-	4	4
Rented from a local authority or new town	93,821	93,690	131	94,194	-	-	130	11	7	-	94,005	39	1	-	1
Persons enumerated but no residents	**2,992**	**2,965**	**27**	**3,051**	**519**	**561**	**1,585**	**80**	**164**	**37**	**97**	-	-	**1**	**7**
Owner occupied	1,079	1,078	1	1,081	519	561	1	-	-	-	-	-	-	-	-
Not owner occupied	1,913	1,887	26	1,970	-	-	1,584	80	164	37	97	-	-	1	7
Vacant accommodation	26,650	26,611	39	26,752	-	-	5	1	-	-	-	26,742	1	-	3
Other unoccupied accommodation	3,340	3,337	3	3,344	-	-	-	-	-	-	-	-	2,476	690	178
Basingstoke & Deane															
ALL TENURES OR OCCUPANCY TYPES	**56,055**	**56,000**	**55**	**56,191**	**8,875**	**29,581**	**1,289**	**1,386**	**2,035**	**1,229**	**9,814**	**1,857**	**108**	**15**	**2**
Dwellings with residents	**53,933**	**53,879**	**54**	**54,068**	**8,847**	**29,549**	**1,238**	**1,373**	**2,018**	**1,228**	**9,808**	**7**	-	-	-
Owner occupied - owned outright	8,846	8,841	5	8,852	8,847	-	5	-	-	-	-	-	-	-	-
- buying	29,545	29,526	19	29,576	-	29,549	16	-	-	-	6	5	-	-	-
Rented privately - furnished	1,138	1,122	16	1,195	-	-	1,195	-	-	-	-	-	-	-	-
- unfurnished	1,370	1,366	4	1,391	-	-	20	1,371	-	-	-	-	-	-	-
Rented with a job or business	2,010	2,006	4	2,015	-	-	-	-	2,014	-	-	1	-	-	-
Rented from a housing association	1,228	1,226	2	1,230	-	-	-	1	-	1,228	-	1	-	-	-
Rented from a local authority or new town	9,796	9,792	4	9,809	-	-	2	1	4	-	9,802	-	-	-	-
Persons enumerated but no residents	**147**	**147**	-	**147**	**28**	**32**	**51**	**12**	**17**	**1**	**6**	-	-	-	-
Owner occupied	60	60	-	60	28	32	-	-	-	-	-	-	-	-	-
Not owner occupied	87	87	-	87	-	-	51	12	17	1	6	-	-	-	-
Vacant accommodation	1,850	1,849	1	1,851	-	-	-	-	-	-	-	1,850	-	-	-
Other unoccupied accommodation	125	125	-	125	-	-	-	-	-	-	-	-	108	15	2

Table 64 Tenure of dwellings and household spaces – continued

64. Dwellings; household spaces in dwellings

Columns m, n, o, p fall under "Tenure or occupancy type of household spaces"; columns n, o, p fall under "Accommodation not used as main residence - no persons present".

Tenure or occupancy type of dwelling	TOTAL DWELLINGS	Unshared dwellings	Shared dwellings	TOTAL HOUSE-HOLD SPACES	Owner occupied — Owned outright	Owner occupied — Buying	Rented privately — Furnished	Rented privately — Unfurnished	Rented with a job or business	Rented from a housing association	Rented from a local authority or new town	Vacant accommodation	Second residences	Holiday accommodation	Student accommodation
a	b	c	d	e	f	g	h	i	j	k	l	m	n	o	p
East Hampshire															
ALL TENURES OR OCCUPANCY TYPES	40,479	40,436	43	40,568	9,899	20,249	985	1,242	1,627	439	4,349	1,624	142	12	-
Dwellings with residents	38,576	38,533	43	38,665	9,857	20,212	959	1,238	1,611	435	4,346	7	-	-	-
Owner occupied - owned outright	9,856	9,847	9	9,866	9,857	1	7	1							
- buying	20,209	20,201	8	20,218		20,211	2	1			4				
Rented privately - furnished	917	909	8	940			938					2			
- unfurnished	1,236	1,233	3	1,243			7	1,236							
Rented with a job or business	1,608	1,606	2	1,610					1,610						
Rented from a housing association	430	426	4	436					1	435					
Rented from a local authority or new town	4,320	4,311	9	4,352			5				4,342	5			
Persons enumerated but no residents	132	132	-	132	42	37	26	4	16	4	3	-	-	-	-
Owner occupied	79	79	-	79	42	37									
Not owner occupied	53	53	-	53			26	4	16	4	3				
Vacant accommodation	1,617	1,617	-	1,617								1,617			
Other unoccupied accommodation	154	154	-	154									142	12	-
Eastleigh															
ALL TENURES OR OCCUPANCY TYPES	42,578	42,525	53	42,698	9,225	23,971	959	878	332	770	4,713	1,756	91	-	3
Dwellings with residents	40,654	40,605	49	40,767	9,212	23,936	925	877	328	769	4,709	11	-	-	-
Owner occupied - owned outright	9,210	9,202	8	9,232	9,212		16		4						
- buying	23,933	23,926	7	23,942		23,936	5					1			
Rented privately - furnished	843	821	22	900			892					8			
- unfurnished	875	870	5	890			12	877				1			
Rented with a job or business	321	320	1	325					324	1					
Rented from a housing association	768	768	-	768						768					
Rented from a local authority or new town	4,704	4,698	6	4,710							4,709	1			
Persons enumerated but no residents	90	89	1	92	13	35	34	1	4	1	4	-	-	-	-
Owner occupied	48	48	-	48	13	35									
Not owner occupied	42	41	1	44			34	1	4	1	4				
Vacant accommodation	1,740	1,737	3	1,745								1,745			
Other unoccupied accommodation	94	94	-	94									91	-	3

64. Dwellings; household spaces in dwellings

Tenure or occupancy type of dwelling	TOTAL DWELLINGS	Unshared dwellings	Shared dwellings	TOTAL HOUSE-HOLD SPACES	Owner occupied — Owned outright	Owner occupied — Buying	Rented privately — Furnished	Rented privately — Unfurnished	Rented with a job or business	Rented from a housing assoc- iation	Rented from a local authority or new town	Vacant accomm- odation	Second residences	Holiday accomm- odation	Student accomm- odation
a	b	c	d	e	f	g	h	i	j	k	l	m	n	o	p
Fareham															
ALL TENURES OR OCCUPANCY TYPES	**39,654**	**39,628**	**26**	**39,696**	**11,156**	**21,670**	**777**	**710**	**544**	**254**	**3,072**	**1,402**	**107**	**3**	**1**
Dwellings with residents	**38,038**	**38,012**	**26**	**38,080**	**11,125**	**21,636**	**751**	**708**	**537**	**254**	**3,068**	**1**	-	-	-
Owner occupied - owned outright	11,123	11,118	5	11,129	11,125		1	2							
- buying	21,633	21,629	4	21,637		21,635	2								
Rented privately - furnished	726	719	7	746			744		2						
- unfurnished	704	699	5	710			4	706							
Rented with a job or business	535	535	-	535					535						
Rented from a housing association	252	251	1	254						254					
Rented from a local authority or new town	3,065	3,061	4	3,069							3,068				
Persons enumerated but no residents	**104**	**104**	-	**104**	**31**	**34**	**26**	**2**	**7**		**4**				
Owner occupied	65	65	-	65	31	34									
Not owner occupied	39	39	-	39			26	2	7		4				
Vacant accommodation	1,401	1,401	-	1,401								1,401	107		
Other unoccupied accommodation	111	111	-	111										3	1
Gosport															
ALL TENURES OR OCCUPANCY TYPES	**31,258**	**31,234**	**24**	**31,315**	**6,435**	**14,100**	**872**	**779**	**1,394**	**633**	**5,118**	**1,890**	**75**	**19**	-
Dwellings with residents	**29,208**	**29,185**	**23**	**29,259**	**6,418**	**14,076**	**859**	**779**	**1,380**	**631**	**5,112**	**4**	-	-	-
Owner occupied - owned outright	6,418	6,417	1	6,419	6,418		1								
- buying	14,075	14,071	4	14,082		14,076	6								
Rented privately - furnished	817	806	11	846			844					2			
- unfurnished	776	772	4	785			7	778							
Rented with a job or business	1,380	1,380	-	1,380					1,380						
Rented from a housing association	631	631	-	631						631					
Rented from a local authority or new town	5,111	5,108	3	5,116				1			5,112	2			
Persons enumerated but no residents	**76**	**76**	-	**76**	**17**	**24**	**13**	-	**14**	**2**	**6**				
Owner occupied	41	41	-	41	17	24									
Not owner occupied	35	35	-	35			13		14	2	6				
Vacant accommodation	1,880	1,879	1	1,886								1,886	75		
Other unoccupied accommodation	94	94	-	94										19	

64. Dwellings; household spaces in dwellings

Tenure or occupancy type of dwelling	TOTAL DWELLINGS	Unshared dwellings	Shared dwellings	TOTAL HOUSE-HOLD SPACES	Tenure or occupancy type of household spaces								Accommodation not used as main residence - no persons present		
					Owner occupied		Rented privately		Rented with a job or business	Rented from a housing association	Rented from a local authority or new town	Vacant accommodation	Second residences	Holiday accommodation	Student accommodation
					Owned outright	Buying	Furnished	Unfurnished							
a	b	c	d	e	f	g	h	i	j	k	l	m	n	o	p
Hart															
ALL TENURES OR OCCUPANCY TYPES	29,903	29,883	20	29,945	5,853	17,491	909	707	1,259	299	2,308	1,064	53	2	-
Dwellings with residents	28,701	28,682	19	28,739	5,833	17,464	892	701	1,240	299	2,308	2	-	-	-
Owner occupied - owned outright	5,833	5,827	6	5,839	5,833	1	4	1							
- buying	17,461	17,454	7	17,469		17,463	5	1							
Rented privately - furnished	862	858	4	884			882					2			
- unfurnished	699	698	1	700			1	699							
Rented with a job or business	1,240	1,240	-	1,240					1,240						
Rented from a housing association	299	299	-	299						299					
Rented from a local authority or new town	2,307	2,306	1	2,308							2,308				
Persons enumerated but no residents	87	87	-	87	20	27	15	6	19						
Owner occupied	47	47	-	47	20	27									
Not owner occupied	40	40	-	40			15	6	19						
Vacant accommodation	1,060	1,059	1	1,064								1,062	53		
Other unoccupied accommodation	55	55	-	55										2	-
Havant															
ALL TENURES OR OCCUPANCY TYPES	48,043	47,983	60	48,172	11,427	22,061	1,200	710	484	401	9,850	1,583	273	181	2
Dwellings with residents	45,913	45,854	59	46,041	11,395	22,024	1,177	708	481	399	9,844	13	-	-	-
Owner occupied - owned outright	11,395	11,388	7	11,402	11,395	3	3	1							
- buying	22,019	22,012	7	22,029		22,021	3	2		1		2			
Rented privately - furnished	1,117	1,101	16	1,173			1,163					10			
- unfurnished	703	701	2	709			4	705							
Rented with a job or business	481	481	-	481					481						
Rented from a housing association	398	396	2	403			4			398		1			
Rented from a local authority or new town	9,800	9,775	25	9,844							9,838				
Persons enumerated but no residents	105	105	-	105	32	37	23	2	3	2	6				
Owner occupied	69	69	-	69	32	37									
Not owner occupied	36	36	-	36			23	2	3	2	6				
Vacant accommodation	1,569	1,568	1	1,570								1,570	273		
Other unoccupied accommodation	456	456	-	456										181	2

Table 64 Tenure of dwellings and household spaces – continued

64 Dwellings; household spaces in dwellings

Tenure or occupancy type of dwelling	TOTAL DWELLINGS	Unshared dwellings	Shared dwellings	TOTAL HOUSE-HOLD SPACES	Owner occupied – Owned outright	Owner occupied – Buying	Rented privately – Furnished	Rented privately – Un-furnished	Rented with a job or business	Rented from a housing assoc-iation	Rented from a local authority or new town	Vacant accomm-odation	Accomm. not used as main residence – no persons present – Second residences	Holiday accomm-odation	Student accomm-odation
a	b	c	d	e	f	g	h	i	j	k	l	m	n	o	p
New Forest															
ALL TENURES OR OCCUPANCY TYPES	68,872	68,810	62	69,009	23,204	29,042	1,647	2,161	1,492	857	6,229	3,108	928	341	-
Dwellings with residents	64,092	64,032	60	64,222	23,030	28,929	1,545	2,151	1,477	855	6,220	14	1	-	-
Owner occupied – owned outright	23,028	23,015	13	23,043	23,030	3	7	1	1	-	-	1	-	-	-
– buying	28,924	28,914	10	28,937		28,926	9	2	2						
Rented privately – furnished	1,481	1,465	16	1,527			1,516					8	1		
– unfurnished	2,145	2,141	4	2,154			7	2,147							
Rented with a job or business	1,474	1,474	-	1,474					1,474						
Rented from a housing association	854	852	2	860			1			855	3				
Rented from a local authority or new town	6,186	6,171	15	6,227			5	1			6,217	4			
Persons enumerated but no residents	423	422	1	425	174	113	102	10	15	2	9	-	-		
Owner occupied	286	285	1	288	174	113	1								
Not owner occupied	137	137	-	137			101	10	15	2	9				
Vacant accommodation	3,089	3,088	1	3,094								3,094	927		
Other unoccupied accommodation	1,268	1,268	-	1,268										341	
Portsmouth															
ALL TENURES OR OCCUPANCY TYPES	76,360	75,841	519	77,755	17,906	30,792	5,534	3,025	1,581	2,256	12,072	4,250	217	57	65
Dwellings with residents	71,154	70,653	501	72,503	17,854	30,717	4,880	3,020	1,566	2,243	12,058	145	3	9	8
Owner occupied – owned outright	17,851	17,786	65	17,947	17,854	3	69	17				4			
– buying	30,709	30,631	78	30,848		30,714	113	6	1			8			3
Rented privately – furnished	3,832	3,563	269	4,650			4,537		3			100	1	5	4
– unfurnished	2,965	2,907	58	3,099			92	2,989	2			15	1		1
Rented with a job or business	1,558	1,557	1	1,560					1,560						
Rented from a housing association	2,188	2,175	13	2,276				3		2,241	2			4	
Rented from a local authority or new town	12,051	12,034	17	12,123			57	5			12,055	4	1		
Persons enumerated but no residents	804	794	10	828	52	75	653	5	15	13	14				
Owner occupied	127	127	-	127	52	75									
Not owner occupied	677	667	10	701			653	5	15	13	14				
Vacant accommodation	4,087	4,079	8	4,109								4,105	214		
Other unoccupied accommodation	315	315	-	315										47	54

Table 64 Tenure of dwellings and household spaces – continued

64. Dwellings: household spaces in dwellings

Tenure or occupancy type of dwelling	TOTAL DWELLINGS	Unshared dwellings	Shared dwellings	TOTAL HOUSE-HOLD SPACES	Owner occupied — Owned outright	Owner occupied — Buying	Rented privately — Furnished	Rented privately — Unfurnished	Rented with a job or business	Rented from a housing association	Rented from a local authority or new town	Vacant accommodation	Second residences	Holiday accommodation	Student accommodation
a	b	c	d	e	f	g	h	i	j	k	l	m	n	o	p

Rushmoor

a	b	c	d	e	f	g	h	i	j	k	l	m	n	o	p
ALL TENURES OR OCCUPANCY TYPES	**31,276**	**31,120**	**156**	**31,740**	**4,679**	**15,588**	**1,425**	**872**	**2,213**	**592**	**5,017**	**1,326**	**26**	**1**	**1**
Dwellings with residents	**29,911**	**29,757**	**154**	**30,373**	**4,674**	**15,570**	**1,393**	**871**	**2,203**	**591**	**5,006**	**61**	**4**	**-**	**-**
Owner occupied - owned outright	4,674	4,672	2	4,676	4,674	-	1	1	-	-	-	-	-	-	-
- buying	15,566	15,550	16	15,596	-	15,570	21	2	-	-	-	3	-	-	-
Rented privately - furnished	1,081	1,006	75	1,301	-	-	1,261	-	-	-	-	30	4	-	-
- unfurnished	855	824	31	948	-	-	67	865	-	-	-	16	-	-	-
Rented with a job or business	2,195	2,195	-	2,195	-	-	-	-	2,195	-	-	-	-	-	-
Rented from a housing association	574	569	5	608	-	-	13	1	-	591	-	3	-	-	-
Rented from a local authority or new town	4,966	4,941	25	5,049	-	-	30	3	2	-	5,005	9	-	-	-
Persons enumerated but no residents	**78**	**78**	**-**	**78**	**5**	**18**	**32**	**1**	**10**	**1**	**11**	**-**	**-**	**-**	**-**
Owner occupied	23	23	-	23	5	18	-	-	-	-	-	-	-	-	-
Not owner occupied	55	55	-	55	-	-	32	1	10	1	11	-	-	-	-
Vacant accommodation	1,263	1,261	2	1,265	-	-	-	-	-	-	-	1,265	-	-	-
Other unoccupied accommodation	24	24	-	24	-	-	-	-	-	-	-	-	22	1	1

Southampton

a	b	c	d	e	f	g	h	i	j	k	l	m	n	o	p
ALL TENURES OR OCCUPANCY TYPES	**84,446**	**83,745**	**701**	**86,363**	**17,831**	**31,584**	**5,911**	**3,497**	**854**	**2,754**	**19,292**	**4,314**	**161**	**21**	**144**
Dwellings with residents	**79,524**	**78,858**	**666**	**81,361**	**17,806**	**31,526**	**5,420**	**3,479**	**835**	**2,749**	**19,267**	**245**	**7**	**-**	**-**
Owner occupied - owned outright	17,796	17,734	62	17,899	17,806	-	70	11	-	-	-	8	-	-	-
- buying	31,517	31,454	63	31,623	-	31,524	80	6	-	-	-	11	-	-	-
Rented privately - furnished	4,009	3,618	391	5,175	-	-	4,968	-	-	-	-	178	7	-	-
- unfurnished	3,414	3,316	98	3,717	-	-	228	3,458	-	-	-	27	-	-	-
Rented with a job or business	825	823	2	829	-	-	-	3	826	-	-	-	-	-	-
Rented from a housing association	2,710	2,679	31	2,820	-	-	49	-	-	2,749	-	14	-	-	-
Rented from a local authority or new town	19,253	19,234	19	19,298	-	-	25	1	1	-	19,264	7	-	-	-
Persons enumerated but no residents	**616**	**602**	**14**	**646**	**25**	**58**	**489**	**18**	**19**	**5**	**25**	**-**	**-**	**-**	**7**
Owner occupied	83	83	-	83	25	58	-	-	-	-	-	-	-	-	-
Not owner occupied	533	519	14	563	-	-	489	18	19	5	25	-	-	-	7
Vacant accommodation	4,026	4,008	18	4,072	-	-	-	-	-	-	-	4,069	1	-	2
Other unoccupied accommodation	280	277	3	284	-	-	-	-	-	-	-	-	153	21	110

Table 64 Tenure of dwellings and household spaces – continued

64. Dwellings; household spaces in dwellings

Tenure or occupancy type of dwelling	TOTAL DWELLINGS	Unshared dwellings	Shared dwellings	TOTAL HOUSE-HOLD SPACES	Owner occupied		Rented privately		Rented with a job or business	Rented from a housing assoc-iation	Rented from a local authority or new town	Vacant accomm-odation	Accommodation not used as main residence - no persons present		
					Owned outright	Buying	Furnished	Un-furnished					Second residences	Holiday accomm-odation	Student accomm-odation
a	b	c	d	e	f	g	h	i	j	k	l	m	n	o	p
Test Valley															
ALL TENURES OR OCCUPANCY TYPES	**39,845**	**39,821**	**24**	**39,896**	**8,240**	**18,509**	**846**	**1,558**	**2,048**	**591**	**6,331**	**1,586**	**158**	**28**	**1**
Dwellings with residents	**37,961**	**37,938**	**23**	**38,008**	**8,197**	**18,481**	**819**	**1,550**	**2,039**	**589**	**6,328**	**5**	**-**	**-**	**-**
Owner occupied - owned outright	8,195	8,190	5	8,200	8,197	-	2	1	-	-	-	-	-	-	-
- buying	18,479	18,474	5	18,485	-	18,481	4	-	-	-	-	-	-	-	-
Rented privately - furnished	787	780	7	813	-	-	808	-	-	-	-	5	-	-	-
- unfurnished	1,547	1,544	3	1,553	-	-	4	1,549	-	-	-	-	-	-	-
Rented with a job or business	2,036	2,034	2	2,039	-	-	-	-	2,039	-	-	-	-	-	-
Rented from a housing association	589	589	-	589	-	-	-	-	-	589	-	-	-	-	-
Rented from a local authority or new town	6,328	6,327	1	6,329	-	-	1	-	-	-	6,328	-	-	-	-
Persons enumerated but no residents	**120**	**120**	**-**	**120**	**43**	**28**	**27**	**8**	**9**	**2**	**3**	**-**	**-**	**-**	**-**
Owner occupied	71	71	-	71	43	28	-	-	-	-	-	-	-	-	-
Not owner occupied	49	49	-	49	-	-	27	8	9	2	3	-	-	-	-
Vacant accommodation	1,577	1,576	1	1,581	-	-	-	-	-	-	-	1,581	-	-	-
Other unoccupied accommodation	187	187	-	187	-	-	-	-	-	-	-	-	158	28	1
Winchester															
ALL TENURES OR OCCUPANCY TYPES	**38,781**	**38,726**	**55**	**38,955**	**9,159**	**16,562**	**1,222**	**1,421**	**2,012**	**897**	**5,964**	**1,541**	**153**	**17**	**7**
Dwellings with residents	**36,903**	**36,851**	**52**	**37,070**	**9,122**	**16,519**	**1,128**	**1,410**	**1,996**	**893**	**5,958**	**44**	**-**	**-**	**-**
Owner occupied - owned outright	9,122	9,117	5	9,128	9,122	1	5	-	-	-	-	-	-	-	-
- buying	16,517	16,504	13	16,534	-	16,518	16	-	-	-	-	-	-	-	-
Rented privately - furnished	1,071	1,053	18	1,129	-	-	1,103	-	7	-	-	19	-	-	-
- unfurnished	1,403	1,399	4	1,416	-	-	2	1,409	1	-	-	4	-	-	-
Rented with a job or business	1,973	1,968	5	2,005	-	-	-	-	1,988	-	-	17	-	-	-
Rented from a housing association	883	878	5	898	-	-	2	1	-	893	1	1	-	-	-
Rented from a local authority or new town	5,934	5,932	2	5,960	-	-	-	-	-	-	5,957	3	-	-	-
Persons enumerated but no residents	**210**	**209**	**1**	**211**	**37**	**43**	**94**	**11**	**16**	**4**	**6**	**-**	**-**	**-**	**-**
Owner occupied	80	80	-	80	37	43	-	-	-	-	-	-	-	-	-
Not owner occupied	130	129	1	131	-	-	94	11	16	4	6	-	-	-	-
Vacant accommodation	1,491	1,489	2	1,497	-	-	-	-	-	-	-	1,497	-	-	-
Other unoccupied accommodation	177	177	-	177	-	-	-	-	-	-	-	-	153	17	7

Table 65 Occupancy of dwellings and household spaces

65. Dwellings: household spaces in dwellings

HAMPSHIRE

					Households with residents		Vacant accommodation			Accommodation not used as main residence — No persons present			Accommodation not used as main residence — Persons enumerated but no residents	
Occupancy type of dwelling	TOTAL DWELLINGS	Unshared dwellings	Shared dwellings	TOTAL HOUSE-HOLD SPACES	Persons present	Absent household	New	Under improve-ment	Other	Second residences	Holiday accomm-odation	Student accomm-odation	Owner occupied	Not owner occupied
a	b	c	d	e	f	g	h	i	j	k	l	m	n	o
ALL TYPES OF OCCUPANCY	627,550	625,752	1,798	632,303	578,083	20,214	4,384	3,005	19,912	2,492	700	223	1,082	2,208
Dwellings with residents	594,568	592,839	1,729	599,156	578,083	20,214	-	20	539	15	9	35	2	239
Dwellings with person(s) present	574,975	573,274	1,701	579,527	578,083	602	-	18	528	15	9	31	2	239
Dwellings with no person(s) present	19,593	19,565	28	19,629		19,612	-	2	11	-	-	4	-	-
Vacant accommodation	26,650	26,611	39	26,752			4,384	2,985	19,373	1		3		6
New, never occupied	4,378	4,376	2	4,384			4,384							
Under improvement	2,968	2,962	6	2,989				2,985	1			3		
Other	19,304	19,273	31	19,379					19,372	1				6
Accommodation not used as main residence	6,332	6,302	30	6,395						2,476	691	185	1,080	1,963
No persons present	3,340	3,337	3	3,344						2,476	690	178	-	-
Second residences	2,476	2,476	-	2,476						2,476	-	-		
Holiday accommodation	690	690	-	690						-	690	-		
Student accommodation	174	171	3	178						-	-	178		
Persons enumerated but no residents	2,992	2,965	27	3,051						-	1	7	1,080	1,963
Owner occupied	1,079	1,078	1	1,081						-	-	-	1,080	1
Not owner occupied	1,913	1,887	26	1,970						-	1	7		1,962

Table 65 Occupancy of dwellings and household spaces – continued

65. Dwellings; household spaces in dwellings

Basingstoke & Deane

Occupancy type of dwelling	TOTAL DWELLINGS	Unshared dwellings	Shared dwellings	TOTAL HOUSE-HOLD SPACES	Households with residents		Vacant accommodation			Accommodation not used as main residence				
										No persons present			Persons enumerated but no residents	
					Persons present	Absent household	New	Under improve-ment	Other	Second residences	Holiday accomm-odation	Student accomm-odation	Owner occupied	Not owner occupied
a	b	c	d	e	f	g	h	i	j	k	l	m	n	o
ALL TYPES OF OCCUPANCY	56,055	56,000	55	56,191	52,385	1,673	391	149	1,317	108	15	2	60	91
Dwellings with residents	53,933	53,879	54	54,068	52,385	1,673	-	-	7	-	-	-	-	3
Dwellings with person(s) present	52,286	52,233	53	52,420	52,385	25	-	-	7	-	-	-	-	3
Dwellings with no person(s) present	1,647	1,646	1	1,648		1,648	-	-	-	-	-	-	-	-
Vacant accommodation	1,850	1,849	1	1,851			391	149	1,310					1
New, never occupied	391	391	-	391			391							-
Under improvement	149	149	-	149				149						-
Other	1,310	1,309	1	1,311				-	1,310					1
Accommodation not used as main residence	272	272	-	272						108	15	2	60	87
No persons present	125	125	-	125						108	15	2		-
Second residences	108	108	-	108						108	-	-		-
Holiday accommodation	15	15	-	15						-	15	-		-
Student accommodation	2	2	-	2						-	-	2		-
Persons enumerated but no residents	147	147	-	147						-	-	-	60	87
Owner occupied	60	60	-	60						-	-	-	60	-
Not owner occupied	87	87	-	87						-	-	-	-	87

Table 65 Occupancy of dwellings and household spaces – **continued**

65. Dwellings; household spaces in dwellings

East Hampshire

Occupancy type of dwelling	TOTAL DWELLINGS	Unshared dwellings	Shared dwellings	TOTAL HOUSE-HOLD SPACES	Households with residents: Persons present	Households with residents: Absent household	Vacant accommodation: New	Vacant accommodation: Under improvement	Vacant accommodation: Other	Not used as main residence — No persons present: Second residences	Not used as main residence — No persons present: Holiday accommodation	Not used as main residence — No persons present: Student accommodation	Not used as main residence — Persons enumerated but no residents: Owner occupied	Not used as main residence — Persons enumerated but no residents: Not owner occupied
a	b	c	d	e	f	g	h	i	j	k	l	m	n	o
ALL TYPES OF OCCUPANCY	**40,479**	**40,436**	**43**	**40,568**	**37,415**	**1,241**	**394**	**152**	**1,078**	**142**	**12**	**-**	**79**	**55**
Dwellings with residents	**38,576**	**38,533**	**43**	**38,665**	**37,415**	**1,241**	**-**	**-**	**7**	**-**	**-**	**-**	**-**	**2**
Dwellings with person(s) present	37,337	37,294	43	37,426	37,415	2	-	-	7	-	-	-	-	2
Dwellings with no person(s) present	1,239	1,239	-	1,239		1,239	-	-	-	-	-	-	-	-
Vacant accommodation	**1,617**	**1,617**	**-**	**1,617**			**394**	**152**	**1,071**					
New, never occupied	394	394	-	394			394							
Under improvement	152	152	-	152				152						
Other	1,071	1,071	-	1,071					1,071					
Accommodation not used as main residence	**286**	**286**	**-**	**286**						**142**	**12**	**-**	**79**	**53**
No persons present	154	154	-	154						142	12	-		
Second residences	142	142	-	142						142	-			
Holiday accommodation	12	12	-	12							12			
Student accommodation	-	-	-	-								-		
Persons enumerated but no residents	132	132	-	132						-	-	-	79	53
Owner occupied	79	79	-	79						-	-	-	79	-
Not owner occupied	53	53	-	53						-	-	-	-	53

Table 65 Occupancy of dwellings and household spaces – continued

65. Dwellings; household spaces in dwellings

Eastleigh

| Occupancy type of dwelling | TOTAL DWELLINGS | Unshared dwellings | Shared dwellings | TOTAL HOUSE-HOLD SPACES | Households with residents | | Vacant accommodation | | | Accommodation not used as main residence | | | | |
| | | | | | Persons present | Absent household | New | Under improve-ment | Other | No persons present — Second residences | No persons present — Holiday accomm-odation | No persons present — Student accomm-odation | Persons enumerated but no residents — Owner occupied | Persons enumerated but no residents — Not owner occupied |
a	b	c	d	e	f	g	h	i	j	k	l	m	n	o
ALL TYPES OF OCCUPANCY	42,578	42,525	53	42,698	39,486	1,267	562	155	1,039	91	3	-	48	47
Dwellings with residents	40,654	40,605	49	40,767	39,486	1,267	-	-	11	-	-	-	-	3
Dwellings with person(s) present	39,403	39,354	49	39,516	39,486	16	-	-	11	-	-	-	-	3
Dwellings with no person(s) present	1,251	1,251	-	1,251		1,251	-	-	-					-
Vacant accommodation	1,740	1,737	3	1,745			562	155	1,028					-
New, never occupied	562	562	-	562			562							
Under improvement	154	153	1	155				155						
Other	1,024	1,022	2	1,028					1,028					
Accommodation not used as main residence	184	183	1	186						91	3		48	44
No persons present	94	94	-	94						91	3	-		
Second residences	91	91	-	91						91				
Holiday accommodation	3	3	-	3							3			
Student accommodation	-	-	-	-								-		
Persons enumerated but no residents	90	89	1	92									48	44
Owner occupied	48	48	-	48									48	-
Not owner occupied	42	41	1	44									-	44

Table 65 Occupancy of dwellings and household spaces – **continued**

65. Dwellings; household spaces in dwellings

Fareham

Occupancy type of dwelling	TOTAL DWELLINGS	Unshared dwellings	Shared dwellings	TOTAL HOUSE-HOLD SPACES	Households with residents: Persons present	Households with residents: Absent household	Vacant accommodation: New	Vacant accommodation: Under improvement	Vacant accommodation: Other	Accom. not used as main res. — No persons present: Second residences	Accom. not used as main res. — No persons present: Holiday accommodation	Accom. not used as main res. — No persons present: Student accommodation	Accom. not used as main res. — Persons enumerated but no residents: Owner occupied	Accom. not used as main res. — Persons enumerated but no residents: Not owner occupied
a	b	c	d	e	f	g	h	i	j	k	l	m	n	o
ALL TYPES OF OCCUPANCY	39,654	39,628	26	39,696	36,975	1,103	301	79	1,022	107	3	1	65	40
Dwellings with residents	38,038	38,012	26	38,080	36,975	1,103	-	-	1	-	-	-	-	1
Dwellings with person(s) present	36,936	36,910	26	36,978	36,975	1	-	-	1	-	-	-	-	1
Dwellings with no person(s) present	1,102	1,102	-	1,102		1,102	-	-	-	-	-	-	-	-
Vacant accommodation	1,401	1,401	-	1,401			301	79	1,021	-	-	-	-	-
New, never occupied	301	301	-	301			301	-	-	-	-	-	-	-
Under improvement	79	79	-	79			-	79	-	-	-	-	-	-
Other	1,021	1,021	-	1,021			-	-	1,021	-	-	-	-	-
Accommodation not used as main residence	215	215	-	215						107	3	1	65	39
No persons present	111	111	-	111						107	3	1	-	-
Second residences	107	107	-	107						107	-	-	-	-
Holiday accommodation	3	3	-	3						-	3	-	-	-
Student accommodation	1	1	-	1						-	-	1	-	-
Persons enumerated but no residents	104	104	-	104						-	-	-	65	39
Owner occupied	65	65	-	65						-	-	-	65	-
Not owner occupied	39	39	-	39						-	-	-	-	39

Table 65 Occupancy of dwellings and household spaces – **continued**

65. Dwellings; household spaces in dwellings

Gosport

Occupancy type of dwelling	TOTAL DWELLINGS	Unshared dwellings	Shared dwellings	TOTAL HOUSE-HOLD SPACES	Households with residents — Persons present	Households with residents — Absent household	Vacant accommodation — New	Vacant accommodation — Under improvement	Vacant accommodation — Other	Accommodation not used as main residence — No persons present — Second residences	Accommodation not used as main residence — No persons present — Holiday accommodation	Accommodation not used as main residence — No persons present — Student accommodation	Accommodation not used as main residence — Persons enumerated but no residents — Owner occupied	Accommodation not used as main residence — Persons enumerated but no residents — Not owner occupied
a	b	c	d	e	f	g	h	i	j	k	l	m	n	o
ALL TYPES OF OCCUPANCY	**31,258**	**31,234**	**24**	**31,315**	**28,265**	**989**	**110**	**117**	**1,663**	**75**	**19**	**-**	**41**	**36**
Dwellings with residents	**29,208**	**29,185**	**23**	**29,259**	**28,265**	**989**	**-**	**-**	**4**	**-**	**-**	**-**	**-**	**1**
Dwellings with person(s) present	28,222	28,200	22	28,272	28,265	2	-	-	4	-	-	-	-	1
Dwellings with no person(s) present	986	985	1	987		987	-	-	-	-	-	-	-	-
Vacant accommodation	**1,880**	**1,879**	**1**	**1,886**			**110**	**117**	**1,659**					
New, never occupied	110	110	-	110			110	-						
Under improvement	117	117	-	117			-	117						
Other	1,653	1,652	1	1,659			-	-	1,659					
Accommodation not used as main residence	**170**	**170**	**-**	**170**			**-**			**75**	**19**	**-**	**41**	**35**
No persons present	94	94	-	94			-	-	-	75	19	-		
Second residences	75	75	-	75			-	-	-	75	-	-		
Holiday accommodation	19	19	-	19			-	-	-	-	19	-		
Student accommodation	-	-	-	-			-	-	-	-	-	-		
Persons enumerated but no residents	76	76	-	76			-	-	-				41	35
Owner occupied	41	41	-	41			-	-	-				41	-
Not owner occupied	35	35	-	35			-	-	-				-	35

Table 65 Occupancy of dwellings and household spaces – **continued**

65. Dwellings; household spaces in dwellings

Hart

Occupancy type of dwelling	TOTAL DWELLINGS	Unshared dwellings	Shared dwellings	TOTAL HOUSE-HOLD SPACES	Occupancy type of household spaces									
					Households with residents		Vacant accommodation			Accommodation not used as main residence					
										No persons present			Persons enumerated but no residents	
					Persons present	Absent household	New	Under improve-ment	Other	Second residences	Holiday accomm-odation	Student accomm-odation	Owner occupied	Not owner occupied
a	b	c	d	e	f	g	h	i	j	k	l	m	n	o
ALL TYPES OF OCCUPANCY	**29,903**	**29,883**	**20**	**29,945**	**27,821**	**915**	**257**	**82**	**725**	**53**	**2**	**-**	**47**	**43**
Dwellings with residents	**28,701**	**28,682**	**19**	**28,739**	**27,821**	**915**	**-**	**-**	**2**	**-**	**-**	**-**	**-**	**1**
Dwellings with person(s) present	27,791	27,772	19	27,829	27,821	5	-	-	2	-	-	-	-	1
Dwellings with no person(s) present	910	910	-	910		910	-	-	-	-	-	-	-	-
Vacant accommodation	**1,060**	**1,059**	**1**	**1,064**			**257**	**82**	**723**					**2**
New, never occupied	257	257	-	257			257	-	-					-
Under improvement	82	82	-	82			-	82	-					-
Other	721	720	1	725			-	-	723					2
Accommodation not used as main residence	**142**	**142**	**-**	**142**						**53**	**2**	**-**	**47**	**40**
No persons present	55	55	-	55						53	2	-		
Second residences	53	53	-	53						53	-	-		
Holiday accommodation	2	2	-	2						-	2	-		
Student accommodation	-	-	-	-						-	-	-		
Persons enumerated but no residents	87	87	-	87									47	40
Owner occupied	47	47	-	47									47	-
Not owner occupied	40	40	-	40									-	40

Table 65 Occupancy of dwellings and household spaces – **continued**

65. Dwellings: household spaces in dwellings

Havant

Occupancy type of dwelling	TOTAL DWELLINGS	Unshared dwellings	Shared dwellings	TOTAL HOUSE-HOLD SPACES	Households with residents — Persons present	Households with residents — Absent household	Vacant accommodation — New	Vacant accommodation — Under improvement	Vacant accommodation — Other	No persons present — Second residences	No persons present — Holiday accommodation	No persons present — Student accommodation	Persons enumerated but no residents — Owner occupied	Persons enumerated but no residents — Not owner occupied
a	b	c	d	e	f	g	h	i	j	k	l	m	n	o
ALL TYPES OF OCCUPANCY	**48,043**	**47,983**	**60**	**48,172**	**44,731**	**1,297**	**198**	**171**	**1,214**	**273**	**181**	**2**	**69**	**36**
Dwellings with residents	**45,913**	**45,854**	**59**	**46,041**	**44,731**	**1,297**	-	**7**	**6**	-	-	-	-	-
Dwellings with person(s) present	44,625	44,566	59	44,753	44,731	9	-	7	6	-	-	-	-	-
Dwellings with no person(s) present	1,288	1,288	-	1,288		1,288	-	-	-	-	-	-	-	-
Vacant accommodation	**1,569**	**1,568**	**1**	**1,570**			**198**	**164**	**1,208**					
New, never occupied	198	198	-	198			198							
Under improvement	164	164	-	164			-	164						
Other	1,207	1,206	1	1,208			-	-	1,208					
Accommodation not used as main residence	**561**	**561**	-	**561**						**273**	**181**	**2**	**69**	**36**
No persons present	456	456	-	456			-	-		273	181	2	-	-
Second residences	273	273	-	273			-	-		273	-	-	-	-
Holiday accommodation	181	181	-	181			-	-		273	181	-	-	-
Student accommodation	2	2	-	2			-	-				2	-	-
Persons enumerated but no residents	105	105	-	105			-	-		-	-	-	69	36
Owner occupied	69	69	-	69			-	-		-	-	-	69	-
Not owner occupied	36	36	-	36			-	-		-	-	-	-	36

Table 65 Occupancy of dwellings and household spaces – **continued**

65. Dwellings; household spaces in dwellings

New Forest

Occupancy type of dwelling	TOTAL DWELLINGS	Unshared dwellings	Shared dwellings	TOTAL HOUSE-HOLD SPACES	Households with residents: Persons present	Households with residents: Absent household	Vacant accommodation: New	Vacant accommodation: Under improvement	Vacant accommodation: Other	Accommodation not used as main residence — No persons present: Second residences	Accommodation not used as main residence — No persons present: Holiday accommodation	Accommodation not used as main residence — No persons present: Student accommodation	Accommodation not used as main residence — Persons enumerated but no residents: Owner occupied	Accommodation not used as main residence — Persons enumerated but no residents: Not owner occupied
a	b	c	d	e	f	g	h	i	j	k	l	m	n	o
ALL TYPES OF OCCUPANCY	68,872	68,810	62	69,009	61,899	2,308	611	349	2,148	928	341	-	287	138
Dwellings with residents	64,092	64,032	60	64,222	61,899	2,308	-	-	14	1	-	-	-	-
Dwellings with person(s) present	61,796	61,737	59	61,925	61,899	11	-	-	14	1	-	-	-	-
Dwellings with no person(s) present	2,296	2,295	1	2,297		2,297	-	-	-	-	-	-	-	-
Vacant accommodation	3,089	3,088	1	3,094			611	349	2,134	-	-	-	-	-
New, never occupied	611	611	-	611			611			-	-	-	-	-
Under improvement	344	343	1	349				349		-	-	-	-	-
Other	2,134	2,134	-	2,134					2,134	-	-	-	-	-
Accommodation not used as main residence	1,691	1,690	1	1,693						927	341	-	287	138
No persons present	1,268	1,268	-	1,268						927	341	-	-	-
Second residences	927	927	-	927						927	-	-	-	-
Holiday accommodation	341	341	-	341						-	341	-	-	-
Student accommodation	-	-	-	-						-	-	-	-	-
Persons enumerated but no residents	423	422	1	425						-	-	-	287	138
Owner occupied	286	285	1	288						-	-	-	287	1
Not owner occupied	137	137	-	137						-	-	-	-	137

Table 65 Occupancy of dwellings and household spaces – continued

65. Dwellings; household spaces in dwellings

Portsmouth

Column groups: b–d under *Occupancy type of dwelling*; e–o under *Occupancy type of household spaces* — f,g *Households with residents*; h,i,j *Vacant accommodation*; k–o *Accommodation not used as main residence* (k,l,m *No persons present*; n,o *Persons enumerated but no residents*).

Occupancy type of dwelling	TOTAL DWELLINGS	Unshared dwellings	Shared dwellings	TOTAL HOUSE-HOLD SPACES	Persons present	Absent household	New	Under improve-ment	Other	Second residences	Holiday accomm-odation	Student accomm-odation	Owner occupied	Not owner occupied
	b	c	d	e	f	g	h	i	j	k	l	m	n	o
ALL TYPES OF OCCUPANCY	**76,360**	**75,841**	**519**	**77,755**	**69,484**	**2,776**	**343**	**541**	**3,366**	**217**	**57**	**65**	**129**	**777**
Dwellings with residents	**71,154**	**70,653**	**501**	**72,503**	**69,484**	**2,776**	-	**4**	**141**	**3**	**9**	**8**	**2**	**76**
Dwellings with person(s) present	68,531	68,034	497	69,875	69,484	151	-	4	139	3	9	7	2	76
Dwellings with no person(s) present	2,623	2,619	4	2,628		2,625	-	-	2	-	-	1	-	-
Vacant accommodation	**4,087**	**4,079**	**8**	**4,109**			**343**	**537**	**3,225**			**3**		**1**
New, never occupied	342	341	1	343			343							-
Under improvement	537	536	1	541				537	1			3		
Other	3,208	3,202	6	3,225					3,224					1
Accommodation not used as main residence	**1,119**	**1,109**	**10**	**1,143**						**214**	**48**	**54**	**127**	**700**
No persons present	315	315	-	315						214	47	54	-	-
Second residences	214	214	-	214						214	-	-	-	-
Holiday accommodation	47	47	-	47						-	47	-	-	-
Student accommodation	54	54	-	54						-	-	54	-	-
Persons enumerated but no residents	804	794	10	828						-	1	-	127	700
Owner occupied	127	127	-	127						-	-	-	127	-
Not owner occupied	677	667	10	701						-	1	-	-	700

Table 65 Occupancy of dwellings and household spaces – continued

65. Dwellings; household spaces in dwellings

Rushmoor

Occupancy type of dwelling	TOTAL DWELLINGS	Unshared dwellings	Shared dwellings	TOTAL HOUSE-HOLD SPACES	Households with residents: Persons present	Households with residents: Absent household	Vacant accommodation: New	Vacant accommodation: Under improvement	Vacant accommodation: Other	No persons present: Second residences	No persons present: Holiday accommodation	No persons present: Student accommodation	Persons enumerated but no residents: Owner occupied	Persons enumerated but no residents: Not owner occupied
a	b	c	d	e	f	g	h	i	j	k	l	m	n	o
ALL TYPES OF OCCUPANCY	**31,276**	**31,120**	**156**	**31,740**	**29,252**	**1,044**	**62**	**204**	**1,060**	**26**	**1**	**1**	**23**	**67**
Dwellings with residents	**29,911**	**29,757**	**154**	**30,373**	**29,252**	**1,044**	**-**	**1**	**60**	**4**	**-**	**-**	**-**	**12**
Dwellings with person(s) present	28,927	28,777	150	29,384	29,252	58	-	1	57	4	-	-	-	12
Dwellings with no person(s) present	984	980	4	989		986	-	-	3	-	-	-	-	-
Vacant accommodation	**1,263**	**1,261**	**2**	**1,265**			**62**	**203**	**1,000**	**-**	**-**	**-**	**-**	**-**
New, never occupied	62	62	-	62			62							
Under improvement	203	203	-	203				203						
Other	998	996	2	1,000					1,000					
Accommodation not used as main residence	**102**	**102**	**-**	**102**			**-**	**-**		**22**	**1**	**1**	**23**	**55**
No persons present	24	24	-	24						22	1	1		
Second residences	22	22	-	22						22				
Holiday accommodation	1	1	-	1							1			
Student accommodation	1	1	-	1								1		
Persons enumerated but no residents	78	78	-	78						-	-	-	23	55
Owner occupied	23	23	-	23									23	-
Not owner occupied	55	55	-	55									-	55

Table 65 Occupancy of dwellings and household spaces – continued

County, districts

65. Dwellings; household spaces in dwellings

Southampton

Occupancy type of dwelling	TOTAL DWELLINGS	Unshared dwellings	Shared dwellings	TOTAL HOUSE-HOLD SPACES	Households with residents — Persons present	Households with residents — Absent household	Vacant accommodation — New	Vacant accommodation — Under improvement	Vacant accommodation — Other	Accommodation not used as main residence — No persons present — Second residences	Accommodation not used as main residence — No persons present — Holiday accommodation	Accommodation not used as main residence — No persons present — Student accommodation	Accommodation not used as main residence — Persons enumerated but no residents — Owner occupied	Accommodation not used as main residence — Persons enumerated but no residents — Not owner occupied
a	b	c	d	e	f	g	h	i	j	k	l	m	n	o
ALL TYPES OF OCCUPANCY	84,446	83,745	701	86,363	77,769	3,189	565	548	3,201	161	21	144	83	682
Dwellings with residents	79,524	78,858	666	81,361	77,769	3,189	-	8	237	7	-	27	-	124
Dwellings with person(s) present	76,644	75,994	650	78,459	77,769	298	-	6	231	7	-	24	-	124
Dwellings with no person(s) present	2,880	2,864	16	2,902	-	2,891	-	2	6	-	-	3	-	-
Vacant accommodation	4,026	4,008	18	4,072	-	-	565	540	2,964	1	-	-	-	2
New, never occupied	565	565	-	565			565			-				-
Under improvement	529	526	3	540				540		-				-
Other	2,932	2,917	15	2,967					2,964	1		-		2
Accommodation not used as main residence	896	879	17	930						153	21	117	83	556
No persons present	280	277	3	284						153	21	110		-
Second residences	153	153	-	153						153				-
Holiday accommodation	21	21	-	21							21			-
Student accommodation	106	103	3	110								110		-
Persons enumerated but no residents	616	602	14	646						-	-	7	83	556
Owner occupied	83	83	-	83						-	-	-	83	-
Not owner occupied	533	519	14	563						-	-	7	-	556

Table 65 Occupancy of dwellings and household spaces – continued

65. Dwellings: household spaces in dwellings

Test Valley

Occupancy type of dwelling	TOTAL DWELLINGS	Unshared dwellings	Shared dwellings	TOTAL HOUSE-HOLD SPACES	Occupancy type of household spaces									
					Households with residents		Vacant accommodation			Accommodation not used as main residence				
										No persons present			Persons enumerated but no residents	
					Persons present	Absent household	New	Under improve-ment	Other	Second residences	Holiday accomm-odation	Student accomm-odation	Owner occupied	Not owner occupied
a	b	c	d	e	f	g	h	i	j	k	l	m	n	o
ALL TYPES OF OCCUPANCY	**39,845**	**39,821**	**24**	**39,896**	**36,796**	**1,206**	**296**	**232**	**1,058**	**158**	**28**	**1**	**71**	**50**
Dwellings with residents	**37,961**	**37,938**	**23**	**38,008**	**36,796**	**1,206**	-	-	**5**	-	-	-	-	**1**
Dwellings with person(s) present	36,764	36,741	23	36,811	36,796	9	-	-	5	-	-	-	-	1
Dwellings with no person(s) present	1,197	1,197	-	1,197		1,197	-	-	-	-	-	-	-	-
Vacant accommodation	**1,577**	**1,576**	**1**	**1,581**			**296**	**232**	**1,053**					
New, never occupied	296	296	-	296			296							
Under improvement	232	232	-	232				232						
Other	1,049	1,048	1	1,053					1,053					
Accommodation not used as main residence	**307**	**307**	-	**307**						**158**	**28**	**1**	**71**	**49**
No persons present	187	187	-	187						158	28	1		
Second residences	158	158	-	158						158				
Holiday accommodation	28	28	-	28							28			
Student accommodation	1	1	-	1								1		
Persons enumerated but no residents	120	120	-	120						-	-	-	71	49
Owner occupied	71	71	-	71									71	
Not owner occupied	49	49	-	49										49

65. Dwellings: household spaces in dwellings

Winchester

Occupancy type of dwelling	TOTAL DWELLINGS	Unshared dwellings	Shared dwellings	TOTAL HOUSE-HOLD SPACES	Households with residents		Vacant accommodation			No persons present			Persons enumerated but no residents	
					Persons present	Absent household	New	Under improvement	Other	Second residences	Holiday accommodation	Student accommodation	Owner occupied	Not owner occupied
a	b	c	d	e	f	g	h	i	j	k	l	m	n	o
ALL TYPES OF OCCUPANCY	38,781	38,726	55	38,955	35,805	1,206	294	226	1,021	153	17	7	80	146
Dwellings with residents	36,903	36,851	52	37,070	35,805	1,206	-	-	44	-	-	-	-	15
Dwellings with person(s) present	35,713	35,662	51	35,879	35,805	15	-	-	44	-	-	-	-	15
Dwellings with no person(s) present	1,190	1,189	1	1,191		1,191	-	-	-	-	-	-	-	-
Vacant accommodation	1,491	1,489	2	1,497			294	226	977	-	-	-	-	-
New, never occupied	289	288	1	294			294							
Under improvement	226	226	-	226				226						
Other	976	975	1	977					977					
Accommodation not used as main residence	387	386	1	388						153	17	7	80	131
No persons present	177	177	-	177						153	17	7		
Second residences	153	153	-	153						153				
Holiday accommodation	17	17	-	17							17			
Student accommodation	7	7	-	7								7		
Persons enumerated but no residents	210	209	1	211						-	-	-	80	131
Owner occupied	80	80	-	80						-	-	-	80	-
Not owner occupied	130	129	1	131						-	-	-	-	131

Table 66 Shared dwellings

66. Shared dwellings; household spaces in shared dwellings

Number of household spaces within dwelling	TOTAL HOUSEHOLD SPACES	Type of not self-contained household space in shared dwellings				TOTAL SHARED DWELLINGS
		Not self-contained flat	Not self-contained 'rooms'	Bedsit	Not self-contained unoccupied	
a	b	c	d	e	f	g
HAMPSHIRE						
TOTAL SHARED DWELLINGS	6,551	863	776	4,789	123	1,798
2	1,472	545	342	532	53	736
3	1,017	119	153	732	13	339
4	1,012	77	75	850	10	253
5	1,015	54	66	882	13	203
6	672	31	61	565	15	112
7	434	16	33	377	8	62
8 or more	929	21	46	851	11	93
Basingstoke & Deane						
TOTAL SHARED DWELLINGS	191	34	23	134	-	55
2	56	24	16	16	-	28
3	24	3	2	19	-	8
4	16	1	1	14	-	4
5	35	2	3	30	-	7
6	24	2	1	21	-	4
7	-	-	-	-	-	-
8 or more	36	2	-	34	-	4
East Hampshire						
TOTAL SHARED DWELLINGS	132	29	15	86	2	43
2	50	25	10	15	-	25
3	15	1	2	12	-	5
4	20	1	2	17	-	5
5	20	-	1	19	-	4
6	6	-	-	6	-	1
7	21	2	-	17	2	3
8 or more	-	-	-	-	-	-
Eastleigh						
TOTAL SHARED DWELLINGS	173	20	25	122	6	53
2	44	14	16	8	6	22
3	42	5	5	32	-	14
4	20	-	1	19	-	5
5	35	1	2	32	-	7
6	18	-	-	18	-	3
7	14	-	1	13	-	2
8 or more	-	-	-	-	-	-
Fareham						
TOTAL SHARED DWELLINGS	68	16	15	36	1	26
2	36	15	12	8	1	18
3	18	1	3	14	-	6
4	-	-	-	-	-	-
5	-	-	-	-	-	-
6	-	-	-	14	-	2
7	14	-	-	-	-	-
8 or more	-	-	-	-	-	-
Gosport						
TOTAL SHARED DWELLINGS	81	16	7	57	1	24
2	24	9	5	9	1	12
3	6	-	-	6	-	2
4	16	4	1	11	-	4
5	15	1	-	14	-	3
6	6	1	-	5	-	1
7	14	1	1	12	-	2
8 or more	-	-	-	-	-	-

Table 66 Shared dwellings – **continued**

County, districts

66. Shared dwellings; household spaces in shared dwellings

Number of household spaces within dwelling	TOTAL HOUSEHOLD SPACES	Type of not self-contained household space in shared dwellings				TOTAL SHARED DWELLINGS
		Not self-contained flat	Not self-contained 'rooms'	Bedsit	Not self-contained unoccupied	
a	b	c	d	e	f	g
Hart						
TOTAL SHARED DWELLINGS	62	15	13	34	-	20
2	30	15	12	3	-	15
3	6	-	1	5	-	2
4	-	-	-	-	-	-
5	5	-	-	5	-	1
6	-	-	-	-	-	-
7	-	-	-	-	-	-
8 or more	21	-	-	21	-	2
Havant						
TOTAL SHARED DWELLINGS	189	29	42	113	5	60
2	74	23	32	15	4	37
3	6	1	1	4	-	2
4	32	3	4	25	-	8
5	40	-	-	39	1	8
6	12	2	-	10	-	2
7	-	-	-	-	-	-
8 or more	25	-	5	20	-	3
New Forest						
TOTAL SHARED DWELLINGS	199	45	42	105	7	62
2	66	32	12	21	1	33
3	30	8	6	16	-	10
4	16	4	7	5	-	4
5	45	1	9	34	1	9
6	24	-	8	11	5	4
7	-	-	-	-	-	-
8 or more	18	-	-	18	-	2
Portsmouth						
TOTAL SHARED DWELLINGS	1,914	318	239	1,307	50	519
2	430	187	89	135	19	215
3	309	39	54	208	8	103
4	256	37	20	194	5	64
5	270	26	21	218	5	54
6	186	12	18	155	1	31
7	140	2	12	125	1	20
8 or more	323	15	25	272	11	32
Rushmoor						
TOTAL SHARED DWELLINGS	620	42	43	528	7	156
2	82	24	12	42	4	41
3	96	3	10	82	1	32
4	136	9	4	123	-	34
5	125	3	7	113	2	25
6	72	1	5	66	-	12
7	35	-	3	32	-	5
8 or more	74	2	2	70	-	7
Southampton						
TOTAL SHARED DWELLINGS	2,618	247	285	2,050	36	701
2	498	142	111	228	17	249
3	420	49	64	303	4	140
4	476	17	35	419	5	119
5	405	16	23	362	4	81
6	288	10	23	254	1	48
7	196	11	16	164	5	28
8 or more	335	2	13	320	-	36

Table 66　Shared dwellings – **continued**

66. Shared dwellings; household spaces in shared dwellings

Number of household spaces within dwelling	TOTAL HOUSEHOLD SPACES	Type of not self-contained household space in shared dwellings				TOTAL SHARED DWELLINGS
		Not self-contained flat	Not self-contained 'rooms'	Bedsit	Not self-contained unoccupied	
a	b	c	d	e	f	g
Test Valley						
TOTAL SHARED DWELLINGS	75	13	10	52	-	24
2	26	10	9	7	-	13
3	6	-	-	6	-	2
4	16	1	-	15	-	4
5	15	-	-	15	-	3
6	12	2	1	9	-	2
7	-	-	-	-	-	-
8 or more	-	-	-	-	-	-
Winchester						
TOTAL SHARED DWELLINGS	229	39	17	165	8	55
2	56	25	6	25	-	28
3	39	9	5	25	-	13
4	8	-	-	8	-	2
5	5	4	-	1	-	1
6	24	1	5	10	8	4
7	-	-	-	-	-	-
8 or more	97	-	1	96	-	7

Date of change	Authority for change	Existing area i.e. as constituted at 21st April 1991 (names or descriptions not existing on 5th April 1981 are marked *)	Composition of existing area in terms of areas as constituted at 5th April 1981 (names or descriptions of counties/districts which have now ceased to exist are marked #)	Present population 1981	Existing areas in which the balance (if any) of the area named in col d is now situated
a	b	c	d	e	f
1st April 1991	The Berkshire, Buckinghamshire, Hampshire, Oxfordshire and Surrey (County Boundaries) Order 1991	HAMPSHIRE	Hampshire except: Basingstoke and Deane (pt) Silchester Ward (pt)	1,467,142 1,466,385 −264	†Berkshire
			Hart (pt) Eversley Ward (pt)	-	†Berkshire
			Berkshire (pt) viz: Newbury (pt) No 7 Ward (pt) No 11 Ward (pt)	- +1,021	†Berkshire
			Wokingham (pt) Finchampstead Ward (pt)	-	†Berkshire
1st April 1985	The Hampshire (Areas) Order 1985	Basingstoke and Deane	Basingstoke and Deane except: North Waltham Ward (pt)	131,264 130,526 −19	Winchester
1st April 1991	The Berkshire, Buckinghamshire, Hampshire, Oxfordshire and Surrey (County Boundaries) Order 1991		Basingstoke and Deane except: Silchester Ward (pt)	−264	Newbury †(Berkshire)
			Newbury (pt) viz: No 7 Ward (pt) No 11 Ward (pt)	- +1,021	Newbury †(Berkshire)
1st April 1984	The East Hampshire and Havant (Areas) Order 1983	East Hampshire	East Hampshire except: Horndean-Hazleton Ward (pt) Horndean-Kings Ward (pt)	90,585 90,613 −8 −45	Havant
			Havant (pt) viz: Cowplain Ward (pt) Hart Plain Ward (pt)	+21 +11	Havant
1st April 1985	The Hampshire (Areas) Order 1985		East Hampshire except: Clanfield and Buriton Ward (pt) Froxfield and Steep Ward (pt) Medstead Ward (pt)	−11 - -	Winchester
			Winchester (pt) viz: Bishops Sutton Ward (pt) Upper Meon Valley Ward (pt)	+2 +2	Winchester

†See relevant County Report

Notes:- Hectare measurements for those areas affected by boundary changes have not been included because the figures are not routinely available.

Changes of boundaries may involve areas of land with no population present in 1981, this is shown by a dash in Column e.

Where changes have affected ward or parish boundaries and/or names, details can be obtained from the Office of Population Censuses and Surveys, Census Customer Services, Titchfield, Fareham, Hants. PO15 5RR.

Date of change	Authority for change	Existing area i.e. as constituted at 21st April 1991 (names or descriptions not existing on 5th April 1981 are marked *)	Composition of existing area in terms of areas as constituted at 5th April 1981 (names or descriptions of counties/districts which have now ceased to exist are marked #)	Present population 1981	Existing areas in which the balance (if any) of the area named in col d is now situated
a	b	c	d	e	f
1st April 1985	The Hampshire (Areas) Order 1985	Eastleigh		92,952	
			Eastleigh except:	92,954	Winchester
			Eastleigh North Ward (pt)	− 6	
			Winchester (pt) viz:		Winchester
			Otterbourne and Hursley Ward (pt)	+4	
1st April 1990	The Hampshire (District Boundaries) Order 1990	Hart		72,717	
			Hart except:	76,158	Rushmoor
			Hawley Ward (pt)	− 3,441	
			Rushmoor (pt) viz:		Rushmoor
			Cove Ward (pt)	-	
1st April 1991	The Berkshire, Buckinghamshire, Hampshire, Oxfordshire and Surrey (County Boundaries) Order 1991		Hart except:		Wokingham †(Berkshire)
			Eversley Ward (pt)	-	
			Wokingham (pt) viz:		Wokingham †(Berkshire)
			Finchampstead Ward (pt)	-	
1st April 1984	The East Hampshire and Havant (Areas) Order 1983	Havant		117,449	
			Havant except:	117,428	East Hampshire
			Cowplain Ward (pt)	− 21	
			Hart Plain Ward (pt)	− 11	
			East Hampshire (pt) viz:		East Hampshire
			Horndean-Hazleton Ward (pt)	+8	
			Horndean-Kings Ward (pt)	+45	
1st April 1990	The Hampshire (District Boundaries) Order 1990	Rushmoor		81,684	
			Rushmoor except:	78,243	Hart
			Cove Ward (pt)	-	
			Hart (pt) viz:		Hart
			Hawley Ward (pt)	+3,441	
1st April 1985	The Hampshire (Areas) Order 1985	Test Valley		91,436	
			Test Valley	91,407	
			Winchester (pt) viz:		Winchester
			Sparsholt Ward (pt)	+29	

†See relevant County Report

Notes:- Hectare measurements for those areas affected by boundary changes have not been included because the figures are not routinely available.
Changes of boundaries may involve areas of land with no population present in 1981, this is shown by a dash in Column e.
Where changes have affected ward or parish boundaries and/or names, details can be obtained from the Office of Population Censuses and Surveys, Census Customer Services, Titchfield, Fareham, Hants. PO15 5RR.

Date of change	Authority for change	Existing area i.e. as constituted at 21st April 1991 (names or descriptions not existing on 5th April 1981 are marked *)	Composition of existing area in terms of areas as constituted at 5th April 1981 (names or descriptions of counties/districts which have now ceased to exist are marked #)	Present population 1981	Existing areas in which the balance (if any) of the area named in col d is now situated
a	b	c	d	e	f
1st April 1985	The Hampshire (Areas) Order 1985	Winchester		90,826	
			Winchester	90,827	East Hampshire, Eastleigh,
			except:		Test Valley
			Bishops Sutton Ward (pt)	− 2	
			Otterbourne and Hursley Ward (pt)	− 4	
			Sparsholt Ward (pt)	− 29	
			Upper Meon Valley Ward (pt)	− 2	
			Basingstoke and Deane (pt)		Basingstoke
			viz:		and Deane
			North Waltham Ward (pt)	+19	
			East Hampshire (pt)		East Hampshire
			viz:		
			Clanfield and Buriton Ward (pt)	+11	
			Froxfield and Steep Ward (pt)	-	
			Medstead Ward (pt)	-	
			Eastleigh (pt)		Eastleigh
			viz:		
			Eastleigh North Ward (pt)	+6	

Notes:- Hectare measurements for those areas affected by boundary changes have not been included because the figures are not routinely available.

Changes of boundaries may involve areas of land with no population present in 1981, this is shown by a dash in Column e.

Where changes have affected ward or parish boundaries and/or names, details can be obtained from the Office of Population Censuses and Surveys, Census Customer Services, Titchfield, Fareham, Hants. PO15 5RR.

The products described in this Annex become available in the period May 1992 until mid-1994. Dates of availability are not given, to avoid any confusion as this Report continues to be used during and after the period 1992-94. All products are described as if available, but, in any case of doubt, a check should be made with OPCS Census Customer Services at the address given at the end of this Annex.

The form of results

The statistical results of the Census are made available in two ways:

(a)   in printed *reports* sold by HMSO bookshops (or, in a few cases, directly from the Census Offices); or

(b)   in *statistical abstracts* available, on request and for a charge, from the Census offices.

The *reports* take three general forms:

- volumes - such as this Report - containing substantial and detailed tables;

- *key statistics*, which give around 200 summary statistics for particular types of areas throughout the country, with national and regional figures, laid out for easy comparison between areas; and

- *Monitors*, pamphlets which either give between 20 and 60 summary statistics for particular types of area in parts of the country, sometimes issued before main reports to give early results, or provide summaries for the country as a whole.

Statistical abstracts are supplied mainly in machine-readable form, although small quantities can be supplied as hard copies, and are generally either:

- in a standard form, commissioned by a number of customers sharing costs, particularly to provide results for areas and populations smaller than those covered in reports; or

- specially designed output commissioned by individual customers.

The Census Offices also supply supplementary products, for example to provide information on the geographical base of the Census, and documentation in a series of OPCS/GRO(S) *1991 Census User Guides*.

There are two broad types of results:

(a)   *local statistics*, which cover the full range of census topics - such as this Report; and

(b)   *topic statistics*, which focus on particular census topics in more detail, mainly at national and regional level.

All the main statistical results and products are described in *Prospectuses* in the *User Guides* series, available from the addresses given in section 13 and at the end of this Annex. Prospectuses for reports and abstracts contain complete outlines of the tables which will become available.

All areas for which results are provided in reports and abstracts are as at the time of the 1991 Census (unless otherwise indicated).

Local statistics

Local authorities

Results for smaller areas within the local authorities covered in this Report, or within local authorities elsewhere, are available as:

Ward and Civil Parish Monitors (England) or *Ward and Community Monitors* (Wales): pamphlets for each county in England and Wales which give some 30 statistics for each ward and civil parish/community, with figures for counties and districts/boroughs for comparison (see *Prospectus/User Guide 32*).

Local and Small Area Statistics are standard abstracts available from a variety of areas throughout Britain from the smallest - the Census Enumeration District - upwards. They are introduced in section 3 of this Report, and further information is available in *Prospectus/User Guide 3*. Further *User Guides* give: the file specification (number 21); the cell numbering system (24 and 25); and explanatory notes (38).

Results for local authorities in other parts of the country are available, with full comparability, as:

County Reports (England and Wales) and *Region Reports* (Scotland): issued separately in two parts for each County in England and Wales and for each Region in Scotland.

Key Statistics (Great Britain): a single report giving around 200 summary statistics, with some 1981/91 comparisons, for each local authority (see *Prospectus/User Guide 29*).

County Monitors (England and Wales) and *Region Monitors* (Scotland): pamphlets issued separately for each County or Region in advance of the main *Reports*, with contents as section 15 of this Report. Welsh County Monitors will be produced in bi-lingual format (Welsh and English).

Local and Small Area Statistics are also available at local authority level.

Results for other types of area, in forms comparable with those for local authorities listed above, are available for:

Health authority areas

Health Regions Report: a single report, in the form of a County Report, for Regional Health Authorities in England (elsewhere in Britain health authority boundaries coincided with those of local authorities at the time of the 1991 Census).

Key Statistics: a single report giving some 200 summary statistics for each Regional and District Health Authority in England (see *Prospectus/User Guide 30*).

Health Authority Monitors: pamphlets, in the form of County Monitors, for Regional and District Health Authorities.

Local and Small Area Statistics are also available at health authority level.

Urban and Rural Areas

Key Statistics: a single report for the larger urban areas and the rural areas in Great Britain, giving some 200 summary statistics for each area, with six 'regional' reports covering urban areas of all sizes and the rural areas in various parts of England and, separately, for Wales and Scotland (see *User Guide/Prospectus 31*).

Urban and rural areas have been specially defined for both the 1981 and 1991 Censuses, and a further report will give figures on change over the decade. 'Urban areas' cover conurbations, cities and towns of all sizes defined on a land use ('bricks and mortar') basis, so, for example, Census results are available for smaller towns *within* the larger local authority areas.

Small Area Statistics are also available for each urban and rural area.

Parliamentary and European Constituencies

Parliamentary Constituency Monitors: pamphlets, in the form of County Monitors, but with some additional '10 per cent' statistics, with results for each Parliamentary Constituency (and with figures for Britain for comparison). There are separate Monitors for each standard statistical region in England, and for Wales and Scotland (see *User Guide/Prospectus 34*). A single pamphlet in the same form is available for the European Parliamentary Constituencies in Great Britain.

Postcode areas

Postcode Sector Monitors: pamphlets for counties or groups of counties in England and Wales, giving some 30 '100 per cent' and '10 per cent' summary statistics at postcode sector level (see *Prospectus/User Guide 33*).

Small Area Statistics are also available for postcode sectors.

The 1991 Census records for England and Wales are re-sorted to give exact counts for postcode sectors. Results for a wide range of postcode based areas are available in Scotland.

National versions of local results

Results for Great Britain, regions in England, and Wales and Scotland, for these areas as a whole in forms comparable with those for local authorities and other types of area listed above, are available as:

National Reports: issued in two parts, on the lines of this Report, for Great Britain as a whole, including results for standard statistical regions in England and for Wales and Scotland; there is also a *Report for Wales*, bi-lingual in Welsh and English, and a *Report for Scotland*.

National and Regional Summary Monitor: pamphlet for Great Britain, including results for standard statistical regions in England and for Wales and Scotland, with contents as section 15 of this Report. Similar summary Monitors will be issued for Wales (bi-lingual) and Scotland, including summary results at County/Region level.

Topic statistics

Results for particular census topics are available in a series of reports summarised in the table on the following page. The reports present results mainly at the national level, but the following table shows those which have results at regional level, or at a county or district (or equivalent) level. Prospectuses should be checked for detailed information. The Regional Migration Reports comprise separate volumes for each standard statistical region of England, and for Wales and for Scotland.

Workplace and migration statistics

The analysis of the Census questions on 'address of workplace' and 'usual address one year before the Census' gives results on journeys from residences to workplaces and on migration moves, together with figures on people with workplaces in an area and out-migrants from an area, not only for the larger areas covered by the Reports listed above but also for smaller local areas. The latter are:

Special Migration Statistics: which provide information (in machine-readable form only) on migrants within and between local areas (see *Prospectus/User Guide 35*).

Special Workplace Statistics: which provide information (in machine-readable form only) on workforces in areas of workplace and residence for customer defined zones, and on journeys from residence to workplace between the zones (see *Prospectus/User Guide 36*).

Other products
Commissioned tables

In addition to the standard tables prepared for the local and topic statistics, the Census Offices also supply tables, on request, to a customer's own specification, at a charge which meets the marginal cost of production. *Prospectus/User Guide 14* explains how customers may specify and order commissioned tables, and provides guidance on estimation of costs.

Topic	Processing level (per cent)	Prospectus (number)	With some results for:		
			Standard Statistical Regions*	Counties/ Scottish regions	Districts
Sex, Age and Marital Status (GB)	100	2	yes	yes	no
Historical Tables (GB)	100	4	yes	yes	no
Usual Residence (GB)	100	7	yes	yes	yes
Persons Aged 60 and Over (GB)	100	6	yes	no	no
Housing and Availability of Cars (GB and S)	100	12	yes	yes	yes
Communal Establishments (GB)	100	15	yes	no	no
Household Composition (GB)	100	11	yes	no	no
Limiting Long-term Illness (GB)	100	5	yes	no	no
Ethnic Group and Country of Birth (GB)	100/10	9	yes	yes	yes
Welsh Language in Wales	100/10	10	n/a	yes	yes
Gaelic Language in Scotland	100/10	18	n/a	yes	yes
National Migration (Part 1) (GB)	100	17	yes**	no	no
National Migration (Part 2) (GB)	10	17	yes**	no	no
Regional Migration (Part 1)	100	22	yes**	yes	yes
Regional Migration (Part 2)	10	22	yes**	yes	no
Report for Health Areas (GB)	100	39	n/a	n/a	n/a
Economic Activity (GB and S)	10	16	yes	no	no
Workplace and Transport to Work (GB and S)	10	20	yes	yes	yes***
Household and Family Composition (GB)	10	23	no	no	no
Qualified Manpower (GB)	10	8	yes	no	no
Children and Young Adults (GB)	100/10	13	yes	no	no

GB   Volumes for Great Britain
GB and S   Volumes for Great Britain together with additional volumes for Scotland

*   includes Metropolitan Counties in England
**   includes main urban areas
***   includes city centres

Enumeration District/Postcode Directory

This Directory provides a means of associating enumeration districts to postcodes to enable users to undertake their own linkage between census and other datasets. It is available, on magnetic media only, separately for each county. Alternatively, customers may purchase a National Directory. Further details of the file specification, information on availability, cost and ordering are provided in *Prospectus 26*.

User Guide Catalogue

This catalogue is available from the Census Customer Services at the address given below. The catalogue is regularly revised to provide up-to-date information on all Prospectuses/User Guides.

Census Newsletter

The Newsletter is published several times a year to provide a link with users. It gives information on many aspects of the 1991 Census, including details of relevant publications and census-related activities. The Newsletter is a major source of information about the availability of census results and also reports on the main findings from evaluations of coverage and quality. Customers wishing to be included on the mailing list for future copies of the Newsletter should contact Census Customer Services.

Information on all products described in this Annex may be obtained from

Census Customer Services
OPCS
Segensworth Road
Titchfield
Fareham
Hampshire
PO15 5RR

Telephone 0329 813800

Please mention this Report when making an enquiry.

Summary tables

References to the '*Definitions* volume' are to the publication described in section 7.

Tables A and B

Tables A and B are the only summary tables which refer to the present population. In Tables A and B, and in the accompanying diagram, *preliminary counts of the population present* for 1981 have been used because they are felt to be generally more accurate than the final 1981 counts of the population present which were inflated by a processing error (see *1981 Census Monitor CEN 82/3*). The 1981 preliminary counts have been corrected for a few errors (also reported in *1981 Census Monitor CEN 82/3*), and for boundary changes between 1981 and 1991. Because of the preliminary nature of these figures, they have been rounded to the nearest hundred before presentation.

Tables C, E, F, G, I, K, L, and M

Tables C, E, F, G, I, K and L (also M - Wales only) include comparisons between the numbers of residents, and households with residents, in 1981 and 1991. These comparisons are made using the 1981 resident population base (that is, the 1991 statistics used in the comparisons exclude wholly absent households in the same way that the 1981 statistics do) to give a valid picture of intercensal changes.

Tables F and K

The 1981-91 comparisons in Tables F and K use the 1981 definition of students, in which all students are categorised as economically inactive. The remaining sections of these tables use the 1991 definition, in which students who were in employment or seeking work in the week before the Census are categorised as economically active and are included in the relevant economically active categories.

The 1981-91 comparisons of residents and households with residents in section 15 also use the 1981 population base. Some intercensal changes are expressed in terms of '*percentage points*'. This is the arithmetic difference between the 1991 percentage and the 1981 percentage.

All Tables

The following terms appear in the *Summary* tables - see the *Definitions* volume for full details:

(i)   A 'hectare' is equivalent to 2.471 acres.

(ii) A 'household' is either one person living alone; or a group of people (who may or may not be related), living, or staying temporarily, at the same address with common housekeeping - that is, sharing at least one meal a day or sharing a living room or sitting room.

(iii) 'Communal establishments' comprise:

- NHS and non-NHS hospitals,
- local authority homes,
- housing association homes and hostels,
- nursing homes,
- residential homes,
- children's homes,
- prison service establishments,
- defence establishments,
- educational establishments,
- hotels and boarding houses,
- hostels and lodging houses,
- other miscellaneous establishments,
- campers and people sleeping rough, and
- civilian ships, boats, and barges.

(iv) A 'person of pensionable age' is a man aged 65 or over or a woman aged 60 or over.

(v)   'Economically inactive' includes:

- students without a job in the week before the Census,
- permanently sick people,
- retired people, and
- people looking after the home or family and not in paid employment.

(vi) A 'dwelling' consists of one or more household spaces, which may be occupied or unoccupied. A *shared dwelling* consists of two or more household spaces in a multi-occupied building which share access and are not self-contained.

(vii) A 'lone parent' in the Summary tables is a person who is the only adult (person aged 16 or over) in a household with children aged 15 or under.

(viii) A 'dependant' is either a dependent child, or a person with limiting long-term illness *and* permanently sick or retired.

(ix) A 'dependent child' is defined as either a person aged 0-15 in a household; or one aged 16-18, never married, in full-time education, *and* economically inactive.

Percentages in the tables do not necessarily add up to exactly 100 per cent, because each is individually rounded.

Vertical lines in the tables separate different analyses. Percentages or counts should only be summed *within* vertical lines.

In the tables a count or percentage of zero is shown by a dash (-). In Tables A and B percentages of less than 0.005 per cent are shown as 0.00 per cent. In other tables percentages of less than 0.05 per cent are shown as 0.0 per cent.

In Tables E, F, I, K, and L a blank means that no relevant 1981 Census data exist.

In Table G the 1981 percentages for household amenities straddle two columns because no information on central heating was collected in the 1981 Census.

Main tables

References to the '*Definitions* volume' are to the publication described in section 7.

I Demographic and economic characteristics

Table 1

Definitions of populations counted on rows 1 to 5 are:

1. Present residents - residents and persons of no fixed abode or no usual residence who were present on Census night (that is, for whom the response to Question 6, whereabouts, was 'at this address').

2. Absent residents (part of household present) - residents for whom the response to Question 6, whereabouts, was not 'at this address' in households where one or more persons were enumerated as present 'at that address' on Census night.

3. Absent residents (wholly absent household - enumerated) - residents in households where nobody was enumerated as present at that address on Census night (wholly absent households), where a Census form was returned under the voluntary arrangements for the enumeration of such wholly absent households.

4. Absent residents (wholly absent household - imputed) - residents in households where nobody was enumerated as present at that address on Census night (wholly absent households), but where no Census form was returned. Details for the households and residents have been imputed - see the *Definitions* volume paragraphs 1.48-1.54. This category also includes imputed residents of households reported to have residents but where no contact could be made, and also imputed residents in households that refused to complete a Census form.

5. Visitors - persons present at an address for whom the response to Question 7, usual address, was 'elsewhere'.

The components in rows 1 to 5 are used to compile counts on three population bases - those used in the 1971, 1981, and 1991 Censuses. This allows comparison with Small Area Statistics (SAS) results from previous censuses:

PERSONS PRESENT 1991: 1971 BASE (1+5) - this is the sum of lines 1 and 5; that is all present residents plus all visitors. This is equivalent to the count 'Total population present' in 1971 SAS Table 1, from which other sub-populations of persons were drawn for the 1971 SAS.

RESIDENTS 1991: 1981 BASE (1+2) - this is the sum of lines 1 and 2; that is all present residents plus all

absent residents in households where someone was enumerated as present on Census night. This is equivalent to the count ALL RESIDENT 1981: 1981 BASE in 1981 SAS Table 1, which formed the base for most 1981 SAS Tables, most tables in the 1981 Reports, and many other 1981 Census Tables.

RESIDENTS 1991: 1991 BASE (1+2+3+4) - this is the sum of lines 1, 2, 3, and 4; that is all present and absent residents. This is the count which forms the base for most 1991 100 per cent tables in the Reports/LBS, SAS, and most other 100 per cent tables.

Table 3

(i) 'Persons present not in households' are all persons enumerated in communal establishments, plus persons sleeping rough and campers.

(ii) 'Number of establishments' is the total number of each type of establishment in the area at which persons were enumerated on Census night. No counts of 'establishments' are given for persons sleeping rough or for campers.

(iii) 'Residents: Staff' includes residents returned on the Census form as relatives of the manager or other staff, and other people who are not guests (in hotels, etc) or inmates. It should be noted that staff **on duty** in an establishment on Census night whose usual addresses were elsewhere were **not** enumerated in the establishment unless they were temporarily residing in the establishment.

(iv) 'Residents: Other' will, in general, include only those persons who were resident guests (in hotels, etc) or resident inmates. However, **all** persons resident on ships and all persons resident in defence establishments are included in this category.

(v) 'Non-NHS/LA/HA' means that the establishments are not under the management of the National Health Service, a local authority, or a housing association. 'Non-HA' means not under the management of a housing association.

(vi) For the full definition and classification of communal establishments see Chapter 4 of the *Definitions* volume.

Table 4

(i) 'Residents (non-staff) present not in households' will, in general, include only those persons who were resident guests (in hotels, etc) or resident inmates. However, **all** persons resident on ships and all persons resident in defence establishments are included in this category.

(ii) 'Non-NHS/LA/HA' means that the establishments are not under the management of the National Health Service, a local authority, or a housing association.

Table 5

(i) See note (i) to Table 4.

(ii) 'Non-HA' means not under the management of a housing association.

Table 7

(i) The 'Europe' sub-total comprises UK, Channel Islands, Isle of Man, Irish Republic, Ireland (part not stated), and all countries under 'Remainder of Europe'.

(ii) The 'European Community' sub-total comprises UK and all countries listed under 'European Community'.

Table 10

Because the County Reports are published for each county soon after processing of the Census data for each is completed, this table counts only those students who are resident in the area and those who are not residents but were present on Census night. Students who normally live in the area during term-time but are not residents of the area and were not present in the area on Census night are excluded from the table. A complete matrix of area of residence and area of term-time address for students is being prepared by the Census Offices when processing all areas of Great Britain is complete. More information on the availability of statistics from this matrix can be obtained from the Census Offices at the addresses shown in section 13.

Table 11

(i) 'Residents: Staff' includes residents returned on the Census form as relatives of the manager or other staff, and other people who are not guests (in hotels, etc) or inmates. It should be noted that staff **on duty** in an establishment on Census night whose usual addresses were elsewhere were **not** enumerated in the establishment unless they were temporarily residing in the establishment.

(ii) 'Residents: Other' will, in general, include only those persons who were resident guests (in hotels, etc) or resident inmates. However, **all** persons resident on ships and all persons resident in defence establishments are included in this category.

Table 13

(i) 'Other' establishments comprises 'Detention, defence, and education' establishments, and 'Other groups' including persons sleeping rough and campers.

(ii) For the full definition and classification of communal establishments see Chapter 4 of the *Definitions* volume.

Table 15

'Neighbouring counties/neighbouring districts' are areas with common boundaries. This concept is used in tables counting 'migrants' (usual residents of an area with a different usual address one year before the Census). The counts in these columns represent the number of migrants resident in an area who lived in neighbouring areas one year before Census night. For each local government district the counts represent those migrants who formerly lived in the counties/Scottish regions neighbouring the county containing the area in question, or those formerly living in the local government districts neighbouring the district in question. For the county as a whole the counts will represent the sum of all migrants who moved from neighbouring counties/ Scottish regions and neighbouring districts. (All areas/boundaries are as on 21 April 1991.)

All areas which share a section of land boundary, including those which touch at a point, are included as neighbours. Areas which are separated by water (a river, or larger body of water) are included as neighbours if there is a transport link (rail or road bridge, or tunnel, or vehicle ferry) between the two areas. Areas which are separated by land belonging to a third area are not included as neighbours, no matter how close together the areas are. The lists of neighbouring areas were compiled in consultation with the local authorities.

The full lists of neighbouring counties/Scottish regions and neighbouring districts are shown in a *User Guide* available from the Census Offices.

Table 16

(i) See note to Table 15.

(ii) Counts of persons and households in the section for 'Wholly moving households with dependent children' may include a small number of households with no adults.

Table 18

(i) This table includes counts of all imputed residents in wholly absent households which did not return a form under the voluntary arrangements for the enumeration of wholly absent households, plus imputed residents in households where people were reported to live, but where no contact could be made, plus imputed residents of households which refused to complete a Census form.

(ii) 'Other ethnic groups' comprises Black-Caribbean, Black-African, Black-Other, Indian, Pakistani, Bangladeshi, Chinese, and Other groups.

(iii) See paragraphs 1.48-1.54 of the *Definitions* volume for details of the imputation of wholly absent households.

II Housing

Table 19

(i) This table gives imputed counts of all wholly absent households which did not return a form under the voluntary arrangements for the enumeration of such wholly absent households, plus households where people were reported to live, but where no contact could be made, plus households which refused to complete a Census form.

(ii) See paragraphs 1.48-1.54 of the *Definitions* volume for details of the imputation of wholly absent households.

(iii) The range of tenure categories in this table is incomplete; the category 'rented with a job or business' is omitted because it would contain only very small numbers. The counts can be derived by subtracting the sum of the given tenure categories from the table total.

Table 21

(i) 'Number of persons aged 17 and over (with and without others)' is a classification of residents aged 17 and over in households regardless of whether any other residents in the household are aged under 17.

(ii) The rows 'ALL HOUSEHOLDS' and 'TOTAL PERSONS (ALL AGES)' may include a small number of households with no person aged 17 and over, and residents in such households. Such households and residents are not included elsewhere in the table.

Table 22

(i) 'Households with the following rooms' counts the number of households with the stated number of rooms.

(ii) 'Households with the following . . . persons' counts the number of households with the stated number of residents.

Table 24

(i) 'Households with the following persons' and 'Households with the following number of persons aged 18 and over' count the number of households with the stated number of residents, and residents aged 18 and over respectively.

(ii) The column 'TOTAL HOUSEHOLDS' may include a small number of households with no person aged 18 and over, and residents in such households. Such households and residents are not included elsewhere in the table.

Table 25

(i) This table counts households which were enumerated with persons present but which had no residents, whether present or absent; that is households consisting entirely of visitors. The table will include occupied second homes, holiday accommodation, and student residences (excluding halls of residence and other communal student accommodation).

(ii) 'Students' in this table are defined as those aged 18 and over to exclude schoolchildren enumerated with their parents.

(iii) The range of tenure categories in this table is incomplete; the category 'rented with a job or business' is omitted because it would contain only very small numbers. The counts can be derived by subtracting the sum of the given tenure categories from the table total.

Table 26

(i) This table counts households enumerated with residents (whether present or absent) in which at least one student (aged 18 or over) was resident (whether present or absent) or a visitor.

(ii) 'Students' in this table are defined as those aged 18 and over, to exclude schoolchildren enumerated with their parents.

(iii) The range of tenure categories in this table is incomplete; the category 'rented with a job or business' is omitted because it would contain only very small numbers. The counts can be derived by subtracting the sum of the given tenure categories from the table total.

Table 27

(i) This table counts households, persons in households, and rooms, according to the population bases used in the 1971, 1981, and 1991 Censuses.

(ii) Row 1 counts households with at least one person present on Census night 1991, whether a resident or not, sub-divided by the number of persons present on Census night. The 'TOTAL PERSONS' column counts the total number of persons present in households.

(iii) Row 2 counts households with at least one person present on Census night 1991, whether a resident or not, sub-divided by the number of residents, whether present or absent on Census night. The entry in the column headed '0' counts households with no residents but at least one person present on Census night. The 'TOTAL PERSONS' column counts the total number of residents present in households, and absent residents in households where at least one person was present.

(iv) Row 3 counts households with at least one person present (whether a resident or not), plus wholly absent households (enumerated and imputed), plus imputed counts for households where people were reported to live, but where no contact could be made, or which refused to complete a Census form, sub-divided by the number of residents, whether present or absent on Census night. The entry in the column headed '0' counts households with no residents but at least one person present on Census night. The 'TOTAL PERSONS' column counts the total number of residents in households, whether present or absent.

III Households and household composition

Table 30

In the columns classifying households by the age of the youngest and oldest dependant, households with only one dependant are classified by taking the dependant as both the youngest and the oldest in the household.

Table 31

The row 'ALL HOUSEHOLDS' may include a small number of households with no adults, and residents in such households. Such households and residents are not included elsewhere in the table.

Table 32

(i) This table is given alongside Table 31 to provide comparative statistics with 1981 County Report Table 34.

(ii) The row 'ALL HOUSEHOLDS' may include a small number of households with no persons aged 16 and over, and residents in such households. Such households and residents are not included elsewhere in the table.

Table 33

(i) A 'couple' is a male aged 16 and over and a female aged 16 and over, whether or not both were returned as 'married' (whether to each other or not), resident in a household with no other residents aged 16 and over.

(ii) 'Other' economically active females comprise females on a Government scheme, and those unemployed.

Table 36

'Households with the following adults' and 'Households with the following dependent children' count respectively households with the stated number of resident adults, and resident dependent children.

Table 37

(i) Lone 'parents' are the sole *residents* aged 16-24 (with no residents aged 25 or over) in households with a child or children aged 0-15 in the household. The 'lone parent' is not necessarily a parent of the child, for example, a woman aged 21 living alone with her 15 year old sister will be included in the counts. The counts will not include all lone parent families; those in households with other adults will be excluded - see Table 87 in Part 2 of the County Report for 10 per cent sample counts of *lone parent families*.

(ii) The range of employment position categories in this table is incomplete; the category 'self-employed' is omitted because it contains only very small numbers. The counts can be derived by subtracting the sum of the given economic position categories from the table total.

Table 39

The two total rows 'All ages 16 and over' may include a small number of heads and residents in households where the head is aged under 16. Such households and residents are also included in the rows for ages 16-19.

Table 40

(i) Lone 'parents' are the sole *residents* aged 16 or over in households with a child or children aged 0-15 in the household. The 'lone parent' is not necessarily a parent of the child, for example, a woman aged 21 living alone with her 15 year old sister will be included in the counts. The counts will not include all lone parent families; those in households with other adults will be excluded (see Table 87 in Part 2 of the County Report for 10 per cent sample counts of all *lone parent families*).

(ii) 'Other' economically active comprises those on a Government scheme, and those unemployed.

Table 42

(i) The range of 'persons per room' categories in this table is incomplete; the categories 'up to 0.5 persons per room' and 'over 0.5 and up to 1 person per room' are omitted. A total for these two counts can be derived by subtracting the sum of the given 'persons per room' categories from the table total.

(ii) The range of categories of dependent children by age in this table is incomplete; the category 'dependent children aged 18' is omitted. The counts can be derived by subtracting the sum of the given categories from the total for all dependent children.

(iii) The range of categories of cars in this table is incomplete; the categories '1 car' and '2 cars' are omitted. A total for these counts can be derived by subtracting the sum of the given categories from the table total.

(iv) The total row 'ALL HOUSEHOLDS' may include a small number of households with no resident adults. Such households are not included in the other household composition categories.

Table 43

(i) The total row 'ALL HOUSEHOLDS' may include a small number of households with no resident adults. Such households are not included in the other household composition categories.

(ii) The range of categories of residents by age in this table is incomplete; ages 19 up to pensionable age are omitted. A total for these ages can be derived by subtracting the sum of the given categories from the total. (**Note**: the age categories 0-4, 5-15 and 0-17 are all sub-categories of 'All dependent children aged 0-18' and therefore should be omitted from any calculation of the number of residents aged 19 up to pensionable age.)

Table 44

The total row 'ALL HOUSEHOLDS' may include a small number of households with no resident adults. Such households are not included in the other household composition categories.

Table 45

The columns 'Total migrant heads' and 'TOTAL HOUSEHOLD HEADS' may include a small number of households where the head is aged under 16. Such households are also included in the age 16-19 columns.

Table 46

(i) The range of 'persons per room' categories in this table is incomplete; the categories 'up to 0.5 persons per room' and 'over 0.5 and up to 1 person per room' are omitted. A total for these two counts can be derived by subtracting the sum of the given 'persons per room' categories from the table total.

(ii) The range of tenure categories in this table is incomplete; the category 'rented with a job or business' is omitted because it would contain only very small numbers. The counts can be derived by subtracting the sum of the given tenure categories from the table total.

Table 47

The final six cells in the last column of this table are blank to avoid needless repetition of the counts in the last three cells of the first column.

Table 49

(i) The range of 'persons per room' categories in this table is incomplete; the categories 'up to 0.5 persons per room' and 'over 0.5 and up to 1 person per room' are omitted. A total for these two counts can be derived by subtracting the sum of the given 'persons per room' categories from the table total.

(ii) The range of tenure categories in this table is incomplete; the category 'rented with a job or business' is omitted because it would contain only very small counts for most ethnic groups. The counts can be derived by subtracting the sum of the given tenure categories from the table total.

(iii) Counts for households with head born in the New Commonwealth are included to provide some statistics to compare with 1981 Report Table 33.

Table 50

In the columns, 'Inside UK' **does not** include Channel Islands and the Isle of Man.

Table 52

This table is included as a proxy measure of the population not having English as a first language.

Table 53

A 'couple' household is a household with one male resident aged 16 and over and one female resident aged 16 and over, whether or not both were returned as 'married' (whether to each other or not), with no other residents aged 16 and over in the household.

IV Household spaces and dwellings

Table 54

(i) 'TOTAL HOUSEHOLD SPACES' for households with residents, and with persons enumerated but no residents, include as 'household spaces' the accommodation of any households living in non-permanent accommodation. The other occupancy types shown comprise only accommodation in permanent buildings.

(ii) 'TOTAL ROOMS' in 'Hotels and boarding houses' include only those rooms used by guests or staff for living, eating or sleeping.

(iii) 'TOTAL ROOMS' in absent households (imputed), in vacant accommodation, and in accommodation not used as main residence in which no persons were present (that is, second residences, holiday accommodation, and student accommodation), are totals of estimates made in each such case by the enumerator.

Table 56

(i) 'Absent households' includes both enumerated and imputed absent households.

(ii) 'Other' vacant accommodation includes vacant accommodation 'under improvement'.

(iii) The distinction between 'not self-contained flat' and 'not self-contained 'rooms'' in columns j and k, and columns m and n is made with reference to whether basic household amenities are shared. For household spaces where nobody was enumerated (vacant accommodation etc), this distinction is not possible, and only a single count can be given to cover 'not self-contained flat' and 'not self-contained 'rooms''. This also affects any totals which incorporate unoccupied accommodation. Some counts in this table therefore straddle columns.

Table 57

'Households with the following rooms', 'Households with the following persons', and 'Households with the following persons per room' count the number of households with the stated number of rooms, residents, and residents per room respectively.

Table 59

(i) The range of categories of residents by age in this table is incomplete; adults up to pensionable age are omitted. A total for this group can be derived by subtracting the sum of the given categories from the total. (**Note**: the age categories 0-4 and 5-15 are all sub-categories of 'All dependent children' and therefore should be omitted from any calculation of the number of resident adults up to pensionable age.)

(ii) The total row 'ALL HOUSEHOLDS' may include a small number of households with no resident adults. Such households are not included in the other household composition categories.

Table 60

'TOTAL CONVERTED OR SHARED ACCOMMODATION' is a count of buildings containing converted or shared household spaces; that is, a count of multi-occupied buildings.

Table 61

The distinction between 'not self-contained flat' and 'not self-contained 'rooms'' in columns k and l is made with reference to whether basic household amenities are shared. For dwellings where nobody was enumerated (vacant accommodation, etc), this distinction is not possible, and only a single count can be given to cover 'not self-contained flat' and 'not self-contained 'rooms''. This also affects any totals which incorporate unoccupied accommodation. Some counts in this table therefore straddle columns.

Table 64

(i) The tenure of a dwelling is chosen with reference to the tenure(s) of the household space(s) making up the dwelling. For a dwelling of one household space the tenure will be the same for both the dwelling and the household space. For a multi-household space dwelling the tenure is chosen according to a priority order:

1 Owner occupied - owned outright
2 Owner occupied - buying
3 Rented from a housing association
4 Rented from a new town
5 Rented from a local authority
6 Rented privately - unfurnished
7 Rented privately - furnished
8 Rented with a job or business

(Items 4 and 5 are always taken together in England and Wales.)

The highest ranked tenure among the household spaces becomes the tenure for the dwelling. For example, a dwelling consisting of one 'owner occupied - buying' household space and one 'rented privately - furnished' household space will be classified as an 'owner occupied - buying' dwelling.

Impossible combinations of dwelling and household space tenures (where the dwelling would have a lower priority tenure than a household space) are shown in the table as blank cells.

(ii) 'Other unoccupied accommodation' comprises second residences, holiday accommodation and student accommodation.

Table 65

The occupancy type of a dwelling is chosen with reference to the occupancy type(s) of the household space(s) making up the dwelling. For a dwelling of one household space the occupancy type will be the same for both the dwelling and the household space. For a multi-household space dwelling the occupancy type is chosen according to a priority order:

1 With residents - persons present
2 With residents - absent household (no persons present)
3 Vacant - under improvement
4 Vacant - other
5 Persons enumerated but no residents - owner occupied
6 Second residences
7 Persons enumerated but no residents - not owner occupied
8 Holiday accommodation
9 Student accommodation
10 Vacant - new, never occupied

The highest ranked occupancy type among the household spaces becomes the occupancy type for the dwelling. For example, a dwelling consisting of one 'second residence' household space and one household space 'with residents - persons present' will be classified as a dwelling 'with residents - persons present'.

Impossible combinations of dwelling and household space occupancy types (where the dwelling would have a lower priority occupancy type than a household space) are shown in the table as blank cells.

V Wales only table

Table 67

The question on the Welsh language is asked only of persons aged 3 and over.

Imputed data

A Tables 18 and 19 show counts of residents in imputed households, and imputed households for a selection of key variables (these tables include imputed wholly absent households and the other categories of imputed households and residents described in section 5). Table 71 in part 2 of the Report shows a comparison of the numbers of households processed at 100 per cent, and the number included in the 10 per cent sample.

B These counts will aid any comparison of grossed-up estimates from 10 per cent sample tables with 100 per cent processed tables, and to calculate percentage distributions of 10 per cent items based on an estimate of the total population. The imputed households and imputed residents form, in effect, 'not stated' cases for each census topic in the 10 per cent sample tables.

Printed in the United Kingdom for HMSO
Dd295878 1/93 C7 G3397 10170